SO-AJD-084

Tracing the Multinationals

A Sourcebook on U.S.-based Enterprises

Tracing the Multinationals

A Sourcebook on U.S.-based Enterprises

Joan P. Curhan
William H. Davidson
Rajan Suri

This book was published
under the auspices
of the Division of Research,
Graduate School of
Business Administration,
Harvard University.

Ballinger Publishing Company • Cambridge, Massachusetts
A Subsidiary of J.B. Lippincott Company

338.8
C 975

168411

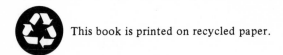 This book is printed on recycled paper.

Copyright © 1977 by Ballinger Publishing Company. All rights reserved. No part of this publication may be reproduced, stored in a retrieval system, or transmitted in any form or by any means, electronic mechanical photocopy, recording or otherwise, without the prior written consent of the publisher.

International Standard Book Number: 0-88410-655-1

Library of Congress Catalog Card Number: 77-9979

Printed in the United States of America

Library of Congress Cataloging in Publication Data

Curhan, Joan P
  Tracing the Multinationals.
  Bibliography: p.
  1. Corporations, American—Statistics.
I. Davidson, William, 1951-   joint author.
II. Suri, Rajan, joint author. III. Title.
HD2785.C89   338.8'8'0973   77-9979
ISBN 0-88410-655-1

This book is warmly dedicated to:

Ronald

Anneke

Catherine

Overview of Tables

Chapter One   Introduction   1

Background   3
Data Gathering Process   4
Compiling the Tables   10
Sample of Companies   11
Size of Sample   12
Revised Figures from Previous Books   15
Direct Access to the Data Bank   16

Chapter Two   The Proliferation of Foreign Subsidiaries   17

Section 1   An Overview   19
Section 2   Flow of Manufacturing Subsidiaries   28
Section 3   Flow of Subsidiary-Industries   44
Section 4   Geographical Spread in Specific Industries   56

Chapter Three   The Maturing of Foreign Subsidiaries   141

Section 1   Changes in Subsidiary Characteristics   142
Section 2   Stock of Manufacturing Subsidiaries at January 1, 1976   148
Section 3   Mergers Within Parent System   160
Section 4   Exits Excluding Mergers Within Parent System   165
Section 5   "Expropriations"   178
Section 6   Methods of Exit by Period   182

Chapter Four   Financial Statistics of Foreign Subsidiaries   189

Section 1   Sales of Subsidiaries Active at January 1, 1976   190
Section 2   Assets of Subsidiaries Active at January 1, 1976   198
Section 3   Equity of Subsidiaries Active at January 1, 1976   206
Section 4   Financial Statistics in Specific Industries   214

Chapter Five   Employment Statistics of Foreign Subsidiaries   257

Section 1   Overview of all Subsidiaries Active at January 1, 1976   258
Section 2   Employment in Specific Industries   266

Chapter Six   Ownership Patterns   309

Section 1   An Overview   310
Section 2   Comparison of Net Flow and Stock   312
Section 3   In Specific Industries, By Region and Entry Period   320
Section 4   Flow of Joint Ventures   362
Section 5   Outside Owners in 1975   374

Chapter Seven   Exports and Intrasystem Sales   383

Section 1   Overview of all Subsidiaries Active at January 1, 1976   385
Section 2   Manufacturing Subsidiaries Active at January 1, 1976   392
Section 3   By Region and Principal Industry in 1975   400

Chapter Eight   Extraction and Exploration Activity   409

Section 1   Extraction Subsidiaries   410
Section 2   Exploration Subsidiaries   417

Table of Contents

FOREWORD   xix

CHAPTER ONE   INTRODUCTION   1

  Background   3

  Data Gathering Process   4

    Questionnaire   4
    Definition of Variables   4
    Collecting the Data   9
    Processing the Data   10

  Compiling the Tables   10

    Flow and Stock Tabulations   10
    Industry Compilations   10

  Sample of Companies   11

  Size of Sample   12

  Revised Figures from Previous Books   15

  Direct Access to the Data Bank   16

CHAPTER TWO   THE PROLIFERATION OF FOREIGN SUBSIDIARIES   17

  Section One   An Overview   19

2.1.1   Of Principal Activities   19
2.1.2   Of Ownership Patterns   20
2.1.3   Of Methods of Entry   21
2.1.4   By Geographical Region   22
2.1.5   By Geographical Region and Ownership at Entry   24
2.1.6   By Geographical Region and Entry Method   26

  Section Two   Flow of Manufacturing Subsidiaries   28

2.2.1   Overview by Principal Industry   28
2.2.2   By Principal Industry and Ownership at Entry   30
2.2.3   By Principal Industry and Entry Method   32
2.2.4   By Geographical Region   34
2.2.5   By Geographical Region and Ownership at Entry   36
2.2.6   By Geographical Region and Entry Method   38
2.2.7   Net Flow by Region and Principal Industry   40

  Section Three   Flow of Subsidiary-Industries   44

2.3.1   Overview By Industry   44
2.3.2   By Geographical Region   46

2.3.3   Net Flow by Region and Industry   48
2.3.4   New Flow By Principal Industry Of Subsidiary   52

   Section Four   Geographical Spread in Specific Industries   56
2.4.1   The Beverages Industry (SIC 208)   56
2.4.2   The Tobacco Industry (SIC 21)   58
2.4.3   The Food Industry (SIC 20, Excluding 208)   60
2.4.4   The Textiles and Apparel Industries (SIC 22 and 23)   62
2.4.5   The Wood and Furniture Industries (SIC 24 and 25)   64
2.4.6   The Paper Industry (SIC 26)   66
2.4.7   The Printing Industry (SIC 27)   68
2.4.8   The Industrial Chemicals Industry (SIC 281)   70
2.4.9   The Plastics Industry (SIC 282)   72
2.4.10 The Agricultural Chemicals Industry (SIC 287)   74
2.4.11 The Cosmetics and Soap Industries (SIC 284)   76
2.4.12 The Drugs Industry (SIC 283)   78
2.4.13 Other Chemical Industries (Other SIC 28)   80
2.4.14 Fabricated Plastics Industries (SIC 306 and 307)   82
2.4.15 The Tires Industry (SIC 301)   84
2.4.16 The Petroleum Refining Industry (SIC 291)   86
2.4.17 Other Petroleum Industries (Other SIC 29)   88
2.4.18 The Leather Industry (SIC 31)   90
2.4.19 Stone, Clay and Cement Industries (SIC 324 to 328)   92
2.4.20 Abrasives and Asbestos Industries (SIC 329)   94
2.4.21 The Glass Industry (SIC 321–323)   96
2.4.22 The Iron and Steel Industry (SIC 331–332)   98
2.4.23 Non-ferrous Metal Industries (Other SIC 33)   100
2.4.24 The Metal Cans Industry (SIC 341)   102
2.4.25 Other Fabricated Metal Industries (Other SIC 34)   104
2.4.26 The Engines and Turbines Industry (SIC 351)   106
2.4.27 The Construction Machinery Industry (SIC 353)   108
2.4.28 The Farm Machinery Industry (SIC 352)   110
2.4.29 The Office Machines and Computers Industry (SIC 357)   112
2.4.30 The Special Machinery Industry (SIC 355)   114
2.4.31 The General Machinery Industry (SIC 356)   116
2.4.32 Other Non-electrical Machinery Industries (Other SIC 35)   118
2.4.33 Electric Light and Wiring Industry (SIC 364)   120
2.4.34 Electric Transmission Equipment Industry (SIC 361)   122
2.4.35 Radio, TV and Appliances Industries (SIC 363 and 365)   124
2.4.36 The Electronics Industry (SIC 367)   126
2.4.37 Other Electrical Industries (Other SIC 36)   128
2.4.38 Communication Equipment Industry (SIC 366)   130
2.4.39 The Motor Vehicles Industry (SIC 371)   132
2.4.40 Other Transportation Industries (SIC 37)   134

2.4.41 Precision Instruments Industries (SIC 38)   136
2.4.42 Miscellaneous Industries (SIC 39)   138

CHAPTER THREE   THE MATURING OF FOREIGN SUBSIDIARIES   141

Section One   Changes in Subsidiary Characteristics   142

3.1.1   By Principal Activity   142
3.1.2   By Parent Ownership   143
3.1.3   By Principal Industry   144

Section Two   Stock of Manufacturing Subsidiaries at January 1, 1976   148

3.2.1   By Region and Principal Industry in 1975   148
3.2.2   By Region and Subsidiary-Industries in 1975   152
3.2.3   By Principal Industry and Subsidiary Industries   156

Section Three   Exits via Merger and Reorganization   160

3.3.1   By Year and Geographical Region   160
3.3.2   By Year and Principal Industry   162

Section Four   Exits Excluding Mergers   165

3.4.1   Overview, By Method of Exit   165
3.4.2   By Activity of Subsidiary   166
3.4.3   By Ownership of Subsidiary   167
3.4.4   By Entry Method of Subsidiary   168
3.4.5   By Entry Date of Subsidiary   169
3.4.6   By Geographical Region   170
3.4.7   By Principal Industry   172
3.4.8   Total Exits Excluding Mergers 1967–75, By Country and Industry   174

Section Five   "Expropriations"   178

3.5.1   By Year and Geographical Region   178
3.5.2   By Year and Principal Industry   180

Section Six   Methods of Exit by Period   182

3.6.1   By Principal Activity of Subsidiary   182
3.6.2   By Parent Ownership of Subsidiary   183
3.6.3   By Geographical Region   184
3.6.4   By Principal Industry of Subsidiary   186

CHAPTER FOUR   FINANCIAL STATISTICS OF FOREIGN SUBSIDI-
   ARIES   189

Section One   Sales of Subsidiaries Active at January 1, 1976   190

4.1.1   By Principal Activities   190
4.1.2   By Ownership Patterns   191
4.2.3   By Method of Entry   192

4.1.4   By Entry Date   193
4.1.5   By Geographical Region   194
4.1.6   By Principal Industry of Subsidiary   196

   Section Two   Assets of Subsidiaries Active at January 1, 1976   198

4.2.1   By Principal Activities   198
4.2.2   By Ownership Patterns   199
4.2.3   By Method of Entry   200
4.2.4   By Entry Date   201
4.2.5   By Geographical Region   202
4.2.6   By Principal Industry of Subsidiary   204

   Section Three   Equity of Subsidiaries Active at January 1, 1976   206

4.3.1   By Principal Activities   206
4.3.2   By Ownership Patterns   207
4.3.3   By Method of Entry   208
4.3.4   By Entry Date   209
4.3.5   By Geographical Region   210
4.3.6   By Principal Industry of Subsidiary   212

   Section Four   Financial Statistics in Specific Industries   214

4.4.1   The Beverages Industry (SIC 208)   214
4.4.2   The Tobacco Industry (SIC 21)   215
4.4.3   The Food Industry (SIC 20, Excluding 208)   216
4.4.4   The Textiles and Apparel Industries (SIC 22 and 23)   217
4.4.5   The Wood and Furniture Industries (SIC 24 and 25)   218
4.4.6   The Paper Industry (SIC 26)   219
4.4.7   The Printing Industry (SIC 27)   220
4.4.8   The Industrial Chemicals Industry (SIC 281)   221
4.4.9   The Plastics Industry (SIC 282)   222
4.4.10 The Agricultural Chemicals Industry (SIC 287)   223
4.4.11 The Cosmetics and Soap Industries (SIC 284)   224
4.4.12 The Drugs Industry (SIC 283)   225
4.4.13 Other Chemical Industries (Other SIC 28)   226
4.4.14 Fabricated Plastics Industries (SIC 306 and 307)   227
4.4.15 The Tires Industry (SIC 301)   228
4.4.16 The Petroleum Refining Industry (SIC 291)   229
4.4.17 Other Petroleum Industries (Other SIC 29)   230
4.4.18 The Leather Industry (SIC 31)   231
4.4.19 Stone, Clay and Cement Industries (SIC 324 to 328)   232
4.4.20 Abrasives and Asbestos Industries (SIC 329)   233
4.4.21 The Glass Industry (SIC 321–323)   234
4.4.22 The Iron and Steel Industry (SIC 331–332)   235
4.4.23 Non-ferrous Metal Industries (Other SIC 33)   236
4.4.24 The Metal Cans Industry (SIC 341)   237

4.4.25 Other Fabricated Metal Industries (Other SIC 34)   238
4.4.26 The Engines and Turbines Industry (SIC 351)   239
4.4.27 The Construction Machinery Industry (SIC 353)   240
4.4.28 The Farm Machinery Industry (SIC 352)   241
4.4.29 The Office Machines and Computers Industry (SIC 357)   242
4.4.30 The Special Machinery Industry (SIC 355)   243
4.4.31 The General Machinery Industry (SIC 356)   244
4.4.32 Other Non-Electrical Machinery Industries (Other SIC 35)   245
4.4.33 Electric Light and Wiring Industry (SIC 364)   246
4.4.34 Electric Transmission Equipment Industry (SIC 361)   247
4.4.35 Radio, TV and Appliances Industries (SIC 363 and 365)   248
4.4.36 The Electronics Industry (SIC 367)   249
4.4.37 Other Electrical Industries (Other SIC 36)   250
4.4.38 Communication Equipment Industry (SIC 366)   251
4.4.39 The Motor Vehicles Industry (SIC 371)   252
4.4.40 Other Transportation Industries (SIC 37)   253
4.4.41 Precision Instruments Industries (SIC 38)   254
4.4.42 Miscellaneous Industries (SIC 39)   255

CHAPTER FIVE   EMPLOYMENT STATISTICS OF FOREIGN SUB-
     SIDIARIES   257

   Section One   Overview of All Subsidiaries Active at January 1, 1976   258

5.1.1   By Principal Activities   258
5.1.2   By Ownership Patterns   259
5.1.3   By Method of Entry   260
5.1.4   By Entry Date   261
5.1.5   By Geographical Region   262
5.1.6   By Principal Industry of Subsidiary   264

   Section Two   Employment Data in Specific Industries   266

5.2.1   The Beverages Industry (SIC 208)   266
5.2.2   The Tobacco Industry (SIC 21)   267
5.2.3   The Food Industry (SIC 20, Excluding 208)   268
5.2.4   The Textiles and Apparel Industries (SIC 22 and 23)   269
5.2.5   The Wood and Furniture Industries (SIC 24 and 25)   270
5.2.6   The Paper Industry (SIC 26)   271
5.2.7   The Printing Industry (SIC 27)   272
5.2.8   The Industrial Chemicals Industry (SIC 281)   273
5.2.9   The Plastics Industry (SIC 282)   274
5.2.10 The Agricultural Chemicals Industry (SIC 287)   275
5.2.11 The Cosmetics and Soap Industries (SIC 284)   276
5.2.12 The Drugs Industry (SIC 283)   277
5.2.13 Other Chemical Industries (Other SIC 28)   278
5.2.14 Fabricated Plastics Industries (SIC 306 and 307)   279

5.2.15 The Tires Industry (SIC 301)   280
5.2.16 The Petroleum Refining Industry (SIC 291)   281
5.2.17 Other Petroleum Industries (Other SIC 29)   282
5.2.18 The Leather Industry (SIC 31)   283
5.2.19 Stone, Clay and Cement Industries (SIC 324 to 328)   284
5.2.20 Abrasives and Asbestos Industries (SIC 329)   285
5.2.21 The Glass Industry (SIC 321–323)   286
5.2.22 The Iron and Steel Industry (SIC 331–332)   287
5.2.23 Non-ferrous Metal Industries (Other SIC 33)   288
5.2.24 The Metal Cans Industry (SIC 341)   289
5.2.25 Other Fabricated Metal Industries (Other SIC 34)   290
5.2.26 The Engines and Turbines Industry (SIC 351)   291
5.2.27 The Construction Machinery Industry (SIC 353)   292
5.2.28 The Farm Machinery Industry (SIC 352)   293
5.2.29 The Office Machines and Computers Industry (SIC 357)   294
5.2.30 The Special Machinery Industry (SIC 355)   295
5.2.31 The General Machinery Industry (SIC 356)   296
5.2.32 Other Non-electrical Machinery Industries (Other SIC 35)   297
5.2.33 Electric Light and Wiring Industry (SIC 364)   298
5.2.34 Electric Transmission Equipment Industry (SIC 361)   299
5.2.35 Radio, TV and Appliances Industries (SIC 363 and 365)   300
5.2.36 The Electronics Industry (SIC 367)   301
5.2.37 Other Electrical Industries (Other SIC 36)   302
5.2.38 Communication Equipment Industry (SIC 366)   303
5.2.39 The Motor Vehicles Industry (SIC 371)   304
5.2.40 Other Transportation Industries (SIC 37)   305
5.2.41 Precision Instruments Industries (SIC 38)   306
5.2.42 Miscellaneous Industries (SIC 39)   307

CHAPTER SIX   OWNERSHIP PATTERNS   309

  Section One   An Overview   310

6.1.1   By Principal Activity at Entry Date   310
6.1.2   By Method of Entry   311

  Section Two   Comparison of Net Flow and Stock   312

6.2.1   By Principal Activity in 1975   312
6.2.2   By Method of Entry   313
6.2.3   By Geographical Region   314
6.2.4   For Manufacturing Subsidiaries, By Region   316
6.2.5   By Principal Industry   318

  Section Three   In Specific Industries, By Region and Entry Period 320

6.3.1   The Beverages Industry (SIC 208)   320
6.3.2   The Tobacco Industry (SIC 21)   321

6.3.3   The Food Industry (SIC 20, Excluding 208)   322
6.3.4   The Textiles and Apparel Industries (SIC 22 and 23)   323
6.3.5   The Wood and Furniture Industries (SIC 24 and 25)   324
6.3.6   The Paper Industry (SIC 26)   325
6.3.7   The Printing Industry (SIC 27)   326
6.3.8   The Industrial Chemicals Industry (SIC 281)   327
6.3.9   The Plastics Industry (SIC 282)   328
6.3.10   The Agricultural Chemicals Industry (SIC 287)   329
6.3.11   The Cosmetics and Soap Industries (SIC 284)   330
6.3.12   The Drugs Industry (SIC 283)   331
6.3.13   Other Chemical Industries (Other SIC 28)   332
6.3.14   Fabricated Plastics Industries (SIC 306 and 307)   333
6.3.15   The Tires Industry (SIC 301)   334
6.3.16   The Petroleum Refining Industry (SIC 291)   335
6.3.17   Other Petroleum Industries (Other SIC 29)   336
6.3.18   The Leather Industry (SIC 31)   337
6.3.19   Stone, Clay and Cement Industries (SIC 324 to 328)   338
6.3.20   Abrasives and Asbestos Industries (SIC 329)   339
6.3.21   The Glass Industry (SIC 321–323)   340
6.3.22   The Iron and Steel Industry (SIC 331–332)   341
6.3.23   Non-ferrous Metal Industries (Other SIC 33)   342
6.3.24   The Metal Cans Industry (SIC 341)   343
6.3.25   Other Fabricated Metal Industries (Other SIC 34)   344
6.3.26   The Engines and Turbines Industry (SIC 351)   345
6.3.27   The Construction Machinery Industry (SIC 353)   346
6.3.28   The Farm Machinery Industry (SIC 352)   347
6.3.29   The Office Machines and Computers Industry (SIC 357)   348
6.3.30   The Special Machinery Industry (SIC 355)   349
6.3.31   The General Machinery Industry (SIC 356)   350
6.3.32   Other Non-electrical Machinery Industries (Other SIC 35)   351
6.3.33   Electric Light and Wiring Industry (SIC 364)   352
6.3.34   Electric Transmission Equipment Industry (SIC 361)   353
6.3.35   Radio, TV and Appliances Industries (SIC 363 and 365)   354
6.3.36   The Electronics Industry (SIC 367) ·   355
6.3.37   Other Electrical Industries (Other SIC 36)   356
6.3.38   Communication Equipment Industry (SIC 366)   357
6.3.39   The Motor Vehicles Industry (SIC 371)   358
6.3.40   Other Transportation Industries (SIC 37)   359
6.3.41   Precision Instruments Industries (SIC 38)   360
6.3.42   Miscellaneous Industries (SIC 39)   361

Section Four   Flow of Joint Ventures   362

6.4.1   Majority-Owned (51–94%) by Parent, at Entry Date   362
6.4.2   Co-owned (50%) by Parent, at Entry Date   364

6.4.3   Minority-Owned (5–49%) by Parent, at Entry Date   366
6.4.4   Manufacturing Subsidiaries, Majority-Owned at Entry   368
6.4.5   Manufacturing Subsidiaries, Co-owned at Entry   370
6.4.6   Manufacturing Subsidiaries, Minority-Owned at Entry   372

   Section Five   Outside Owners in 1975   374

6.5.1   By Principal Activity in 1975   374
6.5.2   By Method of Entry   375
6.5.3   By Geographical Region   376
6.5.4   For Manufacturing Subsidiaries, by Region   380
6.5.5   By Principal Industry   380
6.5.6   By Sales of Subsidiary in 1975   382

CHAPTER SEVEN   EXPORTS AND INTRA-SYSTEM SALES   383

   Section One   Overview of All Subsidiaries Active at January 1, 1976   385

7.1.1   By Principal Activities   385
7.1.2   By Ownership Patterns   386
7.1.3   By Method of Entry   387
7.1.4   By Entry Date   388
7.1.5   By Sales of Subsidiary in 1975   389
7.1.6   By Geographical Region   390

   Section Two   Manufacturing Subsidiaries Active at January 1, 1976   392

7.2.1   By Principal Industry   392
7.2.2   By Ownership Patterns   394
7.2.3   By Method of Entry   395
7.2.4   By Entry Date   396
7.2.5   By Slaes of Subsidiary in 1975   397
7.2.6   By Geographical Region   398

   Section Three   By Region and Principal Industry in 1975   400

7.3.1   "Export Subsidiaries"   400
7.3.2   "Intra-system Sales Subsidiaries"   404

CHAPTER EIGHT   EXTRACTION AND EXPLORATION ACTIVITY   409

   Section One   Extraction Subsidiaries   410

8.1.1   Proliferation by Geographical Region   410
8.1.2   Proliferation by Ownership Pattersn   411
8.1.3   Exits Excluding Mergers by Region   412
8.1.4   By Region and Ownership Changes   413
8.1.5   By Region and Outside Ownership in 1975   414
8.1.6   By Region and Financial Data for 1975   415
8.1.7   By Parent Ownership and Financial Data for 1975   416

Section Two   Exploration Subsidiaries   417

8.2.1   Proliferation by Geographical Region   417
8.2.2   By Region and Assets in 1975   418

Appendix I   Questionnaires   419

Appendix II   Information Sources   427

Appendix III   Industry Groups   429

Foreword

This book of tables is the third in a series produced over the past eight years by the Multinational Enterprise Project of the Harvard Business School. Like those before it, this work offers data that allow the user to trace in detail the growth and overseas spread of several hundred very large U.S.-based multinational enterprises.

In recent years, publications on the subject of the multinational enterprise have reached flood proportions. Statistics on the subject are being produced in great quantities, not only by national governments but also by many international organizations, including notably those of the United Nations. As a rule, however, the available data have been unsatisfying in one critical respect: statistics from government sources on the whole have been quite highly aggregated, being presented in broad industry totals or national aggregates. Statistics from private sources, on the other hand, have been very narrow in focus, often covering only single firms or small groups of firms.

From the first, the data bases and the related analyses of the Multinational Enterprise Project have sought to occupy the middle ground. The object has been to record the growth and spread of individual enterprises in rich detail, while covering a universe of enterprises sufficiently large to warrant major generalizations with respect to those patterns. Accordingly, the project has developed a body of data for U.S.-based multinational enterprises that includes all the largest of such enterprises, together with their 19,000 subsidiaries in foreign countries.

In 1969, 500 pages of data based on these materials were published by J.W. Vaupel and J.P. Curhan in a book called *The Making of Multinational Enterprise*. Then, in 1973, Vaupel and Curhan produced a second book, *The World's Multinational Enterprises*. That second book afforded a first detailed glimpse of the growth and spread of over 200 multinational enterprises based in countries other than the United States, together with comparative data for the U.S. group. The present volume shifts the focus back to the largest U.S. enterprises, recording their growth and spread up to the close of the year 1975.

The tabulations in this volume, however, do more than bring the record up to date. Since the time when this data bank was first developed, there has been a dramatic improvement in public data sources with regard to individual enterprises. By using these public sources and by obtaining the unstinting cooperation of nearly all the firms in the sample, the project has been able measurably to improve the range and quality of its descriptive data. That work has been achieved at some considerable cost to the cooperating enterprises, inasmuch as about 500 man days were spent at various corporate headquarters, checking and completing data on individual foreign subsidiaries.

The most important advance that this compilation incorporates over its predecessors is a series of measures of the size of individual foreign subsidiaries. In previous compilations, the researchers had to content themselves with recording the growth and spread of U.S.-based enterprises mainly by counts of the number of subsidiaries that were included in relevant categories. The tables carried in this volume, however, fill in a critical piece of the mosaic that has heretofore been lacking, by providing measures of size for the various categories of subsidiaries covered in the tables.

The tabulations presented here have been selected from the data bank with an eye to their general utility for researchers. In some cases, our obligations to co-operating companies have imposed limits on the data that could be published. We have followed the practice, however, of making the underlying data available to academic researchers under suitable conditions that would guarantee the preservation of confidentiality. Moreover, an on-line program is available at the Harvard Business School that will allow such researchers to extract data directly from the data bank to suit their particular needs. The programs used in these on-line systems, like the tables presented in this publication, also are designed to satisfy the confidentiality commitment.

The library work and the preparation of the new data bank were done by 60 undergraduate and graduate students working more than 20,000 hours over an eighteen month period. The field interviews at firm headquarters were conducted by interview teams (directed by author Davidson) that included Michael Barlowe, Gary Crocker, Michael Elliott, Nathan Fagre, Lawrence Goodstein, Gary Jakaitis, Regina Pisa, and Laurence Ronan. In the computer aspects of the work, author Suri was assisted by G. Anandalingam, Peter Gennis, and Gregory Hammett.

The principal administrator for this phase of the project was author Curhan. Curhan and Davidson trained the student researchers and interviewers; Davidson managed their data-collecting activities, and data preparation. Suri's main contribution was in designing the necessary data storage and data processing systems, and, in collaboration with the other authors, developing the form and structure of the tables in this volume.

The funding for this phase of the work of the Multinational Enterprise Project came from a number of different sources. The College Work-Study Program (sponsored by the U.S. Department of Health, Education, and Welfare) supported the student contingent. The Division of Research of the Harvard Business School provided indispensable funds in a time of acute need, besides authorizing my own continued participation in the project.

The staff of Baker Library at the Harvard Business School, including notably Lorna Daniells and Shirley Wayne, labored unstintingly to make available the resources at that extraordinary institution. The Harvard Business School's Division of Computer Services also extended valuable assistance. To all these sources of support, we express our appreciation.

Soldiers Field
Boston, Mass.
May 1977

Raymond Vernon
Coordinator
Multinational Enterprise
     Project
Harvard Business School

Chapter One

Introduction

BACKGROUND

The Multinational enterprise project at the Harvard Business School was initiated in 1965. Since that time, researchers under the direction of Professor Raymond Vernon have been involved in an analysis of the problems and practices of multinational enterprises—that is, of large business firms having extensive interests in subsidiaries outside their home countries. As an important part of this study, statistical data have been collected on more than 35,000 "foreign" subsidiaries of the world's largest multinational manufacturing enterprises—"foreign" subsidiaries being defined as those subsidiaries located outside the home country of the parent enterprise.

The project's first data bank, dubbed EMY 1, was completed in 1969. This bank contains information on the foreign subsidiaries of the largest U.S.-based manufacturing enterprises. Over a four year period, information was collected from published sources and company interviews on over 10,000 foreign subsidiaries of 187 U.S. parent firms. Coverage spans the period from 1900 until January 1, 1968. A book of tables generated from the initial data base was published in 1969.*

The U.S. study was followed by a second major data-gathering effort when a study of the 226 largest manufacturing enterprises based *outside* the United States was initiated in 1970. The 226 enterprises included all companies that appeared on *Fortune's* list of the "200 Largest Non-U.S. Industrial Corporations" for the year 1970, plus 26 additional companies. This project resulted in a second data bank, EMY 2, completed in 1973. The data bank includes descriptions of over 15,000 foreign subsidiaries and covers the period from 1900 until January 1, 1971. A second data book was published in 1973.**

As numerous researchers throughout the world have made continued use of the data banks, a decision to update EMY 1 was made to insure its usefulness in the future. This effort began in 1975 and culminated in a new data bank, EMY 11. The same group of 187 U.S.-based manufacturing enterprises included in the EMY 1 study was the basis for the new data bank. However, due to various consolidations and other events, the sample has been reduced to 180 firms, as detailed in the section on Sample of Companies. On the other hand, the number of foreign subsidiaries covered has increased from a little over 10,000 to over 19,000.

This current book of tables is derived from the new EMY 11 data base. As in the case of its two predecessors, this book of tables is designed to facilitate recognition of significant patterns in the structure and development of multinational

---

*James W. Vaupel and Joan P. Curhan, *The Making of Multinational Enterprise: A Sourcebook of Tables Based on a Study of 187 Major U.S. Manufacturing Corporations* (Boston: Division of Research, Harvard Business School, 1969).

**James W. Vaupel and Joan P. Curhan, *The World's Multinational Enterprises: A Sourcebook of Tables Based on a Study of the Largest U.S. and Non-U.S. Manufacturing Corporations* (Boston: Division of Research, Harvard Business School, 1973).

3

enterprises, to permit testing of a wide range of hypotheses about multinational enterprises, and to provide an overview of the master data bank.

The Harvard Business School has taken measures to limit access to the data banks to academic researchers and has established safeguards to insure the confidentiality of privileged data. However, academic researchers requiring specific information not contained in the published tables may arrange for direct access to the data bank. The procedure for obtaining customized data is described in the section on Direct Access to the Data Bank.

DATA-GATHERING PROCESS

Questionnaire

The first step in the data collection process was the development of a questionnaire. The basis for the questionnaire was the format used in the previous EMY 1 and EMY 2 studies. However, from the experience of the Multinational Enterprise Project over a period of years, it has become apparent that certain variables are of special interest to researchers in the international business field. These variables include financial statistics for sales, assets, and equity; employment figures; level of exports; and level of intrasystem sales for individual subsidiaries. They have been included and given special emphasis in the newest study. All data collected from any of the various sources used in the project were entered on the questionnaire, which appears in Appendix I.

Definitions of Variables

The variables used in this book relate to individual foreign subsidiaries of U.S. parent systems. A "foreign subsidiary," as defined in this book, represents an entity incorporated in a country other than the United States; however, foreign branches of U.S. corporations are also covered if such branches were engaged in exploration, extraction, or manufacturing. To qualify for the sample used to generate the tables in this book, 5 percent or more of a subsidiary's equity had to be held by one of the 180 parent systems in the sample. "Parent system" is here defined as the ultimate U.S. parent corporation and its affiliates throughout the world. In the event that a foreign subsidiary qualified for inclusion in more than one parent system, that subsidiary was counted only once in those tables in which double counting might otherwise have occurred.

The tables in this book do not use all of the variables contained in the EMY data bank. Those variables used in the book are listed below. Similarly, not all of the values for each variable in the data bank appear in the tables. Definitions of specific values for each variable are given below.

Variable 1: Subsidiary's Country. Each subsidiary is classified in the data base according to the country in which it is legally incorporated and the country in which it performs its principal activity. In the book, subsidiaries are counted according to their country of principal activity alone. For 95 percent of the subsidiaries studied, the country of principal activity is also the nation in which the subsidiary is incorporated. Branches of U.S. corporations active in other countries provide the principal exception.

Variable 2: Subsidiary's Year of Entry. The date of entry into a parent system is recorded as the first year in which one of the parent systems in the sample forms or acquires the subsidiary. A subsidiary is considered to have entered a parent system when more than 5 percent of its equity is held by the parent system.

Variable 3: Subsidiary's Method of Entry. Three principal methods were defined by which subsidiaries enter a parent system. The category "newly formed" applies when a subsidiary is established directly by a parent system. If a subsidiary was formed as a result of the reorganization of one or more subsidiaries already in a parent system, the category "descendent" is used. In the event that an existing company's equity was purchased directly by a parent system, or if a parent system, in acquiring an existing company, thereby acquired the subsidiaries of the company, the category "acquired" is used to denote the subsidiary's method of entry. A distinction between the direct and indirect methods of acquisition is made in the data base but the two are combined to form one category in the book.

Variable 4: Subsidiary's Year of Departure. This variable records the year in which a subsidiary leaves its parent system by any method. In the event that a parent system's ownership of a foreign subsidiary drops below 5 percent but some equity is still held by the parent system, the subsidiary is considered to have left the system. The year in which this occurs is classified as the year of departure for that subsidiary.

Variable 5: Subsidiary's Method of Departure. As with method of entry, four categories of departure are defined. If a subsidiary's equity is sold to an independent party, the "sold" category applies. Foreign subsidiaries reported by the parent as confiscated or expropriated are classified as "expropriated." A subsidiary that ceases to exist as a legal entity as a result of a decision of the parent, and whose activities cease, is classified as "liquidated." When the activities of a liquidated company are continued by a successor subsidiary within the parent system, the subsidiary is considered to have been "merged or reorganized." The category "merged or reorganized" applies when subsidiaries are merged to form a single entity, and when a subsidiary is broken into one or more new subsidiaries. It also applies to the case where a subsidiary is merged with an independent firm, but only if the resulting new company qualifies as a member of the original parent system (e.g., is owned more than 5 percent). If the resulting company does not qualify as a member of the parent system, the original subsidiary would be considered to have left the system by some method other than "merged or reorganized."

Tables in Chapter Three distinguish the departure of a subsidiary via merger or reorganization as opposed to other methods of departure from the parent system. In cases of merger or reorganization, the departure of a subsidiary does not involve the exit of the function performed by the subsidiary. The other methods of departure involve the exit of both the legal entity and its function from the parent system.

Variable 6: Nature of Subsidiary's Principal Activity at Entry Date.   This variable classifies a subsidiary into one of four categories, according to the nature of the subsidiary's principal activity in the year the subsidiary entered its parent system. "Manufacturing" applies if a subsidiary did *any* manufacturing, assembling, or packaging. "Sales and Service" includes marketing, repair and maintenance, transport, storage, or finance. "Extraction" embraces all raw material extraction, as well as farming and fishing. The fourth category, "Other," is an aggregate of a number of other activities that appear in the data base under separate principal activity categories. These are holding, research and development, exploration, inactive, and other.

Variable 7: Latest Principal Activity of Subsidiary.   This variable takes the same values as Variable 6, but is based on the most recent principal activity of a subsidiary. If a subsidiary did not leave the parent system, this variable would apply to 1975. In the event that a subsidiary did leave the system, this variable applies to the year of departure.

Variable 8: Products Manufactured at Entry by Industry, and

Variable 9: Products Manufactured, Most Recent, by Industry.   These two variables refer to final products manufactured, assembled, or packaged by a subsidiary. The products are recorded in the form of "Standard Industrial Classification" (SIC) codes.* Data before 1967 are recorded in three digit SIC codes, while data for 1967–1976 are recorded in four digit codes. For each subsidiary, the products are listed in order of contribution to total sales revenue. The product group contributing the greatest single share is considered the "principal industry" of the subsidiary. As previously noted, "entry" refers to the subsidiary's first year of membership in a parent system; "most recent" applies to 1975 or to the year of departure.

Variable 10: Ownership of the Subsidiary at Entry, and

Variable 11: Ownership of the Subsidiary, Most Recent.   These variables refer to the ownership of a subsidiary by its immediate parent(s) in its parent system. The

---

*For complete source, see Statistical Policy Division of the Executive Office of the President: Office of Management and Budget, *Standard Industrial Classification Manual* (Washington, D.C.: U.S. Government Printing Office, 1972). Also see Appendix III in this book.

phrase "immediate parent(s)" means the company or companies that directly hold the subsidiary's equity. These may include the ultimate U.S. parent, its subsidiaries, or any combination of owners including both the U.S. parent and its subsidiaries. Ownership information is collected for the subsidiary's year of entry into its parent system, and also for 1975 or the year of departure.

Variable 12: Outside Owners at Entry, and

Variable 13: Outside Owners, Most Recent. The phrase "outside owner" refers to local or foreign private enterprises, state agencies, and members of the public that hold equity in a subsidiary and are not a part of its parent system. Outside owners are classified into one of three categories: "a locally controlled private enterprise"; "a local state agency or state enterprise"; and "a foreign-controlled private enterprise." A fourth category, "stock is widely dispersed among the public," represents the case where a large number of portfolio investors hold equity in the subsidiary. When a subsidiary's stock is held by more than five independent parties, its ownership is considered to be widely dispersed. If there are less than five outside owners, the two largest owners are ranked according to percentage of equity held in the subsidiary listed. The outside owner listed first is considered the "principal outside owner." If there are more than five outside owners, and no one party holds a significant share of the equity, the category "stock is widely dispersed" is used to classify the outside owners. Again, data are recorded for year of entry and also for 1975 or year of departure. Data are recorded for two outside owners both at entry and for the most recent dates, although tables in this book include only the principal outside owner.

Variable 14: Percentage of Subsidiary's Equity Held by Outside Owner(s) at Entry, and

Variable 15: Percentage of Subsidiary's Equity Held by Outside Owner(s), Most Recent. These variables list the percentage of the subsidiary's equity owned by each outside owner noted under Variables 12 and 13.

Variable 16: Sales of Subsidiary, Most Recent. These data are for 1974 or 1975, depending on the fiscal year of the corporation. Sales are recorded in dollars, as translated from local currency at year end rates for the year in which the data apply. The sales level of the subsidiary is recorded in one of five categories: less than $1 million, $1 to $10 million, $10 to $25 million, $25 to $100 million, and greater than $100 million. If the subsidiary left the system, sales in year of departure are recorded.

Variable 17: Total Assets of Subsidiary, Most Recent. The total assets of the subsidiary are translated into U.S. dollars for the most recent fiscal year. If the

Table 1.1   Variables Used and Their Response Rate

Variables	# of Responses	Response Rate*
Subsidiary's Nation of Incorporation	11,198	1.0000
Subsidiary's Nation of Primary Activity (if not that of incorporation)	354	0.0316
Entry Year (year subsidiary entered system)	11,198	1.0000
Entry Code (method of entry)	10,374	0.9264
Primary Activity At Entry	10,457	0.9338
Primary Activity, Most Recent	10,941	0.9770
Ownership % by Main System Owner At Entry	10,770	0.9618
Ownership % by Main System Owner (latest)	10,860	0.9698
Exports Level	6,070	0.5421
Intra-System Sales Level	5,942	0.5306
Sales Category	7,316	0.6533
Assets Category	7,248	0.6473
Equity Category	5,829	0.5205
Number of Employees	5,084	0.4540
Joint Venture Code (designates joint venture between EMY parents)	293	0.0262
Branch Code (foreign branch of U.S. company)	224	0.0200
Outside Ownership at Entry: First Owner Category	1,659	0.4677
Outside Ownership at Entry: Second Owner Category	259	0.0730
Ownership % by First Outside Owner	1,582	0.9536
Ownership % by Second Outside Owner	209	0.8069
Outside Ownership, Most Recent: First Owner Category	1,419	0.4000
Outside Ownership, Most Recent: Second Owner Category	302	0.0851
Ownership % by First Outside Owner	1,356	0.9556
Ownership % by Second Outside Owner	265	0.8775
Year of Earliest Available Product List	5,674	0.9825
Number of Earliest Available Products	5,674	0.9825
Earliest Product 1	5,674	0.9825
Earliest Product 2	1,347	0.2332
Earliest Product 3	447	0.0774
Earliest Product 4	161	0.0278
Earliest Product 5	67	0.0116
Earliest Product 6	26	0.0045
Year of Latest Available Product List	5,710	0.9887
Number of Latest Available Products	5,719	0.9903
Latest Product 1	5,719	0.9903
Latest Product 2	2,666	0.4616
Latest Product 3	1,427	0.2471
Latest Product 4	781	0.1352
Latest Product 5	425	0.0736
Latest Product 6	255	0.0442

*The response rate is calculated as a percentage of the 11,198 subsidiaries that were in existence as members of a parent system in 1975, except that outside ownership response rates are reflected as a percentage of subsidiaries not wholly owned and product list response rates as a percentage of manufacturing subsidiaries.

subsidiary did not leave the system, this would be 1974 or 1975. The five categories employed for Variable 16 were also used here.

Variable 18: Subsidiary's Equity, Most Recent. This variable covers owner's equity for the subsidiary's most recent fiscal year. Owner's equity is paid-in capital and retained earnings. It is recorded under the five categories used for Variables 16 and 17. If the subsidiary left the system, data are recorded for year of departure.

Variable 19: Subsidiary's Number of Employees, Most Recent. The total number of employees, including managerial, clerical, staff, and production workers, was entered for each subsidiary, as of most recent year or year of departure. This figure is entered as an exact number and is classified as to year of applicability.

Variable 20: Subsidiary's Export Sales, Most Recent. The subsidiary's sales are broken down into local and export sales. The percentage of exports to total sales is then classified into one of three categories: less than 10 percent, 10 to 50 percent, and more than 50 percent. These data are for the subsidiary's most recent fiscal year (1974 or 1975), or year of departure.

Variable 21: Subsidiary's Intra-system Sales, Most Recent. This variable records the percentage of the subsidiary's sales made to other members of its parent system. The level of intercompany sales is recorded in one of three categories: less than 10 percent, 10 to 50 percent, and more than 50 percent. This variable covers the subsidiary's most recent fiscal year (1974 or 1975), or year of departure.

Additional variables employed in the book, which are not mentioned here, are defined in footnotes to relevant tables in which they appear. Table 1.1 lists variables used in this book, and the response rate in the data base for each variable.

Collecting the Data

Data for this study were collected in a manner consistent with procedures used for the previous two studies. First, a detailed library search of published materials was conducted, and second, an interview was arranged with most of the companies. Some 60 students, primarily from Harvard University and supported mainly by the College Work-Study Program (sponsored by the U.S. Department of Health, Education, and Welfare), carried out the library research, and a smaller group conducted the company interviews. These students were carefully trained and supervised by the authors.

The principal sources of published information were corporate annual reports, company reports to the Securities and Exchange Commission, other government documents, business histories, articles in business periodicals, and various directories of foreign companies. Indeed, these foreign directories, especially the *Kompass* directories and Dun & Bradstreet's *Principal International Businesses*, were the source of a larger proportion of data than in previous studies and were second in importance only to annual reports and 10-K Reports to the Securities and Exchange Commission. (A complete list of sources appears in Appendix II.)

Following the intensive library search of the aforementioned data sources, arrangements were made for researchers to spend a day at corporate headquarters. Of the 180 companies in the sample, 169 were interviewed. These interviews were generally with an officer familiar with international operations and served to verify data collected in the library search as well as to fill gaps in information.

Processing the Data
Once the questionnaires were returned from the participating companies, the data were coded, keypunched, and computerized. Extensive tests were then conducted to detect the presence of errors in keypunching and coding. Inevitably, in a data base of this size, some errors and inaccuracies will remain undetected.

COMPILING THE TABLES

Flow and Stock Tabulations
Two distinct types of tables are to be found in this book. One type counts subsidiary entries by year of entry and characteristics at entry date. This type is called a *flow* table. The second type of table counts the number of subsidiaries in a category as of 1975. This is a *stock* table.

For tables in this book, the net flow in a category (such as the number of manufacturing subsidiary entries up to 1976) will not be equal to the stock total in 1975. This happens because changes in subsidiary characteristics occur between entry date and 1975. If a subsidiary that entered as a sales subsidiary later becomes a manufacturing subsidiary, for instance, it appears in the stock table as a manufacturing company in 1975, but it appears in the flow table only as a sales subsidiary.

In Chapter Three, section 1, a set of tables identifies changes in subsidiary characteristics between entry date and 1975. The user can reconcile differences between net flow and stock totals by referring to this section.

Industry Compilations
In addition to the difference between flow and stock totals, a second distinction is important for manufacturing subsidiaries. In Chapter Two, a distinction is made between *principal industry* and *subsidiary-industry* tables.

A subsidiary's "principal industry" is the broad product line (as defined in Appendix III) that accounts for the single largest share of the subsidiary's sales. Tables in section 2 of Chapter Two are based on the principal industry of each of the 5,622 manufacturing subsidiaries in the sample at the end of 1975. The total number of principal industry observations is 5,622, one for each of the manufacturing subsidiaries.

Tables in section 3 of Chapter Two are compiled on a different basis. Here, in addition to its principal industry, all other industries in which a subsidiary manufactures are counted in the tables. The term "subsidiary-industries" is used to denote this basis of compilation.

A "subsidiary-industry" is the presence through manufacturing of a subsidiary in an industry. A subsidiary may be present in more than one industry group, so that the number of subsidiary-industries will be greater than the total number of manufacturing subsidiaries.

Subsidiary-industry and principal industry tables were compiled in both flow and stock form. Sections 2 and 3 of Chapter Two are flow tables for these two methods of compilation, while section 2 of Chapter Three presents stock tables.

SAMPLE OF COMPANIES

As described earlier, the original sample of 187 major U.S. manufacturing enterprises on which *The Making of Multinational Enterprise* is based was used for this data book. It may be recalled that initially the 187 companies were selected by two rules:*

1. The enterprise was listed in *Fortune's* "500 Largest U.S. Industrial Corporations" for the year 1964, published in 1965, or for the year 1963, published in 1964.
2. At the end of 1963, the U.S. parent system held equity interests in manufacturing enterprises located in six or more foreign countries, such equity interest in each case amounting to 25 percent or more of the total equity of the foreign enterprise. "Manufacturing" is used here to include assembly and packaging plants.

Once a U.S. parent system qualified for the study, all foreign enterprises in which it owned 5 percent or more of the equity, non-manufacturing as well as manufacturing, were included in the study. If a parent corporation in the study was merged with a corporation outside the sample after 1963, then all the foreign enterprises of the successor corporations were included in the study.

Various consolidations have occurred since the sample was drawn in 1965, so that the list now consists of 180 companies. The following changes account for the reduction in number of companies covered in the new sample.

1. A number of firms merged or were acquired by other companies already in the sample. In such a case, the records of the two companies were merged to form one corporate record retroactive to the origins of both firms. Five cases fall into this category:

   Beech Nut Life Savers, Inc., merged with Squibb.
   Container Corporation of America was acquired by Marcor, which was acquired by Mobil.
   Kendall Co. was acquired by Colgate-Palmolive.
   Parke, Davis & Co. was acquired by Warner-Lambert.
   Westinghouse Air Brake Company was acquired by American Standard.

2. In three cases, companies in the sample were acquired by firms in the non-U.S. sample. In these cases, the records of the U.S. companies were deleted from the U.S. sample, and will be assigned to their foreign parents in EMY 2:

   Atlas Chemical Industries, Inc., was acquired by I.C.I.
   International Packers Ltd. was acquired by Deltec.
   Libby, McNeill & Libby was acquired by Nestlé.

*Vaupel and Curhan, *The Making of Multinational Enterprise*, p. 3.

3. Six companies merged or were acquired by other manufacturing companies not in the original sample. In these cases, the new parent firm entered the sample, and assumed the records of the merged or acquired company;

ABEX Corp. was acquired by IC Industries.
Armour & Co. was acquired by Greyhound.
Clevite Corp. was acquired by Gould Inc.
Federal Pacific Electric Co. was acquired by U.V. Industries.
Glen Alden Corp. was acquired by Rapid American.
Swift & Co. was acquired by ESMARK.

4. In one case, a firm on the original sample was acquired by a non-manufacturing company. The new parent was not included in the current sample:

Rheem Manufacturing Company was acquired by City Investing Co.

There were major name changes for several companies still in the sample:

American Metal Climax, Inc., changed to Amax Inc.
American Smelting and Refining Company changed to ASARCO.
Standard Oil Company (New Jersey) changed to Exxon Corporation.
General American Transportation Corporation changed to GATX.
Interchemical Corp. changed to Inmont Corp.
National Dairy Products Corp. changed to Kraftco.
National Lead Company changed to NL Industries.
Pennsalt Chemicals Corp. changed to Pennwalt.
Pittsburgh Plate Glass Company changed to PPG Industries, Inc.
Schering Corp. changed to Schering-Plough, Inc.

With all such changes accounted for, the list of sample companies is shown in Table 1.2.

SIZE OF SAMPLE

The U.S. Department of Commerce is perhaps the major source of information on the foreign activities of U.S.-based enterprises. The sample used in this book can best be evaluated in comparison with the sample used by the Commerce Department.

In the February 1977 issue of the Department's *Survey of Current Business*, sales of majority-owned foreign manufacturing affiliates of U.S. companies were estimated at a total of $192 billion in 1975. This estimate is intended to describe the universe of all foreign manufacturing companies that are owned 50 percent or more by an American parent corporation. The estimate is based on a sample of 282 U.S. parent systems and their 5,900 majority-owned foreign manufacturing affiliates.

The sample used in this book contains 168 U.S. manufacturing parents (plus 12 extractive firms) and approximately 5,400 foreign manufacturing affiliates. Of this

Table 1.2   List of U.S.-Based Companies

Abbott Laboratories
Addressograph Multigraph Corporation
Allied Chemical Corporation
Allis-Chalmers Corporation
Aluminium Company of America
American Can Company
American Cyanamid Company
American Home Products Corporation
AMF Incorporated
AMAX Inc.
ASARCO Incorporated
American Standard Inc.
Archer Daniels Midland Company
Armco Steel Corporation
Armstrong Cork Company

Beatrice Foods Co.
Bendix Corporation
Black and Decker Manufacturing Company
Borden, Inc.
Borg-Warner Corporation
Bristol-Myers Company
Brunswick Corporation
Budd Company
Burlington Industries, Inc.

Cabot Corporation
Campbell Soup Company
Carborundum Company
Carnation Company
Caterpillar Tractor Co.
Celanese Corporation
Champion Spark Plug Company
Chemetron Corporation
Chesebrough-Pond's Inc.
Chicago Pneumatic Tool Company
Chrysler Corporation
Cities Service Company
Clark Equipment Company
Coca-Cola Company
Colgate-Palmolive Company
Combustion Engineering, Inc.
Continental Can Company, Inc.
Continental Oil Company
Corning Glass Works
CPC International Inc.
Crane Co.
Crown Cork & Seal Company, Inc.

Dana Corporation
Deere & Company
Del Monte Corporation
Dow Chemical Company
Dresser Industries, Inc.

E.I. du Pont de Nemours & Company
Eli Lilly and Company
ESB Incorporated
Eastman Kodak Company
Eaton Corporation
Eltra Corporation
Emhart Corporation

Englehard Minerals & Chemicals Corporation
Esmark, Inc.
Exxon Corporation

FMC Corporation
Federal-Mogul Corporation
Firestone Tire & Rubber Company
Ford Motor Company
Foremost-McKesson, Inc.
Fruehauf Corporation

GATX Corporation
General Dynamics Corporation
General Electric Company
General Foods Corporation
General Mills, Inc.
General Motors Corporation
General Telephone & Electronics Corporation
General Tire & Rubber Company
Genesco Inc.
The Gillette Company
B.F. Goodrich Company
Goodyear Tire & Rubber Company
Gould Inc.
W.R. Grace & Co.
Greyhound Corporation
Gulf Oil Corporation

H.J. Heinz Company
Hercules Incorporated
Hobart Corporation
Honeywell Inc.
Hoover Company
Hygrade Food Products Corporation

IC Industries, Inc.
Ingersoll-Rand Company
Inmont Corporation
International Business Machines Corporation
International Harvester Company
International Paper Company
International Telephone and Telegraph Corporation

Johns-Manville Corporation
Johnson & Johnson
JOY Manufacturing Company

Kaiser Industries Corporation
Kellogg Company
Kimberly-Clark Corporation
Koppers Company, Incorporated
Kraftco Corporation

Litton Industries, Inc.
Lockheed Aircraft Corporation

P.R. Mallory & Co. Inc.
Marcor Inc.
Maremont Corporation
Martin Marietta Corporation
Merck & Co., Inc.
Miles Laboratories, Inc.
Minnesota Mining and Manufacturing Company
Mobil Oil Corporation

Table 1–2 continued

Monsanto Company

Nabisco, Inc.
NCR Corporation
National Distillers & Chemical Corporation
NL Industries, Inc.
Norton Company

Olin Corporation
Otis Elevator Company
Owens-Corning Fiberglas Corporation
Owens-Illinois, Inc.

PPG Industries, Inc.
Pennwalt Corporation
PepsiCo Inc.
Pet Incorporated
Pfizer Inc.
Phelps Dodge Corporation
Philip Morris Incorporated
Phillips Petroleum Company
Pillsbury Company
H.K. Porter Company, Inc.
Procter & Gamble Company
Purex Corporation

Quaker Oats Company

RCA Corporation
Ralston Purina Company
Rapid-American Corporation
Raytheon Company
Revlon, Inc.
Reynolds Metals Company
Richardson-Merrell Inc.
H.H. Robertson Company
Rockwell International Corporation
Rohm and Haas Company

Schering-Plough Corporation
SCM Corporation
St. Regis Paper Company
Scott Paper Company
Scovill Manufacturing Company
Simmons Company
Singer Company
SmithKline Corporation
Sperry Rand Corporation
Squibb Corporation
A.E. Staley Manufacturing Company
Standard Brands Incorporated
Standard Oil Company of California
Standard Oil Company (Indiana)
Stauffer Chemical Company
Sterling Drug Inc.
Studebaker-Worthington, Inc.
Sunbeam Corporation

TRW Inc.
Texaco Inc.
Texas Instruments Incorporated
Time Incorporated
Timken Company

USM Corporation
Union Carbide Corporation
UNIROYAL, Inc.
United Merchants and Manufacturers, Inc.
Upjohn Company
UV Industries, Inc.

Warner-Lambert Company
Westinghouse Electric Corporation
Weyerhaeuser Company
Wm. Wrigley Jr. Company

total, 4,600 are owned 50 percent or more by U.S. parent systems in the sample and approximately 750 foreign manufacturing affiliates are owned 5 to 50 percent by the parent systems in the sample.

Our estimate of aggregate sales by the 5,400 manufacturing affiliates in the sample for 1975 is approximately $155 billion.* Aggregate sales for foreign minority-owned manufacturing affiliates in our sample were calculated as $19 billion, so that our estimate for sales by foreign manufacturing affiliates owned 50 percent or more by U.S. parents is $136 billion. This figure represents about 71 percent of the Commerce Department's estimate for the total sales of all foreign manufacturing affiliates owned 50 percent or more by U.S. parent systems.

Our estimates are derived by a two step process. The exact sales figures for all manufacturing affiliates whose sales were reported as greater than $100 million

---

*It should be noted that approximately 10 percent of the subsidiaries in the sample have sales data as of 1974, due to varying fiscal years and the time schedule of the data collection and interview process.

were aggregated. Exact figures were secured for these larger subsidiaries because of their impact on total sales estimates. For subsidiaries whose sales are reported under our format as less than $1 million, $1 to 10 million, $10 to 25 million, or $25 to 100 million, an estimated mean for each range is used to record those subsidiaries' sales. The means were estimated on the basis of a sample of about 10 percent of the total for which exact sales figures were known. The sales figures were then aggregated to yield a total figure.

Table 1.3 compares Department of Commerce totals for sales in different countries and regions with sales figures derived from the sample used in this book. It should be noted that outside of the western hemisphere, the sample used in this book represents a high percentage of the Commerce Department's estimates. Such a trend could be anticipated, since Canada, Latin America, and to a similar degree the U.K., are areas where smaller U.S. firms have higher propensities to invest.

REVISED FIGURES FROM PREVIOUS BOOKS

In the course of gathering data on the 180 U.S. enterprises, it was found that public information sources had improved dramatically in the last decade. For this reason, and because of the high degree of cooperation afforded us by the companies covered in the study, a number of revisions were made in the original EMY 1 data. Errors were corrected, redundancies eliminated, and missing information supplied. As a result, pre-1967 data in EMY 11 do not directly correspond to the EMY 1 tape from which the Vaupel and Curhan book, *The Making of Multinational Enterprise*, was drawn. Therefore, any comparison of figures from this book with the above Vaupel and Curhan book will reveal inconsistencies.

The reader will note that the tables in this book begin as of 1950. Data prior to 1950 are available in the first Vaupel and Curhan book.

Table 1.3. Comparison Between Department of Commerce Totals and Harvard Multinational Enterprise Project Sample Totals (Sales of Foreign Manufacturing Affiliates in 1975)

Country or Region	Commerce Totals	Harvard Sample	Harvard/ Commerce
	($ million)	($ million)	%
Canada	43,598	27,800	63.8
France	16,134	13,839	83.0
West Germany	24,590	20,522	83.5
United Kingdom	26,526	19,862	74.9
Other Western Europe	34,337	33,320	97.0
Japan	5,640	4,810	85.3
Australia, New Zealand S. Africa, and Rhodesia	11,548	10,378	89.9
Latin America	23,962	17,864	74.6
Other	5,916	6,895	116.5
TOTAL	192,251	155,290	80.8

DIRECT ACCESS TO THE DATA BANK

Since the publication of *The Making of Multinational Enterprise* in 1969, researchers from various institutions throughout the world have made use of the data obtained directly from the EMY 1 and EMY 2 computerized data banks. Within the limits of confidentiality imposed on the data by participating companies, researchers can now obtain additional customized data from the new data bank. *Tracing the Multinationals* is intended to provide an overview of the data available; however, specific needs of researchers may best be satisfied by tables and other data produced to their specifications. Inquiries for specific data from the master tape should be made to:

> Multinational Enterprise Project
> Harvard Business School
> Soldiers Field
> Boston, MA 02163

The Proliferation
of Foreign Subsidiaries

CHAPTER 2 - THE PROLIFERATION OF FOREIGN SUBSIDIARIES
SECTION 1 -- AN OVERVIEW
TABLE 1 --- OF PRINCIPAL ACTIVITIES

NO. OF SUBSIDIARIES, BY ACTIVITY AT ENTRY DATE

PRINCIPAL ACTIVITY	NET FLOW UP TO 31-DEC-50	NO. OF ENTRIES DURING YEAR(S)													TOTAL ENTRIES 1951-75	TOTAL EXITS 1951-75	NET FLOW UP TO 1-JAN-76
		51-55	56-60	61-65	1966	1967	1968	1969	1970	1971	1972	1973	1974	1975			
MANUFACTURING	947	419	960	1612	343	437	546	471	416	446	381	375	269	204	6879	2204	5622
SALES	638	237	480	810	149	299	271	240	233	263	159	187	200	101	3629	1040	3227
EXTRACTION	108	58	67	73	14	27	29	44	19	30	11	12	32	14	430	190	348
OTHER	109	124	181	272	64	85	120	125	134	124	81	104	95	54	1563	412	1260
UNKNOWN	394	151	269	458	99	64	40	65	51	42	14	15	23	3	1294	947	741
TOTAL	2196	989	1957	3225	669	912	1006	945	853	905	646	693	619	376	13795	4793	11198

CHAPTER 2 - THE PROLIFERATION OF FOREIGN SUBSIDIARIES
SECTION 1 -- AN OVERVIEW
TABLE 2 --- OF OWNERSHIP PATTERNS

NO. OF SUBSIDIARIES, BY PARENT OWNERSHIP AT ENTRY

OWNERSHIP AT ENTRY	NET FLOW UP TO 31-DEC-50	NO. OF ENTRIES DURING YEAR(S)													TOTAL ENTRIES 1951-75	TOTAL EXITS 1951-75	NET FLOW UP TO 1-JAN-76
		51-55	56-60	61-65	1966	1967	1968	1969	1970	1971	1972	1973	1974	1975			
WHL OWNED: 95-100%	1538	693	1303	1959	413	617	771	705	614	669	467	478	433	246	9368	3165	7741
MAJ OWNED: 51- 94%	185	99	190	377	71	94	96	63	88	77	62	68	48	32	1365	460	1090
CO- OWNED: 50%	90	56	150	307	61	71	61	63	63	72	56	56	50	40	1106	350	846
MIN OWNED: 5- 49%	143	82	173	338	77	80	58	77	80	75	58	81	82	58	1319	383	1079
UNKNOWN	240	59	141	244	47	50	20	37	8	12	3	10	6	0	637	435	442
TOTAL	2196	989	1957	3225	669	912	1006	945	853	905	646	693	619	376	13795	4793	11198

CHAPTER 2 - THE PROLIFERATION OF FOREIGN SUBSIDIARIES
SECTION 1 -- AN OVERVIEW
TABLE 3 --- OF METHODS OF ENTRY

NO. OF SUBSIDIARIES, BY METHODS OF ENTRY

METHOD OF ENTRY	NET FLOW UP TO 31-DEC-50	NO. OF ENTRIES DURING YEAR(S)													TOTAL ENTRIES 1951-75	TOTAL EXITS 1951-75	NET FLOW UP TO 1-JAN-76
		51-55	56-60	61-65	1966	1967	1968	1969	1970	1971	1972	1973	1974	1975			
NEWLY FORMED	1230	507	1009	1430	288	366	423	437	402	388	282	307	365	234	6438	1652	6016
ACQUIRED	465	301	645	1314	309	457	534	452	403	479	319	354	212	135	5914	2237	4142
DESCENDENT	30	7	20	36	2	19	29	15	17	16	23	11	30	7	232	46	216
UNKNOWN	471	174	283	445	70	70	20	41	31	22	22	21	12	0	1211	858	824
TOTAL	2196	989	1957	3225	669	912	1006	945	853	905	646	693	619	376	13795	4793	11198

CHAPTER 2 - THE PROLIFERATION OF FOREIGN SUBSIDIARIES
SECTION 1 -- AN OVERVIEW
TABLE 4 --- BY GEOGRAPHICAL REGION

NO. OF SUBSIDIARIES, BY COUNTRY OR REGION

COUNTRY OR REGION	NET FLOW UP TO 31-DEC-50	NO. OF ENTRIES DURING YEAR(S)													TOTAL ENTRIES 1951-75	TOTAL EXITS 1951-75	NET FLOW UP TO 1-JAN-76
		51-55	56-60	61-65	1966	1967	1968	1969	1970	1971	1972	1973	1974	1975			
CANADA	441	176	246	345	72	98	144	121	90	78	63	57	49	27	1566	844	1163
LATIN AMER. (TOTAL)	616	292	573	696	128	183	195	149	151	170	128	143	120	85	3013	1167	2462
C.AM.+CARIB.(TOTAL)	235	121	272	311	61	81	90	77	86	108	78	61	61	43	1450	505	1180
BAHAMAS	6	6	15	11	3	3	7	4	8	3	5	4	0	2	71	21	56
BERMUDA	1	0	10	12	0	5	4	8	5	11	8	11	3	4	81	10	72
COSTA RICA	2	0	3	13	2	5	4	5	5	5	5	5	3	1	53	10	45
GUATEMALA	8	1	13	19	5	4	2	5	5	4	5	2	3	0	74	17	65
JAMAICA	4	1	8	8	4	4	3	5	5	2	0	2	1	0	42	8	38
MEXICO	133	63	117	161	34	43	39	32	31	49	31	25	26	18	669	250	552
NETH.ANTILLES	0	0	1	4	1	3	6	7	17	11	7	2	5	0	66	11	55
NICARAGUA	3	0	2	9	5	0	1	1	1	3	3	0	0	1	26	6	23
PANAMA	17	25	68	48	9	10	16	2	6	10	8	7	8	12	215	62	170
OTHER C.AM+CAR.	61	24	35	26	2	6	5	8	6	8	6	3	12	12	153	110	104
S.AMERICA (TOTAL)	381	171	301	385	67	102	105	72	65	62	50	82	59	42	1563	662	1282
BOLIVIA	11	5	3	5	0	2	7	1	2	0	0	0	1	2	16	17	10
CHILE	28	5	6	22	4	12	7	2	3	0	2	2	2	4	69	45	52
COLOMBIA	58	30	37	67	8	6	9	6	6	10	3	4	4	6	192	89	161
ECUADOR	5	1	6	15	2	5	4	2	5	4	1	2	4	1	52	14	43
PERU	24	19	24	36	5	14	6	4	2	6	0	3	1	0	120	64	80
ARGENTINA	87	27	42	67	12	16	25	17	12	4	5	3	3	1	235	115	207
BRAZIL	87	43	79	70	18	30	30	20	22	24	25	41	36	19	457	169	375
URUGUAY	21	8	9	9	1	2	2	0	2	0	2	2	2	0	32	32	39
VENEZUELA	55	37	95	91	16	15	20	19	14	14	16	22	8	0	375	130	300
OTHER S.AMER.	5	1	7	3	2	6	5	1	0	0	0	1	1	0	15	5	15
EUROPE (TOTAL)	813	288	782	1469	319	418	469	440	411	430	296	307	278	171	6078	2062	4829
BELGIUM	50	12	42	79	13	31	31	46	28	22	21	15	15	17	372	113	309
FRANCE	110	35	116	204	37	60	60	52	62	37	45	49	38	15	810	303	617
GERMANY	90	49	113	203	50	53	71	78	57	60	48	42	47	22	893	295	688
ITALY	51	28	74	156	27	22	36	35	35	31	36	25	16	8	529	198	382
LUXEMBOURG	1	1	1	2	2	5	3	3	6	0	2	2	2	0	47	9	39
NETHERLANDS	46	11	44	102	20	26	21	22	26	40	14	16	20	10	378	118	306
DENMARK	21	7	14	41	6	14	18	7	8	9	6	9	5	3	137	43	115
IRELAND	10	9	6	26	6	16	16	3	7	10	8	3	9	9	118	24	104
U.K.	276	72	174	300	62	106	115	105	91	123	58	88	55	43	1392	584	1084
AUSTRIA	15	0	16	17	8	11	9	4	6	8	5	2	7	5	100	25	90
FINLAND	9	3	1	13	3	3	3	4	4	4	0	3	4	2	48	11	46
GREECE	1	3	7	17	4	4	6	9	9	9	6	2	5	1	73	20	54
NORWAY	21	4	17	23	6	6	4	6	3	5	5	7	3	0	97	26	92
PORTUGAL	14	8	10	12	3	4	2	9	11	3	3	6	3	1	78	21	71
SPAIN	32	14	25	86	29	32	36	13	17	27	17	18	22	13	349	83	298
SWEDEN	36	9	18	52	14	25	24	12	14	13	10	8	11	6	204	49	191
SWITZERLAND	25	15	96	100	18	19	21	28	23	19	7	10	9	10	375	122	278
TURKEY	2	6	0	16	1	1	2	1	0	0	0	0	0	0	41	9	34
OTHER EUROPE	3	2	0	3	3	1	1	1	1	2	5	1	5	5	37	9	31

TABLE 2.1.4 (CONTINUED)

COUNTRY OR REGION	NET FLOW UP TO 31-DEC-50	51-55	56-60	61-65	1966	1967	1968	1969	1970	1971	1972	1973	1974	1975	TOTAL ENTRIES 1951-75	TOTAL EXITS 1951-75	NET FLOW UP TO 1-JAN-76
					NO. OF ENTRIES DURING YEAR(S)												
N.AFR+M.EAST (TOTAL)	45	37	43	60	16	21	14	18	13	21	8	25	26	16	318	99	264
ALGERIA	5	4	4	2	0	4	1	1	0	1	0	2	3	0	19	10	14
EGYPT	7	6	1	2	0	3	0	1	1	0	0	0	0	3	20	7	20
IRAN	0	10	7	15	6	3	4	4	2	5	3	4	11	6	80	13	67
ISRAEL	4	1	3	4	1	1	2	2	0	2	0	2	1	0	22	6	20
LEBANON	0	2	2	11	1	2	1	4	2	2	0	3	2	0	30	8	22
MOROCCO	6	2	6	8	1	2	2	1	2	4	2	2	2	1	36	13	29
SAUDI ARABIA	6	1	0	0	1	3	0	3	3	1	0	2	4	5	20	4	22
OTHER N.AF+M.E.	17	12	20	18	5	4	4	4	4	3	3	9	6	1	91	38	70
E.+W.AFRICA (TOTAL)	15	33	25	77	21	23	20	35	32	20	18	21	29	12	366	60	321
GHANA	1	0	1	5	0	5	3	1	0	0	2	2	0	1	20	4	17
IVORY COAST	0	0	1	5	0	2	0	3	1	1	0	0	1	0	14	1	13
KENYA	1	3	4	7	0	2	1	5	2	1	0	1	2	1	32	6	27
LIBERIA	6	4	4	5	2	2	3	5	5	3	3	6	6	1	46	7	45
NIGERIA	1	2	2	17	2	3	2	7	6	3	0	6	5	4	59	3	57
ZAIRE	1	2	2	2	0	4	1	4	2	6	4	4	2	0	27	2	26
ZAMBIA	3	15	4	16	9	4	4	2	2	1	1	0	1	1	61	17	47
OTHER E.+W.AFR.	2	6	7	20	8	4	6	8	14	6	4	9	12	3	107	20	89
SOUTH ASIA (TOTAL)	29	10	35	50	8	5	10	8	6	6	1	8	3	3	153	38	144
INDIA	22	6	25	35	6	4	6	3	5	5	0	6	1	3	104	25	101
PAKISTAN	4	4	8	13	2	0	3	4	1	1	1	1	1	2	40	11	33
SRI LANKA	3	0	2	2	0	1	1	1	0	0	0	0	1	1	8	2	9
OTHER S.ASIA	0	0	0	0	0	0	0	0	0	0	0	1	0	0	1	0	1
EAST ASIA (TOTAL)	63	57	93	239	53	73	64	89	76	97	78	78	75	42	1114	173	1004
HONG KONG	1	3	13	24	4	8	6	11	9	16	9	9	7	2	115	19	97
INDONESIA	13	3	2	8	1	1	3	8	4	11	6	6	8	2	59	11	61
JAPAN	12	28	40	131	18	31	18	34	26	45	31	37	21	17	477	63	426
MALAYSIA	4	4	7	16	8	3	5	5	5	1	6	6	6	3	68	11	61
PHILIPPINES	23	15	19	24	6	8	5	5	4	9	9	9	11	5	108	23	108
SINGAPORE	5	1	1	8	6	1	4	8	9	8	7	6	8	6	76	7	74
S.KOREA	0	1	0	3	0	5	5	4	5	2	6	6	0	1	39	2	37
THAILAND	1	2	5	11	5	7	11	8	12	5	2	2	3	3	76	15	62
TAIWAN	3	0	5	8	4	7	7	7	5	6	3	7	7	3	64	8	59
OTHER E.ASIA	1	0	1	6	1	2	0	5	1	2	6	6	6	0	32	14	19
S.DOMINIONS (TOTAL)	174	96	160	289	52	91	90	85	74	83	54	54	39	20	1187	350	1011
AUSTRALIA	77	53	110	157	30	49	53	53	44	46	28	22	23	13	681	214	544
NEW ZEALAND	30	14	10	34	4	18	9	6	3	0	0	9	1	3	127	25	132
RHODESIA	7	3	6	15	2	2	1	3	1	0	7	2	0	0	36	17	26
S.AFRICA	60	26	34	83	16	22	27	23	26	28	19	22	13	4	343	94	309
OUTSIDE U.S. (TOTAL)	2196	989	1957	3225	669	912	1006	945	853	905	646	693	619	376	13795	4793	11198

CHAPTER 2 — THE PROLIFERATION OF FOREIGN SUBSIDIARIES
SECTION 1 — AN OVERVIEW
TABLE 5 — BY GEOGRAPHICAL REGION AND OWNERSHIP AT ENTRY

NO. OF ENTRIES, BY PERIOD AND OWNERSHIP AT ENTRY

(WHL=WHOLLY OWNED, 95-100%   MA=MAJORITY, 51-94%   CO=50%   MI=MINORITY, 5-49%   UN=UNKNOWN   ALL=TOTAL FOR PERIOD)

Column groups (each with WHL, MA, CO, MI, UN, ALL): 1951-1966 | 1967-1969 | 1970-1972 | 1973-1975

COUNTRY OR REGION	WHL	MA	CO	MI	UN	ALL	WHL	MA	CO	MI	UN	ALL	WHL	MA	CO	MI	UN	ALL	WHL	MA	CO	MI	UN	ALL
CANADA	674	52	27	47	39	839	322	9	11	8	13	363	204	7	12	7	1	231	110	5	6	9	3	133
LATIN AMER. (TOTAL)	1034	198	116	202	139	1689	355	68	38	47	19	527	317	47	27	56	2	449	218	36	26	65	3	348
C.AM.+CARIB.(TOTAL)	496	77	47	89	56	765	166	25	18	26	13	248	204	18	15	35	0	272	114	12	13	25	1	165
BAHAMAS	30	0	2	3	0	35	12	2	0	0	0	14	11	2	2	1	0	16	6	0	0	0	0	6
BERMUDA	18	1	2	1	0	22	15	2	0	0	0	17	23	0	1	0	0	24	17	0	1	0	0	18
COSTA RICA	8	2	3	2	3	18	11	4	0	1	0	16	12	1	0	0	0	13	3	2	0	1	0	6
GUATEMALA	17	2	3	4	1	27	9	1	0	2	0	12	13	0	0	1	0	14	8	0	1	1	0	11
JAMAICA	12	3	2	4	1	22	5	2	1	1	0	9	5	2	1	0	0	8	2	0	0	1	0	3
MEXICO	216	47	22	58	32	375	63	12	15	16	8	114	65	8	9	29	0	111	39	4	5	20	1	69
NETH.ANTILLES	6	1	1	0	0	8	14	0	0	1	2	17	34	0	0	1	0	35	6	0	0	0	1	7
NICARAGUA	3	5	1	4	2	15	2	0	1	0	0	3	5	1	0	1	0	7	0	0	1	0	0	1
PANAMA	126	8	5	6	11	156	24	3	1	3	2	33	22	1	1	0	0	24	15	1	1	0	0	17
OTHER C.AM+CAR.	60	8	7	7	5	87	11	0	0	4	1	16	16	1	0	3	0	20	18	3	2	4	0	27
S.AMERICA (TOTAL)	538	121	69	113	83	924	189	43	20	21	6	279	113	29	12	21	2	177	104	24	13	40	2	183
BOLIVIA	4	2	0	1	1	8	2	2	1	2	0	7	0	1	0	1	0	2	1	1	0	1	0	3
CHILE	20	8	5	3	1	37	11	6	1	2	1	21	7	1	1	4	0	13	4	3	0	1	0	8
COLOMBIA	75	20	13	23	11	142	17	1	2	1	1	22	7	3	3	1	1	15	7	3	1	3	0	14
ECUADOR	10	3	1	8	2	24	9	1	2	1	0	13	7	1	1	0	0	9	3	2	0	1	0	6
PERU	57	8	6	7	6	84	16	5	2	1	0	24	4	2	0	0	1	7	3	0	0	1	0	4
ARGENTINA	83	18	16	22	9	148	47	5	2	1	3	58	15	3	0	4	1	23	4	0	0	1	1	6
BRAZIL	128	27	16	19	20	210	52	16	7	4	1	80	50	11	5	1	4	71	51	11	10	23	1	96
URUGUAY	17	1	0	1	1	20	4	0	0	0	1	5	3	0	0	0	0	3	1	0	0	1	0	2
VENEZUELA	135	33	14	28	29	239	30	7	5	11	1	54	26	10	2	6	0	44	28	1	1	8	0	38
OTHER S.AMER.	9	1	0	0	2	12	1	0	0	0	1	2	2	0	0	0	0	2	2	0	0	0	0	2
EUROPE (TOTAL)	1829	314	283	229	203	2858	997	112	81	78	59	1327	867	112	68	79	11	1137	563	62	54	71	6	756
BELGIUM	95	14	14	10	13	146	85	10	10	2	0	107	51	5	6	8	1	71	38	4	2	4	0	48
FRANCE	190	79	40	58	25	392	104	39	8	16	5	172	88	33	3	17	3	144	52	23	11	15	1	102
GERMANY	250	49	40	36	40	415	153	17	11	18	3	202	125	22	11	7	0	165	90	7	8	5	1	111
ITALY	173	38	27	25	22	285	65	10	8	6	4	93	78	14	4	6	0	102	38	3	5	3	0	49
LUXEMBOURG	18	1	3	3	3	28	10	0	0	0	0	10	8	0	0	0	0	8	2	0	0	0	0	2
NETHERLANDS	119	15	21	9	23	177	51	3	7	3	5	69	71	3	0	5	1	80	44	3	0	5	0	52
DENMARK	51	2	8	2	9	69	27	0	0	0	2	29	20	1	0	1	1	23	13	0	0	3	0	16
IRELAND	35	3	2	5	6	47	23	0	1	0	1	25	22	0	1	1	1	25	20	0	0	1	0	21
U.K.	438	32	70	32	36	608	266	8	18	10	24	326	231	10	19	9	3	272	157	5	6	17	1	186
AUSTRIA	27	4	2	1	5	41	20	0	0	3	3	26	14	3	0	2	0	19	13	0	1	0	0	14
FINLAND	16	2	0	1	1	20	8	0	0	2	0	10	8	0	0	1	0	9	8	0	0	1	0	9
GREECE	16	7	2	1	2	31	10	1	0	2	1	21	10	1	0	2	0	13	4	2	1	1	0	8
NORWAY	37	3	1	1	5	50	10	0	2	0	1	13	18	0	1	4	0	23	7	0	3	1	0	11
PORTUGAL	23	4	1	3	4	35	10	2	2	0	1	15	10	4	1	3	1	19	5	2	0	2	0	9
SPAIN	51	30	40	28	5	154	42	16	9	9	5	81	35	7	16	4	0	61	22	4	14	11	2	53
SWEDEN	74	6	4	2	6	93	43	2	5	2	0	52	28	1	4	4	0	37	17	4	1	3	0	25
SWITZERLAND	197	14	4	3	11	229	59	4	2	2	0	68	38	0	2	2	2	49	26	1	1	1	0	29
TURKEY	15	9	0	1	0	30	5	2	0	2	0	9	3	0	0	2	0	5	0	0	0	0	0	0
OTHER EUROPE	4	2	1	1	0	8	2	0	0	1	0	3	10	0	0	5	0	15	7	0	0	4	0	11

TABLE 2.1.5 (CONTINUED)

(WHL=WHOLLY OWNED,95-100% MA=MAJORITY,51-94% CO=50% MI=MINORITY,5-49% UN=UNKNOWN ALL=TOTAL FOR PERIOD)

COUNTRY OR REGION	1951-1966 WHL	MA	CO	MI	UN	ALL	1967-1969 WHL	MA	CO	MI	UN	ALL	1970-1972 WHL	MA	CO	MI	UN	ALL	1973-1975 WHL	MA	CO	MI	UN	ALL
N.AFR+M.EAST(TOTAL)	91	24	15	18	8	156	32	7	4	10	0	53	23	8	2	8	1	42	29	11	6	21	0	67
ALGERIA	7	1	0	2	0	10	5	0	0	1	0	6	0	0	0	1	0	1	0	2	0	0	0	2
EGYPT	8	1	0	0	0	9	1	1	1	1	0	4	6	0	0	3	1	10	3	1	2	0	0	6
IRAN	19	5	7	4	3	38	7	0	2	2	0	11	2	1	0	0	0	3	6	1	2	12	0	21
ISRAEL	4	3	1	1	0	9	4	1	0	0	0	5	3	2	1	1	0	7	2	0	1	0	0	3
LEBANON	7	5	1	1	2	16	3	0	0	3	0	6	3	0	0	2	0	5	3	0	0	1	0	4
MOROCCO	11	5	1	0	0	17	4	1	0	0	0	5	1	2	0	0	0	3	2	2	1	0	0	5
SAUDI ARABIA	2	0	0	0	0	2	0	4	0	2	0	6	1	1	0	0	0	2	3	2	2	3	0	10
OTHER N.AF+M.E.	34	4	5	9	3	55	8	0	1	1	0	10	7	2	1	1	0	11	10	3	0	3	0	16
E.+W.AFRICA (TOTAL)	95	20	9	23	9	156	48	13	3	11	3	78	50	7	5	8	0	70	49	5	1	6	1	62
GHANA	3	1	1	0	2	7	4	1	3	1	0	9	1	0	1	0	0	2	2	0	0	0	0	2
IVORY COAST	1	1	2	1	1	6	4	1	0	0	0	5	1	0	0	0	0	1	2	0	0	0	0	2
KENYA	10	1	1	1	1	14	3	2	0	2	0	7	3	1	0	0	0	4	5	0	0	0	0	5
LIBERIA	12	1	1	1	0	15	8	0	0	0	2	10	7	1	0	2	0	10	10	0	0	3	0	13
NIGERIA	17	3	0	2	1	23	5	3	0	4	0	12	7	0	1	1	0	9	7	3	0	1	0	11
ZAIRE	5	0	0	1	0	6	6	0	0	1	0	7	9	0	1	0	0	10	2	0	0	0	0	2
ZAMBIA	22	10	2	8	2	44	9	1	0	0	0	10	2	0	0	0	0	2	3	0	0	0	0	3
OTHER E.+W.AFR.	25	3	2	9	2	41	9	5	0	3	1	18	20	5	2	5	0	32	18	2	1	2	1	24
SOUTH ASIA (TOTAL)	34	23	11	30	5	103	14	2	0	7	0	23	5	2	4	2	0	13	4	3	0	7	0	14
INDIA	19	10	11	27	5	72	9	1	0	3	0	13	4	0	4	2	0	10	0	2	0	7	0	9
PAKISTAN	13	11	0	3	0	27	4	0	0	3	0	7	1	2	0	0	0	3	3	1	0	0	0	4
SRI LANKA	2	2	0	0	0	4	1	1	0	1	0	3	0	0	0	0	0	0	1	0	0	0	0	1
OTHER S.ASIA	0	0	0	0	0	0	0	0	0	0	0	0	0	0	0	0	0	0	0	0	0	0	0	0
EAST ASIA (TOTAL)	222	40	58	80	42	442	117	22	41	38	8	226	128	26	56	36	5	251	105	15	47	27	1	195
HONG KONG	33	3	0	3	5	44	19	1	1	3	1	25	28	2	4	0	0	34	11	0	0	1	0	12
INDONESIA	11	1	0	1	1	14	8	1	2	1	0	12	7	1	3	6	0	17	9	0	5	2	0	16
JAPAN	69	8	52	65	23	217	26	5	27	19	6	83	28	7	45	22	0	102	25	8	32	10	0	75
MALAYSIA	27	4	1	2	1	35	9	2	0	2	0	13	6	2	0	0	0	8	9	1	0	2	0	12
PHILIPPINES	35	15	3	6	5	64	13	3	0	2	0	18	11	1	0	2	0	14	6	1	0	5	0	12
SINGAPORE	12	3	0	1	0	16	10	1	1	1	0	13	19	2	2	1	0	24	18	0	2	3	0	23
S.KOREA	2	0	1	0	1	4	4	3	4	3	0	14	6	2	2	0	0	10	6	3	2	0	0	11
THAILAND	13	6	1	0	3	23	15	3	3	4	0	25	17	3	0	3	0	23	4	0	0	1	0	5
TAIWAN	14	0	0	2	1	17	9	3	3	1	0	16	2	5	0	2	5	14	9	1	4	2	1	17
OTHER E ASIA	6	0	0	0	2	8	4	0	0	2	1	7	4	1	0	0	0	5	8	1	2	1	0	12
S.DOMINIONS (TOTAL)	389	66	55	41	46	597	208	20	17	16	5	266	156	18	17	17	3	211	79	11	6	15	2	113
AUSTRALIA	216	46	34	18	36	350	123	10	11	7	4	155	83	10	11	12	2	118	40	7	4	7	0	58
NEW ZEALAND	45	5	7	2	3	62	27	2	0	4	0	33	15	1	2	1	0	19	10	0	1	2	0	13
RHODESIA	20	2	2	0	2	26	5	0	1	0	0	6	1	0	0	0	0	1	2	1	0	0	0	3
S.AFRICA	108	13	12	21	5	159	53	8	5	5	1	72	57	7	4	4	1	73	27	3	1	6	2	39
OUTSIDE U.S. (TOTAL)	4368	737	574	670	491	6840	2093	253	195	215	107	2863	1750	227	191	213	23	2404	1157	148	146	221	16	1688

CHAPTER 2
SECTION 1$_6$
TABLE

- THE PROLIFERATION OF FOREIGN SUBSIDIARIES
-- AN OVERVIEW
--- BY GEOGRAPHICAL REGION AND ENTRY METHOD

NO. OF ENTRIES, BY PERIOD AND METHOD OF ENTRY

Legend: NEW=NEWLY FORMED   ACQ=ACQUIRED   DES=DESCENDENT   UNK=UNKNOWN   ALL=TOTAL FOR PERIOD

COUNTRY OR REGION	1951-1966 NEW	ACQ	DES	UNK	ALL	1967-1969 NEW	ACQ	DES	UNK	ALL	1970-1972 NEW	ACQ	DES	UNK	ALL	1973-1975 NEW	ACQ	DES	UNK	ALL
CANADA	243	456	14	126	839	108	239	7	9	363	63	157	7	4	231	43	80	4	6	133
LATIN AMER. (TOTAL)	917	533	19	220	1689	275	225	7	20	527	246	175	10	18	449	204	123	15	6	348
C.AM.+CARIB. (TOTAL)	402	248	9	106	765	131	104	2	11	248	158	97	3	14	272	104	50	8	3	165
BAHAMAS	20	6	0	9	35	10	3	0	1	14	12	3	0	1	16	3	2	0	1	6
BERMUDA	17	1	0	4	22	15	1	0	1	17	22	0	0	2	24	16	2	0	0	18
COSTA RICA	12	4	0	2	18	6	10	0	0	16	9	4	0	0	13	2	3	0	1	6
GUATEMALA	18	13	1	5	37	8	2	0	1	11	7	2	1	0	10	7	3	1	0	11
JAMAICA	13	5	0	4	22	6	3	0	0	9	7	1	0	0	8	2	1	0	0	3
MEXICO	173	166	4	32	375	44	67	0	3	114	34	72	2	3	111	37	27	4	1	69
NETH.ANTILLES	7	0	0	1	8	12	2	0	2	16	28	4	0	3	35	7	0	0	0	7
NICARAGUA	10	4	0	1	15	3	0	0	0	3	3	3	0	1	7	1	0	0	0	1
PANAMA	85	27	1	33	146	14	11	1	2	28	15	6	0	3	24	10	4	3	0	17
OTHER C.AM+CAR.	47	22	3	15	87	13	5	0	1	19	16	4	0	0	20	19	8	0	0	27
S.AMERICA (TOTAL)	515	285	10	114	924	144	121	5	9	279	88	78	7	4	177	100	73	7	3	183
BOLIVIA	5	2	0	1	8	2	1	0	0	3	3	0	0	0	3	3	0	0	0	3
CHILE	24	8	1	4	37	9	10	0	2	21	1	0	0	1	2	4	1	3	0	8
COLOMBIA	74	43	1	24	142	15	6	0	0	21	5	9	1	0	15	9	5	0	0	14
ECUADOR	16	7	0	1	24	9	2	0	0	11	8	0	0	1	9	7	1	0	0	8
PERU	51	24	0	9	84	12	13	0	0	25	7	0	0	0	7	1	2	1	0	4
ARGENTINA	66	60	3	19	148	31	25	1	1	58	10	12	0	1	23	2	3	0	1	6
BRAZIL	113	74	3	20	210	35	39	3	3	80	29	38	4	0	71	41	52	2	1	96
URUGUAY	8	9	0	3	20	2	3	0	0	5	1	2	0	0	3	3	1	0	0	4
VENEZUELA	151	54	2	32	239	29	22	0	3	54	24	17	2	1	44	28	8	1	1	38
OTHER S.AMER.	7	4	0	1	12	1	0	0	0	1	0	0	0	0	0	2	0	0	0	2
EUROPE (TOTAL)	1252	1153	24	429	2858	483	738	37	69	1327	398	675	30	34	1137	347	375	22	12	756
BELGIUM	76	61	1	8	146	48	53	3	0	104	32	36	2	1	71	31	12	3	2	48
FRANCE	162	180	6	44	392	58	99	5	10	172	44	91	4	5	144	42	54	4	2	102
GERMANY	170	183	3	59	415	68	123	5	6	202	64	86	8	7	165	41	67	3	0	111
ITALY	119	137	3	26	285	41	45	3	4	93	32	60	3	7	102	26	17	3	3	49
LUXEMBOURG	14	6	0	8	28	4	2	0	2	8	6	2	0	0	8	2	0	0	0	2
NETHERLANDS	87	60	1	29	177	30	31	2	6	69	24	51	2	3	80	23	25	1	3	52
DENMARK	31	27	0	11	69	10	14	2	3	29	9	14	0	0	23	11	5	0	0	16
IRELAND	23	18	1	5	47	13	11	2	3	29	14	10	0	1	25	16	5	0	0	21
U.K.	185	289	6	128	608	80	212	9	25	326	59	206	5	2	272	56	127	3	0	186
AUSTRIA	24	13	0	4	41	10	16	0	0	26	8	11	0	0	19	9	4	1	0	14
FINLAND	9	7	0	4	20	4	6	0	0	10	3	5	0	1	9	6	2	1	0	9
GREECE	20	6	0	5	31	13	6	0	2	21	8	3	0	2	13	7	0	0	1	8
NORWAY	23	9	0	18	50	8	5	0	0	13	12	9	1	1	23	10	1	0	0	11
PORTUGAL	22	7	0	6	35	8	7	0	0	15	9	9	0	1	19	8	1	0	0	9
SPAIN	68	71	0	14	153	39	38	2	2	81	30	26	3	2	61	26	23	3	1	53
SWEDEN	54	25	0	14	93	13	30	2	4	49	18	19	0	0	37	12	13	0	0	25
SWITZERLAND	140	48	2	39	229	32	32	2	2	68	16	31	1	1	49	11	18	0	0	29
TURKEY	21	2	0	7	30	3	6	0	0	9	3	6	0	0	9	0	0	0	0	0
OTHER EUROPE	4	4	0	0	8	1	2	0	0	3	7	0	1	0	8	10	1	0	0	11

TABLE 2.1.6 (CONTINUED)

Legend: NEW=NEWLY FORMED ACQ=ACQUIRED DES=DESCENDENT UNK=UNKNOWN ALL=TOTAL FOR PERIOD

COUNTRY OR REGION	1951-1966					1967-1969					1970-1972					1973-1975				
	NEW	ACQ	DES	UNK	ALL	NEW	ACQ	DES	UNK	ALL	NEW	ACQ	DES	UNK	ALL	NEW	ACQ	DES	UNK	ALL
N.AFR+M.EAST(TOTAL)	105	23	1	27	156	42	8	0	3	53	33	8	0	1	42	60	6	0	1	67
ALGERIA	8	1	1	0	10	4	1	0	1	6	1	0	0	0	1	2	0	0	0	2
EGYPT	7	1	0	1	9	4	0	0	0	4	1	0	0	0	1	6	0	0	0	6
IRAN	29	1	0	8	38	9	2	0	0	11	9	1	0	0	10	19	2	0	0	21
ISRAEL	6	2	0	1	9	3	2	0	0	5	4	1	0	0	5	2	1	0	0	3
LEBANON	7	7	0	2	16	5	1	0	0	6	3	1	0	0	4	2	1	0	1	4
MOROCCO	10	4	0	3	17	5	0	0	0	5	6	3	0	0	9	4	1	0	0	5
SAUDI ARABIA	2	0	0	0	2	4	0	0	2	6	1	1	0	0	2	10	0	0	0	10
OTHER N.AF+M.E.	36	7	0	12	55	8	2	0	0	10	8	1	0	1	10	15	1	0	0	16
E.+W.AFRICA (TOTAL)	98	22	0	36	156	62	10	1	5	78	59	8	1	2	70	52	7	0	3	62
GHANA	5	1	0	1	7	9	0	0	0	9	8	0	0	0	8	2	1	0	0	3
IVORY COAST	4	0	0	2	6	3	1	0	1	5	1	0	0	0	1	2	0	0	0	2
KENYA	9	2	0	3	14	5	2	0	0	7	4	2	0	0	6	5	0	0	0	5
LIBERIA	7	2	0	6	15	8	2	0	0	10	7	1	0	0	8	9	3	0	0	12
NIGERIA	10	7	0	6	23	10	2	0	0	12	13	2	0	0	15	10	1	0	0	11
ZAIRE	4	2	0	0	6	7	0	0	0	7	10	0	0	0	10	2	0	0	0	2
ZAMBIA	34	3	0	7	44	7	1	1	1	10	3	0	1	0	4	3	0	0	0	3
OTHER E.+W.AFR.	25	5	0	11	41	13	2	0	3	18	13	3	0	2	18	19	2	0	3	24
SOUTH ASIA (TOTAL)	64	33	0	6	103	10	12	1	0	23	6	5	0	2	13	10	4	0	0	14
INDIA	43	25	0	4	72	6	6	1	0	13	4	4	0	2	10	5	4	0	0	9
PAKISTAN	19	6	0	2	27	2	5	0	0	7	2	1	0	0	3	3	0	0	0	3
SRI LANKA	2	2	0	0	4	2	1	0	0	3	0	0	0	0	0	1	0	0	0	1
OTHER S.ASIA	0	0	0	0	0	0	0	0	0	0	0	0	0	0	0	1	0	0	0	1
EAST ASIA (TOTAL)	289	97	2	54	442	150	58	2	16	226	188	53	4	6	251	153	33	4	5	195
HONG KONG	29	10	0	5	44	16	8	0	1	25	16	17	0	1	34	10	3	0	0	13
INDONESIA	11	1	0	2	14	10	1	0	1	12	13	4	0	0	17	14	2	0	0	16
JAPAN	145	53	2	17	217	46	30	1	7	84	82	15	2	3	102	54	16	2	3	75
MALAYSIA	19	9	0	7	35	10	2	0	0	12	8	0	0	0	8	9	4	0	0	13
PHILIPPINES	38	15	0	11	64	10	6	0	2	18	10	4	0	0	14	11	3	0	0	14
SINGAPORE	10	3	0	3	16	11	1	0	1	13	19	4	0	1	24	18	2	0	0	20
S.KOREA	3	1	0	0	4	9	3	1	1	14	9	4	1	0	14	10	1	0	1	12
THAILAND	14	4	0	5	23	20	4	0	1	25	16	2	0	1	19	3	0	0	1	4
TAIWAN	14	1	0	2	17	12	2	0	2	16	12	2	1	0	15	13	1	1	0	15
OTHER E.ASIA	6	0	0	2	8	6	1	0	0	7	3	1	0	0	4	11	1	0	1	13
S.DOMINIONS (TOTAL)	266	252	5	74	597	96	153	8	9	266	79	120	4	8	211	37	73	2	1	113
AUSTRALIA	155	152	3	40	350	60	86	4	5	155	44	68	4	2	118	17	38	2	1	58
NEW ZEALAND	31	19	1	11	62	10	21	1	1	33	8	10	0	1	19	8	5	0	0	13
RHODESIA	13	9	0	4	26	3	3	0	0	6	1	0	0	0	1	0	3	0	0	3
S.AFRICA	67	72	1	19	159	23	43	3	3	72	26	42	0	5	73	12	27	0	0	39
OUTSIDE U.S. (TOTAL)	3234	2569	65	972	6840	1226	1443	63	131	2863	1072	1201	56	75	2404	906	701	48	33	1688

28

CHAPTER 2   - THE PROLIFERATION OF FOREIGN SUBSIDIARIES
SECTION 2   -- FLOW OF MANUFACTURING SUBSIDIARIES
TABLE 1   --- OVERVIEW BY PRINCIPAL INDUSTRY

NO. OF SUBSIDIARIES, BY PRINCIPAL INDUSTRY OF SUBSIDIARY AT TIME OF ENTRY INTO PARENT SYSTEM

PRINCIPAL INDUSTRY	NET FLOW UP TO 31-DEC-50	NO. OF ENTRIES DURING YEAR(S)													TOTAL ENTRIES 1951-75	TOTAL EXITS 1951-75	NET FLOW UP TO 1-JAN-76
		51-55	56-60	61-65	1966	1967	1968	1969	1970	1971	1972	1973	1974	1975			
BEVERAGES	26	6	12	17	6	3	22	2	8	12	10	5	7	0	110	39	97
TOBACCO	1	1	3	5	2	1	4	2	1	6	1	0	3	0	29	2	28
FOOD	117	44	111	201	50	58	52	80	48	46	51	25	22	21	809	312	614
TEXTILES+APPAREL	23	7	25	44	15	7	14	11	12	18	3	5	7	2	170	85	108
WOOD+FURNITURE	7	1	8	17	4	2	6	9	6	3	8	7	2	2	75	23	59
PAPER	25	29	50	84	14	15	15	13	9	18	4	8	6	9	274	92	207
PRINTING	5	3	6	13	10	7	15	5	3	5	4	2	2	0	75	15	65
INDUSTRIAL CHEM	54	25	73	89	23	14	26	10	10	20	12	6	9	11	328	123	259
PLASTICS	17	24	36	106	10	15	15	11	9	18	13	10	13	8	288	109	196
AGRIC CHEM	5	6	7	27	4	7	5	3	2	4	2	3	3	4	75	31	49
COSMETICS	42	10	51	52	23	21	17	16	8	51	5	25	9	5	293	69	266
DRUGS	74	38	92	121	10	24	60	40	22	26	14	11	19	12	489	85	478
OTHER CHEM	25	19	29	54	15	17	18	16	14	24	18	19	10	20	273	67	231
FABR PLASTICS	6	8	6	22	5	7	9	11	10	14	8	12	6	0	118	43	81
TIRES	45	8	11	14	3	3	2	1	0	3	3	0	0	3	51	19	77
REF PETROLEUM	30	17	25	35	8	6	14	10	9	4	3	2	4	6	143	52	121
OTH PETROLEUM	14	6	12	25	6	8	2	2	6	1	1	2	0	2	73	26	61
LEATHER	6	0	2	6	3	1	4	0	0	1	1	4	1	0	23	8	21
STONE+CLAY+CEMNT	3	3	10	10	4	1	6	8	5	2	6	5	5	0	65	17	51
ABRASIVES	13	15	15	14	8	11	5	5	15	11	7	8	3	4	121	26	108
GLASS	15	3	10	13	5	6	3	6	4	3	4	7	2	1	67	17	65
IRON+STEEL	3	0	1	9	1	6	6	7	3	4	4	7	5	3	56	19	40

TABLE 2.2.1 (CONTINUED)

PRINCIPAL INDUSTRY	NET FLOW UP TO 31-DEC-50	51-55	56-60	61-65	1966	1967	1968	1969	1970	1971	1972	1973	1974	1975	TOTAL ENTRIES 1951-75	TOTAL EXITS 1951-75	NET FLOW UP TO 1-JAN-76
						NO. OF ENTRIES DURING YEAR(S)											
NON-FERROUS	19	6	36	41	4	15	15	19	10	13	5	2	6	7	179	47	151
METAL CANS	9	3	9	15	1	1	6	4	1	1	1	0	2	2	46	13	42
OTHER FAB METAL	41	15	43	77	9	22	31	32	31	29	15	26	15	13	358	103	296
ENGINES+TURBIN	3	3	6	13	2	3	3	3	2	1	0	3	2	1	42	18	27
CONSTR MACH	21	13	22	29	1	22	8	12	13	11	11	5	18	7	172	52	141
FARM MACHINERY	4	3	5	14	2	0	0	3	4	1	0	0	3	2	37	12	29
OFFICE MC+COMPUT	33	9	10	9	3	3	4	3	3	4	1	5	0	1	61	36	58
SPEC MACHINERY	17	7	11	27	8	11	2	4	6	5	5	18	5	4	113	35	95
GENL MACHINERY	20	10	15	18	5	9	19	13	6	9	9	12	5	3	133	41	112
OTH NON-EL MC	15	5	9	27	7	6	12	19	10	4	14	11	3	5	132	37	110
EL LIGHT+WIRING	6	1	10	11	0	5	2	2	3	4	3	3	3	1	48	16	38
EL TRAN EQUIP	1	0	13	9	1	2	4	4	2	3	9	0	3	1	51	17	35
RADIO+TV+APPL	14	6	16	41	6	12	6	7	13	2	1	1	8	5	124	43	95
ELECTRONICS	1	3	11	20	3	9	9	4	14	6	8	13	4	3	107	21	87
OTHER ELEC	32	14	20	34	3	12	13	10	25	7	15	16	11	5	185	62	155
COMMUNICATION	18	5	7	12	1	2	9	4	6	1	0	7	3	1	58	21	55
MOTOR VEHIC	33	13	49	103	25	25	18	16	17	10	42	37	11	15	381	118	296
OTHER TRANSP	4	2	7	3	0	1	8	4	4	1	9	5	3	0	47	18	33
PRECISION	15	0	7	46	19	8	14	11	9	10	33	15	13	6	191	52	154
MISCELLANEOUS	85	28	59	85	14	29	43	29	27	30	18	25	13	9	409	163	331
TOTAL	947	419	960	1612	343	437	546	471	416	446	381	375	269	204	6879	2204	5622

CHAPTER 2   - THE PROLIFERATION OF FOREIGN SUBSIDIARIES
SECTION 2   -- FLOW OF MANUFACTURING SUBSIDIARIES
TABLE 2   --- BY PRINCIPAL INDUSTRY AND OWNERSHIP AT ENTRY

NO. OF MANUFACTURING SUBSIDIARIES ENTERING PARENT SYSTEMS IN EACH PERIOD, BY PARENT OWNERSHIP AT ENTRY

WHL=WHOLLY OWNED,95-100%   MA=MAJORITY,51-94%   CO=50%   MI=MINORITY,5-49%   UN=UNKNOWN   ALL=TOTAL FOR PERIOD

PRINCIPAL INDUSTRY	1951-1966						1967-1969						1970-1972						1973-1975					
	WHL	MA	CO	MI	UN	ALL	WHL	MA	CO	MI	UN	ALL	WHL	MA	CO	MI	UN	ALL	WHL	MA	CO	MI	UN	ALL
BEVERAGES	30	8	2	0	1	41	19	7	1	0	0	27	27	2	1	0	0	30	6	1	2	3	0	12
TOBACCO	6	4	0	0	1	11	3	0	0	3	1	7	2	3	0	3	0	8	1	2	0	0	0	3
FOOD	224	90	40	37	15	406	129	30	14	11	6	190	96	23	14	10	2	145	48	7	9	3	1	68
TEXTILES+APPAREL	49	6	19	9	8	91	25	1	4	2	0	32	21	5	6	1	0	33	8	1	0	5	0	14
WOOD+FURNITURE	17	3	6	3	1	30	13	0	2	1	1	17	14	2	2	0	0	17	9	0	0	2	0	11
PAPER	80	30	29	33	5	177	23	5	8	5	2	43	15	4	7	5	0	31	11	4	4	4	0	23
PRINTING	18	4	3	5	2	32	25	1	0	1	0	27	12	0	0	0	0	12	2	1	0	1	0	4
INDUSTRIAL CHEM	77	38	44	34	17	210	29	3	10	7	1	50	25	3	7	7	0	42	12	2	5	7	0	26
PLASTICS	64	23	30	37	22	176	26	6	5	1	3	41	19	5	7	7	2	40	17	0	5	6	1	31
AGRIC CHEM	16	7	9	9	3	44	7	2	0	3	3	15	5	6	2	1	0	8	5	0	2	1	0	8
COSMETICS	113	3	8	4	8	136	46	4	2	1	1	54	55	6	2	1	0	64	32	4	1	2	0	39
DRUGS	181	40	18	8	14	261	100	11	4	2	7	124	48	9	3	1	1	62	32	5	2	3	0	42
OTHER CHEM	53	23	12	26	3	117	26	7	10	7	1	51	27	11	10	8	0	56	27	4	8	10	0	49
FABR PLASTICS	15	4	11	7	4	41	16	5	3	3	0	27	21	3	6	2	0	32	13	3	1	2	0	18
TIRES	9	8	10	7	2	36	1	4	0	1	0	6	4	2	0	0	0	6	1	1	0	1	0	3
REF PETROLEUM	36	12	12	18	7	85	10	1	4	15	0	30	7	0	2	7	0	16	4	1	2	6	0	12
OTH PETROLEUM	19	3	17	2	8	49	3	1	3	5	0	12	5	1	2	1	0	8	1	0	2	1	0	4
LEATHER	7	1	1	1	1	11	3	0	1	1	0	5	2	0	0	0	0	2	3	0	1	1	0	5
STONE+CLAY+CEMNT	12	2	1	7	5	27	8	3	1	1	2	15	8	1	3	3	0	13	6	1	1	2	0	10
ABRASIVES	24	4	4	16	1	52	9	5	4	4	0	21	18	1	6	4	0	33	9	3	2	1	0	15
GLASS	11	6	5	8	1	31	5	2	6	2	0	15	6	2	1	2	0	11	4	3	2	1	0	10
IRON+STEEL	4	1	2	3	1	11	12	3	2	1	1	19	4	4	2	1	0	11	5	3	1	6	0	15

TABLE 2.2.2 (CONTINUED)

(WHL=WHOLLY OWNED,95-100% MA=MAJORITY,51-94% CO=50% MI=MINORITY,5-49% UN=UNKNOWN ALL=TOTAL FOR PERIOD)

PRINCIPAL INDUSTRY	1951-1966						1967-1969						1970-1972						1973-1975					
	WHL	MA	CO	MI	UN	ALL	WHL	MA	CO	MI	UN	ALL	WHL	MA	CO	MI	UN	ALL	WHL	MA	CO	MI	UN	ALL
NON-FERROUS	34	17	15	17	4	87	23	4	7	13	2	49	18	1	4	5	0	28	7	0	1	7	0	15
METAL CANS	11	5	1	7	4	28	7	1	1	2	0	11	3	0	0	0	0	3	2	0	0	2	0	4
OTHER FAB METAL	79	14	13	23	15	144	57	9	11	5	3	85	56	6	5	8	0	75	31	5	4	13	1	54
ENGINES+TURBIN	13	5	3	1	2	24	7	0	0	2	0	9	2	1	0	0	0	3	2	0	2	2	0	6
CONSTR MACH	36	7	10	7	5	65	26	11	1	3	1	42	17	7	4	7	0	35	16	5	1	8	0	30
FARM MACHINERY	8	6	2	7	1	24	2	0	0	0	1	3	2	0	1	2	0	5	4	0	0	1	0	5
OFFICE MC+COMPUT	21	5	0	5	0	31	8	0	1	1	0	10	12	1	0	1	0	14	4	1	1	0	0	6
SPEC MACHINERY	25	4	6	11	7	53	12	3	1	1	0	17	9	2	2	2	1	16	19	2	1	4	1	27
GENL MACHINERY	31	3	5	5	4	48	26	4	4	5	2	41	13	2	2	7	0	24	10	5	3	2	0	20
OTH NON-EL MC	24	4	5	10	5	48	29	2	2	2	2	37	19	4	3	2	0	28	15	1	1	2	0	19
EL LIGHT+WIRING	10	4	1	4	3	22	5	2	0	2	0	9	7	2	1	0	0	10	2	3	1	1	0	7
EL TRAN EQUIP	13	4	2	1	3	23	8	1	0	1	0	10	13	1	0	0	0	14	3	1	0	0	0	4
RADIO+TV+APPL	43	15	7	1	3	69	16	2	1	6	0	25	12	1	0	3	0	16	10	2	1	1	0	14
ELECTRONICS	17	5	3	11	1	37	15	2	3	2	0	22	21	2	2	3	0	28	14	2	4	0	0	20
OTHER ELEC	32	4	10	9	16	71	22	5	1	3	4	35	31	5	4	7	0	47	19	2	4	7	0	32
COMMUNICATION	20	1	1	1	2	25	13	1	1	0	0	15	5	1	0	1	0	7	8	1	1	1	0	11
MOTOR VEHIC	72	31	21	52	14	190	35	7	4	12	1	59	36	9	10	14	0	69	30	9	8	14	2	63
OTHER TRANSP	2	3	1	4	2	12	9	2	2	0	0	13	11	1	1	1	0	14	5	0	0	3	0	8
PRECISION	54	9	3	4	2	72	23	4	2	3	1	33	42	8	1	1	0	52	20	5	3	6	0	34
MISCELLANEOUS	112	21	20	16	17	186	69	8	10	10	4	101	51	11	4	7	2	75	26	10	6	4	1	47
TOTAL	1722	490	402	476	244	3334	948	169	134	152	51	1454	819	155	127	134	8	1243	503	97	94	146	8	848

CHAPTER 2   - THE PROLIFERATION OF FOREIGN SUBSIDIARIES
SECTION 2   -- FLOW OF MANUFACTURING SUBSIDIARIES
TABLE 3   --- BY PRINCIPAL INDUSTRY AND ENTRY METHOD

NO. OF MANUFACTURING SUBSIDIARIES ENTERING PARENT SYSTEMS IN EACH PERIOD, BY METHOD OF ENTRY

(NEW=NEWLY FORMED)   ACQ=ACQUIRED   DES=DESCENDENT   UNK=UNKNOWN   ALL=TOTAL FOR PERIOD

PRINCIPAL INDUSTRY	1951-1966					1967-1969					1970-1972					1973-1975				
	NEW	ACQ	DES	UNK	ALL	NEW	ACQ	DES	UNK	ALL	NEW	ACQ	DES	UNK	ALL	NEW	ACQ	DES	UNK	ALL
BEVERAGES	21	19	0	1	41	5	22	0	0	27	3	27	0	0	30	5	6	1	0	12
TOBACCO	4	7	0	0	11	0	7	0	0	7	4	4	0	0	8	2	0	1	0	3
FOOD	120	258	7	21	406	37	137	6	10	190	27	114	1	3	145	29	38	1	0	68
TEXTILES+APPAREL	55	32	0	4	91	9	23	0	0	32	11	22	0	0	33	7	7	0	0	14
WOOD+FURNITURE	10	19	0	1	30	5	11	1	0	17	5	12	0	0	17	2	8	0	1	11
PAPER	53	120	1	3	177	16	25	1	1	43	7	20	3	1	31	9	13	1	0	23
PRINTING	15	16	1	0	32	11	15	1	0	27	5	6	1	0	12	3	1	0	0	4
INDUSTRIAL CHEM	114	79	1	16	210	28	19	3	0	50	20	21	1	0	42	17	9	0	0	26
PLASTICS	100	63	3	10	176	17	22	0	2	41	19	21	0	0	40	21	9	1	0	31
AGRIC CHEM	27	12	0	5	44	8	4	0	3	15	5	3	0	0	8	5	3	0	0	8
COSMETICS	71	55	0	10	136	26	24	0	4	54	10	53	1	0	64	13	26	0	0	39
DRUGS	154	93	1	13	261	41	78	2	3	124	33	23	2	4	62	26	13	2	1	42
OTHER CHEM	53	56	1	7	117	20	28	2	1	51	30	24	1	1	56	24	25	0	0	49
FABR PLASTICS	18	20	0	3	41	13	12	1	1	27	12	18	1	1	32	5	13	0	0	18
TIRES	25	10	0	1	36	5	0	1	0	6	3	3	0	0	6	3	0	0	0	3
REF PETROLEUM	39	25	1	20	85	23	5	1	1	30	13	3	0	0	16	7	1	4	0	12
OTH PETROLEUM	35	11	1	2	49	6	5	0	1	12	5	2	0	1	8	3	1	0	0	4
LEATHER	3	8	0	0	11	1	3	0	1	5	1	1	0	0	2	1	4	0	0	5
STONE+CLAY+CEMNT	11	14	0	2	27	3	11	1	0	15	2	10	0	1	13	3	6	0	1	10
ABRASIVES	29	21	1	1	52	8	12	0	1	21	9	20	3	1	33	9	6	0	0	15
GLASS	14	17	0	0	31	3	10	1	1	15	6	5	0	0	11	5	3	2	0	10
IRON+STEEL	5	6	0	0	11	5	14	0	0	19	5	3	2	1	11	2	13	0	0	15

TABLE 2.2.3 (CONTINUED)

Legend: NEW=NEWLY FORMED ACQ=ACQUIRED DES=DESCENDENT UNK=UNKNOWN ALL=TOTAL FOR PERIOD

PRINCIPAL INDUSTRY	1951-1966					1967-1969					1970-1972					1973-1975				
	NEW	ACQ	DES	UNK	ALL	NEW	ACQ	DES	UNK	ALL	NEW	ACQ	DES	UNK	ALL	NEW	ACQ	DES	UNK	ALL
NON-FERROUS	40	43	1	3	87	17	30	1	1	49	7	18	3	0	28	4	10	1	0	15
METAL CANS	11	12	4	1	28	6	5	0	0	11	0	3	0	0	3	1	3	0	0	4
OTHER FAB METAL	42	88	5	9	144	29	50	1	5	85	22	51	2	0	75	25	28	0	1	54
ENGINES+TURBIN	8	13	2	1	24	3	6	0	0	9	2	1	0	0	3	2	1	1	0	6
CONSTR MACH	31	31	2	1	65	9	31	2	0	42	10	22	3	0	35	14	15	1	1	30
FARM MACHINERY	9	14	1	0	24	2	1	0	0	3	3	2	0	0	5	0	5	0	0	5
OFFICE MC+COMPUT	9	21	1	0	31	7	2	1	0	10	6	5	1	2	14	3	2	1	1	6
SPEC MACHINERY	19	32	0	2	53	4	12	0	1	17	5	8	2	1	16	4	23	0	0	27
GENL MACHINERY	20	23	0	5	48	7	32	2	0	41	8	14	2	0	24	11	8	1	0	20
OTH NON-EL MC	12	34	0	2	48	8	28	1	0	37	8	19	1	0	28	7	9	3	0	19
EL LIGHT+WIRING	6	15	0	1	22	3	6	0	0	9	3	6	0	1	10	0	5	2	0	7
EL TRAN EQUIP	14	9	0	0	23	3	7	0	0	10	0	12	2	0	14	0	4	0	0	4
RADIO+TV+APPL	40	27	0	2	69	3	20	1	1	25	7	9	0	0	16	6	8	0	0	14
ELECTRONICS	15	20	0	2	37	14	8	0	0	22	16	11	0	1	28	13	7	0	0	20
OTHER ELEC	33	26	1	11	71	20	12	2	1	35	16	30	1	0	47	16	15	1	0	32
COMMUNICATION	9	16	0	0	25	8	7	0	0	15	4	3	0	0	7	5	4	1	1	11
MOTOR VEHIC	70	111	4	5	190	21	36	2	0	59	24	42	1	2	69	10	52	1	0	63
OTHER TRANSP	5	5	4	1	12	3	10	0	0	13	7	6	0	1	14	3	5	0	0	8
PRECISION	12	56	4	0	72	14	18	1	0	33	12	39	0	1	52	14	20	0	0	34
MISCELLANEOUS	96	66	2	22	186	28	70	1	2	101	9	62	2	2	75	11	31	4	1	47
TOTAL	1477	1623	46	188	3334	499	878	36	41	1454	404	778	36	25	1243	352	460	30	6	848

CHAPTER 2   - THE PROLIFERATION OF FOREIGN SUBSIDIARIES
SECTION 2   -- FLOW OF MANUFACTURING SUBSIDIARIES
TABLE 4   --- BY GEOGRAPHICAL REGION

NO. OF SUBSIDIARIES WITH MANUFACTURING ACTIVITY AT TIME OF ENTRY INTO PARENT SYSTEM

COUNTRY OR REGION	NET FLOW UP TO 31-DEC-50	NO. OF ENTRIES DURING YEAR(S)													TOTAL ENTRIES 1951-75	TOTAL EXITS 1951-75	NET FLOW UP TO 1-JAN-76
		51-55	56-60	61-65	1966	1967	1968	1969	1970	1971	1972	1973	1974	1975			
CANADA	222	92	114	167	35	53	71	70	52	44	45	41	23	18	825	414	633
LATIN AMER. (TOTAL)	254	122	296	383	78	98	102	72	70	75	66	87	54	45	1548	526	1276
C.AM.+CARIB.(TOTAL)	87	43	121	162	38	45	40	34	32	37	29	27	22	21	651	211	527
BAHAMAS	1	0	0	1	1	1	2	0	0	0	0	0	0	0	5	0	6
BERMUDA	0	0	2	1	0	0	0	0	0	0	0	0	0	0	3	1	2
COSTA RICA	1	0	0	9	0	3	2	4	2	1	0	2	2	0	25	5	21
GUATEMALA	2	0	6	14	1	1	2	2	1	4	0	2	1	0	39	9	32
JAMAICA	1	2	3	4	4	0	2	1	1	0	0	2	2	2	23	4	20
MEXICO	59	33	84	99	25	32	27	19	17	27	22	19	14	12	430	134	355
NETH.ANTILLES	0	0	0	1	0	3	0	0	0	1	2	0	0	0	7	2	5
NICARAGUA	0	0	1	7	3	0	2	0	0	2	2	0	0	1	16	3	13
PANAMA	3	5	5	11	3	1	1	1	2	0	0	0	0	1	30	6	27
OTHER C.AM+CAR.	20	3	20	15	0	4	2	5	4	2	3	2	5	6	73	47	46
S.AMERICA (TOTAL)	167	79	175	221	40	53	62	38	38	38	37	60	32	24	897	315	749
BOLIVIA	2	0	0	0	0	0	1	0	0	0	0	1	1	0	3	4	1
CHILE	13	2	4	14	2	8	4	2	1	0	0	2	2	2	41	26	28
COLOMBIA	23	13	24	49	7	3	6	2	2	7	0	4	2	4	126	43	106
ECUADOR	1	0	3	9	0	1	2	2	1	1	1	1	2	2	24	6	19
PERU	13	6	12	17	3	5	3	2	2	1	0	3	0	0	53	26	40
ARGENTINA	41	11	29	45	8	8	12	11	7	5	3	3	0	0	142	55	128
BRAZIL	47	29	54	35	12	18	20	13	14	17	20	32	21	12	297	105	239
URUGUAY	9	2	1	3	0	1	0	0	1	0	0	1	0	1	10	1	18
VENEZUELA	18	16	46	47	7	9	14	10	8	7	10	14	4	4	196	48	166
OTHER S.AMER.	0	0	2	2	1	0	0	0	0	0	0	0	0	0	5	1	4
EUROPE (TOTAL)	346	128	361	684	159	176	259	215	203	214	190	168	119	89	2965	972	2339
BELGIUM	17	3	24	40	8	19	13	26	18	11	10	3	8	12	195	61	151
FRANCE	54	20	69	106	23	25	31	23	30	20	32	30	18	12	439	160	333
GERMANY	49	26	52	100	21	19	43	49	29	30	39	29	18	14	469	141	377
ITALY	17	14	50	91	15	10	20	22	25	21	23	11	7	7	314	106	225
LUXEMBOURG	1	0	0	4	0	0	0	0	0	0	0	1	0	5	12	0	13
NETHERLANDS	17	4	21	40	4	8	10	11	10	18	7	5	8	0	151	49	119
DENMARK	6	1	4	15	5	1	7	2	4	1	5	3	0	4	52	18	40
IRELAND	4	6	14	14	3	1	10	2	4	5	4	2	4	6	65	13	56
U.K.	132	33	90	145	36	63	67	42	50	68	37	62	26	15	734	299	567
AUSTRIA	9	0	4	4	4	1	5	0	1	1	2	0	1	2	31	10	30
FINLAND	0	0	0	5	0	0	0	0	1	1	0	0	2	0	10	2	8
GREECE	0	1	4	8	3	4	3	6	2	2	3	0	4	0	39	7	32
NORWAY	7	0	4	5	3	0	1	2	1	3	1	1	0	0	22	9	20
PORTUGAL	5	3	5	9	2	3	2	5	7	3	2	2	1	9	43	9	39
SPAIN	13	10	16	58	22	16	23	10	10	16	13	12	10	5	225	49	189
SWEDEN	10	3	18	18	3	3	13	3	3	4	4	2	2	3	74	15	69
SWITZERLAND	4	1	5	10	4	0	5	7	3	4	3	2	2	0	49	13	40
TURKEY	0	2	4	10	1	1	1	1	1	0	0	0	0	2	24	6	18
OTHER EUROPE	1	0	0	2	2	1	0	1	0	3	2	1	3	0	17	5	13

TABLE 2 .2 .4 (CONTINUED)

COUNTRY OR REGION	NET FLOW UP TO 31-DEC-50	NO. OF ENTRIES DURING YEAR(S)													TOTAL ENTRIES 1951-75	TOTAL EXITS 1951-75	NET FLOW UP TO 1-JAN-76
		51-55	56-60	61-65	1966	1967	1968	1969	1970	1971	1972	1973	1974	1975			
N.AFR+M.EAST(TOTAL)	7	5	15	27	6	10	8	7	2	8	2	8	11	8	117	19	105
ALGERIA	0	0	1	1	0	1	0	1	0	0	0	0	1	0	4	1	3
EGYPT	0	0	0	0	0	1	0	0	0	0	0	0	0	2	3	0	3
IRAN	2	2	3	8	3	2	2	2	1	0	0	2	7	3	35	2	33
ISRAEL	0	0	3	3	0	1	2	2	0	4	2	2	0	0	17	3	16
LEBANON	2	0	1	3	0	1	1	1	0	0	0	1	1	0	10	2	8
MOROCCO	2	0	5	5	0	1	1	0	1	1	2	2	0	0	18	2	18
SAUDI ARABIA	0	0	0	0	0	1	2	2	0	1	0	0	1	3	8	0	8
OTHER N.AF+M.E.	3	3	2	7	3	2	1	0	0	2	0	1	1	0	22	9	16
E.+W.AFRICA (TOTAL)	0	2	6	25	5	9	7	14	8	6	7	0	4	4	97	7	90
GHANA	0	0	1	2	0	3	0	1	0	0	0	0	0	0	7	1	6
IVORY COAST	0	0	0	2	0	0	0	0	0	0	0	0	0	0	4	0	4
KENYA	0	1	3	4	0	1	1	2	0	2	2	0	1	2	19	3	16
LIBERIA	0	0	0	1	0	1	0	3	0	0	0	1	0	0	1	0	1
NIGERIA	0	0	2	10	1	1	1	0	0	1	4	0	2	2	22	1	21
ZAIRE	0	0	0	0	0	3	0	1	2	3	0	2	0	0	11	0	11
ZAMBIA	0	1	0	3	3	2	2	1	1	0	0	0	1	0	13	1	12
OTHER E.+W.AFR.	0	0	0	3	1	1	3	4	5	1	1	1	1	0	20	1	19
SOUTH ASIA (TOTAL)	9	3	26	42	4	2	9	4	5	4	0	7	1	2	109	18	100
INDIA	7	3	19	32	3	1	5	1	4	3	0	5	1	2	79	14	72
PAKISTAN	1	0	5	8	1	0	3	2	1	1	0	1	0	0	22	3	20
SRI LANKA	1	0	2	2	0	1	1	1	0	0	0	0	0	0	7	1	7
OTHER S.ASIA	0	0	0	0	0	0	0	0	0	0	0	1	0	0	1	0	1
EAST ASIA (TOTAL)	24	24	45	137	25	38	37	52	42	52	41	40	37	22	592	84	532
HONG KONG	5	1	3	6	0	2	3	3	3	10	3	2	2	1	37	7	30
INDONESIA	6	0	0	1	0	0	1	3	2	8	2	3	4	1	25	5	25
JAPAN	1	14	21	78	12	19	12	24	15	26	19	21	13	10	284	41	249
MALAYSIA	10	1	1	1	3	3	3	3	3	1	3	5	1	1	33	4	30
PHILIPPINES	2	8	11	19	3	3	2	3	3	3	3	2	1	2	60	9	61
SINGAPORE	0	0	0	5	0	0	2	4	6	2	2	6	6	4	37	3	36
S.KOREA	0	0	0	5	2	3	5	3	4	1	3	0	0	0	29	1	28
THAILAND	0	0	5	8	8	5	5	5	4	2	3	5	3	1	39	6	33
TAIWAN	0	0	2	7	2	5	4	2	0	1	0	1	0	0	42	5	37
OTHER E.ASIA	0	0	0	2	0	0	0	2	0	0	0	0	0	0	6	3	3
S.DOMINIONS (TOTAL)	85	43	97	147	31	51	53	37	34	43	30	24	20	16	626	164	547
AUSTRALIA	37	25	71	73	18	30	33	18	26	26	13	12	11	10	366	108	295
NEW ZEALAND	15	6	4	16	2	2	0	0	1	5	4	4	1	0	64	6	73
RHODESIA	1	0	2	2	2	0	5	3	1	0	0	1	1	0	16	4	13
S.AFRICA	32	12	20	51	9	11	15	13	6	12	13	8	7	3	180	46	166
OUTSIDE U.S. (TOTAL)	947	419	960	1612	343	437	546	471	416	446	381	375	269	204	6879	2204	5622

CHAPTER 2 - THE PROLIFERATION OF FOREIGN SUBSIDIARIES
SECTION 2 -- FLOW OF MANUFACTURING SUBSIDIARIES
TABLE 5 --- BY GEOGRAPHICAL REGION AND OWNERSHIP AT ENTRY

NO. OF MANUFACTURING SUBSIDIARIES ENTERING PARENT SYSTEMS IN EACH PERIOD, BY PARENT OWNERSHIP AT ENTRY

(WHL=WHOLLY OWNED,95-100% MA=MAJORITY,51-94% CO=50% MI=MINORITY,5-49% UN=UNKNOWN ALL=TOTAL FOR PERIOD)

COUNTRY OR REGION	1951-1966						1967-1969						1970-1972						1973-1975					
	WHL	MA	CO	MI	UN	ALL	WHL	MA	CO	MI	UN	ALL	WHL	MA	CO	MI	UN	ALL	WHL	MA	CO	MI	UN	ALL
CANADA	321	32	18	20	17	408	175	5	8	2	4	194	128	3	7	2	1	141	71	3	4	2	2	82
LATIN AMER. (TOTAL)	408	146	88	158	79	879	148	50	26	38	10	272	123	38	19	29	2	211	97	26	16	46	1	186
C.AM.+CARIB.(TOTAL)	169	57	35	73	30	364	61	17	13	20	8	119	61	13	10	14	0	98	39	9	4	18	0	70
BAHAMAS	0	0	0	2	0	2	3	0	0	0	0	3	0	0	0	0	0	0	0	0	0	0	0	0
BERMUDA	2	0	0	1	0	3	0	0	0	0	0	0	0	0	0	0	0	0	0	0	0	0	0	0
COSTA RICA	2	2	3	2	1	10	5	3	0	1	0	9	3	0	0	0	0	3	1	2	0	0	0	3
GUATEMALA	5	7	2	3	4	21	7	0	0	2	0	9	3	0	0	0	0	3	5	1	0	0	0	6
JAMAICA	4	3	1	4	0	12	2	2	0	0	0	4	1	4	0	0	0	5	1	0	1	0	0	2
MEXICO	119	35	20	50	17	241	37	9	12	14	6	78	40	6	9	11	0	66	27	3	1	14	0	45
NETH.ANTILLES	0	0	0	0	1	1	0	0	0	0	1	1	5	0	0	0	0	5	0	0	0	0	0	0
NICARAGUA	0	4	1	4	2	11	1	0	1	0	0	2	1	1	1	0	0	3	0	0	0	0	0	0
PANAMA	16	0	2	3	1	22	2	0	0	0	0	2	4	1	0	0	0	5	1	0	0	0	0	1
OTHER C.AM+CAR.	21	6	6	4	4	41	4	3	0	3	1	11	4	1	0	3	0	8	4	3	2	4	0	13
S.AMERICA (TOTAL)	239	89	53	85	49	515	87	33	13	18	2	153	62	25	9	15	2	113	58	17	12	28	1	116
BOLIVIA	0	0	0	0	0	0	0	0	0	0	0	0	0	2	0	0	0	2	0	1	0	0	0	1
CHILE	9	7	4	0	2	22	5	6	0	1	0	12	0	0	1	0	0	1	3	2	0	1	0	6
COLOMBIA	38	17	10	17	11	93	7	1	2	1	0	11	5	1	3	3	0	12	4	2	1	3	0	10
ECUADOR	3	2	0	6	1	12	4	0	0	1	0	5	2	0	0	0	0	2	1	2	1	1	0	5
PERU	22	4	4	6	2	38	3	3	1	1	0	8	1	2	0	1	0	4	2	1	0	0	0	3
ARGENTINA	43	14	11	20	5	93	24	3	1	1	2	31	8	2	0	4	1	15	2	0	0	0	1	3
BRAZIL	69	20	13	16	12	130	28	14	5	4	0	51	32	11	4	3	1	51	31	8	9	17	0	65
URUGUAY	5	0	0	1	0	6	1	1	0	0	0	2	1	0	0	0	0	1	0	0	0	1	0	1
VENEZUELA	48	24	11	17	16	116	15	5	4	9	0	33	13	7	1	4	0	25	15	1	1	5	0	22
OTHER S.AMER.	2	1	0	2	0	5	0	0	0	0	0	0	0	0	0	0	0	0	0	0	0	0	0	0
EUROPE (TOTAL)	692	201	183	157	99	1332	461	67	52	46	24	650	432	78	41	52	4	607	251	44	31	46	4	376
BELGIUM	40	11	12	6	6	75	45	3	7	3	0	58	26	4	2	7	0	39	16	3	3	1	0	23
FRANCE	92	45	28	34	19	218	44	18	6	10	1	79	44	24	1	12	1	82	23	17	7	12	1	60
GERMANY	103	29	26	25	16	199	81	11	7	7	5	111	67	18	7	6	0	98	48	7	4	2	0	61
ITALY	89	32	19	16	14	170	32	8	6	3	3	52	51	13	2	3	0	69	15	5	1	2	0	23
LUXEMBOURG	4	0	0	0	0	4	2	0	0	0	0	2	5	0	0	0	0	5	1	0	0	0	0	1
NETHERLANDS	39	8	11	4	7	69	22	2	2	1	1	28	32	1	1	2	1	37	14	0	1	2	0	17
DENMARK	18	1	2	2	1	24	12	0	0	0	0	12	8	1	0	1	0	10	5	1	0	0	0	6
IRELAND	18	2	2	2	3	27	12	0	1	0	0	13	11	0	1	0	1	13	11	0	0	1	0	12
U.K.	199	22	38	27	18	304	138	6	14	8	6	172	133	2	14	5	1	155	86	4	4	8	1	103
AUSTRIA	7	2	0	2	1	12	6	1	0	2	0	9	3	2	0	1	0	6	3	0	1	0	0	4
FINLAND	3	2	0	0	1	6	0	0	0	0	0	0	1	0	0	1	0	2	1	0	0	1	0	2
GREECE	7	3	0	4	2	16	6	1	1	2	3	13	4	2	0	0	0	6	1	1	1	1	0	4
NORWAY	6	1	3	1	1	12	1	1	0	1	0	3	5	0	0	1	0	6	1	0	0	0	0	1
PORTUGAL	8	3	1	3	4	19	7	1	1	0	1	10	7	1	0	3	0	11	1	1	0	1	0	3
SPAIN	22	24	34	25	1	106	23	11	4	7	4	49	17	7	12	3	0	39	13	2	4	10	2	31
SWEDEN	17	5	4	1	3	30	17	0	1	1	0	19	10	1	1	1	0	13	4	2	5	1	0	12
SWITZERLAND	13	4	2	0	1	20	9	2	1	0	0	12	8	2	0	0	0	10	6	1	0	0	0	7
TURKEY	5	7	0	4	1	17	3	2	1	0	0	6	0	0	0	1	0	1	0	0	0	0	0	0
OTHER EUROPE	2	0	1	1	0	4	1	0	0	1	0	2	0	0	0	5	0	5	2	0	0	4	0	6

TABLE 2 . 2 . 5 (CONTINUED)

(WHL=WHOLLY OWNED,95-100% MA=MAJORITY,51-94% CO=50% MI=MINORITY,5-49% UN=UNKNOWN ALL=TOTAL FOR PERIOD)

COUNTRY OR REGION	1951-1966						1967-1969						1970-1972						1973-1975					
	WHL	MA	CO	MI	UN	ALL	WHL	MA	CO	MI	UN	ALL	WHL	MA	CO	MI	UN	ALL	WHL	MA	CO	MI	UN	ALL
N.AFR+M.EAST(TOTAL)	19	11	10	9	4	53	10	5	2	8	0	25	3	4	1	4	0	12	3	6	4	14	0	27
ALGERIA	0	0	0	2	0	2	2	0	0	0	0	2	0	0	0	0	0	0	0	0	0	0	0	0
EGYPT	0	0	0	0	0	0	0	0	1	0	0	1	0	0	0	0	0	0	2	0	0	0	0	2
IRAN	5	4	3	1	3	16	3	1	1	2	0	6	0	0	0	1	0	1	2	0	0	10	0	12
ISRAEL	3	1	1	1	0	6	1	0	1	1	0	4	0	2	0	1	0	4	0	1	2	0	0	3
LEBANON	3	3	0	1	0	6	0	1	0	1	0	3	1	0	1	0	0	4	0	1	0	1	0	1
MOROCCO	4	2	0	0	0	8	0	1	0	1	0	3	0	2	0	2	0	4	0	1	1	2	0	3
SAUDI ARABIA	0	0	0	0	0	0	0	1	0	1	0	3	0	1	0	1	0	1	0	2	1	1	0	4
OTHER N.AF+M.E.	4	1	5	4	1	15	1	0	0	2	0	3	2	0	0	0	0	2	1	1	0	1	0	2
E.+W.AFRICA (TOTAL)	20	5	4	7	2	38	11	8	1	7	3	30	14	1	2	4	0	21	6	3	0	1	0	8
GHANA	1	1	0	0	0	2	1	0	1	0	1	4	0	0	0	0	0	0	0	0	0	0	0	0
IVORY COAST	0	1	0	2	0	3	2	2	0	0	1	2	0	0	2	0	0	0	0	0	0	0	0	0
KENYA	4	1	2	1	0	8	1	0	0	0	0	5	1	0	2	0	0	3	3	0	0	1	0	3
LIBERIA	1	0	0	0	1	2	0	0	0	1	0	0	0	0	0	0	0	0	0	0	0	0	0	0
NIGERIA	9	1	0	2	1	13	1	1	2	0	0	4	8	0	0	1	0	9	3	1	0	0	0	4
ZAIRE	0	0	1	0	0	0	1	0	0	0	0	2	0	1	0	1	0	1	0	0	0	0	0	0
ZAMBIA	4	1	1	1	0	7	2	2	0	2	0	5	0	0	0	1	0	9	0	0	0	0	0	0
OTHER E.+W.AFR.	1	1	1	1	0	4	3	1	1	3	0	8	5	0	0	0	0	7	0	0	0	1	0	1
SOUTH ASIA (TOTAL)	15	20	11	26	3	75	6	2	0	7	0	15	1	2	4	2	0	9	1	3	0	6	0	10
INDIA	11	9	11	23	3	57	3	1	0	3	0	7	1	0	4	2	0	7	0	2	0	6	0	8
PAKISTAN	2	9	0	3	0	14	2	0	0	3	0	5	0	2	0	0	0	2	1	0	0	0	0	1
SRI LANKA	2	2	2	0	0	4	1	1	0	1	0	3	0	0	0	0	0	0	0	0	0	0	0	1
OTHER S.ASIA	0	0	0	0	0	0	0	0	0	0	0	0	0	0	0	0	0	0	0	1	0	0	0	1
EAST ASIA (TOTAL)	67	30	46	66	22	231	39	17	31	35	5	127	48	15	42	29	1	135	37	6	34	21	1	99
HONG KONG	6	0	0	0	2	10	6	2	1	1	0	8	11	1	3	2	1	16	2	2	1	0	1	3
INDONESIA	0	0	0	0	1	1	0	2	0	0	0	4	3	6	1	1	1	12	4	2	0	2	0	8
JAPAN	15	41	41	53	12	125	5	2	20	27	2	55	6	1	34	19	0	60	8	3	26	7	0	44
MALAYSIA	8	4	1	2	1	14	3	3	0	0	0	7	4	1	0	0	0	5	4	0	3	2	0	7
PHILIPPINES	19	12	3	6	1	41	6	2	0	0	0	8	4	1	0	1	0	6	2	0	0	3	0	5
SINGAPORE	4	0	0	2	2	8	4	1	0	0	0	6	9	0	0	1	0	10	1	0	0	0	0	1
S.KOREA	1	1	1	1	0	3	1	1	6	6	0	11	2	2	2	2	0	8	1	3	1	2	0	13
THAILAND	5	6	1	1	2	15	5	6	3	3	0	15	6	1	3	1	0	8	3	1	2	2	0	7
TAIWAN	9	2	1	1	0	12	6	1	1	1	0	15	3	1	0	1	0	8	2	0	4	3	0	10
OTHER E.ASIA	0	1	0	1	1	2	1	0	0	0	0	2	1	0	0	2	0	1	0	1	0	1	0	1
S.DOMINIONS (TOTAL)	180	45	42	33	18	318	98	15	14	9	5	141	70	14	11	12	0	107	37	8	5	10	0	60
AUSTRALIA	97	30	27	18	15	187	58	7	9	3	4	81	43	7	7	8	0	65	22	5	3	5	0	33
NEW ZEALAND	14	5	6	1	2	28	12	2	2	2	1	18	8	1	1	0	0	10	5	3	0	3	0	8
RHODESIA	9	1	0	0	1	11	2	0	1	0	0	3	1	0	0	0	0	1	0	0	0	1	0	1
S.AFRICA	60	9	9	14	0	92	26	6	2	4	0	39	18	6	3	4	0	31	10	0	2	4	0	18
OUTSIDE U.S.(TOTAL)	1722	490	402	476	244	3334	948	169	134	152	51	1454	819	155	127	134	8	1243	503	97	94	146	8	848

CHAPTER 2   - THE PROLIFERATION OF FOREIGN SUBSIDIARIES
SECTION 2   -- FLOW OF MANUFACTURING SUBSIDIARIES
TABLE 6   --- BY GEOGRAPHICAL REGION AND ENTRY METHOD

NO. OF MANUFACTURING SUBSIDIARIES ENTERING PARENT SYSTEMS IN EACH PERIOD, BY METHOD OF ENTRY

(NEW=NEWLY FORMED   ACQ=ACQUIRED   DES=DESCENDENT   UNK=UNKNOWN   ALL=TOTAL FOR PERIOD)

COUNTRY OR REGION	1951-1966					1967-1969					1970-1972					1973-1975				
	NEW	ACQ	DES	UNK	ALL	NEW	ACQ	DES	UNK	ALL	NEW	ACQ	DES	UNK	ALL	NEW	ACQ	DES	UNK	ALL
CANADA	97	280	11	20	408	40	144	6	4	194	17	118	4	2	141	17	58	4	3	82
LATIN AMER. (TOTAL)	458	363	13	45	879	113	151	3	5	272	86	114	7	4	211	86	93	7	0	186
C.AM.+CARIB.(TOTAL)	176	167	7	14	364	46	69	1	3	119	37	58	1	2	98	34	33	3	0	70
BAHAMAS	2	2	0	0	4	1	1	0	0	2	0	0	0	0	0	0	0	0	0	0
BERMUDA	2	1	0	0	3	0	2	0	0	2	0	0	0	0	0	0	0	0	0	0
COSTA RICA	6	3	0	1	10	3	0	0	0	3	0	3	0	0	3	1	2	0	0	3
GUATEMALA	8	10	1	2	21	5	6	1	1	13	0	3	0	0	3	4	2	0	0	6
JAMAICA	7	5	0	0	12	1	2	0	0	3	4	1	0	0	5	1	1	0	0	2
MEXICO	108	125	3	5	241	25	52	0	1	78	18	47	1	0	66	19	23	3	0	45
NETH.ANTILLES	1	0	0	0	1	1	0	0	0	1	2	3	0	0	5	0	0	0	0	0
NICARAGUA	6	4	0	1	11	2	0	0	0	2	1	2	0	0	3	0	0	0	0	0
PANAMA	11	8	1	2	22	2	0	0	0	2	2	2	0	1	5	1	0	0	0	1
OTHER C.AM+CAR.	25	11	2	3	41	6	4	0	1	11	7	0	0	1	8	8	5	0	0	13
S.AMERICA (TOTAL)	282	196	6	31	515	67	82	2	2	153	49	56	6	2	113	52	60	4	0	116
BOLIVIA	0	0	0	0	0	0	0	0	0	0	1	0	0	0	1	0	2	0	0	2
CHILE	14	6	0	2	22	5	6	0	1	12	1	0	0	0	1	3	1	2	0	6
COLOMBIA	49	35	1	8	93	6	5	0	0	11	4	7	1	0	12	6	4	0	0	10
ECUADOR	7	5	0	0	12	4	1	0	0	5	1	0	0	0	1	2	3	0	0	5
PERU	23	12	0	3	38	3	5	0	0	8	4	0	0	1	5	2	1	0	0	3
ARGENTINA	42	43	2	6	93	13	18	0	0	31	8	6	1	0	15	21	43	1	0	65
BRAZIL	64	61	2	3	130	19	29	2	1	51	17	31	3	0	51	1	1	0	0	2
URUGUAY	2	3	0	1	6	1	1	0	0	2	1	0	0	0	1	1	0	0	0	1
VENEZUELA	78	29	1	8	116	16	17	0	0	33	12	12	1	0	25	16	6	0	0	22
OTHER S.AMER.	3	2	0	0	5	0	0	0	0	0	0	0	0	1	1	0	0	0	0	0
EUROPE (TOTAL)	522	713	19	78	1332	184	432	17	17	650	141	432	21	13	607	125	235	14	2	376
BELGIUM	37	34	0	4	75	19	38	1	0	58	14	24	1	0	39	14	7	2	0	23
FRANCE	79	122	1	11	218	13	59	3	1	79	19	60	3	0	82	21	35	3	1	60
GERMANY	73	114	3	9	199	30	78	2	1	111	26	64	5	3	98	15	44	2	0	61
ITALY	71	90	2	7	170	22	27	1	0	52	10	51	2	6	69	9	11	2	1	23
LUXEMBOURG	3	1	0	0	4	1	1	0	0	2	3	0	0	0	2	1	0	0	0	1
NETHERLANDS	31	31	1	6	69	10	17	1	0	28	6	29	2	2	37	5	12	0	0	17
DENMARK	11	12	0	1	24	3	7	1	1	12	2	8	2	0	10	2	4	0	0	6
IRELAND	12	13	1	1	27	6	6	0	1	13	7	5	0	0	13	9	3	0	0	12
U.K.	86	193	5	20	304	36	124	7	5	172	19	131	5	0	155	19	81	3	0	103
AUSTRIA	4	7	0	1	12	2	7	0	0	9	0	6	0	0	6	1	3	0	0	4
FINLAND	4	2	0	0	6	0	0	0	0	0	2	0	0	0	2	1	1	0	0	2
GREECE	11	3	0	2	16	10	3	0	0	13	3	3	0	0	6	4	0	0	0	4
NORWAY	5	5	0	2	12	0	7	0	0	7	5	1	0	0	6	0	1	0	0	1
PORTUGAL	14	3	0	2	19	3	7	0	0	10	5	6	0	0	11	2	1	0	0	3
SPAIN	41	59	1	5	106	19	28	2	0	49	15	19	3	2	39	11	18	2	0	31
SWEDEN	18	10	0	2	30	4	14	0	1	19	0	13	0	0	13	5	7	0	0	12
SWITZERLAND	7	10	0	3	20	4	7	0	1	12	1	9	0	0	10	1	6	0	0	7
TURKEY	13	2	0	2	17	2	4	0	0	6	0	1	0	0	1	0	6	0	0	6
OTHER EUROPE	2	2	0	0	4	0	2	0	0	2	0	5	0	0	5	1	5	0	0	6

TABLE 2 . 2 .6   (CONTINUED)

NEW=NEWLY FORMED ACQ=ACQUIRED DES=DESCENDENT UNK=UNKNOWN ALL=TOTAL FOR PERIOD

COUNTRY OR REGION	1951-1966					1967-1969					1970-1972					1973-1975				
	NEW	ACQ	DES	UNK	ALL	NEW	ACQ	DES	UNK	ALL	NEW	ACQ	DES	UNK	ALL	NEW	ACQ	DES	UNK	ALL
N.AFR+M.EAST (TOTAL)	42	7	0	4	53	18	5	0	2	25	8	4	0	0	12	22	5	0	0	27
ALGERIA	2	0	0	0	2	1	0	0	1	2	0	0	0	0	0	0	0	0	0	0
EGYPT	0	0	0	0	0	1	0	0	0	1	0	0	0	0	0	2	0	0	0	2
IRAN	14	0	0	2	16	4	2	0	0	6	1	0	0	0	1	10	2	0	0	12
ISRAEL	5	1	0	0	6	2	2	0	0	4	3	1	0	0	4	2	1	0	0	3
LEBANON	3	2	0	1	6	2	1	0	0	3	0	0	0	0	0	1	0	0	0	1
MOROCCO	7	1	0	0	8	3	0	0	0	3	3	1	0	0	4	2	1	0	0	3
SAUDI ARABIA	0	0	0	0	0	2	0	0	1	3	0	1	0	0	1	4	0	0	0	4
OTHER N.AF+M.E.	11	3	0	1	15	3	0	0	0	3	1	1	0	0	2	1	1	0	0	2
E.+W.AFRICA (TOTAL)	24	8	0	6	38	23	3	0	4	30	15	4	1	1	21	8	0	0	0	8
GHANA	2	0	0	1	3	4	0	0	0	4	0	0	0	0	0	0	0	0	0	0
IVORY COAST	2	0	0	0	2	1	0	0	1	2	0	0	0	0	0	0	0	0	0	0
KENYA	5	1	0	2	8	4	1	0	0	5	2	1	0	0	3	3	0	0	0	3
LIBERIA	0	1	0	0	1	0	0	0	0	0	0	0	0	0	0	0	0	0	0	0
NIGERIA	7	4	0	2	13	3	1	0	0	4	1	0	0	0	1	4	0	0	0	4
ZAIRE	0	0	0	0	0	2	0	0	0	2	7	2	0	0	9	0	0	0	0	0
ZAMBIA	5	2	0	0	7	4	0	0	1	5	0	0	0	1	1	0	0	0	0	0
OTHER E.+W.AFR.	3	0	0	1	4	5	1	0	2	8	5	1	1	0	7	1	0	0	0	1
SOUTH ASIA (TOTAL)	47	27	0	1	75	4	10	0	1	15	4	4	0	1	9	7	3	0	0	10
INDIA	35	21	0	1	57	1	6	0	0	7	3	3	0	1	7	5	3	0	0	8
PAKISTAN	10	4	0	0	14	1	3	1	0	5	1	1	0	0	2	1	0	0	0	1
SRI LANKA	2	2	0	0	4	2	1	0	0	3	0	0	0	0	0	0	0	0	0	0
OTHER S.ASIA	0	0	0	0	0	0	0	0	0	0	0	0	0	0	0	1	0	0	0	1
EAST ASIA (TOTAL)	150	60	0	21	231	84	36	2	5	127	102	31	0	2	135	75	21	3	0	99
HONG KONG	3	6	0	1	10	4	4	0	0	8	5	11	0	0	16	2	1	0	0	3
INDONESIA	1	0	0	0	1	3	1	0	0	4	10	2	0	0	12	7	1	0	0	8
JAPAN	84	34	0	7	125	34	20	1	0	55	47	12	0	1	60	31	10	3	0	44
MALAYSIA	8	2	0	4	14	4	2	0	1	7	5	0	0	0	5	5	2	0	0	7
PHILIPPINES	25	12	0	4	41	4	4	0	0	8	5	1	0	0	6	4	1	0	0	5
SINGAPORE	5	2	0	1	8	5	0	0	1	6	8	1	0	1	10	10	3	0	0	13
S.KOREA	2	1	0	0	3	8	2	0	1	11	7	1	0	0	8	6	1	0	0	7
THAILAND	10	3	0	2	15	11	3	1	0	15	7	1	0	0	8	1	0	0	0	1
TAIWAN	11	0	0	1	12	9	0	0	2	11	8	1	0	0	9	8	2	0	0	10
OTHER E.ASIA	1	0	0	1	2	2	0	0	0	2	0	1	0	0	1	1	0	0	0	1
S.DOMINIONS (TOTAL)	137	165	3	13	318	33	97	7	4	141	31	71	3	2	107	12	45	2	1	60
AUSTRALIA	80	95	1	11	187	18	55	4	4	81	16	44	3	2	65	4	26	2	1	33
NEW ZEALAND	18	9	1	0	28	4	13	1	0	18	4	6	0	0	10	4	4	0	0	8
RHODESIA	3	7	0	1	11	2	1	0	0	3	1	0	0	0	1	0	1	0	0	1
S.AFRICA	36	54	1	1	92	9	28	2	0	39	10	21	0	0	31	4	14	0	0	18
OUTSIDE U.S. (TOTAL)	1477	1623	46	188	3334	499	878	36	41	1454	404	778	36	25	1243	352	460	30	6	848

CHAPTER 2   - THE PROLIFERATION OF FOREIGN SUBSIDIARIES
SECTION 2   -- FLOW OF MANUFACTURING SUBSIDIARIES
TABLE 7   --- NET FLOW BY REGION AND PRINCIPAL INDUSTRY

NET FLOW (ENTRIES MINUS EXITS) UP TO 1-JAN-76, BY PRINCIPAL INDUSTRY OF SUBSIDIARY AT TIME OF ENTRY INTO PARENT SYSTEM

COUNTRY OR REGION	BEVERAGES	TOBACCO	FOOD	TXTL+APPRL	WOOD+FURNI	PAPER	PRINTING	INDUS-CHEM	PLASTIC	AGRIC-CHEM	COSMETICS	DRUGS	OTHER-CHEM	FABR-PLSTCS	TIRES	REF-PETRLM	OTH-PETRLM	LEATHER	STONE+CLAY+CEMNT	ABRASIVES	GLASS	IRON
CANADA	20	1	76	27	17	22	10	31	14	3	21	26	25	8	6	7	4	3	5	6	5	4
LATIN AMER. (TOTAL)	28	11	173	24	11	60	9	57	50	17	64	128	49	15	25	20	14	3	12	24	19	4
C.AM.+CARIB. (TOTAL)	10	0	86	7	5	19	4	35	24	10	30	46	19	4	8	13	5	1	2	8	9	1
BAHAMAS	0	1	2	0	0	0	0	0	2	0	0	1	0	0	0	0	0	0	0	0	0	0
BERMUDA	1	0	0	0	0	0	0	0	1	0	0	1	0	0	0	0	0	0	0	0	0	0
COSTA RICA	0	0	5	0	0	2	0	0	1	1	0	2	1	0	1	0	0	0	0	0	0	0
GUATEMALA	0	1	11	0	0	1	0	0	1	0	5	5	1	1	0	0	0	0	0	0	0	0
JAMAICA	0	0	8	2	1	9	4	28	19	2	16	4	0	0	0	2	0	1	4	8	4	1
MEXICO	8	1	43	7	1	2	0	1	1	1	0	24	14	3	6	1	4	0	4	0	4	0
NETH.ANTILLES	0	0	0	0	0	0	0	1	0	1	0	0	3	0	0	0	0	0	0	0	0	0
NICARAGUA	0	0	4	0	0	2	0	0	1	0	4	0	2	0	0	1	0	0	0	0	0	0
PANAMA	0	1	6	0	1	1	0	1	1	0	2	3	1	0	0	3	1	0	1	1	0	0
OTHER C.AM+CAR.	0	1	7	0	3	3	0	2	1	4	2	7	0	0	0	6	0	0	0	0	0	0
S.AMERICA (TOTAL)	18	7	87	17	6	41	5	22	26	7	34	82	30	11	17	7	9	2	6	15	15	3
BOLIVIA	0	0	0	0	0	0	0	0	2	0	0	0	0	0	1	0	1	1	0	0	0	0
CHILE	0	0	4	0	1	0	0	0	2	0	0	5	0	0	3	0	1	0	1	0	0	0
COLOMBIA	5	0	16	3	0	8	0	3	6	4	4	12	4	1	2	3	1	0	0	1	2	1
ECUADOR	1	0	3	0	0	1	0	0	1	0	0	5	2	0	1	1	0	0	0	0	0	0
PERU	1	1	7	1	1	2	0	0	0	0	6	9	0	1	2	1	0	0	0	3	0	0
ARGENTINA	3	1	11	1	1	4	2	2	8	0	7	13	5	2	3	2	2	1	1	4	3	1
BRAZIL	5	1	23	4	2	11	3	10	5	2	6	17	13	4	3	2	4	0	1	4	5	1
URUGUAY	2	0	2	2	0	1	0	1	1	1	2	2	0	0	3	0	0	0	0	2	0	0
VENEZUELA	2	5	19	3	1	14	0	6	4	0	9	19	6	4	2	1	1	0	0	7	5	1
OTHER S.AMER.	0	0	2	0	0	1	0	0	0	0	0	0	0	0	0	1	0	0	0	0	0	0
EUROPE (TOTAL)	25	8	245	42	23	67	35	112	69	9	106	177	105	40	21	48	28	12	25	52	27	24
BELGIUM	1	1	12	7	1	5	3	13	7	2	5	9	8	2	3	2	3	1	2	6	2	1
FRANCE	2	1	23	4	5	17	6	13	8	1	23	28	14	4	3	8	7	3	1	8	1	4
GERMANY	4	1	43	6	5	9	7	17	7	2	15	22	14	9	2	12	6	3	2	12	8	4
ITALY	3	0	19	1	5	5	1	16	2	2	8	22	15	0	1	6	2	1	5	5	4	3
LUXEMBOURG	0	0	0	4	0	0	0	1	1	0	0	0	0	0	1	0	0	0	0	0	0	0
NETHERLANDS	1	1	22	2	0	2	0	7	0	0	4	5	11	2	1	2	0	0	1	1	0	0
DENMARK	1	0	15	2	2	1	1	0	3	0	0	1	2	0	0	1	1	1	0	1	0	0
IRELAND	1	0	1	1	1	1	0	3	1	0	2	1	2	3	2	0	1	2	2	2	3	0
U.K.	7	1	42	10	5	9	9	23	26	0	23	25	18	12	2	4	4	3	11	9	7	8
AUSTRIA	0	0	3	0	0	1	1	2	0	0	1	3	2	0	0	4	0	0	0	0	1	0
FINLAND	0	0	0	0	0	1	0	0	0	0	1	1	0	0	0	0	1	0	0	1	0	0
GREECE	0	0	5	0	0	2	0	1	1	0	2	8	0	0	0	3	0	0	2	0	1	0
NORWAY	0	0	0	1	0	0	0	0	1	0	0	0	1	0	0	1	0	0	0	0	0	2
PORTUGAL	0	0	4	0	0	1	0	2	3	0	2	9	1	0	3	0	0	0	3	0	0	1
SPAIN	4	2	30	2	3	9	2	12	3	4	11	15	12	4	2	2	1	1	2	3	3	0
SWEDEN	0	0	12	2	0	3	1	0	1	0	3	6	4	1	0	1	0	0	1	0	0	1
SWITZERLAND	1	1	6	2	0	3	0	0	3	0	2	4	3	2	0	2	2	0	0	2	0	0
TURKEY	0	0	1	3	0	0	0	0	0	0	2	4	0	0	0	1	0	0	2	0	0	1
OTHER EUROPE	0	0	0	1	0	1	0	1	1	0	2	0	0	0	0	0	0	0	0	0	0	0

TABLE 2.2.7 (CONTINUED)

COUNTRY OR REGION	BEVERAGES	TOBACCO	FOOD	TXTL+APPRL	WOOD+FURNI	PAPER	PRINTING	INDUS-CHEM PLASTIC	PLASTIC	AGRIC-CHEM	COSMETICS	DRUGS	OTHER-CHEM	FABR-PLSTCS TIRES	REF-PETRLM	OTH-PETRLM	LEATHER	STONE+CLAY+CEMNT	ABRASIVES	GLASS	IRON
N.AFR+M.EAST (TOTAL)	0	0	11	2	1	4	0	5	5	2	8	14	3	0	6	5	3	1	1	2	1
ALGERIA	0	0	1	0	0	0	0	0	0	0	0	0	0	0	0	0	1	0	0	0	0
EGYPT	0	0	0	0	0	0	0	1	0	0	0	0	0	0	0	0	0	0	0	0	0
IRAN	0	0	1	0	0	1	0	0	1	0	2	9	2	0	3	1	1	1	0	1	0
ISRAEL	0	0	1	1	0	0	0	1	0	0	2	1	1	0	0	0	0	0	0	0	1
LEBANON	0	0	2	0	0	2	0	1	4	0	1	2	0	0	0	0	1	0	1	0	0
MOROCCO	0	0	2	0	1	0	0	0	0	0	1	2	0	0	2	2	0	0	0	0	0
SAUDI ARABIA	0	0	3	0	0	0	0	1	0	0	2	0	0	0	0	2	0	0	0	0	0
OTHER N.AF+M.E.	0	0	1	1	0	1	0	1	0	2	1	0	0	0	1	0	0	0	0	1	0
E.+W.AFRICA (TOTAL)	3	1	10	1	0	5	0	1	1	2	8	10	0	2	4	9	2	0	1	1	0
GHANA	0	0	1	0	0	0	0	0	1	0	1	1	0	0	1	0	0	0	0	0	0
IVORY COAST	1	0	1	0	0	0	0	0	0	0	0	0	0	0	0	2	1	0	0	0	0
KENYA	0	0	3	0	0	0	0	0	0	1	2	3	0	1	1	2	0	0	1	0	0
LIBERIA	0	1	0	0	0	0	0	0	0	0	0	0	0	0	0	0	1	0	0	0	0
NIGERIA	0	0	2	0	0	0	0	0	0	0	3	4	0	0	0	2	0	0	0	1	0
ZAIRE	0	0	0	0	0	0	0	1	0	0	0	2	0	0	0	0	0	0	0	0	0
ZAMBIA	1	0	0	0	0	3	0	0	0	0	1	1	0	1	0	0	0	0	0	0	0
OTHER E.+W.AFR.	1	0	3	0	0	2	0	0	0	1	1	0	0	1	3	3	0	0	0	0	0
SOUTH ASIA (TOTAL)	2	1	3	3	0	2	0	3	3	5	3	21	3	2	2	4	1	1	0	1	2
INDIA	1	1	2	1	0	1	0	2	3	4	1	12	3	2	1	2	1	1	0	1	2
PAKISTAN	1	0	1	1	0	0	0	1	0	1	1	7	0	0	0	1	0	0	0	0	0
SRI LANKA	0	0	0	1	0	1	0	0	0	0	1	1	0	0	1	1	0	0	0	0	0
OTHER S.ASIA	0	0	0	0	0	0	0	0	0	0	0	1	0	0	0	0	0	0	0	0	0
EAST ASIA (TOTAL)	10	1	41	6	4	12	3	29	34	10	21	49	25	5	7	16	4	4	5	9	1
HONG KONG	0	0	2	0	1	0	0	0	1	0	2	2	4	0	0	0	0	0	0	0	0
INDONESIA	0	1	1	0	0	0	0	0	0	1	1	1	1	0	0	0	0	0	0	0	0
JAPAN	4	0	18	5	2	3	3	20	20	1	7	10	11	2	1	8	1	1	1	8	0
MALAYSIA	3	0	3	0	0	1	0	0	1	2	1	1	1	1	1	1	0	0	0	0	0
PHILIPPINES	0	0	8	0	1	0	0	1	3	1	4	3	1	1	2	1	0	0	1	0	0
SINGAPORE	1	0	2	0	0	0	0	4	0	0	3	12	3	2	0	3	1	0	0	0	0
S.KOREA	1	0	2	1	0	0	0	0	3	5	1	1	0	0	0	3	0	0	0	1	0
THAILAND	1	0	4	0	0	2	0	1	1	0	1	5	1	1	2	0	1	1	0	0	1
TAIWAN	0	0	1	0	0	2	0	0	5	0	1	5	2	2	1	0	1	0	1	0	0
OTHER E.ASIA	1	0	0	0	0	0	0	3	0	0	0	0	2	0	0	0	0	0	0	0	0
S.DOMINIONS (TOTAL)	9	4	55	6	3	36	8	21	20	1	35	53	21	9	6	12	5	3	5	12	4
AUSTRALIA	7	3	26	2	3	9	2	13	13	1	17	25	11	4	4	7	3	2	2	5	3
NEW ZEALAND	1	1	9	1	0	0	1	6	3	0	2	1	4	0	1	1	0	1	1	2	3
RHODESIA	0	0	0	1	0	3	1	0	0	0	1	1	3	1	0	1	0	0	1	0	0
S.AFRICA	2	0	20	2	0	21	4	2	4	0	9	18	7	4	1	3	2	0	1	5	1
OUTSIDE U.S.(TOTAL)	97	28	614	108	59	207	65	259	196	49	266	478	231	81	77	121	61	21	51	108	40

(TABLE CONTINUED ON FOLLOWING PAGES)

TABLE 2 . 2 . 7 (CONTINUED)

COUNTRY OR REGION	NON-FERROUS METAL CANS	FAB-MET	ENGINES CONSTR-MC	FARM-MC	OFF-MC+COMPUT SPECL-MC	GENL-MC	OTH-NON-EL-MC EL-LT+WIRING EL-TRAN		RAD+TV+APPL ELECTRONICS OTH-ELE		COMMUNICATION MOTOR-VEHIC OTH-TRN		PRECISION MISC	TOTAL
CANADA	21	8	41	4	20	3	7	9	6	12	13	17	45	633
LATIN AMER. (TOTAL)	19	15	42	2	33	4	9	12	24	13	17	18	59	1276
C.AM.+CARIB.(TOTAL)	5	7	17	0	13	0	5	4	14	6	2	3	22	527
BAHAMAS	0	0	0	0	0	0	0	0	0	0	0	0	0	6
BERMUDA	0	0	0	0	0	0	0	0	0	0	0	0	0	2
COSTA RICA	0	0	0	0	0	1	0	0	0	0	0	0	0	21
GUATEMALA	0	1	1	0	0	0	1	0	1	1	0	0	3	32
JAMAICA	0	0	0	0	0	3	0	0	0	0	0	0	1	20
MEXICO	4	3	14	0	13	5	5	14	4	2	2	8	15	355
NETH.ANTILLES	0	0	0	0	0	0	4	0	0	0	8	3	5	5
NICARAGUA	0	0	0	0	0	0	0	0	0	0	0	0	0	13
PANAMA	0	1	0	0	0	0	1	0	0	1	0	1	0	27
OTHER C.AM+CAR.	1	2	1	0	1	0	1	0	1	1	1	0	3	46
S.AMERICA (TOTAL)	14	8	25	2	20	4	4	8	10	12	7	1	37	749
BOLIVIA	0	0	0	0	1	0	0	0	0	0	0	0	0	1
CHILE	0	0	4	0	1	0	0	0	0	1	0	3	3	28
COLOMBIA	1	1	1	2	1	1	2	0	1	1	7	0	6	106
ECUADOR	0	0	1	0	0	0	0	0	0	0	0	0	1	19
PERU	0	0	1	0	0	0	0	0	0	1	2	1	1	40
ARGENTINA	6	2	2	2	4	1	7	5	4	2	14	1	4	128
BRAZIL	5	5	3	0	0	0	1	5	3	0	25	5	11	239
URUGUAY	1	1	11	0	2	1	3	5	0	1	3	3	1	18
VENEZUELA	2	3	1	0	1	0	0	0	3	0	1	0	11	166
OTHER S.AMER.	0	0	0	0	0	0	1	0	4	0	2	2	10	4
EUROPE (TOTAL)	62	10	136	14	52	13	31	63	54	53	16	36	154	2339
BELGIUM	3	0	5	4	5	1	3	6	2	8	0	3	2	151
FRANCE	2	1	13	4	13	1	3	8	8	3	1	3	22	333
GERMANY	9	4	23	3	3	1	7	6	0	7	5	7	22	377
ITALY	3	0	1	1	6	0	1	7	2	5	2	4	14	225
LUXEMBOURG	0	0	1	0	1	0	1	1	1	2	1	0	0	13
NETHERLANDS	4	1	6	1	0	1	0	4	0	1	0	1	10	119
DENMARK	1	6	3	0	1	1	2	2	0	0	0	0	2	40
IRELAND	0	0	0	1	0	0	1	1	4	0	3	1	1	56
U.K.	32	1	47	0	14	6	22	18	14	9	10	11	46	567
AUSTRIA	0	0	2	0	1	0	0	1	0	0	2	0	2	30
FINLAND	0	0	0	0	1	0	0	0	0	0	1	0	1	8
GREECE	0	1	0	0	1	0	2	0	0	1	1	1	1	32
NORWAY	4	0	1	0	0	0	1	1	0	1	1	0	1	20
PORTUGAL	0	1	1	0	3	1	0	0	0	0	0	3	4	39
SPAIN	3	0	13	2	3	1	2	4	3	3	8	4	10	189
SWEDEN	1	2	4	1	1	0	3	1	1	0	2	0	7	69
SWITZERLAND	0	0	1	0	1	0	1	1	0	1	0	1	4	40
TURKEY	0	0	0	2	0	0	0	1	1	1	1	0	4	18
OTHER EUROPE	1	1	1	0	0	0	1	1	0	0	0	1	0	13

TABLE 2 .2 .7 (CONTINUED)

COUNTRY OR REGION	NON-FERROUS	METAL CANS	FAB-MET	ENGINES	CONSTR-MC	FARM-MC	OFF-MC+COMPUT	SPECL-MC	GENL-MC	OTH-NON-EL-MC	EL-LT+WIRING	EL-TRAN	RAD+TV+APPL	ELECTRONICS	OTH-ELE	COMMUNICATION	MOTOR-VEHIC	OTH-TRN	PRECISION	MISC	TOTAL
N.AFR+M.EAST(TOTAL)	3	1	3	0	5	1	0	2	1	0	0	0	2	0	3	0	4	0	2	4	105
ALGERIA	0	0	0	0	0	0	0	0	0	0	0	0	0	0	0	0	1	0	0	0	3
EGYPT	0	0	0	0	2	0	0	0	0	0	0	0	0	0	0	0	0	0	0	0	3
IRAN	2	0	1	0	1	1	0	0	1	0	0	0	0	0	2	0	1	0	0	1	33
ISRAEL	0	1	0	0	0	0	0	0	0	0	0	0	1	0	0	0	0	0	1	1	16
LEBANON	0	0	0	0	1	0	0	1	0	0	0	0	0	0	0	0	0	0	0	0	8
MOROCCO	0	0	2	0	0	0	0	1	0	0	0	0	0	0	0	0	1	0	1	1	18
SAUDI ARABIA	0	0	0	0	0	0	0	0	0	0	0	0	0	0	0	0	1	0	0	0	8
OTHER N.AF+M.E.	1	0	0	0	1	0	0	0	0	0	0	0	1	0	1	0	0	0	0	1	16
E.+W.AFRICA (TOTAL)	6	1	4	0	0	0	0	0	0	0	0	0	4	2	5	1	1	0	1	6	90
GHANA	1	0	0	0	0	0	0	0	0	0	0	0	0	0	1	0	0	0	0	0	6
IVORY COAST	0	0	0	0	0	0	0	0	0	0	0	0	0	0	1	0	0	0	0	0	4
KENYA	0	0	0	0	0	0	0	0	0	0	0	0	0	0	1	0	0	0	0	1	16
LIBERIA	0	0	0	0	0	0	0	0	0	0	0	0	0	0	0	0	0	0	0	1	1
NIGERIA	0	0	0	0	0	0	0	0	0	0	0	0	2	1	1	1	0	0	0	3	21
ZAIRE	1	0	1	0	0	0	0	0	0	0	0	0	1	1	1	0	1	0	1	0	11
ZAMBIA	3	0	1	0	0	0	0	0	0	0	0	0	0	0	0	0	0	0	0	1	12
OTHER E.+W.AFR.	1	1	2	0	0	0	0	0	0	0	0	0	1	0	0	0	0	0	0	0	19
SOUTH ASIA (TOTAL)	2	0	6	0	2	2	1	0	0	3	3	0	3	0	7	0	4	0	2	2	100
INDIA	2	0	5	0	2	2	1	0	0	3	3	0	1	0	5	0	4	0	1	1	72
PAKISTAN	0	0	0	0	0	0	0	0	0	0	0	0	1	0	1	0	0	0	1	0	20
SRI LANKA	0	0	1	0	0	0	0	0	0	0	0	0	1	0	1	0	0	0	0	1	7
OTHER S.ASIA	0	0	0	0	0	0	0	0	0	0	0	0	0	0	0	0	0	0	0	0	1
EAST ASIA (TOTAL)	16	4	26	5	12	1	9	5	15	5	4	2	13	25	22	6	26	0	10	28	532
HONG KONG	4	0	2	0	1	0	1	0	0	0	0	0	1	2	2	1	0	0	1	3	30
INDONESIA	0	0	3	0	1	0	0	0	0	0	0	0	0	0	1	0	0	0	1	2	25
JAPAN	5	3	9	4	6	0	6	4	14	5	2	2	2	7	10	0	17	0	8	14	249
MALAYSIA	0	0	2	0	0	0	0	0	0	0	0	0	2	4	3	0	1	0	0	3	30
PHILIPPINES	0	1	4	0	1	0	0	1	1	0	2	0	4	0	0	2	2	0	0	0	61
SINGAPORE	3	0	2	1	3	1	1	0	0	0	0	0	1	3	4	1	0	0	0	2	36
S.KOREA	1	0	1	0	0	0	1	0	0	0	0	0	0	2	0	0	2	0	0	1	28
THAILAND	2	0	2	0	0	0	0	0	0	0	0	0	1	1	1	1	3	0	0	1	33
TAIWAN	1	0	0	0	0	0	0	0	0	0	0	0	2	6	1	1	1	0	0	2	37
OTHER E.ASIA	0	0	1	0	0	0	0	0	0	0	0	0	0	0	0	0	0	0	0	0	3
S.DOMINIONS (TOTAL)	22	3	38	2	17	5	1	7	5	14	0	6	1	3	10	3	36	2	9	33	547
AUSTRALIA	18	2	21	1	9	3	1	4	4	8	0	5	0	3	5	2	17	2	8	20	295
NEW ZEALAND	2	0	9	0	1	0	0	1	1	0	0	0	0	0	1	0	5	0	0	4	73
RHODESIA	0	0	1	0	0	0	0	0	0	0	0	0	0	0	0	0	1	0	0	1	13
S.AFRICA	2	1	7	1	7	2	0	2	0	6	0	1	1	0	4	1	13	0	1	8	166
OUTSIDE U.S.(TOTAL)	151	42	296	27	141	29	58	95	112	110	38	35	95	87	155	55	296	33	154	331	5622

44

NO. OF SUBSIDIARY-INDUSTRIES

INDUSTRY	NET FLOW UP TO 31-DEC-50	NO. OF ENTRIES DURING YEAR(S)													TOTAL ENTRIES 1951-75	TOTAL EXITS 1951-75	NET FLOW UP TO 1-JAN-76
		51-55	56-60	61-65	1966	1967	1968	1969	1970	1971	1972	1973	1974	1975			
BEVERAGES	33	6	15	19	6	3	24	3	8	13	10	5	7	0	119	44	108
TOBACCO	1	1	4	5	2	1	4	2	1	6	1	0	3	0	30	2	29
FOOD	122	45	113	207	55	58	55	80	49	48	53	26	23	21	833	319	636
TEXTILES+APPAREL	25	9	27	45	15	7	15	11	13	21	5	5	8	3	184	87	122
WOOD+FURNITURE	14	2	10	18	5	2	8	9	7	5	9	7	2	2	86	26	74
PAPER	33	29	53	88	15	16	15	14	11	22	5	8	8	10	294	95	232
PRINTING	5	3	6	13	11	7	16	7	3	6	4	2	2	1	81	17	69
INDUSTRIAL CHEM	66	28	76	102	25	16	30	15	11	26	16	8	12	15	380	140	306
PLASTICS	28	32	51	121	13	18	18	13	10	21	16	15	14	9	351	121	258
AGRIC CHEM	7	7	14	32	6	7	9	6	3	6	2	2	3	4	101	37	71
COSMETICS	65	20	59	68	24	22	23	20	10	56	13	32	11	5	363	74	354
DRUGS	79	43	98	129	11	27	67	45	23	30	14	11	20	12	530	94	515
OTHER CHEM	38	22	34	63	18	28	22	20	20	32	24	26	17	22	348	79	307
FABR PLASTICS	20	13	11	29	5	8	15	19	14	22	13	17	9	2	177	53	144
TIRES	48	8	11	14	3	3	2	1	0	4	3	0	0	3	52	19	81
REF PETROLEUM	30	17	25	36	8	8	15	11	11	5	4	2	4	6	152	53	129
OTH PETROLEUM	16	7	15	32	7	8	4	4	8	1	3	3	1	2	95	34	77
LEATHER	6	0	3	6	4	1	4	0	0	1	1	4	1	0	25	8	23
STONE+CLAY+CEMNT	10	4	12	11	4	3	7	9	6	2	6	5	5	0	74	21	63
ABRASIVES	15	21	15	15	9	13	7	7	17	14	13	10	3	4	148	30	133
GLASS	15	3	10	17	5	6	4	6	5	4	6	7	2	1	76	17	74
IRON+STEEL	4	1	3	9	1	6	8	9	3	5	5	9	5	3	67	22	49

TABLE 2.3.1 (CONTINUED)

INDUSTRY	NET FLOW UP TO 31-DEC-50	NO. OF ENTRIES DURING YEAR(S)													TOTAL ENTRIES 1951-75	TOTAL EXITS 1951-75	NET FLOW UP TO 1-JAN-76
		51-55	56-60	61-65	1966	1967	1968	1969	1970	1971	1972	1973	1974	1975			
NON-FERROUS	21	6	39	44	4	15	19	24	12	17	9	3	7	8	207	52	176
METAL CANS	9	3	10	17	2	2	9	6	2	1	1	0	2	2	57	13	53
OTHER FAB METAL	49	16	49	82	10	28	40	42	36	32	21	30	21	17	424	122	351
ENGINES+TURBIN	4	3	7	17	2	3	3	5	3	1	3	3	2	1	51	18	37
CONSTR MACH	31	17	23	34	2	22	14	15	15	12	12	6	19	8	199	59	171
FARM MACHINERY	6	4	7	20	2	1	0	3	5	2	0	1	4	2	51	16	41
OFFICE MC+COMPUT	33	9	10	9	3	4	7	6	10	5	2	9	1	2	77	37	73
SPEC MACHINERY	23	9	12	28	10	11	5	5	7	5	7	21	5	6	131	42	112
GENL MACHINERY	26	12	17	28	5	15	23	22	8	13	19	14	8	7	191	54	163
OTH NON-EL MC	18	6	13	36	7	9	15	23	14	4	20	13	8	5	173	47	144
EL LIGHT+WIRING	7	2	14	14	2	6	3	4	4	5	4	4	3	1	65	19	53
EL TRAN EQUIP	1	3	15	9	1	2	5	4	5	3	11	0	4	1	63	20	44
RADIO+TV+APPL	17	7	18	48	6	17	8	9	17	3	5	2	11	5	156	47	126
ELECTRONICS	2	3	12	23	3	9	15	6	17	7	9	17	8	5	134	25	111
OTHER ELEC	39	15	21	40	4	15	23	11	27	9	26	18	13	5	227	72	194
COMMUNICATION	18	6	7	13	1	5	12	6	10	1	1	9	4	1	76	23	71
MOTOR VEHIC	42	13	53	106	28	27	23	19	23	13	44	41	13	15	418	132	328
OTHER TRANSP	4	2	9	4	1	2	10	4	4	1	10	8	4	2	61	22	43
PRECISION	19	1	17	53	22	12	21	14	14	14	38	22	17	9	254	63	210
MISCELLANEOUS	87	28	66	90	15	29	44	30	27	30	24	27	14	10	434	167	354
TOTAL	1136	486	1084	1794	382	502	671	568	493	528	490	452	328	237	8015	2442	6709

(A SUBSIDIARY MANUFACTURING IN SEVERAL INDUSTRIES, AT TIME OF ENTRY INTO PARENT SYSTEM, IS COUNTED ONCE FOR EACH INDUSTRY)

CHAPTER 2 — THE PROLIFERATION OF FOREIGN SUBSIDIARIES
SECTION 3 -- FLOW OF SUBSIDIARY-INDUSTRIES
TABLE 2 --- BY GEOGRAPHICAL REGION

NO. OF SUBSIDIARY-INDUSTRIES, BY REGION

COUNTRY OR REGION	NET FLOW UP TO 31-DEC-50	NO. OF ENTRIES DURING YEAR(S) 51-55	56-60	61-65	1966	1967	1968	1969	1970	1971	1972	1973	1974	1975	TOTAL ENTRIES 1951-75	TOTAL EXITS 1951-75	NET FLOW UP TO 1-JAN-76
CANADA	267	105	130	185	40	66	77	84	60	52	54	57	29	21	960	460	767
LATIN AMER. (TOTAL)	314	139	329	414	88	105	127	81	78	89	79	100	64	54	1747	583	1478
C.AM.+CARIB.(TOTAL)	109	47	134	175	42	46	44	36	34	46	31	30	26	26	717	227	599
BAHAMAS	1	0	0	1	1	0	1	0	0	0	0	0	0	0	3	0	6
BERMUDA	0	0	2	1	0	1	0	0	0	0	0	0	0	0	3	1	2
COSTA RICA	1	0	0	9	1	3	3	4	2	0	2	2	1	0	27	5	23
GUATEMALA	3	0	8	14	1	3	3	4	3	0	0	2	2	2	42	10	35
JAMAICA	3	0	2	5	4	0	3	2	3	0	0	2	2	0	24	4	21
MEXICO	75	37	93	108	28	33	29	21	19	34	24	22	17	17	482	143	414
NETH.ANTILLES	0	0	1	1	0	1	0	0	0	3	2	0	0	0	8	3	5
NICARAGUA	0	0	1	7	4	0	2	0	0	1	0	0	0	0	17	3	14
PANAMA	4	3	5	12	3	1	1	0	2	0	3	0	0	1	31	6	29
OTHER C.AM+CAR.	24	6	22	17	0	4	2	5	4	2	2	2	6	6	78	52	50
S.AMERICA (TOTAL)	205	92	195	239	46	59	83	45	44	43	48	70	38	28	1030	356	879
BOLIVIA	2	0	0	1	0	0	0	0	3	0	0	2	1	0	4	5	1
CHILE	16	2	5	14	2	8	4	0	2	0	0	0	2	2	43	29	30
COLOMBIA	28	14	29	52	9	3	7	2	1	7	0	2	4	4	140	44	124
ECUADOR	1	0	3	9	0	1	2	2	1	1	0	4	3	2	24	6	19
PERU	19	7	12	19	4	5	6	0	0	6	1	1	0	0	60	29	50
ARGENTINA	51	13	34	52	10	9	17	14	9	21	31	3	0	0	170	65	156
BRAZIL	56	34	59	36	12	23	27	15	16	7	0	40	25	16	355	122	289
URUGUAY	10	2	3	3	0	1	1	1	0	0	0	0	5	4	10	19	19
VENEZUELA	22	20	50	52	8	9	19	11	8	7	10	16	0	0	219	54	187
OTHER S.AMER.	0	0	2	2	1	0	0	0	0	0	0	0	0	0	5	1	4
EUROPE (TOTAL)	397	154	409	778	173	205	330	247	238	249	263	207	145	102	3500	1070	2827
BELGIUM	19	5	26	44	9	21	19	28	21	14	13	3	10	14	227	65	181
FRANCE	61	22	78	124	23	30	40	26	35	20	48	33	21	16	516	179	398
GERMANY	55	33	58	110	22	25	60	54	36	36	48	40	23	15	560	153	462
ITALY	18	14	61	105	19	12	27	29	31	26	31	13	7	6	381	117	282
LUXEMBOURG	1	0	0	0	0	0	1	1	0	0	0	0	0	0	13	14	14
NETHERLANDS	18	4	21	45	4	8	16	10	18	22	13	6	8	4	179	53	144
DENMARK	6	1	3	16	5	4	8	2	4	4	2	3	3	0	55	18	43
IRELAND	7	7	5	15	3	1	11	2	5	6	7	3	4	6	75	14	68
U.K.	158	40	103	170	40	72	84	45	54	73	58	78	39	19	875	337	696
AUSTRIA	9	0	4	4	4	0	0	0	0	4	3	1	1	2	34	10	33
FINLAND	0	1	0	6	0	4	0	0	2	2	0	0	2	0	13	3	10
GREECE	0	1	4	10	4	0	3	8	2	1	4	0	5	0	46	7	39
NORWAY	7	4	5	5	3	2	2	2	1	2	4	1	1	0	24	10	21
PORTUGAL	5	4	10	10	2	3	2	8	7	3	1	2	1	0	48	9	44
SPAIN	17	13	19	67	24	20	27	13	12	19	17	14	10	10	265	55	227
SWEDEN	10	5	5	19	3	3	3	5	3	12	4	2	4	5	90	15	85
SWITZERLAND	5	2	4	11	1	0	6	7	3	5	3	2	2	3	56	14	47
TURKEY	0	2	0	11	1	2	1	1	1	0	2	0	0	0	25	6	19
OTHER EUROPE	1	0	0	2	2	1	0	1	0	3	2	2	3	2	18	5	14

TABLE 2 .3 .2 (CONTINUED)

COUNTRY OR REGION	NET FLOW UP TO 31-DEC-50	NO. OF ENTRIES DURING YEAR(S)													TOTAL ENTRIES 1951-75	TOTAL EXITS 1951-75	NET FLOW UP TO 1-JAN-76
		51-55	56-60	61-65	1966	1967	1968	1969	1970	1971	1972	1973	1974	1975			
N.AFR+M.EAST (TOTAL)	7	5	16	29	6	10	10	9	2	9	2	8	11	10	127	19	115
ALGERIA	0	0	1	1	0	1	0	1	0	0	0	0	0	0	4	1	3
EGYPT	0	0	0	0	0	1	0	0	0	0	0	0	0	3	4	0	4
IRAN	2	2	3	10	3	2	2	2	1	0	0	2	7	3	37	2	35
ISRAEL	2	0	3	3	1	1	3	2	0	0	0	2	0	0	19	3	18
LEBANON	0	0	1	5	0	1	1	0	0	0	2	1	1	0	11	2	9
MOROCCO	2	0	6	3	0	1	3	2	1	2	1	1	1	0	20	0	20
SAUDI ARABIA	2	0	0	0	0	1	0	0	0	0	0	2	1	4	10	0	10
OTHER N.AF+M.E.	3	3	2	7	3	2	1	0	0	2	0	1	1	0	22	9	16
E.+W.AFRICA (TOTAL)	0	2	8	26	7	11	7	18	10	8	7	0	5	5	114	8	106
GHANA	0	0	1	3	0	3	0	1	0	0	0	0	0	0	8	1	7
IVORY COAST	0	0	0	2	0	0	0	2	0	0	0	0	0	0	4	0	4
KENYA	0	1	3	4	1	1	1	3	0	0	2	0	1	3	20	3	17
LIBERIA	0	0	0	1	0	0	0	0	0	1	0	0	0	0	1	0	1
NIGERIA	0	0	4	10	1	1	1	0	0	1	0	0	3	2	25	1	24
ZAIRE	0	0	0	0	0	3	0	2	2	2	4	0	0	0	16	0	16
ZAMBIA	0	1	0	3	4	2	2	2	1	5	0	0	0	0	15	1	14
OTHER E.+W.AFR.	0	0	0	3	2	1	3	6	7	1	1	0	1	0	25	2	23
SOUTH ASIA (TOTAL)	12	4	27	47	6	2	11	6	13	4	0	7	1	4	132	22	122
INDIA	10	4	20	36	3	2	7	2	12	3	0	5	1	4	98	18	90
PAKISTAN	1	0	5	9	3	0	3	3	1	1	0	1	0	0	26	3	24
SRI LANKA	1	0	2	2	0	1	1	1	0	0	0	0	0	0	7	1	7
OTHER S.ASIA	0	0	0	0	0	0	0	0	0	0	0	1	0	0	1	0	1
EAST ASIA (TOTAL)	29	28	51	150	28	44	45	63	51	68	46	42	50	25	691	94	626
HONG KONG	0	2	3	6	0	2	4	4	3	15	3	0	4	1	47	7	40
INDONESIA	5	0	0	0	0	2	4	4	2	10	3	3	4	1	27	5	27
JAPAN	8	16	21	88	13	21	17	32	17	29	21	22	18	12	327	47	288
MALAYSIA	1	1	3	9	2	1	3	3	3	0	4	5	4	1	35	4	32
PHILIPPINES	13	9	16	19	4	5	2	3	3	0	2	3	7	2	73	12	74
SINGAPORE	2	0	0	5	3	0	5	4	4	2	4	3	7	5	42	3	41
S.KOREA	0	0	0	8	6	3	5	4	6	1	3	0	8	1	34	1	33
THAILAND	0	0	5	7	3	6	6	6	6	7	3	6	4	6	45	6	39
TAIWAN	0	0	3	5	6	6	4	6	2	7	3	1	0	0	54	5	49
OTHER E.ASIA	0	0	0	3	0	0	0	2	0	1	0	1	0	0	7	4	3
S.DOMINIONS (TOTAL)	110	49	114	165	34	59	64	60	41	49	39	31	23	16	744	186	668
AUSTRALIA	49	27	86	86	21	38	43	30	33	31	16	17	13	10	451	126	374
NEW ZEALAND	17	9	5	17	2	10	5	3	1	5	8	6	1	3	75	8	84
RHODESIA	1	0	2	7	2	0	0	7	1	0	0	0	0	1	20	4	17
S.AFRICA	43	13	21	55	9	11	16	20	6	13	15	8	8	3	198	48	193
OUTSIDE U.S. (TOTAL)	1136	486	1084	1794	382	502	671	568	493	528	490	452	328	237	8015	2442	6709

(A SUBSIDIARY MANUFACTURING IN SEVERAL INDUSTRIES, AT TIME OF ENTRY INTO PARENT SYSTEM, IS COUNTED ONCE FOR EACH INDUSTRY)

CHAPTER 2 — THE PROLIFERATION OF FOREIGN SUBSIDIARIES
SECTION 3 — FLOW OF SUBSIDIARY-INDUSTRIES
TABLE 3 — NET FLOW BY REGION AND INDUSTRY

NET FLOW (ENTRIES MINUS EXITS) OF SUBSIDIARY-INDUSTRIES UP TO 1-JAN-76

COUNTRY OR REGION	BEVERAGES	TOBACCO	FOOD	TXTL+APPRL	WOOD+FURNI	PAPER	PRINTING	INDUS-CHEM	PLASTIC	AGRIC-CHEM	COSMETICS	DRUGS	OTHER-CHEM	FABR-PLSTCS	TIRES	REF-PETRLM	OTH-PETRLM	LEATHER	STONE+CLAY+CEMNT	LEATHER	ABRASIVES	GLASS	IRON	GLASS
CANADA	20	1	78	27	21	26	10	32	23	6	26	29	35	19	7	7	21	14	6	3	6	10	6	6
LATIN AMER. (TOTAL)	34	11	177	30	12	67	9	67	59	21	86	134	67	27	21	14	21	14	6	3	15	29	21	6
C.AM.+CARIB.(TOTAL)	13	4	86	10	6	22	4	40	29	11	37	48	24	10	8	8	14	5	1	7	9	4	2	
BAHAMAS	0	0	2	0	0	0	0	0	0	1	1	0	2	0	0	0	5	1	0	0	7	9	4	
BERMUDA	1	1	2	0	0	0	0	1	1	0	0	1	0	0	0	0	0	0	0	0	0	0	0	
COSTA RICA	0	0	0	0	0	0	0	1	1	1	0	1	0	0	0	0	0	0	0	0	0	0	0	
GUATEMALA	1	0	5	0	2	1	0	1	0	0	6	2	2	0	1	1	0	0	0	0	0	0	0	
JAMAICA	1	0	11	0	1	1	0	1	0	0	2	5	5	0	1	0	0	0	0	0	0	0	0	
MEXICO	10	1	8	9	2	12	4	32	24	2	20	24	18	9	6	3	4	1	1	0	5	8	4	
NETH.ANTILLES	0	0	43	0	0	0	0	1	1	2	0	0	0	0	0	1	3	0	0	0	8	0	0	
NICARAGUA	0	0	0	0	0	0	0	1	1	2	0	0	2	0	0	0	1	0	0	0	0	0	0	
PANAMA	0	1	4	0	2	2	0	0	0	0	5	4	4	0	0	0	3	1	0	0	1	1	0	
OTHER C.AM+CAR.	0	1	6	1	0	1	0	3	1	4	3	8	0	0	0	6	6	0	0	0	0	0	0	
S.AMERICA (TOTAL)	21	7	91	20	6	45	5	27	30	10	49	86	43	17	19	9	7	9	2	8	20	17	4	
BOLIVIA	0	0	0	0	0	0	0	0	0	0	0	0	0	0	0	0	0	0	0	0	0	0	0	
CHILE	0	0	4	0	0	0	0	0	2	0	0	5	2	0	3	0	1	1	0	1	0	0	0	
COLOMBIA	6	0	18	3	1	8	0	4	7	4	5	13	8	1	3	1	1	0	1	2	1	0	1	
ECUADOR	1	0	3	0	0	0	0	0	1	0	0	5	0	0	3	1	1	0	0	1	0	0	0	
PERU	2	0	8	0	1	2	0	0	0	3	9	9	0	2	2	0	1	2	0	0	4	0	1	
ARGENTINA	3	1	12	2	1	5	2	5	9	0	11	14	6	3	3	2	2	4	1	0	4	4	2	
BRAZIL	5	1	23	5	2	13	3	11	6	2	9	19	16	6	3	3	4	1	0	2	8	6	1	
URUGUAY	2	0	2	0	1	0	0	1	1	1	3	3	0	0	1	1	0	0	0	0	0	0	0	
VENEZUELA	2	5	19	6	0	15	0	6	5	0	12	19	9	5	3	0	6	0	0	0	7	7	6	
OTHER S.AMER.	0	0	2	0	0	1	0	0	0	0	0	0	0	0	0	0	0	1	0	0	0	0	0	
EUROPE (TOTAL)	27	9	254	49	29	75	37	134	97	17	145	192	134	67	22	52	37	13	30	64	31	29		
BELGIUM	2	1	12	7	1	5	3	15	9	0	7	12	9	3	0	2	3	1	2	8	3	1		
FRANCE	4	0	23	7	2	18	6	15	11	4	27	28	17	4	3	8	10	1	4	11	1	5		
GERMANY	4	1	46	6	2	9	7	19	13	1	25	26	19	11	3	13	8	3	1	14	9	4		
ITALY	3	2	20	7	5	7	5	21	3	4	13	24	21	4	2	7	3	2	6	4	4	4		
LUXEMBOURG	0	0	0	2	0	0	0	0	1	0	0	0	0	1	2	1	0	0	1	0	0	0		
NETHERLANDS	1	1	23	4	2	2	1	8	5	1	6	5	12	4	4	0	1	0	1	1	0	0		
DENMARK	1	0	15	2	2	0	1	0	1	0	5	5	2	1	0	2	0	1	1	1	0	0		
IRELAND	1	0	8	1	1	3	0	3	1	0	4	12	2	5	0	0	6	2	0	2	0	0		
U.K.	7	1	43	12	7	12	10	27	35	2	27	27	28	19	2	5	6	3	14	11	9	10		
AUSTRIA	0	0	3	0	0	1	1	2	0	0	2	3	2	1	0	4	0	0	0	1	0	0		
FINLAND	0	0	0	0	0	1	0	0	0	0	2	0	0	1	0	0	0	0	0	0	1	0		
GREECE	1	0	5	0	0	2	0	2	2	0	2	9	0	0	0	3	0	0	0	2	1	0		
NORWAY	0	0	1	0	1	0	0	2	1	0	0	0	1	1	0	1	0	0	0	0	0	0		
PORTUGAL	0	0	4	2	0	1	0	0	3	0	3	1	0	0	0	0	3	0	3	0	3	0		
SPAIN	4	2	30	4	4	9	2	14	6	5	13	16	14	6	3	3	4	1	3	3	3	3		
SWEDEN	1	0	13	3	3	3	1	4	1	1	6	7	3	3	1	1	2	0	1	2	0	1		
SWITZERLAND	0	1	6	3	0	0	1	1	4	0	4	4	4	2	2	2	0	0	2	0	0	0		
TURKEY	1	0	2	0	0	0	0	0	1	0	0	4	0	1	1	2	0	0	0	0	0	1		
OTHER EUROPE	0	0	0	1	1	1	0	1	1	0	2	0	0	0	0	0	2	0	0	2	0	0		

48

TABLE   2 .3 .3   (CONTINUED)

COUNTRY OR REGION	BEVERAGES	TOBACCO	FOOD	TXTL+APPRL	WOOD+FURNI	PAPER	PRINTING	INDUS-CHEM	PLASTIC	AGRIC-CHEM	COSMETICS	DRUGS	OTHER-CHEM	FABR-PLSTCS TIRES	TIRES	REF-PETRLM	OTH-PETRLM	LEATHER	STONE+CLAY+CEMNT	ABRASIVES	GLASS	IRON
N.AFR+M.EAST (TOTAL)	0	0	11	2	1	4	0	7	5	2	10	14	6	1	6	5	3	1	1	2	0	1
ALGERIA	0	0	1	0	0	0	0	1	0	0	0	0	0	0	0	0	1	1	1	0	0	1
EGYPT	0	0	0	0	0	0	0	0	0	0	0	0	0	0	0	0	0	0	0	0	0	0
IRAN	0	0	1	0	0	1	0	2	1	0	2	9	3	0	3	0	1	0	0	1	0	0
ISRAEL	0	0	1	1	0	0	0	0	4	0	2	2	2	0	0	1	0	0	0	0	0	0
LEBANON	0	0	2	0	1	0	0	1	0	0	2	2	1	1	0	0	0	0	0	0	0	0
MOROCCO	0	0	2	0	0	2	0	1	0	0	2	1	0	0	2	0	0	0	0	0	0	0
SAUDI ARABIA	0	0	3	0	0	0	0	1	0	0	1	0	0	0	0	2	1	0	0	0	0	0
OTHER N.AF+M.E.	0	0	1	1	0	1	0	1	0	2	1	0	0	0	1	2	0	0	0	1	0	0
E.+W.AFRICA (TOTAL)	3	1	10	0	0	5	1	1	3	3	9	11	0	4	4	9	3	0	1	1	0	0
GHANA	0	1	1	0	0	0	0	1	1	0	1	0	0	0	1	3	1	0	0	1	0	0
IVORY COAST	0	0	1	0	0	0	0	0	0	0	0	1	0	0	1	2	0	0	0	0	0	0
KENYA	1	0	3	0	0	0	0	0	0	1	2	3	0	1	1	2	1	0	0	0	0	0
LIBERIA	0	0	0	0	0	0	0	0	0	0	0	0	0	0	0	0	0	0	0	0	0	0
NIGERIA	0	0	2	0	0	0	0	0	0	1	3	3	0	0	0	2	1	0	0	0	0	0
ZAIRE	0	0	0	0	0	0	0	0	2	0	1	3	0	0	0	0	0	0	0	0	0	0
ZAMBIA	1	0	0	0	0	3	0	0	0	0	1	1	0	1	0	0	0	0	0	0	0	0
OTHER E.+W.AFR.	1	0	3	0	0	2	1	0	0	1	1	0	0	2	1	0	0	0	1	0	0	0
SOUTH ASIA (TOTAL)	3	2	6	1	0	1	0	3	4	5	6	25	4	2	2	4	1	0	2	2	3	2
INDIA	2	1	3	1	0	0	0	2	4	4	2	15	4	2	1	2	1	0	2	2	2	2
PAKISTAN	1	1	2	0	0	0	0	1	0	1	2	8	0	0	1	1	0	0	0	0	1	0
SRI LANKA	0	0	1	0	0	1	0	0	0	0	1	1	0	0	0	1	0	0	0	0	0	0
OTHER S.ASIA	0	0	0	0	0	0	0	0	0	0	1	1	0	0	0	0	0	0	0	0	0	0
EAST ASIA (TOTAL)	10	1	46	6	4	16	4	37	40	11	27	52	27	9	7	18	8	0	4	12	7	1
HONG KONG	0	0	2	0	1	0	0	1	1	1	3	2	4	0	0	0	0	0	0	0	0	1
INDONESIA	0	1	2	0	0	0	0	0	0	1	2	2	4	0	0	0	0	0	0	0	1	0
JAPAN	4	0	20	5	2	5	2	23	25	1	8	10	11	5	1	8	4	0	1	8	5	0
MALAYSIA	0	0	3	0	0	1	0	0	1	2	2	13	0	1	1	1	0	0	1	1	0	0
PHILIPPINES	3	0	10	0	1	4	1	3	3	1	6	13	3	1	2	1	2	0	1	1	0	0
SINGAPORE	1	0	2	1	0	0	0	4	3	0	3	1	3	0	1	3	0	0	0	0	1	0
S.KOREA	0	0	2	0	0	0	0	2	3	5	1	1	1	0	0	3	1	0	0	0	0	0
THAILAND	0	0	4	0	0	2	0	1	1	0	1	5	1	1	1	1	0	0	0	1	0	0
TAIWAN	1	0	1	0	0	0	1	3	3	0	1	5	0	1	1	1	1	0	1	1	0	0
OTHER E.ASIA	1	0	0	0	0	4	0	0	0	0	0	0	0	0	0	0	0	0	0	0	0	0
S.DOMINIONS (TOTAL)	11	4	57	7	7	38	8	25	27	6	45	58	34	15	6	13	5	2	5	13	6	4
AUSTRALIA	8	3	28	3	4	10	2	16	19	3	22	27	18	8	4	8	3	2	3	6	4	3
NEW ZEALAND	0	1	9	1	2	4	1	6	3	1	9	10	5	0	1	1	0	0	1	4	0	0
RHODESIA	0	0	0	1	0	3	1	0	0	1	2	1	1	1	0	1	0	0	0	1	1	0
S.AFRICA	3	0	20	2	1	21	4	3	5	1	12	20	10	6	1	3	2	0	1	2	1	1
OUTSIDE U.S. (TOTAL)	108	29	636	122	74	232	69	306	258	71	354	515	307	144	81	129	77	23	63	133	74	49

(TABLE CONTINUED ON FOLLOWING PAGES)

TABLE   2 .3 .3   (CONTINUED)

COUNTRY OR REGION	NON-FERROUS METAL	CANS FAB-MET	ENGINES FAB-MET	CONSTR-MC FARM-MC	OFF-MC+COMPUT FARM-MC	SPECL-MC GENL-MC	OTH-NON-EL-MC GENL-MC	EL-LT+WIRING EL-TRAN	RAD+TV+APPL EL-TRAN	ELECTRONICS OTH-ELE	COMMUNICATION OTH-ELE	MOTOR-VEHIC OTH-TRN	PRECISION OTH-TRN	MISC	TOTAL
CANADA	22	8	52	4	23	4	9	11	25	25	8	10	17	14	9	39	9	24	46	767
LATIN AMER. (TOTAL)	27	17	54	3	37	6	9	15	31	23	18	5	28	54	9	87	8	31	60	1478
C.AM.+CARIB. (TOTAL)	6	7	23	0	14	0	5	6	16	7	9	2	12	25	3	20	3	9	22	599
BAHAMAS	0	0	0	0	0	0	0	0	0	0	0	0	0	0	0	0	0	0	0	6
BERMUDA	0	0	0	0	0	0	0	0	0	0	0	0	0	0	0	0	0	0	0	2
COSTA RICA	0	1	1	0	0	0	0	0	0	0	0	0	0	0	0	0	0	0	0	23
GUATEMALA	0	0	1	0	0	0	0	0	0	0	0	0	1	1	0	0	0	0	3	35
JAMAICA	0	0	1	0	0	0	0	0	0	0	0	2	0	2	0	0	0	7	1	21
MEXICO	5	3	19	0	14	5	5	16	6	7	2	10	13	18	3	20	3	7	15	414
NETH.ANTILLES	0	0	0	0	0	0	0	0	0	0	0	0	1	0	0	0	0	0	0	5
NICARAGUA	0	0	0	0	0	0	0	0	0	0	0	0	0	0	0	0	0	0	0	14
PANAMA	0	1	0	0	0	0	0	0	0	0	0	0	0	2	0	1	0	1	0	29
OTHER C.AM+CAR.	1	2	1	0	0	0	1	0	1	0	1	0	1	1	0	0	0	0	3	50
S.AMERICA (TOTAL)	21	10	31	3	23	6	4	9	16	9	3	16	29	67	6	67	5	22	38	879
BOLIVIA	0	0	0	0	1	0	0	0	0	0	0	0	0	0	0	0	0	0	0	1
CHILE	0	2	1	0	1	0	1	0	1	0	1	1	0	1	1	0	0	0	3	30
COLOMBIA	2	2	5	0	0	2	1	0	1	0	0	0	2	8	0	0	0	1	7	124
ECUADOR	0	1	1	0	2	0	1	0	0	0	0	1	0	0	0	0	0	0	1	19
PERU	0	0	2	0	0	0	0	0	0	0	0	2	0	2	0	0	1	1	1	50
ARGENTINA	7	0	2	2	4	3	0	0	6	1	1	4	3	14	6	4	1	6	4	156
BRAZIL	7	3	7	1	12	2	5	10	8	1	0	4	19	28	2	12	4	12	11	289
URUGUAY	0	0	0	0	0	0	1	0	0	1	1	0	0	2	0	0	0	0	1	19
VENEZUELA	5	2	12	0	2	0	1	1	2	0	1	4	4	12	1	12	0	3	10	187
OTHER S.AMER.	0	0	0	0	0	0	0	0	0	1	0	0	0	0	1	0	0	0	0	4
EUROPE (TOTAL)	69	14	161	22	65	20	38	71	72	67	15	21	49	72	39	127	23	117	168	2827
BELGIUM	3	2	7	5	7	1	4	6	2	6	1	2	2	4	4	7	1	7	6	181
FRANCE	2	2	15	5	14	3	3	10	6	10	1	8	12	9	6	20	8	23	24	398
GERMANY	11	5	26	4	7	4	10	11	12	2	2	7	11	11	7	22	2	29	23	462
ITALY	3	0	13	1	6	10	10	8	10	5	3	7	2	11	3	16	2	8	15	282
LUXEMBOURG	0	0	0	0	1	0	0	1	0	0	0	0	1	0	0	0	0	2	0	14
NETHERLANDS	5	1	7	1	2	3	2	4	4	0	2	2	5	0	2	6	1	8	11	144
DENMARK	1	0	3	1	1	0	0	2	2	2	0	1	1	1	0	4	0	8	2	43
IRELAND	0	0	0	0	2	1	0	1	1	0	0	0	1	0	2	3	0	2	2	68
U.K.	33	2	56	2	17	6	25	21	15	21	10	13	15	25	7	35	7	28	53	696
AUSTRIA	0	0	2	0	1	1	1	0	0	1	1	1	0	1	2	1	0	1	2	33
FINLAND	0	0	0	0	1	0	0	1	0	0	0	0	0	0	1	0	0	2	2	10
GREECE	0	1	0	0	1	1	1	0	0	1	0	1	0	1	1	0	0	1	1	39
NORWAY	4	0	2	0	0	0	0	1	2	0	0	0	0	1	0	0	0	0	1	21
PORTUGAL	0	2	0	0	0	1	0	0	0	1	0	1	0	1	0	1	0	0	4	44
SPAIN	5	1	16	2	5	3	2	7	4	3	1	3	4	4	4	8	3	3	10	227
SWEDEN	1	2	4	1	1	1	0	2	2	1	0	0	1	4	1	2	1	2	7	85
SWITZERLAND	1	0	1	1	1	3	0	2	1	1	1	0	1	4	0	0	0	2	1	47
TURKEY	0	0	0	0	0	2	0	1	0	0	0	1	1	0	0	1	0	0	0	19
OTHER EUROPE	1	0	1	0	0	0	0	0	1	1	0	0	1	1	0	0	0	1	1	14

TABLE 2 .3 .3 (CONTINUED)

COUNTRY OR REGION	NON-FERROUS	METAL CANS	FAB-MET	ENGINES	CONSTR-MC	FARM-MC	OFF-MC+COMPUT	SPECL-MC	GENL-MC	OTH-NON-EL-MC	EL-LT+WIRING	EL-TRAN	RAD+TV+APPL	ELECTRONICS	OTH-ELE	COMMUNICATION	MOTOR-VEHIC	OTH-TRN	PRECISION	MISC	TOTAL
N.AFR+M.EAST (TOTAL)	3	1	3	0	5	1	0	2	1	0	0	2	0	0	3	1	4	0	3	4	115
ALGERIA	0	0	0	0	0	1	0	0	0	0	0	0	0	0	0	0	1	0	0	0	3
EGYPT	0	0	1	0	2	0	0	0	0	0	0	0	0	0	1	0	0	0	1	0	4
IRAN	2	1	0	0	1	1	0	0	1	0	0	1	0	0	2	0	0	0	1	1	35
ISRAEL	0	0	0	0	0	0	0	0	0	0	0	0	0	0	0	1	0	0	1	1	18
LEBANON	0	0	2	0	1	0	0	1	0	0	0	0	0	0	0	0	1	0	0	0	9
MOROCCO	0	0	0	0	0	0	0	0	3	0	0	0	0	0	0	0	1	0	0	1	20
SAUDI ARABIA	0	0	0	0	0	0	0	0	0	0	0	0	1	0	1	1	1	0	0	0	10
OTHER N.AF+M.E.	1	0	0	0	1	0	0	0	0	0	1	1	0	0	1	0	1	0	0	1	16
E.+W.AFRICA (TOTAL)	7	4	4	0	0	0	0	0	0	0	5	5	2	5	5	2	1	0	1	6	106
GHANA	1	1	0	0	0	0	0	0	0	0	2	0	2	1	0	0	0	0	0	0	7
IVORY COAST	0	0	0	0	0	0	0	0	0	0	0	0	0	1	1	0	0	0	0	0	4
KENYA	0	0	0	0	0	0	0	0	0	0	0	0	0	1	1	0	0	0	1	1	17
LIBERIA	0	0	0	0	0	0	0	0	0	0	0	0	0	0	0	0	0	0	0	1	1
NIGERIA	0	0	0	0	0	0	0	0	0	0	2	2	1	1	1	1	0	0	0	3	24
ZAIRE	2	0	1	0	0	0	0	0	0	0	0	2	1	0	1	1	1	0	0	1	16
ZAMBIA	3	1	1	0	0	0	0	0	0	0	1	0	0	0	0	1	0	0	0	0	14
OTHER E.+W.AFR.	1	3	2	0	0	0	0	0	0	0	1	1	1	0	0	0	0	0	0	0	23
SOUTH ASIA (TOTAL)	3	0	0	0	2	2	1	0	4	3	5	5	5	0	7	0	4	1	3	2	122
INDIA	3	0	0	0	2	2	1	0	4	3	3	3	3	0	5	0	4	1	1	1	90
PAKISTAN	0	0	0	0	0	0	0	0	0	0	1	1	0	0	1	0	0	0	2	0	24
SRI LANKA	0	0	0	0	0	0	0	0	0	0	0	1	0	0	1	0	0	0	0	1	7
OTHER S.ASIA	0	0	0	0	0	0	0	0	0	0	0	0	0	0	0	0	0	0	0	0	1
EAST ASIA (TOTAL)	20	5	27	6	15	3	13	5	18	6	7	2	19	29	25	8	28	0	13	30	626
HONG KONG	5	0	2	0	1	1	1	0	0	0	3	3	3	2	3	1	0	0	2	1	40
INDONESIA	6	3	3	0	1	0	0	0	5	0	2	0	0	8	1	0	0	0	1	2	27
JAPAN	6	0	10	4	9	8	8	4	15	5	2	2	0	4	12	0	18	0	9	15	288
MALAYSIA	0	0	2	0	0	0	0	1	0	1	2	0	2	4	3	1	1	0	1	3	32
PHILIPPINES	1	4	4	2	1	2	2	0	1	0	2	0	2	3	0	3	3	0	3	2	74
SINGAPORE	3	0	2	0	3	1	0	0	0	0	5	0	3	0	4	1	0	0	0	0	41
S.KOREA	2	1	1	0	0	0	0	0	0	0	2	0	0	3	1	1	2	0	0	1	33
THAILAND	3	0	2	0	0	1	0	1	0	0	1	0	1	1	1	2	3	0	1	2	39
TAIWAN	1	0	0	0	0	0	0	0	1	0	4	0	8	0	1	2	1	0	1	0	49
OTHER E.ASIA	0	1	1	0	0	0	0	0	0	0	0	0	0	0	0	0	0	0	0	0	3
S.DOMINIONS (TOTAL)	25	4	43	2	24	3	3	8	12	20	2	6	1	4	14	2	38	2	18	38	668
AUSTRALIA	21	3	23	1	13	2	2	4	9	13	5	5	1	4	9	2	18	2	15	23	374
NEW ZEALAND	2	0	9	0	2	1	1	1	1	1	0	0	0	0	1	0	5	0	1	0	84
RHODESIA	0	0	1	0	0	0	0	0	0	0	0	0	0	0	0	0	1	0	2	5	17
S.AFRICA	2	1	10	1	9	2	3	3	2	7	1	1	1	0	4	1	14	0	2	9	193
OUTSIDE U.S. (TOTAL)	176	53	351	37	171	41	73	112	163	144	53	44	126	111	194	71	328	43	210	354	6709

CHAPTER 2   - THE PROLIFERATION OF FOREIGN SUBSIDIARIES
SECTION 3   -- FLOW OF SUBSIDIARY-INDUSTRIES
TABLE 4   --- NET FLOW BY PRINCIPAL INDUSTRY OF SUBSIDIARY

NET FLOW (ENTRIES MINUS EXITS) UP TO 1-JAN-76

NO. OF SUBSIDIARY-INDUSTRIES, BY PRINCIPAL INDUSTRY OF SUBSIDIARY, AT TIME OF ENTRY INTO PARENT SYSTEM

PRINCIPAL INDUSTRY	BEVERAGES	TOBACCO	FOOD	TXTL+APPRL	WOOD+FURNI	PAPER	PRINTING	INDUS-CHEM	PLASTIC	AGRIC-CHEM	COSMETICS	DRUGS	OTHER-CHEM	FABR-PLSTCS	TIRES	REF-PETRLM	OTH-PETRLM	LEATHER	STONE+CLAY+CEMNT	ABRASIVES	GLASS	IRON
BEVERAGES	97	0	10	0	0	0	0	0	0	0	0	0	0	0	0	0	0	0	0	0	0	0
TOBACCO	0	28	0	0	0	0	0	0	0	0	0	0	0	0	0	0	0	0	0	0	0	0
FOOD	11	0	614	1	0	0	0	1	3	1	7	2	13	0	0	1	0	0	0	0	0	0
TEXTILES+APPAREL	0	0	0	108	1	1	0	0	5	0	0	0	1	1	0	0	0	0	0	0	1	1
WOOD+FURNITURE	0	0	0	1	59	0	0	0	1	0	0	0	5	0	0	0	0	0	2	1	0	0
PAPER	1	0	0	1	2	207	1	1	2	0	3	0	0	3	0	0	1	1	0	0	1	1
PRINTING	0	0	0	0	0	0	65	0	0	0	0	0	0	0	0	0	0	0	0	0	0	0
INDUSTRIAL CHEM	0	1	0	0	1	2	0	259	14	5	2	6	18	3	0	1	4	1	0	3	1	2
PLASTICS	0	2	0	2	1	0	0	3	196	1	2	2	7	9	1	0	1	0	1	0	1	0
AGRIC CHEM	0	0	0	0	0	0	0	3	3	49	1	4	3	0	0	0	0	0	0	0	0	0
COSMETICS	0	4	0	4	4	2	0	1	5	0	266	14	1	2	0	0	2	1	0	3	0	2
DRUGS	0	4	0	0	4	2	0	4	4	8	46	478	6	1	0	0	0	0	0	0	1	0
OTHER CHEM	0	0	13	1	1	2	0	14	12	4	15	2	231	2	1	2	2	0	0	5	0	2
FABR PLASTICS	0	0	0	0	0	2	0	0	2	2	0	0	2	81	1	1	0	0	5	0	2	2
TIRES	0	0	0	0	0	0	0	0	3	1	0	0	1	17	77	0	0	0	0	0	0	0
REF PETROLEUM	0	0	0	0	0	0	0	6	1	0	0	1	1	0	0	121	6	0	0	0	0	0
OTH PETROLEUM	0	0	0	0	0	0	0	5	3	0	1	0	0	0	0	3	61	21	0	0	0	0
LEATHER	0	0	0	0	0	0	0	0	0	0	0	0	2	3	0	0	0	0	0	0	0	0
STONE+CLAY+CEMNT	0	0	0	0	0	0	0	1	1	0	0	0	1	0	0	0	1	0	51	7	1	0
ABRASIVES	0	0	0	0	1	1	0	3	1	0	0	6	6	1	0	1	0	0	2	108	0	1
GLASS	0	0	0	0	0	0	0	1	0	0	0	1	1	0	0	0	0	0	0	1	65	0
IRON+STEEL	0	0	0	1	0	0	0	0	0	0	0	0	1	0	0	0	0	0	0	0	0	40

TABLE 2.3.4 (CONTINUED)

PRINCIPAL INDUSTRY	BEVERAGES	TOBACCO	FOOD	TXTL+APPRL	WOOD+FURNI	PAPER	PRINTING	INDUS-CHEM	PLASTIC	AGRIC-CHEM	COSMETICS	DRUGS	OTHER-CHEM	FABR-PLSTCS	TIRES	REF-PETRLM	OTH-PETRLM	LEATHER	STONE+CLAY+CEMNT	ABRASIVES	GLASS	IRON
NON-FERROUS	0	0	0	0	0	0	1	1	2	0	0	1	0	2	0	0	0	0	1	0	0	0
METAL CANS	0	0	0	0	0	2	0	0	0	0	0	0	0	0	0	0	0	0	0	0	0	0
OTHER FAB METAL	0	0	0	0	2	3	1	0	0	0	1	0	1	3	0	0	0	0	2	2	0	1
ENGINES+TURBIN	0	0	0	0	0	0	0	1	0	0	0	0	0	0	0	0	0	0	0	0	0	0
CONSTR MACH	0	0	0	0	0	0	0	0	0	0	0	0	0	0	0	0	0	0	0	2	0	0
FARM MACHINERY	0	0	0	1	1	0	0	0	0	0	0	0	0	0	0	0	0	0	0	0	0	0
OFFICE MC+COMPUT	0	0	0	0	0	1	0	0	0	0	0	0	0	0	0	0	0	0	0	0	0	0
SPEC MACHINERY	0	0	0	0	7	0	0	0	0	0	0	0	0	0	0	0	0	0	0	0	0	0
GENL MACHINERY	0	0	0	0	0	0	1	0	1	1	1	0	1	2	0	0	0	0	1	1	0	0
OTH NON-EL MC	0	0	0	0	0	0	0	0	0	0	0	0	0	1	0	0	0	0	3	0	1	0
EL LIGHT+WIRING	0	0	0	0	0	0	0	0	0	0	0	0	0	0	0	0	0	0	0	0	1	0
EL TRAN EQUIP	0	0	0	0	0	0	0	0	0	0	0	0	0	0	0	0	0	0	0	0	0	0
RADIO+TV+APPL	0	0	0	0	0	0	0	0	0	0	0	0	0	0	0	0	0	0	0	0	0	0
ELECTRONICS	0	0	0	0	0	0	0	0	0	0	0	0	0	1	0	0	0	0	0	1	1	0
OTHER ELEC	0	1	0	0	0	0	0	3	3	0	0	0	1	2	0	0	0	0	0	1	0	0
COMMUNICATION	0	1	0	0	0	1	0	0	0	0	0	0	0	0	0	0	0	0	0	0	1	0
MOTOR VEHIC	0	0	0	0	1	0	0	0	0	0	0	0	0	3	0	0	0	0	0	1	0	1
OTHER TRANSP	0	0	0	0	0	0	0	0	0	0	0	0	0	1	0	0	0	0	0	0	0	1
PRECISION	0	0	0	3	0	4	0	0	0	1	8	3	5	4	0	0	0	0	0	0	1	0
MISCELLANEOUS	0	0	0	0	0	1	0	0	0	0	0	1	0	1	0	0	0	0	1	1	0	0
TOTAL	108	29	636	122	74	232	69	306	258	71	354	515	307	144	81	129	77	23	63	133	74	49

(TABLE CONTINUED ON FOLLOWING PAGES)

TABLE   2 .3 .4   (CONTINUED)

PRINCIPAL INDUSTRY	NON-FERROUS METAL	CANS FAB-MET	ENGINES CONSTR-MC	ENGINES FARM-MC	OFF-MC+COMPUT SPECL-MC	OFF-MC+COMPUT GENL-MC	OTH-NON-EL-MC EL-LT+WIRING	OTH-NON-EL-MC EL-TRAN	RAD+TV+APPL ELECTRONICS	RAD+TV+APPL OTH-ELE	COMMUNICATION MOTOR-VEHIC	COMMUNICATION OTH-TRN	PRECISION MISC	TOTAL
BEVERAGES	0	0	0	0	0	0	0	0	0	0	0	0	0	107
TOBACCO	0	0	0	0	0	0	0	0	0	0	0	0	0	28
FOOD	0	0	0	0	0	0	0	0	0	0	0	0	0	652
TEXTILES+APPAREL	0	0	0	0	1	1	0	0	0	0	0	1	0	120
WOOD+FURNITURE	0	4	0	0	0	1	0	0	0	0	0	0	0	74
PAPER	2	0	0	0	0	0	0	0	0	0	0	3	0	227
PRINTING	0	2	0	0	0	0	0	0	0	0	0	0	2	69
INDUSTRIAL CHEM	2	2	0	0	1	0	0	1	0	5	0	1	1	335
PLASTICS	0	0	0	0	0	0	0	0	1	0	0	0	1	230
AGRIC CHEM	0	0	0	0	0	0	0	0	0	0	0	0	0	62
COSMETICS	0	0	0	0	0	0	0	1	0	1	1	1	2	302
DRUGS	0	0	0	0	1	1	0	0	0	0	0	12	1	568
OTHER CHEM	1	1	0	0	1	0	0	0	0	0	1	1	0	300
FABR PLASTICS	0	2	0	0	0	0	0	0	0	0	1	0	0	97
TIRES	0	0	0	0	0	0	0	0	0	0	1	0	0	100
REF PETROLEUM	0	0	0	0	0	0	0	0	0	1	0	0	0	136
OTH PETROLEUM	0	0	0	0	0	0	0	0	0	0	0	0	0	73
LEATHER	0	0	0	0	0	0	0	0	0	0	0	0	1	27
STONE+CLAY+CEMNT	0	2	0	0	0	2	1	1	0	1	0	0	2	69
ABRASIVES	2	1	0	0	1	2	4	0	0	0	1	1	1	141
GLASS	0	3	0	0	0	0	0	0	0	0	0	1	0	78
IRON+STEEL	6	5	0	1	0	1	1	0	0	1	1	0	1	61

55

TABLE 2 . 3 . 4 (CONTINUED)

Column groups: NON-FERROUS [NON-FERROUS, METAL CANS]; ENGINES [FAB-MET, ENGINES, CONSTR-MC]; OFF-MC+COMPUT [FARM-MC, OFF-MC+COMPUT, SPECL-MC]; OTH-NON-EL-MC [GENL-MC, OTH-NON-EL-MC]; RAD+TV+APPL [EL-LT+WIRING, EL-TRAN, RAD+TV+APPL]; COMMUNICATION [ELECTRONICS, OTH-ELE, COMMUNICATION]; [MOTOR-VEHIC, OTH-TRN]; PRECISION [PRECISION, MISC].

PRINCIPAL INDUSTRY	NON-FERROUS	METAL CANS	FAB-MET	ENGINES	CONSTR-MC	FARM-MC	OFF-MC+COMPUT	SPECL-MC	GENL-MC	OTH-NON-EL-MC	EL-LT+WIRING	EL-TRAN	RAD+TV+APPL	ELECTRONICS	OTH-ELE	COMMUNICATION	MOTOR-VEHIC	OTH-TRN	PRECISION	MISC	TOTAL
NON-FERROUS	151	2	2	0	0	0	0	0	0	1	3	0	1	0	0	0	1	0	0	2	171
METAL CANS	0	42	1	0	0	0	0	0	0	1	0	0	0	0	0	0	1	0	0	0	47
OTHER FAB METAL	6	6	296	0	2	1	1	3	12	5	2	0	2	1	2	0	5	2	6	4	372
ENGINES+TURBIN	0	0	1	27	2	0	0	2	2	3	0	0	0	0	0	0	3	0	2	0	43
CONSTR MACH	0	0	1	2	141	1	0	3	9	1	0	0	1	0	0	1	3	0	2	0	167
FARM MACHINERY	0	0	0	0	1	29	0	0	0	0	0	0	1	0	1	0	1	0	0	0	35
OFFICE MC+COMPUT	0	0	0	0	0	0	58	0	1	0	0	0	1	5	1	0	0	0	1	0	68
SPEC MACHINERY	0	0	4	0	12	2	2	95	2	2	0	0	2	0	1	0	1	0	1	1	132
GENL MACHINERY	1	0	4	1	6	1	1	3	112	2	0	2	0	0	4	1	2	2	3	2	155
OTH NON-EL MC	0	0	2	1	1	0	1	0	11	110	1	2	1	1	0	0	0	2	3	0	140
EL LIGHT+WIRING	0	0	0	0	0	0	0	0	0	1	38	0	4	2	1	1	0	0	2	0	50
EL TRAN EQUIP	1	0	1	0	0	0	0	0	1	1	2	35	0	1	7	1	0	0	0	0	50
RADIO+TV+APPL	0	0	3	0	0	0	2	0	0	3	0	0	95	3	2	3	0	0	0	0	111
ELECTRONICS	0	0	0	0	0	0	2	0	0	0	0	1	4	87	3	2	1	0	2	0	105
OTHER ELEC	4	0	4	2	2	1	2	0	2	0	6	1	7	3	155	1	5	1	4	0	210
COMMUNICATION	0	0	1	1	1	0	0	1	0	0	0	1	2	5	1	55	0	0	1	0	70
MOTOR VEHIC	2	0	7	3	1	5	0	0	1	6	0	0	3	0	2	1	296	3	3	1	340
OTHER TRANSP	0	0	0	0	1	1	0	0	0	0	0	0	0	0	3	0	2	33	2	0	43
PRECISION	0	0	1	0	1	0	1	0	2	1	0	0	0	2	3	3	1	0	154	1	199
MISCELLANEOUS	0	0	3	0	0	0	0	1	1	1	0	0	0	0	1	0	1	0	1	331	345
TOTAL	176	53	351	37	171	41	73	112	163	144	53	44	126	111	194	71	328	43	210	354	6709

CHAPTER 2   – THE PROLIFERATION OF FOREIGN SUBSIDIARIES
SECTION 4   -- GEOGRAPHICAL SPREAD IN SPECIFIC INDUSTRIES
TABLE 1 --- THE BEVERAGES INDUSTRY (SIC 208)

NO. OF SUBSIDIARIES MANUFACTURING IN THIS INDUSTRY AT TIME OF ENTRY INTO PARENT SYSTEM

COUNTRY OR REGION	NET FLOW UP TO 31-DEC-50	NO. OF ENTRIES DURING YEAR(S)													TOTAL ENTRIES 1951-75	TOTAL EXITS 1951-75	NET FLOW UP TO 1-JAN-76
		51-55	56-60	61-65	1966	1967	1968	1969	1970	1971	1972	1973	1974	1975			
CANADA	5	0	1	2	0	1	5	1	3	7	1	1	1	0	23	8	20
LATIN AMER. (TOTAL)	11	2	3	6	4	1	7	1	1	1	2	6	1	0	35	12	34
C.AM.+CARIB.(TOTAL)	3	0	1	1	1	0	1	0	0	1	1	6	0	0	12	2	13
BAHAMAS	0	0	0	0	0	0	0	0	0	0	0	0	0	0	0	0	0
BERMUDA	0	0	0	1	0	0	0	0	0	0	0	0	0	0	1	0	1
COSTA RICA	0	0	0	0	0	0	0	0	0	0	0	0	0	0	0	0	0
GUATEMALA	0	0	1	0	0	0	0	0	0	0	0	0	0	0	1	0	1
JAMAICA	0	0	0	0	0	0	1	0	0	0	0	0	0	0	1	0	1
MEXICO	1	0	0	0	1	0	0	0	0	1	1	6	0	0	9	0	10
NETH.ANTILLES	0	0	0	0	0	0	0	0	0	0	0	0	0	0	0	0	0
NICARAGUA	0	0	0	0	0	0	0	0	0	0	0	0	0	0	0	0	0
PANAMA	0	0	0	0	0	0	0	0	0	0	0	0	0	0	0	0	0
OTHER C.AM+CAR.	2	0	0	0	0	0	0	0	0	0	0	0	0	0	0	2	0
S.AMERICA (TOTAL)	8	2	2	5	3	1	6	1	1	0	1	0	1	0	23	10	21
BOLIVIA	0	0	0	0	0	0	1	0	0	0	0	0	0	0	1	1	0
CHILE	0	0	0	0	0	0	2	0	0	0	0	0	0	0	2	2	0
COLOMBIA	1	1	0	0	2	0	1	0	1	0	0	0	0	0	5	0	6
ECUADOR	0	0	0	0	0	0	1	0	0	0	0	0	0	0	1	0	1
PERU	3	0	0	0	0	1	0	0	0	0	0	0	0	0	1	2	2
ARGENTINA	2	0	0	2	0	0	1	0	0	0	1	0	0	0	4	3	3
BRAZIL	2	0	1	2	0	0	0	1	0	0	0	0	1	0	5	2	5
URUGUAY	0	1	0	1	0	0	0	0	0	0	0	0	0	0	2	0	2
VENEZUELA	0	0	1	0	1	0	0	0	0	0	0	0	0	0	2	0	2
OTHER S.AMER.	0	0	0	0	0	0	0	0	0	0	0	0	0	0	0	0	0
EUROPE (TOTAL)	14	2	1	7	0	1	9	1	2	0	1	1	2	0	27	14	27
BELGIUM	1	0	0	2	0	0	0	0	0	0	0	0	0	0	2	1	2
FRANCE	1	0	0	0	0	0	0	0	0	0	1	0	0	0	1	0	2
GERMANY	1	0	0	1	0	0	2	0	0	0	0	0	0	0	3	0	4
ITALY	0	0	0	1	0	0	3	0	0	0	0	1	0	0	5	2	3
LUXEMBOURG	0	0	0	0	0	0	0	0	0	0	0	0	0	0	0	0	0
NETHERLANDS	0	0	0	1	0	0	0	0	0	0	0	0	0	0	1	0	1
DENMARK	0	0	0	0	0	1	0	0	0	0	0	0	0	0	1	0	1
IRELAND	0	0	0	0	0	0	1	0	0	0	0	0	0	0	1	0	1
U.K.	11	2	1	2	0	0	1	0	1	0	0	0	0	0	7	11	7
AUSTRIA	0	0	0	0	0	0	0	0	0	0	0	0	0	0	0	0	0
FINLAND	0	0	0	0	0	0	0	0	0	0	0	0	0	0	0	0	0
GREECE	0	0	0	0	0	0	0	1	0	0	0	0	0	0	1	0	1
NORWAY	0	0	0	0	0	0	0	0	0	0	0	0	0	0	0	0	0
PORTUGAL	0	0	0	0	0	0	0	0	0	0	0	0	0	0	0	0	0
SPAIN	0	0	0	0	0	0	2	0	1	0	0	0	0	0	3	0	3
SWEDEN	0	0	0	0	0	0	0	0	0	0	0	0	1	0	1	0	1
SWITZERLAND	0	0	0	0	0	0	0	0	0	0	0	0	0	0	0	0	0
TURKEY	0	0	0	0	0	0	0	0	0	0	0	0	1	0	1	0	1
OTHER EUROPE	0	0	0	0	0	0	0	0	0	0	0	0	0	0	0	0	0

TABLE 2.4.1 (CONTINUED)

COUNTRY OR REGION	NET FLOW UP TO 31-DEC-50	NO. OF ENTRIES DURING YEAR(S)													TOTAL ENTRIES 1951-75	TOTAL EXITS 1951-75	NET FLOW UP TO 1-JAN-76
		51-55	56-60	61-65	1966	1967	1968	1969	1970	1971	1972	1973	1974	1975			
N.AFR+M.EAST (TOTAL)	0	0	0	0	0	0	0	0	0	0	0	0	0	0	0	0	0
ALGERIA	0	0	0	0	0	0	0	0	0	0	0	0	0	0	0	0	0
EGYPT	0	0	0	0	0	0	0	0	0	0	0	0	0	0	0	0	0
IRAN	0	0	0	0	0	0	0	0	0	0	0	0	0	0	0	0	0
ISRAEL	0	0	0	0	0	0	0	0	0	0	0	0	0	0	0	0	0
LEBANON	0	0	0	0	0	0	0	0	0	0	0	0	0	0	0	0	0
MOROCCO	0	0	0	0	0	0	0	0	0	0	0	0	0	0	0	0	0
SAUDI ARABIA	0	0	0	0	0	0	0	0	0	0	0	0	0	0	0	0	0
OTHER N.AF+M.E.	0	0	0	0	0	0	0	0	0	0	0	0	0	0	0	0	0
E.+W.AFRICA (TOTAL)	0	0	1	1	0	0	0	0	0	1	0	0	0	0	3	0	3
GHANA	0	0	0	0	0	0	0	0	0	0	0	0	0	0	0	0	0
IVORY COAST	0	0	0	0	0	0	0	0	0	0	0	0	0	0	0	0	0
KENYA	0	0	1	0	0	0	0	0	0	0	0	0	0	0	1	0	1
LIBERIA	0	0	0	0	0	0	0	0	0	0	0	0	0	0	0	0	0
NIGERIA	0	0	0	0	0	0	0	0	0	0	0	0	0	0	0	0	0
ZAIRE	0	0	0	0	0	0	0	0	0	0	0	0	0	0	0	0	0
ZAMBIA	0	0	0	1	0	0	0	0	0	0	0	0	0	0	1	0	1
OTHER E.+W.AFR.	0	0	0	0	0	0	0	0	0	1	0	0	0	0	1	0	1
SOUTH ASIA (TOTAL)	1	0	1	1	0	0	0	0	0	0	0	0	0	0	2	0	3
INDIA	1	0	1	0	0	0	0	0	0	0	0	0	0	0	1	0	2
PAKISTAN	0	0	0	1	0	0	0	0	0	0	0	0	0	0	1	0	1
SRI LANKA	0	0	0	0	0	0	0	0	0	0	0	0	0	0	0	0	0
OTHER S.ASIA	0	0	0	0	0	0	0	0	0	0	0	0	0	0	0	0	0
EAST ASIA (TOTAL)	0	1	5	0	1	0	1	0	0	0	0	1	3	0	12	2	10
HONG KONG	0	0	0	0	0	0	0	0	0	0	0	0	0	0	0	0	0
INDONESIA	0	0	0	0	0	0	0	0	0	0	0	0	0	0	0	0	0
JAPAN	0	1	2	0	0	0	0	0	0	0	0	0	2	0	5	1	4
MALAYSIA	0	0	0	0	0	0	0	0	0	0	0	0	0	0	0	0	0
PHILIPPINES	0	0	3	0	1	0	0	0	0	0	0	0	0	0	4	1	3
SINGAPORE	0	0	0	0	0	0	0	0	0	0	0	0	0	0	0	0	0
S.KOREA	0	0	0	0	0	0	0	0	0	0	0	1	0	0	1	0	1
THAILAND	0	0	0	0	0	0	1	0	0	0	0	0	0	0	1	0	1
TAIWAN	0	0	0	0	0	0	0	0	0	0	0	0	0	0	0	0	0
OTHER E.ASIA	0	0	0	0	0	0	0	0	0	0	0	0	1	0	1	0	1
S.DOMINIONS (TOTAL)	2	1	3	2	1	0	2	0	2	3	2	1	0	0	17	8	11
AUSTRALIA	0	1	1	1	0	0	2	0	2	3	1	1	0	0	12	4	8
NEW ZEALAND	0	0	0	0	0	0	0	0	0	0	0	0	0	0	0	0	0
RHODESIA	0	0	0	0	0	0	0	0	0	0	0	0	0	0	0	0	0
S.AFRICA	2	0	2	1	1	0	0	0	0	0	1	0	0	0	5	4	3
OUTSIDE U.S. (TOTAL)	33	6	15	19	6	3	24	3	8	13	10	5	7	0	119	44	108

CHAPTER 2 - THE PROLIFERATION OF FOREIGN SUBSIDIARIES
SECTION 4 -- GEOGRAPHICAL SPREAD IN SPECIFIC INDUSTRIES
TABLE 2 --- THE TOBACCO INDUSTRY (SIC 21)

NO. OF SUBSIDIARIES MANUFACTURING IN THIS INDUSTRY AT TIME OF ENTRY INTO PARENT SYSTEM

COUNTRY OR REGION	NET FLOW UP TO 31-DEC-50	NO. OF ENTRIES DURING YEAR(S)													TOTAL ENTRIES 1951-75	TOTAL EXITS 1951-75	NET FLOW UP TO 1-JAN-76
		51-55	56-60	61-65	1966	1967	1968	1969	1970	1971	1972	1973	1974	1975			
CANADA	0	0	1	1	0	0	0	0	0	0	0	0	0	0	2	1	1
LATIN AMER. (TOTAL)	0	0	2	3	1	0	1	0	0	1	1	0	3	0	12	1	11
C.AM.+CARIB. (TOTAL)	0	0	0	0	0	0	1	0	0	0	1	0	3	0	5	1	4
BAHAMAS	0	0	0	0	0	0	0	0	0	0	0	0	0	0	0	0	0
BERMUDA	0	0	0	0	0	0	0	0	0	0	0	0	0	0	0	0	0
COSTA RICA	0	0	0	0	0	0	0	0	0	0	0	0	1	0	1	0	1
GUATEMALA	0	0	0	0	0	0	0	0	0	0	0	0	0	0	0	0	0
JAMAICA	0	0	0	0	0	0	0	0	0	0	0	0	0	0	0	0	0
MEXICO	0	0	0	0	0	0	1	0	0	0	0	0	1	0	2	1	1
NETH.ANTILLES	0	0	0	0	0	0	0	0	0	0	0	0	0	0	0	0	0
NICARAGUA	0	0	0	0	0	0	0	0	0	0	1	0	0	0	1	0	1
PANAMA	0	0	0	0	0	0	0	0	0	0	0	0	0	0	0	0	0
OTHER C.AM+CAR.	0	0	0	0	0	0	0	0	0	0	0	0	1	0	1	0	1
S.AMERICA (TOTAL)	0	0	2	3	1	0	0	0	0	1	0	0	0	0	7	0	7
BOLIVIA	0	0	0	0	0	0	0	0	0	0	0	0	0	0	0	0	0
CHILE	0	0	0	0	0	0	0	0	0	0	0	0	0	0	0	0	0
COLOMBIA	0	0	0	0	0	0	0	0	0	0	0	0	0	0	0	0	0
ECUADOR	0	0	0	0	0	0	0	0	0	0	0	0	0	0	0	0	0
PERU	0	0	0	0	0	0	0	0	0	0	0	0	0	0	0	0	0
ARGENTINA	0	0	0	0	1	0	0	0	0	0	0	0	0	0	1	0	1
BRAZIL	0	0	0	0	0	0	0	0	0	1	0	0	0	0	1	0	1
URUGUAY	0	0	0	0	0	0	0	0	0	0	0	0	0	0	0	0	0
VENEZUELA	0	0	2	3	0	0	0	0	0	0	0	0	0	0	5	0	5
OTHER S.AMER.	0	0	0	0	0	0	0	0	0	0	0	0	0	0	0	0	0
EUROPE (TOTAL)	1	1	0	0	0	0	0	2	1	3	0	0	1	0	8	0	9
BELGIUM	0	1	0	0	0	0	0	0	0	0	0	0	0	0	1	0	1
FRANCE	0	0	0	0	0	0	0	0	0	0	0	0	0	0	0	0	0
GERMANY	0	0	0	0	0	0	0	0	0	1	0	0	0	0	1	0	1
ITALY	0	0	0	0	0	0	0	1	1	0	0	0	0	0	2	0	2
LUXEMBOURG	0	0	0	0	0	0	0	0	0	0	0	0	0	0	0	0	0
NETHERLANDS	0	0	0	0	0	0	0	1	0	0	0	0	0	0	1	0	1
DENMARK	0	0	0	0	0	0	0	0	0	0	0	0	0	0	0	0	0
IRELAND	0	0	0	0	0	0	0	0	0	0	0	0	0	0	0	0	0
U.K.	1	0	0	0	0	0	0	0	0	0	0	0	0	0	0	0	1
AUSTRIA	0	0	0	0	0	0	0	0	0	0	0	0	0	0	0	0	0
FINLAND	0	0	0	0	0	0	0	0	0	0	0	0	0	0	0	0	0
GREECE	0	0	0	0	0	0	0	0	0	0	0	0	0	0	0	0	0
NORWAY	0	0	0	0	0	0	0	0	0	0	0	0	0	0	0	0	0
PORTUGAL	0	0	0	0	0	0	0	0	0	0	0	0	0	0	0	0	0
SPAIN	0	0	0	0	0	0	0	0	0	2	0	0	0	0	2	0	2
SWEDEN	0	0	0	0	0	0	0	0	0	0	0	0	0	0	0	0	0
SWITZERLAND	0	0	0	0	0	0	0	0	0	0	0	0	1	0	1	0	1
TURKEY	0	0	0	0	0	0	0	0	0	0	0	0	0	0	0	0	0
OTHER EUROPE	0	0	0	0	0	0	0	0	0	0	0	0	0	0	0	0	0

TABLE 2.4.2 (CONTINUED)

COUNTRY OR REGION	NET FLOW UP TO 31-DEC-50	NO. OF ENTRIES DURING YEAR(S)													TOTAL ENTRIES 1951-75	TOTAL EXITS 1951-75	NET FLOW UP TO 1-JAN-76
		51-55	56-60	61-65	1966	1967	1968	1969	1970	1971	1972	1973	1974	1975			
N.AFR+M.EAST (TOTAL)	0	0	0	0	0	0	0	0	0	0	0	0	0	0	0	0	0
ALGERIA	0	0	0	0	0	0	0	0	0	0	0	0	0	0	0	0	0
EGYPT	0	0	0	0	0	0	0	0	0	0	0	0	0	0	0	0	0
IRAN	0	0	0	0	0	0	0	0	0	0	0	0	0	0	0	0	0
ISRAEL	0	0	0	0	0	0	0	0	0	0	0	0	0	0	0	0	0
LEBANON	0	0	0	0	0	0	0	0	0	0	0	0	0	0	0	0	0
MOROCCO	0	0	0	0	0	0	0	0	0	0	0	0	0	0	0	0	0
SAUDI ARABIA	0	0	0	0	0	0	0	0	0	0	0	0	0	0	0	0	0
OTHER N.AF+M.E.	0	0	0	0	0	0	0	0	0	0	0	0	0	0	0	0	0
E.+W.AFRICA (TOTAL)	0	0	0	0	0	1	0	0	0	0	0	0	0	0	1	0	1
GHANA	0	0	0	0	0	0	0	0	0	0	0	0	0	0	0	0	0
IVORY COAST	0	0	0	0	0	0	0	0	0	0	0	0	0	0	0	0	0
KENYA	0	0	0	0	0	0	0	0	0	0	0	0	0	0	0	0	0
LIBERIA	0	0	0	0	0	0	0	0	0	0	0	0	0	0	0	0	0
NIGERIA	0	0	0	0	0	1	0	0	0	0	0	0	0	0	1	0	1
ZAIRE	0	0	0	0	0	0	0	0	0	0	0	0	0	0	0	0	0
ZAMBIA	0	0	0	0	0	0	0	0	0	0	0	0	0	0	0	0	0
OTHER E.+W.AFR.	0	0	0	0	0	0	0	0	0	0	0	0	0	0	0	0	0
SOUTH ASIA (TOTAL)	0	0	0	0	0	0	2	0	0	0	0	0	0	0	2	0	2
INDIA	0	0	0	0	0	0	1	0	0	0	0	0	0	0	1	0	1
PAKISTAN	0	0	0	0	0	0	1	0	0	0	0	0	0	0	1	0	1
SRI LANKA	0	0	0	0	0	0	0	0	0	0	0	0	0	0	0	0	0
OTHER S.ASIA	0	0	0	0	0	0	0	0	0	0	0	0	0	0	0	0	0
EAST ASIA (TOTAL)	0	0	0	0	0	0	0	0	0	1	0	0	0	0	1	0	1
HONG KONG	0	0	0	0	0	0	0	0	0	0	0	0	0	0	0	0	0
INDONESIA	0	0	0	0	0	0	0	0	0	1	0	0	0	0	1	0	1
JAPAN	0	0	0	0	0	0	0	0	0	0	0	0	0	0	0	0	0
MALAYSIA	0	0	0	0	0	0	0	0	0	0	0	0	0	0	0	0	0
PHILIPPINES	0	0	0	0	0	0	0	0	0	0	0	0	0	0	0	0	0
SINGAPORE	0	0	0	0	0	0	0	0	0	0	0	0	0	0	0	0	0
S.KOREA	0	0	0	0	0	0	0	0	0	0	0	0	0	0	0	0	0
THAILAND	0	0	0	0	0	0	0	0	0	0	0	0	0	0	0	0	0
TAIWAN	0	0	0	0	0	0	0	0	0	0	0	0	0	0	0	0	0
OTHER E.ASIA	0	0	0	0	0	0	0	0	0	0	0	0	0	0	0	0	0
S.DOMINIONS (TOTAL)	0	1	0	0	1	0	0	0	1	1	0	0	0	0	4	0	4
AUSTRALIA	0	1	0	0	1	0	0	0	1	0	0	0	0	0	3	0	3
NEW ZEALAND	0	0	0	0	0	0	0	0	0	1	0	0	0	0	1	0	1
RHODESIA	0	0	0	0	0	0	0	0	0	0	0	0	0	0	0	0	0
S.AFRICA	0	0	0	0	0	0	0	0	0	0	0	0	0	0	0	0	0
OUTSIDE U.S. (TOTAL)	1	1	4	5	2	1	4	2	1	6	1	0	3	0	30	2	29

CHAPTER 2 - THE PROLIFERATION OF FOREIGN SUBSIDIARIES
SECTION 4 -- GEOGRAPHICAL SPREAD IN SPECIFIC INDUSTRIES
TABLE 3 --- THE FOOD INDUSTRY (SIC 20, EXCLUDING 208)

NO. OF SUBSIDIARIES MANUFACTURING IN THIS INDUSTRY AT TIME OF ENTRY INTO PARENT SYSTEM

COUNTRY OR REGION	NET FLOW UP TO 31-DEC-50	NO. OF ENTRIES DURING YEAR(S)													TOTAL ENTRIES 1951-75	TOTAL EXITS 1951-75	NET FLOW UP TO 1-JAN-76
		51-55	56-60	61-65	1966	1967	1968	1969	1970	1971	1972	1973	1974	1975			
CANADA	27	16	12	18	12	9	5	21	16	8	11	4	2	2	136	83	80
LATIN AMER. (TOTAL)	42	13	45	64	21	17	11	10	7	6	17	5	6	7	229	91	180
C.AM.+CARIB.(TOTAL)	13	5	21	34	13	15	4	5	5	2	14	1	3	4	126	50	89
BAHAMAS	1	0	0	1	0	0	0	0	0	0	0	0	0	0	1	0	2
BERMUDA	0	0	0	1	0	0	0	0	0	0	0	0	0	0	1	1	0
COSTA RICA	0	0	0	2	1	1	0	2	0	1	0	0	0	0	7	2	5
GUATEMALA	0	0	3	5	2	2	1	1	1	0	1	0	0	0	16	5	11
JAMAICA	1	0	1	1	2	1	0	1	1	0	0	0	0	0	7	0	8
MEXICO	4	4	9	19	7	11	3	1	1	1	12	0	0	1	69	29	44
NETH.ANTILLES	0	0	0	0	0	0	0	0	0	0	0	0	0	0	0	0	0
NICARAGUA	0	0	0	2	1	0	0	1	0	0	0	0	0	0	4	0	4
PANAMA	2	1	0	2	1	0	0	0	1	0	1	0	0	0	6	1	7
OTHER C.AM+CAR.	5	0	8	1	0	0	0	0	1	0	0	1	3	1	15	12	8
S.AMERICA (TOTAL)	29	8	24	30	8	2	7	5	2	4	3	4	3	3	103	41	91
BOLIVIA	1	0	0	0	0	0	0	0	0	0	0	0	0	0	0	1	0
CHILE	1	0	0	6	0	0	0	0	0	1	0	0	0	0	8	5	4
COLOMBIA	5	3	4	6	3	0	1	0	0	0	0	2	0	0	19	6	18
ECUADOR	1	0	0	1	0	0	0	1	0	0	0	0	0	1	3	1	3
PERU	7	1	2	7	2	0	0	1	0	0	0	0	0	0	13	12	8
ARGENTINA	4	1	1	2	1	1	1	2	0	0	0	0	0	0	9	1	12
BRAZIL	5	1	6	6	0	0	3	2	0	0	3	2	0	3	26	8	23
URUGUAY	2	0	1	2	0	0	0	0	0	0	0	0	0	0	1	1	2
VENEZUELA	3	2	9	5	1	1	0	1	0	2	0	0	0	0	22	6	19
OTHER S.AMER.	0	0	1	1	0	0	0	0	0	0	0	0	0	0	2	0	2
EUROPE (TOTAL)	35	10	37	93	14	27	31	38	18	23	16	14	12	8	341	120	256
BELGIUM	0	0	4	5	2	2	3	3	3	0	1	0	2	3	25	13	12
FRANCE	2	0	4	14	1	1	3	4	3	0	1	2	2	1	37	15	24
GERMANY	8	5	7	18	0	3	6	7	2	2	2	3	2	2	57	19	46
ITALY	1	0	3	10	0	3	0	0	3	5	0	1	0	0	26	7	20
LUXEMBOURG	0	0	0	0	0	0	0	0	0	0	0	0	0	0	0	0	0
NETHERLANDS	5	0	5	6	1	0	0	6	2	4	0	2	2	2	31	13	23
DENMARK	2	2	3	4	1	1	1	2	1	1	4	0	2	0	21	8	15
IRELAND	1	0	0	6	1	1	0	1	1	0	0	0	2	1	12	5	8
U.K.	14	1	5	11	5	3	5	10	3	5	0	6	2	1	57	28	43
AUSTRIA	0	0	2	0	0	0	0	0	0	0	0	0	1	0	3	0	3
FINLAND	0	0	0	0	0	0	0	0	0	0	0	0	0	0	0	0	0
GREECE	0	0	0	1	0	0	1	1	0	0	0	0	2	0	5	0	5
NORWAY	1	0	0	1	0	0	0	0	0	1	0	0	0	0	2	2	1
PORTUGAL	0	1	1	2	1	0	0	0	0	0	0	0	1	0	6	2	4
SPAIN	1	0	2	4	1	3	3	3	2	3	3	0	1	1	33	4	30
SWEDEN	0	0	1	1	0	2	6	0	0	1	1	0	0	0	17	3	14
SWITZERLAND	0	0	0	1	0	0	1	2	0	0	0	2	0	0	6	0	6
TURKEY	0	0	0	1	0	1	0	0	0	0	0	0	0	0	2	0	2
OTHER EUROPE	0	0	0	0	0	0	0	0	0	1	0	0	0	0	1	1	0

TABLE 2.4.3 (CONTINUED)

COUNTRY OR REGION	NET FLOW UP TO 31-DEC-50	51-55	56-60	61-65	1966	1967	1968	1969	1970	1971	1972	1973	1974	1975	TOTAL ENTRIES 1951-75	TOTAL EXITS 1951-75	NET FLOW UP TO 1-JAN-76
					NO. OF ENTRIES DURING YEAR(S)												
N.AFR+M.EAST(TOTAL)	0	1	1	3	0	0	0	2	0	1	0	0	2	1	11	0	11
ALGERIA	0	0	0	0	0	0	0	1	0	0	0	0	0	1	1	0	1
EGYPT	0	0	0	0	0	0	0	0	0	0	0	0	0	0	0	0	0
IRAN	0	0	0	1	0	0	0	0	0	1	0	0	0	0	1	0	1
ISRAEL	0	1	1	0	0	0	0	0	0	0	0	0	1	0	1	0	1
LEBANON	0	0	0	2	0	0	0	0	0	0	0	0	0	0	2	0	2
MOROCCO	0	0	0	1	0	0	0	0	0	0	0	0	1	0	2	0	2
SAUDI ARABIA	0	0	0	0	0	0	0	1	0	1	0	0	0	1	3	0	3
OTHER N.AF+M.E.	0	1	0	0	0	0	0	0	0	0	0	0	0	0	1	0	1
E.+W.AFRICA (TOTAL)	0	0	0	2	0	1	1	5	0	1	0	0	0	0	10	0	10
GHANA	0	0	0	0	0	0	0	1	0	0	0	0	0	1	1	0	1
IVORY COAST	0	0	0	0	0	0	0	1	0	1	0	0	0	0	1	0	1
KENYA	0	0	0	2	0	0	1	1	0	0	0	0	0	0	3	0	3
LIBERIA	0	0	0	0	0	0	0	0	0	0	0	0	0	0	0	0	0
NIGERIA	0	0	0	0	0	0	0	1	0	1	0	0	0	0	2	0	2
ZAIRE	0	0	0	0	0	0	0	0	0	0	0	0	0	0	0	0	0
ZAMBIA	0	0	0	0	0	0	0	0	0	0	0	0	0	0	0	0	0
OTHER E.+W.AFR.	0	0	0	0	0	0	0	2	0	0	1	0	0	0	3	0	3
SOUTH ASIA (TOTAL)	1	0	0	0	0	0	0	0	1	2	0	0	0	0	4	2	3
INDIA	1	0	0	0	0	0	0	0	1	1	0	0	0	0	2	1	2
PAKISTAN	0	0	0	0	0	0	0	0	0	1	1	0	0	0	2	1	1
SRI LANKA	0	0	0	0	0	0	0	0	0	0	0	0	0	0	0	0	0
OTHER S.ASIA	0	0	0	0	0	0	0	0	0	0	0	0	0	0	0	0	0
EAST ASIA (TOTAL)	3	1	7	14	6	4	1	3	5	2	3	1	3	3	53	10	46
HONG KONG	0	0	0	0	0	0	0	0	0	0	0	0	1	1	2	0	2
INDONESIA	0	0	2	0	0	0	0	0	0	0	0	0	0	0	2	0	2
JAPAN	0	1	5	7	2	1	0	1	2	0	1	0	0	2	22	2	20
MALAYSIA	0	0	0	2	1	1	0	0	1	0	1	0	0	0	6	3	3
PHILIPPINES	0	0	0	4	2	1	0	1	0	1	0	0	0	0	9	2	10
SINGAPORE	0	0	0	0	0	0	0	0	1	0	1	1	0	0	3	1	2
S.KOREA	0	0	0	0	1	0	0	0	0	0	0	0	1	0	2	0	2
THAILAND	0	0	0	1	0	1	0	0	1	1	0	0	1	0	5	1	4
TAIWAN	0	0	0	0	0	0	1	0	0	0	0	0	0	0	1	0	1
OTHER E.ASIA	0	0	0	0	0	0	0	1	0	0	0	0	0	0	1	1	0
S.DOMINIONS (TOTAL)	15	4	13	17	3	2	6	2	2	5	5	3	0	0	62	18	59
AUSTRALIA	8	1	10	11	2	2	2	1	1	2	2	1	0	0	35	13	30
NEW ZEALAND	3	2	0	2	0	0	2	0	0	0	0	0	0	0	6	0	9
RHODESIA	0	0	0	0	0	0	0	0	0	0	0	0	0	0	0	0	0
S.AFRICA	4	1	3	4	1	0	2	1	1	3	3	2	0	0	21	5	20
OUTSIDE U.S.(TOTAL)	123	45	115	212	56	59	55	81	49	48	53	27	25	21	846	324	645

CHAPTER 2 - THE PROLIFERATION OF FOREIGN SUBSIDIARIES
SECTION 4 -- GEOGRAPHICAL SPREAD IN SPECIFIC INDUSTRIES
TABLE 4 --- THE TEXTILES & APPAREL INDUSTRIES (SIC 22 AND 23)

NO. OF SUBSIDIARIES MANUFACTURING IN THIS INDUSTRY AT TIME OF ENTRY INTO PARENT SYSTEM

COUNTRY OR REGION	NET FLOW UP TO 31-DEC-50	NO. OF ENTRIES DURING YEAR(S)													TOTAL ENTRIES 1951-75	TOTAL EXITS 1951-75	NET FLOW UP TO 1-JAN-76
		51-55	56-60	61-65	1966	1967	1968	1969	1970	1971	1972	1973	1974	1975			
CANADA	11	1	2	5	5	2	1	1	3	2	2	0	1	0	25	9	27
LATIN AMER. (TOTAL)	13	6	9	12	2	0	1	1	0	3	1	3	2	0	40	22	31
C.AM.+CARIB.(TOTAL)	3	2	3	4	1	0	0	1	0	2	1	0	1	0	15	8	10
BAHAMAS	0	0	0	0	0	0	0	0	0	0	0	0	0	0	0	0	0
BERMUDA	0	0	0	0	0	0	0	0	0	0	0	0	0	0	0	0	0
COSTA RICA	0	0	0	0	0	0	0	0	0	0	0	0	0	0	0	0	0
GUATEMALA	0	0	0	1	0	0	0	0	0	0	0	0	0	0	1	1	0
JAMAICA	0	0	0	0	0	0	0	0	0	0	0	0	0	0	0	1	0
MEXICO	3	2	3	3	1	0	1	1	0	0	0	0	0	0	11	5	9
NETH.ANTILLES	0	0	0	0	0	0	0	0	0	0	0	0	0	0	0	0	0
NICARAGUA	0	0	0	0	0	0	0	0	0	1	0	0	0	0	1	0	0
PANAMA	0	0	0	0	0	0	0	0	0	0	0	0	0	0	0	0	0
OTHER C.AM+CAR.	0	0	0	0	0	0	0	0	0	1	0	0	1	0	2	1	1
S.AMERICA (TOTAL)	10	4	6	8	1	0	1	0	0	1	0	3	1	0	25	14	21
BOLIVIA	0	0	0	0	0	0	0	0	0	0	0	0	0	0	0	0	0
CHILE	0	0	0	0	1	0	0	0	0	0	0	0	0	0	1	1	0
COLOMBIA	1	0	0	2	0	0	0	0	0	1	0	1	0	0	5	3	3
ECUADOR	1	0	0	0	0	0	0	0	0	0	0	0	0	0	0	0	0
PERU	1	0	0	0	0	0	0	0	0	0	0	0	0	0	0	1	0
ARGENTINA	2	0	1	0	0	0	0	0	0	0	0	0	1	0	1	0	3
BRAZIL	2	1	0	1	0	0	0	0	0	1	0	2	0	0	5	2	5
URUGUAY	1	1	1	0	0	0	0	0	0	0	0	0	0	0	2	0	3
VENEZUELA	3	2	3	5	0	0	1	0	0	0	0	0	0	0	11	7	7
OTHER S.AMER.	0	0	0	0	0	0	0	0	0	0	0	0	0	0	0	0	0
EUROPE (TOTAL)	0	2	12	29	8	5	13	6	9	12	2	1	3	2	104	55	49
BELGIUM	0	0	0	2	0	0	1	4	0	2	0	0	0	0	9	2	7
FRANCE	0	0	1	3	0	0	1	0	1	1	0	1	0	2	15	9	6
GERMANY	0	1	3	5	5	0	2	1	1	5	0	0	1	0	14	7	7
ITALY	0	0	2	2	0	0	2	1	3	2	0	0	1	0	10	8	2
LUXEMBOURG	0	0	0	3	0	0	1	0	0	0	0	0	0	0	4	0	4
NETHERLANDS	0	0	0	2	0	0	1	0	2	2	0	0	1	0	6	4	2
DENMARK	0	0	0	1	0	0	0	0	0	0	0	0	0	0	1	1	0
IRELAND	0	0	0	0	0	0	1	0	1	0	0	0	0	0	2	1	1
U.K.	0	0	8	6	3	3	3	0	1	1	1	1	0	0	23	11	12
AUSTRIA	0	0	0	0	0	0	2	0	0	0	0	0	0	0	3	3	0
FINLAND	0	0	0	0	0	0	0	0	0	0	0	0	0	0	0	1	0
GREECE	0	0	0	0	0	0	0	0	0	0	0	0	0	0	0	0	0
NORWAY	0	0	0	0	0	0	0	0	0	0	0	0	0	0	0	0	0
PORTUGAL	0	2	0	2	0	0	0	0	0	0	0	0	0	0	2	2	2
SPAIN	0	0	0	1	0	1	0	0	0	0	0	0	0	0	4	4	0
SWEDEN	0	0	0	3	0	0	1	0	0	0	0	1	0	0	4	2	2
SWITZERLAND	0	0	1	3	0	0	1	0	0	0	0	0	0	0	5	2	3
TURKEY	0	0	0	0	0	0	0	0	0	0	0	0	0	0	0	0	0
OTHER EUROPE	0	0	0	0	0	1	0	0	0	0	0	0	0	0	1	0	1

TABLE 2 . 4 . 4 (CONTINUED)

COUNTRY OR REGION	NET FLOW UP TO 31-DEC-50	NO. OF ENTRIES DURING YEAR(S)													TOTAL ENTRIES 1951-75	TOTAL EXITS 1951-75	NET FLOW UP TO 1-JAN-76
		51-55	56-60	61-65	1966	1967	1968	1969	1970	1971	1972	1973	1974	1975			
N.AFR+M.EAST (TOTAL)	0	0	0	0	0	0	1	0	1	1	0	0	0	0	3	1	2
ALGERIA	0	0	0	0	0	0	0	0	0	0	0	0	0	0	0	0	0
EGYPT	0	0	0	0	0	0	0	0	0	0	0	0	0	0	0	0	0
IRAN	0	0	0	0	0	0	0	0	0	0	0	0	0	0	0	0	0
ISRAEL	0	0	0	0	0	0	0	0	0	1	0	0	0	0	1	0	1
LEBANON	0	0	0	0	0	0	0	0	0	0	0	0	0	0	0	0	0
MOROCCO	0	0	0	0	0	0	1	0	0	0	0	0	0	0	1	1	0
SAUDI ARABIA	0	0	0	0	0	0	0	0	0	0	0	0	0	0	0	0	0
OTHER N.AF+M.E.	0	0	0	0	0	0	0	0	1	0	0	0	0	0	1	0	1
E.+W.AFRICA (TOTAL)	0	0	0	0	0	0	0	0	0	0	0	0	0	0	0	0	0
GHANA	0	0	0	0	0	0	0	0	0	0	0	0	0	0	0	0	0
IVORY COAST	0	0	0	0	0	0	0	0	0	0	0	0	0	0	0	0	0
KENYA	0	0	0	0	0	0	0	0	0	0	0	0	0	0	0	0	0
LIBERIA	0	0	0	0	0	0	0	0	0	0	0	0	0	0	0	0	0
NIGERIA	0	0	0	0	0	0	0	0	0	0	0	0	0	0	0	0	0
ZAIRE	0	0	0	0	0	0	0	0	0	0	0	0	0	0	0	0	0
ZAMBIA	0	0	0	0	0	0	0	0	0	0	0	0	0	0	0	0	0
OTHER E.+W.AFR.	0	0	0	0	0	0	0	0	0	0	0	0	0	0	0	0	0
SOUTH ASIA (TOTAL)	0	0	0	0	0	0	0	0	0	1	0	0	0	0	1	0	1
INDIA	0	0	0	0	0	0	0	0	0	1	0	0	0	0	1	0	1
PAKISTAN	0	0	0	0	0	0	0	0	0	0	0	0	0	0	0	0	0
SRI LANKA	0	0	0	0	0	0	0	0	0	0	0	0	0	0	0	0	0
OTHER S.ASIA	0	0	0	0	0	0	0	0	0	0	0	0	0	0	0	0	0
EAST ASIA (TOTAL)	0	0	0	1	0	0	0	2	2	3	0	0	0	0	8	2	6
HONG KONG	0	0	0	0	0	0	0	0	0	0	0	0	0	0	0	0	0
INDONESIA	0	0	0	0	0	0	0	0	0	0	0	0	0	0	0	0	0
JAPAN	0	0	0	1	0	0	0	2	1	3	0	0	0	0	7	2	5
MALAYSIA	0	0	0	0	0	0	0	0	0	0	0	0	0	0	0	0	0
PHILIPPINES	0	0	0	0	0	0	0	0	0	0	0	0	0	0	0	0	0
SINGAPORE	0	0	0	0	0	0	0	0	0	0	0	0	0	0	0	0	0
S.KOREA	0	0	0	0	0	0	0	0	1	0	0	0	0	0	1	0	1
THAILAND	0	0	0	0	0	0	0	0	0	0	0	0	0	0	0	0	0
TAIWAN	0	0	0	0	0	0	0	0	0	0	0	0	0	0	0	0	0
OTHER E.ASIA	0	0	0	0	0	0	0	0	0	0	0	0	0	0	0	0	0
S.DOMINIONS (TOTAL)	1	0	2	2	0	0	1	1	0	0	0	0	2	1	9	3	7
AUSTRALIA	1	0	2	1	0	0	0	0	0	0	0	0	1	0	4	2	3
NEW ZEALAND	0	0	0	0	0	0	0	0	0	0	0	0	0	1	1	0	1
RHODESIA	0	0	0	0	0	0	0	0	0	0	0	0	1	0	1	0	1
S.AFRICA	0	0	0	1	0	0	1	1	0	0	0	0	0	0	3	1	2
OUTSIDE U.S.(TOTAL)	25	9	28	49	15	7	16	11	13	21	5	5	8	3	190	92	123

CHAPTER 2   - THE PROLIFERATION OF FOREIGN SUBSIDIARIES
SECTION 4   -- GEOGRAPHICAL SPREAD IN SPECIFIC INDUSTRIES
TABLE 5   --- THE WOOD AND FURNITURE INDUSTRIES (SIC 24 AND 25)

NO. OF SUBSIDIARIES MANUFACTURING IN THIS INDUSTRY AT TIME OF ENTRY INTO PARENT SYSTEM

COUNTRY OR REGION	NET FLOW UP TO 31-DEC-50	51-55	56-60	61-65	1966	1967	1968	1969	1970	1971	1972	1973	1974	1975	TOTAL ENTRIES 1951-75	TOTAL EXITS 1951-75	NET FLOW UP TO 1-JAN-76
		NO. OF ENTRIES DURING YEAR(S)															
CANADA	4	0	2	6	1	0	3	7	2	1	5	1	0	1	29	12	21
LATIN AMER. (TOTAL)	2	1	2	4	0	1	2	1	1	0	0	0	1	1	14	4	12
C.AM.+CARIB.(TOTAL)	2	0	2	2	0	1	0	0	0	0	0	0	1	0	7	3	6
BAHAMAS	0	0	0	0	0	0	0	0	0	0	0	0	0	0	0	0	0
BERMUDA	0	0	0	0	0	1	0	0	0	0	0	0	0	0	0	0	0
COSTA RICA	0	0	0	1	0	0	0	1	0	0	0	0	1	0	3	0	2
GUATEMALA	0	0	1	0	0	0	0	0	0	0	0	0	0	0	1	0	1
JAMAICA	0	0	0	0	0	0	0	1	0	0	0	0	0	0	1	1	0
MEXICO	2	0	0	1	0	0	1	0	0	0	0	0	0	0	0	0	2
NETH.ANTILLES	0	0	0	0	0	0	0	0	0	0	0	0	0	0	0	0	0
NICARAGUA	0	0	0	0	0	0	0	0	0	0	0	0	0	0	0	0	0
PANAMA	0	0	0	1	0	0	0	1	0	0	0	0	0	0	2	1	1
S.AMERICA (TOTAL)	0	1	0	2	0	0	2	0	1	0	0	0	1	0	7	1	6
BOLIVIA	0	0	0	0	0	0	0	0	0	0	0	0	0	0	0	0	0
CHILE	0	0	0	0	0	0	0	1	0	0	0	0	0	0	1	0	1
COLOMBIA	0	0	0	0	0	0	0	0	0	0	0	0	0	0	0	0	0
ECUADOR	0	0	0	1	0	0	0	0	0	0	0	0	0	0	1	0	1
PERU	0	0	0	0	0	1	0	1	0	0	0	0	0	0	1	0	1
ARGENTINA	0	0	0	1	0	0	1	0	0	0	0	0	0	0	2	0	2
BRAZIL	0	1	0	0	0	0	1	0	0	0	0	0	1	0	1	0	1
URUGUAY	0	0	0	1	0	0	0	0	0	0	0	0	0	0	0	1	0
VENEZUELA	0	0	0	0	0	0	0	0	0	0	0	0	0	0	2	0	1
OTHER S.AMER.	0	0	0	0	0	0	0	0	0	0	0	0	0	0	0	0	0
EUROPE (TOTAL)	6	4	7	7	3	1	2	2	1	3	3	3	1	0	29	5	30
BELGIUM	0	1	0	0	0	0	1	1	0	0	0	0	0	0	1	1	1
FRANCE	1	1	1	1	0	0	1	0	1	0	0	0	1	0	7	1	7
GERMANY	0	0	1	1	1	0	0	0	0	0	0	0	0	0	3	1	2
ITALY	0	0	1	2	2	0	0	0	0	0	0	0	0	0	5	0	5
LUXEMBOURG	0	0	0	0	0	0	0	0	0	0	0	0	0	0	0	0	0
NETHERLANDS	0	0	0	0	0	0	0	0	0	0	2	0	0	0	2	0	2
DENMARK	0	0	0	0	0	0	0	0	0	0	0	0	0	0	0	0	0
IRELAND	2	0	1	1	0	1	0	1	0	1	0	0	0	1	1	2	1
U.K.	2	1	2	2	0	0	0	0	0	1	1	0	0	0	7	2	7
AUSTRIA	0	0	0	0	0	0	0	0	0	0	0	0	0	0	0	0	0
FINLAND	0	0	0	0	0	0	0	0	0	0	0	0	0	0	0	0	0
GREECE	0	0	0	0	0	0	0	0	0	0	0	0	0	0	0	0	0
NORWAY	0	0	1	0	0	1	0	0	0	0	0	0	0	0	1	0	1
PORTUGAL	3	0	0	1	0	0	0	0	0	0	0	0	0	0	0	1	0
SPAIN	0	0	0	0	0	0	0	0	0	0	0	0	0	0	2	0	4
SWEDEN	0	0	0	0	0	0	0	0	0	0	0	0	0	0	0	0	0
SWITZERLAND	0	0	0	0	0	0	0	0	0	0	0	0	0	0	0	0	0
TURKEY	0	0	0	0	0	0	0	0	0	0	0	0	0	0	0	0	0
OTHER EUROPE	0	0	0	0	0	0	0	0	0	0	0	0	0	0	0	0	0

TABLE 2 . 4 . 5 (CONTINUED)

COUNTRY OR REGION	NET FLOW UP TO 31-DEC-50	NO. OF ENTRIES DURING YEAR(S)													TOTAL ENTRIES 1951-75	TOTAL EXITS 1951-75	NET FLOW UP TO 1-JAN-76
		51-55	56-60	61-65	1966	1967	1968	1969	1970	1971	1972	1973	1974	1975			
N.AFR+M.EAST (TOTAL)	0	0	0	0	0	0	0	0	0	0	0	1	0	0	1	0	1
ALGERIA	0	0	0	0	0	0	0	0	0	0	0	0	0	0	0	0	0
EGYPT	0	0	0	0	0	0	0	0	0	0	0	0	0	0	0	0	0
IRAN	0	0	0	0	0	0	0	0	0	0	0	1	0	0	1	0	1
ISRAEL	0	0	0	0	0	0	0	0	0	0	0	0	0	0	0	0	0
LEBANON	0	0	0	0	0	0	0	0	0	0	0	0	0	0	0	0	0
MOROCCO	0	0	0	0	0	0	0	0	0	0	0	0	0	0	0	0	0
SAUDI ARABIA	0	0	0	0	0	0	0	0	0	0	0	0	0	0	0	0	0
OTHER N.AF+M.E.	0	0	0	0	0	0	0	0	0	0	0	0	0	0	0	0	0
E.+W.AFRICA (TOTAL)	0	0	0	0	0	0	0	0	0	0	0	0	0	0	0	0	0
GHANA	0	0	0	0	0	0	0	0	0	0	0	0	0	0	0	0	0
IVORY COAST	0	0	0	0	0	0	0	0	0	0	0	0	0	0	0	0	0
KENYA	0	0	0	0	0	0	0	0	0	0	0	0	0	0	0	0	0
LIBERIA	0	0	0	0	0	0	0	0	0	0	0	0	0	0	0	0	0
NIGERIA	0	0	0	0	0	0	0	0	0	0	0	0	0	0	0	0	0
ZAIRE	0	0	0	0	0	0	0	0	0	0	0	0	0	0	0	0	0
ZAMBIA	0	0	0	0	0	0	0	0	0	0	0	0	0	0	0	0	0
OTHER E.+W.AFR.	0	0	0	0	0	0	0	0	0	0	0	0	0	0	0	0	0
SOUTH ASIA (TOTAL)	0	0	0	0	0	0	0	0	0	0	0	0	0	0	1	1	0
INDIA	0	0	0	0	0	0	0	0	0	0	0	0	0	0	1	1	0
PAKISTAN	0	0	0	0	0	0	0	0	0	0	0	0	0	0	0	0	0
SRI LANKA	0	0	0	0	0	0	0	0	0	0	0	0	0	0	0	0	0
OTHER S.ASIA	0	0	0	0	0	0	0	0	0	0	0	0	0	0	0	0	0
EAST ASIA (TOTAL)	0	0	1	1	1	0	0	0	1	0	0	0	0	0	6	1	5
HONG KONG	0	0	0	0	1	0	0	0	0	0	0	0	0	0	1	0	1
INDONESIA	0	0	0	0	0	0	0	0	1	0	0	0	0	0	1	0	1
JAPAN	0	0	1	1	0	0	0	0	0	0	0	0	0	0	2	0	2
MALAYSIA	0	0	0	0	0	0	0	0	0	0	0	0	0	0	0	0	0
PHILIPPINES	0	0	0	0	1	0	0	0	1	0	0	0	0	0	2	1	1
SINGAPORE	0	0	0	0	0	0	0	0	0	0	0	0	0	0	0	0	0
S.KOREA	0	0	0	0	0	0	0	0	0	0	0	0	0	0	0	0	0
THAILAND	0	0	0	0	0	0	0	0	0	0	0	0	0	0	0	0	0
TAIWAN	0	0	0	0	0	0	0	0	0	0	0	0	0	0	0	0	0
OTHER E.ASIA	0	0	0	0	0	0	0	0	0	0	0	0	0	0	0	0	0
S.DOMINIONS (TOTAL)	2	1	2	2	0	0	1	1	1	1	0	0	0	0	9	4	7
AUSTRALIA	1	0	2	2	0	0	1	1	1	0	0	0	0	0	7	4	4
NEW ZEALAND	0	1	0	0	0	0	0	0	0	1	0	0	0	0	2	0	2
RHODESIA	0	0	0	0	0	0	0	0	0	0	0	0	0	0	0	0	0
S.AFRICA	1	0	0	0	0	0	0	0	0	0	0	0	0	0	0	0	1
OUTSIDE U.S. (TOTAL)	14	2	11	18	5	2	8	10	8	5	9	7	2	2	89	27	76

CHAPTER 2 — THE PROLIFERATION OF FOREIGN SUBSIDIARIES
SECTION 4 —— GEOGRAPHICAL SPREAD IN SPECIFIC INDUSTRIES
TABLE 6 ——— THE PAPER INDUSTRY (SIC 26)

NO. OF SUBSIDIARIES MANUFACTURING IN THIS INDUSTRY AT TIME OF ENTRY INTO PARENT SYSTEM

COUNTRY OR REGION	NET FLOW UP TO 31-DEC-50	NO. OF ENTRIES DURING YEAR(S)													TOTAL ENTRIES 1951-75	TOTAL EXITS 1951-75	NET FLOW UP TO 1-JAN-76
		51-55	56-60	61-65	1966	1967	1968	1969	1970	1971	1972	1973	1974	1975			
CANADA	12	8	14	5	1	1	4	0	0	2	0	0	0	0	35	21	26
LATIN AMER. (TOTAL)	12	12	17	18	4	4	2	3	2	6	1	3	2	5	79	24	67
C.AM.+CARIB. (TOTAL)	4	4	5	7	2	2	0	1	1	4	0	2	1	1	30	12	22
BAHAMAS	0	0	0	0	0	0	0	0	0	0	0	0	0	0	0	0	0
BERMUDA	0	0	0	0	0	0	0	0	0	0	0	0	0	0	0	0	0
COSTA RICA	0	0	0	0	0	0	0	0	0	1	0	0	0	1	2	0	2
GUATEMALA	0	0	0	0	0	0	0	0	0	1	0	0	0	0	1	0	1
JAMAICA	0	0	0	1	0	0	0	0	0	0	0	1	0	0	2	1	1
MEXICO	2	3	5	4	1	1	0	1	1	0	0	0	0	0	16	6	12
NETH.ANTILLES	0	0	0	0	0	0	0	0	0	1	0	0	0	0	1	1	0
NICARAGUA	0	0	0	1	1	1	0	0	0	0	0	0	0	0	3	1	2
PANAMA	0	0	0	1	0	0	0	0	0	1	0	1	0	0	3	2	1
OTHER C.AM+CAR.	2	1	0	0	0	0	0	0	0	0	0	0	1	0	2	1	3
S.AMERICA (TOTAL)	8	8	12	11	2	2	2	2	1	2	1	1	1	4	49	12	45
BOLIVIA	0	0	0	0	0	0	0	0	0	0	0	0	0	0	0	0	0
CHILE	2	0	0	0	0	0	0	0	0	0	0	0	0	0	0	1	1
COLOMBIA	0	1	2	3	0	0	0	0	0	0	0	0	0	1	7	2	5
ECUADOR	1	0	0	1	0	1	0	1	0	0	0	0	0	0	3	2	2
PERU	0	1	0	1	1	0	0	0	0	0	0	0	0	0	3	0	3
ARGENTINA	3	0	0	0	1	0	1	0	0	0	0	0	0	0	2	0	5
BRAZIL	2	2	3	2	0	1	1	1	0	1	0	1	1	1	14	3	13
URUGUAY	0	0	0	0	0	0	0	0	0	0	0	0	0	0	0	0	0
VENEZUELA	0	4	7	4	0	0	0	0	1	0	1	0	0	2	19	4	15
OTHER S.AMER.	0	0	0	0	0	0	0	0	0	1	0	0	0	0	1	0	1
EUROPE (TOTAL)	4	16	27	...	5	4	5	6	6	13	...	5	6	4	103	32	75
BELGIUM	2	3	0	1	1	0	1	0	0	2	0	0	0	0	8	5	5
FRANCE	0	0	4	5	1	0	2	2	2	4	2	1	0	0	21	3	18
GERMANY	0	2	3	2	1	0	2	3	0	1	2	1	1	0	16	7	9
ITALY	0	0	5	3	0	0	0	0	0	0	0	0	1	1	10	3	7
LUXEMBOURG	0	0	0	0	0	0	0	0	0	0	0	0	0	0	0	0	0
NETHERLANDS	0	0	1	0	0	0	1	0	0	0	0	0	0	1	3	1	2
DENMARK	0	0	0	0	0	0	0	0	0	0	0	1	0	0	1	0	1
IRELAND	1	0	0	1	0	0	1	0	0	0	0	0	0	0	2	0	3
U.K.	1	3	3	4	1	1	0	0	1	4	0	0	1	0	16	5	12
AUSTRIA	0	0	0	0	0	0	0	0	0	1	0	0	0	0	1	0	1
FINLAND	0	0	0	1	0	0	0	0	0	0	0	0	0	0	1	0	1
GREECE	0	0	0	0	0	0	0	0	1	1	0	0	1	0	3	1	2
NORWAY	0	0	0	0	0	0	0	0	0	0	0	0	0	0	0	0	0
PORTUGAL	0	0	0	1	0	1	0	0	1	0	0	0	0	0	1	0	1
SPAIN	0	0	0	7	1	1	0	0	3	3	0	0	1	0	16	7	9
SWEDEN	0	0	1	1	0	0	0	0	0	0	0	1	0	0	3	0	3
SWITZERLAND	0	0	0	0	0	0	0	0	0	0	0	0	0	0	0	0	0
TURKEY	0	0	0	0	0	0	0	0	0	0	0	0	0	0	0	0	0
OTHER EUROPE	0	0	0	0	0	0	0	0	0	1	0	0	0	0	1	0	1

TABLE   2 . 4 . 6   (CONTINUED)

COUNTRY OR REGION	NET FLOW UP TO 31-DEC-50	NO. OF ENTRIES DURING YEAR(S)													TOTAL ENTRIES 1951-75	TOTAL EXITS 1951-75	NET FLOW UP TO 1-JAN-76
		51-55	56-60	61-65	1966	1967	1968	1969	1970	1971	1972	1973	1974	1975			
N.AFR+M.EAST (TOTAL)	1	0	1	1	0	0	0	0	1	0	0	0	0	0	3	0	4
ALGERIA	0	0	0	0	0	0	0	0	0	0	0	0	0	0	0	0	0
EGYPT	0	0	0	0	0	0	0	0	0	0	0	0	0	0	0	0	0
IRAN	0	0	0	0	0	0	0	0	0	0	0	0	0	0	0	0	0
ISRAEL	0	0	1	0	0	0	0	0	0	0	0	0	0	0	1	0	1
LEBANON	0	0	0	0	0	0	0	0	0	0	0	0	0	0	0	0	0
MOROCCO	1	0	0	0	0	0	0	0	1	0	0	0	0	0	1	0	2
SAUDI ARABIA	0	0	0	0	0	0	0	0	0	0	0	0	0	0	0	0	0
OTHER N.AF+M.E.	0	0	0	1	0	0	0	0	0	0	0	0	0	0	1	0	1
E.+W.AFRICA (TOTAL)	0	0	0	1	0	1	1	1	0	0	1	0	0	0	5	0	5
GHANA	0	0	0	0	0	0	0	0	0	0	0	0	0	0	0	0	0
IVORY COAST	0	0	0	0	0	0	0	0	0	0	0	0	0	0	0	0	0
KENYA	0	0	0	0	0	0	0	0	0	0	0	0	0	0	0	0	0
LIBERIA	0	0	0	0	0	0	0	0	0	0	0	0	0	0	0	0	0
NIGERIA	0	0	0	0	0	0	0	0	0	0	0	0	0	0	0	0	0
ZAIRE	0	0	0	0	0	0	0	0	0	0	0	0	0	0	0	0	0
ZAMBIA	0	0	0	1	0	1	0	0	0	0	1	0	0	0	3	0	3
OTHER E.+W.AFR.	0	0	0	0	0	0	1	1	0	0	0	0	0	0	2	0	2
SOUTH ASIA (TOTAL)	0	0	0	0	0	0	0	0	1	0	0	0	0	0	1	0	1
INDIA	0	0	0	0	0	0	0	0	0	0	0	0	0	0	0	0	0
PAKISTAN	0	0	0	0	0	0	0	0	1	0	0	0	0	0	1	0	1
SRI LANKA	0	0	0	0	0	0	0	0	0	0	0	0	0	0	0	0	0
OTHER S.ASIA	0	0	0	0	0	0	0	0	0	0	0	0	0	0	0	0	0
EAST ASIA (TOTAL)	0	1	1	8	1	1	1	2	2	1	0	0	0	1	18	2	16
HONG KONG	0	0	0	1	0	0	0	0	0	0	0	0	0	0	1	1	0
INDONESIA	0	0	0	0	0	0	0	0	0	0	0	0	0	0	0	0	0
JAPAN	0	0	1	4	0	0	0	0	0	0	0	0	0	0	5	0	5
MALAYSIA	0	1	0	0	0	0	0	0	0	0	0	0	0	0	1	0	1
PHILIPPINES	0	0	0	3	1	1	0	0	0	0	0	0	0	0	5	1	4
SINGAPORE	0	0	0	0	0	0	0	0	0	0	0	0	0	0	0	0	0
S.KOREA	0	0	0	0	0	0	0	0	0	0	0	0	0	0	0	0	0
THAILAND	0	0	0	0	0	0	0	1	1	0	0	0	0	0	2	0	2
TAIWAN	0	0	0	0	0	0	1	1	1	0	0	0	0	0	3	0	3
OTHER E.ASIA	0	0	0	0	0	0	0	0	0	1	0	0	0	1	3	0	1
S.DOMINIONS (TOTAL)	4	5	4	28	1	6	2	2	2	0	0	0	0	0	50	16	38
AUSTRALIA	3	2	2	4	1	2	2	1	1	0	0	0	0	0	15	8	10
NEW ZEALAND	1	1	1	1	0	0	0	0	0	0	0	0	0	0	3	0	4
RHODESIA	0	0	0	3	0	0	0	0	0	0	0	0	0	0	3	0	3
S.AFRICA	0	2	1	20	0	4	0	1	1	0	0	0	0	0	29	8	21
OUTSIDE U.S. (TOTAL)	33	29	53	88	15	16	15	14	11	22	5	8	8	10	294	95	232

CHAPTER 2   - THE PROLIFERATION OF FOREIGN SUBSIDIARIES
SECTION 4   -- GEOGRAPHICAL SPREAD IN SPECIFIC INDUSTRIES
TABLE 7   --- THE PRINTING INDUSTRY (SIC 27)

NO. OF SUBSIDIARIES MANUFACTURING IN THIS INDUSTRY AT TIME OF ENTRY INTO PARENT SYSTEM

COUNTRY OR REGION	NET FLOW UP TO 31-DEC-50	NO. OF ENTRIES DURING YEAR(S)													TOTAL ENTRIES 1951-75	TOTAL EXITS 1951-75	NET FLOW UP TO 1-JAN-76
		51-55	56-60	61-65	1966	1967	1968	1969	1970	1971	1972	1973	1974	1975			
CANADA	2	1	0	1	1	0	3	2	2	1	0	0	0	0	11	3	10
LATIN AMER. (TOTAL)	1	1	1	2	2	2	1	1	1	1	0	1	0	0	13	5	9
C.AM.+CARIB. (TOTAL)	0	1	0	1	1	0	0	1	0	1	0	1	0	0	6	2	4
BAHAMAS	0	0	0	0	0	0	0	0	0	0	0	0	0	0	0	0	0
BERMUDA	0	0	0	0	0	0	0	0	0	0	0	0	0	0	0	0	0
COSTA RICA	0	0	0	0	0	0	0	0	0	0	0	0	0	0	0	0	0
GUATEMALA	0	0	0	0	0	0	0	0	0	0	0	0	0	0	0	0	0
JAMAICA	0	0	0	0	0	0	0	0	0	0	0	0	0	0	0	0	0
MEXICO	0	1	0	1	1	0	0	1	0	0	0	0	0	0	4	0	4
NETH.ANTILLES	0	0	0	0	0	0	0	0	0	1	0	0	0	0	1	1	0
NICARAGUA	0	0	0	0	0	0	0	0	0	0	0	0	0	0	0	0	0
PANAMA	0	0	0	0	0	0	0	0	0	0	0	0	0	0	0	0	0
OTHER C.AM+CAR.	0	0	0	0	0	0	0	0	0	0	0	1	0	0	1	1	0
S.AMERICA (TOTAL)	1	0	1	1	1	2	1	0	1	0	0	0	0	0	7	3	5
BOLIVIA	0	0	0	0	0	0	0	0	0	0	0	0	0	0	0	0	0
CHILE	0	0	0	0	0	0	0	0	0	0	0	0	0	0	0	0	0
COLOMBIA	0	0	0	0	0	0	0	0	0	0	0	0	0	0	0	0	0
ECUADOR	0	0	0	0	0	0	0	0	0	0	0	0	0	0	0	0	0
PERU	0	0	0	0	0	0	0	0	0	0	0	0	0	0	0	0	0
ARGENTINA	0	0	1	1	1	1	0	0	0	0	0	0	0	0	4	2	2
BRAZIL	1	0	0	0	0	1	1	0	1	0	0	0	0	0	3	1	3
URUGUAY	0	0	0	0	0	0	0	0	0	0	0	0	0	0	0	0	0
VENEZUELA	0	0	0	0	0	0	0	0	0	0	0	0	0	0	0	0	0
OTHER S.AMER.	0	0	0	0	0	0	0	0	0	0	0	0	0	0	0	0	0
EUROPE (TOTAL)	2	5	5	5	6	5	8	3	0	4	4	1	1	0	43	8	37
BELGIUM	0	1	0	0	0	1	0	0	0	0	0	1	0	0	3	0	3
FRANCE	0	0	1	1	1	0	1	1	0	1	1	0	0	0	7	1	6
GERMANY	1	0	1	1	2	0	1	0	0	1	1	0	0	0	8	2	7
ITALY	0	1	1	0	2	1	1	0	0	0	0	0	0	0	6	1	5
LUXEMBOURG	0	0	0	0	0	0	0	0	0	0	0	0	0	0	0	0	0
NETHERLANDS	0	1	0	0	0	0	0	0	0	0	0	0	0	0	1	1	0
DENMARK	0	0	1	0	0	0	0	0	0	0	0	0	0	0	1	0	1
IRELAND	0	0	0	0	0	0	0	0	0	0	0	0	0	0	0	0	0
U.K.	1	1	0	1	0	1	4	1	0	0	0	0	0	0	12	3	10
AUSTRIA	0	0	0	1	0	0	0	0	0	0	0	0	0	0	1	0	1
FINLAND	0	0	0	0	0	0	0	0	0	0	0	0	0	0	0	0	0
GREECE	0	0	0	0	0	0	0	0	0	0	0	0	0	0	0	0	0
NORWAY	0	0	0	0	0	0	0	0	0	0	0	0	0	0	0	0	0
PORTUGAL	0	0	0	0	0	0	0	0	0	0	0	0	0	0	0	0	0
SPAIN	0	0	1	0	0	0	0	0	0	0	0	1	0	0	2	2	0
SWEDEN	0	0	0	0	0	0	0	0	0	0	1	0	0	0	1	1	0
SWITZERLAND	0	0	0	0	1	0	0	0	0	0	0	0	0	0	1	1	1
TURKEY	0	0	0	0	0	0	0	0	0	1	0	0	0	0	1	0	0
OTHER EUROPE	0	0	0	0	0	0	0	0	0	0	0	0	0	0	0	0	0

TABLE 2 . 4 . 7 (CONTINUED)

NO. OF ENTRIES DURING YEAR(S)

COUNTRY OR REGION	NET FLOW UP TO 31-DEC-50	51-55	56-60	61-65	1966	1967	1968	1969	1970	1971	1972	1973	1974	1975	TOTAL ENTRIES 1951-75	TOTAL EXITS 1951-75	NET FLOW UP TO 1-JAN-76
N.AFR+M.EAST (TOTAL)	3	0	0	0	0	0	0	0	0	0	0	0	0	0	0	0	3
ALGERIA	0	0	0	0	0	0	0	0	0	0	0	0	0	0	0	0	0
EGYPT	0	0	0	0	0	0	0	0	0	0	0	0	0	0	0	0	0
IRAN	3	0	0	0	0	0	0	0	0	0	0	0	0	0	0	0	3
ISRAEL	0	0	0	0	0	0	0	0	0	0	0	0	0	0	0	0	0
LEBANON	0	0	0	0	0	0	0	0	0	0	0	0	0	0	0	0	0
MOROCCO	0	0	0	0	0	0	0	0	0	0	0	0	0	0	0	0	0
SAUDI ARABIA	0	0	0	0	0	0	0	0	0	0	0	0	0	0	0	0	0
OTHER N.AF+M.E.	0	0	0	0	0	0	0	0	0	0	0	0	0	0	0	0	0
E.+W.AFRICA (TOTAL)	0	0	0	0	0	0	0	1	0	0	0	0	0	0	1	0	1
GHANA	0	0	0	0	0	0	0	0	0	0	0	0	0	0	0	0	0
IVORY COAST	0	0	0	0	0	0	0	0	0	0	0	0	0	0	0	0	0
KENYA	0	0	0	0	0	0	0	0	0	0	0	0	0	0	0	0	0
LIBERIA	0	0	0	0	0	0	0	0	0	0	0	0	0	0	0	0	0
NIGERIA	0	0	0	0	0	0	0	0	0	0	0	0	0	0	0	0	0
ZAIRE	0	0	0	0	0	0	0	0	0	0	0	0	0	0	0	0	0
ZAMBIA	0	0	0	0	0	0	0	0	0	0	0	0	0	0	0	0	0
OTHER E.+W.AFR.	0	0	0	0	0	0	0	1	0	0	0	0	0	0	1	0	1
SOUTH ASIA (TOTAL)	0	0	0	0	0	0	0	0	0	0	0	0	0	0	0	0	0
INDIA	0	0	0	0	0	0	0	0	0	0	0	0	0	0	0	0	0
PAKISTAN	0	0	0	0	0	0	0	0	0	0	0	0	0	0	0	0	0
SRI LANKA	0	0	0	0	0	0	0	0	0	0	0	0	0	0	0	0	0
OTHER S.ASIA	0	0	0	0	0	0	0	0	0	0	0	0	0	0	0	0	0
EAST ASIA (TOTAL)	0	0	0	1	1	0	0	0	1	0	0	0	1	1	5	1	4
HONG KONG	0	0	0	0	0	0	0	0	0	0	0	0	0	0	0	0	0
INDONESIA	0	0	0	0	0	0	0	0	0	0	0	0	0	0	0	0	0
JAPAN	0	0	0	1	1	0	0	0	1	0	0	0	1	0	4	0	4
MALAYSIA	0	0	0	0	0	0	0	0	0	0	0	0	0	0	0	0	0
PHILIPPINES	0	0	0	0	0	0	0	0	0	0	0	0	0	0	0	0	0
SINGAPORE	0	0	0	0	0	0	0	0	0	0	0	0	0	1	1	1	0
S.KOREA	0	0	0	0	0	0	0	0	0	0	0	0	0	0	0	0	0
THAILAND	0	0	0	0	0	0	0	0	0	0	0	0	0	0	0	0	0
TAIWAN	0	0	0	0	0	0	0	0	0	0	0	0	0	0	0	0	0
OTHER E.ASIA	0	0	0	0	0	0	0	0	0	0	0	0	0	0	0	0	0
S.DOMINIONS (TOTAL)	0	0	0	4	1	0	4	0	0	0	0	0	0	0	9	1	8
AUSTRALIA	0	0	0	0	0	0	2	0	0	0	0	0	0	0	2	0	2
NEW ZEALAND	0	0	0	0	0	0	1	0	0	0	0	0	0	0	1	0	1
RHODESIA	0	0	0	1	0	0	0	0	0	0	0	0	0	0	1	0	1
S.AFRICA	0	0	0	3	1	0	1	0	0	0	0	0	0	0	5	1	4
OUTSIDE U.S. (TOTAL)	5	3	6	13	11	7	16	7	3	7	4	2	2	1	82	18	69

CHAPTER 2 - THE PROLIFERATION OF FOREIGN SUBSIDIARIES
SECTION 4 -- GEOGRAPHICAL SPREAD IN SPECIFIC INDUSTRIES
TABLE 8 --- THE INDUSTRIAL CHEMICALS INDUSTRY (SIC 281)

NO. OF SUBSIDIARIES MANUFACTURING IN THIS INDUSTRY AT TIME OF ENTRY INTO PARENT SYSTEM

COUNTRY OR REGION	NET FLOW UP TO 31-DEC-50	51-55	56-60	61-65	NO. OF ENTRIES DURING YEAR(S)										TOTAL ENTRIES 1951-75	TOTAL EXITS 1951-75	NET FLOW UP TO 1-JAN-76
					1966	1967	1968	1969	1970	1971	1972	1973	1974	1975			
CANADA	23	7	3	13	2	0	6	1	1	1	0	1	1	0	36	27	32
LATIN AMER. (TOTAL)	19	9	35	17	8	1	10	0	2	3	1	2	3	5	96	45	70
C.AM.+CARIB. (TOTAL)	8	4	21	6	5	0	4	0	1	2	1	1	2	4	51	17	42
BAHAMAS	0	0	0	0	0	0	1	0	0	0	0	0	0	0	1	0	1
BERMUDA	0	0	0	0	0	0	0	0	0	0	0	0	0	0	0	0	0
COSTA RICA	0	0	0	0	0	0	0	0	0	0	0	0	0	0	0	0	0
GUATEMALA	1	0	0	0	0	0	0	0	0	0	0	0	0	0	0	1	1
JAMAICA	0	0	0	1	1	0	0	0	0	0	0	0	0	0	2	1	1
MEXICO	7	3	17	5	3	0	3	0	1	2	1	2	0	0	40	13	34
NETH.ANTILLES	0	0	0	1	0	0	0	0	0	0	0	0	0	0	1	0	1
NICARAGUA	0	0	0	0	1	0	0	0	0	0	0	0	0	0	1	1	0
PANAMA	0	0	1	0	0	0	0	0	0	0	0	0	0	0	1	0	1
OTHER C.AM+CAR.	0	0	2	0	0	0	0	0	0	1	0	0	0	1	4	1	3
S.AMERICA (TOTAL)	11	5	14	11	3	1	6	0	1	1	0	1	1	1	45	28	28
BOLIVIA	0	0	0	0	0	0	0	0	0	0	0	0	0	0	0	0	0
CHILE	0	0	1	1	0	0	0	0	0	0	0	0	0	0	2	2	0
COLOMBIA	2	0	4	1	0	0	0	0	1	1	0	0	1	0	8	6	4
ECUADOR	0	0	0	2	0	1	0	0	0	0	0	0	0	0	3	0	0
PERU	1	0	3	0	0	0	0	0	0	0	0	0	0	0	3	4	0
ARGENTINA	3	2	4	3	1	0	2	0	0	0	0	0	0	0	12	9	6
BRAZIL	2	2	2	3	0	0	3	0	0	0	0	1	0	0	13	4	11
URUGUAY	1	0	0	1	0	0	0	0	0	0	0	0	0	0	1	0	1
VENEZUELA	3	1	0	0	2	0	1	0	0	1	0	0	0	1	6	3	6
OTHER S.AMER.	0	0	0	0	0	0	0	0	0	0	0	0	0	0	0	0	0
EUROPE (TOTAL)	18	8	26	51	11	10	9	6	6	18	10	4	5	7	171	55	134
BELGIUM	1	1	3	9	2	2	1	3	1	2	1	1	2	0	19	5	15
FRANCE	2	2	2	9	2	2	0	0	1	2	1	1	0	0	22	9	15
GERMANY	4	2	6	4	1	0	2	1	1	3	2	1	1	1	24	9	19
ITALY	1	1	3	12	2	0	3	0	2	6	2	1	1	1	30	10	21
LUXEMBOURG	0	0	0	0	0	0	0	0	0	0	0	0	0	0	0	0	0
NETHERLANDS	2	0	1	5	1	1	0	0	0	0	0	0	0	0	9	3	8
DENMARK	0	1	0	0	0	0	0	0	0	0	0	0	0	0	1	1	0
IRELAND	0	0	0	1	0	1	1	0	0	0	0	0	0	1	3	0	3
U.K.	5	2	7	7	1	3	2	2	0	3	2	1	2	2	34	12	27
AUSTRIA	0	0	0	0	0	0	0	0	0	0	1	0	0	0	2	0	2
FINLAND	0	0	0	0	1	0	0	0	0	0	0	0	0	0	2	0	2
GREECE	0	0	0	1	0	1	0	0	0	0	0	0	0	0	1	0	2
NORWAY	1	0	0	1	0	0	0	0	0	0	0	0	0	0	1	1	2
PORTUGAL	0	1	0	1	0	1	0	0	0	0	0	1	0	0	1	1	0
SPAIN	2	1	3	7	1	0	0	0	0	1	0	1	0	0	16	4	14
SWEDEN	1	1	1	2	0	0	0	0	0	1	0	0	0	0	5	1	4
SWITZERLAND	0	0	0	0	0	0	0	0	0	1	0	0	0	0	1	0	1
TURKEY	0	0	0	0	0	0	0	0	0	0	0	0	0	0	0	0	0
OTHER EUROPE	0	0	0	1	0	0	0	0	0	0	0	0	0	0	1	0	1

TABLE 2 .4 . 8 (CONTINUED)

Columns under **NO. OF ENTRIES DURING YEAR(S)**: 51-55 through 1975.

COUNTRY OR REGION	NET FLOW UP TO 31-DEC-50	51-55	56-60	61-65	1966	1967	1968	1969	1970	1971	1972	1973	1974	1975	TOTAL ENTRIES 1951-75	TOTAL EXITS 1951-75	NET FLOW UP TO 1-JAN-76
N.AFR+M.EAST (TOTAL)	1	0	1	3	1	0	1	0	0	0	0	1	0	1	8	2	7
ALGERIA	0	0	0	1	0	0	0	0	0	0	0	0	0	0	1	0	1
EGYPT	0	0	0	0	0	0	0	0	0	0	0	0	0	0	0	0	0
IRAN	0	0	0	1	0	0	0	0	0	0	0	1	0	0	2	0	2
ISRAEL	0	0	0	0	0	0	0	0	0	0	0	0	0	0	0	0	0
LEBANON	0	0	0	1	0	0	0	0	0	0	0	0	0	0	1	0	1
MOROCCO	0	0	0	0	1	0	0	0	0	0	0	0	0	0	1	0	1
SAUDI ARABIA	0	0	0	0	0	0	1	0	0	0	0	0	0	0	1	0	1
OTHER N.AF+M.E.	1	0	1	0	0	0	0	0	0	0	0	0	0	1	2	2	1
E.+W.AFRICA (TOTAL)	1	0	0	0	0	0	0	1	0	0	0	0	0	0	1	1	1
GHANA	1	0	0	0	0	0	0	0	0	0	0	0	0	0	0	1	0
IVORY COAST	0	0	0	0	0	0	0	0	0	0	0	0	0	0	0	0	0
KENYA	0	0	0	0	0	0	0	0	0	0	0	0	0	0	0	0	0
LIBERIA	0	0	0	0	0	0	0	0	0	0	0	0	0	0	0	0	0
NIGERIA	0	0	0	0	0	0	0	0	0	0	0	0	0	0	0	0	0
ZAIRE	0	0	0	0	0	0	0	0	0	0	0	0	0	0	0	0	0
ZAMBIA	0	0	0	0	0	0	0	1	0	0	0	0	0	0	1	0	1
OTHER E.+W.AFR.	0	0	0	0	0	0	0	0	0	0	0	0	0	0	0	0	0
SOUTH ASIA (TOTAL)	0	0	1	1	0	0	0	1	0	0	0	0	0	0	3	0	3
INDIA	0	0	0	1	0	0	0	1	0	0	0	0	0	0	2	0	2
PAKISTAN	0	0	1	0	0	0	0	0	0	0	0	0	0	0	1	0	1
SRI LANKA	0	0	0	0	0	0	0	0	0	0	0	0	0	0	0	0	0
OTHER S.ASIA	0	0	0	0	0	0	0	0	0	0	0	0	0	0	0	0	0
EAST ASIA (TOTAL)	1	3	2	11	2	3	3	4	2	2	3	0	3	1	39	3	37
HONG KONG	0	0	0	0	0	0	0	1	0	0	0	0	0	0	1	0	1
INDONESIA	0	0	0	0	0	0	0	0	0	0	0	0	0	0	0	0	0
JAPAN	0	2	2	8	1	3	1	2	1	2	1	0	2	0	25	2	23
MALAYSIA	1	0	0	0	0	0	0	0	0	0	0	0	0	0	0	1	0
PHILIPPINES	0	0	0	2	0	0	0	0	0	0	1	0	0	0	3	0	3
SINGAPORE	0	1	0	0	0	0	1	0	0	0	1	0	1	0	4	0	4
S.KOREA	0	0	0	0	1	0	0	0	0	0	0	0	0	1	2	0	2
THAILAND	0	0	0	0	0	0	1	0	0	0	0	0	0	0	1	0	1
TAIWAN	0	0	0	0	0	0	0	0	0	0	0	0	0	0	0	0	0
OTHER E.ASIA	0	0	0	1	0	0	0	1	1	0	0	0	0	0	3	0	3
S.DOMINIONS (TOTAL)	5	2	9	8	1	2	0	3	0	2	2	0	1	0	30	10	25
AUSTRALIA	4	2	8	5	1	2	0	1	0	2	0	0	0	0	21	9	16
NEW ZEALAND	0	0	1	2	0	0	0	1	0	0	1	0	1	0	6	0	6
RHODESIA	0	0	0	0	0	0	0	0	0	0	0	0	0	0	0	0	0
S.AFRICA	1	0	0	1	0	0	0	1	0	0	1	0	0	0	3	1	3
OUTSIDE U.S. (TOTAL)	68	29	77	104	25	16	30	15	11	26	16	8	12	15	384	143	309

CHAPTER 2 - THE PROLIFERATION OF FOREIGN SUBSIDIARIES
SECTION 4 -- GEOGRAPHICAL SPREAD IN SPECIFIC INDUSTRIES
TABLE 9 --- THE PLASTICS INDUSTRY (SIC 282)

NO. OF SUBSIDIARIES MANUFACTURING IN THIS INDUSTRY AT TIME OF ENTRY INTO PARENT SYSTEM

COUNTRY OR REGION	NET FLOW UP TO 31-DEC-50	NO. OF ENTRIES DURING YEAR(S)													TOTAL ENTRIES 1951-75	TOTAL EXITS 1951-75	NET FLOW UP TO 1-JAN-76
		51-55	56-60	61-65	1966	1967	1968	1969	1970	1971	1972	1973	1974	1975			
CANADA	9	3	6	8	0	1	1	0	0	3	1	4	0	1	28	14	23
LATIN AMER. (TOTAL)	10	11	12	30	2	5	3	2	3	9	3	2	2	1	85	36	59
C.AM.+CARIB.(TOTAL)	5	3	5	12	1	1	1	0	2	5	1	0	1	1	35	11	29
BAHAMAS	0	0	0	0	1	0	0	0	0	0	0	0	0	0	1	0	1
BERMUDA	0	0	0	0	0	0	0	0	0	0	0	0	0	0	0	0	0
COSTA RICA	0	0	0	0	0	0	0	1	0	0	0	0	0	0	1	0	1
GUATEMALA	0	0	0	0	0	0	0	0	0	0	0	0	0	0	0	0	0
JAMAICA	0	0	0	0	0	0	0	0	0	0	0	0	0	0	0	0	0
MEXICO	5	3	5	10	0	1	1	0	2	5	1	0	1	1	30	11	24
NETH.ANTILLES	0	0	0	0	0	0	0	0	0	0	1	0	0	0	1	0	1
NICARAGUA	0	0	0	1	0	0	0	0	0	0	0	0	0	0	1	0	1
PANAMA	0	0	0	0	0	0	0	0	0	0	0	1	0	0	1	0	1
OTHER C.AM+CAR.	0	0	0	1	0	0	0	0	0	0	0	0	0	0	1	0	1
S.AMERICA (TOTAL)	5	8	7	18	1	4	2	0	1	4	2	2	1	0	50	25	30
BOLIVIA	0	0	0	0	0	0	0	0	0	0	0	0	0	0	0	0	0
CHILE	1	0	0	0	0	2	0	0	0	0	0	0	0	0	2	1	2
COLOMBIA	0	1	1	6	0	0	1	0	0	1	0	0	0	0	10	3	7
ECUADOR	0	0	0	0	0	0	0	0	0	1	0	0	0	0	1	0	1
PERU	3	0	0	0	0	0	0	0	0	0	0	1	0	0	1	4	0
ARGENTINA	1	2	1	4	0	0	1	0	1	0	0	0	0	0	9	1	9
BRAZIL	0	4	3	5	0	1	0	1	0	3	2	2	0	0	19	13	6
URUGUAY	0	0	0	0	0	0	0	0	0	0	0	0	0	0	0	0	0
VENEZUELA	0	1	2	2	1	1	0	0	0	0	0	0	0	0	8	3	5
OTHER S.AMER.	0	0	0	0	0	0	0	0	0	0	0	0	0	0	0	0	0
EUROPE (TOTAL)	8	15	21	49	7	8	11	7	3	4	9	7	4	3	148	58	98
BELGIUM	0	0	2	5	2	1	1	0	0	0	0	0	1	1	13	4	9
FRANCE	0	4	3	5	0	1	2	0	0	0	0	0	0	0	15	4	11
GERMANY	1	2	2	5	1	0	0	3	0	1	3	4	0	0	21	9	13
ITALY	0	0	0	4	0	0	0	1	0	0	0	0	0	0	6	3	3
LUXEMBOURG	0	0	0	0	0	0	0	0	0	1	0	0	0	0	1	0	1
NETHERLANDS	0	0	3	5	0	0	0	1	1	0	0	0	0	0	10	5	5
DENMARK	0	0	0	1	0	0	0	0	0	0	0	0	0	0	1	0	1
IRELAND	0	0	0	0	0	0	0	0	1	0	0	0	0	0	1	0	1
U.K.	7	7	6	18	0	4	8	2	1	1	2	3	1	1	54	25	36
AUSTRIA	0	0	0	0	0	0	0	0	0	0	0	0	0	0	0	0	0
FINLAND	0	0	0	0	0	0	0	0	0	0	0	0	0	0	0	1	0
GREECE	0	0	1	0	2	0	0	0	0	0	0	0	0	0	3	1	2
NORWAY	0	1	0	1	1	0	0	0	0	0	0	0	0	0	1	0	1
PORTUGAL	0	1	3	2	0	1	1	0	0	0	1	0	0	0	3	0	3
SPAIN	0	0	0	3	1	0	0	0	1	1	1	0	0	1	11	5	6
SWEDEN	0	0	1	2	0	0	1	0	0	0	0	0	2	0	2	1	1
SWITZERLAND	0	0	0	1	0	1	0	0	1	0	1	0	0	0	5	1	4
TURKEY	0	0	0	0	0	0	0	0	0	0	0	0	0	0	0	0	0
OTHER EUROPE	0	0	0	0	0	0	0	0	1	0	0	0	0	0	1	0	1

TABLE 2.4.9 (CONTINUED)

COUNTRY OR REGION	NET FLOW UP TO 31-DEC-50	NO. OF ENTRIES DURING YEAR(S)													TOTAL ENTRIES 1951-75	TOTAL EXITS 1951-75	NET FLOW UP TO 1-JAN-76
		51-55	56-60	61-65	1966	1967	1968	1969	1970	1971	1972	1973	1974	1975			
N.AFR+M.EAST (TOTAL)	0	0	0	1	0	0	1	0	0	2	0	0	1	0	5	0	5
ALGERIA	0	0	0	0	0	0	0	0	0	0	0	0	0	0	0	0	0
EGYPT	0	0	0	0	0	0	0	0	0	0	0	0	0	0	0	0	0
IRAN	0	0	0	0	0	0	1	0	0	0	0	0	0	0	1	0	1
ISRAEL	0	0	0	1	0	0	0	0	0	2	0	0	1	0	4	0	4
LEBANON	0	0	0	0	0	0	0	0	0	0	0	0	0	0	0	0	0
MOROCCO	0	0	0	0	0	0	0	0	0	0	0	0	0	0	0	0	0
SAUDI ARABIA	0	0	0	0	0	0	0	0	0	0	0	0	0	0	0	0	0
OTHER N.AF+M.E.	0	0	0	0	0	0	0	0	0	0	0	0	0	0	0	0	0
E.+W.AFRICA (TOTAL)	0	0	1	1	0	0	0	0	1	0	0	0	0	0	3	0	3
GHANA	0	0	1	0	0	0	0	0	0	0	0	0	0	0	1	0	1
IVORY COAST	0	0	0	0	0	0	0	0	0	0	0	0	0	0	0	0	0
KENYA	0	0	0	0	0	0	0	0	0	0	0	0	0	0	0	0	0
LIBERIA	0	0	0	0	0	0	0	0	0	0	0	0	0	0	0	0	0
NIGERIA	0	0	0	1	0	0	0	0	1	0	0	0	0	0	2	0	2
ZAIRE	0	0	0	0	0	0	0	0	0	0	0	0	0	0	0	0	0
ZAMBIA	0	0	0	0	0	0	0	0	0	0	0	0	0	0	0	0	0
OTHER E.+W.AFR.	0	0	0	0	0	0	0	0	0	0	0	0	0	0	0	0	0
SOUTH ASIA (TOTAL)	0	0	1	3	0	0	0	0	0	0	0	0	0	0	4	0	4
INDIA	0	0	1	3	0	0	0	0	0	0	0	0	0	0	4	0	4
PAKISTAN	0	0	0	0	0	0	0	0	0	0	0	0	0	0	0	0	0
SRI LANKA	0	0	0	0	0	0	0	0	0	0	0	0	0	0	0	0	0
OTHER S.ASIA	0	0	0	0	0	0	0	0	0	0	0	0	0	0	0	0	0
EAST ASIA (TOTAL)	0	3	4	14	2	2	1	2	2	3	1	2	6	3	45	5	40
HONG KONG	0	0	0	1	0	0	0	0	0	0	0	0	0	0	1	0	1
INDONESIA	0	0	0	0	0	0	0	0	0	0	0	0	0	0	0	0	0
JAPAN	0	2	4	13	2	2	1	2	2	1	1	0	0	0	30	5	25
MALAYSIA	0	1	0	0	0	0	0	0	0	0	0	0	0	0	1	0	1
PHILIPPINES	0	0	0	0	0	0	0	0	0	2	0	1	0	0	3	0	3
SINGAPORE	0	0	0	0	0	0	0	0	0	0	0	0	0	0	0	0	0
S.KOREA	0	0	0	0	0	0	0	0	0	0	0	1	0	2	3	0	3
THAILAND	0	0	0	0	0	0	0	0	0	0	0	0	0	1	1	0	1
TAIWAN	0	0	0	0	0	0	0	0	0	0	0	0	6	0	6	0	6
OTHER E.ASIA	0	0	0	0	0	0	0	0	0	0	0	0	0	0	0	0	0
S.DOMINIONS (TOTAL)	1	8	15	2	2	2	1	2	3	0	2	0	0	1	36	10	27
AUSTRALIA	0	7	10	2	2	2	1	1	3	0	2	0	0	1	29	10	19
NEW ZEALAND	0	1	2	0	0	0	0	0	0	0	0	0	0	0	3	0	3
RHODESIA	0	0	0	0	0	0	0	0	0	0	0	0	0	0	0	0	0
S.AFRICA	1	0	3	0	0	0	0	1	0	0	0	0	0	0	4	0	5
OUTSIDE U.S. (TOTAL)	28	32	53	121	13	18	18	13	11	21	16	15	14	9	354	123	259

CHAPTER 2 - THE PROLIFERATION OF FOREIGN SUBSIDIARIES
SECTION 4 -- GEOGRAPHICAL SPREAD IN SPECIFIC INDUSTRIES
TABLE 10 --- THE AGRICULTURAL CHEMICALS INDUSTRY (SIC 287)

NO. OF SUBSIDIARIES MANUFACTURING IN THIS INDUSTRY AT TIME OF ENTRY INTO PARENT SYSTEM

COUNTRY OR REGION	NET FLOW UP TO 31-DEC-50	NO. OF ENTRIES DURING YEAR(S)													TOTAL ENTRIES 1951-75	TOTAL EXITS 1951-75	NET FLOW UP TO 1-JAN-76
		51-55	56-60	61-65	1966	1967	1968	1969	1970	1971	1972	1973	1974	1975			
CANADA	3	0	0	3	0	0	1	1	0	0	0	0	0	1	6	3	6
LATIN AMER. (TOTAL)	2	4	5	7	4	2	2	2	3	3	0	1	1	3	37	18	21
C.AM.+CARIB. (TOTAL)	1	2	2	2	2	1	1	1	2	2	0	1	1	1	18	8	11
BAHAMAS	0	0	0	0	0	0	0	0	0	0	0	0	0	0	0	0	0
BERMUDA	0	0	0	0	0	0	0	0	0	0	0	0	0	0	0	0	0
COSTA RICA	0	0	0	0	0	0	0	0	0	1	0	0	0	0	1	0	1
GUATEMALA	0	0	0	0	0	0	0	0	0	0	0	0	0	0	0	0	0
JAMAICA	0	0	0	0	0	0	0	0	0	0	0	0	0	0	0	0	0
MEXICO	0	2	1	0	0	1	0	0	1	0	0	0	1	0	6	4	2
NETH.ANTILLES	0	0	0	1	0	0	0	0	0	1	0	0	0	0	2	0	2
NICARAGUA	0	0	0	0	2	0	1	0	0	0	0	0	0	1	4	2	2
PANAMA	0	0	0	0	0	0	0	0	0	0	0	0	0	0	0	0	0
OTHER C.AM+CAR.	1	0	1	1	0	0	0	1	1	0	0	1	0	0	5	2	4
S.AMERICA (TOTAL)	1	2	3	5	2	1	1	1	1	1	0	0	0	2	19	10	10
BOLIVIA	0	0	0	0	0	0	0	0	0	0	0	0	0	0	0	0	0
CHILE	0	0	0	0	0	0	0	0	0	0	0	0	0	0	0	0	0
COLOMBIA	0	0	1	2	0	0	1	0	0	0	0	0	0	1	5	1	4
ECUADOR	0	0	0	0	0	0	0	0	0	0	0	0	0	0	0	0	0
PERU	0	0	0	0	0	0	0	0	0	0	0	0	0	0	0	0	0
ARGENTINA	1	0	1	2	0	1	0	1	0	0	0	0	0	0	5	3	3
BRAZIL	0	2	1	1	1	0	0	0	0	1	0	0	0	0	6	4	2
URUGUAY	0	0	0	0	0	0	0	0	0	0	0	0	0	0	0	0	0
VENEZUELA	0	0	0	0	1	0	0	0	1	0	0	0	0	1	3	2	1
OTHER S.AMER.	0	0	0	0	0	0	0	0	0	0	0	0	0	0	0	0	0
EUROPE (TOTAL)	1	2	2	7	3	1	3	0	2	1	1	2	0	1	25	9	17
BELGIUM	0	1	1	1	0	0	1	0	1	0	0	0	0	0	5	1	4
FRANCE	0	0	0	1	0	0	0	0	0	0	0	1	0	0	2	1	1
GERMANY	0	0	1	1	0	1	0	0	0	1	0	0	0	0	4	0	4
ITALY	0	0	0	0	0	0	0	0	0	0	0	0	0	0	0	0	0
LUXEMBOURG	0	0	0	0	0	0	0	0	0	0	1	0	0	0	1	0	1
NETHERLANDS	0	0	0	0	0	0	0	0	0	0	0	0	0	0	0	0	0
DENMARK	0	0	0	0	0	0	0	0	0	0	0	0	0	0	0	0	0
IRELAND	0	0	0	0	0	0	0	0	0	0	0	0	0	0	0	0	0
U.K.	0	1	0	0	1	0	1	0	0	0	0	0	0	1	4	2	2
AUSTRIA	0	0	0	0	0	0	0	0	0	0	0	0	0	0	0	0	0
FINLAND	0	0	0	1	0	0	0	0	0	0	0	0	0	0	1	1	0
GREECE	0	0	0	0	0	0	0	0	0	0	0	0	0	0	0	0	0
NORWAY	0	0	0	0	0	0	0	0	0	0	0	0	0	0	0	0	0
PORTUGAL	0	0	0	0	0	0	0	0	0	0	0	0	0	0	0	0	0
SPAIN	1	0	0	3	2	0	1	0	1	0	0	1	0	0	8	4	5
SWEDEN	0	0	0	0	0	0	0	0	0	0	0	0	0	0	0	0	0
SWITZERLAND	0	0	0	0	0	0	0	0	0	0	0	0	0	0	0	0	0
TURKEY	0	0	0	0	0	0	0	0	0	0	0	0	0	0	0	0	0
OTHER EUROPE	0	0	0	0	0	0	0	0	0	0	0	0	0	0	0	0	0

TABLE 2.4.10 (CONTINUED)

COUNTRY OR REGION	NET FLOW UP TO 31-DEC-50	NO. OF ENTRIES DURING YEAR(S)													TOTAL ENTRIES 1951-75	TOTAL EXITS 1951-75	NET FLOW UP TO 1-JAN-76
		51-55	56-60	61-65	1966	1967	1968	1969	1970	1971	1972	1973	1974	1975			
N.AFR+M.EAST (TOTAL)	0	0	0	3	0	0	0	0	0	0	0	0	0	0	3	1	2
ALGERIA	0	0	0	0	0	0	0	0	0	0	0	0	0	0	0	0	0
EGYPT	0	0	0	0	0	0	0	0	0	0	0	0	0	0	0	0	0
IRAN	0	0	0	0	0	0	0	0	0	0	0	0	0	0	0	0	0
ISRAEL	0	0	0	0	0	0	0	0	0	0	0	0	0	0	0	0	0
LEBANON	0	0	0	1	0	0	0	0	0	0	0	0	0	0	1	1	0
MOROCCO	0	0	0	0	0	0	0	0	0	0	0	0	0	0	0	0	0
SAUDI ARABIA	0	0	0	0	0	0	0	0	0	0	0	0	0	0	0	0	0
OTHER N.AF+M.E.	0	0	0	2	0	0	0	0	0	0	0	0	0	0	2	0	2
E.+W.AFRICA (TOTAL)	0	0	2	1	0	0	0	0	0	0	0	0	0	0	3	0	3
GHANA	0	0	0	0	0	0	0	0	0	0	0	0	0	0	0	0	0
IVORY COAST	0	0	0	0	0	0	0	0	0	0	0	0	0	0	0	0	0
KENYA	0	0	1	0	0	0	0	0	0	0	0	0	0	0	1	0	1
LIBERIA	0	0	0	0	0	0	0	0	0	0	0	0	0	0	0	0	0
NIGERIA	0	0	1	0	0	0	0	0	0	0	0	0	0	0	1	0	1
ZAIRE	0	0	0	0	0	0	0	0	0	0	0	0	0	0	0	0	0
ZAMBIA	0	0	0	0	0	0	0	0	0	0	0	0	0	0	0	0	0
OTHER E.+W.AFR.	0	0	0	1	0	0	0	0	0	0	0	0	0	0	1	0	1
SOUTH ASIA (TOTAL)	1	1	0	3	0	0	0	0	0	0	0	0	0	0	4	0	5
INDIA	1	1	0	2	0	0	0	0	0	0	0	0	0	0	3	0	4
PAKISTAN	0	0	0	1	0	0	0	0	0	0	0	0	0	0	1	0	1
SRI LANKA	0	0	0	0	0	0	0	0	0	0	0	0	0	0	0	0	0
OTHER S.ASIA	0	0	0	0	0	0	0	0	0	0	0	0	0	0	0	0	0
EAST ASIA (TOTAL)	0	1	0	1	0	3	2	1	0	1	1	0	2	0	12	1	11
HONG KONG	0	0	0	0	0	0	0	0	0	0	0	0	0	0	0	0	0
INDONESIA	0	0	0	0	0	0	0	0	0	0	0	0	1	0	1	0	1
JAPAN	0	1	0	0	0	0	0	0	0	0	0	0	0	0	1	0	1
MALAYSIA	0	0	0	1	0	1	0	0	0	0	0	0	0	0	2	0	2
PHILIPPINES	0	0	0	0	0	0	1	0	0	0	0	0	0	0	1	0	1
SINGAPORE	0	0	0	0	0	0	0	0	0	0	0	0	0	0	0	0	0
S.KOREA	0	0	0	0	0	1	1	1	0	1	1	0	0	0	5	0	5
THAILAND	0	0	0	0	0	0	0	0	0	0	0	0	0	0	0	0	0
TAIWAN	0	0	0	0	0	1	0	0	0	0	0	0	1	0	2	1	1
OTHER E.ASIA	0	0	0	0	0	0	0	0	0	0	0	0	0	0	0	0	0
S.DOMINIONS (TOTAL)	0	0	3	3	0	1	1	1	0	2	0	0	0	0	11	5	6
AUSTRALIA	0	0	3	2	0	1	1	0	0	0	0	0	0	0	7	4	3
NEW ZEALAND	0	0	0	1	0	0	0	0	0	0	0	0	0	0	1	0	1
RHODESIA	0	0	0	0	0	0	0	0	0	2	0	0	0	0	2	1	1
S.AFRICA	0	0	0	0	0	0	0	1	0	0	0	0	0	0	1	0	1
OUTSIDE U.S. (TOTAL)	7	7	14	32	6	7	9	6	3	6	2	2	3	4	101	37	71

CHAPTER 2 - THE PROLIFERATION OF FOREIGN SUBSIDIARIES
SECTION 4 -- GEOGRAPHICAL SPREAD IN SPECIFIC INDUSTRIES
TABLE 11 --- THE COSMETICS AND SOAP INDUSTRIES (SIC 284)

NO. OF SUBSIDIARIES MANUFACTURING IN THIS INDUSTRY AT TIME OF ENTRY INTO PARENT SYSTEM

COUNTRY OR REGION	NET FLOW UP TO 31-DEC-50	NO. OF ENTRIES DURING YEAR(S)													TOTAL ENTRIES 1951-75	TOTAL EXITS 1951-75	NET FLOW UP TO 1-JAN-76
		51-55	56-60	61-65	1966	1967	1968	1969	1970	1971	1972	1973	1974	1975			
CANADA	9	2	8	3	1	3	2	1	0	6	1	2	0	0	29	12	26
LATIN AMER. (TOTAL)	21	8	16	15	4	5	5	4	2	10	1	11	3	0	84	18	87
C.AM.+CARIB. (TOTAL)	9	3	8	6	2	2	4	3	1	4	1	2	1	0	37	8	38
BAHAMAS	0	0	0	0	0	0	1	0	0	0	0	0	0	0	1	0	1
BERMUDA	0	0	0	0	0	0	0	0	0	0	0	0	0	0	0	0	0
COSTA RICA	0	0	0	0	0	0	0	0	0	0	0	0	0	0	0	0	0
GUATEMALA	1	0	1	1	0	1	0	0	0	0	0	2	0	0	5	0	6
JAMAICA	0	0	0	0	1	0	0	1	0	0	0	0	0	0	2	0	2
MEXICO	4	2	4	4	0	1	3	1	0	3	1	0	0	0	19	3	20
NETH.ANTILLES	0	0	0	0	0	0	0	0	0	0	0	0	0	0	0	0	0
NICARAGUA	0	0	0	0	0	0	0	0	0	0	0	0	0	0	0	0	0
PANAMA	1	0	1	1	1	0	0	0	0	0	0	0	1	0	4	0	5
OTHER C.AM+CAR.	3	1	2	0	0	0	0	1	1	1	0	0	0	0	6	5	4
S.AMERICA (TOTAL)	12	5	8	9	2	3	1	1	1	6	0	9	2	0	47	10	49
BOLIVIA	0	0	0	0	0	0	0	0	0	0	0	0	0	0	0	0	0
CHILE	0	0	0	0	0	0	0	0	0	0	0	0	0	0	0	0	0
COLOMBIA	2	0	1	2	0	0	0	0	0	0	0	1	0	0	4	1	5
ECUADOR	0	0	0	0	0	0	0	0	0	0	0	0	0	0	0	0	0
PERU	1	1	1	1	0	1	0	0	1	1	0	2	1	0	9	1	9
ARGENTINA	4	1	2	2	0	1	0	1	0	2	0	1	0	0	10	3	11
BRAZIL	2	2	0	2	1	1	0	0	0	1	0	3	0	0	10	3	9
URUGUAY	2	0	0	0	0	0	0	0	0	0	0	1	0	0	1	0	3
VENEZUELA	1	1	4	2	1	0	1	0	0	2	0	1	1	0	13	2	12
OTHER S.AMER.	0	0	0	0	0	0	0	0	0	0	0	0	0	0	0	0	0
EUROPE (TOTAL)	23	8	25	26	12	10	8	7	7	7	11	27	7	1	156	34	145
BELGIUM	1	2	2	1	0	0	0	1	0	1	0	0	0	0	7	1	7
FRANCE	5	1	7	2	4	2	0	1	2	7	1	1	1	0	29	7	27
GERMANY	6	2	3	2	0	2	1	2	1	2	1	2	2	0	20	7	25
ITALY	1	0	4	6	0	1	1	0	1	2	1	2	1	0	19	7	13
LUXEMBOURG	0	0	0	0	0	0	0	0	0	0	0	0	0	0	0	0	0
NETHERLANDS	1	0	0	1	0	1	1	0	0	2	0	1	0	0	6	1	6
DENMARK	0	0	0	1	0	1	0	0	0	0	0	1	2	0	5	2	3
IRELAND	0	1	0	0	0	1	0	0	0	1	1	0	0	0	4	0	4
U.K.	9	0	4	8	2	1	2	0	1	7	3	0	1	0	29	11	27
AUSTRIA	0	0	1	0	0	0	0	0	0	0	1	0	0	0	2	0	2
FINLAND	0	0	0	0	0	0	0	1	0	1	0	0	0	0	2	0	2
GREECE	0	0	1	0	0	0	0	0	0	0	0	0	1	0	2	0	2
NORWAY	0	0	0	0	0	0	0	0	0	0	0	0	0	0	0	0	0
PORTUGAL	0	0	0	0	0	0	0	0	1	0	0	1	1	0	3	0	3
SPAIN	0	1	1	1	4	3	1	0	1	1	0	1	0	0	14	1	13
SWEDEN	0	1	1	3	1	0	0	1	0	2	0	0	0	0	9	3	6
SWITZERLAND	0	0	1	0	0	0	0	0	1	0	0	1	0	0	3	0	3
TURKEY	0	0	0	0	0	0	0	0	0	0	0	0	0	0	0	0	0
OTHER EUROPE	0	0	0	0	0	0	1	1	0	0	0	0	0	0	2	0	2

TABLE   2 .4 .11   (CONTINUED)

COUNTRY OR REGION	NET FLOW UP TO 31-DEC-50	NO. OF ENTRIES DURING YEAR(S)													TOTAL ENTRIES 1951-75	TOTAL EXITS 1951-75	NET FLOW UP TO 1-JAN-76
		51-55	56-60	61-65	1966	1967	1968	1969	1970	1971	1972	1973	1974	1975			
N.AFR+M.EAST (TOTAL)	0	0	4	2	0	0	0	1	0	2	0	1	0	0	10	0	10
ALGERIA	0	0	0	0	0	0	0	0	0	0	0	0	0	0	0	0	0
EGYPT	0	0	0	0	0	0	0	0	0	0	0	0	0	0	0	0	0
IRAN	0	0	0	2	0	0	0	0	0	0	0	0	0	0	2	0	2
ISRAEL	0	0	1	0	0	0	0	0	0	0	0	1	0	0	2	0	2
LEBANON	0	0	1	0	0	0	0	0	0	0	0	0	0	0	2	0	2
MOROCCO	0	0	2	0	0	0	0	1	0	0	0	0	0	0	1	0	1
SAUDI ARABIA	0	0	0	0	0	0	0	0	0	1	0	0	0	0	1	0	1
OTHER N.AF+M.E.	0	0	0	0	0	0	0	0	0	1	0	0	0	0	1	0	1
E.+W.AFRICA (TOTAL)	0	0	0	3	0	1	1	2	0	1	0	0	0	1	9	0	9
GHANA	0	0	0	1	0	0	1	0	0	0	0	0	0	1	1	0	1
IVORY COAST	0	0	0	0	0	0	0	0	0	0	0	0	0	0	0	0	0
KENYA	0	0	0	1	0	0	0	0	0	0	0	0	0	0	2	0	2
LIBERIA	0	0	0	0	0	0	0	0	0	0	0	0	0	0	0	0	0
NIGERIA	0	0	0	1	0	0	0	1	0	0	0	0	0	0	3	0	3
ZAIRE	0	0	0	0	0	1	0	0	0	0	0	0	0	0	1	0	1
ZAMBIA	0	0	0	0	0	0	0	0	0	1	0	0	0	0	1	0	1
OTHER E.+W.AFR.	0	0	0	0	0	0	0	1	0	0	0	0	0	0	1	0	1
SOUTH ASIA (TOTAL)	0	0	0	2	2	0	2	0	0	0	0	0	0	0	6	0	6
INDIA	0	0	0	0	1	0	1	0	0	0	0	0	0	0	2	0	2
PAKISTAN	0	0	0	2	1	0	0	0	0	0	0	0	0	0	3	0	3
SRI LANKA	0	0	0	0	0	0	1	0	0	0	0	0	0	0	1	0	1
OTHER S.ASIA	0	0	0	0	0	0	0	0	0	0	0	0	0	0	0	0	0
EAST ASIA (TOTAL)	2	0	2	10	0	2	3	2	0	1	3	3	0	2	28	3	27
HONG KONG	0	0	0	1	0	0	1	0	0	0	1	0	0	0	3	0	3
INDONESIA	0	0	0	0	0	0	0	1	0	1	0	0	0	0	2	0	2
JAPAN	0	0	0	4	0	1	0	0	0	0	1	2	0	1	9	1	8
MALAYSIA	0	0	1	1	0	0	0	0	0	0	0	0	0	0	2	0	2
PHILIPPINES	2	0	1	0	0	1	0	1	0	0	1	0	0	0	4	0	6
SINGAPORE	0	0	0	1	0	0	0	0	0	0	0	1	0	1	3	0	3
S.KOREA	0	0	0	0	0	0	1	0	0	0	0	0	0	0	1	0	1
THAILAND	0	0	0	1	0	0	1	0	0	0	0	0	0	0	2	1	1
TAIWAN	0	0	0	2	0	0	0	0	0	0	0	0	0	0	2	1	1
OTHER E.ASIA	0	0	0	0	0	0	0	0	0	0	0	0	0	0	0	0	0
S.DOMINIONS (TOTAL)	12	2	4	7	5	1	2	3	1	9	1	4	1	1	41	7	46
AUSTRALIA	3	2	3	3	3	1	1	2	1	4	0	2	1	1	24	4	23
NEW ZEALAND	3	0	0	2	0	0	1	0	0	1	1	1	0	0	6	0	9
RHODESIA	0	0	0	1	0	0	0	1	0	0	0	0	0	0	2	0	2
S.AFRICA	6	0	1	1	2	0	0	0	0	4	0	1	0	0	9	3	12
OUTSIDE U.S. (TOTAL)	67	20	59	68	24	22	23	20	10	56	13	32	11	5	363	74	356

CHAPTER 2 - THE PROLIFERATION OF FOREIGN SUBSIDIARIES
SECTION 4 -- GEOGRAPHICAL SPREAD IN SPECIFIC INDUSTRIES
TABLE 12 --- THE DRUGS INDUSTRY (SIC 283)

NO. OF SUBSIDIARIES MANUFACTURING IN THIS INDUSTRY AT TIME OF ENTRY INTO PARENT SYSTEM

COUNTRY OR REGION	NET FLOW UP TO 31-DEC-50	NO. OF ENTRIES DURING YEAR(S)													TOTAL ENTRIES 1951-75	TOTAL EXITS 1951-75	NET FLOW UP TO 1-JAN-76
		51-55	56-60	61-65	1966	1967	1968	1969	1970	1971	1972	1973	1974	1975			
CANADA	11	5	6	9	1	3	2	4	1	0	0	0	0	0	31	13	29
LATIN AMER. (TOTAL)	33	11	29	40	1	8	15	6	4	8	2	2	7	1	134	31	136
C.AM.+CARIB.(TOTAL)	15	3	7	19	0	5	5	3	3	2	1	0	0	0	46	11	50
BAHAMAS	0	0	0	0	0	0	0	0	0	0	0	0	0	0	0	0	0
BERMUDA	0	0	0	0	0	0	0	0	1	0	0	0	0	0	1	0	1
COSTA RICA	1	0	1	0	0	0	0	0	0	0	1	0	0	0	2	1	2
GUATEMALA	1	0	0	2	0	0	1	0	2	0	0	0	0	0	4	0	5
JAMAICA	0	0	0	2	0	1	1	0	0	0	0	0	0	0	4	0	4
MEXICO	8	1	5	11	0	3	2	2	0	2	0	0	0	0	25	8	25
NETH.ANTILLES	0	0	0	0	0	0	0	0	0	0	0	0	0	0	0	0	0
NICARAGUA	0	0	0	0	0	0	0	0	0	0	0	0	0	0	0	0	0
PANAMA	1	1	0	2	0	0	0	0	0	0	0	0	0	0	3	0	4
OTHER C.AM+CAR.	4	1	1	3	0	1	0	1	0	0	0	0	0	0	7	2	9
S.AMERICA (TOTAL)	18	8	22	21	1	3	10	3	3	6	1	2	7	1	88	20	86
BOLIVIA	0	0	1	0	0	0	0	0	0	0	0	0	0	0	0	0	0
CHILE	0	0	1	2	0	1	1	0	0	0	0	0	0	0	5	0	5
COLOMBIA	3	2	4	5	1	0	1	0	3	0	0	1	0	0	16	6	13
ECUADOR	0	0	0	1	0	1	1	1	0	3	0	1	1	0	6	1	5
PERU	2	0	3	2	0	0	1	0	0	1	0	0	0	0	7	0	9
ARGENTINA	8	1	2	3	0	1	2	1	0	0	0	0	0	1	11	5	14
BRAZIL	3	4	6	3	0	1	4	0	0	2	0	3	0	0	23	7	19
URUGUAY	1	0	1	0	0	0	0	0	1	0	0	0	0	0	1	0	2
VENEZUELA	1	1	6	5	0	0	1	0	1	0	1	0	1	0	19	1	19
OTHER S.AMER.	0	0	0	0	0	0	0	0	0	0	0	0	0	0	0	0	0
EUROPE (TOTAL)	19	16	34	47	4	11	32	19	12	10	6	5	8	8	212	38	193
BELGIUM	1	1	4	5	0	0	1	0	1	1	0	0	0	0	14	2	13
FRANCE	1	1	5	5	0	6	5	4	3	2	0	1	0	1	31	4	28
GERMANY	1	2	4	7	1	6	2	5	1	0	3	2	2	1	30	5	26
ITALY	0	4	8	11	1	0	3	2	1	0	0	1	1	2	34	10	24
LUXEMBOURG	0	0	0	0	0	0	0	0	0	0	0	0	0	0	0	0	0
NETHERLANDS	1	1	1	0	0	0	0	0	0	0	0	0	1	0	4	0	5
DENMARK	0	0	1	0	0	2	0	1	0	0	0	0	0	0	5	5	0
IRELAND	1	0	1	1	0	0	2	1	0	1	2	0	1	2	11	0	12
U.K.	13	4	3	6	1	3	3	2	2	2	0	1	1	0	26	12	27
AUSTRIA	1	0	1	0	0	0	0	0	0	1	0	0	0	0	2	0	3
FINLAND	0	0	0	0	0	0	0	0	0	0	0	0	0	0	1	1	1
GREECE	0	0	1	3	0	0	1	2	0	1	0	0	2	0	10	0	9
NORWAY	0	0	0	0	0	0	0	0	0	0	0	0	0	0	0	2	0
PORTUGAL	0	0	1	3	0	0	2	1	2	1	0	0	1	0	11	1	9
SPAIN	0	0	1	4	2	0	6	1	2	1	0	0	0	1	17	1	16
SWEDEN	1	1	1	1	0	0	1	1	1	0	0	0	0	1	7	0	7
SWITZERLAND	1	1	1	1	0	0	1	0	0	0	0	0	0	0	4	1	4
TURKEY	0	1	1	1	0	0	2	0	0	0	0	0	0	0	5	0	4
OTHER EUROPE	0	0	0	0	0	0	0	0	0	0	0	0	0	0	0	0	0

TABLE 2 .4 .12 (CONTINUED)

COUNTRY OR REGION	NET FLOW UP TO 31-DEC-50	NO. OF ENTRIES DURING YEAR(S) 51-55	56-60	61-65	1966	1967	1968	1969	1970	1971	1972	1973	1974	1975	TOTAL ENTRIES 1951-75	TOTAL EXITS 1951-75	NET FLOW UP TO 1-JAN-76
N.AFR+M.EAST (TOTAL)	0	0	0	6	1	2	3	1	0	0	0	0	1	1	15	1	14
ALGERIA	0	0	0	0	0	0	0	0	0	0	0	0	0	0	0	0	0
EGYPT	0	0	0	0	0	0	0	0	0	0	0	0	0	0	0	0	0
IRAN	0	0	0	4	1	0	2	0	0	0	0	0	1	1	9	0	9
ISRAEL	0	0	0	0	0	1	0	0	0	0	0	0	0	0	1	0	1
LEBANON	0	0	0	1	0	0	0	1	0	0	0	0	0	0	2	0	2
MOROCCO	0	0	0	0	0	1	1	0	0	0	0	0	0	0	2	0	2
SAUDI ARABIA	0	0	0	0	0	0	0	0	0	0	0	0	0	0	0	0	0
OTHER N.AF+M.E.	0	0	0	1	0	0	0	0	0	0	0	0	0	0	1	1	0
E.+W.AFRICA (TOTAL)	0	0	1	1	1	0	0	1	0	2	2	0	2	1	11	0	11
GHANA	0	0	1	0	0	0	0	0	0	0	0	0	0	0	1	0	1
IVORY COAST	0	0	0	0	0	0	0	0	0	0	0	0	0	0	0	0	0
KENYA	0	0	0	0	0	0	0	0	0	0	0	0	0	0	0	0	0
LIBERIA	0	0	0	1	0	0	0	0	0	1	1	0	0	0	3	0	3
NIGERIA	0	0	0	0	0	0	0	0	0	0	0	0	0	0	0	0	0
ZAIRE	0	0	0	0	0	0	0	0	0	1	1	0	2	0	4	0	4
ZAMBIA	0	0	0	0	1	0	0	1	0	0	0	0	0	1	3	0	3
OTHER E.+W.AFR.	0	0	0	0	0	0	0	0	0	0	0	0	0	0	0	0	0
SOUTH ASIA (TOTAL)	2	1	11	7	0	0	4	1	1	0	0	2	0	0	27	3	26
INDIA	2	1	7	4	0	0	3	0	1	0	0	0	0	0	16	3	15
PAKISTAN	0	0	4	2	0	0	1	1	0	0	0	1	0	0	9	0	9
SRI LANKA	0	0	0	1	0	0	0	0	0	0	0	0	0	0	1	0	1
OTHER S.ASIA	0	0	0	0	0	0	0	0	0	0	0	1	0	0	1	0	1
EAST ASIA (TOTAL)	3	4	7	10	1	2	6	7	4	4	3	2	2	1	53	4	52
HONG KONG	0	0	0	0	0	0	2	0	0	0	0	0	0	0	2	0	2
INDONESIA	1	0	0	0	0	0	0	1	2	2	2	1	1	1	10	1	10
JAPAN	0	2	1	3	0	2	1	2	0	1	1	0	1	0	14	1	13
MALAYSIA	2	0	0	2	0	0	0	1	0	0	0	0	0	0	3	0	5
PHILIPPINES	0	2	3	2	0	0	2	0	1	0	0	0	0	0	10	0	10
SINGAPORE	0	0	1	0	0	0	0	0	0	0	0	0	0	0	1	1	0
S.KOREA	0	0	1	0	0	0	0	0	0	0	0	0	0	0	1	0	1
THAILAND	0	0	0	1	1	0	0	1	1	0	0	1	0	0	5	0	5
TAIWAN	0	0	1	1	0	0	1	1	0	1	0	0	0	0	5	0	5
OTHER E.ASIA	0	0	0	1	0	0	0	1	0	0	0	0	0	0	2	1	1
S.DOMINIONS (TOTAL)	13	6	11	12	2	1	5	6	1	2	0	0	2	3	51	5	59
AUSTRALIA	5	3	7	5	1	1	2	1	1	2	0	0	0	2	25	2	28
NEW ZEALAND	3	0	0	3	1	0	1	1	0	0	0	0	1	0	7	0	10
RHODESIA	0	0	0	0	0	0	0	1	0	0	0	0	0	0	1	0	1
S.AFRICA	5	3	4	4	0	0	2	3	0	0	0	0	1	1	18	3	20
OUTSIDE U.S. (TOTAL)	81	43	99	132	11	27	67	45	23	30	14	11	20	12	534	95	520

CHAPTER 2 - THE PROLIFERATION OF FOREIGN SUBSIDIARIES
SECTION 4 -- GEOGRAPHICAL SPREAD IN SPECIFIC INDUSTRIES
TABLE 13 --- OTHER CHEMICAL INDUSTRIES (OTHER SIC 28)

NO. OF SUBSIDIARIES MANUFACTURING IN THIS INDUSTRY AT TIME OF ENTRY INTO PARENT SYSTEM

COUNTRY OR REGION	NET FLOW UP TO 31-DEC-50	NO. OF ENTRIES DURING YEAR(S)													TOTAL ENTRIES 1951-75	TOTAL EXITS 1951-75	NET FLOW UP TO 1-JAN-76
		51-55	56-60	61-65	1966	1967	1968	1969	1970	1971	1972	1973	1974	1975			
CANADA	12	3	3	6	1	3	2	2	4	2	3	3	1	2	35	11	36
LATIN AMER. (TOTAL)	11	8	13	14	2	6	3	3	6	7	4	5	6	3	80	24	67
C.AM.+CARIB.(TOTAL)	3	4	3	7	0	2	0	2	3	5	2	0	0	0	28	7	24
BAHAMAS	0	0	0	0	0	0	0	0	0	0	0	0	0	0	0	0	0
BERMUDA	0	0	0	0	0	0	0	0	0	0	0	0	0	0	0	0	0
COSTA RICA	0	0	0	1	0	1	0	0	0	0	0	0	0	0	2	0	2
GUATEMALA	0	0	1	0	0	0	0	0	0	0	0	0	0	0	1	0	1
JAMAICA	3	3	2	3	0	0	0	2	3	4	2	0	0	0	19	4	18
MEXICO	0	0	0	0	0	0	0	0	0	0	0	0	0	0	0	0	0
NETH.ANTILLES	0	0	0	1	0	0	0	0	0	1	0	0	0	0	2	0	2
NICARAGUA	0	0	0	2	0	0	0	0	0	0	0	0	0	0	2	1	1
PANAMA	0	1	0	0	0	1	0	0	0	0	0	0	0	0	2	2	0
OTHER C.AM+CAR.	0	0	0	0	0	0	0	0	0	0	0	0	0	0	0	0	0
S.AMERICA (TOTAL)	8	4	10	7	2	4	3	1	3	2	2	5	6	3	52	17	43
BOLIVIA	0	0	0	0	0	0	0	1	0	0	0	0	0	0	1	1	0
CHILE	2	0	0	0	0	0	0	0	0	0	0	0	0	1	1	1	2
COLOMBIA	2	1	1	3	0	0	0	0	1	0	0	0	1	0	7	1	8
ECUADOR	0	0	3	0	0	0	0	0	0	0	0	0	0	1	4	2	2
PERU	0	0	0	0	0	1	0	0	0	0	0	0	0	0	1	1	0
ARGENTINA	3	0	3	0	1	0	1	0	1	0	0	0	0	0	6	3	6
BRAZIL	1	3	1	2	1	3	1	0	0	1	2	4	3	1	22	7	16
URUGUAY	0	0	0	0	0	0	0	0	0	0	0	0	0	0	0	0	0
VENEZUELA	0	0	2	2	0	0	1	0	1	1	0	1	2	0	10	1	9
OTHER S.AMER.	0	0	0	0	0	0	0	0	0	0	0	0	0	0	0	0	0
EUROPE (TOTAL)	9	9	11	31	14	13	11	9	7	12	12	12	5	15	161	34	136
BELGIUM	0	0	2	2	0	0	0	0	1	0	2	2	0	3	12	3	9
FRANCE	1	1	3	4	0	3	2	1	0	2	2	2	2	1	23	7	17
GERMANY	2	3	3	5	0	0	2	2	0	0	4	0	1	0	20	3	19
ITALY	1	1	3	7	2	1	1	3	0	1	1	2	1	2	25	3	23
LUXEMBOURG	0	0	0	0	0	0	1	0	0	0	0	0	0	0	1	0	1
NETHERLANDS	0	0	0	4	0	1	0	2	1	2	0	0	0	3	13	1	12
DENMARK	0	0	0	0	1	0	0	0	0	0	0	0	0	0	1	0	1
IRELAND	0	1	0	0	1	0	0	0	0	0	0	0	1	0	3	1	2
U.K.	3	3	0	7	2	6	3	1	3	3	3	5	0	2	38	13	28
AUSTRIA	0	0	0	0	0	0	2	0	0	0	0	0	0	0	2	0	2
FINLAND	0	0	0	0	0	0	0	0	0	0	0	0	0	0	0	0	0
GREECE	0	0	0	0	1	0	0	0	0	0	0	0	0	0	1	0	1
NORWAY	0	0	0	0	1	0	0	0	0	0	0	0	0	0	1	0	1
PORTUGAL	1	0	0	1	5	2	0	0	2	3	0	0	0	2	15	2	14
SPAIN	1	0	0	1	0	0	0	0	0	0	0	0	0	1	2	0	3
SWEDEN	0	0	0	0	1	0	0	0	0	1	0	1	0	1	4	1	3
SWITZERLAND	0	0	0	0	0	0	0	0	0	0	0	0	0	0	0	0	0
TURKEY	0	0	0	0	0	0	0	0	0	0	0	0	0	0	0	0	0
OTHER EUROPE	0	0	0	0	0	0	0	0	0	0	0	0	0	0	0	0	0

TABLE   2 .4 .13   (CONTINUED)

COUNTRY OR REGION	NET FLOW UP TO 31-DEC-50	51-55	56-60	61-65	1966	1967	1968	1969	1970	1971	1972	1973	1974	1975	TOTAL ENTRIES 1951-75	TOTAL EXITS 1951-75	NET FLOW UP TO 1-JAN-76
		NO. OF ENTRIES DURING YEAR(S)															
N.AFR+M.EAST(TOTAL)	0	0	0	1	0	0	2	0	0	1	0	0	1	1	6	0	6
ALGERIA	0	0	0	0	0	0	0	0	0	0	0	0	0	0	0	0	0
EGYPT	0	0	0	0	0	0	0	0	0	0	0	0	0	0	0	0	0
IRAN	0	0	0	0	0	0	1	0	0	1	0	0	0	1	3	0	3
ISRAEL	0	0	0	1	0	0	0	0	0	0	0	0	1	0	2	0	2
LEBANON	0	0	0	0	0	0	0	0	0	0	0	0	0	0	0	0	0
MOROCCO	0	0	0	0	0	0	1	0	0	0	0	0	0	0	1	0	1
SAUDI ARABIA	0	0	0	0	0	0	0	0	0	0	0	0	0	0	0	0	0
OTHER N.AF+M.E.	0	0	0	0	0	0	0	0	0	0	0	0	0	0	0	0	0
E.+W.AFRICA (TOTAL)	0	0	0	0	0	0	0	0	0	0	0	0	0	0	0	0	0
GHANA	0	0	0	0	0	0	0	0	0	0	0	0	0	0	0	0	0
IVORY COAST	0	0	0	0	0	0	0	0	0	0	0	0	0	0	0	0	0
KENYA	0	0	0	0	0	0	0	0	0	0	0	0	0	0	0	0	0
LIBERIA	0	0	0	0	0	0	0	0	0	0	0	0	0	0	0	0	0
NIGERIA	0	0	0	0	0	0	0	0	0	0	0	0	0	0	0	0	0
ZAIRE	0	0	0	0	0	0	0	0	0	0	0	0	0	0	0	0	0
ZAMBIA	0	0	0	0	0	0	0	0	0	0	0	0	0	0	0	0	0
OTHER E.+W.AFR.	0	0	0	0	0	0	0	0	0	0	0	0	0	0	0	0	0
SOUTH ASIA (TOTAL)	1	0	0	1	0	0	0	0	0	0	0	1	1	0	3	0	4
INDIA	1	0	0	1	0	0	0	0	0	0	0	1	1	0	3	0	4
PAKISTAN	0	0	0	0	0	0	0	0	0	0	0	0	0	0	0	0	0
SRI LANKA	0	0	0	0	0	0	0	0	0	0	0	0	0	0	0	0	0
OTHER S.ASIA	0	0	0	0	0	0	0	0	0	0	0	0	0	0	0	0	0
EAST ASIA (TOTAL)	1	2	2	8	1	3	1	1	4	5	2	1	2	0	32	6	27
HONG KONG	0	0	0	1	1	0	0	0	1	1	0	0	0	0	4	0	4
INDONESIA	0	0	0	1	0	0	0	0	0	0	0	0	0	0	1	0	1
JAPAN	0	1	1	6	0	2	0	0	0	2	2	1	0	0	15	4	11
MALAYSIA	0	0	0	0	0	0	0	0	1	0	0	0	0	0	1	1	1
PHILIPPINES	1	1	0	0	0	0	0	0	1	1	0	0	0	0	3	1	3
SINGAPORE	0	0	0	0	0	0	0	0	0	1	0	0	0	0	1	0	1
S.KOREA	0	0	0	0	0	1	0	1	1	0	0	0	0	0	3	1	3
THAILAND	0	0	1	0	0	0	1	0	0	0	0	0	0	0	2	1	1
TAIWAN	0	0	0	0	0	0	0	0	0	0	0	0	2	0	2	0	2
OTHER E.ASIA	0	0	0	0	0	0	0	0	0	0	0	0	0	0	0	0	0
S.DOMINIONS (TOTAL)	4	0	5	3	1	3	3	3	1	5	3	5	1	1	34	4	34
AUSTRALIA	1	0	4	2	1	2	3	0	1	4	2	3	0	1	21	4	18
NEW ZEALAND	0	0	1	0	0	0	0	0	0	0	2	2	0	0	5	0	5
RHODESIA	0	0	0	0	0	0	0	1	0	0	0	0	0	0	1	0	1
S.AFRICA	3	0	0	1	0	1	0	2	0	1	0	0	1	0	7	0	10
OUTSIDE U.S.(TOTAL)	38	22	34	64	19	28	22	20	20	32	24	27	17	22	351	79	310

CHAPTER 2 - THE PROLIFERATION OF FOREIGN SUBSIDIARIES
SECTION 4 -- GEOGRAPHICAL SPREAD IN SPECIFIC INDUSTRIES
TABLE 14 --- FABRICATED PLASTICS INDUSTRIES (SIC 306 AND 307)

NO. OF SUBSIDIARIES MANUFACTURING IN THIS INDUSTRY AT TIME OF ENTRY INTO PARENT SYSTEM

COUNTRY OR REGION	NET FLOW UP TO 31-DEC-50	NO. OF ENTRIES DURING YEAR(S)													TOTAL ENTRIES 1951-75	TOTAL EXITS 1951-75	NET FLOW UP TO 1-JAN-76
		51-55	56-60	61-65	1966	1967	1968	1969	1970	1971	1972	1973	1974	1975			
CANADA	2	4	1	3	0	3	1	1	0	3	2	4	1	0	23	6	19
LATIN AMER. (TOTAL)	9	5	3	4	1	2	1	4	2	4	1	3	0	0	30	12	27
C.AM.+CARIB.(TOTAL)	3	3	1	3	0	0	0	2	1	3	0	0	0	0	13	6	10
BAHAMAS	0	0	0	0	0	0	0	0	0	0	0	0	0	0	0	0	0
BERMUDA	0	0	0	0	0	0	0	0	0	0	0	0	0	0	0	0	0
COSTA RICA	0	0	0	1	0	0	0	1	0	0	0	0	0	0	2	1	1
GUATEMALA	0	0	1	0	0	0	0	0	0	0	0	0	0	0	1	1	0
JAMAICA	0	0	0	0	0	0	0	0	0	0	0	0	0	0	0	1	0
MEXICO	3	3	0	2	0	0	0	1	1	3	0	0	0	0	10	4	9
NETH.ANTILLES	0	0	0	0	0	0	0	0	0	0	0	0	0	0	0	0	0
NICARAGUA	0	0	0	0	0	0	0	0	0	0	0	0	0	0	0	0	0
PANAMA	0	0	0	0	0	0	0	0	0	0	0	0	0	0	0	0	0
OTHER C.AM+CAR.	0	0	0	0	0	0	0	0	0	0	0	0	0	0	0	0	0
S.AMERICA (TOTAL)	6	2	2	1	1	2	1	2	1	1	1	3	0	0	17	6	17
BOLIVIA	0	0	0	0	0	0	1	0	0	0	0	0	0	0	1	1	0
CHILE	0	0	0	1	0	0	0	0	0	0	0	0	0	0	1	1	0
COLOMBIA	1	0	0	0	0	1	0	0	0	0	0	0	0	0	1	1	1
ECUADOR	0	0	0	0	0	0	0	0	0	0	0	0	0	0	0	0	0
PERU	1	1	0	0	0	0	0	0	0	0	0	0	0	0	1	0	2
ARGENTINA	1	1	0	0	0	0	0	0	0	0	0	1	0	0	2	0	3
BRAZIL	1	0	1	0	0	0	0	2	0	1	0	2	0	0	6	1	6
URUGUAY	0	0	0	0	0	0	0	0	0	0	0	0	0	0	0	0	0
VENEZUELA	2	0	1	0	1	1	0	0	1	0	1	0	0	0	5	2	5
OTHER S.AMER.	0	0	0	0	0	0	0	0	0	0	0	0	0	0	0	0	0
EUROPE (TOTAL)	6	3	4	16	2	2	11	7	6	11	9	10	4	1	86	25	67
BELGIUM	0	0	0	2	0	0	0	0	0	0	0	0	0	1	3	0	3
FRANCE	1	0	1	1	0	0	0	0	0	0	2	0	0	0	4	1	4
GERMANY	0	1	1	2	0	0	0	2	1	2	3	0	0	0	12	1	11
ITALY	0	0	0	2	0	0	2	1	1	1	0	0	0	0	7	3	4
LUXEMBOURG	0	0	0	0	0	0	0	1	0	0	0	0	0	0	1	0	1
NETHERLANDS	0	0	0	1	0	0	2	0	0	0	1	1	0	0	5	1	4
DENMARK	0	0	0	0	0	0	0	0	0	0	0	0	1	0	1	0	1
IRELAND	1	1	1	1	0	0	0	0	0	0	0	0	1	0	4	0	5
U.K.	3	1	1	3	0	1	8	1	3	2	3	7	1	0	31	15	19
AUSTRIA	0	0	0	0	0	0	1	0	0	0	0	0	0	0	1	0	1
FINLAND	0	0	0	0	0	0	0	1	0	0	0	0	0	0	1	0	1
GREECE	0	0	0	0	0	0	0	0	0	0	0	0	0	0	0	1	0
NORWAY	0	0	0	0	1	0	0	0	0	0	0	0	0	0	1	1	0
PORTUGAL	0	0	0	1	0	0	0	0	0	0	0	0	0	0	1	0	0
SPAIN	0	1	0	3	0	0	2	0	0	1	0	1	0	0	8	2	6
SWEDEN	1	0	0	0	0	0	0	0	0	1	0	1	0	0	2	0	3
SWITZERLAND	0	0	0	1	0	0	0	1	0	0	0	2	0	0	4	0	4
TURKEY	0	0	0	0	0	0	0	0	0	0	0	0	0	0	0	0	0
OTHER EUROPE	0	0	0	0	0	0	0	0	0	0	0	0	0	0	0	0	0

TABLE 2 .4 .14 (CONTINUED)

COUNTRY OR REGION	NET FLOW UP TO 31-DEC-50	51-55	56-60	61-65	1966	1967	1968	1969	1970	1971	1972	1973	1974	1975	TOTAL ENTRIES 1951-75	TOTAL EXITS 1951-75	NET FLOW UP TO 1-JAN-76
N.AFR+M.EAST (TOTAL)	0	0	1	1	0	0	0	0	0	0	0	0	0	0	2	1	1
ALGERIA	0	0	0	0	0	0	0	0	0	0	0	0	0	0	0	0	0
EGYPT	0	0	0	0	0	0	0	0	0	0	0	0	0	0	0	0	0
IRAN	0	0	0	0	0	0	0	0	0	0	0	0	0	0	0	0	0
ISRAEL	0	0	0	0	0	0	0	0	0	0	0	0	0	0	0	0	0
LEBANON	0	0	1	0	0	0	0	0	0	0	0	0	0	0	1	1	0
MOROCCO	0	0	0	1	0	0	0	0	0	0	0	0	0	0	1	0	1
SAUDI ARABIA	0	0	0	0	0	0	0	0	0	0	0	0	0	0	0	0	0
OTHER N.AF+M.E.	0	0	0	0	0	0	0	0	0	0	0	0	0	0	0	0	0
E.+W.AFRICA (TOTAL)	0	0	0	1	0	0	0	1	0	1	0	0	0	2	5	1	4
GHANA	0	0	0	0	0	0	0	0	0	0	0	0	0	0	0	0	0
IVORY COAST	0	0	0	0	0	0	0	0	0	0	0	0	0	0	0	0	0
KENYA	0	0	0	1	0	0	0	0	0	1	0	0	0	0	2	1	1
LIBERIA	0	0	0	0	0	0	0	0	0	0	0	0	0	0	0	0	0
NIGERIA	0	0	0	0	0	0	0	0	0	0	0	0	0	0	0	0	0
ZAIRE	0	0	0	0	0	0	0	0	0	0	0	0	0	0	0	0	0
ZAMBIA	0	0	0	0	0	0	0	0	0	0	0	0	0	1	1	0	1
OTHER E.+W.AFR.	0	0	0	0	0	0	0	1	0	0	0	0	0	1	2	0	2
SOUTH ASIA (TOTAL)	0	0	0	1	0	0	0	0	0	1	0	0	0	0	2	0	2
INDIA	0	0	0	1	0	0	0	0	0	1	0	0	0	0	2	0	2
PAKISTAN	0	0	0	0	0	0	0	0	0	0	0	0	0	0	0	0	0
SRI LANKA	0	0	0	0	0	0	0	0	0	0	0	0	0	0	0	0	0
OTHER S.ASIA	0	0	0	0	0	0	0	0	0	0	0	0	0	0	0	0	0
EAST ASIA (TOTAL)	1	1	1	3	1	0	1	2	2	2	0	0	0	0	13	5	9
HONG KONG	0	0	0	1	0	0	0	0	0	0	0	0	0	0	1	1	0
INDONESIA	0	0	0	0	0	0	0	0	0	0	0	0	0	0	0	0	0
JAPAN	1	1	1	1	1	0	0	1	1	1	0	0	0	0	7	3	5
MALAYSIA	0	0	0	1	0	0	0	0	0	0	0	0	0	0	1	0	1
PHILIPPINES	0	0	0	0	0	0	0	0	0	0	0	0	0	0	0	0	0
SINGAPORE	0	0	0	0	0	0	0	1	0	0	0	0	0	0	1	1	0
S.KOREA	0	0	0	0	0	0	0	0	0	1	0	0	0	0	1	0	1
THAILAND	0	0	0	0	0	0	0	0	1	0	0	0	0	0	1	0	1
TAIWAN	0	0	0	0	0	0	1	0	0	0	0	0	0	0	1	0	1
OTHER E.ASIA	0	0	0	0	0	0	0	0	0	0	0	0	0	0	0	0	0
S.DOMINIONS (TOTAL)	2	0	2	2	1	0	1	3	3	2	0	0	2	0	16	3	15
AUSTRALIA	1	0	2	2	0	0	0	1	1	2	0	0	0	0	8	1	8
NEW ZEALAND	1	0	0	0	0	0	0	0	0	0	0	0	0	0	0	1	0
RHODESIA	0	0	0	0	0	0	0	0	0	0	0	0	1	0	1	0	1
S.AFRICA	0	0	0	0	1	0	1	2	2	0	0	0	1	0	7	1	6
OUTSIDE U.S. (TOTAL)	20	13	11	29	5	8	15	19	14	22	13	17	9	2	177	53	144

CHAPTER 2   - THE PROLIFERATION OF FOREIGN SUBSIDIARIES
SECTION 4   -- GEOGRAPHICAL SPREAD IN SPECIFIC INDUSTRIES
TABLE 15 --- THE TIRES INDUSTRY (SIC 301)

NO. OF SUBSIDIARIES MANUFACTURING IN THIS INDUSTRY AT TIME OF ENTRY INTO PARENT SYSTEM

COUNTRY OR REGION	NET FLOW UP TO 31-DEC-50	NO. OF ENTRIES DURING YEAR(S)													TOTAL ENTRIES 1951-75	TOTAL EXITS 1951-75	NET FLOW UP TO 1-JAN-76
		51-55	56-60	61-65	1966	1967	1968	1969	1970	1971	1972	1973	1974	1975			
CANADA	5	0	0	1	0	0	1	0	0	0	0	0	0	0	2	0	7
LATIN AMER. (TOTAL)	24	4	3	3	0	0	0	0	0	0	0	0	0	2	12	9	27
C.AM.+CARIB. (TOTAL)	8	1	2	2	0	0	0	0	0	0	0	0	0	0	5	5	8
BAHAMAS	0	0	0	0	0	0	0	0	0	0	0	0	0	0	0	0	0
BERMUDA	0	0	0	0	0	0	0	0	0	0	0	0	0	0	0	0	0
COSTA RICA	0	0	0	1	0	0	0	0	0	0	0	0	0	0	1	0	1
GUATEMALA	0	0	1	0	0	0	0	0	0	0	0	0	0	0	1	1	0
JAMAICA	0	0	1	0	0	0	0	0	0	0	0	0	0	0	1	0	1
MEXICO	5	0	0	1	0	0	0	0	0	0	0	0	0	0	1	0	6
NETH.ANTILLES	0	0	0	0	0	0	0	0	0	0	0	0	0	0	0	0	0
NICARAGUA	0	0	0	0	0	0	0	0	0	0	0	0	0	0	0	0	0
PANAMA	0	0	0	0	0	0	0	0	0	0	0	0	0	0	0	0	0
OTHER C.AM+CAR.	3	1	0	0	0	0	0	0	0	0	0	0	0	0	1	4	0
S.AMERICA (TOTAL)	16	3	1	1	0	0	0	0	0	0	0	0	0	2	7	4	19
BOLIVIA	2	0	0	1	0	0	0	0	0	0	0	0	0	0	1	0	3
CHILE	3	0	0	0	0	0	0	0	0	0	0	0	0	0	0	0	3
COLOMBIA	0	0	0	0	0	0	0	0	0	0	0	0	0	1	1	0	1
ECUADOR	1	0	0	0	0	0	0	0	0	0	0	0	0	1	1	0	2
PERU	4	1	0	0	0	0	0	0	0	0	0	0	0	0	1	2	3
ARGENTINA	2	0	1	0	0	0	0	0	0	0	0	0	0	0	1	2	1
BRAZIL	1	2	0	0	0	0	0	0	0	0	0	0	0	0	2	0	3
URUGUAY	0	0	0	0	0	0	0	0	0	0	0	0	0	0	0	0	0
VENEZUELA	3	0	0	0	0	0	0	0	0	0	0	0	0	0	0	0	3
OTHER S.AMER.	0	0	0	0	0	0	0	0	0	0	0	0	0	0	0	0	0
EUROPE (TOTAL)	10	5	5	4	1	0	0	0	0	4	0	0	0	0	19	7	22
BELGIUM	0	0	0	0	1	0	0	0	0	0	0	0	0	0	1	0	1
FRANCE	1	1	1	1	0	0	0	0	0	0	0	0	0	0	3	1	3
GERMANY	1	2	1	0	0	0	0	0	0	0	0	0	0	0	3	2	2
ITALY	0	0	2	0	0	0	0	0	0	0	0	0	0	0	2	2	0
LUXEMBOURG	1	0	0	0	0	0	0	0	0	0	0	0	0	0	0	0	1
NETHERLANDS	1	1	0	0	0	0	0	0	0	3	0	0	0	0	4	1	4
DENMARK	0	0	0	0	0	0	0	0	0	0	0	0	0	0	0	0	0
IRELAND	0	0	0	0	0	0	0	0	0	1	0	0	0	0	1	0	1
U.K.	2	0	1	0	0	0	0	0	0	0	0	0	0	0	1	1	2
AUSTRIA	0	0	0	0	0	0	0	0	0	0	0	0	0	0	0	0	0
FINLAND	0	0	0	0	0	0	0	0	0	0	0	0	0	0	0	0	0
GREECE	0	0	0	0	0	0	0	0	0	0	0	0	0	0	0	0	0
NORWAY	0	0	0	0	0	0	0	0	0	0	0	0	0	0	0	0	0
PORTUGAL	2	1	0	0	0	0	0	0	0	0	0	0	0	0	1	0	3
SPAIN	1	0	0	1	0	0	0	0	0	0	0	0	0	0	1	0	2
SWEDEN	0	0	0	0	0	0	0	0	0	0	0	0	0	0	0	0	0
SWITZERLAND	1	0	0	0	0	0	0	0	0	0	0	0	0	0	0	0	1
TURKEY	0	0	0	2	0	0	0	0	0	0	0	0	0	0	2	0	2
OTHER EUROPE	0	0	0	0	0	0	0	0	0	0	0	0	0	0	0	0	0

TABLE 2.4.15 (CONTINUED)

COUNTRY OR REGION	NET FLOW UP TO 31-DEC-50	51-55	56-60	61-65	1966	1967	1968	1969	1970	1971	1972	1973	1974	1975	TOTAL ENTRIES 1951-75	TOTAL EXITS 1951-75	NET FLOW UP TO 1-JAN-76
		NO. OF ENTRIES DURING YEAR(S)															
N.AFR+M.EAST (TOTAL)	1	0	2	1	1	0	0	0	0	0	1	0	0	1	6	1	6
ALGERIA	0	0	0	0	0	0	0	0	0	0	0	0	0	0	0	0	0
EGYPT	0	0	0	0	0	0	0	0	0	0	0	0	0	0	0	0	0
IRAN	1	0	0	1	1	0	0	0	0	0	0	0	0	1	3	1	3
ISRAEL	0	0	0	0	0	0	0	0	0	0	0	0	0	0	0	0	0
LEBANON	0	0	0	0	0	0	0	0	0	0	0	0	0	0	0	0	0
MOROCCO	0	0	1	0	0	0	0	0	0	0	1	0	0	0	2	0	2
SAUDI ARABIA	0	0	0	0	0	0	0	0	0	0	0	0	0	0	0	0	0
OTHER N.AF+M.E.	0	0	1	0	0	0	0	0	0	0	0	0	0	0	1	0	1
E.+W.AFRICA (TOTAL)	0	0	0	1	0	2	0	1	0	0	0	0	0	1	5	1	4
GHANA	0	0	0	1	0	0	0	0	0	0	0	0	0	0	1	0	1
IVORY COAST	0	0	0	0	0	1	0	0	0	0	0	0	0	0	0	1	0
KENYA	0	0	0	0	0	1	0	1	0	0	0	0	0	0	2	0	1
LIBERIA	0	0	0	0	0	0	0	0	0	0	0	0	0	0	0	0	0
NIGERIA	0	0	0	0	0	0	0	0	0	0	0	0	0	0	0	0	0
ZAIRE	0	0	0	0	0	0	0	1	0	0	0	0	0	0	1	0	1
ZAMBIA	0	0	0	0	0	0	0	0	0	0	0	0	0	0	0	0	0
OTHER E.+W.AFR.	0	0	0	0	0	1	0	0	0	0	0	0	0	1	1	0	1
SOUTH ASIA (TOTAL)	1	0	0	1	0	0	0	0	0	0	0	0	0	0	1	0	2
INDIA	1	0	0	0	0	0	0	0	0	0	0	0	0	0	0	0	1
PAKISTAN	0	0	0	1	0	0	0	0	0	0	0	0	0	0	1	0	1
SRI LANKA	0	0	0	0	0	0	0	0	0	0	0	0	0	0	0	0	0
OTHER S.ASIA	0	0	0	0	0	0	0	0	0	0	0	0	0	0	0	0	0
EAST ASIA (TOTAL)	3	0	0	2	1	0	1	0	0	1	0	0	0	0	5	1	7
HONG KONG	0	0	0	0	1	0	0	0	0	0	0	0	0	0	1	1	0
INDONESIA	0	0	0	0	0	0	0	0	0	0	0	0	0	0	0	0	0
JAPAN	1	0	0	0	0	0	0	0	0	0	0	0	0	0	0	0	1
MALAYSIA	0	0	0	1	0	0	0	0	0	0	0	0	0	0	1	0	1
PHILIPPINES	2	0	0	0	0	0	0	0	0	0	0	0	0	0	0	0	2
SINGAPORE	0	0	0	0	0	0	0	0	0	0	0	0	0	0	0	0	0
S.KOREA	0	0	0	0	0	0	0	0	0	0	0	0	0	0	0	0	0
THAILAND	0	0	0	1	0	0	1	0	0	0	0	0	0	0	2	0	2
TAIWAN	0	0	0	0	0	0	0	0	0	1	0	0	0	0	1	0	1
OTHER E.ASIA	0	0	0	0	0	0	0	0	0	0	0	0	0	0	0	0	0
S.DOMINIONS (TOTAL)	4	0	1	1	1	0	0	0	0	0	0	0	0	0	3	1	6
AUSTRALIA	1	0	1	1	1	0	0	0	0	0	0	0	0	0	3	0	4
NEW ZEALAND	2	0	0	0	0	0	0	0	0	0	0	0	0	0	0	1	1
RHODESIA	0	0	0	0	0	0	0	0	0	0	0	0	0	0	0	0	0
S.AFRICA	1	0	0	0	0	0	0	0	0	0	0	0	0	0	0	0	1
OUTSIDE U.S. (TOTAL)	48	9	11	14	3	3	2	1	0	4	3	0	0	3	53	20	81

CHAPTER 2 — THE PROLIFERATION OF FOREIGN SUBSIDIARIES
SECTION 4 —— GEOGRAPHICAL SPREAD IN SPECIFIC INDUSTRIES
TABLE 16 ——— THE PETROLEUM REFINING INDUSTRY (SIC 291)

NO. OF SUBSIDIARIES MANUFACTURING IN THIS INDUSTRY AT TIME OF ENTRY INTO PARENT SYSTEM

COUNTRY OR REGION	NET FLOW UP TO 31-DEC-50	NO. OF ENTRIES DURING YEAR(S)													TOTAL ENTRIES 1951-75	TOTAL EXITS 1951-75	NET FLOW UP TO 1-JAN-76
		51-55	56-60	61-65	1966	1967	1968	1969	1970	1971	1972	1973	1974	1975			
CANADA	4	0	4	1	0	1	0	0	0	0	0	0	0	1	7	4	7
LATIN AMER. (TOTAL)	6	3	3	4	0	1	5	1	1	2	1	0	0	2	23	8	21
C.AM.+CARIB. (TOTAL)	2	1	2	1	0	1	3	1	1	2	0	0	0	2	14	2	14
BAHAMAS	0	0	0	0	0	0	1	0	0	0	0	0	0	0	1	0	1
BERMUDA	0	0	0	0	0	0	0	0	0	0	0	0	0	0	0	0	0
COSTA RICA	0	0	0	0	0	0	0	0	0	0	0	0	0	0	0	0	0
GUATEMALA	0	0	0	0	0	0	0	0	0	0	0	0	0	0	0	0	0
JAMAICA	0	0	0	0	0	0	0	0	0	0	0	0	0	0	0	0	0
MEXICO	0	0	0	0	0	1	1	0	1	0	0	0	0	0	3	0	3
NETH.ANTILLES	0	0	0	0	0	0	0	0	0	1	0	0	0	0	1	0	1
NICARAGUA	0	0	0	0	0	0	0	0	0	0	0	0	0	0	0	0	0
PANAMA	0	0	1	0	0	0	1	0	0	1	0	0	0	0	3	0	3
OTHER C.AM+CAR.	2	1	1	1	0	0	0	1	0	0	0	0	0	2	6	2	6
S.AMERICA (TOTAL)	4	2	1	3	0	0	2	0	0	0	1	0	0	0	9	6	7
BOLIVIA	0	0	0	0	0	0	0	0	0	0	0	0	0	0	0	0	0
CHILE	0	0	0	0	0	0	0	0	0	0	0	0	0	0	0	0	0
COLOMBIA	1	1	1	0	0	0	0	0	0	0	0	0	0	0	2	0	3
ECUADOR	0	0	0	0	0	0	0	0	0	0	0	0	0	0	0	0	0
PERU	0	0	0	1	0	0	0	0	0	0	0	0	0	0	1	1	0
ARGENTINA	1	0	0	0	0	0	1	0	0	0	1	0	0	0	2	0	3
BRAZIL	0	0	0	0	0	0	0	0	0	0	0	0	0	0	0	0	0
URUGUAY	0	0	0	0	0	0	0	0	0	0	0	0	0	0	0	0	0
VENEZUELA	2	1	0	2	0	0	1	0	0	0	0	0	0	0	4	5	1
OTHER S.AMER.	0	0	0	0	0	0	0	0	0	0	0	0	0	0	0	0	0
EUROPE (TOTAL)	15	6	9	18	7	4	5	4	4	4	3	2	1	1	68	31	52
BELGIUM	1	0	0	0	0	0	0	1	0	0	0	0	0	0	1	0	2
FRANCE	2	0	1	0	0	1	0	1	1	1	1	1	1	0	8	2	8
GERMANY	0	2	2	6	5	1	1	2	0	0	1	0	0	0	20	7	13
ITALY	2	2	2	3	1	1	2	0	0	0	0	0	0	0	11	6	7
LUXEMBOURG	0	0	0	0	0	0	0	0	0	0	0	0	0	0	0	0	0
NETHERLANDS	0	0	2	1	0	0	1	0	0	0	0	0	0	0	4	2	2
DENMARK	0	0	0	0	1	0	0	0	0	0	0	0	0	0	1	0	1
IRELAND	0	0	0	0	0	0	0	0	0	0	0	0	0	0	0	0	0
U.K.	5	1	1	4	0	1	1	0	0	0	0	0	0	0	8	8	5
AUSTRIA	3	0	0	0	0	0	0	0	0	0	0	0	0	1	1	0	4
FINLAND	0	0	0	0	0	0	0	0	0	0	0	0	0	0	0	0	0
GREECE	0	0	1	1	0	0	1	0	0	0	0	0	0	0	3	0	3
NORWAY	0	0	0	0	0	0	0	1	1	0	0	0	0	0	2	1	1
PORTUGAL	0	0	0	0	0	0	0	0	0	0	0	0	0	0	0	0	0
SPAIN	1	0	0	0	0	1	1	1	1	1	1	0	0	0	6	4	3
SWEDEN	1	1	0	0	0	0	0	0	0	0	0	0	0	0	1	1	1
SWITZERLAND	0	0	0	0	0	0	0	0	0	0	0	0	0	0	0	0	0
TURKEY	0	0	0	0	0	0	0	1	0	1	0	0	0	0	2	0	2
OTHER EUROPE	0	0	0	0	0	0	0	0	0	0	0	0	0	0	0	0	0

TABLE 2.4.16 (CONTINUED)

COUNTRY OR REGION	NET FLOW UP TO 31-DEC-50	NO. OF ENTRIES DURING YEAR(S)													TOTAL ENTRIES 1951-75	TOTAL EXITS 1951-75	NET FLOW UP TO 1-JAN-76
		51-55	56-60	61-65	1966	1967	1968	1969	1970	1971	1972	1973	1974	1975			
N.AFR+M.EAST (TOTAL)	2	4	2	0	0	0	0	0	0	0	0	0	0	2	8	5	5
ALGERIA	0	0	1	0	0	0	0	0	0	0	0	0	0	0	1	1	0
EGYPT	0	0	0	0	0	0	0	0	0	0	0	0	0	0	0	0	0
IRAN	0	2	0	0	0	0	0	0	0	0	0	0	0	0	2	1	1
ISRAEL	0	0	0	0	0	0	0	0	0	0	0	0	0	0	0	0	0
LEBANON	0	0	0	0	0	0	0	0	0	0	0	0	0	0	0	0	0
MOROCCO	0	0	0	0	0	0	0	0	0	0	0	0	0	0	0	0	0
SAUDI ARABIA	0	0	0	0	0	0	0	0	0	0	0	0	0	2	2	0	2
OTHER N.AF+M.E.	2	2	1	0	0	0	0	0	0	0	0	0	0	0	3	3	2
E.+W.AFRICA (TOTAL)	0	0	1	3	1	0	1	2	1	0	1	0	0	0	10	1	9
GHANA	0	0	0	0	0	0	0	0	0	0	0	0	0	0	0	0	0
IVORY COAST	0	0	0	2	0	0	0	0	0	0	0	0	0	0	2	0	2
KENYA	0	0	0	0	0	0	1	1	0	0	0	0	0	0	2	0	2
LIBERIA	0	0	0	0	0	0	0	0	0	0	0	0	0	0	0	0	0
NIGERIA	0	0	1	1	0	0	0	0	0	0	0	0	0	0	2	0	2
ZAIRE	0	0	0	0	0	0	0	0	0	0	0	0	0	0	0	0	0
ZAMBIA	0	0	0	0	0	0	0	0	0	0	0	0	0	0	0	0	0
OTHER E.+W.AFR.	0	0	0	1	0	0	1	1	0	1	0	0	0	0	4	1	3
SOUTH ASIA (TOTAL)	1	0	1	2	0	0	0	0	0	0	0	0	0	0	3	0	4
INDIA	0	0	1	1	0	0	0	0	0	0	0	0	0	0	2	0	2
PAKISTAN	0	0	0	1	0	0	0	0	0	0	0	0	0	0	1	0	1
SRI LANKA	1	0	0	0	0	0	0	0	0	0	0	0	0	0	0	0	1
OTHER S.ASIA	0	0	0	0	0	0	0	0	0	0	0	0	0	0	0	0	0
EAST ASIA (TOTAL)	0	2	4	5	1	1	3	3	3	1	0	0	0	0	22	4	18
HONG KONG	0	0	0	0	0	0	0	0	0	0	0	0	0	0	0	0	0
INDONESIA	0	0	0	0	0	0	0	0	0	0	0	0	0	0	0	0	0
JAPAN	0	2	2	2	0	0	1	1	1	0	0	0	0	0	9	1	8
MALAYSIA	0	0	1	1	0	0	0	0	0	0	0	0	0	0	2	1	1
PHILIPPINES	0	0	1	1	0	0	0	0	0	0	0	0	0	0	2	1	1
SINGAPORE	0	0	0	1	0	0	1	1	0	0	0	0	0	0	3	0	3
S.KOREA	0	0	0	0	1	1	0	1	1	0	0	0	0	0	4	1	3
THAILAND	0	0	0	0	0	0	0	0	1	0	0	0	0	0	1	0	1
TAIWAN	0	0	0	0	0	0	1	0	0	0	0	0	0	0	1	0	1
OTHER E.ASIA	0	0	0	0	0	0	0	0	0	0	0	0	0	0	0	0	0
S.DOMINIONS (TOTAL)	2	2	1	3	0	1	1	1	2	0	0	0	0	0	11	0	13
AUSTRALIA	2	2	1	1	0	0	1	1	0	0	0	0	0	0	6	0	8
NEW ZEALAND	0	0	0	1	0	0	0	0	0	0	0	0	0	0	1	0	1
RHODESIA	0	0	0	0	0	1	0	0	0	0	0	0	0	0	1	0	1
S.AFRICA	0	0	0	1	0	0	0	0	2	0	0	0	0	0	3	0	3
OUTSIDE U.S. (TOTAL)	30	17	25	36	8	8	15	11	11	5	4	2	4	6	152	53	129

CHAPTER 2 - THE PROLIFERATION OF FOREIGN SUBSIDIARIES
SECTION 4 -- GEOGRAPHICAL SPREAD IN SPECIFIC INDUSTRIES
TABLE 17 --- OTHER PETROLEUM INDUSTRIES (OTHER SIC 29)

NO. OF SUBSIDIARIES MANUFACTURING IN THIS INDUSTRY AT TIME OF ENTRY INTO PARENT SYSTEM

COUNTRY OR REGION	NET FLOW UP TO 31-DEC-50	51-55	56-60	61-65	1966	1967	1968	1969	1970	1971	1972	1973	1974	1975	TOTAL ENTRIES 1951-75	TOTAL EXITS 1951-75	NET FLOW UP TO 1-JAN-76
CANADA	5	1	2	3	0	0	0	0	0	0	0	1	0	0	7	6	6
LATIN AMER. (TOTAL)	2	3	3	3	4	1	0	3	0	0	0	1	0	0	18	6	14
C.AM.+CARIB. (TOTAL)	0	0	1	1	1	0	0	2	0	0	0	1	0	0	6	1	5
BAHAMAS	0	0	0	0	0	0	0	0	0	0	0	0	0	0	0	0	0
BERMUDA	0	0	0	0	0	0	0	0	0	0	0	0	0	0	0	0	0
COSTA RICA	0	0	0	0	0	0	0	0	0	0	0	0	0	0	0	0	0
GUATEMALA	0	0	0	0	0	0	0	0	0	0	0	0	0	0	0	0	0
JAMAICA	0	0	0	1	0	0	0	0	0	0	0	0	0	0	1	1	0
MEXICO	0	0	1	0	1	0	0	1	0	0	0	1	0	0	4	0	4
NETH.ANTILLES	0	0	0	0	0	0	0	0	0	0	0	0	0	0	0	0	0
NICARAGUA	0	0	0	0	0	0	0	1	0	0	0	0	0	0	1	0	1
PANAMA	0	0	0	0	0	0	0	0	0	0	0	0	0	0	0	0	0
OTHER C.AM+CAR.	0	0	0	0	0	0	0	0	0	0	0	0	0	0	0	0	0
S.AMERICA (TOTAL)	2	3	2	2	3	0	0	1	1	0	0	0	0	0	12	5	9
BOLIVIA	0	0	0	0	0	0	0	0	0	0	0	0	0	0	0	0	0
CHILE	0	0	0	1	0	0	0	0	0	0	0	0	0	0	1	0	1
COLOMBIA	0	0	0	0	1	0	0	0	0	0	0	0	0	0	1	0	1
ECUADOR	0	0	0	0	0	0	0	0	1	0	0	0	0	0	1	0	1
PERU	0	0	0	0	0	0	0	0	0	0	0	0	0	0	0	0	0
ARGENTINA	1	0	0	0	0	0	0	1	0	0	0	0	0	0	1	0	2
BRAZIL	0	3	1	1	1	0	0	0	0	0	0	0	0	0	6	2	4
URUGUAY	0	0	0	0	0	0	0	0	0	0	0	0	0	0	0	0	0
VENEZUELA	1	0	1	0	1	0	0	0	0	0	0	0	0	0	2	3	0
OTHER S.AMER.	0	0	0	0	0	0	0	0	0	0	0	0	0	0	0	0	0
EUROPE (TOTAL)	8	2	6	18	2	0	1	3	1	1	2	1	1	1	39	10	37
BELGIUM	1	0	1	2	0	0	0	1	0	0	0	0	0	0	3	1	3
FRANCE	2	1	3	2	1	0	0	1	0	0	1	0	0	0	9	1	10
GERMANY	2	0	1	2	0	0	1	0	1	0	1	1	0	0	6	0	8
ITALY	0	0	1	1	0	0	0	0	0	0	1	0	0	0	3	0	3
LUXEMBOURG	0	0	0	0	0	0	0	0	0	0	0	0	0	0	0	0	0
NETHERLANDS	0	0	0	1	0	0	0	0	0	0	0	0	0	1	2	1	1
DENMARK	0	0	0	4	0	0	0	0	0	0	0	0	0	0	4	4	0
IRELAND	0	0	1	0	0	0	0	0	0	0	0	0	0	0	1	1	0
U.K.	3	0	0	5	0	0	0	0	0	0	0	0	0	0	5	2	6
AUSTRIA	0	0	0	0	0	0	0	0	0	0	0	0	0	0	0	0	0
FINLAND	0	0	0	0	0	0	0	0	0	0	0	0	0	0	0	0	0
GREECE	0	0	0	0	0	0	0	0	0	0	0	0	0	0	0	0	0
NORWAY	0	0	0	0	0	0	0	0	0	0	0	0	0	0	0	0	0
PORTUGAL	0	1	0	0	1	0	0	0	0	1	0	0	1	0	4	0	4
SPAIN	0	0	0	0	0	0	0	2	0	0	0	0	0	0	2	0	2
SWEDEN	0	0	0	0	0	0	0	0	0	0	0	0	0	0	0	0	0
SWITZERLAND	0	0	0	0	0	0	0	0	0	0	0	0	0	0	0	0	0
TURKEY	0	0	0	0	0	0	0	0	0	0	0	0	0	0	0	0	0
OTHER EUROPE	0	0	0	0	0	0	0	0	0	0	0	0	0	0	0	0	0

TABLE 2 .4 .17 (CONTINUED)

COUNTRY OR REGION	NET FLOW UP TO 31-DEC-50	51-55	56-60	61-65	1966	1967	1968	1969	1970	1971	1972	1973	1974	1975	TOTAL ENTRIES 1951-75	TOTAL EXITS 1951-75	NET FLOW UP TO 1-JAN-76
		NO. OF ENTRIES DURING YEAR(S)															
N.AFR+M.EAST (TOTAL)	0	0	0	0	0	2	0	1	0	0	0	0	0	0	3	0	3
ALGERIA	0	0	0	0	0	0	0	0	0	0	0	0	0	0	0	0	0
EGYPT	0	0	0	0	0	0	0	1	0	0	0	0	0	0	1	0	1
IRAN	0	0	0	0	0	0	0	0	0	0	0	0	0	0	0	0	0
ISRAEL	0	0	0	0	0	0	0	0	0	0	0	0	0	0	0	0	0
LEBANON	0	0	0	0	0	0	0	0	0	0	0	0	0	0	0	0	0
MOROCCO	0	0	0	0	0	0	0	0	0	0	0	0	0	0	0	0	0
SAUDI ARABIA	0	0	0	0	0	2	0	0	0	0	0	0	0	0	2	0	2
OTHER N.AF+M.E.	0	0	0	0	0	0	0	0	0	0	0	0	0	0	0	0	0
E.+W.AFRICA (TOTAL)	0	0	0	1	0	0	1	1	1	0	0	0	0	0	4	1	3
GHANA	0	0	0	1	0	0	0	0	0	0	0	0	0	0	1	0	1
IVORY COAST	0	0	0	0	0	0	0	0	0	0	0	0	0	0	0	0	0
KENYA	0	0	0	0	0	0	0	0	1	0	0	0	0	0	1	0	1
LIBERIA	0	0	0	0	0	0	0	0	0	0	0	0	0	0	0	0	0
NIGERIA	0	0	0	0	0	0	0	0	0	0	0	0	0	0	0	0	0
ZAIRE	0	0	0	0	0	0	0	0	0	0	0	0	0	0	0	0	0
ZAMBIA	0	0	0	0	0	0	0	0	0	0	0	0	0	0	0	0	0
OTHER E.+W.AFR.	0	0	0	0	0	0	1	1	0	0	0	0	0	0	2	1	1
SOUTH ASIA (TOTAL)	0	0	0	1	1	0	0	0	0	1	0	0	0	0	3	2	1
INDIA	0	0	0	1	1	0	0	0	0	1	0	0	0	0	3	2	1
PAKISTAN	0	0	0	0	0	0	0	0	0	0	0	0	0	0	0	0	0
SRI LANKA	0	0	0	0	0	0	0	0	0	0	0	0	0	0	0	0	0
OTHER S.ASIA	0	0	0	0	0	0	0	0	0	0	0	0	0	0	0	0	0
EAST ASIA (TOTAL)	0	0	1	5	0	4	1	1	1	0	0	0	0	0	13	5	8
HONG KONG	0	0	0	0	0	0	0	0	0	0	0	0	0	0	0	0	0
INDONESIA	0	0	0	0	0	0	0	0	0	0	0	0	0	0	0	0	0
JAPAN	0	0	0	4	0	3	0	1	0	0	0	0	0	0	8	4	4
MALAYSIA	0	0	0	0	0	0	0	0	0	0	0	0	0	0	0	0	0
PHILIPPINES	0	0	0	0	0	0	1	0	0	0	0	0	0	0	1	0	1
SINGAPORE	0	0	1	1	0	0	0	0	0	0	0	0	0	0	2	1	1
S.KOREA	0	0	0	0	0	0	0	0	0	0	0	0	0	0	0	0	0
THAILAND	0	0	0	0	0	1	0	0	0	0	0	0	0	0	1	0	1
TAIWAN	0	0	0	0	0	0	0	0	1	0	0	0	0	0	1	0	1
OTHER E.ASIA	0	0	0	0	0	0	0	0	0	0	0	0	0	0	0	0	0
S.DOMINIONS (TOTAL)	1	1	2	1	0	1	1	1	0	0	0	0	0	1	8	4	5
AUSTRALIA	0	1	1	1	0	1	1	1	0	0	0	0	0	1	7	4	3
NEW ZEALAND	0	0	0	0	0	0	0	0	0	0	0	0	0	0	0	0	0
RHODESIA	0	0	0	0	0	0	0	0	0	0	0	0	0	0	0	0	0
S.AFRICA	1	0	1	0	0	0	0	0	0	0	0	0	0	0	1	0	2
OUTSIDE U.S. (TOTAL)	16	7	15	32	7	8	4	4	8	1	3	3	1	2	95	34	77

CHAPTER 2 - THE PROLIFERATION OF FOREIGN SUBSIDIARIES
SECTION 4 -- GEOGRAPHICAL SPREAD IN SPECIFIC INDUSTRIES
TABLE 18 --- THE LEATHER INDUSTRY (SIC 31)

NO. OF SUBSIDIARIES MANUFACTURING IN THIS INDUSTRY AT TIME OF ENTRY INTO PARENT SYSTEM

COUNTRY OR REGION	NET FLOW UP TO 31-DEC-50	51-55	56-60	61-65	1966	1967	1968	1969	1970	1971	1972	1973	1974	1975	TOTAL ENTRIES 1951-75	TOTAL EXITS 1951-75	NET FLOW UP TO 1-JAN-76
CANADA	0	0	0	2	0	0	1	0	0	0	0	1	1	0	5	2	3
LATIN AMER. (TOTAL)	4	0	0	0	0	0	1	0	0	0	0	0	0	0	1	2	3
C.AM.+CARIB. (TOTAL)	1	0	0	0	0	0	1	0	0	0	0	0	0	0	1	1	1
BAHAMAS	0	0	0	0	0	0	0	0	0	0	0	0	0	0	0	0	0
BERMUDA	0	0	0	0	0	0	0	0	0	0	0	0	0	0	0	0	0
COSTA RICA	0	0	0	0	0	0	0	0	0	0	0	0	0	0	0	0	0
GUATEMALA	0	0	0	0	0	0	0	0	0	0	0	0	0	0	0	0	0
JAMAICA	0	0	0	0	0	0	0	0	0	0	0	0	0	0	0	0	0
MEXICO	1	0	0	0	0	0	1	0	0	0	0	0	0	0	1	1	1
NETH.ANTILLES	0	0	0	0	0	0	0	0	0	0	0	0	0	0	0	0	0
NICARAGUA	0	0	0	0	0	0	0	0	0	0	0	0	0	0	0	0	0
PANAMA	0	0	0	0	0	0	0	0	0	0	0	0	0	0	0	0	0
OTHER C.AM+CAR.	0	0	0	0	0	0	0	0	0	0	0	0	0	0	0	0	0
S.AMERICA (TOTAL)	3	0	0	0	0	0	0	0	0	0	0	0	0	0	0	1	2
BOLIVIA	0	0	0	0	0	0	0	0	0	0	0	0	0	0	0	0	0
CHILE	1	0	0	0	0	0	0	0	0	0	0	0	0	0	0	0	1
COLOMBIA	0	0	0	0	0	0	0	0	0	0	0	0	0	0	0	0	0
ECUADOR	0	0	0	0	0	0	0	0	0	0	0	0	0	0	0	0	0
PERU	1	0	0	0	0	0	0	0	0	0	0	0	0	0	0	1	0
ARGENTINA	0	0	0	0	0	0	0	0	0	0	0	0	0	0	0	0	0
BRAZIL	1	0	0	0	0	0	0	0	0	0	0	0	0	0	0	0	1
URUGUAY	0	0	0	0	0	0	0	0	0	0	0	0	0	0	0	0	0
VENEZUELA	0	0	0	0	0	0	0	0	0	0	0	0	0	0	0	0	0
OTHER S.AMER.	0	0	0	0	0	0	0	0	0	0	0	0	0	0	0	0	0
EUROPE (TOTAL)	2	3	3	3	3	1	2	0	0	0	0	0	0	0	15	4	13
BELGIUM	0	0	1	0	1	0	0	0	0	0	0	0	0	0	2	1	1
FRANCE	0	0	0	1	0	0	0	0	0	0	0	0	0	0	1	1	0
GERMANY	0	1	1	1	0	0	0	0	0	0	0	0	0	0	3	0	3
ITALY	0	1	0	0	1	0	0	0	0	0	0	0	0	0	2	0	2
LUXEMBOURG	0	0	0	0	0	0	0	0	0	0	0	0	0	0	0	0	0
NETHERLANDS	1	0	0	0	0	0	0	0	0	0	0	0	0	0	0	0	1
DENMARK	0	0	0	0	0	0	0	0	0	0	0	0	0	0	0	0	0
IRELAND	0	0	0	0	0	0	2	0	0	0	0	0	0	0	2	0	2
U.K.	1	1	1	1	1	0	0	0	0	0	0	0	0	0	4	2	3
AUSTRIA	0	0	0	0	0	0	0	0	0	0	0	0	0	0	0	0	0
FINLAND	0	0	0	0	0	0	0	0	0	0	0	0	0	0	0	0	0
GREECE	0	0	0	0	0	0	0	0	0	0	0	0	0	0	0	0	0
NORWAY	0	0	0	0	0	0	0	0	0	0	0	0	0	0	0	0	0
PORTUGAL	0	0	0	0	0	1	0	0	0	0	0	0	0	0	1	0	1
SPAIN	0	0	0	0	0	0	0	0	0	0	0	0	0	0	0	0	0
SWEDEN	0	0	0	0	0	0	0	0	0	0	0	0	0	0	0	0	0
SWITZERLAND	0	0	0	0	0	0	0	0	0	0	0	0	0	0	0	0	0
TURKEY	0	0	0	0	0	0	0	0	0	0	0	0	0	0	0	0	0
OTHER EUROPE	0	0	0	0	0	0	0	0	0	0	0	0	0	0	0	0	0

TABLE   2 .4 .18   (CONTINUED)

COUNTRY OR REGION	NET FLOW UP TO 31-DEC-50	NO. OF ENTRIES DURING YEAR(S)													TOTAL ENTRIES 1951-75	TOTAL EXITS 1951-75	NET FLOW UP TO 1-JAN-76
		51-55	56-60	61-65	1966	1967	1968	1969	1970	1971	1972	1973	1974	1975			
N.AFR+M.EAST(TOTAL)	0	0	0	0	0	0	0	0	0	1	0	0	0	0	1	0	1
ALGERIA	0	0	0	0	0	0	0	0	0	0	0	0	0	0	0	0	0
EGYPT	0	0	0	0	0	0	0	0	0	0	0	0	0	0	0	0	0
IRAN	0	0	0	0	0	0	0	0	0	0	0	0	0	0	0	0	0
ISRAEL	0	0	0	0	0	0	0	0	0	1	0	0	0	0	1	0	1
LEBANON	0	0	0	0	0	0	0	0	0	0	0	0	0	0	0	0	0
MOROCCO	0	0	0	0	0	0	0	0	0	0	0	0	0	0	0	0	0
SAUDI ARABIA	0	0	0	0	0	0	0	0	0	0	0	0	0	0	0	0	0
OTHER N.AF+M.E.	0	0	0	0	0	0	0	0	0	0	0	0	0	0	0	0	0
E.+W.AFRICA (TOTAL)	0	0	0	0	1	0	0	0	0	0	0	0	0	0	1	0	1
GHANA	0	0	0	0	0	0	0	0	0	0	0	0	0	0	0	0	0
IVORY COAST	0	0	0	0	0	0	0	0	0	0	0	0	0	0	0	0	0
KENYA	0	0	0	0	0	0	0	0	0	0	0	0	0	0	0	0	0
LIBERIA	0	0	0	0	0	0	0	0	0	0	0	0	0	0	0	0	0
NIGERIA	0	0	0	0	0	0	0	0	0	0	0	0	0	0	0	0	0
ZAIRE	0	0	0	0	0	0	0	0	0	0	0	0	0	0	0	0	0
ZAMBIA	0	0	0	0	0	0	0	0	0	0	0	0	0	0	0	0	0
OTHER E.+W.AFR.	0	0	0	0	1	0	0	0	0	0	0	0	0	0	1	0	1
SOUTH ASIA (TOTAL)	0	0	0	0	0	0	0	0	0	0	0	0	0	0	0	0	0
INDIA	0	0	0	0	0	0	0	0	0	0	0	0	0	0	0	0	0
PAKISTAN	0	0	0	0	0	0	0	0	0	0	0	0	0	0	0	0	0
SRI LANKA	0	0	0	0	0	0	0	0	0	0	0	0	0	0	0	0	0
OTHER S.ASIA	0	0	0	0	0	0	0	0	0	0	0	0	0	0	0	0	0
EAST ASIA (TOTAL)	0	0	0	0	0	0	0	0	0	0	0	0	0	0	0	0	0
HONG KONG	0	0	0	0	0	0	0	0	0	0	0	0	0	0	0	0	0
INDONESIA	0	0	0	0	0	0	0	0	0	0	0	0	0	0	0	0	0
JAPAN	0	0	0	0	0	0	0	0	0	0	0	0	0	0	0	0	0
MALAYSIA	0	0	0	0	0	0	0	0	0	0	0	0	0	0	0	0	0
PHILIPPINES	0	0	0	0	0	0	0	0	0	0	0	0	0	0	0	0	0
SINGAPORE	0	0	0	0	0	0	0	0	0	0	0	0	0	0	0	0	0
S.KOREA	0	0	0	0	0	0	0	0	0	0	0	0	0	0	0	0	0
THAILAND	0	0	0	0	0	0	0	0	0	0	0	0	0	0	0	0	0
TAIWAN	0	0	0	0	0	0	0	0	0	0	0	0	0	0	0	0	0
OTHER E.ASIA	0	0	0	0	0	0	0	0	0	0	0	0	0	0	0	0	0
S.DOMINIONS (TOTAL)	0	0	0	1	0	0	0	0	0	0	0	1	0	0	2	0	2
AUSTRALIA	0	0	0	0	0	0	0	0	0	0	0	0	0	0	0	0	0
NEW ZEALAND	0	0	0	0	0	0	0	0	0	0	0	0	0	0	0	0	0
RHODESIA	0	0	0	0	0	0	0	0	0	0	0	0	0	0	0	0	0
S.AFRICA	0	0	0	1	0	0	0	0	0	0	0	1	0	0	2	0	2
OUTSIDE U.S. (TOTAL)	6	0	3	6	4	1	4	0	0	1	1	4	1	0	25	8	23

CHAPTER 2 - THE PROLIFERATION OF FOREIGN SUBSIDIARIES
SECTION 4 -- GEOGRAPHICAL SPREAD IN SPECIFIC INDUSTRIES
TABLE 19 --- STONE,CLAY AND CEMENT INDUSTRIES (SIC 324 TO 328)

NO. OF SUBSIDIARIES MANUFACTURING IN THIS INDUSTRY AT TIME OF ENTRY INTO PARENT SYSTEM

COUNTRY OR REGION	NET FLOW UP TO 31-DEC-50	NO. OF ENTRIES DURING YEAR(S)													TOTAL ENTRIES 1951-75	TOTAL EXITS 1951-75	NET FLOW UP TO 1-JAN-76
		51-55	56-60	61-65	1966	1967	1968	1969	1970	1971	1972	1973	1974	1975			
CANADA	1	1	2	0	0	0	1	0	0	0	0	1	3	0	8	3	6
LATIN AMER. (TOTAL)	5	2	4	4	0	1	2	4	1	0	0	0	1	0	19	9	15
C.AM.+CARIB.(TOTAL)	2	1	1	2	0	0	2	0	0	0	0	0	1	0	7	2	7
BAHAMAS	0	0	0	0	0	0	0	0	0	0	0	0	0	0	0	0	0
BERMUDA	0	0	0	0	0	0	0	0	0	0	0	0	0	0	0	0	0
COSTA RICA	0	0	0	0	0	0	0	0	0	0	0	0	0	0	0	0	0
GUATEMALA	0	0	0	0	0	0	0	0	0	0	0	0	1	0	1	0	1
JAMAICA	0	0	0	0	0	0	0	0	0	0	0	0	0	0	0	0	0
MEXICO	2	1	1	2	0	0	1	0	0	0	0	0	0	0	5	2	5
NETH.ANTILLES	0	0	0	0	0	0	0	0	0	0	0	0	0	0	0	0	0
NICARAGUA	0	0	0	0	0	0	1	0	0	0	0	0	0	0	1	0	1
PANAMA	0	0	0	0	0	0	0	0	0	0	0	0	0	0	0	0	0
OTHER C.AM+CAR.	0	0	0	0	0	0	0	0	0	0	0	0	0	0	0	0	0
S.AMERICA (TOTAL)	3	1	3	2	0	1	0	4	1	0	0	0	0	0	12	7	8
BOLIVIA	1	0	0	0	0	0	0	0	0	0	0	0	0	0	0	1	0
CHILE	2	0	1	0	0	0	0	0	0	0	0	0	0	0	1	2	1
COLOMBIA	0	0	0	1	0	0	0	0	0	0	0	0	0	0	1	0	1
ECUADOR	0	0	0	0	0	0	0	0	0	0	0	0	0	0	0	0	0
PERU	0	1	0	0	0	0	0	0	0	0	0	0	0	0	1	1	0
ARGENTINA	0	0	2	0	0	0	0	1	0	0	0	0	0	0	3	1	2
BRAZIL	0	0	0	0	0	1	0	2	0	0	0	0	0	0	3	1	2
URUGUAY	0	0	0	0	0	0	0	0	0	0	0	0	0	0	0	1	0
VENEZUELA	0	0	0	1	0	0	0	1	1	0	0	0	0	0	3	0	2
OTHER S.AMER.	0	0	0	0	0	0	0	0	0	0	0	0	0	0	0	0	0
EUROPE (TOTAL)	3	0	4	4	2	2	4	4	4	2	5	3	0	0	34	7	30
BELGIUM	1	0	1	0	0	0	0	1	0	0	1	0	0	0	3	1	2
FRANCE	0	0	0	1	2	0	0	1	0	0	0	0	0	0	3	0	4
GERMANY	1	0	0	0	0	0	0	0	0	0	1	0	0	0	1	0	1
ITALY	0	0	2	1	0	0	1	2	0	0	0	0	0	0	5	3	2
LUXEMBOURG	0	0	0	0	0	0	0	0	0	0	0	0	0	0	0	0	0
NETHERLANDS	0	0	0	1	0	0	0	0	0	0	0	0	0	0	1	1	1
DENMARK	0	0	0	0	0	1	0	1	0	0	0	1	0	0	1	0	0
IRELAND	0	0	0	0	0	0	0	0	0	0	0	1	0	0	1	0	0
U.K.	2	0	0	1	1	1	3	0	2	2	2	0	0	0	14	2	14
AUSTRIA	0	0	0	0	0	0	0	0	0	0	0	0	0	0	0	0	0
FINLAND	0	0	0	0	0	0	0	0	0	0	0	0	0	0	0	0	0
GREECE	0	0	0	0	1	0	0	0	0	0	0	0	0	0	2	0	2
NORWAY	0	0	0	0	0	0	0	0	0	0	0	0	0	0	0	0	0
PORTUGAL	0	0	0	0	0	0	0	0	0	0	0	0	0	0	0	0	0
SPAIN	0	0	0	1	0	0	0	0	0	0	0	0	0	0	3	0	3
SWEDEN	0	0	0	0	0	0	0	0	0	0	0	1	0	0	1	0	1
SWITZERLAND	0	0	0	0	0	0	0	1	0	0	0	1	0	0	0	0	0
TURKEY	0	0	0	0	0	0	0	0	0	0	0	0	0	0	0	0	0
OTHER EUROPE	0	0	0	0	0	0	0	0	0	0	0	0	0	0	0	0	0

TABLE 2 .4 .19 (CONTINUED)

COUNTRY OR REGION	NET FLOW UP TO 31-DEC-50	NO. OF ENTRIES DURING YEAR(S)													TOTAL ENTRIES 1951-75	TOTAL EXITS 1951-75	NET FLOW UP TO 1-JAN-76
		51-55	56-60	61-65	1966	1967	1968	1969	1970	1971	1972	1973	1974	1975			
N.AFR+M.EAST (TOTAL)	0	0	0	0	0	0	0	0	0	0	0	1	0	0	1	0	1
ALGERIA	0	0	0	0	0	0	0	0	0	0	0	0	0	0	0	0	0
EGYPT	0	0	0	0	0	0	0	0	0	0	0	0	0	0	0	0	0
IRAN	0	0	0	0	0	0	0	0	0	0	0	1	0	0	1	0	1
ISRAEL	0	0	0	0	0	0	0	0	0	0	0	0	0	0	0	0	0
LEBANON	0	0	0	0	0	0	0	0	0	0	0	0	0	0	0	0	0
MOROCCO	0	0	0	0	0	0	0	0	0	0	0	0	0	0	0	0	0
SAUDI ARABIA	0	0	0	0	0	0	0	0	0	0	0	0	0	0	0	0	0
OTHER N.AF+M.E.	0	0	0	0	0	0	0	0	0	0	0	0	0	0	0	0	0
E.+W.AFRICA (TOTAL)	0	0	0	0	0	0	0	0	0	0	0	0	0	0	0	0	0
GHANA	0	0	0	0	0	0	0	0	0	0	0	0	0	0	0	0	0
IVORY COAST	0	0	0	0	0	0	0	0	0	0	0	0	0	0	0	0	0
KENYA	0	0	0	0	0	0	0	0	0	0	0	0	0	0	0	0	0
LIBERIA	0	0	0	0	0	0	0	0	0	0	0	0	0	0	0	0	0
NIGERIA	0	0	0	0	0	0	0	0	0	0	0	0	0	0	0	0	0
ZAIRE	0	0	0	0	0	0	0	0	0	0	0	0	0	0	0	0	0
ZAMBIA	0	0	0	0	0	0	0	0	0	0	0	0	0	0	0	0	0
OTHER E.+W.AFR.	0	0	0	0	0	0	0	0	0	0	0	0	0	0	0	0	0
SOUTH ASIA (TOTAL)	0	0	2	0	0	0	0	1	0	0	0	0	0	0	3	1	2
INDIA	0	0	2	0	0	0	0	1	0	0	0	0	0	0	3	1	2
PAKISTAN	0	0	0	0	0	0	0	0	0	0	0	0	0	0	0	0	0
SRI LANKA	0	0	0	0	0	0	0	0	0	0	0	0	0	0	0	0	0
OTHER S.ASIA	0	0	0	0	0	0	0	0	0	0	0	0	0	0	0	0	0
EAST ASIA (TOTAL)	0	0	0	0	1	0	0	1	0	0	1	0	1	0	4	0	4
HONG KONG	0	0	0	0	0	0	0	0	0	0	0	0	0	0	0	0	0
INDONESIA	0	0	0	0	0	0	0	1	0	0	0	0	0	0	1	0	1
JAPAN	0	0	0	0	0	0	0	0	0	0	0	0	1	0	1	0	1
MALAYSIA	0	0	0	0	1	0	0	0	0	0	0	0	0	0	1	0	1
PHILIPPINES	0	0	0	0	0	0	0	0	0	0	0	0	0	0	0	0	0
SINGAPORE	0	0	0	0	0	0	0	0	0	0	1	0	0	0	1	0	1
S.KOREA	0	0	0	0	0	0	0	0	0	0	0	0	0	0	0	0	0
THAILAND	0	0	0	0	0	0	0	0	0	0	0	0	0	0	0	0	0
TAIWAN	0	0	0	0	0	0	0	0	0	0	0	0	0	0	0	0	0
OTHER E.ASIA	0	0	0	0	0	0	0	0	0	0	0	0	0	0	0	0	0
S.DOMINIONS (TOTAL)	1	1	0	2	1	0	0	0	0	0	1	0	0	0	5	1	5
AUSTRALIA	1	0	0	2	0	0	0	0	0	0	0	0	0	0	2	0	3
NEW ZEALAND	0	1	0	0	0	0	0	0	0	0	1	0	0	0	2	1	1
RHODESIA	0	0	0	0	0	0	0	0	0	0	0	0	0	0	0	0	0
S.AFRICA	0	0	0	0	1	0	0	0	0	0	0	0	0	0	1	0	1
OUTSIDE U.S. (TOTAL)	10	4	12	11	4	3	7	9	6	2	6	5	5	0	74	21	63

CHAPTER 2 - THE PROLIFERATION OF FOREIGN SUBSIDIARIES
SECTION 4 -- GEOGRAPHICAL SPREAD IN SPECIFIC INDUSTRIES
TABLE 20 --- ABRASIVES AND ASBESTOS INDUSTRIES (SIC 329)

NO. OF SUBSIDIARIES MANUFACTURING IN THIS INDUSTRY AT TIME OF ENTRY INTO PARENT SYSTEM

COUNTRY OR REGION	NET FLOW UP TO 31-DEC-50	NO. OF ENTRIES DURING YEAR(S)													TOTAL ENTRIES 1951-75	TOTAL EXITS 1951-75	NET FLOW UP TO 1-JAN-76
		51-55	56-60	61-65	1966	1967	1968	1969	1970	1971	1972	1973	1974	1975			
CANADA	3	4	0	0	0	3	1	0	1	1	2	0	0	0	12	3	12
LATIN AMER. (TOTAL)	1	6	6	3	0	2	2	1	5	3	0	3	0	0	31	3	29
C.AM.+CARIB. (TOTAL)	1	2	2	2	0	1	0	0	2	0	0	0	0	0	9	1	9
BAHAMAS	0	0	0	0	0	0	0	0	0	0	0	0	0	0	0	0	0
BERMUDA	0	0	0	0	0	0	0	0	0	0	0	0	0	0	0	0	0
COSTA RICA	0	0	0	0	0	0	0	0	0	0	0	0	0	0	0	0	0
GUATEMALA	0	0	0	0	0	0	0	0	0	0	0	0	0	0	0	0	0
JAMAICA	0	0	0	0	0	0	0	0	0	0	0	0	0	0	0	0	0
MEXICO	1	2	1	2	0	1	0	0	1	0	0	0	0	0	7	0	8
NETH.ANTILLES	0	0	0	0	0	0	0	0	0	0	0	0	0	0	0	0	0
NICARAGUA	0	0	0	0	0	0	0	0	1	0	0	0	0	0	1	0	1
PANAMA	0	0	1	0	0	0	0	0	0	0	0	0	0	0	1	1	0
OTHER C.AM+CAR.	0	0	0	0	0	0	0	0	0	0	0	0	0	0	0	0	0
S.AMERICA (TOTAL)	0	4	4	1	0	1	2	1	3	3	0	3	0	0	22	2	20
BOLIVIA	0	0	0	0	0	0	0	0	0	0	0	0	0	0	0	0	0
CHILE	0	0	0	0	0	0	0	0	0	0	0	0	0	0	0	0	0
COLOMBIA	0	1	0	0	0	0	0	0	0	0	0	0	0	0	1	0	1
ECUADOR	0	0	0	0	0	0	0	0	0	0	0	0	0	0	0	0	0
PERU	0	1	0	0	0	0	2	0	1	1	0	1	0	0	6	2	4
ARGENTINA	0	1	3	1	0	0	0	1	1	1	0	0	0	0	8	0	8
BRAZIL	0	0	0	0	0	0	0	0	0	0	0	0	0	0	0	0	0
URUGUAY	0	0	0	0	0	0	0	0	0	0	0	0	0	0	0	0	0
VENEZUELA	0	1	1	0	0	1	0	0	1	1	0	2	0	0	7	0	7
OTHER S.AMER.	0	0	0	0	0	0	0	0	0	0	0	0	0	0	0	0	0
EUROPE (TOTAL)	8	10	6	8	5	4	4	5	7	9	8	5	2	3	76	20	64
BELGIUM	1	0	1	0	0	0	1	0	0	2	2	1	0	0	7	0	8
FRANCE	2	4	3	5	1	1	0	1	2	1	0	1	0	1	20	11	11
GERMANY	1	3	0	1	1	1	0	1	1	3	2	2	0	0	15	2	14
ITALY	0	0	0	0	1	0	1	1	1	1	1	0	0	1	7	1	6
LUXEMBOURG	0	0	0	1	0	0	0	0	0	0	0	0	0	0	1	0	1
NETHERLANDS	0	0	0	0	0	1	0	0	0	0	1	0	0	0	2	1	1
DENMARK	0	0	0	0	0	0	0	0	0	0	0	0	0	0	0	0	0
IRELAND	0	0	0	0	0	0	1	0	1	1	1	1	0	0	5	3	2
U.K.	3	2	0	1	1	1	0	1	1	0	1	0	1	0	9	1	11
AUSTRIA	0	0	0	0	0	0	0	0	0	0	0	0	0	0	0	0	0
FINLAND	0	0	0	0	0	0	0	0	0	0	0	0	0	0	0	0	0
GREECE	0	0	0	0	0	0	0	0	0	0	0	0	0	0	0	0	0
NORWAY	1	0	1	0	0	0	0	0	0	0	0	0	1	0	2	0	3
PORTUGAL	0	0	0	0	0	0	0	0	0	0	0	0	0	0	0	0	0
SPAIN	0	0	1	0	0	0	0	0	1	1	0	0	0	1	4	1	3
SWEDEN	0	0	0	0	0	0	1	1	0	0	0	0	0	0	2	0	2
SWITZERLAND	0	0	0	0	0	0	0	0	0	0	0	0	0	0	0	0	0
TURKEY	0	0	0	0	0	0	0	0	0	0	0	0	0	0	0	0	0
OTHER EUROPE	0	1	0	1	1	0	0	0	0	0	0	0	0	0	2	0	2

TABLE 2 . 4 . 20   (CONTINUED)

COUNTRY OR REGION	NET FLOW UP TO 31-DEC-50	NO. OF ENTRIES DURING YEAR(S)													TOTAL ENTRIES 1951-75	TOTAL EXITS 1951-75	NET FLOW UP TO 1-JAN-76
		51-55	56-60	61-65	1966	1967	1968	1969	1970	1971	1972	1973	1974	1975			
N.AFR+M.EAST (TOTAL)	0	0	1	0	1	0	0	0	0	0	0	0	0	0	2	0	2
ALGERIA	0	0	0	0	0	0	0	0	0	0	0	0	0	0	0	0	0
EGYPT	0	0	0	0	0	0	0	0	0	0	0	0	0	0	0	0	0
IRAN	0	0	1	0	0	0	0	0	0	0	0	0	0	0	1	0	1
ISRAEL	0	0	0	0	0	0	0	0	0	0	0	0	0	0	0	0	0
LEBANON	0	0	0	0	0	0	0	0	0	0	0	0	0	0	0	0	0
MOROCCO	0	0	0	0	0	0	0	0	0	0	0	0	0	0	0	0	0
SAUDI ARABIA	0	0	0	0	0	0	0	0	0	0	0	0	0	0	0	0	0
OTHER N.AF+M.E.	0	0	0	0	1	0	0	0	0	0	0	0	0	0	1	0	1
E.+W.AFRICA (TOTAL)	0	0	1	0	0	0	0	0	0	0	0	0	0	0	1	0	1
GHANA	0	0	0	0	0	0	0	0	0	0	0	0	0	0	0	0	0
IVORY COAST	0	0	0	0	0	0	0	0	0	0	0	0	0	0	0	0	0
KENYA	0	0	0	0	0	0	0	0	0	0	0	0	0	0	0	0	0
LIBERIA	0	0	0	0	0	0	0	0	0	0	0	0	0	0	0	0	0
NIGERIA	0	0	1	0	0	0	0	0	0	0	0	0	0	0	1	0	1
ZAIRE	0	0	0	0	0	0	0	0	0	0	0	0	0	0	0	0	0
ZAMBIA	0	0	0	0	0	0	0	0	0	0	0	0	0	0	0	0	0
OTHER E.+W.AFR.	0	0	0	0	0	0	0	0	0	0	0	0	0	0	0	0	0
SOUTH ASIA (TOTAL)	0	1	0	0	0	0	0	0	1	0	0	0	0	0	2	0	2
INDIA	0	1	0	0	0	0	0	0	1	0	0	0	0	0	2	0	2
PAKISTAN	0	0	0	0	0	0	0	0	0	0	0	0	0	0	0	0	0
SRI LANKA	0	0	0	0	0	0	0	0	0	0	0	0	0	0	0	0	0
OTHER S.ASIA	0	0	0	0	0	0	0	0	0	0	0	0	0	0	0	0	0
EAST ASIA (TOTAL)	0	0	2	2	2	0	0	1	1	2	2	0	0	0	12	0	12
HONG KONG	0	0	0	0	0	0	0	0	0	0	0	0	0	0	0	0	0
INDONESIA	0	0	0	0	0	0	0	0	0	0	0	0	0	0	0	0	0
JAPAN	0	0	2	2	2	0	0	1	1	0	0	0	0	0	8	0	8
MALAYSIA	0	0	0	0	0	0	0	0	0	1	0	0	0	0	1	0	1
PHILIPPINES	0	0	0	0	0	0	0	0	0	1	0	0	0	0	1	0	1
SINGAPORE	0	0	0	0	0	0	0	0	0	0	0	0	0	0	0	0	0
S.KOREA	0	0	0	0	0	0	0	0	0	0	0	0	0	0	0	0	0
THAILAND	0	0	0	0	0	0	0	0	0	0	1	0	0	0	1	0	1
TAIWAN	0	0	0	0	0	0	0	0	0	0	1	0	0	0	1	0	1
OTHER E.ASIA	0	0	0	0	0	0	0	0	0	0	0	0	0	0	0	0	0
S.DOMINIONS (TOTAL)	4	1	2	1	2	0	0	1	2	1	1	1	0	1	13	4	13
AUSTRALIA	3	0	1	1	1	0	0	1	0	1	0	1	0	0	6	3	6
NEW ZEALAND	0	0	1	0	0	0	0	0	1	0	0	0	0	0	2	0	2
RHODESIA	0	0	0	0	0	0	0	0	0	0	0	0	0	0	0	0	0
S.AFRICA	1	1	0	0	1	0	0	0	1	0	1	0	0	1	5	1	5
OUTSIDE U.S. (TOTAL)	16	22	15	15	9	13	7	7	17	14	13	10	3	4	149	30	135

CHAPTER 2 - THE PROLIFERATION OF FOREIGN SUBSIDIARIES
SECTION 4 -- GEOGRAPHICAL SPREAD IN SPECIFIC INDUSTRIES
TABLE 21 --- THE GLASS INDUSTRY (SIC 321 TO 323)

NO. OF SUBSIDIARIES MANUFACTURING IN THIS INDUSTRY AT TIME OF ENTRY INTO PARENT SYSTEM

COUNTRY OR REGION	NET FLOW UP TO 31-DEC-50	NO. OF ENTRIES DURING YEAR(S)													TOTAL ENTRIES 1951-75	TOTAL EXITS 1951-75	NET FLOW UP TO 1-JAN-76
		51-55	56-60	61-65	1966	1967	1968	1969	1970	1971	1972	1973	1974	1975			
CANADA	3	0	1	0	0	0	1	1	0	0	0	1	0	1	5	2	6
LATIN AMER. (TOTAL)	8	2	4	6	0	3	1	1	0	1	3	2	0	0	23	10	21
C.AM.+CARIB. (TOTAL)	0	1	1	0	0	3	1	0	0	0	0	0	0	0	6	2	4
BAHAMAS	0	0	0	0	0	0	0	0	0	0	0	0	0	0	0	0	0
BERMUDA	0	0	0	0	0	0	0	0	0	0	0	0	0	0	0	0	0
COSTA RICA	0	0	0	0	0	0	0	0	0	0	0	0	0	0	0	0	0
GUATEMALA	0	0	0	0	0	0	0	0	0	0	0	0	0	0	0	0	0
JAMAICA	0	0	1	0	0	3	1	0	0	0	0	0	0	0	5	1	4
MEXICO	0	0	0	0	0	0	0	0	0	0	0	0	0	0	0	0	0
NETH.ANTILLES	0	0	0	0	0	0	0	0	0	0	0	0	0	0	0	0	0
NICARAGUA	0	0	0	0	0	0	0	0	0	0	0	0	0	0	0	0	0
PANAMA	0	1	0	0	0	0	0	0	0	0	0	0	0	0	1	1	0
OTHER C.AM+CAR.	0	0	0	0	0	0	0	0	0	0	0	0	0	0	0	0	0
S.AMERICA (TOTAL)	8	1	3	6	0	0	0	1	0	1	3	2	0	0	17	8	17
BOLIVIA	0	0	0	0	0	0	0	0	0	0	0	0	0	0	0	0	0
CHILE	2	1	0	1	0	0	0	0	0	0	0	0	0	0	2	2	2
COLOMBIA	1	0	1	0	0	0	0	0	0	0	1	0	0	0	2	3	0
ECUADOR	0	0	0	0	0	0	0	0	0	0	0	0	0	0	0	0	0
PERU	0	0	0	0	0	0	0	1	0	1	1	0	0	0	3	0	3
ARGENTINA	2	0	1	1	0	0	0	0	0	0	0	2	0	0	4	0	6
BRAZIL	3	0	0	0	0	0	0	0	0	0	0	0	0	0	0	3	0
URUGUAY	0	0	1	4	0	0	0	0	0	0	1	0	0	0	6	0	6
VENEZUELA	0	0	0	0	0	0	0	0	0	0	0	0	0	0	0	0	0
OTHER S.AMER.	0	0	0	0	0	0	0	0	0	0	0	0	0	0	0	0	0
EUROPE (TOTAL)	4	1	3	7	2	3	2	3	3	2	2	2	1	0	31	4	31
BELGIUM	2	1	0	0	0	0	0	0	0	0	0	0	0	0	1	0	3
FRANCE	2	0	0	0	0	0	0	0	0	0	0	0	0	0	0	1	1
GERMANY	0	0	1	2	1	0	1	1	1	0	0	1	1	0	9	0	9
ITALY	0	0	1	2	0	0	0	0	0	0	1	1	0	0	5	1	4
LUXEMBOURG	0	0	0	0	0	0	0	0	0	0	0	0	0	0	0	0	0
NETHERLANDS	0	0	0	0	0	0	0	0	0	0	0	0	0	0	0	0	0
DENMARK	0	0	0	0	0	0	0	0	0	0	0	0	0	0	0	0	0
IRELAND	0	0	0	0	0	0	0	0	0	0	0	0	0	0	0	0	0
U.K.	0	0	1	3	1	1	0	1	1	2	0	0	0	0	10	1	9
AUSTRIA	0	0	0	0	0	0	0	1	0	0	0	0	0	0	1	0	1
FINLAND	0	0	0	0	0	0	0	0	0	0	1	0	0	0	1	1	0
GREECE	0	0	0	0	0	1	0	0	0	0	0	0	0	0	1	0	1
NORWAY	0	0	0	0	0	0	0	0	0	0	0	0	0	0	0	0	0
PORTUGAL	0	0	0	0	0	0	0	0	0	0	0	0	0	0	0	0	0
SPAIN	0	0	0	0	0	1	1	0	1	0	0	0	0	0	3	0	3
SWEDEN	0	0	0	0	0	0	0	0	0	0	0	0	0	0	0	0	0
SWITZERLAND	0	0	0	0	0	0	0	0	0	0	0	0	0	0	0	0	0
TURKEY	0	0	0	0	0	0	0	0	0	0	0	0	0	0	0	0	0
OTHER EUROPE	0	0	0	0	0	0	0	0	0	0	0	0	0	0	0	0	0

TABLE 2 .4 .21 (CONTINUED)

COUNTRY OR REGION	NET FLOW UP TO 31-DEC-50	51-55	56-60	61-65	1966	1967	1968	1969	1970	1971	1972	1973	1974	1975	TOTAL ENTRIES 1951-75	TOTAL EXITS 1951-75	NET FLOW UP TO 1-JAN-76
N.AFR+M.EAST (TOTAL)	0	0	0	0	0	0	0	0	0	0	0	0	0	0	0	0	0
ALGERIA	0	0	0	0	0	0	0	0	0	0	0	0	0	0	0	0	0
EGYPT	0	0	0	0	0	0	0	0	0	0	0	0	0	0	0	0	0
IRAN	0	0	0	0	0	0	0	0	0	0	0	0	0	0	0	0	0
ISRAEL	0	0	0	0	0	0	0	0	0	0	0	0	0	0	0	0	0
LEBANON	0	0	0	0	0	0	0	0	0	0	0	0	0	0	0	0	0
MOROCCO	0	0	0	0	0	0	0	0	0	0	0	0	0	0	0	0	0
SAUDI ARABIA	0	0	0	0	0	0	0	0	0	0	0	0	0	0	0	0	0
OTHER N.AF+M.E.	0	0	0	0	0	0	0	0	0	0	0	0	0	0	0	0	0
E.+W.AFRICA (TOTAL)	0	0	0	0	0	0	0	0	0	0	0	0	0	0	0	0	0
GHANA	0	0	0	0	0	0	0	0	0	0	0	0	0	0	0	0	0
IVORY COAST	0	0	0	0	0	0	0	0	0	0	0	0	0	0	0	0	0
KENYA	0	0	0	0	0	0	0	0	0	0	0	0	0	0	0	0	0
LIBERIA	0	0	0	0	0	0	0	0	0	0	0	0	0	0	0	0	0
NIGERIA	0	0	0	0	0	0	0	0	0	0	0	0	0	0	0	0	0
ZAIRE	0	0	0	0	0	0	0	0	0	0	0	0	0	0	0	0	0
ZAMBIA	0	0	0	0	0	0	0	0	0	0	0	0	0	0	0	0	0
OTHER E.+W.AFR.	0	0	0	0	0	0	0	0	0	0	0	0	0	0	0	0	0
SOUTH ASIA (TOTAL)	0	0	0	2	0	0	0	1	0	0	0	0	0	0	3	0	3
INDIA	0	0	0	2	0	0	0	0	0	0	0	0	0	0	2	0	2
PAKISTAN	0	0	0	0	0	0	0	1	0	0	0	0	0	0	1	0	1
SRI LANKA	0	0	0	0	0	0	0	0	0	0	0	0	0	0	0	0	0
OTHER S.ASIA	0	0	0	0	0	0	0	0	0	0	0	0	0	0	0	0	0
EAST ASIA (TOTAL)	0	0	2	2	1	0	0	0	0	1	0	1	0	0	7	0	7
HONG KONG	0	0	0	0	0	0	0	0	0	0	0	0	0	0	0	0	0
INDONESIA	0	0	0	0	0	0	0	0	0	1	0	0	0	0	1	0	1
JAPAN	0	0	0	0	0	0	0	0	0	0	0	0	0	0	0	0	0
MALAYSIA	0	0	0	0	0	0	0	0	0	0	0	1	0	0	1	0	1
PHILIPPINES	0	0	2	2	1	0	0	0	0	0	0	0	0	0	5	0	5
SINGAPORE	0	0	0	0	0	0	0	0	0	0	0	0	0	0	0	0	0
S.KOREA	0	0	0	0	0	0	0	0	0	0	0	0	0	0	0	0	0
THAILAND	0	0	0	0	0	0	0	0	0	0	0	0	0	0	0	0	0
TAIWAN	0	0	0	0	0	0	0	0	0	0	0	0	0	0	0	0	0
OTHER E.ASIA	0	0	0	0	0	0	0	0	0	0	0	0	0	0	0	0	0
S.DOMINIONS (TOTAL)	0	0	2	2	2	0	0	0	1	0	0	0	0	0	7	1	6
AUSTRALIA	0	0	2	2	0	0	0	0	1	0	0	0	0	0	5	1	4
NEW ZEALAND	0	0	0	0	0	0	0	0	0	0	0	0	0	0	0	0	0
RHODESIA	0	0	0	0	1	0	0	0	0	0	0	0	0	0	1	0	1
S.AFRICA	0	0	0	0	1	0	0	0	0	0	0	0	0	0	1	0	1
OUTSIDE U.S.(TOTAL)	15	3	10	17	5	6	4	6	5	4	6	7	2	1	76	17	74

CHAPTER 2 - THE PROLIFERATION OF FOREIGN SUBSIDIARIES
SECTION 4 -- GEOGRAPHICAL SPREAD IN SPECIFIC INDUSTRIES
TABLE 22 --- THE IRON AND STEEL INDUSTRY (SIC 331 AND 332)

NO. OF SUBSIDIARIES MANUFACTURING IN THIS INDUSTRY AT TIME OF ENTRY INTO PARENT SYSTEM

COUNTRY OR REGION	NET FLOW UP TO 31-DEC-50	NO. OF ENTRIES DURING YEAR(S)													TOTAL ENTRIES 1951-75	TOTAL EXITS 1951-75	NET FLOW UP TO 1-JAN-76
		51-55	56-60	61-65	1966	1967	1968	1969	1970	1971	1972	1973	1974	1975			
CANADA	1	1	0	0	1	1	0	1	0	1	1	1	1	0	8	3	6
LATIN AMER. (TOTAL)	2	0	2	2	0	2	0	3	0	0	2	1	0	1	13	9	6
C.AM.+CARIB. (TOTAL)	1	0	0	0	0	0	0	0	0	0	0	0	0	1	1	0	2
BAHAMAS	0	0	0	0	0	0	0	0	0	0	0	0	0	0	0	0	0
BERMUDA	0	0	0	0	0	0	0	0	0	0	0	0	0	0	0	0	0
COSTA RICA	0	0	0	0	0	0	0	0	0	0	0	0	0	0	0	0	0
GUATEMALA	0	0	0	0	0	0	0	0	0	0	0	0	0	0	0	0	0
JAMAICA	0	0	0	0	0	0	0	0	0	0	0	0	0	0	0	0	0
MEXICO	1	0	0	0	0	0	0	0	0	0	0	0	0	1	1	0	2
NETH.ANTILLES	0	0	0	0	0	0	0	0	0	0	0	0	0	0	0	0	0
NICARAGUA	0	0	0	0	0	0	0	0	0	0	0	0	0	0	0	0	0
PANAMA	0	0	0	0	0	0	0	0	0	0	0	0	0	0	0	0	0
OTHER C.AM+CAR.	0	0	0	0	0	0	0	0	0	0	0	0	0	0	0	0	0
S.AMERICA (TOTAL)	1	0	2	2	0	2	0	3	0	0	2	1	0	0	12	9	4
BOLIVIA	0	0	0	0	0	0	0	0	0	0	0	0	0	0	0	0	0
CHILE	1	0	1	0	0	0	0	0	0	0	0	0	0	0	1	2	0
COLOMBIA	0	0	0	0	0	0	0	1	0	0	0	0	0	0	1	0	1
ECUADOR	0	0	0	0	0	0	0	0	0	0	0	0	0	0	0	0	0
PERU	0	0	0	1	0	0	0	0	0	0	0	0	0	0	1	1	0
ARGENTINA	0	0	0	1	0	0	0	0	0	0	0	0	0	0	1	0	1
BRAZIL	0	0	1	0	0	2	0	2	0	0	2	1	0	0	8	6	2
URUGUAY	0	0	0	0	0	0	0	0	0	0	0	0	0	0	0	0	0
VENEZUELA	0	0	0	0	0	0	0	0	0	0	0	0	0	0	0	0	0
OTHER S.AMER.	0	0	0	0	0	0	0	0	0	0	0	0	0	0	0	0	0
EUROPE (TOTAL)	1	0	1	5	0	4	6	3	2	3	2	5	3	1	35	7	29
BELGIUM	0	0	1	0	0	0	1	0	0	0	0	0	0	0	2	1	1
FRANCE	0	0	0	0	0	1	1	0	0	0	0	2	1	0	5	0	5
GERMANY	0	0	0	1	0	0	1	1	0	1	0	1	0	0	5	1	4
ITALY	0	0	0	1	0	1	0	0	0	1	0	1	0	0	4	0	4
LUXEMBOURG	0	0	0	0	0	0	0	0	0	0	0	0	0	0	0	0	0
NETHERLANDS	0	0	0	0	0	0	0	0	1	0	0	0	0	0	1	1	0
DENMARK	0	0	0	0	0	0	0	0	0	0	0	0	0	0	0	0	0
IRELAND	0	0	0	0	0	0	0	0	0	0	0	0	0	0	0	0	0
U.K.	1	0	0	3	0	1	2	1	1	1	1	1	1	0	12	3	10
AUSTRIA	0	0	0	0	0	0	0	0	0	0	0	0	0	0	0	0	0
FINLAND	0	0	0	0	0	0	0	0	0	0	0	0	0	0	0	0	0
GREECE	0	0	0	0	0	0	0	0	0	0	0	0	0	0	0	0	0
NORWAY	0	0	0	0	0	0	0	0	0	0	0	0	0	0	0	0	0
PORTUGAL	0	0	0	0	0	0	0	0	0	0	1	0	1	1	3	0	3
SPAIN	0	0	0	0	0	0	0	1	0	0	0	0	0	0	1	0	1
SWEDEN	0	0	0	0	0	0	1	0	0	0	0	0	0	0	1	1	0
SWITZERLAND	0	0	0	0	0	1	0	0	0	0	0	0	0	0	1	0	1
TURKEY	0	0	0	0	0	0	0	0	0	0	0	0	0	0	0	0	0
OTHER EUROPE	0	0	0	0	0	0	0	0	0	0	0	0	0	0	0	0	0

TABLE 2 .4 .22 (CONTINUED)

Columns under "NO. OF ENTRIES DURING YEAR(S)" span 51-55 through 1975.

COUNTRY OR REGION	NET FLOW UP TO 31-DEC-50	51-55	56-60	61-65	1966	1967	1968	1969	1970	1971	1972	1973	1974	1975	TOTAL ENTRIES 1951-75	TOTAL EXITS 1951-75	NET FLOW UP TO 1-JAN-76
N.AFR+M.EAST (TOTAL)	0	0	0	0	0	0	0	0	0	0	0	0	1	0	1	0	1
ALGERIA	0	0	0	0	0	0	0	0	0	0	0	0	0	0	0	0	0
EGYPT	0	0	0	0	0	0	0	0	0	0	0	0	0	0	0	0	0
IRAN	0	0	0	0	0	0	0	0	0	0	0	0	0	0	0	0	0
ISRAEL	0	0	0	0	0	0	0	0	0	0	0	0	1	0	1	0	1
LEBANON	0	0	0	0	0	0	0	0	0	0	0	0	0	0	0	0	0
MOROCCO	0	0	0	0	0	0	0	0	0	0	0	0	0	0	0	0	0
SAUDI ARABIA	0	0	0	0	0	0	0	0	0	0	0	0	0	0	0	0	0
OTHER N.AF+M.E.	0	0	0	0	0	0	0	0	0	0	0	0	0	0	0	0	0
E.+W.AFRICA (TOTAL)	0	0	0	1	0	0	0	0	0	0	0	0	0	0	1	1	0
GHANA	0	0	0	0	0	0	0	0	0	0	0	0	0	0	0	0	0
IVORY COAST	0	0	0	0	0	0	0	0	0	0	0	0	0	0	0	0	0
KENYA	0	0	0	0	0	0	0	0	0	0	0	0	0	0	0	0	0
LIBERIA	0	0	0	0	0	0	0	0	0	0	0	0	0	0	0	0	0
NIGERIA	0	0	0	1	0	0	0	0	0	0	0	0	0	0	1	1	0
ZAIRE	0	0	0	0	0	0	0	0	0	0	0	0	0	0	0	0	0
ZAMBIA	0	0	0	0	0	0	0	0	0	0	0	0	0	0	0	0	0
OTHER E.+W.AFR.	0	0	0	0	0	0	0	0	0	0	0	0	0	0	0	0	0
SOUTH ASIA (TOTAL)	0	0	0	0	0	0	0	0	0	0	0	2	0	0	2	0	2
INDIA	0	0	0	0	0	0	0	0	0	0	0	2	0	0	2	0	2
PAKISTAN	0	0	0	0	0	0	0	0	0	0	0	0	0	0	0	0	0
SRI LANKA	0	0	0	0	0	0	0	0	0	0	0	0	0	0	0	0	0
OTHER S.ASIA	0	0	0	0	0	0	0	0	0	0	0	0	0	0	0	0	0
EAST ASIA (TOTAL)	0	0	0	0	0	0	1	0	0	1	0	0	0	0	2	1	1
HONG KONG	0	0	0	0	0	0	0	0	0	0	0	0	0	0	0	0	0
INDONESIA	0	0	0	0	0	0	0	0	0	0	0	0	0	0	0	0	0
JAPAN	0	0	0	0	0	0	0	0	0	1	0	0	0	0	1	1	0
MALAYSIA	0	0	0	0	0	0	0	0	0	0	0	0	0	0	0	0	0
PHILIPPINES	0	0	0	0	0	0	0	0	0	0	0	0	0	0	0	0	0
SINGAPORE	0	0	0	0	0	0	0	0	0	0	0	0	0	0	0	0	0
S.KOREA	0	0	0	0	0	0	0	0	0	0	0	0	0	0	0	0	0
THAILAND	0	0	0	0	0	0	0	0	0	0	0	0	0	0	0	0	0
TAIWAN	0	0	0	0	0	0	1	0	0	0	0	0	0	0	1	0	1
OTHER E.ASIA	0	0	0	0	0	0	0	0	0	0	0	0	0	0	0	0	0
S.DOMINIONS (TOTAL)	0	0	0	1	0	0	1	1	1	0	0	0	0	1	5	1	4
AUSTRALIA	0	0	0	0	0	0	1	1	1	0	0	0	0	1	4	1	3
NEW ZEALAND	0	0	0	0	0	0	0	0	0	0	0	0	0	0	0	0	0
RHODESIA	0	0	0	0	0	0	0	0	0	0	0	0	0	0	0	0	0
S.AFRICA	0	0	0	1	0	0	0	0	0	0	0	0	0	0	1	0	1
OUTSIDE U.S. (TOTAL)	4	1	3	9	1	6	8	9	3	5	5	9	5	3	67	22	49

CHAPTER 2 - THE PROLIFERATION OF FOREIGN SUBSIDIARIES
SECTION 4 -- GEOGRAPHICAL SPREAD IN SPECIFIC INDUSTRIES
TABLE 23 --- NON-FERROUS METAL INDUSTRIES (OTHER SIC 33)

NO. OF SUBSIDIARIES MANUFACTURING IN THIS INDUSTRY AT TIME OF ENTRY INTO PARENT SYSTEM

COUNTRY OR REGION	NET FLOW UP TO 31-DEC-50	NO. OF ENTRIES DURING YEAR(S)													TOTAL ENTRIES 1951-75	TOTAL EXITS 1951-75	NET FLOW UP TO 1-JAN-76
		51-55	56-60	61-65	1966	1967	1968	1969	1970	1971	1972	1973	1974	1975			
CANADA	10	3	5	8	0	2	1	2	2	0	1	1	0	0	25	13	22
LATIN AMER. (TOTAL)	7	1	10	6	1	0	4	4	2	0	1	0	1	3	31	11	27
C.AM.+CARIB.(TOTAL)	4	0	3	2	0	0	0	1	0	0	0	0	1	1	8	6	6
BAHAMAS	0	0	0	0	0	0	0	0	0	0	0	0	0	0	0	0	0
BERMUDA	0	0	0	0	0	0	0	0	0	0	0	0	0	0	0	0	0
COSTA RICA	0	0	0	0	0	0	0	0	0	0	0	0	0	0	0	0	0
GUATEMALA	0	0	0	0	0	0	0	0	0	0	0	0	0	0	0	0	0
JAMAICA	0	0	0	0	0	0	0	0	0	0	0	0	0	0	0	0	0
MEXICO	4	0	3	2	0	0	0	1	0	0	0	0	0	1	7	6	5
NETH.ANTILLES	0	0	0	0	0	0	0	0	0	0	0	0	0	0	0	0	0
NICARAGUA	0	0	0	0	0	0	0	0	0	0	0	0	0	0	0	0	0
PANAMA	0	0	0	0	0	0	0	0	0	0	0	0	0	0	0	0	0
OTHER C.AM+CAR.	0	0	0	0	0	0	0	0	0	0	0	0	1	0	1	0	1
S.AMERICA (TOTAL)	3	1	7	4	0	0	3	3	2	1	0	1	0	1	23	5	21
BOLIVIA	0	0	0	0	0	0	0	0	0	0	0	0	0	0	0	0	0
CHILE	0	0	0	0	0	0	0	0	0	0	0	0	0	0	0	1	0
COLOMBIA	0	0	1	2	0	0	0	0	0	0	0	0	0	0	3	1	2
ECUADOR	0	0	0	0	0	0	0	0	0	0	0	0	0	0	0	0	0
PERU	0	0	0	0	0	0	0	0	0	0	0	0	0	0	0	0	0
ARGENTINA	2	0	1	1	0	0	1	1	0	1	0	0	0	0	5	0	7
BRAZIL	1	1	1	1	0	0	1	1	1	0	0	1	0	1	8	2	7
URUGUAY	0	0	0	0	0	0	0	0	0	0	0	0	0	0	0	0	0
VENEZUELA	0	0	3	0	0	0	1	1	1	0	0	0	0	0	6	1	5
OTHER S.AMER.	0	0	1	0	0	0	0	0	0	0	0	0	0	0	1	1	0
EUROPE (TOTAL)	2	0	16	17	2	4	10	13	4	10	4	1	3	3	87	19	70
BELGIUM	1	0	0	2	0	1	1	0	0	0	0	0	0	0	4	2	3
FRANCE	0	0	1	1	0	0	0	1	0	0	0	0	0	0	3	2	2
GERMANY	0	0	2	3	0	0	0	2	0	1	0	1	1	0	13	2	11
ITALY	0	0	1	1	0	0	0	1	0	0	0	0	0	0	3	2	3
LUXEMBOURG	0	0	0	0	0	0	0	0	0	0	0	0	0	0	0	0	0
NETHERLANDS	0	0	0	0	0	0	1	0	1	1	1	0	0	0	5	0	5
DENMARK	0	0	0	0	0	0	0	0	0	0	0	0	0	0	0	0	0
IRELAND	0	0	0	0	0	0	0	0	0	0	0	0	0	0	0	0	0
U.K.	1	0	8	7	0	3	4	5	1	7	2	0	1	2	41	9	33
AUSTRIA	0	0	0	0	0	0	0	0	0	0	0	0	0	0	0	0	0
FINLAND	0	0	0	0	0	0	0	0	0	0	0	0	0	0	0	0	0
GREECE	0	0	3	0	0	0	0	0	0	0	0	0	0	0	0	4	0
NORWAY	0	0	0	2	0	0	0	2	0	0	0	0	1	0	8	4	4
PORTUGAL	0	0	1	0	1	0	0	0	0	0	0	0	0	0	0	0	0
SPAIN	0	0	0	1	0	0	0	0	0	1	1	0	0	0	5	0	5
SWEDEN	0	0	1	0	0	0	0	1	1	0	0	0	0	0	1	2	1
SWITZERLAND	0	0	0	0	1	0	0	0	0	0	0	0	0	1	1	0	1
TURKEY	0	0	0	0	0	0	0	0	0	0	0	0	0	1	1	1	1
OTHER EUROPE	0	0	0	0	0	0	0	0	0	0	0	0	0	1	1	0	1

TABLE 2 .4 .23 (CONTINUED)

COUNTRY OR REGION	NET FLOW UP TO 31-DEC-50	NO. OF ENTRIES DURING YEAR(S)													TOTAL ENTRIES 1951-75	TOTAL EXITS 1951-75	NET FLOW UP TO 1-JAN-76
		51-55	56-60	61-65	1966	1967	1968	1969	1970	1971	1972	1973	1974	1975			
N.AFR+M.EAST (TOTAL)	0	0	0	1	1	1	1	0	0	0	0	0	1	0	5	2	3
ALGERIA	0	0	0	0	0	0	0	0	0	0	0	0	0	0	0	0	0
EGYPT	0	0	0	0	0	0	0	0	0	0	0	0	0	0	0	0	0
IRAN	0	0	0	1	0	1	0	0	0	0	0	0	0	0	2	0	2
ISRAEL	0	0	0	0	0	0	0	0	0	0	0	0	0	0	0	0	0
LEBANON	0	0	0	0	0	0	0	0	0	0	0	0	0	0	0	0	0
MOROCCO	0	0	0	0	0	0	0	0	0	0	0	0	0	0	0	0	0
SAUDI ARABIA	0	0	0	0	0	0	0	0	0	0	0	0	0	0	0	0	0
OTHER N.AF+M.E.	0	0	0	0	1	0	1	0	0	0	0	0	1	0	3	2	1
E.+W.AFRICA (TOTAL)	0	1	1	0	0	0	1	0	3	0	0	0	1	0	7	0	7
GHANA	0	1	0	0	0	0	0	0	0	0	0	0	0	0	1	0	1
IVORY COAST	0	0	0	0	0	0	0	0	0	0	0	0	0	0	0	0	0
KENYA	0	0	0	0	0	0	0	0	0	0	0	0	0	0	0	0	0
LIBERIA	0	0	0	0	0	0	0	0	0	0	0	0	0	0	0	0	0
NIGERIA	0	0	0	0	0	0	0	0	1	0	0	0	0	0	1	0	1
ZAIRE	0	0	0	0	0	0	0	0	0	0	0	0	0	0	0	0	0
ZAMBIA	0	0	1	0	0	0	0	0	1	0	0	0	0	0	2	0	2
OTHER E.+W.AFR.	0	0	0	0	0	0	1	0	1	0	0	0	1	0	3	0	3
SOUTH ASIA (TOTAL)	0	0	0	0	0	0	1	0	1	1	0	0	0	0	3	0	3
INDIA	0	0	0	0	0	0	1	0	1	1	0	0	0	0	3	0	3
PAKISTAN	0	0	0	0	0	0	0	0	0	0	0	0	0	0	0	0	0
SRI LANKA	0	0	0	0	0	0	0	0	0	0	0	0	0	0	0	0	0
OTHER S.ASIA	0	0	0	0	0	0	0	0	0	0	0	0	0	0	0	0	0
EAST ASIA (TOTAL)	0	0	0	6	0	1	2	2	4	4	2	1	2	0	24	4	20
HONG KONG	0	0	0	0	0	1	2	2	0	0	0	0	0	0	5	0	5
INDONESIA	0	0	0	0	0	0	0	0	0	0	0	0	0	0	0	0	0
JAPAN	0	0	0	3	0	0	0	0	2	2	1	0	1	0	9	3	6
MALAYSIA	0	0	0	0	0	0	0	0	0	0	0	0	0	0	0	0	0
PHILIPPINES	0	0	0	0	0	0	0	0	0	0	0	0	0	0	0	0	0
SINGAPORE	0	0	0	3	0	0	0	0	0	0	0	0	0	0	3	0	3
S.KOREA	0	0	0	0	0	0	0	0	1	0	1	0	0	0	2	0	2
THAILAND	0	0	0	0	0	0	0	0	1	1	0	1	1	0	4	1	3
TAIWAN	0	0	0	0	0	0	0	0	0	1	0	0	0	0	1	0	1
OTHER E.ASIA	0	0	0	0	0	0	0	0	0	0	0	0	0	0	0	0	0
S.DOMINIONS (TOTAL)	2	1	5	7	0	7	0	2	2	1	1	0	0	1	27	3	26
AUSTRALIA	1	1	5	5	0	6	0	1	2	1	1	0	0	1	23	2	22
NEW ZEALAND	0	0	0	1	0	0	0	1	0	0	0	0	0	0	2	0	2
RHODESIA	0	0	0	0	0	1	0	0	0	0	0	0	0	0	1	1	0
S.AFRICA	1	0	0	1	0	0	0	0	0	0	0	0	0	0	1	0	2
OUTSIDE U.S. (TOTAL)	21	6	40	45	4	15	19	24	12	17	9	3	7	8	209	52	178

CHAPTER 2 - THE PROLIFERATION OF FOREIGN SUBSIDIARIES
SECTION 4 -- GEOGRAPHICAL SPREAD IN SPECIFIC INDUSTRIES
TABLE 24 --- THE METAL CANS INDUSTRY (SIC 341)

NO. OF SUBSIDIARIES MANUFACTURING IN THIS INDUSTRY AT TIME OF ENTRY INTO PARENT SYSTEM

COUNTRY OR REGION	NET FLOW UP TO 31-DEC-50	NO. OF ENTRIES DURING YEAR(S)													TOTAL ENTRIES 1951-75	TOTAL EXITS 1951-75	NET FLOW UP TO 1-JAN-76
		51-55	56-60	61-65	1966	1967	1968	1969	1970	1971	1972	1973	1974	1975			
CANADA	1	1	1	4	1	0	0	1	0	0	0	0	1	0	9	2	8
LATIN AMER. (TOTAL)	3	1	9	4	0	0	4	0	0	0	0	0	1	2	21	7	17
C.AM.+CARIB. (TOTAL)	1	0	5	3	0	0	2	0	0	0	0	0	1	0	11	5	7
BAHAMAS	0	0	0	0	0	0	0	0	0	0	0	0	0	0	0	0	0
BERMUDA	0	0	0	0	0	0	0	0	0	0	0	0	0	0	0	0	0
COSTA RICA	0	0	0	0	0	0	1	0	0	0	0	0	0	0	1	0	1
GUATEMALA	0	0	0	0	0	0	0	0	0	0	0	0	0	0	0	0	0
JAMAICA	0	0	0	0	0	0	0	0	0	0	0	0	0	0	0	0	0
MEXICO	0	0	4	2	0	0	0	0	0	0	0	0	0	0	6	3	3
NETH.ANTILLES	0	0	0	0	0	0	0	0	0	0	0	0	0	0	0	0	0
NICARAGUA	0	0	0	0	0	0	0	0	0	0	0	0	0	0	0	0	0
PANAMA	0	0	0	1	0	0	0	0	0	0	0	0	0	0	1	0	1
OTHER C.AM+CAR.	1	0	1	0	0	0	1	0	0	0	0	0	1	0	3	2	2
S.AMERICA (TOTAL)	2	1	4	1	0	0	2	0	0	0	0	0	0	2	10	2	10
BOLIVIA	0	0	0	0	0	0	0	0	0	0	0	0	0	0	0	0	0
CHILE	0	0	0	0	0	0	0	0	0	0	0	0	0	0	0	0	0
COLOMBIA	0	0	1	0	0	0	0	0	0	0	0	0	0	0	1	1	0
ECUADOR	0	0	0	0	0	0	1	0	0	0	0	0	0	1	2	0	2
PERU	0	0	0	0	0	0	0	0	0	0	0	0	0	0	0	0	0
ARGENTINA	1	0	0	0	0	0	0	0	0	0	0	0	0	0	0	0	1
BRAZIL	1	0	0	0	0	0	0	0	0	0	0	0	0	0	0	1	0
URUGUAY	0	0	1	0	0	0	1	0	0	0	0	0	0	1	3	0	3
VENEZUELA	0	1	0	0	0	0	0	0	0	0	0	0	0	0	1	0	1
OTHER S.AMER.	0	0	2	1	0	0	0	0	0	0	0	0	0	0	3	0	3
EUROPE (TOTAL)	3	0	0	0	0	0	5	2	2	0	1	0	3	0	13	2	14
BELGIUM	0	0	0	0	0	0	0	0	0	0	0	0	0	0	0	0	0
FRANCE	0	0	0	0	0	0	1	0	0	0	1	0	0	0	2	0	2
GERMANY	0	0	0	0	0	0	2	2	1	0	0	0	0	0	5	0	5
ITALY	1	0	0	0	0	0	0	0	0	0	0	0	0	0	0	1	0
LUXEMBOURG	0	0	0	0	0	0	0	0	0	0	0	0	0	0	0	0	0
NETHERLANDS	0	0	0	0	0	0	1	0	0	0	0	0	0	0	1	0	1
DENMARK	1	0	0	0	0	0	0	0	0	0	0	0	0	0	0	1	0
IRELAND	0	0	0	0	0	0	0	0	0	0	0	0	0	0	0	0	0
U.K.	1	0	0	0	0	0	1	0	0	0	0	0	0	0	1	0	2
AUSTRIA	0	0	0	0	0	0	0	0	0	0	0	0	0	0	0	0	0
FINLAND	0	0	0	0	0	0	0	0	0	0	0	0	0	0	0	0	0
GREECE	0	0	0	0	0	0	0	0	0	0	0	0	1	0	1	0	1
NORWAY	0	0	0	0	0	0	0	0	0	0	0	0	0	0	0	0	0
PORTUGAL	0	0	0	0	0	0	0	0	0	0	0	0	0	0	0	0	0
SPAIN	0	0	0	0	0	0	0	0	0	0	0	0	1	0	1	0	1
SWEDEN	0	0	0	0	0	0	0	0	1	0	0	0	1	0	2	0	2
SWITZERLAND	0	0	0	0	0	0	0	0	0	0	0	0	0	0	0	0	0
TURKEY	0	0	0	0	0	0	0	0	0	0	0	0	0	0	0	0	0
OTHER EUROPE	0	0	0	0	0	0	0	0	0	0	0	0	0	0	0	0	0

TABLE 2 .4 .24 (CONTINUED)

COUNTRY OR REGION	NET FLOW UP TO 31-DEC-50	NO. OF ENTRIES DURING YEAR(S)													TOTAL ENTRIES 1951-75	TOTAL EXITS 1951-75	NET FLOW UP TO 1-JAN-76
		51-55	56-60	61-65	1966	1967	1968	1969	1970	1971	1972	1973	1974	1975			
N.AFR+M.EAST (TOTAL)	0	0	0	1	0	0	0	0	0	0	0	0	0	0	1	0	1
ALGERIA	0	0	0	0	0	0	0	0	0	0	0	0	0	0	0	0	0
EGYPT	0	0	0	0	0	0	0	0	0	0	0	0	0	0	0	0	0
IRAN	0	0	0	0	0	0	0	0	0	0	0	0	0	0	0	0	0
ISRAEL	0	0	0	0	0	0	0	0	0	0	0	0	0	0	0	0	0
LEBANON	0	0	0	1	0	0	0	0	0	0	0	0	0	0	1	0	1
MOROCCO	0	0	0	0	0	0	0	0	0	0	0	0	0	0	0	0	0
SAUDI ARABIA	0	0	0	0	0	0	0	0	0	0	0	0	0	0	0	0	0
OTHER N.AF+M.E.	0	0	0	0	0	0	0	0	0	0	0	0	0	0	0	0	0
E.+W.AFRICA (TOTAL)	0	0	0	0	1	0	0	1	2	0	0	0	0	0	4	0	4
GHANA	0	0	0	0	0	0	0	0	0	0	0	0	0	0	0	0	0
IVORY COAST	0	0	0	0	0	0	0	0	0	0	0	0	0	0	0	0	0
KENYA	0	0	0	0	0	0	0	0	0	0	0	0	0	0	0	0	0
LIBERIA	0	0	0	0	0	0	0	0	0	0	0	0	0	0	0	0	0
NIGERIA	0	0	0	0	0	0	0	0	0	0	0	0	0	0	0	0	0
ZAIRE	0	0	0	0	0	0	0	0	0	0	0	0	0	0	0	0	0
ZAMBIA	0	0	0	0	1	0	0	0	0	0	0	0	0	0	1	0	1
OTHER E.+W.AFR.	0	0	0	0	0	0	0	1	2	0	0	0	0	0	3	0	3
SOUTH ASIA (TOTAL)	0	0	0	0	0	0	0	0	0	0	0	0	0	0	0	0	0
INDIA	0	0	0	0	0	0	0	0	0	0	0	0	0	0	0	0	0
PAKISTAN	0	0	0	0	0	0	0	0	0	0	0	0	0	0	0	0	0
SRI LANKA	0	0	0	0	0	0	0	0	0	0	0	0	0	0	0	0	0
OTHER S.ASIA	0	0	0	0	0	0	0	0	0	0	0	0	0	0	0	0	0
EAST ASIA (TOTAL)	1	0	1	2	0	1	1	0	0	0	0	0	0	0	5	1	5
HONG KONG	1	0	0	0	0	0	0	0	0	0	0	0	0	0	0	0	1
INDONESIA	0	0	0	0	0	0	0	0	0	0	0	0	0	0	0	0	0
JAPAN	0	0	0	2	0	0	1	0	0	0	0	0	0	0	3	0	3
MALAYSIA	0	0	0	0	0	0	0	0	0	0	0	0	0	0	0	0	0
PHILIPPINES	0	0	0	0	0	1	0	0	0	0	0	0	0	0	1	0	1
SINGAPORE	0	0	0	0	0	0	0	0	0	0	0	0	0	0	0	0	0
S.KOREA	0	0	0	0	0	0	0	0	0	0	0	0	0	0	0	0	0
THAILAND	0	0	0	0	0	0	0	0	0	0	0	0	0	0	0	0	0
TAIWAN	0	0	0	0	0	0	0	0	0	0	0	0	0	0	0	0	0
OTHER E.ASIA	0	0	1	0	0	0	0	0	0	0	0	0	0	0	1	1	0
S.DOMINIONS (TOTAL)	1	1	1	1	0	1	0	0	0	0	0	0	0	0	4	1	4
AUSTRALIA	0	1	0	1	0	1	0	0	0	0	0	0	0	0	3	0	3
NEW ZEALAND	0	0	0	0	0	0	0	0	0	0	0	0	0	0	0	0	0
RHODESIA	0	0	0	0	0	0	0	0	0	0	0	0	0	0	0	0	0
S.AFRICA	1	0	1	0	0	0	0	0	0	0	0	0	0	0	1	1	1
OUTSIDE U.S. (TOTAL)	9	3	10	17	2	2	9	6	2	1	1	0	2	2	57	13	53

CHAPTER 2   - THE PROLIFERATION OF FOREIGN SUBSIDIARIES
SECTION 4 -- GEOGRAPHICAL SPREAD IN SPECIFIC INDUSTRIES
TABLE 25 --- OTHER FABRICATED METAL INDUSTRIES (OTHER SIC 34)

NO. OF SUBSIDIARIES MANUFACTURING IN THIS INDUSTRY AT TIME OF ENTRY INTO PARENT SYSTEM

COUNTRY OR REGION	NET FLOW UP TO 31-DEC-50	NO. OF ENTRIES DURING YEAR(S)													TOTAL ENTRIES 1951-75	TOTAL EXITS 1951-75	NET FLOW UP TO 1-JAN-76
		51-55	56-60	61-65	1966	1967	1968	1969	1970	1971	1972	1973	1974	1975			
CANADA	20	8	13	12	1	3	7	8	6	3	0	5	4	3	73	40	53
LATIN AMER. (TOTAL)	8	2	11	15	2	3	6	4	4	3	2	7	1	2	62	15	55
C.AM.+CARIB.(TOTAL)	3	1	5	9	1	2	2	0	3	2	0	0	1	0	26	6	23
BAHAMAS	0	0	0	0	0	0	0	0	0	0	0	0	0	0	0	0	0
BERMUDA	0	0	0	0	0	0	0	0	0	0	0	0	0	0	0	0	0
COSTA RICA	0	0	0	0	0	0	0	0	0	0	0	0	1	0	1	0	1
GUATEMALA	0	0	0	0	0	1	0	0	0	0	0	0	0	0	1	0	1
JAMAICA	0	0	0	1	0	0	0	0	0	0	0	0	0	0	1	0	1
MEXICO	2	1	4	7	0	2	0	3	0	1	1	0	1	1	21	4	19
NETH.ANTILLES	0	0	0	0	0	0	0	0	0	0	0	0	0	0	0	0	0
NICARAGUA	0	0	0	0	0	0	0	0	0	0	0	0	0	0	0	0	0
PANAMA	0	0	0	0	0	0	0	0	0	0	0	0	0	0	0	0	0
OTHER C.AM+CAR.	1	0	1	1	0	0	0	0	0	0	0	0	0	0	2	2	1
S.AMERICA (TOTAL)	5	1	6	6	1	1	4	4	1	1	2	7	0	2	36	9	32
BOLIVIA	0	0	0	0	0	0	0	0	0	0	0	0	0	0	0	0	0
CHILE	0	0	0	0	0	0	0	0	0	0	0	1	0	0	1	0	1
COLOMBIA	0	0	2	2	0	0	1	0	1	0	0	0	0	0	6	1	5
ECUADOR	0	0	0	0	0	0	0	0	0	0	0	1	0	0	1	0	1
PERU	1	1	1	0	1	0	0	0	0	0	0	0	0	0	4	2	2
ARGENTINA	2	0	1	2	1	0	1	0	0	0	0	2	0	0	3	4	3
BRAZIL	1	0	2	2	0	0	1	1	0	1	0	3	0	0	9	0	7
URUGUAY	1	0	0	0	0	0	0	0	0	0	0	0	0	0	0	1	1
VENEZUELA	1	0	2	0	0	0	0	2	0	0	1	3	0	0	12	1	12
OTHER S.AMER.	0	0	0	0	0	0	0	0	0	0	0	0	0	0	0	0	0
EUROPE (TOTAL)	20	7	20	46	4	10	19	18	17	17	13	15	13	6	205	59	166
BELGIUM	1	0	2	2	0	0	2	1	1	1	1	3	2	0	12	6	7
FRANCE	4	0	2	5	0	2	2	1	1	0	3	3	1	0	19	7	16
GERMANY	2	4	2	12	0	2	2	3	3	3	3	0	2	0	35	9	28
ITALY	0	0	5	2	0	0	2	1	0	3	3	0	0	1	17	4	13
LUXEMBOURG	0	0	0	0	0	0	0	1	0	0	0	0	0	0	1	0	1
NETHERLANDS	1	0	0	1	0	0	0	0	2	0	0	1	0	1	9	3	7
DENMARK	0	0	0	0	0	0	1	0	0	0	1	1	1	0	3	0	3
IRELAND	1	0	0	1	0	3	1	0	0	1	0	1	1	1	5	0	6
U.K.	8	2	10	13	2	6	5	4	6	9	2	5	4	2	70	21	57
AUSTRIA	1	0	0	1	0	0	0	0	0	0	0	0	1	0	2	1	2
FINLAND	0	0	0	0	0	0	0	0	0	0	1	0	0	0	0	0	0
GREECE	0	0	0	1	0	0	1	0	0	0	0	0	0	0	3	1	2
NORWAY	0	0	1	0	0	0	1	0	0	1	0	0	0	0	2	1	2
PORTUGAL	0	0	0	0	0	0	0	0	0	0	0	0	0	0	2	2	1
SPAIN	0	0	0	7	0	1	1	0	2	2	2	2	0	0	17	1	16
SWEDEN	1	0	0	0	0	0	1	1	0	0	0	0	0	1	5	1	4
SWITZERLAND	0	0	0	0	1	0	1	1	0	0	0	0	0	1	1	1	1
TURKEY	1	0	0	0	0	0	0	0	0	0	0	0	0	0	1	1	0
OTHER EUROPE	0	0	0	0	0	0	0	0	0	1	0	1	0	0	2	1	1

TABLE 2 .4 .25 (CONTINUED)

COUNTRY OR REGION	NET FLOW UP TO 31-DEC-50	NO. OF ENTRIES DURING YEAR(S) 51-55	56-60	61-65	1966	1967	1968	1969	1970	1971	1972	1973	1974	1975	TOTAL ENTRIES 1951-75	TOTAL EXITS 1951-75	NET FLOW UP TO 1-JAN-76
N.AFR+M.EAST(TOTAL)	0	0	0	0	0	0	1	0	1	0	1	0	0	0	3	0	3
ALGERIA	0	0	0	0	0	0	0	0	0	0	0	0	0	0	0	0	0
EGYPT	0	0	0	0	0	0	0	0	0	0	0	0	0	0	0	0	0
IRAN	0	0	0	0	0	0	0	0	0	0	1	0	0	0	1	0	1
ISRAEL	0	0	0	0	0	0	0	0	0	0	0	0	0	0	0	0	0
LEBANON	0	0	0	0	0	0	0	0	0	0	0	0	0	0	0	0	0
MOROCCO	0	0	0	0	0	0	1	0	1	0	0	0	0	0	2	0	2
SAUDI ARABIA	0	0	0	0	0	0	0	0	0	0	0	0	0	0	0	0	0
OTHER N.AF+M.E.	0	0	0	0	0	0	0	0	0	0	0	0	0	0	0	0	0
E.+W.AFRICA (TOTAL)	0	0	0	0	1	0	0	1	0	0	0	1	1	0	4	0	4
GHANA	0	0	0	0	0	0	0	0	0	0	0	0	0	0	0	0	0
IVORY COAST	0	0	0	0	0	0	0	0	0	0	0	0	0	0	0	0	0
KENYA	0	0	0	0	0	0	0	0	0	0	0	0	0	0	0	0	0
LIBERIA	0	0	0	0	0	0	0	0	0	0	0	0	0	0	0	0	0
NIGERIA	0	0	0	0	1	0	0	0	0	0	0	0	0	0	0	0	0
ZAIRE	0	0	0	0	0	0	0	0	0	0	0	0	0	0	0	0	0
ZAMBIA	0	0	0	0	0	0	0	0	0	0	0	1	0	0	1	0	1
OTHER E.+W.AFR.	0	0	0	0	0	0	0	1	0	0	0	0	1	0	1	0	2
SOUTH ASIA (TOTAL)	0	0	2	2	0	0	0	0	1	0	0	1	0	2	8	1	7
INDIA	0	0	2	2	0	0	0	1	1	0	0	1	0	0	7	1	6
PAKISTAN	0	0	1	2	0	0	0	0	0	0	0	0	0	0	0	0	0
SRI LANKA	0	0	0	0	0	0	0	0	0	0	0	0	0	0	1	0	1
OTHER S.ASIA	0	0	1	0	0	0	0	0	0	0	0	0	0	0	0	0	0
EAST ASIA (TOTAL)	0	1	4	4	2	2	3	5	2	4	1	2	1	3	28	1	27
HONG KONG	0	0	0	0	0	0	0	0	0	0	0	0	0	0	2	0	2
INDONESIA	0	0	0	0	0	0	0	0	0	0	0	0	0	0	3	0	3
JAPAN	0	0	4	4	0	1	1	0	0	0	0	1	0	0	11	1	10
MALAYSIA	0	0	0	0	0	1	1	0	0	0	0	0	0	0	2	0	2
PHILIPPINES	0	0	0	0	0	0	1	1	1	0	0	0	0	0	4	0	4
SINGAPORE	0	0	0	0	0	0	0	1	1	0	0	0	0	0	2	0	2
S.KOREA	0	0	0	0	0	0	0	1	0	0	0	0	0	0	1	0	1
THAILAND	0	0	0	0	0	0	1	2	0	0	0	0	0	0	2	0	2
TAIWAN	0	0	0	0	0	0	0	0	0	1	0	0	0	0	0	0	0
OTHER E.ASIA	0	0	0	0	0	0	0	0	0	1	0	0	0	0	1	0	1
S.DOMINIONS (TOTAL)	3	0	5	4	2	10	5	6	5	4	4	0	2	1	48	7	44
AUSTRALIA	0	0	4	3	2	4	3	2	1	3	3	0	1	1	27	3	24
NEW ZEALAND	0	0	0	0	0	4	2	0	2	1	0	0	0	0	9	0	9
RHODESIA	0	0	0	0	0	0	0	1	0	0	0	0	0	0	1	0	1
S.AFRICA	3	0	1	1	0	2	0	3	2	0	1	0	1	0	11	4	10
OUTSIDE U.S. (TOTAL)	51	18	51	84	10	28	40	42	37	32	21	30	21	17	431	123	359

CHAPTER 2 — THE PROLIFERATION OF FOREIGN SUBSIDIARIES
SECTION 4 —— GEOGRAPHICAL SPREAD IN SPECIFIC INDUSTRIES
TABLE 26 ——— THE ENGINES AND TURBINES INDUSTRY (SIC 351)

NO. OF SUBSIDIARIES MANUFACTURING IN THIS INDUSTRY AT TIME OF ENTRY INTO PARENT SYSTEM

COUNTRY OR REGION	NET FLOW UP TO 31-DEC-50	NO. OF ENTRIES DURING YEAR(S)													TOTAL ENTRIES 1951-75	TOTAL EXITS 1951-75	NET FLOW UP TO 1-JAN-76
		51-55	56-60	61-65	1966	1967	1968	1969	1970	1971	1972	1973	1974	1975			
CANADA	1	1	0	5	0	0	0	0	0	0	0	0	0	0	6	3	4
LATIN AMER. (TOTAL)	1	0	1	1	1	0	0	2	0	0	0	0	0	0	5	3	3
C.AM.+CARIB. (TOTAL)	0	0	0	0	1	0	0	0	0	0	0	0	0	0	1	1	0
BAHAMAS	0	0	0	0	0	0	0	0	0	0	0	0	0	0	0	0	0
BERMUDA	0	0	0	0	0	0	0	0	0	0	0	0	0	0	0	0	0
COSTA RICA	0	0	0	0	0	0	0	0	0	0	0	0	0	0	0	0	0
GUATEMALA	0	0	0	0	0	0	0	0	0	0	0	0	0	0	0	0	0
JAMAICA	0	0	0	0	0	0	0	0	0	0	0	0	0	0	0	0	0
MEXICO	0	0	0	0	1	0	0	0	0	0	0	0	0	0	1	1	0
NETH.ANTILLES	0	0	0	0	0	0	0	0	0	0	0	0	0	0	0	0	0
NICARAGUA	0	0	0	0	0	0	0	0	0	0	0	0	0	0	0	0	0
PANAMA	0	0	0	0	0	0	0	0	0	0	0	0	0	0	0	0	0
OTHER C.AM+CAR.	0	0	0	0	0	0	0	0	0	0	0	0	0	0	0	0	0
S.AMERICA (TOTAL)	1	0	1	1	0	0	0	2	0	0	0	0	0	0	4	2	3
BOLIVIA	0	0	0	0	0	0	0	0	0	0	0	0	0	0	0	0	0
CHILE	0	0	0	0	0	0	0	0	0	0	0	0	0	0	0	0	0
COLOMBIA	0	0	0	0	0	0	0	0	0	0	0	0	0	0	0	0	0
ECUADOR	0	0	0	0	0	0	0	0	0	0	0	0	0	0	0	0	0
PERU	0	0	0	0	0	0	0	0	0	0	0	0	0	0	0	0	0
ARGENTINA	0	0	0	1	0	0	0	2	0	0	0	0	0	0	3	1	2
BRAZIL	1	0	1	0	0	0	0	0	0	0	0	0	0	0	1	1	1
URUGUAY	0	0	0	0	0	0	0	0	0	0	0	0	0	0	0	0	0
VENEZUELA	0	0	0	0	0	0	0	0	0	0	0	0	0	0	0	0	0
OTHER S.AMER.	0	0	0	0	0	0	0	0	0	0	0	0	0	0	0	0	0
EUROPE (TOTAL)	2	1	6	10	1	3	2	2	1	1	1	2	1	1	32	12	22
BELGIUM	0	0	1	1	0	1	0	0	1	1	0	0	0	0	5	0	5
FRANCE	1	0	2	5	1	1	0	0	0	0	1	0	0	0	10	6	5
GERMANY	1	0	1	1	0	0	2	0	0	0	0	0	0	0	4	1	4
ITALY	0	0	0	1	0	0	0	0	0	0	0	0	0	0	1	0	1
LUXEMBOURG	0	0	0	0	0	0	0	0	0	0	0	0	0	0	0	0	0
NETHERLANDS	0	0	0	0	0	0	0	0	0	0	0	1	0	0	1	0	1
DENMARK	0	0	0	0	0	0	0	0	0	0	0	0	0	0	0	0	0
IRELAND	0	0	0	0	0	0	0	0	0	0	0	0	0	0	0	0	0
U.K.	0	0	2	2	0	1	0	2	0	0	0	0	0	0	7	5	2
AUSTRIA	0	0	0	0	0	0	0	0	0	0	0	0	0	0	0	0	0
FINLAND	0	0	0	0	0	0	0	0	0	0	0	0	0	0	0	0	0
GREECE	0	0	0	0	0	0	0	0	0	0	0	0	0	0	0	0	0
NORWAY	0	0	0	0	0	0	0	0	0	0	0	0	0	0	0	0	0
PORTUGAL	0	0	0	0	0	0	0	0	0	0	0	1	0	1	2	0	2
SPAIN	0	0	0	0	0	0	0	0	0	0	0	0	1	0	1	0	1
SWEDEN	0	1	0	0	0	0	0	0	0	0	0	0	0	0	1	0	1
SWITZERLAND	0	0	0	0	0	0	0	0	0	0	0	0	0	0	0	0	0
TURKEY	0	0	0	0	0	0	0	0	0	0	0	0	0	0	0	0	0
OTHER EUROPE	0	0	0	0	0	0	0	0	0	0	0	0	0	0	0	0	0

TABLE 2 .4 .26 (CONTINUED)

COUNTRY OR REGION	NET FLOW UP TO 31-DEC-50	51-55	56-60	61-65	1966	1967	1968	1969	1970	1971	1972	1973	1974	1975	TOTAL ENTRIES 1951-75	TOTAL EXITS 1951-75	NET FLOW UP TO 1-JAN-76
							NO. OF ENTRIES DURING YEAR(S)										
N.AFR+M.EAST (TOTAL)	0	0	0	0	0	0	0	0	0	0	0	0	0	0	0	0	0
ALGERIA	0	0	0	0	0	0	0	0	0	0	0	0	0	0	0	0	0
EGYPT	0	0	0	0	0	0	0	0	0	0	0	0	0	0	0	0	0
IRAN	0	0	0	0	0	0	0	0	0	0	0	0	0	0	0	0	0
ISRAEL	0	0	0	0	0	0	0	0	0	0	0	0	0	0	0	0	0
LEBANON	0	0	0	0	0	0	0	0	0	0	0	0	0	0	0	0	0
MOROCCO	0	0	0	0	0	0	0	0	0	0	0	0	0	0	0	0	0
SAUDI ARABIA	0	0	0	0	0	0	0	0	0	0	0	0	0	0	0	0	0
OTHER N.AF+M.E.	0	0	0	0	0	0	0	0	0	0	0	0	0	0	0	0	0
E.+W.AFRICA (TOTAL)	0	0	0	0	0	0	0	0	0	0	0	0	0	0	0	0	0
GHANA	0	0	0	0	0	0	0	0	0	0	0	0	0	0	0	0	0
IVORY COAST	0	0	0	0	0	0	0	0	0	0	0	0	0	0	0	0	0
KENYA	0	0	0	0	0	0	0	0	0	0	0	0	0	0	0	0	0
LIBERIA	0	0	0	0	0	0	0	0	0	0	0	0	0	0	0	0	0
NIGERIA	0	0	0	0	0	0	0	0	0	0	0	0	0	0	0	0	0
ZAIRE	0	0	0	0	0	0	0	0	0	0	0	0	0	0	0	0	0
ZAMBIA	0	0	0	0	0	0	0	0	0	0	0	0	0	0	0	0	0
OTHER E.+W.AFR.	0	0	0	0	0	0	0	0	0	0	0	0	0	0	0	0	0
SOUTH ASIA (TOTAL)	0	0	0	0	0	0	0	0	0	0	0	0	0	0	0	0	0
INDIA	0	0	0	0	0	0	0	0	0	0	0	0	0	0	0	0	0
PAKISTAN	0	0	0	0	0	0	0	0	0	0	0	0	0	0	0	0	0
SRI LANKA	0	0	0	0	0	0	0	0	0	0	0	0	0	0	0	0	0
OTHER S.ASIA	0	0	0	0	0	0	0	0	0	0	0	0	0	0	0	0	0
EAST ASIA (TOTAL)	0	0	0	0	0	0	1	1	2	0	0	1	1	0	6	0	6
HONG KONG	0	0	0	0	0	0	0	0	0	0	0	0	0	0	0	0	0
INDONESIA	0	0	0	0	0	0	0	0	0	0	0	0	0	0	0	0	0
JAPAN	0	0	0	0	0	0	1	1	0	0	0	1	1	0	4	0	4
MALAYSIA	0	0	0	0	0	0	0	0	0	0	0	0	0	0	0	0	0
PHILIPPINES	0	0	0	0	0	0	0	0	2	0	0	0	0	0	2	0	2
SINGAPORE	0	0	0	0	0	0	0	0	0	0	0	0	0	0	0	0	0
S.KOREA	0	0	0	0	0	0	0	0	0	0	0	0	0	0	0	0	0
THAILAND	0	0	0	0	0	0	0	0	0	0	0	0	0	0	0	0	0
TAIWAN	0	0	0	0	0	0	0	0	0	0	0	0	0	0	0	0	0
OTHER E.ASIA	0	0	0	0	0	0	0	0	0	0	0	0	0	0	0	0	0
S.DOMINIONS (TOTAL)	0	1	0	0	0	0	0	1	0	0	0	0	0	0	2	0	2
AUSTRALIA	0	1	0	0	0	0	0	0	0	0	0	0	0	0	1	0	1
NEW ZEALAND	0	0	0	0	0	0	0	0	0	0	0	0	0	0	0	0	0
RHODESIA	0	0	0	0	0	0	0	0	0	0	0	0	0	0	0	0	0
S.AFRICA	0	0	0	0	0	0	0	1	0	0	0	0	0	0	1	0	1
OUTSIDE U.S. (TOTAL)	4	3	7	17	2	3	3	5	3	1	1	3	2	1	51	18	37

CHAPTER 2 — THE PROLIFERATION OF FOREIGN SUBSIDIARIES
SECTION 4 — GEOGRAPHICAL SPREAD IN SPECIFIC INDUSTRIES
TABLE 27 —— THE CONSTRUCTION MACHINERY INDUSTRY (SIC 353)

NO. OF SUBSIDIARIES MANUFACTURING IN THIS INDUSTRY AT TIME OF ENTRY INTO PARENT SYSTEM

COUNTRY OR REGION	NET FLOW UP TO 31-DEC-50	NO. OF ENTRIES DURING YEAR(S)													TOTAL ENTRIES 1951-75	TOTAL EXITS 1951-75	NET FLOW UP TO 1-JAN-76
		51-55	56-60	61-65	1966	1967	1968	1969	1970	1971	1972	1973	1974	1975			
CANADA	8	5	4	6	0	8	2	4	2	1	1	1	0	1	35	20	23
LATIN AMER. (TOTAL)	3	3	2	8	1	6	4	3	3	3	2	0	4	1	40	6	37
C.AM.+CARIB. (TOTAL)	1	2	0	4	1	1	1	1	1	2	2	0	0	0	15	2	14
BAHAMAS	0	0	0	0	0	0	0	0	0	0	0	0	0	0	0	0	0
BERMUDA	0	0	0	0	0	0	0	0	0	0	0	0	0	0	0	0	0
COSTA RICA	0	0	0	0	0	0	0	0	0	0	0	0	0	0	0	0	0
GUATEMALA	0	0	0	0	0	0	0	0	0	0	0	0	0	0	0	0	0
JAMAICA	0	0	0	0	0	0	0	0	0	0	0	0	0	0	0	2	0
MEXICO	1	2	0	4	1	1	1	1	1	2	2	0	0	0	15	2	14
NETH.ANTILLES	0	0	0	0	0	0	0	0	0	0	0	0	0	0	0	0	0
NICARAGUA	0	0	0	0	0	0	0	0	0	0	0	0	0	0	0	0	0
PANAMA	0	0	0	0	0	0	0	0	0	0	0	0	0	0	0	0	0
OTHER C.AM+CAR.	0	0	0	0	0	0	0	0	0	0	0	0	0	0	0	0	0
S.AMERICA (TOTAL)	2	1	2	4	0	5	3	2	2	1	0	0	4	1	25	4	23
BOLIVIA	0	0	0	0	0	0	0	0	0	1	0	0	0	0	1	0	1
CHILE	0	0	0	0	0	1	0	0	0	0	0	0	0	0	1	0	1
COLOMBIA	0	0	0	0	0	0	0	0	0	0	0	0	0	0	0	0	0
ECUADOR	0	0	0	0	0	0	0	1	0	0	0	0	1	0	2	0	2
PERU	0	0	0	2	0	2	1	0	1	0	0	0	0	0	4	2	4
ARGENTINA	2	1	1	2	0	2	1	1	1	0	0	0	1	1	12	2	12
BRAZIL	0	0	0	0	0	0	0	0	0	0	0	0	0	0	0	0	2
URUGUAY	0	0	0	0	0	0	0	0	0	0	0	0	0	0	0	0	0
VENEZUELA	0	0	1	1	0	0	1	0	0	0	0	0	2	0	4	2	2
OTHER S.AMER.	0	0	0	0	0	0	0	0	0	0	0	0	0	0	0	0	0
EUROPE (TOTAL)	12	6	12	13	1	5	4	4	7	5	6	3	6	2	74	21	65
BELGIUM	1	0	1	1	1	0	1	1	2	1	1	1	1	0	15	3	14
FRANCE	2	0	4	4	1	1	0	0	2	1	1	1	0	1	8	2	7
GERMANY	1	0	2	1	0	0	1	0	2	1	1	1	0	1	8	2	6
ITALY	1	0	1	2	0	0	0	0	0	0	0	0	0	0	5	0	1
LUXEMBOURG	0	0	0	0	0	0	0	0	0	0	0	0	1	0	1	0	2
NETHERLANDS	1	0	0	2	0	0	1	1	0	0	0	0	0	0	4	0	1
DENMARK	0	0	0	0	0	0	0	0	0	0	0	0	0	0	1	0	0
IRELAND	0	0	2	2	0	3	3	0	3	0	0	0	3	0	21	8	17
U.K.	4	4	2	2	0	0	0	0	0	0	2	0	0	0	21	8	1
AUSTRIA	0	0	0	0	0	0	0	0	0	0	0	0	0	1	1	0	1
FINLAND	0	0	0	0	1	0	1	0	1	1	1	1	1	1	1	0	1
GREECE	0	0	0	0	0	0	0	0	0	0	0	0	0	0	1	0	1
NORWAY	0	0	0	0	0	0	0	0	0	0	0	0	0	0	0	0	0
PORTUGAL	0	0	0	1	0	0	0	0	0	1	0	0	2	0	2	2	0
SPAIN	1	1	1	0	0	0	0	1	0	0	0	0	0	0	5	0	5
SWEDEN	0	0	0	0	0	0	0	0	0	0	0	0	0	0	1	1	1
SWITZERLAND	1	0	0	0	0	0	0	0	0	0	0	0	0	0	0	0	1
TURKEY	0	0	0	0	0	0	0	0	0	0	0	0	0	0	0	0	0
OTHER EUROPE	0	0	0	0	0	0	0	0	0	0	0	0	0	0	0	0	0

TABLE 2 .4 .27 (CONTINUED)

COUNTRY OR REGION	NET FLOW UP TO 31-DEC-50	NO. OF ENTRIES DURING YEAR(S)													TOTAL ENTRIES 1951-75	TOTAL EXITS 1951-75	NET FLOW UP TO 1-JAN-76
		51-55	56-60	61-65	1966	1967	1968	1969	1970	1971	1972	1973	1974	1975			
N.AFR+M.EAST(TOTAL)	0	0	0	0	0	0	1	0	0	0	0	1	1	3	6	0	6
ALGERIA	0	0	0	0	0	0	0	0	0	0	0	0	0	0	0	0	0
EGYPT	0	0	0	0	0	0	0	0	0	0	0	0	0	3	3	0	3
IRAN	0	0	0	0	0	0	0	0	0	0	0	1	0	0	1	0	1
ISRAEL	0	0	0	0	0	0	0	0	0	0	0	0	0	0	0	0	0
LEBANON	0	0	0	0	0	0	1	0	0	0	0	0	0	0	1	0	1
MOROCCO	0	0	0	0	0	0	0	0	0	0	0	0	0	0	0	0	0
SAUDI ARABIA	0	0	0	0	0	0	0	0	0	0	0	0	0	0	0	0	0
OTHER N.AF+M.E.	0	0	0	0	0	0	0	0	0	0	0	0	1	0	1	0	1
E.+W.AFRICA (TOTAL)	0	0	0	0	0	0	0	0	0	0	0	0	0	0	0	0	0
GHANA	0	0	0	0	0	0	0	0	0	0	0	0	0	0	0	0	0
IVORY COAST	0	0	0	0	0	0	0	0	0	0	0	0	0	0	0	0	0
KENYA	0	0	0	0	0	0	0	0	0	0	0	0	0	0	0	0	0
LIBERIA	0	0	0	0	0	0	0	0	0	0	0	0	0	0	0	0	0
NIGERIA	0	0	0	0	0	0	0	0	0	0	0	0	0	0	0	0	0
ZAIRE	0	0	0	0	0	0	0	0	0	0	0	0	0	0	0	0	0
ZAMBIA	0	0	0	0	0	0	0	0	0	0	0	0	0	0	0	0	0
OTHER E.+W.AFR.	0	0	0	0	0	0	0	0	0	0	0	0	0	0	0	0	0
SOUTH ASIA (TOTAL)	0	0	0	2	0	0	0	0	0	0	0	0	0	0	2	0	2
INDIA	0	0	0	2	0	0	0	0	0	0	0	0	0	0	2	0	2
PAKISTAN	0	0	0	0	0	0	0	0	0	0	0	0	0	0	0	0	0
SRI LANKA	0	0	0	0	0	0	0	0	0	0	0	0	0	0	0	0	0
OTHER S.ASIA	0	0	0	0	0	0	0	0	0	0	0	0	0	0	0	0	0
EAST ASIA (TOTAL)	1	1	1	2	0	0	2	1	1	2	2	1	1	2	16	2	15
HONG KONG	0	0	0	0	0	0	0	0	0	0	0	0	0	1	1	0	1
INDONESIA	0	0	0	0	0	0	1	0	0	0	0	0	0	0	1	0	1
JAPAN	1	1	1	2	0	0	1	1	1	2	1	0	0	0	10	2	9
MALAYSIA	0	0	0	0	0	0	0	0	0	0	0	0	0	0	0	0	0
PHILIPPINES	0	0	0	0	0	0	0	0	0	0	0	1	0	0	1	0	1
SINGAPORE	0	0	0	0	0	0	0	0	0	0	1	0	1	1	3	0	3
S.KOREA	0	0	0	0	0	0	0	0	0	0	0	0	0	0	0	0	0
THAILAND	0	0	0	0	0	0	0	0	0	0	0	0	0	0	0	0	0
TAIWAN	0	0	0	0	0	0	0	0	0	0	0	0	0	0	0	0	0
OTHER E.ASIA	0	0	0	0	0	0	0	0	0	0	0	0	0	0	0	0	0
S.DOMINIONS (TOTAL)	7	4	4	4	0	3	2	2	2	1	1	0	5	0	28	11	24
AUSTRALIA	3	4	4	4	0	2	1	1	1	1	0	0	1	0	19	9	13
NEW ZEALAND	0	0	0	0	0	0	0	1	0	0	1	0	0	0	2	0	2
RHODESIA	0	0	0	0	0	0	0	0	0	0	0	0	0	0	0	0	0
S.AFRICA	4	0	0	0	0	1	1	0	1	0	0	0	4	0	7	2	9
OUTSIDE U.S.(TOTAL)	31	17	23	35	2	22	14	15	15	12	12	6	19	9	201	60	172

CHAPTER 2 - THE PROLIFERATION OF FOREIGN SUBSIDIARIES
SECTION 4 -- GEOGRAPHICAL SPREAD IN SPECIFIC INDUSTRIES
TABLE 28 --- THE FARM MACHINERY INDUSTRY (SIC 352)

NO. OF SUBSIDIARIES MANUFACTURING IN THIS INDUSTRY AT TIME OF ENTRY INTO PARENT SYSTEM

COUNTRY OR REGION	NET FLOW UP TO 31-DEC-50	NO. OF ENTRIES DURING YEAR(S)													TOTAL ENTRIES 1951-75	TOTAL EXITS 1951-75	NET FLOW UP TO 1-JAN-76
		51-55	56-60	61-65	1966	1967	1968	1969	1970	1971	1972	1973	1974	1975			
CANADA	3	0	0	1	0	1	0	0	0	0	0	0	0	0	2	1	4
LATIN AMER. (TOTAL)	0	0	1	4	1	0	0	1	0	0	0	1	0	0	8	2	6
C.AM.+CARIB. (TOTAL)	0	0	0	1	0	0	0	0	0	0	0	0	0	0	1	1	0
BAHAMAS	0	0	0	0	0	0	0	0	0	0	0	0	0	0	0	0	0
BERMUDA	0	0	0	0	0	0	0	0	0	0	0	0	0	0	0	0	0
COSTA RICA	0	0	0	0	0	0	0	0	0	0	0	0	0	0	0	0	0
GUATEMALA	0	0	0	0	0	0	0	0	0	0	0	0	0	0	0	0	0
JAMAICA	0	0	0	0	0	0	0	0	0	0	0	0	0	0	0	0	0
MEXICO	0	0	0	0	0	0	0	0	0	0	0	0	0	0	0	0	0
NETH.ANTILLES	0	0	0	0	0	0	0	0	0	0	0	0	0	0	0	0	0
NICARAGUA	0	0	0	0	0	0	0	0	0	0	0	0	0	0	0	0	0
PANAMA	0	0	0	0	0	0	0	0	0	0	0	0	0	0	0	0	0
OTHER C.AM+CAR.	0	0	0	1	0	0	0	0	0	0	0	0	0	0	1	1	0
S.AMERICA (TOTAL)	0	0	1	3	1	0	0	1	0	0	0	1	0	0	7	1	6
BOLIVIA	0	0	0	0	0	0	0	0	0	0	0	0	0	0	0	0	0
CHILE	0	0	0	0	0	0	0	0	0	0	0	0	0	0	0	0	0
COLOMBIA	0	0	0	2	0	0	0	0	0	0	0	0	0	0	2	0	2
ECUADOR	0	0	0	0	0	0	0	0	0	0	0	0	0	0	0	0	0
PERU	0	0	0	0	0	0	0	0	0	0	0	0	0	0	0	0	0
ARGENTINA	0	0	1	1	0	0	0	1	0	0	0	1	0	0	4	1	3
BRAZIL	0	0	0	0	1	0	0	0	0	0	0	0	0	0	1	0	1
URUGUAY	0	0	0	0	0	0	0	0	0	0	0	0	0	0	0	0	0
VENEZUELA	0	0	0	0	0	0	0	0	0	0	0	0	0	0	0	0	0
OTHER S.AMER.	0	0	0	0	0	0	0	0	0	0	0	0	0	0	0	0	0
EUROPE (TOTAL)	2	2	5	11	0	0	0	1	2	1	0	0	3	2	27	9	20
BELGIUM	0	0	0	1	0	0	0	1	0	0	0	0	0	0	2	1	1
FRANCE	1	0	3	5	0	0	0	0	0	0	0	0	0	0	8	6	3
GERMANY	1	0	1	2	0	0	0	0	0	0	0	0	0	0	3	0	4
ITALY	0	0	1	0	0	0	0	0	0	0	0	0	0	0	1	0	1
LUXEMBOURG	0	0	0	0	0	0	0	0	0	0	0	0	0	0	0	0	0
NETHERLANDS	0	0	0	0	0	0	0	0	1	0	0	0	0	0	1	0	1
DENMARK	0	0	0	0	0	0	0	0	0	0	0	0	0	0	0	0	0
IRELAND	0	0	0	0	0	0	0	0	1	0	0	0	0	0	1	0	1
U.K.	0	1	0	3	0	0	0	0	0	1	0	0	0	0	5	2	3
AUSTRIA	0	0	0	0	0	0	0	0	0	0	0	0	0	0	0	0	0
FINLAND	0	0	0	0	0	0	0	0	0	0	0	0	0	0	0	0	0
GREECE	0	0	0	0	0	0	0	0	0	0	0	0	0	0	0	0	0
NORWAY	0	0	0	0	0	0	0	0	0	0	0	0	0	0	0	0	0
PORTUGAL	0	0	0	0	0	0	0	0	0	0	0	0	0	0	0	0	0
SPAIN	0	1	0	0	0	0	0	0	0	0	0	0	1	1	3	0	3
SWEDEN	0	0	0	0	0	0	0	0	0	0	0	0	1	0	1	0	1
SWITZERLAND	0	0	0	0	0	0	0	0	0	0	0	0	0	0	0	0	0
TURKEY	0	0	0	0	0	0	0	0	0	0	0	0	1	1	2	0	2
OTHER EUROPE	0	0	0	0	0	0	0	0	0	0	0	0	0	0	0	0	0

TABLE   2 .4 .28   (CONTINUED)

COUNTRY OR REGION	NET FLOW UP TO 31-DEC-50	NO. OF ENTRIES DURING YEAR(S)													TOTAL ENTRIES 1951-75	TOTAL EXITS 1951-75	NET FLOW UP TO 1-JAN-76
		51-55	56-60	61-65	1966	1967	1968	1969	1970	1971	1972	1973	1974	1975			
N.AFR+M.EAST (TOTAL)	0	0	0	1	0	0	0	1	0	0	0	0	0	0	2	1	1
ALGERIA	0	0	0	0	0	0	0	0	0	0	0	0	0	0	0	0	0
EGYPT	0	0	0	0	0	0	0	0	0	0	0	0	0	0	0	0	0
IRAN	0	0	0	0	0	0	0	1	0	0	0	0	0	0	1	0	1
ISRAEL	0	0	0	0	0	0	0	0	0	0	0	0	0	0	0	0	0
LEBANON	0	0	0	0	0	0	0	0	0	0	0	0	0	0	0	0	0
MOROCCO	0	0	0	0	0	0	0	0	0	0	0	0	0	0	0	0	0
SAUDI ARABIA	0	0	0	0	0	0	0	0	0	0	0	0	0	0	0	0	0
OTHER N.AF+M.E.	0	0	0	1	0	0	0	0	0	0	0	0	0	0	1	1	0
E.+W.AFRICA (TOTAL)	0	0	0	0	0	0	0	0	0	0	0	0	0	0	0	0	0
GHANA	0	0	0	0	0	0	0	0	0	0	0	0	0	0	0	0	0
IVORY COAST	0	0	0	0	0	0	0	0	0	0	0	0	0	0	0	0	0
KENYA	0	0	0	0	0	0	0	0	0	0	0	0	0	0	0	0	0
LIBERIA	0	0	0	0	0	0	0	0	0	0	0	0	0	0	0	0	0
NIGERIA	0	0	0	0	0	0	0	0	0	0	0	0	0	0	0	0	0
ZAIRE	0	0	0	0	0	0	0	0	0	0	0	0	0	0	0	0	0
ZAMBIA	0	0	0	0	0	0	0	0	0	0	0	0	0	0	0	0	0
OTHER E.+W.AFR.	0	0	0	0	0	0	0	0	0	0	0	0	0	0	0	0	0
SOUTH ASIA (TOTAL)	0	0	0	1	0	0	0	0	0	1	0	0	0	0	2	0	2
INDIA	0	0	0	1	0	0	0	0	0	1	0	0	0	0	2	0	2
PAKISTAN	0	0	0	0	0	0	0	0	0	0	0	0	0	0	0	0	0
SRI LANKA	0	0	0	0	0	0	0	0	0	0	0	0	0	0	0	0	0
OTHER S.ASIA	0	0	0	0	0	0	0	0	0	0	0	0	0	0	0	0	0
EAST ASIA (TOTAL)	1	0	0	0	0	0	0	0	1	0	0	0	1	0	2	0	3
HONG KONG	0	0	0	0	0	0	0	0	0	0	0	0	0	0	0	0	0
INDONESIA	1	0	0	0	0	0	0	0	0	0	0	0	0	0	0	0	1
JAPAN	0	0	0	0	0	0	0	0	0	0	0	0	0	0	0	0	0
MALAYSIA	0	0	0	0	0	0	0	0	0	0	0	0	0	0	0	0	0
PHILIPPINES	0	0	0	0	0	0	0	0	0	0	0	0	0	0	0	0	0
SINGAPORE	0	0	0	0	0	0	0	0	0	0	0	0	0	0	0	0	0
S.KOREA	0	0	0	0	0	0	0	0	1	0	0	0	0	0	1	0	1
THAILAND	0	0	0	0	0	0	0	0	0	0	0	0	0	0	0	0	0
TAIWAN	0	0	0	0	0	0	0	0	0	0	0	0	1	0	1	0	1
OTHER E.ASIA	0	0	0	0	0	0	0	0	0	0	0	0	0	0	0	0	0
S.DOMINIONS (TOTAL)	0	2	1	2	1	0	0	0	2	0	0	0	0	0	8	3	5
AUSTRALIA	0	1	1	0	1	0	0	0	2	0	0	0	0	0	5	2	3
NEW ZEALAND	0	0	0	0	0	0	0	0	0	0	0	0	0	0	0	0	0
RHODESIA	0	0	0	0	0	0	0	0	0	0	0	0	0	0	0	0	0
S.AFRICA	0	1	0	2	0	0	0	0	0	0	0	0	0	0	3	1	2
OUTSIDE U.S. (TOTAL)	6	4	7	20	2	1	0	3	5	2	0	1	4	2	51	16	41

CHAPTER 2 - THE PROLIFERATION OF FOREIGN SUBSIDIARIES
SECTION 4 -- GEOGRAPHICAL SPREAD IN SPECIFIC INDUSTRIES
TABLE 29 --- THE OFFICE MACHINES & COMPUTERS INDUSTRY (SIC 357)

NO. OF SUBSIDIARIES MANUFACTURING IN THIS INDUSTRY AT TIME OF ENTRY INTO PARENT SYSTEM

COUNTRY OR REGION	NET FLOW UP TO 31-DEC-50	NO. OF ENTRIES DURING YEAR(S)													TOTAL ENTRIES 1951-75	TOTAL EXITS 1951-75	NET FLOW UP TO 1-JAN-76
		51-55	56-60	61-65	1966	1967	1968	1969	1970	1971	1972	1973	1974	1975			
CANADA	4	1	2	1	1	1	1	0	0	1	0	1	0	0	9	4	9
LATIN AMER. (TOTAL)	4	3	2	1	1	0	1	0	0	0	0	2	0	1	11	6	9
C.AM.+CARIB.(TOTAL)	1	0	1	1	1	0	1	0	0	0	0	2	0	0	6	2	5
BAHAMAS	0	0	0	0	0	0	0	0	0	0	0	0	0	0	0	0	0
BERMUDA	0	0	0	0	0	0	0	0	0	0	0	0	0	0	0	0	0
COSTA RICA	0	0	0	0	0	0	0	0	0	0	0	0	0	0	0	0	0
GUATEMALA	0	0	0	0	0	0	0	0	0	0	0	0	0	0	0	0	0
JAMAICA	0	0	0	0	0	0	0	0	0	0	0	0	0	0	0	0	0
MEXICO	1	0	1	1	1	0	1	0	0	0	0	2	0	0	6	2	5
NETH.ANTILLES	0	0	0	0	0	0	0	0	0	0	0	0	0	0	0	0	0
NICARAGUA	0	0	0	0	0	0	0	0	0	0	0	0	0	0	0	0	0
PANAMA	0	0	0	0	0	0	0	0	0	0	0	0	0	0	0	0	0
OTHER C.AM+CAR.	0	0	0	0	0	0	0	0	0	0	0	0	0	0	0	0	0
S.AMERICA (TOTAL)	3	3	1	0	0	0	0	0	0	1	0	0	0	0	5	4	4
BOLIVIA	0	0	0	0	0	0	0	0	0	0	0	0	0	0	0	0	0
CHILE	0	1	0	0	0	0	0	0	0	0	0	0	0	0	1	1	0
COLOMBIA	0	0	0	0	0	0	0	0	0	1	0	0	0	0	1	0	1
ECUADOR	0	0	0	0	0	0	0	0	0	0	0	0	0	0	0	0	0
PERU	0	0	0	0	0	0	0	0	0	0	0	0	0	0	0	0	0
ARGENTINA	3	0	0	0	0	0	0	0	0	0	0	0	0	0	0	3	0
BRAZIL	0	1	1	0	0	0	0	0	0	0	0	0	0	0	2	0	2
URUGUAY	0	0	0	0	0	0	0	0	0	0	0	0	0	0	0	0	0
VENEZUELA	0	1	0	0	0	0	0	0	0	0	0	0	0	0	1	0	1
OTHER S.AMER.	0	0	0	0	0	0	0	0	0	0	0	0	0	0	0	0	0
EUROPE (TOTAL)	24	2	7	4	1	2	5	5	8	0	2	1	0	0	37	22	39
BELGIUM	1	0	0	1	1	2	0	0	1	0	0	0	0	0	5	2	4
FRANCE	4	0	1	0	0	0	0	0	1	0	1	0	0	0	3	4	3
GERMANY	6	1	1	1	0	0	1	3	1	0	1	1	0	0	10	5	11
ITALY	2	0	1	1	0	0	1	0	1	0	0	0	0	0	4	2	4
LUXEMBOURG	0	0	0	0	0	0	0	0	0	0	0	0	0	0	0	0	0
NETHERLANDS	1	0	2	0	0	0	1	1	1	0	0	0	0	0	5	3	3
DENMARK	0	0	0	0	0	0	0	0	0	0	0	0	0	0	0	0	0
IRELAND	1	0	0	0	0	0	0	0	0	0	0	0	0	0	0	0	1
U.K.	4	1	2	1	0	0	1	0	2	0	0	0	0	0	7	5	6
AUSTRIA	1	0	0	0	0	0	0	0	0	0	0	0	0	0	0	0	1
FINLAND	0	0	0	0	0	0	0	0	0	0	0	0	0	0	0	0	0
GREECE	0	0	0	0	0	0	0	0	0	0	0	0	0	0	0	0	0
NORWAY	1	0	0	0	0	0	0	0	0	0	0	0	0	0	0	0	1
PORTUGAL	1	0	0	0	0	0	0	0	0	0	0	0	0	0	0	0	1
SPAIN	0	0	0	0	0	0	0	0	1	0	0	0	0	0	1	0	1
SWEDEN	2	0	0	0	0	0	1	1	0	0	0	0	0	0	2	1	3
SWITZERLAND	0	0	0	0	0	0	0	0	0	0	0	0	0	0	0	0	0
TURKEY	0	0	0	0	0	0	0	0	0	0	0	0	0	0	0	0	0
OTHER EUROPE	0	0	0	0	0	0	0	0	0	0	0	0	0	0	0	0	0

TABLE 2 .4 .29 (CONTINUED)

COUNTRY OR REGION	NET FLOW UP TO 31-DEC-50	NO. OF ENTRIES DURING YEAR(S)													TOTAL ENTRIES 1951-75	TOTAL EXITS 1951-75	NET FLOW UP TO 1-JAN-76
		51-55	56-60	61-65	1966	1967	1968	1969	1970	1971	1972	1973	1974	1975			
N.AFR+M.EAST (TOTAL)	0	0	0	0	0	0	0	0	0	0	0	0	0	0	0	0	0
ALGERIA	0	0	0	0	0	0	0	0	0	0	0	0	0	0	0	0	0
EGYPT	0	0	0	0	0	0	0	0	0	0	0	0	0	0	0	0	0
IRAN	0	0	0	0	0	0	0	0	0	0	0	0	0	0	0	0	0
ISRAEL	0	0	0	0	0	0	0	0	0	0	0	0	0	0	0	0	0
LEBANON	0	0	0	0	0	0	0	0	0	0	0	0	0	0	0	0	0
MOROCCO	0	0	0	0	0	0	0	0	0	0	0	0	0	0	0	0	0
SAUDI ARABIA	0	0	0	0	0	0	0	0	0	0	0	0	0	0	0	0	0
OTHER N.AF+M.E.	0	0	0	0	0	0	0	0	0	0	0	0	0	0	0	0	0
E.+W.AFRICA (TOTAL)	0	0	0	0	0	0	0	0	0	0	0	0	0	0	0	0	0
GHANA	0	0	0	0	0	0	0	0	0	0	0	0	0	0	0	0	0
IVORY COAST	0	0	0	0	0	0	0	0	0	0	0	0	0	0	0	0	0
KENYA	0	0	0	0	0	0	0	0	0	0	0	0	0	0	0	0	0
LIBERIA	0	0	0	0	0	0	0	0	0	0	0	0	0	0	0	0	0
NIGERIA	0	0	0	0	0	0	0	0	0	0	0	0	0	0	0	0	0
ZAIRE	0	0	0	0	0	0	0	0	0	0	0	0	0	0	0	0	0
ZAMBIA	0	0	0	0	0	0	0	0	0	0	0	0	0	0	0	0	0
OTHER E.+W.AFR.	0	0	0	0	0	0	0	0	0	0	0	0	0	0	0	0	0
SOUTH ASIA (TOTAL)	0	1	0	1	0	0	0	0	0	0	0	0	0	0	2	1	1
INDIA	0	1	0	1	0	0	0	0	0	0	0	0	0	0	2	1	1
PAKISTAN	0	0	0	0	0	0	0	0	0	0	0	0	0	0	0	0	0
SRI LANKA	0	0	0	0	0	0	0	0	0	0	0	0	0	0	0	0	0
OTHER S.ASIA	0	0	0	0	0	0	0	0	0	0	0	0	0	0	0	0	0
EAST ASIA (TOTAL)	1	0	0	2	0	1	0	1	2	3	0	3	1	1	14	2	13
HONG KONG	0	0	0	0	0	0	0	0	0	0	0	0	0	1	1	0	1
INDONESIA	0	0	0	0	0	0	0	0	0	0	0	0	0	0	0	0	0
JAPAN	1	0	0	2	0	1	0	1	1	1	0	2	1	0	9	2	8
MALAYSIA	0	0	0	0	0	0	0	0	0	0	0	0	0	0	0	0	0
PHILIPPINES	0	0	0	0	0	0	0	0	0	0	0	0	0	0	0	0	0
SINGAPORE	0	0	0	0	0	0	0	0	0	1	0	1	0	0	2	0	2
S.KOREA	0	0	0	0	0	0	0	0	0	0	0	0	0	0	0	0	0
THAILAND	0	0	0	0	0	0	0	0	1	0	0	0	0	0	1	0	1
TAIWAN	0	0	0	0	0	0	0	0	0	0	0	0	0	0	0	0	0
OTHER E.ASIA	0	0	0	0	0	0	0	0	0	1	0	0	0	0	1	0	1
S.DOMINIONS (TOTAL)	0	1	0	0	0	1	0	0	0	1	0	2	0	0	5	2	3
AUSTRALIA	0	1	0	0	0	1	0	0	0	0	0	1	0	0	3	1	2
NEW ZEALAND	0	0	0	0	0	0	0	0	0	0	0	1	0	0	1	0	1
RHODESIA	0	0	0	0	0	0	0	0	0	0	0	0	0	0	0	0	0
S.AFRICA	0	0	0	0	0	0	0	0	0	1	0	0	0	0	1	1	0
OUTSIDE U.S.(TOTAL)	33	9	11	9	3	4	7	6	10	5	2	9	1	2	78	37	74

CHAPTER 2 - THE PROLIFERATION OF FOREIGN SUBSIDIARIES
SECTION 4 -- GEOGRAPHICAL SPREAD IN SPECIFIC INDUSTRIES
TABLE 30 --- THE SPECIAL MACHINERY INDUSTRY (SIC 355)

NO. OF SUBSIDIARIES MANUFACTURING IN THIS INDUSTRY AT TIME OF ENTRY INTO PARENT SYSTEM

COUNTRY OR REGION	NET FLOW UP TO 31-DEC-50	NO. OF ENTRIES DURING YEAR(S)													TOTAL ENTRIES 1951-75	TOTAL EXITS 1951-75	NET FLOW UP TO 1-JAN-76
		51-55	56-60	61-65	1966	1967	1968	1969	1970	1971	1972	1973	1974	1975			
CANADA	3	1	0	3	1	0	2	1	1	0	2	0	0	1	12	4	11
LATIN AMER. (TOTAL)	3	0	4	4	0	3	0	0	0	1	0	4	2	2	20	8	15
C.AM.+CARIB. (TOTAL)	2	0	1	2	0	2	0	0	0	1	0	0	1	1	8	4	6
BAHAMAS	0	0	0	0	0	0	0	0	0	0	0	0	0	0	0	0	0
BERMUDA	0	0	0	0	0	0	0	0	0	0	0	0	0	0	0	0	0
COSTA RICA	0	0	0	0	0	0	0	0	0	0	0	0	0	0	0	0	0
GUATEMALA	0	0	0	0	0	0	0	0	0	0	0	0	0	0	0	0	0
JAMAICA	0	0	0	0	0	0	0	0	0	0	0	0	0	0	0	0	0
MEXICO	2	0	0	1	0	2	0	0	0	1	0	0	1	1	6	3	5
NETH.ANTILLES	0	0	0	0	0	0	0	0	0	0	0	0	0	0	0	0	0
NICARAGUA	0	0	0	0	0	0	0	0	0	0	0	0	0	0	0	0	0
PANAMA	0	0	0	0	0	0	0	0	0	0	0	0	0	0	0	0	0
OTHER C.AM+CAR.	0	0	1	1	0	0	0	0	0	0	0	0	0	0	2	1	1
S.AMERICA (TOTAL)	1	0	3	2	0	1	0	0	0	0	0	4	1	1	12	4	9
BOLIVIA	0	0	0	0	0	0	0	0	0	0	0	0	0	0	0	0	0
CHILE	0	0	0	0	0	1	0	0	0	0	0	0	0	0	1	0	1
COLOMBIA	0	0	1	1	0	0	0	0	0	0	0	1	0	0	3	2	1
ECUADOR	0	0	0	1	0	0	0	0	0	0	0	0	0	0	1	0	1
PERU	0	0	0	0	0	0	0	0	0	0	0	0	0	0	0	0	0
ARGENTINA	0	0	0	0	0	0	0	0	0	0	0	0	0	0	0	0	0
BRAZIL	1	0	1	0	0	0	0	0	0	0	0	3	1	1	6	2	5
URUGUAY	0	0	0	0	0	0	0	0	0	0	0	0	0	0	0	0	0
VENEZUELA	0	0	1	0	0	0	0	0	0	0	0	0	0	0	1	0	1
OTHER S.AMER.	0	0	0	0	0	0	0	0	0	0	0	0	0	0	0	0	0
EUROPE (TOTAL)	14	5	7	18	7	5	2	3	7	2	5	14	3	3	81	23	72
BELGIUM	1	0	0	1	1	0	1	0	1	0	1	0	0	0	5	0	6
FRANCE	3	1	0	3	1	2	0	1	1	0	0	1	0	0	10	3	10
GERMANY	1	1	1	3	0	0	0	1	1	1	1	3	1	0	13	5	9
ITALY	1	0	3	3	2	0	0	0	0	0	0	1	0	1	10	1	10
LUXEMBOURG	0	0	0	0	0	0	0	0	0	0	0	0	0	0	0	0	0
NETHERLANDS	0	0	0	1	0	0	0	0	1	0	1	0	0	1	4	2	2
DENMARK	0	0	0	0	0	0	0	0	0	0	0	0	0	0	0	0	0
IRELAND	0	0	0	0	0	0	1	0	1	0	0	0	0	1	3	0	3
U.K.	6	2	2	6	2	3	0	1	2	1	1	9	1	0	30	10	26
AUSTRIA	0	0	0	0	0	0	0	0	0	0	0	0	0	0	0	0	0
FINLAND	0	0	0	0	0	0	0	0	0	0	0	0	0	0	0	0	0
GREECE	0	0	0	0	1	0	0	0	0	0	0	0	0	0	1	0	1
NORWAY	0	0	0	0	0	0	0	0	0	0	0	0	0	0	0	0	0
PORTUGAL	0	0	0	0	0	0	0	0	0	0	0	0	0	0	0	0	0
SPAIN	1	1	0	1	0	0	0	0	0	0	0	1	0	0	3	2	2
SWEDEN	1	0	0	0	0	0	0	0	0	0	0	0	0	0	0	0	1
SWITZERLAND	0	0	1	0	0	0	0	0	0	0	0	0	1	0	2	0	2
TURKEY	0	0	0	0	0	0	0	0	0	0	0	0	0	0	0	0	0
OTHER EUROPE	0	0	0	0	0	0	0	0	0	0	0	0	0	0	0	0	0

TABLE 2 .4 .30 (CONTINUED)

COUNTRY OR REGION	NET FLOW UP TO 31-DEC-50	NO. OF ENTRIES DURING YEAR(S)													TOTAL ENTRIES 1951-75	TOTAL EXITS 1951-75	NET FLOW UP TO 1-JAN-76
		51-55	56-60	61-65	1966	1967	1968	1969	1970	1971	1972	1973	1974	1975			
N.AFR+M.EAST(TOTAL)	0	0	0	0	0	1	0	0	0	1	0	0	0	0	2	0	2
ALGERIA	0	0	0	0	0	0	0	0	0	0	0	0	0	0	0	0	0
EGYPT	0	0	0	0	0	0	0	0	0	0	0	0	0	0	0	0	0
IRAN	0	0	0	0	0	0	0	0	0	0	0	0	0	0	0	0	0
ISRAEL	0	0	0	0	0	0	0	0	0	0	0	0	0	0	0	0	0
LEBANON	0	0	0	0	0	1	0	0	0	0	0	0	0	0	1	0	1
MOROCCO	0	0	0	0	0	0	0	0	0	1	0	0	0	0	1	0	1
SAUDI ARABIA	0	0	0	0	0	0	0	0	0	0	0	0	0	0	0	0	0
OTHER N.AF+M.E.	0	0	0	0	0	0	0	0	0	0	0	0	0	0	0	0	0
E.+W.AFRICA (TOTAL)	0	0	0	0	0	0	0	0	0	0	0	0	0	0	0	0	0
GHANA	0	0	0	0	0	0	0	0	0	0	0	0	0	0	0	0	0
IVORY COAST	0	0	0	0	0	0	0	0	0	0	0	0	0	0	0	0	0
KENYA	0	0	0	0	0	0	0	0	0	0	0	0	0	0	0	0	0
LIBERIA	0	0	0	0	0	0	0	0	0	0	0	0	0	0	0	0	0
NIGERIA	0	0	0	0	0	0	0	0	0	0	0	0	0	0	0	0	0
ZAIRE	0	0	0	0	0	0	0	0	0	0	0	0	0	0	0	0	0
ZAMBIA	0	0	0	0	0	0	0	0	0	0	0	0	0	0	0	0	0
OTHER E.+W.AFR.	0	0	0	0	0	0	0	0	0	0	0	0	0	0	0	0	0
SOUTH ASIA (TOTAL)	0	0	0	0	0	0	0	1	0	0	0	0	0	0	1	1	0
INDIA	0	0	0	0	0	0	0	1	0	0	0	0	0	0	1	1	0
PAKISTAN	0	0	0	0	0	0	0	0	0	0	0	0	0	0	0	0	0
SRI LANKA	0	0	0	0	0	0	0	0	0	0	0	0	0	0	0	0	0
OTHER S.ASIA	0	0	0	0	0	0	0	0	0	0	0	0	0	0	0	0	0
EAST ASIA (TOTAL)	0	1	0	2	0	1	1	0	0	1	0	0	0	0	6	1	5
HONG KONG	0	0	0	0	0	0	0	0	0	0	0	0	0	0	0	0	0
INDONESIA	0	0	0	0	0	0	0	0	0	0	0	0	0	0	0	0	0
JAPAN	0	1	0	2	0	1	0	0	0	1	0	0	0	0	5	1	4
MALAYSIA	0	0	0	0	0	0	0	0	0	0	0	0	0	0	0	0	0
PHILIPPINES	0	0	0	0	0	0	1	0	0	0	0	0	0	0	1	0	1
SINGAPORE	0	0	0	0	0	0	0	0	0	0	0	0	0	0	0	0	0
S.KOREA	0	0	0	0	0	0	0	0	0	0	0	0	0	0	0	0	0
THAILAND	0	0	0	0	0	0	0	0	0	0	0	0	0	0	0	0	0
TAIWAN	0	0	0	0	0	0	0	0	0	0	0	0	0	0	0	0	0
OTHER E.ASIA	0	0	0	0	0	0	0	0	0	0	0	0	0	0	0	0	0
S.DOMINIONS (TOTAL)	3	2	1	1	2	2	1	0	0	0	0	1	0	0	10	5	8
AUSTRALIA	2	2	1	1	1	1	0	0	0	0	0	0	0	0	6	4	4
NEW ZEALAND	0	0	0	0	0	1	0	0	0	0	0	0	0	0	1	0	1
RHODESIA	0	0	0	0	0	0	0	0	0	0	0	0	0	0	0	0	0
S.AFRICA	1	0	0	0	1	0	1	0	0	0	0	1	0	0	3	1	3
OUTSIDE U.S.(TOTAL)	23	9	12	28	10	11	5	5	8	5	7	21	5	6	132	42	113

CHAPTER 2 - THE PROLIFERATION OF FOREIGN SUBSIDIARIES
SECTION 4 -- GEOGRAPHICAL SPREAD IN SPECIFIC INDUSTRIES
TABLE 31 --- THE GENERAL MACHINERY INDUSTRY (SIC 356)

NO. OF SUBSIDIARIES MANUFACTURING IN THIS INDUSTRY AT TIME OF ENTRY INTO PARENT SYSTEM

COUNTRY OR REGION	NET FLOW UP TO 31-DEC-50	51-55	56-60	61-65	1966	1967	1968	1969	1970	1971	1972	1973	1974	1975	TOTAL ENTRIES 1951-75	TOTAL EXITS 1951-75	NET FLOW UP TO 1-JAN-76
						NO. OF ENTRIES DURING YEAR(S)											
CANADA	6	5	5	6	0	3	3	4	1	1	2	0	1	0	31	12	25
LATIN AMER. (TOTAL)	4	2	3	6	1	4	4	3	0	1	2	3	2	1	32	4	32
C.AM.+CARIB. (TOTAL)	2	1	1	4	1	1	1	3	0	0	1	1	2	1	17	3	16
BAHAMAS	0	0	0	0	0	0	0	0	0	0	0	0	0	0	0	0	0
BERMUDA	0	0	0	0	0	0	0	0	0	0	0	0	0	0	0	0	0
COSTA RICA	0	0	0	0	0	0	0	0	0	0	0	0	0	0	0	0	0
GUATEMALA	0	0	0	0	0	0	0	0	0	0	0	0	0	0	0	0	0
JAMAICA	0	0	0	0	0	0	0	0	0	0	0	0	0	0	0	0	0
MEXICO	2	1	1	3	1	1	1	3	0	0	1	1	2	1	16	0	16
NETH.ANTILLES	0	0	0	0	0	0	0	0	0	0	0	0	0	0	0	0	0
NICARAGUA	0	0	0	0	0	0	0	0	0	0	0	0	0	0	0	0	0
PANAMA	0	0	0	0	0	0	0	0	0	0	0	0	0	0	0	0	0
OTHER C.AM+CAR.	0	0	0	1	0	0	0	0	0	1	0	0	0	0	1	1	0
S.AMERICA (TOTAL)	2	1	2	2	0	3	3	0	0	0	0	2	0	0	15	1	16
BOLIVIA	0	0	0	0	0	0	0	0	0	0	0	0	0	0	0	0	0
CHILE	0	0	0	0	0	0	0	0	0	0	0	0	0	0	0	0	0
COLOMBIA	0	0	0	1	0	0	0	0	0	0	0	0	0	0	2	0	2
ECUADOR	0	0	0	0	0	0	0	0	0	0	0	0	0	0	0	0	0
PERU	0	0	0	1	0	1	0	0	0	0	0	0	0	0	1	0	1
ARGENTINA	0	0	1	0	0	0	0	0	0	0	0	0	0	0	2	0	2
BRAZIL	2	1	1	1	0	2	2	0	0	0	0	2	0	0	9	0	10
URUGUAY	0	0	0	0	0	0	0	0	0	0	0	0	0	0	0	0	0
VENEZUELA	0	0	0	0	0	0	1	0	0	0	0	0	0	0	1	0	1
OTHER S.AMER.	0	0	0	0	0	0	0	0	0	0	0	0	0	0	0	0	0
EUROPE (TOTAL)	15	4	9	12	2	7	10	8	7	5	12	9	4	4	93	33	75
BELGIUM	0	0	1	1	0	2	0	0	0	1	0	0	0	0	3	1	2
FRANCE	2	0	0	4	0	2	0	0	0	0	4	3	2	1	16	6	12
GERMANY	3	1	2	2	0	2	4	1	0	2	2	1	0	0	14	5	12
ITALY	2	0	0	0	0	0	2	1	2	0	1	1	0	0	10	4	8
LUXEMBOURG	0	0	0	1	0	0	0	0	0	0	0	0	0	0	1	0	1
NETHERLANDS	0	0	0	0	1	0	1	0	0	0	0	1	0	0	5	1	4
DENMARK	0	0	0	0	0	0	0	0	0	0	0	0	0	0	0	0	0
IRELAND	0	0	0	0	0	1	0	0	1	1	1	2	0	0	1	0	1
U.K.	5	3	5	0	1	2	2	4	1	2	4	2	2	2	30	14	21
AUSTRIA	1	0	0	0	0	0	0	0	0	0	0	1	1	1	1	1	1
FINLAND	0	0	0	0	0	0	0	0	0	0	0	0	0	0	0	0	0
GREECE	0	0	1	0	0	0	0	0	0	0	0	1	0	0	1	0	1
NORWAY	0	0	0	0	0	0	0	0	0	0	0	1	0	0	1	0	1
PORTUGAL	1	0	0	3	0	1	0	1	0	0	0	0	0	0	6	0	0
SPAIN	0	0	0	0	0	0	1	0	0	1	1	0	0	0	2	0	7
SWEDEN	1	0	0	1	0	0	0	0	0	0	0	1	0	0	1	0	2
SWITZERLAND	0	0	0	0	0	0	1	1	0	0	0	1	0	0	1	1	0
TURKEY	0	0	0	0	0	0	0	0	0	0	0	0	0	0	1	0	0
OTHER EUROPE	0	0	0	0	0	0	0	0	0	0	0	0	0	0	0	0	0

TABLE   2 .4 .31   (CONTINUED)

COUNTRY OR REGION	NET FLOW UP TO 31-DEC-50	NO. OF ENTRIES DURING YEAR(S)													TOTAL ENTRIES 1951-75	TOTAL EXITS 1951-75	NET FLOW UP TO 1-JAN-76
		51-55	56-60	61-65	1966	1967	1968	1969	1970	1971	1972	1973	1974	1975			
N.AFR+M.EAST (TOTAL)	0	0	0	0	1	0	0	0	0	0	0	0	0	0	1	0	1
ALGERIA	0	0	0	0	0	0	0	0	0	0	0	0	0	0	0	0	0
EGYPT	0	0	0	0	0	0	0	0	0	0	0	0	0	0	0	0	0
IRAN	0	0	0	0	1	0	0	0	0	0	0	0	0	0	1	0	1
ISRAEL	0	0	0	0	0	0	0	0	0	0	0	0	0	0	0	0	0
LEBANON	0	0	0	0	0	0	0	0	0	0	0	0	0	0	0	0	0
MOROCCO	0	0	0	0	0	0	0	0	0	0	0	0	0	0	0	0	0
SAUDI ARABIA	0	0	0	0	0	0	0	0	0	0	0	0	0	0	0	0	0
OTHER N.AF+M.E.	0	0	0	0	0	0	0	0	0	0	0	0	0	0	0	0	0
E.+W.AFRICA (TOTAL)	0	0	0	0	0	0	0	0	0	0	0	0	0	0	0	0	0
GHANA	0	0	0	0	0	0	0	0	0	0	0	0	0	0	0	0	0
IVORY COAST	0	0	0	0	0	0	0	0	0	0	0	0	0	0	0	0	0
KENYA	0	0	0	0	0	0	0	0	0	0	0	0	0	0	0	0	0
LIBERIA	0	0	0	0	0	0	0	0	0	0	0	0	0	0	0	0	0
NIGERIA	0	0	0	0	0	0	0	0	0	0	0	0	0	0	0	0	0
ZAIRE	0	0	0	0	0	0	0	0	0	0	0	0	0	0	0	0	0
ZAMBIA	0	0	0	0	0	0	0	0	0	0	0	0	0	0	0	0	0
OTHER E.+W.AFR.	0	0	0	0	0	0	0	0	0	0	0	0	0	0	0	0	0
SOUTH ASIA (TOTAL)	0	1	1	1	0	0	0	1	0	0	0	0	0	0	4	0	4
INDIA	0	1	1	1	0	0	0	1	0	0	0	0	0	0	4	0	4
PAKISTAN	0	0	0	0	0	0	0	0	0	0	0	0	0	0	0	0	0
SRI LANKA	0	0	0	0	0	0	0	0	0	0	0	0	0	0	0	0	0
OTHER S.ASIA	0	0	0	0	0	0	0	0	0	0	0	0	0	0	0	0	0
EAST ASIA (TOTAL)	1	1	0	0	0	0	1	3	0	6	2	2	1	1	17	0	18
HONG KONG	0	0	0	0	0	0	0	0	0	1	0	0	0	0	1	0	1
INDONESIA	0	0	0	0	0	0	0	0	0	0	0	0	0	0	0	0	0
JAPAN	1	1	0	0	0	0	1	3	0	4	1	2	1	1	14	0	15
MALAYSIA	0	0	0	0	0	0	0	0	0	0	0	0	0	0	0	0	0
PHILIPPINES	0	0	0	0	0	0	0	0	0	0	1	0	0	0	1	0	1
SINGAPORE	0	0	0	0	0	0	0	0	0	0	0	0	0	0	0	0	0
S.KOREA	0	0	0	0	0	0	0	0	0	0	0	0	0	0	0	0	0
THAILAND	0	0	0	0	0	0	0	0	0	0	0	0	0	0	0	0	0
TAIWAN	0	0	0	0	0	0	0	0	0	0	0	0	0	0	0	0	0
OTHER E.ASIA	0	0	0	0	0	0	0	0	0	1	0	0	0	0	1	0	1
S.DOMINIONS (TOTAL)	1	3	3	1	1	1	5	3	0	0	1	0	0	0	18	6	13
AUSTRALIA	1	1	3	0	1	1	4	2	0	0	1	0	0	0	13	4	10
NEW ZEALAND	0	1	0	1	0	0	0	0	0	0	0	0	0	0	2	1	1
RHODESIA	0	0	0	0	0	0	0	0	0	0	0	0	0	0	0	0	0
S.AFRICA	0	1	0	0	0	0	1	1	0	0	0	0	0	0	3	1	2
OUTSIDE U.S. (TOTAL)	27	13	21	28	5	15	23	22	8	13	19	14	8	7	196	55	168

CHAPTER 2   - THE PROLIFERATION OF FOREIGN SUBSIDIARIES
SECTION 4   -- GEOGRAPHICAL SPREAD IN SPECIFIC INDUSTRIES
TABLE 32   --- OTHER NON-ELEC MACHINERY INDUSTRIES (OTHER SIC 35)

NO. OF SUBSIDIARIES MANUFACTURING IN THIS INDUSTRY AT TIME OF ENTRY INTO PARENT SYSTEM

COUNTRY OR REGION	NET FLOW UP TO 31-DEC-50	NO. OF ENTRIES DURING YEAR(S)													TOTAL ENTRIES 1951-75	TOTAL EXITS 1951-75	NET FLOW UP TO 1-JAN-76
		51-55	56-60	61-65	1966	1967	1968	1969	1970	1971	1972	1973	1974	1975			
CANADA	4	1	1	7	2	3	0	6	1	0	3	4	2	1	31	9	26
LATIN AMER. (TOTAL)	2	0	2	5	5	2	2	4	1	2	1	3	2	3	32	8	26
C.AM.+CARIB.(TOTAL)	0	0	0	3	4	0	0	2	0	0	0	0	1	2	12	3	9
BAHAMAS	0	0	0	0	0	0	0	0	0	0	0	0	0	0	0	0	0
BERMUDA	0	0	0	0	0	0	0	0	0	0	0	0	0	0	0	0	0
COSTA RICA	0	0	0	1	0	0	0	0	0	0	0	0	0	0	1	0	1
GUATEMALA	0	0	0	0	0	0	0	0	0	0	0	0	0	0	0	0	0
JAMAICA	0	0	0	0	1	0	0	0	0	0	0	0	0	0	1	0	1
MEXICO	0	0	0	2	3	0	0	2	0	0	0	0	1	1	9	2	7
NETH.ANTILLES	0	0	0	0	0	0	0	0	0	0	0	0	0	0	0	0	0
NICARAGUA	0	0	0	0	0	0	0	0	0	0	0	0	0	0	0	0	0
PANAMA	0	0	0	0	0	0	0	0	0	0	0	0	0	0	0	0	0
OTHER C.AM+CAR.	0	0	0	0	0	0	0	0	0	0	0	0	0	1	1	1	0
S.AMERICA (TOTAL)	2	0	2	2	1	2	2	2	1	2	1	3	1	1	20	5	17
BOLIVIA	0	0	0	0	0	0	0	0	0	0	0	0	0	0	0	0	0
CHILE	0	0	0	0	0	0	0	0	0	0	0	1	0	0	1	0	1
COLOMBIA	0	0	0	0	0	0	0	0	0	0	0	0	0	0	0	0	0
ECUADOR	0	0	0	0	0	0	0	0	0	0	0	0	0	0	0	0	0
PERU	0	0	0	0	0	0	0	0	0	0	0	0	0	0	0	0	0
ARGENTINA	0	0	0	0	0	1	0	2	0	1	1	0	1	0	6	0	6
BRAZIL	2	0	2	1	0	1	1	0	1	0	0	2	0	1	9	3	8
URUGUAY	0	0	0	0	0	0	0	0	0	0	0	0	0	0	0	0	0
VENEZUELA	0	0	0	1	1	0	1	0	0	1	0	0	0	0	4	2	2
OTHER S.AMER.	0	0	0	0	0	0	0	0	0	0	0	0	0	0	0	0	0
EUROPE (TOTAL)	9	4	6	18	2	3	11	9	7	2	14	5	3	1	85	26	68
BELGIUM	1	1	1	1	1	0	1	1	1	0	0	1	0	0	8	3	6
FRANCE	2	0	1	5	0	0	2	1	0	0	4	0	0	0	13	5	10
GERMANY	2	1	0	5	0	0	1	1	2	0	2	0	0	0	12	2	12
ITALY	1	0	0	4	0	1	3	2	2	0	4	0	0	0	16	7	10
LUXEMBOURG	0	0	0	0	0	0	0	0	1	0	0	0	0	0	1	0	1
NETHERLANDS	0	0	0	0	0	0	1	0	0	0	1	1	1	0	4	2	2
DENMARK	0	0	0	0	0	0	0	0	0	0	0	1	1	0	2	1	1
IRELAND	0	0	0	1	0	0	0	0	0	0	0	0	0	0	1	1	0
U.K.	3	2	4	2	0	1	3	2	1	0	2	0	0	0	17	5	15
AUSTRIA	0	0	0	0	0	0	0	0	0	0	0	0	0	0	0	0	0
FINLAND	0	0	0	0	0	0	0	0	0	0	0	0	0	0	0	0	0
GREECE	0	0	0	0	0	0	0	0	0	0	0	0	0	0	0	0	0
NORWAY	0	0	0	0	0	0	0	1	0	0	0	1	0	0	2	0	2
PORTUGAL	0	0	0	0	0	0	0	0	0	0	0	0	0	0	0	0	0
SPAIN	0	0	0	0	0	0	0	0	0	1	1	1	1	0	4	0	4
SWEDEN	0	0	0	0	0	0	0	1	0	1	0	0	0	0	2	0	2
SWITZERLAND	0	0	0	0	0	1	0	0	0	0	0	0	0	0	1	0	1
TURKEY	0	0	0	0	1	0	0	0	0	0	0	0	0	0	1	0	1
OTHER EUROPE	0	0	0	0	0	0	0	0	0	0	0	0	0	1	1	0	1

TABLE 2 .4 .32 (CONTINUED)

COUNTRY OR REGION	NET FLOW UP TO 31-DEC-50	NO. OF ENTRIES DURING YEAR(S)													TOTAL ENTRIES 1951-75	TOTAL EXITS 1951-75	NET FLOW UP TO 1-JAN-76
		51-55	56-60	61-65	1966	1967	1968	1969	1970	1971	1972	1973	1974	1975			
N.AFR+M.EAST (TOTAL)	0	0	0	0	0	0	0	0	0	0	0	0	0	0	0	0	0
ALGERIA	0	0	0	0	0	0	0	0	0	0	0	0	0	0	0	0	0
EGYPT	0	0	0	0	0	0	0	0	0	0	0	0	0	0	0	0	0
IRAN	0	0	0	0	0	0	0	0	0	0	0	0	0	0	0	0	0
ISRAEL	0	0	0	0	0	0	0	0	0	0	0	0	0	0	0	0	0
LEBANON	0	0	0	0	0	0	0	0	0	0	0	0	0	0	0	0	0
MOROCCO	0	0	0	0	0	0	0	0	0	0	0	0	0	0	0	0	0
SAUDI ARABIA	0	0	0	0	0	0	0	0	0	0	0	0	0	0	0	0	0
OTHER N.AF+M.E.	0	0	0	0	0	0	0	0	0	0	0	0	0	0	0	0	0
E.+W.AFRICA (TOTAL)	0	0	0	0	0	0	0	0	0	0	0	0	0	0	0	0	0
GHANA	0	0	0	0	0	0	0	0	0	0	0	0	0	0	0	0	0
IVORY COAST	0	0	0	0	0	0	0	0	0	0	0	0	0	0	0	0	0
KENYA	0	0	0	0	0	0	0	0	0	0	0	0	0	0	0	0	0
LIBERIA	0	0	0	0	0	0	0	0	0	0	0	0	0	0	0	0	0
NIGERIA	0	0	0	0	0	0	0	0	0	0	0	0	0	0	0	0	0
ZAIRE	0	0	0	0	0	0	0	0	0	0	0	0	0	0	0	0	0
ZAMBIA	0	0	0	0	0	0	0	0	0	0	0	0	0	0	0	0	0
OTHER E.+W.AFR.	0	0	0	0	0	0	0	0	0	0	0	0	0	0	0	0	0
SOUTH ASIA (TOTAL)	0	0	1	1	0	0	0	1	1	0	0	0	0	0	4	1	3
INDIA	0	0	1	1	0	0	0	1	1	0	0	0	0	0	4	1	3
PAKISTAN	0	0	0	0	0	0	0	0	0	0	0	0	0	0	0	0	0
SRI LANKA	0	0	0	0	0	0	0	0	0	0	0	0	0	0	0	0	0
OTHER S.ASIA	0	0	0	0	0	0	0	0	0	0	0	0	0	0	0	0	0
EAST ASIA (TOTAL)	0	0	0	1	2	0	1	1	0	0	1	0	1	0	7	1	6
HONG KONG	0	0	0	0	0	0	0	0	0	0	0	0	0	0	0	0	0
INDONESIA	0	0	0	0	0	0	0	0	0	0	0	0	0	0	0	0	0
JAPAN	0	0	0	0	0	0	0	0	0	0	0	0	0	0	0	0	0
MALAYSIA	0	0	0	1	2	0	1	1	0	0	0	0	1	0	6	1	5
PHILIPPINES	0	0	0	0	0	0	0	0	0	0	0	0	0	0	0	0	0
SINGAPORE	0	0	0	0	0	0	0	0	0	0	1	0	0	0	1	0	1
S.KOREA	0	0	0	0	0	0	0	0	0	0	0	0	0	0	0	0	0
THAILAND	0	0	0	0	0	0	0	0	0	0	0	0	0	0	0	0	0
TAIWAN	0	0	0	0	0	0	0	0	0	0	0	0	0	0	0	0	0
OTHER E.ASIA	0	0	0	0	0	0	0	0	0	0	0	0	0	0	0	0	0
S.DOMINIONS (TOTAL)	3	1	3	4	0	2	2	2	3	0	2	1	0	0	20	3	20
AUSTRALIA	3	1	3	4	0	1	1	1	1	0	0	1	0	0	13	3	13
NEW ZEALAND	0	0	0	0	0	0	0	0	0	0	0	0	0	0	0	0	0
RHODESIA	0	0	0	0	0	0	0	0	0	0	0	0	0	0	0	0	0
S.AFRICA	0	0	0	0	0	1	1	1	2	0	2	0	0	0	7	0	7
OUTSIDE U.S. (TOTAL)	18	6	13	36	11	10	15	23	14	4	21	13	8	5	179	48	149

CHAPTER 2 — THE PROLIFERATION OF FOREIGN SUBSIDIARIES
SECTION 4 —— GEOGRAPHICAL SPREAD IN SPECIFIC INDUSTRIES
TABLE 33 ——— ELECTRIC LIGHT & WIRING INDUSTRY (SIC 364)

NO. OF SUBSIDIARIES MANUFACTURING IN THIS INDUSTRY AT TIME OF ENTRY INTO PARENT SYSTEM

COUNTRY OR REGION	NET FLOW UP TO 31-DEC-50	NO. OF ENTRIES DURING YEAR(S)													TOTAL ENTRIES 1951-75	TOTAL EXITS 1951-75	NET FLOW UP TO 1-JAN-76
		51-55	56-60	61-65	1966	1967	1968	1969	1970	1971	1972	1973	1974	1975			
CANADA	2	0	4	3	0	0	0	1	0	1	0	0	0	0	9	3	8
LATIN AMER. (TOTAL)	2	1	5	3	1	3	2	0	2	1	1	2	1	0	22	6	18
C.AM.+CARIB.(TOTAL)	1	0	2	1	1	2	0	0	0	1	0	1	0	0	8	0	9
BAHAMAS	0	0	0	0	0	0	0	0	0	0	0	0	0	0	0	0	0
BERMUDA	0	0	0	0	0	0	0	0	0	0	0	0	0	0	0	0	0
COSTA RICA	0	0	0	0	0	0	0	0	0	0	0	0	0	0	0	0	0
GUATEMALA	0	0	0	0	0	0	0	0	0	0	0	0	0	0	0	0	0
JAMAICA	0	0	0	0	0	0	0	0	0	0	0	0	0	0	0	0	0
MEXICO	1	0	2	0	1	2	0	0	0	0	0	1	0	0	6	0	7
NETH.ANTILLES	0	0	0	0	0	0	0	0	0	0	0	0	0	0	0	0	0
NICARAGUA	0	0	0	0	0	0	0	0	0	0	0	0	0	0	0	0	0
PANAMA	0	0	0	1	0	0	0	0	0	0	0	0	0	0	1	0	1
OTHER C.AM+CAR.	0	0	0	0	0	0	0	0	0	1	0	0	0	0	1	0	1
S.AMERICA (TOTAL)	1	1	3	2	0	1	2	0	2	0	1	1	1	0	14	6	9
BOLIVIA	0	0	0	0	0	0	0	0	0	0	0	0	0	0	0	0	0
CHILE	1	0	0	0	0	0	0	0	0	0	0	0	1	0	1	1	1
COLOMBIA	0	0	0	1	0	0	0	0	0	0	0	0	0	0	1	0	1
ECUADOR	0	0	0	0	0	0	0	0	0	0	0	0	0	0	0	0	0
PERU	0	0	0	0	0	0	0	0	0	0	0	0	0	0	0	0	0
ARGENTINA	0	0	1	0	0	0	0	0	0	0	1	0	0	0	2	1	1
BRAZIL	0	1	2	1	0	1	1	0	1	0	0	1	0	0	8	3	5
URUGUAY	0	0	0	0	0	0	0	0	1	0	0	0	0	0	1	1	0
VENEZUELA	0	0	0	0	0	0	1	0	0	0	0	0	0	0	1	0	1
OTHER S.AMER.	0	0	0	0	0	0	0	0	0	0	0	0	0	0	0	0	0
EUROPE (TOTAL)	2	1	2	2	3	2	2	1	1	2	1	2	1	1	21	7	16
BELGIUM	1	0	0	0	0	0	0	0	0	0	0	0	0	0	0	1	0
FRANCE	0	0	1	0	0	1	0	0	0	0	0	0	0	1	3	1	2
GERMANY	0	0	0	1	1	0	1	0	1	1	0	0	1	0	6	1	5
ITALY	0	0	0	0	1	0	0	0	0	0	0	1	0	0	2	1	1
LUXEMBOURG	0	0	0	0	0	0	0	0	0	0	0	0	0	0	0	0	0
NETHERLANDS	0	0	0	0	0	0	0	0	0	0	0	0	0	0	0	0	0
DENMARK	0	0	0	0	0	0	0	0	0	0	0	0	0	0	0	0	0
IRELAND	0	0	0	0	0	0	0	0	0	0	0	0	0	0	0	0	0
U.K.	0	1	1	1	1	1	0	1	0	0	1	1	0	0	8	2	6
AUSTRIA	1	0	0	0	0	0	0	0	0	0	0	0	0	0	0	1	0
FINLAND	0	0	0	0	0	0	0	0	0	0	0	0	0	0	0	0	0
GREECE	0	0	0	0	0	0	0	0	0	0	0	0	0	0	0	0	0
NORWAY	0	0	0	0	0	0	0	0	0	0	0	0	0	0	0	0	0
PORTUGAL	0	0	0	0	0	0	0	0	0	0	0	0	0	0	0	0	0
SPAIN	0	0	0	0	0	0	0	0	0	0	0	0	0	0	0	0	0
SWEDEN	0	0	0	0	0	0	0	0	0	0	0	0	0	0	0	0	0
SWITZERLAND	0	0	0	0	0	0	0	0	0	0	0	0	0	0	0	0	0
TURKEY	0	0	0	0	0	0	0	0	0	0	0	0	0	0	0	0	0
OTHER EUROPE	0	0	0	0	0	0	1	0	0	1	0	0	0	0	2	0	2

TABLE   2 . 4 . 33   (CONTINUED)

COUNTRY OR REGION	NET FLOW UP TO 31-DEC-50	NO. OF ENTRIES DURING YEAR(S)													TOTAL ENTRIES 1951-75	TOTAL EXITS 1951-75	NET FLOW UP TO 1-JAN-76
		51-55	56-60	61-65	1966	1967	1968	1969	1970	1971	1972	1973	1974	1975			
N.AFR+M.EAST (TOTAL)	0	0	0	0	0	0	0	0	0	0	0	0	0	0	0	0	0
ALGERIA	0	0	0	0	0	0	0	0	0	0	0	0	0	0	0	0	0
EGYPT	0	0	0	0	0	0	0	0	0	0	0	0	0	0	0	0	0
IRAN	0	0	0	0	0	0	0	0	0	0	0	0	0	0	0	0	0
ISRAEL	0	0	0	0	0	0	0	0	0	0	0	0	0	0	0	0	0
LEBANON	0	0	0	0	0	0	0	0	0	0	0	0	0	0	0	0	0
MOROCCO	0	0	0	0	0	0	0	0	0	0	0	0	0	0	0	0	0
SAUDI ARABIA	0	0	0	0	0	0	0	0	0	0	0	0	0	0	0	0	0
OTHER N.AF+M.E.	0	0	0	0	0	0	0	0	0	0	0	0	0	0	0	0	0
E.+W.AFRICA (TOTAL)	0	0	0	0	0	0	0	0	0	0	0	0	0	0	0	0	0
GHANA	0	0	0	0	0	0	0	0	0	0	0	0	0	0	0	0	0
IVORY COAST	0	0	0	0	0	0	0	0	0	0	0	0	0	0	0	0	0
KENYA	0	0	0	0	0	0	0	0	0	0	0	0	0	0	0	0	0
LIBERIA	0	0	0	0	0	0	0	0	0	0	0	0	0	0	0	0	0
NIGERIA	0	0	0	0	0	0	0	0	0	0	0	0	0	0	0	0	0
ZAIRE	0	0	0	0	0	0	0	0	0	0	0	0	0	0	0	0	0
ZAMBIA	0	0	0	0	0	0	0	0	0	0	0	0	0	0	0	0	0
OTHER E.+W.AFR.	0	0	0	0	0	0	0	0	0	0	0	0	0	0	0	0	0
SOUTH ASIA (TOTAL)	0	0	1	2	0	0	0	0	0	0	0	0	0	0	3	0	3
INDIA	0	0	1	2	0	0	0	0	0	0	0	0	0	0	3	0	3
PAKISTAN	0	0	0	0	0	0	0	0	0	0	0	0	0	0	0	0	0
SRI LANKA	0	0	0	0	0	0	0	0	0	0	0	0	0	0	0	0	0
OTHER S.ASIA	0	0	0	0	0	0	0	0	0	0	0	0	0	0	0	0	0
EAST ASIA (TOTAL)	1	0	0	2	1	0	0	1	0	2	0	0	1	0	7	1	7
HONG KONG	0	0	0	1	0	0	0	1	0	0	0	0	0	0	2	1	1
INDONESIA	0	0	0	0	0	0	0	0	0	0	0	0	0	0	0	0	0
JAPAN	1	0	0	0	1	0	0	0	0	1	0	0	1	0	3	0	4
MALAYSIA	0	0	0	0	0	0	0	0	0	0	0	0	0	0	0	0	0
PHILIPPINES	0	0	0	1	0	0	0	0	0	1	0	0	0	0	2	0	2
SINGAPORE	0	0	0	0	0	0	0	0	0	0	0	0	0	0	0	0	0
S.KOREA	0	0	0	0	0	0	0	0	0	0	0	0	0	0	0	0	0
THAILAND	0	0	0	0	0	0	0	0	0	0	0	0	0	0	0	0	0
TAIWAN	0	0	0	0	0	0	0	0	0	0	0	0	0	0	0	0	0
OTHER E.ASIA	0	0	0	0	0	0	0	0	0	0	0	0	0	0	0	0	0
S.DOMINIONS (TOTAL)	0	0	3	0	0	0	1	0	0	0	0	0	0	0	4	2	2
AUSTRALIA	0	0	3	0	0	0	1	0	0	0	0	0	0	0	4	2	2
NEW ZEALAND	0	0	0	0	0	0	0	0	0	0	0	0	0	0	0	0	0
RHODESIA	0	0	0	0	0	0	0	0	0	0	0	0	0	0	0	0	0
S.AFRICA	0	0	0	0	0	0	0	0	0	0	0	0	0	0	0	0	0
OUTSIDE U.S. (TOTAL)	7	2	14	15	2	6	3	3	4	5	4	4	3	1	66	19	54

CHAPTER 2   - THE PROLIFERATION OF FOREIGN SUBSIDIARIES
SECTION 4   -- GEOGRAPHICAL SPREAD IN SPECIFIC INDUSTRIES
TABLE 34   --- ELEC TRANSMISSION EQUIP INDUSTRY (SIC 361)

NO. OF SUBSIDIARIES MANUFACTURING IN THIS INDUSTRY AT TIME OF ENTRY INTO PARENT SYSTEM

COUNTRY OR REGION	NET FLOW UP TO 31-DEC-50	NO. OF ENTRIES DURING YEAR(S)													TOTAL ENTRIES 1951-75	TOTAL EXITS 1951-75	NET FLOW UP TO 1-JAN-76
		51-55	56-60	61-65	1966	1967	1968	1969	1970	1971	1972	1973	1974	1975			
CANADA	0	1	5	1	0	0	0	2	0	1	0	0	3	0	13	3	10
LATIN AMER. (TOTAL)	2	0	3	2	0	0	4	0	0	0	1	0	0	0	10	6	6
C.AM.+CARIB. (TOTAL)	0	0	2	2	0	0	2	0	0	0	0	0	0	0	6	4	2
BAHAMAS	0	0	0	0	0	0	0	0	0	0	0	0	0	0	0	0	0
BERMUDA	0	0	0	0	0	0	0	0	0	0	0	0	0	0	0	0	0
COSTA RICA	0	0	0	0	0	0	0	0	0	0	0	0	0	0	0	0	0
GUATEMALA	0	0	0	0	0	0	0	0	0	0	0	0	0	0	0	0	0
JAMAICA	0	0	0	0	0	0	1	0	0	0	0	0	0	0	1	1	0
MEXICO	0	0	2	2	0	0	1	0	0	0	0	0	0	0	5	3	2
NETH.ANTILLES	0	0	0	0	0	0	0	0	0	0	0	0	0	0	0	0	0
NICARAGUA	0	0	0	0	0	0	0	0	0	0	0	0	0	0	0	0	0
PANAMA	0	0	0	0	0	0	0	0	0	0	0	0	0	0	0	0	0
OTHER C.AM+CAR.	0	0	0	0	0	0	0	0	0	0	0	0	0	0	0	0	0
S.AMERICA (TOTAL)	2	0	1	0	0	0	2	0	0	0	1	0	0	0	4	2	4
BOLIVIA	0	0	0	0	0	0	0	0	0	0	0	0	0	0	0	0	0
CHILE	0	0	0	0	0	0	0	0	0	0	0	0	0	0	0	0	0
COLOMBIA	0	0	0	0	0	0	0	0	0	0	0	0	0	0	0	0	0
ECUADOR	0	0	0	0	0	0	0	0	0	0	0	0	0	0	0	0	0
PERU	0	0	0	0	0	0	0	0	0	0	0	0	0	0	0	0	0
ARGENTINA	1	0	0	0	0	0	1	0	0	0	1	0	0	0	2	1	2
BRAZIL	1	0	1	0	0	0	0	0	0	0	0	0	0	0	1	1	1
URUGUAY	0	0	0	0	0	0	0	0	0	0	0	0	0	0	0	0	0
VENEZUELA	0	0	0	0	0	0	1	0	0	0	0	0	0	0	1	0	1
OTHER S.AMER.	0	0	0	0	0	0	0	0	0	0	0	0	0	0	0	0	0
EUROPE (TOTAL)	0	2	6	4	1	2	1	5	2	8	0	0	0	0	31	10	21
BELGIUM	0	2	0	0	0	0	0	0	0	0	0	0	0	0	2	2	0
FRANCE	0	0	1	0	0	0	0	1	0	1	0	0	0	0	3	1	2
GERMANY	0	0	1	0	0	0	1	2	1	0	0	0	0	0	5	3	2
ITALY	0	0	1	2	1	1	0	0	0	0	0	0	0	0	5	2	3
LUXEMBOURG	0	0	0	0	0	0	0	0	0	0	0	0	0	0	0	0	0
NETHERLANDS	0	0	0	2	0	0	0	0	0	0	0	0	0	0	2	0	2
DENMARK	0	0	0	0	0	0	0	0	0	0	0	0	0	0	0	0	0
IRELAND	0	0	0	0	0	0	0	0	0	0	0	0	0	0	0	0	0
U.K.	0	0	2	0	0	1	0	1	1	6	0	0	0	0	11	1	10
AUSTRIA	0	0	1	0	0	0	0	0	0	0	0	0	0	0	1	0	1
FINLAND	0	0	0	0	0	0	0	0	0	0	0	0	0	0	0	0	0
GREECE	0	0	0	0	0	0	0	0	0	0	0	0	0	0	0	0	0
NORWAY	0	0	0	0	0	0	0	0	0	0	0	0	0	0	0	0	0
PORTUGAL	0	0	0	0	0	0	0	0	0	0	0	0	0	0	0	0	0
SPAIN	0	0	0	0	0	0	0	1	0	0	0	0	0	0	1	0	1
SWEDEN	0	0	0	0	0	0	0	0	0	0	0	0	0	0	0	0	0
SWITZERLAND	0	0	0	0	0	0	0	0	0	0	0	0	0	0	0	0	0
TURKEY	0	0	0	0	0	0	0	0	0	1	0	0	0	0	1	1	0
OTHER EUROPE	0	0	0	0	0	0	0	0	0	0	0	0	0	0	0	0	0

TABLE 2 . 4 . 34 (CONTINUED)

COUNTRY OR REGION	NET FLOW UP TO 31-DEC-50	NO. OF ENTRIES DURING YEAR(S)													TOTAL ENTRIES 1951-75	TOTAL EXITS 1951-75	NET FLOW UP TO 1-JAN-76
		51-55	56-60	61-65	1966	1967	1968	1969	1970	1971	1972	1973	1974	1975			
N.AFR+M.EAST (TOTAL)	0	0	0	0	0	0	0	0	0	0	0	0	0	0	0	0	0
ALGERIA	0	0	0	0	0	0	0	0	0	0	0	0	0	0	0	0	0
EGYPT	0	0	0	0	0	0	0	0	0	0	0	0	0	0	0	0	0
IRAN	0	0	0	0	0	0	0	0	0	0	0	0	0	0	0	0	0
ISRAEL	0	0	0	0	0	0	0	0	0	0	0	0	0	0	0	0	0
LEBANON	0	0	0	0	0	0	0	0	0	0	0	0	0	0	0	0	0
MOROCCO	0	0	0	0	0	0	0	0	0	0	0	0	0	0	0	0	0
SAUDI ARABIA	0	0	0	0	0	0	0	0	0	0	0	0	0	0	0	0	0
OTHER N.AF+M.E.	0	0	0	0	0	0	0	0	0	0	0	0	0	0	0	0	0
E.+W.AFRICA (TOTAL)	0	0	0	0	0	0	0	0	0	0	0	0	0	0	0	0	0
GHANA	0	0	0	0	0	0	0	0	0	0	0	0	0	0	0	0	0
IVORY COAST	0	0	0	0	0	0	0	0	0	0	0	0	0	0	0	0	0
KENYA	0	0	0	0	0	0	0	0	0	0	0	0	0	0	0	0	0
LIBERIA	0	0	0	0	0	0	0	0	0	0	0	0	0	0	0	0	0
NIGERIA	0	0	0	0	0	0	0	0	0	0	0	0	0	0	0	0	0
ZAIRE	0	0	0	0	0	0	0	0	0	0	0	0	0	0	0	0	0
ZAMBIA	0	0	0	0	0	0	0	0	0	0	0	0	0	0	0	0	0
OTHER E.+W.AFR.	0	0	0	0	0	0	0	0	0	0	0	0	0	0	0	0	0
SOUTH ASIA (TOTAL)	0	0	0	0	0	0	0	0	0	0	0	0	0	0	0	0	0
INDIA	0	0	0	0	0	0	0	0	0	0	0	0	0	0	0	0	0
PAKISTAN	0	0	0	0	0	0	0	0	0	0	0	0	0	0	0	0	0
SRI LANKA	0	0	0	0	0	0	0	0	0	0	0	0	0	0	0	0	0
OTHER S.ASIA	0	0	0	0	0	0	0	0	0	0	0	0	0	0	0	0	0
EAST ASIA (TOTAL)	0	0	0	1	0	0	0	1	0	0	0	0	0	0	2	0	2
HONG KONG	0	0	0	1	0	0	0	0	0	0	0	0	0	0	1	0	1
INDONESIA	0	0	0	0	0	0	0	0	0	0	0	0	0	0	0	0	0
JAPAN	0	0	0	0	0	0	0	1	0	0	0	0	0	0	1	0	1
MALAYSIA	0	0	0	0	0	0	0	0	0	0	0	0	0	0	0	0	0
PHILIPPINES	0	0	0	0	0	0	0	0	0	0	0	0	0	0	0	0	0
SINGAPORE	0	0	0	0	0	0	0	0	0	0	0	0	0	0	0	0	0
S.KOREA	0	0	0	0	0	0	0	0	0	0	0	0	0	0	0	0	0
THAILAND	0	0	0	0	0	0	0	0	0	0	0	0	0	0	0	0	0
TAIWAN	0	0	0	0	0	0	0	0	0	0	0	0	0	0	0	0	0
OTHER E.ASIA	0	0	0	0	0	0	0	0	0	0	0	0	0	0	0	0	0
S.DOMINIONS (TOTAL)	0	0	1	1	0	0	0	1	0	0	2	0	1	1	7	1	6
AUSTRALIA	0	0	1	1	0	0	0	1	0	0	1	0	1	1	6	1	5
NEW ZEALAND	0	0	0	0	0	0	0	0	0	0	0	0	0	0	0	0	0
RHODESIA	0	0	0	0	0	0	0	0	0	0	0	0	0	0	0	0	0
S.AFRICA	0	0	0	0	0	0	0	0	0	0	1	0	0	0	1	0	1
OUTSIDE U.S. (TOTAL)	2	3	15	9	1	2	5	4	5	3	11	0	4	1	63	20	45

CHAPTER 2 - THE PROLIFERATION OF FOREIGN SUBSIDIARIES
SECTION 4 -- GEOGRAPHICAL SPREAD IN SPECIFIC INDUSTRIES
TABLE 35 --- RADIO,TV & APPLIANCES INDUSTRIES (SIC 365 AND 363)

NO. OF SUBSIDIARIES MANUFACTURING IN THIS INDUSTRY AT TIME OF ENTRY INTO PARENT SYSTEM

COUNTRY OR REGION	NET FLOW UP TO 31-DEC-50	NO. OF ENTRIES DURING YEAR(S)													TOTAL ENTRIES 1951-75	TOTAL EXITS 1951-75	NET FLOW UP TO 1-JAN-76
		51-55	56-60	61-65	1966	1967	1968	1969	1970	1971	1972	1973	1974	1975			
CANADA	5	0	1	5	0	3	2	2	2	0	1	0	2	1	19	7	17
LATIN AMER. (TOTAL)	5	2	7	8	3	4	1	0	2	1	1	0	3	0	32	9	28
C.AM.+CARIB.(TOTAL)	2	1	4	3	2	2	0	0	0	0	0	0	3	0	15	5	12
BAHAMAS	0	0	0	0	0	0	0	0	0	0	0	0	0	0	0	0	0
BERMUDA	0	0	0	0	0	0	0	0	0	0	0	0	0	0	0	0	0
COSTA RICA	0	0	0	0	2	0	0	0	0	0	0	0	0	0	2	1	1
GUATEMALA	0	0	0	0	0	0	0	0	0	0	0	0	0	0	0	0	0
JAMAICA	0	0	0	1	0	0	0	0	0	0	0	0	0	0	1	1	0
MEXICO	2	0	4	2	0	2	0	0	0	0	0	0	3	0	11	3	10
NETH.ANTILLES	0	0	0	0	0	0	0	0	0	0	0	0	0	0	0	0	0
NICARAGUA	0	0	0	0	0	0	0	0	0	0	0	0	0	0	0	0	0
PANAMA	0	1	0	1	0	0	0	0	0	0	0	0	0	0	1	0	1
OTHER C.AM+CAR.	0	0	0	0	0	0	0	0	0	0	0	0	0	0	0	0	0
S.AMERICA (TOTAL)	3	1	3	5	1	2	1	0	2	1	1	0	0	0	17	4	16
BOLIVIA	0	0	0	0	0	0	0	0	0	0	0	0	0	0	0	0	0
CHILE	0	0	0	0	1	0	0	0	0	1	0	0	0	0	1	0	1
COLOMBIA	0	0	1	0	0	0	0	0	0	0	0	0	0	0	1	0	1
ECUADOR	0	0	0	0	0	0	0	0	0	0	0	0	0	0	0	0	0
PERU	1	0	0	1	0	0	0	0	1	0	0	0	0	0	2	2	0
ARGENTINA	2	0	3	1	1	0	1	0	1	0	0	0	0	0	5	1	4
BRAZIL	2	0	0	2	0	2	0	0	0	0	0	0	0	0	3	0	4
URUGUAY	0	0	0	0	0	0	0	0	0	0	0	0	0	0	0	0	0
VENEZUELA	0	0	0	2	0	2	0	0	0	0	1	0	0	0	5	1	4
OTHER S.AMER.	0	0	0	0	0	0	0	0	0	0	0	0	0	0	0	0	0
EUROPE (TOTAL)	6	9	9	20	3	4	5	6	7	1	3	2	3	2	69	26	49
BELGIUM	0	0	0	0	0	0	0	2	2	0	0	0	1	0	2	5	2
FRANCE	0	0	2	5	0	0	0	0	3	3	1	0	1	1	13	5	8
GERMANY	1	2	2	4	3	3	3	1	0	1	0	0	0	0	16	9	7
ITALY	0	1	1	2	3	0	1	1	1	0	0	0	0	0	8	2	7
LUXEMBOURG	0	0	0	0	0	0	0	0	0	0	0	0	0	0	0	0	0
NETHERLANDS	0	0	0	0	0	0	0	0	0	0	0	0	2	0	2	0	2
DENMARK	0	0	0	0	0	0	0	1	0	1	0	0	0	0	2	0	2
IRELAND	0	0	0	0	0	0	0	0	0	0	1	0	0	0	1	0	1
U.K.	5	3	3	8	0	0	1	0	0	0	0	0	0	0	15	7	13
AUSTRIA	0	0	0	0	0	0	0	0	0	0	0	0	0	0	0	0	0
FINLAND	0	1	0	0	1	0	0	0	0	0	0	0	0	0	2	1	1
GREECE	0	1	0	0	0	0	0	0	0	0	0	0	0	0	0	0	1
NORWAY	0	0	0	0	0	0	0	0	0	0	0	0	0	0	1	0	1
PORTUGAL	0	0	2	0	0	0	0	0	1	0	0	0	0	0	0	1	0
SPAIN	0	0	0	0	0	0	0	0	0	0	0	0	4	0	4	0	1
SWEDEN	0	1	0	0	1	0	0	0	0	0	0	1	0	0	0	1	3
SWITZERLAND	0	0	1	0	0	0	0	0	0	0	0	0	0	0	1	0	0
TURKEY	0	0	0	0	0	0	0	0	0	0	0	0	0	0	1	0	0
OTHER EUROPE	0	0	0	0	0	0	0	0	0	0	0	0	0	0	0	0	0

TABLE 2 .4 .35 (CONTINUED)

COUNTRY OR REGION	NET FLOW UP TO 31-DEC-50	NO. OF ENTRIES DURING YEAR(S)													TOTAL ENTRIES 1951-75	TOTAL EXITS 1951-75	NET FLOW UP TO 1-JAN-76
		51-55	56-60	61-65	1966	1967	1968	1969	1970	1971	1972	1973	1974	1975			
N.AFR+M.EAST (TOTAL)	0	0	1	1	0	1	0	1	0	0	0	0	0	0	3	1	2
ALGERIA	0	0	0	0	0	0	0	0	0	0	0	0	0	0	0	0	0
EGYPT	0	0	0	0	0	0	0	0	0	0	0	0	0	0	0	0	0
IRAN	0	0	0	0	0	0	0	0	0	0	0	0	0	0	0	0	0
ISRAEL	0	0	0	0	0	0	0	0	0	0	0	0	0	0	0	0	0
LEBANON	0	0	0	0	0	1	0	1	0	0	0	0	0	0	1	0	1
MOROCCO	0	0	0	0	0	0	0	0	0	0	0	0	0	0	0	0	0
SAUDI ARABIA	0	0	1	1	0	0	0	0	0	0	0	0	0	0	1	1	0
OTHER N.AF+M.E.	0	0	0	0	0	1	0	0	0	0	0	0	0	0	1	0	1
E.+W.AFRICA (TOTAL)	0	1	1	2	0	1	0	1	0	0	0	0	1	0	6	1	5
GHANA	0	1	0	0	0	0	0	0	0	0	0	0	0	0	0	0	0
IVORY COAST	0	0	0	0	0	0	0	0	0	0	0	0	0	0	0	0	0
KENYA	0	0	0	1	0	1	0	0	0	0	0	0	0	0	1	1	0
LIBERIA	0	0	0	0	0	0	0	0	0	0	0	0	0	0	0	0	0
NIGERIA	0	0	1	0	0	0	0	1	0	0	0	0	0	0	2	0	2
ZAIRE	0	0	0	0	0	0	0	0	0	0	0	0	0	0	0	0	0
ZAMBIA	0	0	0	0	0	0	0	0	0	0	0	0	0	0	0	0	0
OTHER E.+W.AFR.	0	0	0	1	0	0	0	0	0	0	0	0	0	0	1	0	1
SOUTH ASIA (TOTAL)	0	0	3	3	0	2	0	0	2	0	0	0	0	0	7	2	5
INDIA	0	0	1	1	0	1	0	0	2	0	0	0	0	0	4	1	3
PAKISTAN	0	0	1	1	0	1	0	0	0	0	0	0	0	0	1	1	1
SRI LANKA	0	0	1	0	0	0	0	0	0	0	0	0	0	0	2	0	1
OTHER S.ASIA	0	0	0	0	0	0	0	0	0	0	0	0	0	0	0	0	0
EAST ASIA (TOTAL)	1	1	1	6	0	2	0	0	3	1	0	3	1	0	18	0	19
HONG KONG	1	0	0	0	0	0	0	0	0	0	0	1	0	0	3	0	3
INDONESIA	0	0	1	0	0	0	0	0	0	0	0	0	0	0	0	0	0
JAPAN	0	0	1	0	0	0	0	0	0	0	0	0	0	0	2	0	2
MALAYSIA	0	0	0	2	0	0	0	0	0	0	0	0	0	0	2	0	2
PHILIPPINES	0	0	0	2	0	0	0	0	1	0	0	0	1	1	4	0	5
SINGAPORE	0	0	0	2	0	0	0	0	2	0	0	0	0	0	2	0	2
S.KOREA	0	0	0	0	0	0	0	0	0	0	0	0	0	0	0	0	0
THAILAND	0	0	0	1	0	1	0	0	0	1	0	0	0	0	1	0	1
TAIWAN	0	0	0	1	0	0	0	0	0	0	0	1	0	0	4	0	4
OTHER E.ASIA	0	0	0	0	0	0	0	0	0	0	0	0	0	0	0	0	0
S.DOMINIONS (TOTAL)	0	0	0	3	0	0	0	0	0	0	0	0	0	0	3	2	1
AUSTRALIA	0	0	0	1	0	0	0	0	0	0	0	0	0	0	1	1	0
NEW ZEALAND	0	0	0	1	0	0	0	0	0	0	0	0	0	0	1	1	0
RHODESIA	0	0	0	0	0	0	0	0	0	0	0	0	0	0	0	0	0
S.AFRICA	0	0	0	1	0	0	0	0	0	0	0	0	0	0	1	0	1
OUTSIDE U.S. (TOTAL)	17	7	19	48	6	17	8	9	17	3	5	2	11	5	157	48	126

CHAPTER 2 — THE PROLIFERATION OF FOREIGN SUBSIDIARIES
SECTION 4 —— GEOGRAPHICAL SPREAD IN SPECIFIC INDUSTRIES
TABLE 36 ——— THE ELECTRONICS INDUSTRY (SIC 367)

NO. OF SUBSIDIARIES MANUFACTURING IN THIS INDUSTRY AT TIME OF ENTRY INTO PARENT SYSTEM

COUNTRY OR REGION	NET FLOW UP TO 31-DEC-50	51-55	56-60	61-65	1966	1967	1968	1969	1970	1971	1972	1973	1974	1975	TOTAL ENTRIES 1951-75	TOTAL EXITS 1951-75	NET FLOW UP TO 1-JAN-76
CANADA	1	0	2	2	0	0	1	0	0	0	0	0	1	1	7	4	4
LATIN AMER. (TOTAL)	0	0	3	4	0	1	3	1	0	4	0	7	2	0	25	6	19
C.AM.+CARIB. (TOTAL)	0	0	1	2	0	1	3	0	0	4	0	6	2	0	19	3	16
BAHAMAS	0	0	0	0	0	0	0	0	0	0	0	0	0	0	0	0	0
BERMUDA	0	0	0	0	0	0	0	0	0	0	0	0	0	0	0	0	0
COSTA RICA	0	0	1	0	0	0	0	0	0	0	0	0	0	0	1	0	1
GUATEMALA	0	0	0	0	0	0	0	0	0	0	0	0	0	0	0	0	0
JAMAICA	0	0	0	0	0	0	1	0	0	0	0	0	0	0	1	0	1
MEXICO	0	0	0	2	0	1	2	0	0	4	0	5	2	0	16	3	13
NETH.ANTILLES	0	0	0	0	0	0	0	0	0	0	0	0	0	0	0	0	0
NICARAGUA	0	0	0	0	0	0	0	0	0	0	0	0	0	0	0	0	0
PANAMA	0	0	0	0	0	0	0	0	0	0	0	1	0	0	1	0	1
OTHER C.AM+CAR.	—	0	0	0	0	0	0	0	0	0	0	0	0	0	—	—	—
S.AMERICA (TOTAL)	0	0	2	2	0	0	0	1	0	0	0	1	0	0	6	3	3
BOLIVIA	0	0	0	0	0	0	0	0	0	0	0	0	0	0	0	0	0
CHILE	0	0	0	0	0	0	0	0	0	0	0	0	0	0	0	0	0
COLOMBIA	0	0	0	0	0	0	0	0	0	0	0	0	0	0	0	0	0
ECUADOR	0	0	0	0	0	0	0	0	0	0	0	0	0	0	0	0	0
PERU	0	0	0	0	0	0	0	0	0	0	0	0	0	0	0	0	0
ARGENTINA	0	0	1	1	0	0	0	0	0	0	0	1	0	0	3	0	3
BRAZIL	0	0	1	1	0	0	0	1	0	0	0	0	0	0	3	3	0
URUGUAY	0	0	0	0	0	0	0	0	0	0	0	0	0	0	0	0	0
VENEZUELA	0	0	0	0	0	0	0	0	0	0	0	0	0	0	0	0	0
OTHER S.AMER.	0	0	0	0	0	0	0	0	0	0	0	0	0	0	0	0	0
EUROPE (TOTAL)	1	0	5	14	2	3	6	4	9	4	5	6	2	2	62	10	53
BELGIUM	0	0	0	0	0	0	1	1	1	0	0	1	0	0	4	1	3
FRANCE	0	0	3	4	0	1	1	1	2	1	0	1	0	0	14	2	12
GERMANY	0	0	2	4	0	0	1	1	1	2	2	0	0	0	13	1	12
ITALY	0	0	0	4	0	0	0	0	0	0	0	0	0	0	4	2	2
LUXEMBOURG	0	0	0	0	0	0	0	0	0	0	0	0	0	0	0	0	0
NETHERLANDS	0	0	0	0	0	0	0	0	0	0	1	0	0	0	1	0	1
DENMARK	0	0	0	0	0	0	0	0	0	0	0	0	0	0	0	0	0
IRELAND	0	0	0	0	0	1	0	0	0	0	0	0	0	1	2	0	2
U.K.	1	0	0	2	2	1	3	1	3	0	1	2	0	1	16	2	15
AUSTRIA	0	0	0	0	0	0	0	0	0	0	0	0	0	0	0	0	0
FINLAND	0	0	0	0	0	0	0	0	0	0	0	0	0	0	0	0	0
GREECE	0	0	0	0	0	0	0	0	0	0	0	0	0	0	0	0	0
NORWAY	0	0	0	0	0	0	0	0	0	0	0	0	0	0	0	0	0
PORTUGAL	0	0	0	0	0	0	0	0	2	0	0	2	0	0	4	0	4
SPAIN	0	0	0	0	0	0	0	0	0	0	0	0	1	0	1	1	0
SWEDEN	0	0	0	0	0	0	0	0	0	0	0	0	0	0	0	0	0
SWITZERLAND	0	0	0	0	0	0	0	0	0	1	0	0	1	0	2	1	1
TURKEY	0	0	0	0	0	0	0	0	0	0	1	0	0	0	1	0	1
OTHER EUROPE	0	0	0	0	0	0	0	0	0	0	0	0	0	0	0	0	0

TABLE 2 .4 .36 (CONTINUED)

COUNTRY OR REGION	NET FLOW UP TO 31-DEC-50	NO. OF ENTRIES DURING YEAR(S)													TOTAL ENTRIES 1951-75	TOTAL EXITS 1951-75	NET FLOW UP TO 1-JAN-76
		51-55	56-60	61-65	1966	1967	1968	1969	1970	1971	1972	1973	1974	1975			
N.AFR+M.EAST(TOTAL)	0	0	0	0	0	0	0	0	0	0	0	0	0	0	0	0	0
ALGERIA	0	0	0	0	0	0	0	0	0	0	0	0	0	0	0	0	0
EGYPT	0	0	0	0	0	0	0	0	0	0	0	0	0	0	0	0	0
IRAN	0	0	0	0	0	0	0	0	0	0	0	0	0	0	0	0	0
ISRAEL	0	0	0	0	0	0	0	0	0	0	0	0	0	0	0	0	0
LEBANON	0	0	0	0	0	0	0	0	0	0	0	0	0	0	0	0	0
MOROCCO	0	0	0	0	0	0	0	0	0	0	0	0	0	0	0	0	0
SAUDI ARABIA	0	0	0	0	0	0	0	0	0	0	0	0	0	0	0	0	0
OTHER N.AF+M.E.	0	0	0	0	0	0	0	0	0	0	0	0	0	0	0	0	0
E.+W.AFRICA (TOTAL)	0	0	0	0	0	1	0	0	0	0	0	1	0	0	2	0	2
GHANA	0	0	0	0	0	0	0	0	0	0	0	0	0	0	0	0	0
IVORY COAST	0	0	0	0	0	0	0	0	0	0	0	0	0	0	0	0	0
KENYA	0	0	0	0	0	0	0	0	0	0	0	0	0	0	0	0	0
LIBERIA	0	0	0	0	0	0	0	0	0	0	0	0	0	0	0	0	0
NIGERIA	0	0	0	0	0	1	0	0	0	0	0	0	0	0	1	0	1
ZAIRE	0	0	0	0	0	0	0	0	0	0	0	1	0	0	1	0	1
ZAMBIA	0	0	0	0	0	0	0	0	0	0	0	0	0	0	0	0	0
OTHER E.+W.AFR.	0	0	0	0	0	0	0	0	0	0	0	0	0	0	0	0	0
SOUTH ASIA (TOTAL)	0	0	0	0	0	0	0	0	0	0	0	0	0	0	0	0	0
INDIA	0	0	0	0	0	0	0	0	0	0	0	0	0	0	0	0	0
PAKISTAN	0	0	0	0	0	0	0	0	0	0	0	0	0	0	0	0	0
SRI LANKA	0	0	0	0	0	0	0	0	0	0	0	0	0	0	0	0	0
OTHER S.ASIA	0	0	0	0	0	0	0	0	0	0	0	0	0	0	0	0	0
EAST ASIA (TOTAL)	0	1	1	2	1	4	4	2	3	3	3	5	3	1	33	4	29
HONG KONG	0	0	0	0	0	0	0	0	0	0	0	1	0	1	2	0	2
INDONESIA	0	0	0	0	0	0	0	0	0	0	0	0	0	0	0	0	0
JAPAN	0	1	1	2	1	1	1	0	1	0	1	1	1	0	11	3	8
MALAYSIA	0	0	0	0	0	1	1	0	0	1	0	0	1	0	4	0	4
PHILIPPINES	0	0	0	0	0	0	0	0	0	0	0	0	0	0	0	0	0
SINGAPORE	0	0	0	0	0	1	0	0	1	0	0	1	0	0	3	0	3
S.KOREA	0	0	0	0	0	0	1	0	0	1	1	0	0	0	3	0	3
THAILAND	0	0	0	0	0	0	0	0	0	0	0	1	0	0	1	0	1
TAIWAN	0	0	0	0	0	1	1	2	1	1	1	1	1	0	9	1	8
OTHER E.ASIA	0	0	0	0	0	0	0	0	0	0	0	0	0	0	0	0	0
S.DOMINIONS (TOTAL)	0	2	2	0	0	0	0	0	0	0	0	0	0	1	5	1	4
AUSTRALIA	0	2	2	0	0	0	0	0	0	0	0	0	0	1	5	1	4
NEW ZEALAND	0	0	0	0	0	0	0	0	0	0	0	0	0	0	0	0	0
RHODESIA	0	0	0	0	0	0	0	0	0	0	0	0	0	0	0	0	0
S.AFRICA	0	0	0	0	0	0	0	0	0	0	0	0	0	0	0	0	0
OUTSIDE U.S.(TOTAL)	2	3	12	23	3	9	15	6	17	7	9	17	8	5	134	25	111

CHAPTER 2 - THE PROLIFERATION OF FOREIGN SUBSIDIARIES
SECTION 4 -- GEOGRAPHICAL SPREAD IN SPECIFIC INDUSTRIES
TABLE 37 --- OTHER ELECTRICAL INDUSTRIES (OTHER SIC 36)

NO. OF SUBSIDIARIES MANUFACTURING IN THIS INDUSTRY AT TIME OF ENTRY INTO PARENT SYSTEM

COUNTRY OR REGION	NET FLOW UP TO 31-DEC-50	NO. OF ENTRIES DURING YEAR(S)													TOTAL ENTRIES 1951-75	TOTAL EXITS 1951-75	NET FLOW UP TO 1-JAN-76
		51-55	56-60	61-65	1966	1967	1968	1969	1970	1971	1972	1973	1974	1975			
CANADA	10	6	4	0	1	2	1	1	1	1	1	1	1	1	21	17	14
LATIN AMER. (TOTAL)	10	5	9	16	0	3	5	2	5	1	8	3	2	1	60	16	54
C.AM.+CARIB.(TOTAL)	2	2	7	10	0	0	1	2	3	0	1	0	1	1	28	5	25
BAHAMAS	0	0	0	0	0	0	0	0	0	0	0	0	0	0	0	0	0
BERMUDA	0	0	0	1	0	0	0	0	1	0	0	0	0	0	2	0	2
COSTA RICA	0	0	0	0	0	0	0	0	0	0	0	0	0	0	0	0	0
GUATEMALA	0	0	0	0	0	0	0	0	0	0	0	0	0	0	0	0	0
JAMAICA	0	0	0	1	0	0	0	0	0	0	0	0	0	0	1	0	1
MEXICO	2	0	4	6	0	0	1	2	2	0	1	0	1	1	18	2	18
NETH.ANTILLES	0	0	0	0	0	0	0	0	0	0	0	0	0	0	0	0	0
NICARAGUA	0	0	0	1	0	0	0	0	0	0	0	0	0	0	1	0	1
PANAMA	0	1	2	0	0	0	0	0	0	0	0	0	0	0	3	1	2
OTHER C.AM+CAR.	0	1	1	1	0	0	0	0	0	0	0	0	0	0	3	2	1
S.AMERICA (TOTAL)	8	3	2	6	0	3	4	0	2	1	7	3	1	0	32	11	29
BOLIVIA	0	0	0	0	0	0	0	0	0	0	0	0	0	0	0	0	0
CHILE	1	0	0	0	0	0	0	0	0	0	0	0	0	0	0	1	0
COLOMBIA	1	0	0	0	0	0	0	0	1	0	0	0	0	0	1	0	2
ECUADOR	0	0	0	0	0	0	0	0	0	0	0	1	0	0	1	0	1
PERU	0	0	0	0	0	0	1	0	0	0	0	0	1	0	2	1	1
ARGENTINA	1	2	0	1	0	0	1	0	0	0	0	0	0	0	4	3	2
BRAZIL	4	0	1	4	0	3	2	0	1	1	5	2	0	0	19	4	19
URUGUAY	0	0	0	0	0	0	0	0	0	0	0	0	0	0	0	0	0
VENEZUELA	1	1	1	1	0	0	0	0	0	0	2	0	0	0	5	2	4
OTHER S.AMER.	0	0	0	0	0	0	0	0	0	0	0	0	0	0	0	0	0
EUROPE (TOTAL)	15	1	3	13	2	5	11	4	14	3	12	8	6	2	84	27	72
BELGIUM	0	0	0	3	2	0	0	0	0	0	0	0	1	0	6	2	4
FRANCE	4	1	1	3	0	1	2	0	4	0	2	0	0	0	14	9	9
GERMANY	1	0	1	3	0	0	2	0	3	1	2	0	0	0	12	2	11
ITALY	2	0	1	2	0	1	2	0	3	0	0	0	0	0	9	6	5
LUXEMBOURG	0	0	0	0	0	0	0	0	0	0	0	0	0	0	0	0	0
NETHERLANDS	0	0	0	0	0	0	0	0	0	0	0	1	0	0	1	0	1
DENMARK	0	0	0	0	0	0	0	0	0	0	0	0	0	0	0	0	0
IRELAND	0	0	0	0	0	0	0	0	1	0	0	0	0	0	1	0	1
U.K.	7	0	0	2	0	3	2	2	3	0	4	4	4	1	25	7	25
AUSTRIA	0	0	0	0	0	0	0	0	0	1	0	0	0	0	1	0	1
FINLAND	0	0	0	0	0	0	0	0	0	0	0	0	0	0	0	0	0
GREECE	0	0	0	0	0	0	0	1	0	0	0	0	0	0	1	0	1
NORWAY	1	0	0	0	0	0	0	0	0	0	0	0	0	0	0	1	0
PORTUGAL	0	0	0	0	0	0	1	0	0	0	0	1	1	0	3	0	3
SPAIN	0	0	0	0	0	0	1	1	0	1	1	1	0	0	5	0	5
SWEDEN	0	0	0	0	0	0	1	0	0	0	2	1	0	0	4	0	4
SWITZERLAND	0	0	0	0	0	0	0	0	0	0	0	0	0	1	1	0	1
TURKEY	0	0	0	0	0	0	0	0	0	0	0	0	0	0	0	0	0
OTHER EUROPE	0	0	0	0	0	0	0	0	0	0	1	0	0	0	1	0	1

TABLE 2 .4 .37 (CONTINUED)

COUNTRY OR REGION	NET FLOW UP TO 31-DEC-50	51-55	56-60	61-65	1966	1967	1968	1969	1970	1971	1972	1973	1974	1975	TOTAL ENTRIES 1951-75	TOTAL EXITS 1951-75	NET FLOW UP TO 1-JAN-76
N.AFR+M.EAST(TOTAL)	0	0	0	0	0	0	0	1	1	0	0	0	2	0	4	1	3
ALGERIA	0	0	0	0	0	0	0	0	0	0	0	0	0	0	0	0	0
EGYPT	0	0	0	0	0	0	0	0	0	0	0	0	0	0	0	0	0
IRAN	0	0	0	0	0	0	0	1	0	0	0	0	1	0	3	1	2
ISRAEL	0	0	0	0	0	0	0	0	0	0	0	0	0	0	0	0	0
LEBANON	0	0	0	0	0	0	0	0	0	0	0	0	0	0	0	0	0
MOROCCO	0	0	0	0	0	0	0	0	0	0	0	0	0	0	0	0	0
SAUDI ARABIA	0	0	0	0	0	0	0	0	0	0	0	0	0	0	0	0	0
OTHER N.AF+M.E.	0	0	0	0	0	0	0	0	1	0	0	0	1	0	1	0	1
E.+W.AFRICA (TOTAL)	0	0	0	0	0	2	0	1	2	0	1	1	1	0	5	0	5
GHANA	0	0	0	0	0	1	0	1	1	0	1	1	0	0	1	0	1
IVORY COAST	0	0	0	0	0	0	0	0	1	0	0	0	0	0	1	0	1
KENYA	0	0	0	0	0	1	0	1	1	0	0	0	1	0	1	0	1
LIBERIA	0	0	0	0	0	0	0	0	0	0	0	0	0	0	0	0	0
NIGERIA	0	0	0	0	0	0	0	0	0	0	0	0	1	0	1	0	1
ZAIRE	0	0	0	0	0	0	0	0	0	1	1	0	0	0	1	0	1
ZAMBIA	0	0	0	0	0	0	0	0	0	0	0	0	0	0	0	0	0
OTHER E.+W.AFR.	0	0	0	0	0	0	0	0	0	0	0	0	0	0	0	0	0
SOUTH ASIA (TOTAL)	1	0	0	3	0	0	0	1	2	0	0	1	0	0	7	1	7
INDIA	1	0	0	3	0	0	0	0	1	0	0	1	0	0	5	1	5
PAKISTAN	0	0	0	0	0	0	0	0	1	0	0	0	0	0	1	0	1
SRI LANKA	0	0	0	0	0	0	0	1	0	0	0	0	0	0	1	0	1
OTHER S.ASIA	0	0	0	0	0	0	0	0	0	0	0	0	0	0	0	0	0
EAST ASIA (TOTAL)	1	3	3	6	1	2	4	1	3	3	2	3	1	1	33	9	25
HONG KONG	0	1	1	0	1	0	0	0	0	0	0	0	1	0	4	1	3
INDONESIA	0	0	0	1	0	0	1	0	0	0	0	0	0	0	2	2	1
JAPAN	0	1	1	2	0	1	2	0	1	0	2	1	1	1	14	2	12
MALAYSIA	0	0	0	0	0	0	0	0	0	0	0	1	0	0	3	0	3
PHILIPPINES	1	1	0	1	0	0	0	0	0	0	0	0	0	0	1	1	0
SINGAPORE	0	0	0	0	0	0	0	1	0	1	0	1	0	0	4	1	4
S.KOREA	0	0	0	0	0	0	0	0	1	0	0	0	0	0	0	0	0
THAILAND	0	0	1	0	0	1	0	0	1	0	0	0	0	0	3	2	1
TAIWAN	0	0	0	1	0	0	0	0	0	0	0	0	0	0	2	1	1
OTHER E.ASIA	0	0	0	0	0	0	0	0	0	0	0	0	0	0	0	0	0
S.DOMINIONS (TOTAL)	3	2	1	2	0	1	2	1	2	1	2	2	0	0	15	4	14
AUSTRALIA	2	1	1	1	0	1	2	1	1	1	1	0	0	0	10	3	9
NEW ZEALAND	1	0	0	1	0	0	0	1	0	0	0	0	0	0	0	0	1
RHODESIA	0	0	0	0	0	0	0	0	0	0	0	0	0	0	1	1	0
S.AFRICA	0	1	0	0	0	0	0	0	1	1	0	0	0	0	4	0	4
OUTSIDE U.S. (TOTAL)	40	16	21	40	4	15	23	12	27	9	26	18	13	5	229	75	194

CHAPTER 2 - THE PROLIFERATION OF FOREIGN SUBSIDIARIES
SECTION 4 -- GEOGRAPHICAL SPREAD IN SPECIFIC INDUSTRIES
TABLE 38 --- COMMUNICATION EQUIP INDUSTRY (SIC 366)

NO. OF SUBSIDIARIES MANUFACTURING IN THIS INDUSTRY AT TIME OF ENTRY INTO PARENT SYSTEM

COUNTRY OR REGION	NET FLOW UP TO 31-DEC-50	NO. OF ENTRIES DURING YEAR(S)													TOTAL ENTRIES 1951-75	TOTAL EXITS 1951-75	NET FLOW UP TO 1-JAN-76
		51-55	56-60	61-65	1966	1967	1968	1969	1970	1971	1972	1973	1974	1975			
CANADA	2	3	0	2	0	0	1	0	0	0	0	2	0	0	8	1	9
LATIN AMER. (TOTAL)	1	0	0	1	0	1	1	1	2	0	1	2	2	0	11	3	9
C.AM.+CARIB.(TOTAL)	0	0	0	0	0	1	0	1	0	0	0	2	0	0	4	1	3
BAHAMAS	0	0	0	0	0	0	0	0	0	0	0	0	0	0	0	0	0
BERMUDA	0	0	0	0	0	0	0	0	0	0	0	0	0	0	0	0	0
COSTA RICA	0	0	0	0	0	0	0	0	0	0	0	0	0	0	0	0	0
GUATEMALA	0	0	0	0	0	0	0	0	0	0	0	0	0	0	0	0	0
JAMAICA	0	0	0	0	0	0	0	0	0	0	0	0	0	0	0	0	0
MEXICO	0	0	0	0	0	1	0	1	0	0	0	2	0	0	4	1	3
NETH.ANTILLES	0	0	0	0	0	0	0	0	0	0	0	0	0	0	0	0	0
NICARAGUA	0	0	0	0	0	0	0	0	0	0	0	0	0	0	0	0	0
PANAMA	0	0	0	0	0	0	0	0	0	0	0	0	0	0	0	0	0
OTHER C.AM+CAR.	0	0	0	0	0	0	0	0	0	0	0	0	0	0	0	0	0
S.AMERICA (TOTAL)	1	0	0	1	0	0	1	0	2	0	1	0	2	0	7	2	6
BOLIVIA	0	0	0	0	0	0	0	0	0	0	0	0	0	0	0	0	0
CHILE	0	0	0	0	0	0	0	0	1	0	0	0	0	0	1	0	1
COLOMBIA	0	0	0	0	0	0	0	0	0	0	0	0	0	0	0	0	0
ECUADOR	0	0	0	0	0	0	0	0	0	0	0	0	0	0	0	0	0
PERU	0	0	0	0	0	0	0	0	0	0	0	0	0	0	0	0	0
ARGENTINA	1	0	0	0	0	0	0	0	0	0	1	0	0	0	1	1	1
BRAZIL	0	0	0	0	0	0	1	0	1	0	0	0	1	0	3	1	2
URUGUAY	0	0	0	0	0	0	0	0	0	0	0	0	0	0	0	0	0
VENEZUELA	0	0	0	0	0	0	0	0	0	0	0	0	1	0	1	0	1
OTHER S.AMER.	0	0	0	1	0	0	0	0	0	0	0	0	0	0	1	0	1
EUROPE (TOTAL)	13	5	5	7	1	2	10	3	8	0	0	0	0	0	41	15	39
BELGIUM	0	3	1	0	0	0	0	0	0	0	0	0	0	0	4	0	4
FRANCE	3	0	1	0	0	0	3	1	1	0	0	0	0	0	6	3	6
GERMANY	2	0	1	1	0	0	2	1	1	0	0	0	0	0	6	1	7
ITALY	0	1	2	1	1	1	0	0	1	0	0	0	0	0	7	4	3
LUXEMBOURG	0	0	0	0	0	0	0	0	0	0	0	0	0	0	0	0	0
NETHERLANDS	1	0	0	0	0	0	1	0	0	0	0	0	0	0	1	0	2
DENMARK	0	0	0	0	0	0	0	0	0	0	0	0	0	0	0	0	0
IRELAND	0	0	0	0	0	0	0	0	0	0	0	0	0	0	0	0	0
U.K.	2	1	0	3	0	0	3	1	1	0	0	0	0	0	9	4	7
AUSTRIA	1	0	0	0	0	0	1	0	1	0	0	0	0	0	2	1	2
FINLAND	0	0	0	0	0	0	0	0	1	0	0	0	0	0	1	0	1
GREECE	0	0	0	1	0	0	0	0	0	0	0	0	0	0	1	0	1
NORWAY	0	0	0	0	0	0	0	0	0	0	0	0	0	0	0	0	0
PORTUGAL	1	0	0	0	0	0	0	0	0	0	0	0	0	0	0	1	0
SPAIN	1	0	0	0	0	1	0	0	2	0	0	0	0	0	3	0	4
SWEDEN	2	0	0	0	0	0	0	0	0	0	0	0	0	0	0	1	1
SWITZERLAND	0	0	0	1	0	0	0	0	0	0	0	0	0	0	1	0	1
TURKEY	0	0	0	0	0	0	0	0	0	0	0	0	0	0	0	0	0
OTHER EUROPE	0	0	0	0	0	0	0	0	0	0	0	0	0	0	0	0	0

TABLE 2 .4 .38 (CONTINUED)

COUNTRY OR REGION	NET FLOW UP TO 31-DEC-50	NO. OF ENTRIES DURING YEAR(S)													TOTAL ENTRIES 1951-75	TOTAL EXITS 1951-75	NET FLOW UP TO 1-JAN-76
		51-55	56-60	61-65	1966	1967	1968	1969	1970	1971	1972	1973	1974	1975			
N.AFR+M.EAST (TOTAL)	0	0	0	0	0	0	0	1	0	0	0	0	0	0	1	0	1
ALGERIA	0	0	0	0	0	0	0	0	0	0	0	0	0	0	0	0	0
EGYPT	0	0	0	0	0	0	0	0	0	0	0	0	0	0	0	0	0
IRAN	0	0	0	0	0	0	0	0	0	0	0	0	0	0	0	0	0
ISRAEL	0	0	0	0	0	0	0	0	0	0	0	0	0	0	0	0	0
LEBANON	0	0	0	0	0	0	0	1	0	0	0	0	0	0	1	0	1
MOROCCO	0	0	0	0	0	0	0	0	0	0	0	0	0	0	0	0	0
SAUDI ARABIA	0	0	0	0	0	0	0	0	0	0	0	0	0	0	0	0	0
OTHER N.AF+M.E.	0	0	0	0	0	0	0	0	0	0	0	0	0	0	0	0	0
E.+W.AFRICA (TOTAL)	0	0	0	0	0	1	0	0	0	0	0	1	0	0	2	0	2
GHANA	0	0	0	0	0	0	0	0	0	0	0	0	0	0	0	0	0
IVORY COAST	0	0	0	0	0	0	0	0	0	0	0	0	0	0	0	0	0
KENYA	0	0	0	0	0	0	0	0	0	0	0	0	0	0	0	0	0
LIBERIA	0	0	0	0	0	0	0	0	0	0	0	0	0	0	0	0	0
NIGERIA	0	0	0	0	0	0	0	0	0	0	0	0	0	0	0	0	0
ZAIRE	0	0	0	0	0	1	0	0	0	0	0	0	0	0	1	0	1
ZAMBIA	0	0	0	0	0	0	0	0	0	0	0	1	0	0	1	0	1
OTHER E.+W.AFR.	0	0	0	0	0	0	0	0	0	0	0	0	0	0	0	0	0
SOUTH ASIA (TOTAL)	0	0	0	0	0	0	0	0	0	0	0	0	0	0	0	0	0
INDIA	0	0	0	0	0	0	0	0	0	0	0	0	0	0	0	0	0
PAKISTAN	0	0	0	0	0	0	0	0	0	0	0	0	0	0	0	0	0
SRI LANKA	0	0	0	0	0	0	0	0	0	0	0	0	0	0	0	0	0
OTHER S.ASIA	0	0	0	0	0	0	0	0	0	0	0	0	0	0	0	0	0
EAST ASIA (TOTAL)	0	0	1	1	0	1	0	1	0	1	0	3	1	1	10	2	8
HONG KONG	0	0	0	0	0	0	0	1	0	0	0	0	0	0	1	0	1
INDONESIA	0	0	0	0	0	0	0	0	0	0	0	0	0	0	0	0	0
JAPAN	0	0	0	1	0	0	0	0	0	0	0	0	0	0	1	1	0
MALAYSIA	0	0	0	0	0	0	0	0	0	0	0	0	0	0	0	0	0
PHILIPPINES	0	0	0	0	0	0	0	0	0	0	0	3	0	0	3	0	3
SINGAPORE	0	0	0	0	0	1	0	0	0	0	0	0	0	0	1	0	1
S.KOREA	0	0	0	0	0	0	0	0	0	0	0	0	0	0	0	0	0
THAILAND	0	0	0	0	0	0	0	0	0	0	0	0	1	0	1	0	1
TAIWAN	0	0	1	0	0	0	0	0	0	1	0	0	0	1	3	1	2
OTHER E.ASIA	0	0	0	0	0	0	0	0	0	0	0	0	0	0	0	0	0
S.DOMINIONS (TOTAL)	2	0	1	1	0	0	0	0	0	0	0	1	0	0	3	2	3
AUSTRALIA	1	0	1	0	0	0	0	0	0	0	0	0	0	0	1	0	2
NEW ZEALAND	1	0	0	0	0	0	0	0	0	0	0	0	0	0	0	1	0
RHODESIA	0	0	0	0	0	0	0	0	0	0	0	1	0	0	1	1	0
S.AFRICA	0	0	0	1	0	0	0	0	0	0	0	0	0	0	1	0	1
OUTSIDE U.S. (TOTAL)	18	6	7	13	1	5	12	6	10	1	1	9	4	1	76	23	71

CHAPTER 2 - THE PROLIFERATION OF FOREIGN SUBSIDIARIES
SECTION 4 -- GEOGRAPHICAL SPREAD IN SPECIFIC INDUSTRIES
TABLE 39 --- THE MOTOR VEHIC INDUSTRY (SIC 371)

NO. OF SUBSIDIARIES MANUFACTURING IN THIS INDUSTRY AT TIME OF ENTRY INTO PARENT SYSTEM

COUNTRY OR REGION	NET FLOW UP TO 31-DEC-50	NO. OF ENTRIES DURING YEAR(S)													TOTAL ENTRIES 1951-75	TOTAL EXITS 1951-75	NET FLOW UP TO 1-JAN-76
		51-55	56-60	61-65	1966	1967	1968	1969	1970	1971	1972	1973	1974	1975			
CANADA	16	2	4	14	4	2	4	0	5	1	5	8	0	0	49	26	39
LATIN AMER. (TOTAL)	3	5	22	40	6	10	4	5	2	3	8	9	3	3	120	36	87
C.AM.+CARIB. (TOTAL)	1	1	8	11	2	0	1	1	0	1	1	2	0	1	29	10	20
BAHAMAS	0	0	0	0	0	0	0	0	0	0	0	0	0	0	0	0	0
BERMUDA	0	0	0	0	0	0	0	0	0	0	0	0	0	1	1	1	0
COSTA RICA	0	0	0	1	0	0	0	0	0	0	0	0	0	0	1	0	0
GUATEMALA	0	0	0	0	0	0	0	0	0	0	0	0	0	0	0	0	0
JAMAICA	0	0	0	0	0	0	0	0	0	0	0	0	0	0	0	0	0
MEXICO	1	1	8	10	2	0	1	1	0	1	1	2	0	0	27	8	20
NETH.ANTILLES	0	0	0	0	0	0	0	0	0	0	0	0	0	0	0	0	0
NICARAGUA	0	0	0	0	0	0	0	0	0	0	0	0	0	0	0	0	0
PANAMA	0	0	0	1	0	0	0	0	0	0	0	0	0	0	1	1	0
OTHER C.AM+CAR.	0	0	0	0	0	0	0	0	0	0	0	0	0	0	0	0	0
S.AMERICA (TOTAL)	2	4	14	29	4	10	3	4	2	2	7	7	3	2	91	26	67
BOLIVIA	0	0	0	0	0	0	0	0	0	0	0	0	0	0	0	0	0
CHILE	0	0	0	1	0	1	0	0	0	0	0	0	0	1	3	2	1
COLOMBIA	0	0	0	5	1	1	1	0	0	0	0	1	0	0	10	2	8
ECUADOR	0	0	0	0	0	0	0	0	0	0	0	0	0	2	2	0	0
PERU	0	1	1	2	4	0	0	0	0	0	4	0	0	1	13	11	2
ARGENTINA	2	2	5	13	2	0	0	1	2	1	4	3	3	0	36	10	14
BRAZIL	0	1	8	4	2	3	1	3	0	1	0	0	0	0	13	0	28
URUGUAY	0	0	0	1	0	0	0	0	0	0	1	0	0	0	2	1	2
VENEZUELA	0	0	1	4	1	0	2	0	0	0	1	0	0	0	12	0	12
OTHER S.AMER.	0	0	0	0	0	0	0	0	0	0	0	0	0	0	0	0	0
EUROPE (TOTAL)	18	4	18	32	16	8	12	6	13	5	20	17	6	7	164	54	128
BELGIUM	1	0	1	1	0	0	2	0	0	0	1	1	0	0	6	0	7
FRANCE	4	2	11	7	1	0	3	0	5	0	2	2	0	0	33	17	20
GERMANY	1	0	2	5	1	2	2	2	5	3	3	1	0	0	26	4	23
ITALY	1	0	2	3	1	2	2	2	2	1	4	3	0	0	21	6	16
LUXEMBOURG	0	0	0	0	0	0	0	0	0	0	0	0	0	0	0	0	0
NETHERLANDS	1	0	0	0	0	0	0	0	0	1	0	0	0	1	6	1	6
DENMARK	1	0	0	1	0	0	0	0	0	0	0	1	0	0	3	0	4
IRELAND	0	1	0	1	0	0	0	0	0	0	0	0	0	0	3	0	3
U.K.	8	1	1	9	12	2	0	1	2	3	3	7	5	0	46	19	35
AUSTRIA	0	0	0	0	0	0	1	0	0	0	0	0	0	0	1	0	1
FINLAND	0	0	0	0	0	0	0	0	0	0	0	0	0	1	1	1	0
GREECE	0	0	0	1	0	0	0	0	0	0	0	0	0	0	1	1	0
NORWAY	0	0	0	0	0	0	0	0	0	1	0	0	0	0	1	0	1
PORTUGAL	1	0	0	0	0	0	0	0	0	0	0	1	1	0	0	0	1
SPAIN	0	0	2	3	0	0	0	1	0	1	1	0	1	0	9	2	8
SWEDEN	0	0	0	1	0	0	0	0	0	0	0	0	0	0	2	2	2
SWITZERLAND	0	0	0	1	0	1	0	0	0	0	0	0	0	0	3	0	0
TURKEY	0	1	1	0	0	0	0	0	0	0	0	0	0	0	0	0	1
OTHER EUROPE	0	0	0	0	0	0	0	0	0	0	0	0	0	0	0	0	0

TABLE 2.4.39 (CONTINUED)

COUNTRY OR REGION	NET FLOW UP TO 31-DEC-50	NO. OF ENTRIES DURING YEAR(S)													TOTAL ENTRIES 1951-75	TOTAL EXITS 1951-75	NET FLOW UP TO 1-JAN-76
		51-55	56-60	61-65	1966	1967	1968	1969	1970	1971	1972	1973	1974	1975			
N.AFR+M.EAST (TOTAL)	1	0	1	0	0	1	0	0	0	0	0	1	1	0	4	1	4
ALGERIA	0	0	1	0	0	0	0	0	0	0	0	0	0	0	1	0	1
EGYPT	0	0	0	0	0	0	0	0	0	0	0	0	0	0	0	0	0
IRAN	0	0	0	0	0	0	0	0	0	0	0	1	0	0	1	0	1
ISRAEL	1	0	0	0	0	0	0	0	0	0	0	0	0	0	0	1	0
LEBANON	0	0	0	0	0	0	0	0	0	0	0	0	0	0	0	0	0
MOROCCO	0	0	0	0	0	1	0	0	0	0	0	0	0	0	1	0	1
SAUDI ARABIA	0	0	0	0	0	0	0	0	0	0	0	0	1	0	1	0	1
OTHER N.AF+M.E.	0	0	0	0	0	0	0	0	0	0	0	0	0	0	0	0	0
E.+W.AFRICA (TOTAL)	0	0	0	0	0	0	0	0	0	1	1	0	0	0	2	1	1
GHANA	0	0	0	0	0	0	0	0	0	0	0	0	0	0	0	0	0
IVORY COAST	0	0	0	0	0	0	0	0	0	0	0	0	0	0	0	0	0
KENYA	0	0	0	0	0	0	0	0	0	0	0	0	0	0	0	0	0
LIBERIA	0	0	0	0	0	0	0	0	0	0	0	0	0	0	0	0	0
NIGERIA	0	0	0	0	0	0	0	0	0	1	0	0	0	0	1	1	0
ZAIRE	0	0	0	0	0	0	0	0	0	0	0	0	0	0	0	0	0
ZAMBIA	0	0	0	0	0	0	0	0	0	0	1	0	0	0	1	0	1
OTHER E.+W.AFR.	0	0	0	0	0	0	0	0	0	0	0	0	0	0	0	0	0
SOUTH ASIA (TOTAL)	1	0	1	3	1	0	0	0	0	0	0	0	0	0	5	2	4
INDIA	1	0	1	3	1	0	0	0	0	0	0	0	0	0	5	2	4
PAKISTAN	0	0	0	0	0	0	0	0	0	0	0	0	0	0	0	0	0
SRI LANKA	0	0	0	0	0	0	0	0	0	0	0	0	0	0	0	0	0
OTHER S.ASIA	0	0	0	0	0	0	0	0	0	0	0	0	0	0	0	0	0
EAST ASIA (TOTAL)	0	0	0	6	0	1	0	4	3	3	8	3	1	0	29	1	28
HONG KONG	0	0	0	0	0	1	0	0	0	0	0	0	0	0	1	1	0
INDONESIA	0	0	0	0	0	0	0	0	0	0	0	0	0	0	0	0	0
JAPAN	0	0	0	6	0	0	0	4	2	1	3	2	0	0	18	0	18
MALAYSIA	0	0	0	0	0	0	0	0	0	1	0	0	0	0	1	0	1
PHILIPPINES	0	0	0	0	0	0	0	0	0	0	3	0	0	0	3	0	3
SINGAPORE	0	0	0	0	0	0	0	0	0	0	0	0	0	0	0	0	0
S.KOREA	0	0	0	0	0	0	0	0	1	0	0	0	1	0	2	0	2
THAILAND	0	0	0	0	0	0	0	0	0	1	2	0	0	0	3	0	3
TAIWAN	0	0	0	0	0	0	0	0	0	0	0	1	0	0	1	0	1
OTHER E.ASIA	0	0	0	0	0	0	0	0	0	0	0	0	0	0	0	0	0
S.DOMINIONS (TOTAL)	3	2	7	10	1	5	3	4	1	1	2	4	1	5	47	12	38
AUSTRALIA	1	2	5	4	1	3	3	4	1	1	0	2	1	0	24	7	18
NEW ZEALAND	1	0	2	1	0	0	0	0	0	1	0	0	0	0	4	0	5
RHODESIA	0	0	0	0	0	0	0	0	0	0	0	0	0	0	1	0	1
S.AFRICA	1	0	0	5	0	2	0	0	0	1	2	2	0	2	18	5	14
OUTSIDE U.S. (TOTAL)	42	13	53	106	28	27	23	19	24	13	44	42	13	15	420	133	329

CHAPTER 2   - THE PROLIFERATION OF FOREIGN SUBSIDIARIES
SECTION 4   -- GEOGRAPHICAL SPREAD IN SPECIFIC INDUSTRIES
TABLE 40   --- OTHER TRANSPORTATION INDUSTRIES (OTHER SIC 37)

NO. OF SUBSIDIARIES MANUFACTURING IN THIS INDUSTRY AT TIME OF ENTRY INTO PARENT SYSTEM

COUNTRY OR REGION	NET FLOW UP TO 31-DEC-50	NO. OF ENTRIES DURING YEAR(S)													TOTAL ENTRIES 1951-75	TOTAL EXITS 1951-75	NET FLOW UP TO 1-JAN-76
		51-55	56-60	61-65	1966	1967	1968	1969	1970	1971	1972	1973	1974	1975			
CANADA	3	1	1	2	1	0	3	0	0	0	1	1	1	0	11	5	9
LATIN AMER. (TOTAL)	0	0	1	0	0	0	2	0	2	0	0	4	0	1	10	2	8
C.AM.+CARIB.(TOTAL)	0	0	1	0	0	0	1	0	0	0	0	2	0	0	4	1	3
BAHAMAS	0	0	0	0	0	0	0	0	0	0	0	0	0	0	0	0	0
BERMUDA	0	0	0	0	0	0	0	0	0	0	0	0	0	0	0	0	0
COSTA RICA	0	0	0	0	0	0	0	0	0	0	0	0	0	0	0	0	0
GUATEMALA	0	0	0	0	0	0	0	0	0	0	0	0	0	0	0	0	0
JAMAICA	0	0	0	0	0	0	0	0	0	0	0	0	0	0	0	0	0
MEXICO	0	0	1	0	0	0	1	0	0	0	0	2	0	0	4	1	3
NETH.ANTILLES	0	0	0	0	0	0	0	0	0	0	0	0	0	0	0	0	0
NICARAGUA	0	0	0	0	0	0	0	0	0	0	0	0	0	0	0	0	0
PANAMA	0	0	0	0	0	0	0	0	0	0	0	0	0	0	0	0	0
OTHER C.AM+CAR.	0	0	0	0	0	0	0	0	0	0	0	0	0	0	0	0	0
S.AMERICA (TOTAL)	0	0	0	0	0	0	1	0	2	0	0	2	0	1	6	1	5
BOLIVIA	0	0	0	0	0	0	0	0	0	0	0	0	0	0	0	0	0
CHILE	0	0	0	0	0	0	0	0	0	0	0	0	0	0	0	0	0
COLOMBIA	0	0	0	0	0	0	0	0	0	0	0	0	0	0	0	0	0
ECUADOR	0	0	0	0	0	0	0	0	0	0	0	0	0	0	0	0	0
PERU	0	0	0	0	0	0	0	0	1	0	0	0	0	0	1	0	1
ARGENTINA	0	0	0	0	0	0	1	0	1	0	0	2	0	1	5	1	4
BRAZIL	0	0	0	0	0	0	0	0	0	0	0	0	0	0	0	0	0
URUGUAY	0	0	0	0	0	0	0	0	0	0	0	0	0	0	0	0	0
VENEZUELA	0	0	0	0	0	0	0	0	0	0	0	0	0	0	0	0	0
OTHER S.AMER.	0	0	0	0	0	0	0	0	0	0	0	0	0	0	0	0	0
EUROPE (TOTAL)	2	1	5	1	0	2	4	3	2	8	0	3	3	1	33	12	23
BELGIUM	0	0	0	0	0	0	1	0	0	0	0	0	0	0	1	0	1
FRANCE	0	0	2	0	0	1	1	0	0	4	0	1	1	0	10	2	8
GERMANY	1	0	1	1	0	0	0	0	0	2	0	0	0	0	4	3	2
ITALY	0	0	1	0	0	0	0	0	2	0	0	0	0	0	3	1	2
LUXEMBOURG	0	0	0	0	0	0	0	0	0	0	0	0	0	0	0	0	0
NETHERLANDS	0	0	0	0	0	0	0	2	0	0	0	0	0	0	2	1	1
DENMARK	0	0	0	0	0	0	0	0	0	0	0	0	0	0	0	0	0
IRELAND	0	0	0	0	0	0	0	0	0	0	0	0	0	0	0	0	0
U.K.	1	1	1	0	0	1	2	0	0	2	0	0	1	1	9	3	7
AUSTRIA	0	0	0	0	0	0	0	0	0	0	0	0	0	0	0	0	0
FINLAND	0	0	0	0	0	0	0	0	0	0	0	0	0	0	0	0	0
GREECE	0	0	0	0	0	0	0	0	0	0	0	0	0	0	0	0	0
NORWAY	0	0	0	0	0	0	0	0	0	0	0	0	0	0	0	0	0
PORTUGAL	0	0	0	0	0	0	0	1	0	0	0	0	0	0	1	1	0
SPAIN	0	0	0	0	0	0	0	0	0	0	0	2	0	0	2	1	1
SWEDEN	0	0	0	0	0	0	0	0	0	0	0	0	1	0	1	0	1
SWITZERLAND	0	0	0	0	0	0	0	0	0	0	0	0	0	0	0	0	0
TURKEY	0	0	0	0	0	0	0	0	0	0	0	0	0	0	0	0	0
OTHER EUROPE	0	0	0	0	0	0	0	0	0	0	0	0	0	0	0	0	0

TABLE 2 .4 .40 (CONTINUED)

Columns under **NO. OF ENTRIES DURING YEAR(S)**: 51-55 through 1975.

COUNTRY OR REGION	NET FLOW UP TO 31-DEC-50	51-55	56-60	61-65	1966	1967	1968	1969	1970	1971	1972	1973	1974	1975	TOTAL ENTRIES 1951-75	TOTAL EXITS 1951-75	NET FLOW UP TO 1-JAN-76
N.AFR+M.EAST (TOTAL)	0	0	0	0	0	0	0	0	0	0	0	0	0	0	0	0	0
ALGERIA	0	0	0	0	0	0	0	0	0	0	0	0	0	0	0	0	0
EGYPT	0	0	0	0	0	0	0	0	0	0	0	0	0	0	0	0	0
IRAN	0	0	0	0	0	0	0	0	0	0	0	0	0	0	0	0	0
ISRAEL	0	0	0	0	0	0	0	0	0	0	0	0	0	0	0	0	0
LEBANON	0	0	0	0	0	0	0	0	0	0	0	0	0	0	0	0	0
MOROCCO	0	0	0	0	0	0	0	0	0	0	0	0	0	0	0	0	0
SAUDI ARABIA	0	0	0	0	0	0	0	0	0	0	0	0	0	0	0	0	0
OTHER N.AF+M.E.	0	0	0	0	0	0	0	0	0	0	0	0	0	0	0	0	0
E.+W.AFRICA (TOTAL)	0	0	0	0	0	0	0	0	0	0	0	0	0	0	0	0	0
GHANA	0	0	0	0	0	0	0	0	0	0	0	0	0	0	0	0	0
IVORY COAST	0	0	0	0	0	0	0	0	0	0	0	0	0	0	0	0	0
KENYA	0	0	0	0	0	0	0	0	0	0	0	0	0	0	0	0	0
LIBERIA	0	0	0	0	0	0	0	0	0	0	0	0	0	0	0	0	0
NIGERIA	0	0	0	0	0	0	0	0	0	0	0	0	0	0	0	0	0
ZAIRE	0	0	0	0	0	0	0	0	0	0	0	0	0	0	0	0	0
ZAMBIA	0	0	0	0	0	0	0	0	0	0	0	0	0	0	0	0	0
OTHER E.+W.AFR.	0	0	0	0	0	0	0	0	0	0	0	0	0	0	0	0	0
SOUTH ASIA (TOTAL)	0	0	0	0	0	0	0	0	0	0	0	0	0	1	1	0	1
INDIA	0	0	0	0	0	0	0	0	0	0	0	0	0	1	1	0	1
PAKISTAN	0	0	0	0	0	0	0	0	0	0	0	0	0	0	0	0	0
SRI LANKA	0	0	0	0	0	0	0	0	0	0	0	0	0	0	0	0	0
OTHER S.ASIA	0	0	0	0	0	0	0	0	0	0	0	0	0	0	0	0	0
EAST ASIA (TOTAL)	0	0	0	0	0	0	1	1	0	0	0	0	0	0	2	2	0
HONG KONG	0	0	0	0	0	0	1	0	0	0	0	0	0	0	1	1	0
INDONESIA	0	0	0	0	0	0	0	0	0	0	0	0	0	0	0	0	0
JAPAN	0	0	0	0	0	0	0	1	0	0	0	0	0	0	1	1	0
MALAYSIA	0	0	0	0	0	0	0	0	0	0	0	0	0	0	0	0	0
PHILIPPINES	0	0	0	0	0	0	0	0	0	0	0	0	0	0	0	0	0
SINGAPORE	0	0	0	0	0	0	0	0	0	0	0	0	0	0	0	0	0
S.KOREA	0	0	0	0	0	0	0	0	0	0	0	0	0	0	0	0	0
THAILAND	0	0	0	0	0	0	0	0	0	0	0	0	0	0	0	0	0
TAIWAN	0	0	0	0	0	0	0	0	0	0	0	0	0	0	0	0	0
OTHER E.ASIA	0	0	0	0	0	0	0	0	0	0	0	0	0	0	0	0	0
S.DOMINIONS (TOTAL)	0	2	1	1	0	0	0	0	0	0	1	0	0	0	4	2	2
AUSTRALIA	0	1	1	1	0	0	0	0	0	0	1	0	0	0	3	1	2
NEW ZEALAND	0	0	0	0	0	0	0	0	0	0	0	0	0	0	0	0	0
RHODESIA	0	0	0	0	0	0	0	0	0	0	0	0	0	0	0	0	0
S.AFRICA	0	1	0	0	0	0	0	0	0	0	0	0	0	0	1	1	0
OUTSIDE U.S. (TOTAL)	5	2	9	4	1	2	10	4	4	1	10	8	4	2	61	23	43

CHAPTER 2 - THE PROLIFERATION OF FOREIGN SUBSIDIARIES
SECTION 4 -- GEOGRAPHICAL SPREAD IN SPECIFIC INDUSTRIES
TABLE 41 --- PRECISION INSTRUMENTS INDUSTRIES (SIC 38)

NO. OF SUBSIDIARIES MANUFACTURING IN THIS INDUSTRY AT TIME OF ENTRY INTO PARENT SYSTEM

COUNTRY OR REGION	NET FLOW UP TO 31-DEC-50	NO. OF ENTRIES DURING YEAR(S)													TOTAL ENTRIES 1951-75	TOTAL EXITS 1951-75	NET FLOW UP TO 1-JAN-76
		51-55	56-60	61-65	1966	1967	1968	1969	1970	1971	1972	1973	1974	1975			
CANADA	3	0	3	4	3	2	1	2	3	0	5	2	0	2	27	6	24
LATIN AMER. (TOTAL)	3	2	4	10	3	1	4	1	2	2	2	6	2	0	39	11	31
C.AM.+CARIB. (TOTAL)	2	0	2	3	0	1	1	0	1	1	1	0	0	0	10	3	9
BAHAMAS	0	0	0	0	0	0	0	0	0	0	0	0	0	0	0	0	0
BERMUDA	0	0	0	0	0	0	0	0	0	0	0	0	0	0	0	0	0
COSTA RICA	0	0	0	0	0	0	0	0	0	0	0	0	0	0	0	0	0
GUATEMALA	0	0	0	0	0	0	0	0	0	0	0	0	0	0	0	0	0
JAMAICA	0	0	0	1	0	0	0	0	0	0	0	0	0	0	1	0	1
MEXICO	2	0	2	1	0	1	1	0	1	0	0	0	0	0	6	1	7
NETH.ANTILLES	0	0	0	1	0	0	0	0	0	0	0	0	0	0	1	1	0
NICARAGUA	0	0	0	0	0	0	0	0	0	1	0	0	0	0	1	1	0
PANAMA	0	0	0	0	0	0	0	0	0	0	1	0	0	0	1	0	1
OTHER C.AM+CAR.	0	0	0	0	0	0	0	0	0	0	0	0	0	0	0	0	0
S.AMERICA (TOTAL)	1	2	2	7	3	1	3	0	2	0	5	2	2	0	29	8	22
BOLIVIA	0	0	0	0	0	0	0	0	0	0	0	0	0	0	0	0	0
CHILE	0	0	0	1	0	0	0	0	0	0	0	0	0	0	1	1	0
COLOMBIA	0	0	1	1	0	0	0	0	0	0	0	0	0	0	2	2	0
ECUADOR	0	0	0	0	0	0	0	0	0	0	0	0	1	0	1	0	1
PERU	1	1	1	2	0	0	0	0	1	0	1	1	0	0	7	2	6
ARGENTINA	0	1	2	2	3	1	2	0	1	0	2	1	0	0	15	3	12
BRAZIL	0	0	0	0	0	0	0	0	0	0	0	0	0	0	0	0	0
URUGUAY	0	0	0	0	0	0	0	0	0	0	1	0	1	0	3	0	3
VENEZUELA	0	0	0	0	0	0	0	0	0	0	0	0	0	0	0	0	0
OTHER S.AMER.	0	0	0	0	0	0	0	0	0	0	0	0	0	0	0	0	0
EUROPE (TOTAL)	10	9	36	13	7	10	7	8	5	23	15	12	6	0	151	44	117
BELGIUM	0	0	2	2	1	0	0	0	1	1	1	1	0	0	9	2	7
FRANCE	2	0	6	2	1	0	1	0	2	1	8	3	2	1	28	7	23
GERMANY	2	3	7	6	2	4	4	4	2	1	4	1	1	0	39	12	29
ITALY	0	0	5	1	1	2	0	1	0	0	0	1	0	0	11	3	8
LUXEMBOURG	0	0	1	1	0	0	0	0	0	0	0	0	0	0	2	0	2
NETHERLANDS	0	0	2	1	0	2	0	0	1	0	1	1	0	0	9	1	8
DENMARK	0	0	0	0	0	0	0	0	0	0	0	0	0	0	0	0	0
IRELAND	1	0	0	0	0	0	0	0	1	0	0	0	0	0	1	0	2
U.K.	5	5	11	3	3	4	2	1	1	1	3	2	2	2	40	17	28
AUSTRIA	0	0	0	0	0	0	0	0	0	0	1	0	0	0	1	0	1
FINLAND	0	0	0	0	0	0	0	0	0	0	0	0	0	0	0	0	0
GREECE	0	0	0	0	0	0	0	0	0	1	0	0	0	0	1	0	1
NORWAY	0	0	0	0	0	0	0	0	0	0	0	0	0	0	0	0	0
PORTUGAL	0	0	0	0	0	0	1	1	0	0	1	0	0	1	4	1	3
SPAIN	0	0	0	0	0	0	0	0	0	0	1	1	0	0	2	0	2
SWEDEN	0	1	0	0	0	0	0	0	0	0	0	1	0	0	2	0	2
SWITZERLAND	0	0	0	0	0	0	0	0	0	0	0	0	0	0	0	0	0
TURKEY	0	0	0	0	0	0	0	0	0	0	1	0	0	1	2	1	1
OTHER EUROPE	0	0	0	0	0	0	0	0	0	0	0	0	0	0	2	0	1

TABLE 2.4.41 (CONTINUED)

COUNTRY OR REGION	NET FLOW UP TO 31-DEC-50	NO. OF ENTRIES DURING YEAR(S)													TOTAL ENTRIES 1951-75	TOTAL EXITS 1951-75	NET FLOW UP TO 1-JAN-76
		51-55	56-60	61-65	1966	1967	1968	1969	1970	1971	1972	1973	1974	1975			
N.AFR+M.EAST (TOTAL)	0	0	0	0	0	0	1	0	0	0	0	1	0	1	3	0	3
ALGERIA	0	0	0	0	0	0	0	0	0	0	0	0	0	0	0	0	0
EGYPT	0	0	0	0	0	0	0	0	0	0	0	0	0	1	1	0	1
IRAN	0	0	0	0	0	0	0	0	0	0	0	0	0	0	0	0	0
ISRAEL	0	0	0	0	0	0	1	0	0	0	0	0	0	0	1	0	1
LEBANON	0	0	0	0	0	0	0	0	0	0	0	0	0	0	0	0	0
MOROCCO	0	0	0	0	0	0	0	0	0	0	0	1	0	0	1	0	1
SAUDI ARABIA	0	0	0	0	0	0	0	0	0	0	0	0	0	0	0	0	0
OTHER N.AF+M.E.	0	0	0	0	0	0	0	0	0	0	0	0	0	0	0	0	0
E.+W.AFRICA (TOTAL)	0	0	0	0	0	0	0	1	0	0	0	0	0	0	1	0	1
GHANA	0	0	0	0	0	0	0	0	0	0	0	0	0	0	0	0	0
IVORY COAST	0	0	0	0	0	0	0	0	0	0	0	0	0	0	0	0	0
KENYA	0	0	0	0	0	0	0	0	0	0	0	0	0	0	0	0	0
LIBERIA	0	0	0	0	0	0	0	0	0	0	0	0	0	0	0	0	0
NIGERIA	0	0	0	0	0	0	0	0	0	0	0	0	0	0	0	0	0
ZAIRE	0	0	0	0	0	0	0	0	0	0	0	0	0	0	0	0	0
ZAMBIA	0	0	0	0	0	0	0	1	0	0	0	0	0	0	1	0	1
OTHER E.+W.AFR.	0	0	0	0	0	0	0	0	0	0	0	0	0	0	0	0	0
SOUTH ASIA (TOTAL)	0	0	1	1	1	0	0	0	1	0	0	0	0	0	4	1	3
INDIA	0	0	1	1	0	0	0	0	0	0	0	0	0	0	2	1	1
PAKISTAN	0	0	0	0	1	0	0	0	1	0	0	0	0	0	2	0	2
SRI LANKA	0	0	0	0	0	0	0	0	0	0	0	0	0	0	0	0	0
OTHER S.ASIA	0	0	0	0	0	0	0	0	0	0	0	0	0	0	0	0	0
EAST ASIA (TOTAL)	0	0	0	0	0	0	3	3	1	2	1	3	1	0	14	1	13
HONG KONG	0	0	0	0	0	0	1	1	0	0	0	0	0	0	2	0	2
INDONESIA	0	0	0	0	0	0	0	0	1	0	0	0	0	0	1	0	1
JAPAN	0	0	0	0	0	0	2	2	0	2	1	2	1	0	10	1	9
MALAYSIA	0	0	0	0	0	0	0	0	0	0	0	0	0	0	0	0	0
PHILIPPINES	0	0	0	0	0	0	0	0	0	0	0	0	0	0	0	0	0
SINGAPORE	0	0	0	0	0	0	0	0	0	0	0	0	0	0	0	0	0
S.KOREA	0	0	0	0	0	0	0	0	0	0	0	0	0	0	0	0	0
THAILAND	0	0	0	0	0	0	0	0	0	0	0	0	0	0	0	0	0
TAIWAN	0	0	0	0	0	0	0	0	0	0	0	1	0	0	1	0	1
OTHER E.ASIA	0	0	0	0	0	0	0	0	0	0	0	0	0	0	0	0	0
S.DOMINIONS (TOTAL)	3	0	1	2	2	2	2	2	0	2	3	0	1	0	16	1	18
AUSTRALIA	2	0	1	2	2	1	2	2	0	2	2	0	0	0	14	1	15
NEW ZEALAND	0	0	0	0	0	0	0	0	0	0	0	0	0	0	0	0	0
RHODESIA	0	0	0	0	0	0	0	0	0	0	0	0	1	0	1	0	1
S.AFRICA	1	0	0	0	0	0	0	0	0	0	1	0	0	0	1	0	2
OUTSIDE U.S. (TOTAL)	19	2	17	53	22	12	21	14	14	14	38	22	17	9	255	64	210

CHAPTER 2 - THE PROLIFERATION OF FOREIGN SUBSIDIARIES
SECTION 4 -- GEOGRAPHICAL SPREAD IN SPECIFIC INDUSTRIES
TABLE 42 --- MISCELLANEOUS INDUSTRIES (SIC 39)

NO. OF SUBSIDIARIES MANUFACTURING IN THIS INDUSTRY AT TIME OF ENTRY INTO PARENT SYSTEM

COUNTRY OR REGION	NET FLOW UP TO 31-DEC-50	NO. OF ENTRIES DURING YEAR(S)													TOTAL ENTRIES 1951-75	TOTAL EXITS 1951-75	NET FLOW UP TO 1-JAN-76
		51-55	56-60	61-65	1966	1967	1968	1969	1970	1971	1972	1973	1974	1975			
CANADA	3	3	0	2	1	2	3	3	3	3	3	4	0	0	27	7	23
LATIN AMER. (TOTAL)	4	0	7	6	2	0	2	1	2	2	0	2	0	0	24	6	22
C.AM.+CARIB. (TOTAL)	2	0	1	1	1	0	1	0	1	0	0	1	0	2	8	2	8
BAHAMAS	0	0	0	0	0	0	0	0	0	0	0	0	0	0	0	0	0
BERMUDA	0	0	0	0	0	0	0	0	0	0	0	0	0	0	0	0	0
COSTA RICA	0	0	0	0	0	0	0	0	0	0	0	0	0	0	0	0	0
GUATEMALA	0	0	0	0	0	0	0	0	0	0	0	0	0	0	0	0	0
JAMAICA	0	0	0	0	0	0	0	0	0	0	0	0	0	0	0	0	0
MEXICO	2	0	1	0	1	0	1	0	1	0	0	1	0	1	6	2	6
NETH.ANTILLES	0	0	0	0	0	0	0	0	0	0	0	0	0	0	0	0	0
NICARAGUA	0	0	0	0	0	0	0	0	0	0	0	0	0	0	0	0	0
PANAMA	0	0	0	0	0	0	0	0	0	0	0	0	0	0	0	0	0
OTHER C.AM+CAR.	0	0	0	1	0	0	0	0	0	0	0	0	0	1	2	0	2
S.AMERICA (TOTAL)	2	0	6	5	1	0	1	1	1	0	0	1	0	0	16	4	14
BOLIVIA	0	0	0	0	0	0	0	0	0	0	0	0	0	0	0	0	0
CHILE	0	0	0	1	0	0	0	0	0	0	0	0	0	0	1	0	1
COLOMBIA	0	0	3	0	1	0	0	0	0	0	0	0	0	0	4	2	2
ECUADOR	0	0	0	1	0	0	0	0	0	0	0	0	0	0	1	0	1
PERU	0	0	1	0	0	0	0	1	0	0	0	0	0	0	2	1	1
ARGENTINA	0	0	0	2	0	0	0	0	1	0	0	1	0	0	4	1	3
BRAZIL	2	0	0	0	0	0	1	0	0	0	0	0	0	0	1	0	3
URUGUAY	0	0	0	0	0	0	0	0	0	0	0	0	0	0	0	0	0
VENEZUELA	0	0	2	1	0	0	0	0	0	0	0	0	0	0	3	0	3
OTHER S.AMER.	0	0	0	0	0	0	0	0	0	0	0	0	0	0	0	0	0
EUROPE (TOTAL)	11	15	10	10	3	3	1	7	5	12	9	5	4	2	86	22	75
BELGIUM	1	1	0	0	0	0	0	0	0	0	0	0	0	0	1	1	1
FRANCE	2	0	2	2	0	0	0	0	0	3	3	1	1	0	12	3	11
GERMANY	0	2	2	2	1	1	0	2	2	2	1	0	0	0	15	4	11
ITALY	0	2	1	1	0	0	0	0	1	0	1	1	1	1	9	3	6
LUXEMBOURG	0	0	0	0	0	0	0	0	0	0	0	0	0	0	0	0	0
NETHERLANDS	1	0	0	0	0	0	0	0	0	1	1	0	1	0	3	0	4
DENMARK	0	0	0	0	0	0	0	0	0	0	0	0	0	0	0	0	0
IRELAND	0	0	0	0	0	1	0	1	1	0	0	0	0	0	3	1	2
U.K.	6	10	5	5	0	0	0	3	0	3	2	1	0	0	29	6	29
AUSTRIA	0	0	0	0	1	0	0	1	0	0	1	0	0	0	3	1	2
FINLAND	0	0	0	0	0	0	0	0	0	0	0	1	0	0	1	0	1
GREECE	0	0	0	0	0	0	0	0	0	0	0	0	0	0	0	0	0
NORWAY	1	0	0	0	0	0	0	0	0	0	0	0	0	0	0	1	0
PORTUGAL	0	0	0	0	1	0	0	0	0	0	0	0	0	0	1	0	1
SPAIN	0	0	0	0	0	1	0	0	1	0	0	0	0	1	3	0	3
SWEDEN	0	0	0	0	0	0	0	0	0	0	0	1	1	0	2	0	2
SWITZERLAND	0	0	0	0	0	0	0	0	0	3	0	0	0	0	3	2	1
TURKEY	0	0	0	0	0	0	0	0	0	0	0	0	0	0	0	0	0
OTHER EUROPE	0	0	0	0	0	0	1	0	0	0	0	0	0	0	1	0	1

TABLE 2 .4 .42 (CONTINUED)

COUNTRY OR REGION	NET FLOW UP TO 31-DEC-50	NO. OF ENTRIES DURING YEAR(S)													TOTAL ENTRIES 1951-75	TOTAL EXITS 1951-75	NET FLOW UP TO 1-JAN-76
		51-55	56-60	61-65	1966	1967	1968	1969	1970	1971	1972	1973	1974	1975			
N.AFR+M.EAST (TOTAL)	1	0	0	0	1	1	0	0	0	0	0	0	0	0	2	1	2
ALGERIA	0	0	0	0	0	0	0	0	0	0	0	0	0	0	0	0	0
EGYPT	0	0	0	0	0	0	0	0	0	0	0	0	0	0	0	0	0
IRAN	0	0	0	0	0	0	0	0	0	0	0	0	0	0	0	0	0
ISRAEL	0	0	0	0	1	0	0	0	0	0	0	0	0	0	1	1	0
LEBANON	1	0	0	0	0	0	0	0	0	0	0	0	0	0	0	0	1
MOROCCO	0	0	0	0	0	0	0	0	0	0	0	0	0	0	0	0	0
SAUDI ARABIA	0	0	0	0	0	0	0	0	0	0	0	0	0	0	0	0	0
OTHER N.AF+M.E.	0	0	0	0	0	1	0	0	0	0	0	0	0	0	1	0	1
E.+W.AFRICA (TOTAL)	0	0	0	2	0	0	0	1	0	0	0	0	0	0	3	0	3
GHANA	0	0	0	0	0	0	0	0	0	0	0	0	0	0	0	0	0
IVORY COAST	0	0	0	0	0	0	0	0	0	0	0	0	0	0	0	0	0
KENYA	0	0	0	0	0	0	0	1	0	0	0	0	0	0	1	0	1
LIBERIA	0	0	0	0	0	0	0	0	0	0	0	0	0	0	0	0	0
NIGERIA	0	0	0	2	0	0	0	0	0	0	0	0	0	0	2	0	2
ZAIRE	0	0	0	0	0	0	0	0	0	0	0	0	0	0	0	0	0
ZAMBIA	0	0	0	0	0	0	0	0	0	0	0	0	0	0	0	0	0
OTHER E.+W.AFR.	0	0	0	0	0	0	0	0	0	0	0	0	0	0	0	0	0
SOUTH ASIA (TOTAL)	0	0	0	1	0	0	0	0	0	0	0	0	0	0	1	0	1
INDIA	0	0	0	1	0	0	0	0	0	0	0	0	0	0	1	0	1
PAKISTAN	0	0	0	0	0	0	0	0	0	0	0	0	0	0	0	0	0
SRI LANKA	0	0	0	0	0	0	0	0	0	0	0	0	0	0	0	0	0
OTHER S.ASIA	0	0	0	0	0	0	0	0	0	0	0	0	0	0	0	0	0
EAST ASIA (TOTAL)	1	2	2	3	0	0	1	1	0	1	1	0	2	1	14	3	12
HONG KONG	0	2	2	3	0	0	0	0	0	0	0	0	0	0	7	3	4
INDONESIA	0	0	0	0	0	0	0	0	0	0	0	0	0	0	0	0	0
JAPAN	0	0	0	0	0	0	0	1	0	1	1	0	2	0	5	0	5
MALAYSIA	0	0	0	0	0	0	1	0	0	0	0	0	0	0	1	0	1
PHILIPPINES	0	0	0	0	0	0	0	0	0	0	0	0	0	0	0	0	0
SINGAPORE	1	0	0	0	0	0	0	0	0	0	0	0	0	1	1	0	2
S.KOREA	0	0	0	0	0	0	0	0	0	0	0	0	0	0	0	0	0
THAILAND	0	0	0	0	0	0	0	0	0	0	0	0	0	0	0	0	0
TAIWAN	0	0	0	0	0	0	0	0	0	0	0	0	0	0	0	0	0
OTHER E.ASIA	0	0	0	0	0	0	0	0	0	0	0	0	0	0	0	0	0
S.DOMINIONS (TOTAL)	3	3	3	4	1	1	5	4	1	0	1	0	0	0	23	7	19
AUSTRALIA	1	3	3	3	1	1	4	3	1	0	1	0	0	0	20	7	14
NEW ZEALAND	0	0	0	0	0	0	1	0	0	0	0	0	0	0	1	0	1
RHODESIA	1	0	0	0	0	0	0	0	0	0	0	0	0	0	0	0	1
S.AFRICA	1	0	0	1	0	0	0	1	0	0	0	0	0	0	2	0	3
OUTSIDE U.S. (TOTAL)	23	6	27	29	7	7	21	15	11	19	14	12	8	4	180	46	157

The Maturing of Foreign Subsidiaries

CHAPTER 3   - THE MATURING OF FOREIGN SUBSIDIARIES
SECTION 1   -- CHANGES IN SUBSIDIARY CHARACTERISTICS
TABLE 1   --- BY PRINCIPAL ACTIVITY

NO. OF SUBSIDIARIES ACTIVE AT 1-JAN-76, BY PRINCIPAL ACTIVITIES AT ENTRY DATE AND IN 1975

PRI.ACT. AT ENTRY	PRINCIPAL ACTIVITY IN 1975					NET FLOW UP TO 1-JAN-76
	MANUFACTURING	SALES	EXTRACTION	OTHER	UNKNOWN	
MANUFACTURING	5075	165	29	276	77	5622
SALES	422	2405	15	353	32	3227
EXTRACTION	19	17	247	61	4	348
OTHER	74	64	46	1066	10	1260
UNKNOWN	185	182	19	221	134	741
STOCK AT 1-JAN-76	5775	2833	356	1977	257	11198

CHAPTER 3   - THE MATURING OF FOREIGN SUBSIDIARIES
SECTION 1   -- CHANGES IN SUBSIDIARY CHARACTERISTICS
TABLE 2   --- BY PARENT OWNERSHIP

NO. OF SUBSIDIARIES ACTIVE AT 1-JAN-76, BY PARENT OWNERSHIP AT ENTRY DATE AND IN 1975

PAR.OWN. AT ENTRY	PARENT OWNERSHIP IN 1975					NET FLOW UP TO 1-JAN-76
	WHL (95-100%)	MAJ (51-94%)	CO (50%)	MIN (5-49%)	UNKNOWN	
WHL OWNED: 95-100%	7216	182	58	62	223	7741
MAJ OWNED: 51- 94%	314	697	19	40	20	1090
CO- OWNED: 50%	148	34	595	49	20	846
MIN OWNED: 5- 49%	119	73	33	831	23	1079
UNKNOWN	262	39	20	54	67	442
STOCK AT 1-JAN-76	8059	1025	725	1036	353	11198

CHAPTER   3   - THE MATURING OF FOREIGN SUBSIDIARIES
SECTION   1   -- CHANGES IN SUBSIDIARY CHARACTERISTICS
TABLE   3   --- BY PRINCIPAL INDUSTRY

NO. OF SUBSIDIARIES ACTIVE AT 1-JAN-76, BY PRINCIPAL INDUSTRY OF SUBSIDIARY AT TIME OF ENTRY INTO PARENT SYSTEM, AND IN 1975

PRINCIPAL INDUSTRY AT ENTRY	PRINCIPAL INDUSTRY IN 1975																					
	BEVERAGES	TOBACCO	FOOD	TXTL+APPRL	WOOD+FURNI	PAPER	PRINTING	INDUS-CHEM	PLASTIC	AGRIC-CHEM	COSMETICS	DRUGS	OTHER-CHEM	FABR-PLSTCS	TIRES	REF-PETRLM	OTH-PETRLM	LEATHER	STONE+CLAY+CEMNT	ABRASIVES	GLASS	IRON
BEVERAGES	77	0	1	0	0	0	0	0	0	0	0	0	0	0	0	0	0	0	0	0	0	0
TOBACCO	0	23	0	0	0	0	0	0	0	0	0	0	0	0	0	0	0	0	0	0	0	0
FOOD	1	0	546	1	0	0	1	0	0	0	1	2	2	0	0	0	0	0	0	0	0	0
TEXTILES+APPAREL	0	0	0	76	0	1	0	0	5	0	0	0	2	0	0	0	0	1	2	0	2	0
WOOD+FURNITURE	0	0	1	0	50	4	1	0	0	0	0	0	0	0	0	0	0	0	0	0	0	0
PAPER	0	0	0	1	1	167	0	1	0	0	0	0	1	0	0	0	0	1	1	1	0	0
PRINTING	0	0	0	0	0	0	51	0	0	0	0	0	0	0	0	0	0	0	0	0	0	0
INDUSTRIAL CHEM	0	5	0	0	0	0	0	147	19	3	2	10	27	6	0	0	1	0	0	0	0	0
PLASTICS	0	0	0	4	0	0	0	6	124	2	1	3	14	14	1	0	0	0	4	0	4	0
AGRIC CHEM	0	0	0	0	0	0	0	0	1	31	0	0	2	0	0	0	0	1	0	0	0	0
COSMETICS	0	0	0	0	0	0	0	0	1	0	200	14	0	0	0	0	1	0	0	0	0	0
DRUGS	0	0	0	0	0	0	0	1	2	2	13	392	0	1	0	0	0	0	1	0	0	0
OTHER CHEM	0	0	0	0	1	1	0	0	2	2	1	0	192	0	0	2	2	1	3	1	3	0
FABR PLASTICS	0	0	0	0	0	0	0	0	7	0	0	0	0	62	3	0	0	1	1	0	1	0
TIRES	0	0	0	0	0	0	0	1	2	0	0	0	0	0	68	0	0	0	0	0	0	0
REF PETROLEUM	0	0	0	0	0	0	0	0	1	0	0	0	0	0	0	94	1	1	0	0	0	0
OTH PETROLEUM	0	0	0	0	0	0	0	11	1	1	0	0	0	0	0	11	23	23	1	0	0	0
LEATHER	0	0	0	0	0	0	0	0	0	0	0	0	0	0	0	0	0	16	0	0	0	0
STONE+CLAY+CEMNT	0	0	0	0	1	1	0	0	0	0	0	0	1	0	0	0	1	0	42	4	2	1
ABRASIVES	0	0	0	0	0	0	0	0	2	0	0	0	0	2	0	0	1	0	4	83	1	1
GLASS	0	0	0	0	0	0	0	0	0	0	0	0	0	0	0	0	0	0	1	0	55	0
IRON+STEEL	0	0	0	0	0	0	0	0	0	0	0	0	0	0	0	0	0	0	0	0	0	35

TABLE 3 .1 .3 (CONTINUED)

PRINCIPAL INDUSTRY IN 1975

PRINCIPAL INDUSTRY AT ENTRY	BEVERAGES	TOBACCO	TXTL+APPRL	FOOD	WOOD+FURNI	PAPER	PRINTING	INDUS-CHEM	PLASTIC	AGRIC-CHEM	COSMETICS	OTHER-CHEM	DRUGS	FABR-PLSTCS	TIRES	REF-PETRLM	OTH-PETRLM	STONE+CLAY+CEMNT	LEATHER	ABRASIVES	GLASS	IRON
NON-FERROUS	0	0	0	0	0	0	1	0	0	0	0	0	0	0	0	0	0	0	0	1	0	3
METAL CANS	0	0	0	0	0	2	0	0	0	0	0	0	0	0	0	0	0	0	0	0	0	0
OTHER FAB METAL	0	0	0	0	1	1	0	0	0	0	1	0	0	3	0	0	0	1	0	0	0	7
ENGINES+TURBIN	0	0	0	0	0	0	0	0	0	0	0	0	0	0	0	0	0	0	0	0	0	2
CONSTR MACH	0	0	0	0	0	0	0	0	0	0	0	0	0	0	0	0	0	3	0	3	0	0
FARM MACHINERY	0	0	0	0	0	0	0	0	0	0	0	0	0	0	0	0	0	0	0	0	0	0
OFFICE MC+COMPUT	0	0	0	0	0	2	0	0	0	0	1	1	0	0	0	0	0	0	0	0	0	0
SPEC MACHINERY	0	0	0	1	0	1	0	0	0	0	0	0	0	0	0	0	0	1	1	0	0	1
GENL MACHINERY	0	0	0	0	0	0	0	0	0	1	1	0	0	0	0	0	0	1	0	0	0	0
OTH NON-EL MC	0	0	0	0	1	0	0	0	0	0	1	1	0	0	0	0	0	0	0	6	0	0
EL LIGHT+WIRING	0	0	0	0	0	0	0	0	0	0	0	0	0	1	0	0	0	0	0	0	0	0
EL TRAN EQUIP	0	0	0	0	0	1	0	0	0	0	0	0	0	0	0	0	0	0	0	0	0	0
RADIO+TV+APPL	0	0	0	0	1	0	1	0	0	0	0	0	0	0	0	0	0	0	0	0	0	0
ELECTRONICS	0	0	0	0	0	0	0	0	0	0	0	0	0	0	0	0	0	0	0	0	0	0
OTHER ELEC	0	0	0	0	0	0	4	4	0	0	0	0	0	0	0	0	0	0	0	0	0	0
COMMUNICATION	0	0	0	0	0	0	0	0	0	0	0	0	0	0	0	0	0	1	0	0	0	0
MOTOR VEHIC	0	0	0	0	0	0	0	0	0	0	0	0	0	1	0	0	0	1	0	6	0	0
OTHER TRANSP	0	0	0	0	0	0	0	0	1	0	2	0	0	0	0	0	0	0	0	0	0	0
PRECISION	0	0	2	0	0	1	0	0	0	0	2	1	1	0	0	0	2	0	0	0	0	0
MISCELLANEOUS	2	1	1	11	1	8	4	0	5	0	6	5	9	0	3	0	2	3	1	4	0	0
NONE	1	1	52	8	13	9	33	12	10	10	44	111	35	3	14	46	11	4	6	16	1	8
STOCK AT 1-JAN-76	81	26	635	95	67	206	64	208	180	51	276	546	309	95	89	155	41	26	63	135	61	57

(TABLE CONTINUED ON FOLLOWING PAGES)

146

TABLE 3.1.3 (CONTINUED)

PRINCIPAL INDUSTRY IN 1975

PRINCIPAL INDUSTRY AT ENTRY	NON-FERROUS	METAL CANS	FAB-MET	ENGINES	CONSTR-MC	FARM-MC	OFF-MC+COMPUT	SPECL-MC	GENL-MC	OTH-NON-EL-MC	EL-LT+WIRING	EL-TRAN	RAD+TV+APPL	ELECTRONICS	OTH-ELE	COMMUNICATION	MOTOR-VEHIC	OTH-TRN	PRECISION	MISC	NONE	NET FLOW
BEVERAGES	0	0	0	0	0	0	0	0	0	0	0	0	0	0	0	0	0	0	0	0	10	97
TOBACCO	0	0	0	0	0	0	0	0	0	0	0	0	0	0	0	0	0	0	0	0	5	28
FOOD	0	1	0	0	0	0	0	0	0	0	0	0	0	0	0	0	0	0	0	5	53	614
TEXTILES+APPAREL	0	0	0	0	0	0	0	1	1	0	0	0	0	0	0	0	0	0	1	2	13	108
WOOD+FURNITURE	0	1	1	0	0	0	0	0	0	0	0	0	0	0	0	0	0	0	0	1	2	59
PAPER	0	5	0	0	0	0	0	0	0	0	0	0	0	0	0	0	0	0	2	0	19	207
PRINTING	0	0	0	0	0	0	0	1	1	0	0	0	0	1	0	0	0	0	0	0	8	65
INDUSTRIAL CHEM	2	0	0	0	0	0	0	1	0	0	0	0	1	1	0	0	0	0	0	3	29	259
PLASTICS	0	0	0	0	0	0	0	0	1	0	0	0	0	0	0	0	0	0	0	3	15	196
AGRIC CHEM	0	0	0	0	1	0	0	0	0	0	0	0	0	0	0	0	0	0	0	0	9	49
COSMETICS	0	0	5	0	0	0	0	0	0	0	0	1	0	0	0	0	0	0	1	2	30	266
DRUGS	0	0	0	0	0	0	0	0	0	0	0	0	0	0	0	0	0	0	6	2	46	478
OTHER CHEM	0	0	1	0	0	0	1	2	0	0	0	0	0	0	0	0	0	0	1	0	14	231
FABR PLASTICS	0	0	0	0	0	0	0	0	0	0	0	0	0	0	0	0	1	0	0	3	7	81
TIRES	0	0	0	0	0	0	0	0	1	0	0	0	0	0	0	0	1	0	0	0	7	77
REF PETROLEUM	0	0	0	0	0	0	0	0	0	0	0	0	0	0	0	0	0	0	0	1	24	121
OTH PETROLEUM	0	0	0	0	0	0	0	0	0	0	0	0	0	0	0	0	1	0	0	0	10	61
LEATHER	0	0	0	0	0	0	0	2	0	0	0	0	0	0	0	0	0	0	0	1	2	21
STONE+CLAY+CEMNT	0	0	0	0	0	0	0	0	0	0	0	0	0	0	0	0	0	0	0	0	5	51
ABRASIVES	0	0	1	0	1	0	0	0	1	0	0	0	0	0	0	0	0	0	1	1	11	108
GLASS	0	0	0	0	0	0	0	0	0	0	0	0	1	0	0	0	0	0	0	0	5	65
IRON+STEEL	1	0	1	0	0	1	0	0	0	0	0	0	0	0	0	0	0	0	0	0	2	40

TABLE 3 .1 .3 (CONTINUED)

PRINCIPAL INDUSTRY IN 1975

PRINCIPAL INDUSTRY AT ENTRY	NON-FERROUS	METAL CANS	FAB-MET	ENGINES	CONSTR-MC	FARM-MC	OFF-MC+COMPUT	SPECL-MC	GENL-MC	OTH-NON-EL-MC	EL-LT+WIRING	EL-TRAN	RAD+TV+APPL	ELECTRONICS	OTH-ELE	COMMUNICATION	MOTOR-VEHIC	OTH-TRN	PRECISION	MISC	NONE	NET FLOW
NON-FERROUS	119	0	6	0	0	0	0	0	1	1	0	0	0	0	0	0	0	0	0	0	16	151
METAL CANS	2	31	3	0	0	0	0	0	0	0	0	0	0	0	0	0	0	0	0	0	4	42
OTHER FAB METAL	19	2	216	0	2	0	0	5	0	0	0	0	0	0	0	0	0	0	0	0	25	296
ENGINES+TURBIN	0	0	0	18	0	0	0	2	0	0	0	0	0	0	0	0	0	0	0	0	1	27
CONSTR MACH	0	0	0	0	117	1	0	1	0	0	0	0	0	0	0	0	0	0	0	0	12	141
FARM MACHINERY	0	0	0	0	0	24	0	0	0	0	0	0	0	0	0	0	0	0	0	0	1	29
OFFICE MC+COMPUT	0	0	0	0	0	0	39	0	1	0	0	0	0	0	0	0	0	0	0	0	9	58
SPEC MACHINERY	8	0	1	0	0	0	0	65	3	0	0	0	0	0	0	0	0	0	0	0	11	95
GENL MACHINERY	0	1	4	2	3	0	0	0	84	0	0	0	0	0	0	0	0	0	0	0	10	112
OTH NON-EL MC	0	0	0	0	2	0	0	0	2	79	3	0	0	0	0	0	0	0	0	0	9	110
EL LIGHT+WIRING	2	0	0	0	0	0	0	0	0	0	28	2	0	0	0	0	0	0	0	0	3	38
EL TRAN EQUIP	0	0	0	0	0	0	0	0	0	0	0	24	1	1	3	0	0	0	0	0	2	35
RADIO+TV+APPL	0	0	0	0	0	0	0	0	0	0	0	0	67	4	1	0	0	0	0	0	12	95
ELECTRONICS	0	0	0	0	0	0	0	0	0	0	0	2	3	66	6	0	0	0	0	0	5	87
OTHER ELEC	0	0	1	0	0	0	0	0	0	0	0	0	1	0	129	0	2	0	0	0	8	155
COMMUNICATION	0	0	0	0	1	0	0	0	0	0	0	0	2	0	1	45	0	0	0	0	7	55
MOTOR VEHIC	0	1	5	3	2	0	0	0	0	0	0	0	5	0	9	0	236	0	0	0	23	296
OTHER TRANSP	1	0	0	2	0	0	0	0	0	0	0	0	0	0	0	0	1	24	0	0	1	33
PRECISION	0	0	0	0	0	0	0	0	0	0	0	0	0	0	0	0	1	2	122	2	12	154
MISCELLANEOUS	5	4	22	1	8	3	4	0	0	0	0	0	0	0	0	0	11	0	1	146	50	331
NONE	16	0	21	2	15	6	29	10	8	15	1	2	26	13	14	13	24	3	15	21	4876	5576
STOCK AT 1-JAN-76	176	46	288	28	153	35	78	91	123	109	34	31	115	90	167	62	286	33	161	203	5423	11198

CHAPTER 3   - THE MATURING OF FOREIGN SUBSIDIARIES
SECTION 2   -- STOCK OF MANUFACTURING SUBSIDIARIES AT 1-JAN-76
TABLE 1   --- BY REGION AND PRINCIPAL INDUSTRY IN 1975

NO. OF MANUFACTURING SUBSIDIARIES ACTIVE AT 1-JAN-76, BY PRINCIPAL INDUSTRY OF SUBSIDIARY IN 1975

COUNTRY OR REGION	BEVERAGES	TOBACCO	FOOD	TXTL+APPRL	WOOD+FURNI	PAPER	PRINTING	INDUS-CHEM	PLASTIC	AGRIC-CHEM	COSMETICS	DRUGS	OTHER-CHEM	FABR-PLSTCS	TIRES	REF-PETRLM	OTH-PETRLM	LEATHER	STONE+CLAY+CEMNT	ABRASIVES	GLASS	IRON
CANADA	18	1	83	18	24	18	11	20	9	4	18	23	32	9	5	26	11	3	7	12	5	6
LATIN AMER. (TOTAL)	24	8	174	18	12	60	7	42	40	25	84	146	65	17	26	23	10	15	3	31	19	11
C.AM.+CARIB. (TOTAL)	9	5	85	6	6	20	4	23	20	13	36	54	26	6	8	15	4	10	1	9	4	4
BAHAMAS	0	0	0	0	0	0	0	0	1	0	1	0	0	0	0	1	0	1	0	0	0	0
BERMUDA	0	0	1	0	0	0	0	0	0	0	0	0	0	0	0	0	0	0	0	0	0	0
COSTA RICA	0	1	0	0	0	2	0	0	1	1	0	2	1	1	0	0	0	0	0	0	0	0
GUATEMALA	0	1	4	0	2	1	0	0	1	1	1	3	1	0	1	1	0	0	0	0	0	0
JAMAICA	1	0	11	0	1	1	0	1	1	0	5	3	0	0	1	0	0	0	0	0	0	0
MEXICO	8	1	41	6	2	9	4	17	16	4	18	33	23	5	5	17	2	5	1	8	4	4
NETH.ANTILLES	0	0	0	0	0	0	0	0	0	2	0	0	0	0	0	2	0	1	0	0	0	0
NICARAGUA	0	0	4	0	0	2	0	0	1	0	0	2	0	0	0	2	0	0	0	0	0	0
PANAMA	0	0	7	0	1	2	0	0	0	2	0	1	1	0	0	4	1	1	0	0	0	0
OTHER C.AM+CAR.	0	1	9	0	1	3	0	2	1	3	5	6	0	0	0	5	1	0	0	0	0	0
S.AMERICA (TOTAL)	15	3	89	12	6	40	3	19	20	12	48	92	39	11	18	8	6	2	8	22	15	7
BOLIVIA	0	0	0	0	0	0	0	0	0	0	0	1	0	0	0	0	0	0	0	0	0	0
CHILE	0	0	3	0	1	0	0	0	2	0	0	6	0	0	3	0	2	0	0	0	0	0
COLOMBIA	4	0	16	0	1	1	0	2	6	6	5	9	5	0	3	0	0	0	2	1	2	2
ECUADOR	1	0	4	0	0	1	0	0	0	0	1	7	2	0	1	1	0	0	0	0	0	0
PERU	2	0	8	0	1	1	0	0	0	0	7	1	0	0	1	1	0	1	0	1	0	0
ARGENTINA	2	1	9	5	2	4	1	10	4	1	10	15	7	2	2	1	1	1	2	2	3	1
BRAZIL	5	0	23	5	1	8	2	1	4	4	6	23	17	4	3	3	0	0	8	8	5	2
URUGUAY	2	1	2	0	1	0	0	1	1	0	3	3	3	0	1	0	0	0	0	0	0	1
VENEZUELA	1	0	23	5	1	14	0	5	3	1	15	21	8	5	4	0	2	0	8	8	5	1
OTHER S.AMER.	0	0	1	0	0	1	0	0	1	0	1	0	0	0	0	0	0	0	0	0	0	0
EUROPE (TOTAL)	20	10	249	43	20	76	35	95	76	10	100	213	135	49	28	74	14	27	15	61	24	30
BELGIUM	2	1	14	6	6	16	3	13	9	3	5	9	4	1	2	5	3	1	3	5	2	3
FRANCE	1	1	20	5	4	16	4	15	7	3	23	36	20	12	4	13	3	1	1	11	6	5
GERMANY	3	1	39	6	5	10	6	19	9	2	13	29	20	1	4	12	2	1	2	12	3	5
ITALY	1	1	23	2	3	10	1	10	4	2	3	23	18	3	1	10	1	1	7	3	2	5
LUXEMBOURG	0	0	0	0	0	0	0	0	1	0	0	0	0	1	0	0	0	0	0	0	0	0
NETHERLANDS	1	1	24	3	0	3	2	2	6	0	9	6	2	1	3	6	3	0	1	1	2	0
DENMARK	0	0	14	0	1	1	0	1	0	0	4	5	14	2	0	3	0	1	1	1	0	0
IRELAND	1	0	7	1	1	1	0	0	2	0	2	12	1	0	0	0	0	0	1	1	1	0
U.K.	6	1	48	12	4	9	13	15	25	0	19	27	26	15	4	10	0	5	13	13	5	7
AUSTRIA	0	0	3	0	0	1	1	2	0	0	2	3	2	0	0	3	0	1	0	0	1	0
FINLAND	0	0	0	0	0	1	0	1	0	0	2	1	0	0	0	0	0	0	0	1	0	0
GREECE	0	0	5	0	0	2	0	5	2	0	1	8	1	2	1	2	0	0	1	1	1	0
NORWAY	0	0	1	1	0	1	0	0	6	0	2	0	0	1	0	2	0	0	1	2	0	0
PORTUGAL	4	2	4	0	2	9	2	8	1	4	8	11	9	0	2	0	3	1	0	4	3	3
SPAIN	0	0	25	3	0	3	1	3	3	0	2	26	5	4	1	3	2	0	1	0	0	1
SWEDEN	0	0	16	0	2	0	0	0	0	0	5	4	2	2	3	2	0	0	1	1	0	1
SWITZERLAND	1	2	5	5	0	1	0	0	3	0	4	5	0	0	1	1	0	0	0	1	0	1
TURKEY	0	0	1	1	0	1	0	0	0	0	0	4	1	0	2	0	0	0	0	0	0	0
OTHER EUROPE	0	0	0	0	0	1	0	0	0	0	2	0	1	0	0	2	0	0	1	1	0	0

TABLE 3.2.1 (CONTINUED)

COUNTRY OR REGION	BEVERAGES	TOBACCO	FOOD	TXTL+APPRL	WOOD+FURNI	PAPER	PRINTING	INDUS-CHEM	PLASTIC	AGRIC-CHEM	COSMETICS	DRUGS	OTHER-CHEM	FABR-PLSTCS	TIRES	REF-PETRLM	OTH-PETRLM	LEATHER	STONE+CLAY+CEMNT	ABRASIVES	GLASS	IRON
N.AFR+M.EAST (TOTAL)	0	0	12	2	1	3	0	1	6	1	6	15	5	0	6	4	2	1	1	0	1	1
ALGERIA	0	0	1	0	0	0	0	0	0	0	0	1	0	0	0	1	0	0	0	0	0	0
EGYPT	0	0	0	0	0	0	0	0	2	0	1	0	0	0	0	0	0	0	0	0	0	0
IRAN	0	0	2	1	0	1	0	0	4	0	0	8	3	0	3	0	0	1	1	0	0	1
ISRAEL	0	0	1	0	0	0	0	1	0	0	2	1	2	0	0	1	1	0	0	0	1	0
LEBANON	0	0	2	0	1	1	0	0	0	0	0	4	0	0	2	0	0	0	0	0	0	0
MOROCCO	0	0	3	0	0	0	0	0	0	0	1	2	0	0	2	0	0	0	1	0	0	0
SAUDI ARABIA	0	0	3	0	0	0	0	0	0	0	0	0	0	0	0	2	1	0	0	0	0	0
OTHER N.AF+M.E.	0	0	0	1	0	1	0	0	0	1	1	0	0	0	1	1	1	0	0	0	0	0
E.+W.AFRICA (TOTAL)	3	0	10	0	0	5	0	2	1	0	9	12	0	2	5	8	3	0	1	1	1	0
GHANA	1	0	1	0	0	0	0	0	1	0	1	1	0	0	1	0	1	0	1	0	0	0
IVORY COAST	0	0	1	0	0	0	0	1	0	0	0	0	0	0	0	1	1	0	1	0	0	0
KENYA	1	0	3	0	0	0	0	0	0	0	3	3	0	0	1	2	0	0	0	0	3	0
LIBERIA	0	0	0	0	0	0	0	0	0	0	0	0	0	0	0	0	0	0	0	0	0	0
NIGERIA	0	1	2	0	0	0	0	0	0	0	3	5	0	0	0	2	0	0	1	0	3	0
ZAIRE	0	0	0	0	0	0	0	0	0	0	0	2	0	0	1	0	0	0	0	0	0	0
ZAMBIA	1	0	0	0	0	3	0	1	0	0	2	1	0	1	1	0	0	0	0	0	0	3
OTHER E.+W.AFR.	1	0	3	0	0	2	0	0	0	1	1	0	0	1	1	3	1	0	0	0	0	0
SOUTH ASIA (TOTAL)	1	2	6	2	0	0	0	2	3	4	5	23	6	2	3	3	0	0	1	3	2	2
INDIA	1	1	3	2	0	0	0	3	3	3	2	13	6	2	2	2	0	0	1	3	1	2
PAKISTAN	0	1	3	0	0	0	0	1	0	1	2	8	0	0	1	1	0	0	0	0	1	0
SRI LANKA	0	0	0	0	0	0	0	0	0	0	1	1	0	0	0	0	0	0	0	0	0	0
OTHER S.ASIA	0	0	0	0	0	0	0	0	0	0	0	1	0	0	0	0	0	0	0	0	0	0
EAST ASIA (TOTAL)	10	1	44	7	6	15	3	31	26	6	23	60	33	7	9	20	7	0	7	2	7	2
HONG KONG	0	0	2	0	1	0	0	0	1	0	1	2	3	0	0	1	0	0	0	0	0	0
INDONESIA	1	0	1	0	0	0	0	0	0	0	1	1	1	0	1	0	0	0	0	0	1	0
JAPAN	4	0	19	6	2	3	3	21	15	1	8	19	18	3	3	9	5	0	5	4	5	1
MALAYSIA	0	0	0	0	1	2	0	0	1	2	2	3	1	1	1	1	0	0	0	0	0	0
PHILIPPINES	2	0	3	0	2	4	0	2	1	0	4	15	3	3	3	2	0	0	1	1	0	0
SINGAPORE	0	0	8	0	0	0	0	3	0	0	3	3	0	0	0	3	0	0	1	0	0	0
S.KOREA	1	0	3	2	0	0	0	1	0	3	1	0	4	0	2	1	0	0	0	0	0	0
THAILAND	1	0	2	1	0	2	0	1	2	0	2	1	2	1	1	3	1	0	1	0	0	1
TAIWAN	0	0	4	0	0	3	0	1	1	0	1	4	1	0	1	1	1	0	0	0	0	0
OTHER E.ASIA	1	0	2	0	0	1	0	3	0	0	0	5	0	2	1	0	0	0	0	0	0	0
S.DOMINIONS (TOTAL)	5	3	57	5	4	29	8	15	19	1	31	54	33	9	7	12	3	3	5	19	4	5
AUSTRALIA	3	2	33	2	4	6	4	10	14	1	16	24	18	4	4	5	3	3	1	4	2	4
NEW ZEALAND	0	1	6	1	0	3	1	3	2	0	5	10	5	0	1	1	0	0	3	3	1	0
RHODESIA	0	0	0	1	0	3	1	0	0	0	1	3	0	1	0	1	0	0	0	0	0	0
S.AFRICA	2	0	18	1	0	17	3	2	3	0	9	17	10	4	2	5	0	3	1	8	1	1
OUTSIDE U.S.(TOTAL)	81	26	635	95	67	206	64	208	180	51	276	546	309	95	89	155	41	26	63	135	61	57

(TABLE CONTINUED ON FOLLOWING PAGES)

TABLE 3.2.1 (CONTINUED)

COUNTRY OR REGION	NON-FERROUS METAL	CANS	FAB-MET	ENGINES	CONSTR-MC	FARM-MC	OFF-MC+COMPUT	SPECL-MC	GENL-MC	OTH-NON-EL-MC	EL-LT+WIRING	EL-TRAN	RAD+TV+APPL	ELECTRONICS	OTH-ELE	COMMUNICATION	MOTOR-VEHIC	OTH-TRN	PRECISION	MISC	TOTAL
CANADA	17	5	35	5	25	2	5	7	15	12	3	10	12	1	12	6	25	4	23	30	594
LATIN AMER. (TOTAL)	28	15	43	2	31	6	19	16	24	18	14	1	26	15	51	9	82	9	25	31	1325
C.AM.+CARIB.(TOTAL)	11	6	15	1	15	2	6	4	11	7	5	0	8	11	24	4	18	3	10	16	542
BAHAMAS	0	0	0	0	0	0	0	0	0	0	0	0	0	0	0	0	0	0	0	5	5
BERMUDA	0	0	0	0	0	0	0	0	0	0	0	0	0	0	0	0	0	0	0	0	0
COSTA RICA	0	0	1	0	0	0	0	0	0	0	0	0	0	0	0	0	0	0	2	1	23
GUATEMALA	0	1	0	0	0	0	0	0	0	1	0	0	0	1	0	0	0	0	0	2	34
JAMAICA	0	0	1	0	0	0	0	0	0	0	0	0	0	0	0	0	0	0	0	2	20
MEXICO	8	3	11	1	15	2	6	4	11	6	3	0	7	8	18	4	18	3	8	3	364
NETH.ANTILLES	0	0	0	0	0	0	0	0	0	0	0	0	0	0	0	0	0	0	0	0	6
NICARAGUA	0	0	0	0	0	0	0	0	0	0	0	0	0	0	0	0	0	0	0	0	13
PANAMA	1	0	0	0	0	0	0	0	0	0	1	0	0	1	0	0	0	0	0	0	27
OTHER C.AM+CAR.	2	2	2	0	0	0	0	0	0	1	1	0	1	1	6	0	0	0	0	3	50
S.AMERICA (TOTAL)	17	9	28	1	16	4	13	12	13	11	9	1	18	4	27	5	64	6	15	15	783
BOLIVIA	1	0	0	0	0	0	1	1	0	0	0	0	0	0	0	0	0	0	0	2	2
CHILE	2	0	2	0	4	0	1	0	2	2	1	0	1	0	1	1	1	0	0	0	30
COLOMBIA	1	2	5	0	2	2	0	1	0	0	1	0	2	0	7	1	17	0	0	1	104
ECUADOR	0	0	0	1	0	0	0	0	0	0	0	0	1	0	0	1	0	0	0	0	23
PERU	0	0	1	0	0	0	2	2	0	0	0	0	0	1	1	1	1	1	3	0	38
ARGENTINA	3	1	4	0	2	2	3	3	5	4	1	1	4	1	15	3	15	1	3	4	130
BRAZIL	5	3	6	0	10	2	5	7	6	2	3	0	5	2	25	3	25	5	10	5	255
URUGUAY	1	1	0	0	0	0	0	0	1	1	0	0	2	0	0	0	2	0	2	0	21
VENEZUELA	4	3	7	0	1	0	0	1	2	2	3	0	4	0	13	0	13	0	2	5	176
OTHER S.AMER.	1	0	0	0	0	0	0	0	0	0	0	0	0	0	0	0	0	0	0	0	4
EUROPE (TOTAL)	74	17	128	15	52	15	35	56	61	59	10	12	45	48	51	36	108	18	81	102	2427
BELGIUM	4	0	5	3	3	1	2	5	3	3	0	0	2	2	5	6	2	6	6	1	159
FRANCE	4	2	12	4	14	2	4	8	13	3	2	0	6	9	4	6	21	2	18	15	354
GERMANY	10	6	20	4	5	4	8	8	6	7	9	2	11	10	9	4	17	2	21	18	398
ITALY	4	0	11	1	6	1	0	9	7	5	7	0	5	2	6	2	13	2	4	6	231
LUXEMBOURG	0	0	0	0	2	0	3	0	0	0	0	0	2	0	0	0	0	0	0	0	128
NETHERLANDS	6	1	7	0	0	1	0	3	0	2	0	0	0	1	0	1	0	0	5	5	13
DENMARK	1	1	2	0	1	0	1	0	3	0	1	0	0	0	0	1	2	0	1	1	40
IRELAND	0	0	5	0	0	1	1	0	0	2	0	0	2	1	0	1	3	0	1	3	61
U.K.	32	1	40	2	13	4	4	17	25	20	2	7	11	15	14	5	27	4	12	34	565
AUSTRIA	0	0	1	0	1	0	1	0	1	1	0	0	0	0	1	2	1	0	1	3	32
FINLAND	0	1	0	0	1	0	0	0	0	0	0	0	0	0	1	1	0	1	0	0	7
GREECE	1	1	0	0	1	1	0	0	0	0	0	0	0	0	1	1	0	0	0	0	31
NORWAY	5	0	3	0	0	0	1	0	0	0	0	0	0	1	0	1	0	1	1	0	26
PORTUGAL	0	1	0	1	1	2	1	0	0	0	1	1	4	3	3	1	2	1	1	1	37
SPAIN	4	1	13	0	3	0	4	2	2	2	0	0	4	1	3	4	7	0	5	7	192
SWEDEN	2	1	5	0	1	2	0	3	1	1	1	0	1	0	3	3	3	1	3	4	73
SWITZERLAND	1	1	2	0	1	1	0	2	1	1	1	0	1	1	1	1	1	0	3	4	47
TURKEY	1	0	0	0	0	1	0	0	0	0	0	2	1	0	2	1	2	0	0	0	21
OTHER EUROPE	1	0	2	2	0	0	0	0	1	1	0	0	0	0	0	0	0	0	1	0	12

TABLE 3.2.1 (CONTINUED)

COUNTRY OR REGION	NON-FERROUS	METAL CANS	FAB-MET	ENGINES	CONSTR-MC	FARM-MC	OFF-MC+COMPUT	SPECL-MC	GENL-MC	OTH-NON-EL-MC	EL-LT+WIRING	EL-TRAN	RAD+TV+APPL	ELECTRONICS	COMMUNICATION	OTH-ELE	MOTOR-VEHIC	OTH-TRN	PRECISION	MISC	TOTAL
N.AFR+M.EAST (TOTAL)	4	2	5	0	7	1	0	1	0	0	0	2	0	0	3	0	3	0	3	1	100
ALGERIA	0	0	0	0	0	1	0	0	0	0	0	0	0	0	1	0	1	0	0	1	4
EGYPT	2	0	0	0	0	0	0	0	0	0	0	0	0	0	0	0	0	0	0	0	2
IRAN	0	0	2	0	2	0	0	0	0	0	0	0	0	0	0	0	1	0	1	0	33
ISRAEL	1	1	0	0	2	0	0	0	0	0	0	1	0	0	0	0	0	0	1	0	16
LEBANON	0	0	0	0	0	0	0	0	0	0	0	0	0	0	0	0	0	0	0	0	10
MOROCCO	0	1	3	0	1	0	0	1	0	0	0	0	0	0	1	0	1	0	0	0	17
SAUDI ARABIA	0	0	0	0	0	0	0	0	0	0	0	0	0	0	0	0	0	0	0	0	6
OTHER N.AF+M.E.	1	0	0	0	2	0	0	0	0	0	0	1	0	0	1	0	0	0	1	0	12
E.+W.AFRICA (TOTAL)	7	1	6	0	1	0	0	0	1	3	3	3	1	1	5	0	2	1	3	0	91
GHANA	1	1	0	0	0	0	0	0	1	0	1	0	1	1	1	0	1	0	1	0	6
IVORY COAST	1	0	0	0	0	0	0	0	0	0	1	0	0	0	1	0	0	0	0	0	6
KENYA	0	0	1	0	0	0	0	0	0	0	0	0	0	0	1	0	0	0	0	0	16
LIBERIA	0	0	0	0	0	0	0	0	0	0	0	0	0	0	0	0	0	0	0	0	0
NIGERIA	0	0	1	0	1	0	0	0	0	2	1	2	0	0	1	0	1	1	1	0	20
ZAIRE	1	0	1	0	0	0	0	0	0	1	0	1	0	0	1	0	0	0	1	0	11
ZAMBIA	3	0	1	0	0	0	0	0	0	0	0	0	0	0	0	0	0	0	0	0	15
OTHER E.+W.AFR.	1	1	2	0	0	0	0	0	0	0	0	0	0	0	0	0	0	0	0	0	17
SOUTH ASIA (TOTAL)	6	0	2	0	3	2	1	0	1	3	2	2	1	1	9	0	2	1	3	1	111
INDIA	4	0	2	0	3	2	1	0	1	3	2	1	1	1	7	0	2	1	3	1	82
PAKISTAN	1	0	0	0	0	1	0	0	0	0	0	1	0	0	1	0	0	0	1	0	23
SRI LANKA	1	0	0	0	0	0	0	0	0	0	0	0	0	0	1	0	0	0	0	0	5
OTHER S.ASIA	0	0	0	0	0	0	0	0	0	0	0	0	0	0	0	0	0	0	0	0	1
EAST ASIA (TOTAL)	19	3	26	3	12	2	13	4	17	6	4	2	15	23	22	5	29	0	13	19	568
HONG KONG	3	0	2	0	1	0	2	0	0	0	0	0	1	0	5	0	0	0	1	2	27
INDONESIA	0	0	3	0	1	1	0	0	0	0	0	0	0	0	1	0	0	0	0	0	27
JAPAN	7	2	10	2	6	0	9	3	16	5	2	1	3	6	9	0	19	0	9	14	275
MALAYSIA	0	0	2	0	0	1	0	0	0	0	0	0	3	3	1	0	1	0	1	0	30
PHILIPPINES	2	1	3	0	1	0	0	1	1	1	1	0	3	4	2	1	3	0	1	0	68
SINGAPORE	3	0	2	0	1	1	1	0	0	0	0	1	0	0	0	1	2	0	0	1	35
S.KOREA	1	0	1	0	3	0	1	0	0	0	1	0	3	4	2	1	3	0	0	1	28
THAILAND	2	0	2	0	0	0	1	0	0	0	0	0	1	1	1	0	1	0	1	1	35
TAIWAN	1	0	0	0	0	0	1	0	0	0	0	2	1	5	1	2	0	0	0	1	40
OTHER E.ASIA	0	0	1	1	0	0	0	0	0	0	0	0	0	0	0	0	0	0	0	0	3
S.DOMINIONS (TOTAL)	21	3	43	3	22	7	5	7	4	11	6	9	1	1	14	4	36	1	12	19	559
AUSTRALIA	18	3	23	2	12	3	3	4	3	6	6	7	1	1	7	2	18	1	9	13	310
NEW ZEALAND	2	0	9	0	2	1	1	0	0	0	0	0	0	0	2	1	6	0	0	3	70
RHODESIA	0	0	2	0	0	0	0	0	0	0	0	0	0	0	0	0	0	0	0	0	13
S.AFRICA	1	0	9	1	8	3	1	3	1	5	1	2	0	0	5	1	12	0	3	3	166
OUTSIDE U.S. (TOTAL)	176	46	288	28	153	35	78	91	123	109	34	31	115	90	167	62	286	33	161	203	5775

CHAPTER 3 — THE MATURING OF FOREIGN SUBSIDIARIES
SECTION 2 —— STOCK OF MANUFACTURING SUBSIDIARIES AT 1-JAN-76
TABLE 2 ——— BY REGION AND SUBSIDIARY-INDUSTRIES IN 1975

NO. OF SUBSIDIARY-INDUSTRIES IN 1975, FOR MANUFACTURING SUBSIDIARIES ACTIVE AT 1-JAN-76

COUNTRY OR REGION	BEVERAGES	TOBACCO	FOOD	TXTL+APPRL	WOOD+FURNI	PAPER	PRINTING	INDUS-CHEM	PLASTIC	AGRIC-CHEM	COSMETICS	DRUGS	OTHER-CHEM	FABR-PLSTCS	REF-PETRLM	TIRES	OTH-PETRLM	LEATHER	STONE+CLAY+CEMNT	ABRASIVES	GLASS	IRON
CANADA	21	1	86	27	34	31	15	32	25	11	28	30	54	27	5	12	7	6	12	21	7	9
LATIN AMER. (TOTAL)	30	10	185	34	15	77	11	69	65	44	118	167	115	48	28	25	12	6	22	40	23	17
C.AM.+CARIB. (TOTAL)	12	5	89	13	9	27	6	33	26	22	50	61	40	17	8	17	4	2	8	10	6	4
BAHAMAS	0	0	1	0	0	0	0	0	1	0	1	0	0	0	0	1	0	0	0	0	0	0
BERMUDA	0	0	0	1	0	0	0	0	0	0	0	0	0	0	0	0	0	0	1	0	0	0
COSTA RICA	1	1	4	0	0	2	0	0	1	0	2	0	3	0	0	0	0	0	0	0	0	0
GUATEMALA	1	1	11	0	4	2	0	1	1	2	5	4	2	1	1	0	0	0	1	0	0	0
JAMAICA	1	0	8	0	1	1	0	1	0	0	3	4	2	0	1	0	0	2	0	0	0	0
MEXICO	10	0	45	14	3	14	6	27	22	12	28	37	32	15	5	4	2	0	6	9	6	4
NETH.ANTILLES	0	0	0	0	0	0	0	1	0	2	0	0	0	0	0	2	0	0	0	0	0	0
NICARAGUA	0	0	4	1	0	3	0	0	1	2	4	2	1	0	0	4	0	0	1	1	0	0
PANAMA	0	1	7	0	0	2	0	0	0	0	7	5	1	0	0	4	1	0	0	1	0	0
OTHER C.AM+CAR.	0	1	9	1	1	4	0	2	2	3	9	6	1	0	1	5	1	0	1	0	0	0
S.AMERICA (TOTAL)	18	5	96	21	6	50	5	36	39	22	68	106	75	31	20	8	8	4	14	30	17	13
BOLIVIA	1	0	3	0	0	0	0	2	3	0	2	6	3	1	0	0	2	0	1	1	0	0
CHILE	5	0	16	3	1	14	0	2	3	7	6	10	12	4	3	2	1	1	4	4	0	2
COLOMBIA	1	1	4	3	0	1	0	5	8	0	6	7	2	1	1	1	0	0	0	1	2	0
ECUADOR	0	0	9	0	1	1	0	1	1	0	7	8	0	1	1	1	0	1	0	0	0	0
PERU	2	0	10	3	1	5	2	3	9	4	7	8	16	2	2	1	1	0	1	3	3	2
ARGENTINA	2	1	10	7	2	12	3	18	13	7	16	19	16	6	2	2	3	2	5	4	3	5
BRAZIL	6	2	26	7	1	12	3	18	13	7	13	29	27	9	4	4	3	0	11	11	7	1
URUGUAY	2	0	2	2	0	0	0	6	4	0	3	4	4	4	1	0	0	0	5	0	0	3
VENEZUELA	2	2	25	6	1	16	1	6	4	4	18	22	14	8	8	2	0	0	9	9	5	3
OTHER S.AMER.	0	0	1	0	0	1	0	0	0	0	1	0	0	0	0	0	0	0	0	0	0	0
EUROPE (TOTAL)	35	13	267	61	27	100	47	148	132	35	150	240	236	102	31	79	34	23	38	82	34	38
BELGIUM	3	2	15	7	0	9	2	19	17	5	6	16	20	9	1	5	4	2	7	6	3	4
FRANCE	1	1	23	8	4	24	5	22	12	5	28	41	35	6	2	13	8	5	14	14	1	6
GERMANY	5	1	45	8	6	13	9	27	23	4	25	31	33	17	4	13	7	5	6	14	8	5
ITALY	2	2	24	4	3	11	5	18	8	6	12	28	28	9	2	12	3	3	3	11	3	6
LUXEMBOURG	0	0	0	0	0	0	0	0	2	0	0	0	0	0	0	0	0	0	0	1	0	0
NETHERLANDS	0	1	24	3	4	3	3	5	9	1	5	6	23	5	1	6	2	2	5	2	2	0
DENMARK	0	0	14	0	0	0	0	1	1	0	6	13	2	3	5	3	0	1	3	3	0	0
IRELAND	2	0	8	1	1	2	1	3	3	0	7	13	3	1	0	3	1	0	3	3	0	0
U.K.	8	2	53	18	5	15	16	26	37	6	31	30	53	28	4	10	4	5	15	16	9	9
AUSTRIA	0	0	3	0	0	0	1	2	1	0	3	3	3	1	0	3	0	1	1	1	0	0
FINLAND	0	0	0	0	1	1	0	1	0	0	2	2	1	1	0	2	1	0	0	0	1	1
GREECE	1	0	6	0	0	2	0	0	0	0	2	9	2	2	1	2	0	0	0	1	1	1
NORWAY	0	0	1	1	0	0	0	6	0	0	1	1	2	0	0	2	0	0	1	1	0	0
PORTUGAL	1	2	4	2	0	10	3	12	2	2	3	11	0	0	2	3	0	0	0	0	3	5
SPAIN	6	2	25	2	3	3	1	4	9	0	13	27	18	7	2	3	4	1	2	6	3	1
SWEDEN	1	0	16	2	0	0	1	3	3	1	4	7	7	5	3	1	1	0	6	2	2	0
SWITZERLAND	2	2	5	1	1	3	0	2	3	0	2	6	2	4	2	2	0	0	2	1	0	1
TURKEY	0	0	1	1	0	1	0	0	0	0	0	4	1	0	1	0	0	0	1	0	0	0
OTHER EUROPE	0	0	0	1	0	1	0	0	1	0	2	0	1	1	2	0	0	0	0	1	0	0

TABLE 3 . 2 . 2 (CONTINUED)

COUNTRY OR REGION	BEVERAGES	TOBACCO	FOOD	TXTL+APPRL	WOOD+FURNI	PAPER	PRINTING	INDUS-CHEM	PLASTIC	AGRIC-CHEM	COSMETICS	DRUGS	OTHER-CHEM	FABR-PLSTCS	TIRES	REF-PETRLM	OTH-PETRLM	LEATHER	STONE+CLAY+CEMNT	ABRASIVES	GLASS	IRON
N.AFR+M.EAST (TOTAL)	0	0	13	3	1	3	0	4	7	1	11	15	9	3	6	5	2	1	1	1	1	1
ALGERIA	0	0	1	0	0	0	0	0	0	0	1	1	0	0	0	1	0	1	1	1	0	1
EGYPT	0	0	0	0	0	0	0	0	0	0	0	0	0	0	0	0	0	0	0	0	0	0
IRAN	0	0	2	0	0	1	0	2	3	0	2	8	4	3	3	0	0	0	0	0	0	0
ISRAEL	0	0	1	1	0	1	0	0	4	0	2	1	4	0	0	0	0	0	0	0	1	0
LEBANON	0	0	3	1	1	0	0	0	0	0	3	3	1	0	1	0	1	0	0	0	0	0
MOROCCO	0	0	3	1	0	1	0	1	0	0	1	2	0	0	2	0	0	0	0	0	0	0
SAUDI ARABIA	0	0	0	0	0	0	0	0	0	0	1	0	0	0	0	2	1	0	0	0	0	0
OTHER N.AF+M.E.	0	0	3	0	0	0	0	1	0	1	1	0	0	0	0	2	0	0	0	0	0	0
E.+W.AFRICA (TOTAL)	3	1	10	0	0	5	3	8	2	0	10	13	1	1	5	8	5	1	1	1	1	0
GHANA	0	1	1	0	0	0	0	3	0	0	0	1	1	0	0	0	0	0	1	1	1	0
IVORY COAST	0	0	1	0	0	0	0	0	2	0	0	0	0	0	1	1	1	0	0	0	0	0
KENYA	1	0	3	0	0	0	1	2	0	0	3	3	0	1	0	2	2	0	0	0	0	0
LIBERIA	0	0	0	0	0	0	0	0	0	0	0	0	0	0	1	2	0	0	0	0	0	0
NIGERIA	0	0	2	0	0	0	0	1	0	0	3	5	0	0	0	0	1	0	0	0	0	0
ZAIRE	0	0	0	0	0	0	0	0	0	0	1	3	0	0	0	0	0	0	0	0	0	0
ZAMBIA	1	0	0	0	0	3	2	0	0	0	2	1	0	0	1	0	0	0	0	0	0	0
OTHER E.+W.AFR.	1	0	3	0	0	2	0	2	0	0	1	0	0	0	2	3	1	1	0	0	0	0
SOUTH ASIA (TOTAL)	4	2	7	3	0	1	0	8	6	9	9	27	11	4	3	3	0	0	3	3	3	2
INDIA	3	1	2	3	0	1	0	7	6	6	5	15	10	2	2	2	0	0	3	3	3	2
PAKISTAN	1	1	2	0	0	0	0	1	0	2	3	10	1	1	1	1	0	0	0	0	0	0
SRI LANKA	0	0	0	0	0	0	0	0	0	0	1	1	0	1	0	0	0	0	0	0	0	0
OTHER S.ASIA	0	0	3	0	0	0	0	0	0	1	0	1	0	0	0	0	0	0	0	0	0	0
EAST ASIA (TOTAL)	13	1	51	9	9	21	13	45	38	17	36	64	53	20	9	22	10	0	8	17	8	3
HONG KONG	0	0	2	2	1	0	5	1	1	0	1	2	3	0	0	0	0	0	0	0	0	0
INDONESIA	1	1	2	0	0	0	0	1	0	1	4	11	1	0	1	0	0	0	1	1	1	0
JAPAN	5	0	22	0	2	5	5	29	24	3	11	21	24	9	1	9	7	0	5	9	6	1
MALAYSIA	1	0	3	0	1	2	0	0	1	3	5	4	5	1	3	1	0	0	0	3	0	0
PHILIPPINES	3	0	11	0	5	5	0	2	1	4	8	16	8	4	0	3	0	0	0	3	0	0
SINGAPORE	0	0	3	5	0	0	0	4	0	0	3	3	2	0	0	3	2	0	0	0	0	1
S.KOREA	1	0	2	0	0	1	0	4	4	5	1	2	5	2	2	2	0	0	1	0	1	0
THAILAND	1	0	4	1	0	3	3	1	1	0	1	5	2	2	2	2	1	0	0	1	0	1
OTHER E.ASIA	1	0	2	1	0	5	0	3	6	1	2	0	3	2	0	2	0	0	1	0	0	0
S.DOMINIONS (TOTAL)	9	3	60	12	6	36	13	29	26	16	51	64	62	30	7	12	6	6	7	23	7	7
AUSTRALIA	6	2	36	5	5	11	4	21	20	11	28	31	36	18	4	5	5	2	5	12	4	6
NEW ZEALAND	0	1	6	1	1	1	1	4	2	1	7	11	9	0	1	1	0	0	1	3	1	0
RHODESIA	0	0	0	2	0	3	1	0	0	1	2	3	1	1	0	1	0	0	0	0	0	0
S.AFRICA	3	0	18	4	0	21	7	4	4	3	14	19	16	11	2	5	1	4	1	8	2	1
OUTSIDE U.S. (TOTAL)	115	31	679	149	92	274	94	338	301	133	413	620	541	241	94	166	76	43	91	188	82	77

(TABLE CONTINUED ON FOLLOWING PAGES)

TABLE 3.2.2 (CONTINUED)

COUNTRY OR REGION	NON-FERROUS METAL	METAL CANS	FAB-MET	ENGINES	CONSTR-MC	FARM-MC	OFF-MC+COMPUT	SPECL-MC	GENL-MC	OTH-NON-EL-MC	EL-LT+WIRING	EL-TRAN	RAD+TV+APPL	ELECTRONICS	OTH-ELE	COMMUNICATION	OTH-TRAN	MOTOR-VEHIC	OTH-TRN	PRECISION	MISC	TOTAL
CANADA	20	7	61	6	28	3	18	9	16	34	21	5	13	20	6	22	11	35	8	30	37	893
LATIN AMER. (TOTAL)	36	19	76	11	45	18	22	26	16	42	36	26	4	47	32	64	13	93	14	51	41	1877
C.AM.+CARIB. (TOTAL)	13	6	30	4	19	5	8	8	19	13	17	9	2	19	30	30	5	22	6	12	20	735
BAHAMAS	0	0	0	0	0	0	0	0	0	0	0	0	0	0	0	0	0	0	0	0	0	6
BERMUDA	0	0	0	0	0	0	0	0	0	0	0	0	0	0	0	0	0	0	0	0	0	0
COSTA RICA	0	1	1	0	0	0	0	0	0	0	1	1	0	1	1	1	0	0	0	2	1	29
GUATEMALA	0	0	1	0	0	0	0	0	0	1	0	0	0	0	2	2	0	0	0	0	2	40
JAMAICA	0	1	0	0	0	0	0	0	0	0	1	0	0	0	0	0	0	0	0	0	0	22
MEXICO	10	3	25	4	19	5	8	8	19	12	7	7	2	14	16	24	5	22	6	10	14	533
NETH.ANTILLES	0	0	0	0	0	0	0	0	0	0	0	0	0	0	0	1	0	0	0	0	0	6
NICARAGUA	0	0	0	0	0	0	0	0	0	0	0	0	0	0	0	1	0	0	0	0	0	16
PANAMA	1	0	0	0	0	0	0	0	0	0	1	0	0	0	0	0	0	0	0	0	0	28
OTHER C.AM+CAR.	2	2	0	0	0	0	0	0	0	0	1	1	0	0	1	1	0	0	0	0	3	55
S.AMERICA (TOTAL)	23	13	46	7	26	13	14	18	23	23	17	2	2	31	13	34	8	71	8	39	21	1142
BOLIVIA	0	1	0	0	1	0	0	0	2	0	1	0	0	0	0	0	0	0	0	0	0	2
CHILE	1	2	2	0	0	2	0	1	0	2	1	1	0	1	0	0	0	1	0	0	1	42
COLOMBIA	3	2	9	1	2	2	4	2	1	2	0	3	0	3	2	2	1	8	0	0	1	153
ECUADOR	1	0	2	0	0	0	0	0	2	0	2	0	0	0	2	2	0	0	0	0	0	28
PERU	0	2	2	0	2	0	3	0	0	2	0	2	0	2	0	0	0	0	0	0	0	47
ARGENTINA	4	1	6	3	6	4	3	4	5	9	4	7	1	7	3	3	1	16	1	9	6	214
BRAZIL	6	3	13	2	14	5	6	10	12	10	6	10	1	10	6	21	5	30	7	25	7	404
URUGUAY	0	1	1	1	0	2	0	0	1	0	1	2	0	2	0	0	0	0	0	0	0	26
VENEZUELA	7	3	11	1	1	2	0	1	0	2	3	3	0	6	3	5	0	13	0	3	6	222
OTHER S.AMER.	1	0	0	0	0	0	0	0	0	0	0	0	0	0	0	0	0	0	0	0	0	4
EUROPE (TOTAL)	91	26	195	30	80	28	51	83	111	91	21	27	89	84	90	47	139	40	140	129	3544	3544
BELGIUM	6	1	10	4	6	2	4	6	9	8	2	3	5	7	8	3	6	5	7	2	261	261
FRANCE	5	4	21	6	16	5	5	14	21	18	8	13	2	18	11	9	13	24	30	19	513	513
GERMANY	13	8	29	7	11	5	12	13	16	16	8	15	4	15	18	6	7	25	7	32	24	590
ITALY	4	0	17	3	8	2	6	12	10	9	1	11	2	11	4	9	5	14	2	8	7	336
LUXEMBOURG	0	0	1	0	2	0	0	0	1	1	0	0	0	0	0	0	0	0	0	1	0	18
NETHERLANDS	7	2	13	1	2	2	3	3	4	4	2	3	3	3	1	2	8	3	9	6	189	189
DENMARK	0	1	3	0	2	0	1	0	2	2	0	3	0	3	2	1	2	1	1	1	61
IRELAND	0	0	5	0	1	1	1	3	0	2	0	0	0	0	0	2	3	1	1	4	81
U.K.	37	4	62	3	20	4	9	28	38	25	3	21	11	25	24	6	41	10	31	41	843
AUSTRIA	0	0	2	0	2	0	1	0	3	1	0	0	0	0	2	2	1	0	1	3	42
FINLAND	0	1	1	0	0	0	0	1	0	1	1	0	0	1	1	1	0	0	0	0	14
GREECE	1	0	3	1	1	1	1	0	1	0	2	0	0	1	0	1	0	0	0	0	37
NORWAY	0	1	2	2	2	0	1	0	2	2	0	0	2	3	1	1	2	0	1	1	39
PORTUGAL	0	1	0	0	0	5	2	2	0	0	0	0	4	7	1	1	0	1	2	45
SPAIN	6	2	16	2	3	1	4	1	5	8	2	5	2	3	3	4	3	1	3	7	12	274
SWEDEN	2	2	6	0	2	1	4	2	1	1	1	3	0	1	1	1	1	1	3	4	104
SWITZERLAND	2	1	0	0	1	2	1	0	2	1	2	1	0	2	1	1	1	2	0	3	0	54
TURKEY	1	0	0	1	0	0	0	0	1	1	0	1	0	2	1	0	1	0	1	1	27
OTHER EUROPE	1	0	2	0	0	0	0	0	1	1	1	0	1	1	0	0	0	0	1	1	16

TABLE 3.2.2 (CONTINUED)

COUNTRY OR REGION	NON-FERROUS	METAL CANS FAB-MET	ENGINES	OFF-MC+COMPUT	CONSTR-MC	FARM-MC	SPECL-MC	GENL-MC	OTH-NON-EL-MC	EL-LT+WIRING	EL-TRAN	RAD-TV+APPL	ELECTRONICS	OTH-ELE	COMMUNICATION	MOTOR-VEHIC	OTH-TRN	PRECISION	MISC	TOTAL
N.AFR+M.EAST (TOTAL)	4	2	5	0	7	1	2	1	0	0	2	1	3	3	0	3	2	0	5	127
ALGERIA	0	0	0	0	0	0	0	0	0	0	0	0	0	0	0	1	0	0	1	4
EGYPT	0	0	0	0	2	0	0	0	0	0	0	0	0	0	0	0	1	0	0	3
IRAN	2	0	1	0	2	0	0	1	0	0	0	0	2	1	0	1	1	0	0	40
ISRAEL	0	1	0	0	1	0	0	0	0	0	1	0	0	0	1	0	1	0	1	20
LEBANON	1	0	0	0	0	0	0	0	0	0	0	0	0	0	0	0	1	0	0	19
MOROCCO	0	1	3	0	0	0	1	0	0	0	0	0	0	0	0	1	1	0	0	20
SAUDI ARABIA	0	0	0	0	0	0	0	0	0	0	0	0	0	0	0	0	0	0	0	8
OTHER N.AF+M.E.	1	0	0	0	2	0	1	0	0	0	1	0	1	1	0	0	0	0	0	13
E.+W.AFRICA (TOTAL)	8	5	7	0	2	0	0	1	0	0	5	5	5	1	3	1	0	0	0	120
GHANA	1	0	0	0	0	0	0	1	0	0	0	0	0	1	0	1	0	0	0	8
IVORY COAST	0	0	0	0	0	0	0	0	0	0	0	0	1	1	0	0	0	0	0	7
KENYA	0	1	1	0	0	0	0	0	0	0	0	1	1	0	0	0	1	0	0	21
LIBERIA	0	0	0	0	0	0	0	0	0	0	0	0	0	0	0	0	0	0	0	0
NIGERIA	0	0	0	0	1	0	0	0	0	0	0	1	0	0	1	0	0	0	0	25
ZAIRE	2	0	2	0	1	0	0	0	0	0	2	1	2	0	1	1	0	0	0	19
ZAMBIA	3	1	1	0	1	0	0	0	0	0	0	1	3	0	1	0	0	0	0	19
OTHER E.+W.AFR.	1	3	2	0	0	0	0	0	0	0	1	0	0	0	0	0	0	0	0	21
SOUTH ASIA (TOTAL)	7	7	0	0	5	2	2	4	4	4	6	1	9	1	0	2	2	5	1	169
INDIA	5	7	0	0	5	2	2	4	4	4	4	1	7	1	0	2	2	3	1	131
PAKISTAN	1	0	0	0	0	0	0	0	0	0	1	0	1	0	0	0	0	0	0	31
SRI LANKA	1	0	0	0	0	0	0	0	0	0	1	0	1	1	0	0	0	0	0	5
OTHER S.ASIA	0	0	0	0	0	0	0	0	0	0	0	0	0	0	0	0	0	0	0	2
EAST ASIA (TOTAL)	26	4	32	9	19	5	18	4	22	12	24	38	27	7	2	31	1	19	21	790
HONG KONG	4	0	2	0	2	0	3	0	1	0	3	4	2	0	0	0	0	2	2	38
INDONESIA	0	0	3	0	1	0	0	0	0	0	0	4	1	0	0	0	1	2	0	32
JAPAN	10	2	15	7	11	2	11	3	19	8	4	12	11	2	0	20	0	2	16	377
MALAYSIA	1	1	2	0	1	0	0	1	0	0	3	4	3	0	1	1	0	1	0	46
PHILIPPINES	2	4	2	2	2	1	2	0	0	0	4	5	3	2	0	4	0	2	0	106
SINGAPORE	3	2	1	0	3	1	0	1	0	2	5	5	5	1	1	0	0	0	0	49
S.KOREA	2	1	0	0	2	0	1	0	0	1	1	3	0	0	0	2	0	0	1	39
THAILAND	3	2	1	0	3	0	1	0	1	0	4	1	1	1	1	3	0	1	1	43
TAIWAN	1	0	0	0	0	0	0	1	0	1	0	9	2	3	0	1	0	1	1	57
OTHER E.ASIA	0	1	0	0	0	0	1	0	0	0	0	0	0	0	0	0	0	0	0	3
S.DOMINIONS (TOTAL)	25	7	58	8	34	15	11	10	19	20	14	3	25	6	4	39	6	27	29	856
AUSTRALIA	22	5	33	5	19	9	6	7	14	13	9	3	16	4	1	20	5	20	22	516
NEW ZEALAND	2	0	10	0	4	3	2	0	1	0	2	0	2	1	0	2	0	1	2	91
RHODESIA	0	1	0	0	0	0	0	0	0	0	0	0	0	0	0	0	0	1	0	20
S.AFRICA	1	1	13	3	11	3	3	3	4	7	3	0	7	1	1	13	1	5	3	229
OUTSIDE U.S. (TOTAL)	217	70	441	64	220	72	114	141	234	185	66	54	207	166	245	89	343	71	280	259	8376

CHAPTER 3 - THE MATURING OF FOREIGN SUBSIDIARIES
SECTION 2 -- STOCK OF MANUFACTURING SUBSIDIARIES AT 1-JAN-76
TABLE 3 --- BY PRINCIPAL INDUSTRY AND SUBSIDIARY-INDUSTRIES

FOR MANUFACTURING SUBSIDIARIES ACTIVE AT 1-JAN-76

NO. OF SUBSIDIARY-INDUSTRIES IN 1975, BY PRINCIPAL INDUSTRY OF SUBSIDIARY IN 1975

PRINCIPAL INDUSTRY	BEVERAGES	TOBACCO	FOOD	TXTL+APPRL	WOOD+FURNI	PAPER	PRINTING	INDUS-CHEM	PLASTIC	AGRIC-CHEM	COSMETICS	DRUGS	OTHER-CHEM	FABR-PLSTCS	TIRES	REF-PETRLM	OTH-PETRLM	LEATHER	STONE+CLAY+CEMNT	ABRASIVES	GLASS	IRON
BEVERAGES	81	0	8	0	0	0	0	0	0	0	0	0	0	0	0	0	0	0	0	0	0	0
TOBACCO	0	26	0	0	0	0	0	0	0	0	0	0	0	0	0	0	0	0	0	0	1	0
FOOD	32	1	635	0	0	1	1	3	1	5	11	7	24	0	0	1	0	2	1	0	0	0
TEXTILES+APPAREL	0	0	1	95	1	3	0	0	2	0	1	0	2	3	0	0	0	0	0	2	2	1
WOOD+FURNITURE	0	0	0	4	67	5	0	0	2	0	1	0	6	1	0	0	0	0	0	0	0	2
PAPER	0	0	0	5	5	206	11	1	4	0	3	1	8	8	0	0	0	1	1	7	1	0
PRINTING	0	0	0	0	0	2	64	0	0	0	0	0	2	0	0	0	0	0	0	0	0	0
INDUSTRIAL CHEM	0	0	0	2	3	1	0	208	20	8	5	10	41	4	0	2	3	0	0	5	0	3
PLASTICS	1	2	2	5	1	5	0	16	180	7	0	1	35	26	1	2	0	0	0	0	0	0
AGRIC CHEM	0	0	1	0	0	0	0	4	2	51	2	8	8	1	0	0	2	0	0	0	0	0
COSMETICS	1	0	11	11	0	6	0	1	2	4	276	27	2	2	0	0	0	0	0	0	0	0
DRUGS	0	0	18	0	0	1	0	16	2	30	71	546	35	3	0	0	0	2	0	0	0	0
OTHER CHEM	0	0	1	3	1	7	1	31	39	16	11	8	309	7	1	4	6	1	1	4	0	0
FABR PLASTICS	0	0	0	2	0	2	0	5	9	9	0	1	5	95	1	1	0	0	0	0	2	2
TIRES	0	0	0	2	0	0	0	0	5	1	0	0	3	35	89	0	0	0	0	0	0	0
REF PETROLEUM	0	0	0	2	0	0	0	18	9	3	0	0	16	0	0	155	21	0	0	1	0	0
OTH PETROLEUM	0	0	0	0	0	0	0	4	5	0	1	0	3	1	0	1	41	0	0	1	0	0
LEATHER	0	0	0	1	0	0	0	1	1	0	1	1	1	4	0	0	0	26	0	0	0	0
STONE+CLAY+CEMNT	0	0	0	0	1	0	0	1	1	0	0	0	6	2	0	0	0	0	63	12	2	1
ABRASIVES	0	0	0	8	1	6	2	7	1	1	3	1	10	5	0	0	3	0	13	135	6	1
GLASS	0	0	0	5	0	1	0	0	0	0	0	1	1	4	0	0	0	0	3	3	61	0
IRON+STEEL	0	0	0	0	2	0	0	0	0	0	1	0	0	3	0	0	0	0	1	0	0	57

TABLE 3.2.3 (CONTINUED)

PRINCIPAL INDUSTRY	BEVERAGES	TOBACCO	FOOD	TXTL+APPRL	WOOD+FURNI	PAPER	PRINTING	INDUS-CHEM	PLASTIC	AGRIC-CHEM	COSMETICS	DRUGS	OTHER-CHEM	FABR-PLSTCS TIRES		REF-PETRLM OTH-PETRLM	LEATHER	STONE+CLAY+CEMNT	ABRASIVES	GLASS	IRON
NON-FERROUS	0	0	0	0	0	0	0	6	1	0	0	1	2	2	0	0	0	1	2	0	1
METAL CANS	0	0	1	1	0	7	0	0	0	0	0	0	0	8	0	0	0	0	0	1	0
OTHER FAB METAL	0	0	0	1	2	7	2	3	0	0	8	0	3	6	1	0	2	0	2	0	3
ENGINES+TURBIN	0	0	0	0	0	0	0	1	0	0	0	0	0	0	0	0	0	0	0	0	0
CONSTR MACH	0	0	0	0	0	0	0	2	0	1	0	0	0	0	0	0	0	0	1	0	1
FARM MACHINERY	0	0	0	0	0	0	0	0	0	0	0	0	0	0	0	0	0	0	0	0	0
OFFICE MC+COMPUT	0	0	0	0	1	4	8	0	1	0	0	0	2	1	0	0	0	0	0	0	0
SPEC MACHINERY	0	0	0	1	1	1	0	3	2	1	0	0	5	0	1	0	8	0	0	0	1
GENL MACHINERY	0	0	0	2	0	0	1	0	1	0	0	1	0	3	0	0	0	1	2	0	0
OTH NON-EL MC	0	0	0	0	3	0	0	0	1	0	0	0	0	0	0	0	0	0	1	0	0
EL LIGHT+WIRING	0	0	0	0	0	0	1	0	0	0	0	0	0	0	0	0	0	0	0	1	0
EL TRAN EQUIP	0	0	0	0	0	0	0	1	0	0	0	0	0	0	0	0	0	0	0	0	0
RADIO+TV+APPL	0	0	0	0	2	0	2	0	0	0	0	0	0	0	0	0	0	0	0	0	0
ELECTRONICS	0	0	0	0	0	0	0	0	0	0	0	0	0	0	0	0	0	0	2	4	0
OTHER ELEC	0	0	0	0	0	0	0	3	3	2	0	0	3	3	0	0	0	3	2	0	0
COMMUNICATION	0	1	0	0	0	1	0	0	4	0	0	0	0	3	0	0	0	0	0	0	0
MOTOR VEHIC	0	0	0	1	1	0	0	1	1	0	0	0	2	4	1	0	1	0	2	0	4
OTHER TRANSP	0	0	0	0	1	0	0	0	0	0	0	0	0	0	0	0	0	0	0	0	0
PRECISION	0	0	0	3	0	5	1	0	3	2	18	6	5	4	0	0	0	0	2	1	0
MISCELLANEOUS	0	0	0	3	1	3	0	2	2	0	0	0	2	2	0	0	0	0	2	0	0
TOTAL	115	31	679	149	92	274	94	338	301	133	413	620	541	241	94	166	76	43	91	188	82	77

(TABLE CONTINUED ON FOLLOWING PAGES)

TABLE 3 .2 .3   (CONTINUED)

PRINCIPAL INDUSTRY	NON-FERROUS METAL	METAL CANS FAB-MET	ENGINES	CONSTR-MC	FARM-MC	OFF-MC+COMPUT	SPECL-MC	GENL-MC	OTH-NON-EL-MC	EL-LT+WIRING	EL-TRAN	RAD+TV+APPL	ELECTRONICS	OTH-ELE	COMMUNICATION OTH-ELE	MOTOR-VEHIC	OTH-TRN	PRECISION	MISC	TOTAL
BEVERAGES	0	0	0	0	0	0	0	0	0	0	0	0	0	0	0	0	0	0	0	91
TOBACCO	0	0	0	0	0	0	0	0	0	0	0	0	0	0	0	0	0	0	0	26
FOOD	0	2	0	1	0	0	2	0	0	0	0	0	0	0	0	0	0	0	1	732
TEXTILES+APPAREL	0	1	0	0	0	0	1	1	0	0	0	0	0	0	0	0	0	1	0	119
WOOD+FURNITURE	0	4	0	1	0	0	0	0	0	0	0	0	0	0	0	0	1	0	0	94
PAPER	0	1	0	0	0	2	1	2	0	0	0	2	2	1	1	0	0	6	1	281
PRINTING	0	0	0	0	0	3	1	1	0	0	0	1	0	0	0	0	0	2	2	82
INDUSTRIAL CHEM	6	1	0	0	0	0	1	0	2	1	0	0	0	3	0	1	0	3	7	335
PLASTICS	0	2	0	0	0	0	0	0	0	1	0	0	2	0	0	0	0	2	0	291
AGRIC CHEM	0	0	0	0	0	0	0	1	0	0	0	0	0	0	0	0	0	0	0	79
COSMETICS	0	5	0	0	0	0	0	1	1	0	0	0	0	0	0	0	0	7	3	352
DRUGS	0	2	0	0	0	0	1	1	1	0	0	1	0	0	0	0	0	20	3	753
OTHER CHEM	4	7	0	0	0	2	1	1	0	1	0	2	3	5	0	0	0	5	5	482
FABR PLASTICS	0	3	0	0	0	0	0	0	0	1	0	0	1	1	0	2	0	1	1	135
TIRES	0	1	0	0	0	0	1	1	0	0	0	0	0	1	0	3	0	0	0	142
REF PETROLEUM	0	0	0	0	0	0	0	0	0	0	0	0	0	0	0	0	0	0	0	225
OTH PETROLEUM	0	0	0	0	0	0	0	0	0	0	0	0	0	0	0	0	0	0	0	58
LEATHER	0	1	0	0	0	0	1	0	0	0	0	0	0	0	0	1	0	1	1	41
STONE+CLAY+CEMNT	0	6	1	0	0	0	0	1	3	0	1	3	1	0	0	0	1	1	1	107
ABRASIVES	2	7	0	0	0	4	3	3	2	0	0	0	5	1	0	2	0	6	0	238
GLASS	1	5	0	0	0	0	1	0	0	0	0	2	1	0	0	0	0	2	0	91
IRON+STEEL	8	10	0	3	0	0	0	2	2	1	0	0	1	3	1	1	0	0	0	95

TABLE 3.2.3 (CONTINUED)

PRINCIPAL INDUSTRY	NON-FERROUS	METAL CANS	FAB-MET	ENGINES	CONSTR-MC	FARM-MC	OFF-MC+COMPUT	SPECL-MC	GENL-MC	OTH-NON-EL-MC	EL-LT+WIRING	EL-TRAN	RAD+TV+APPL	ELECTRONICS	OTH-ELE	COMMUNICATION	MOTOR-VEHIC	OTH-TRN	PRECISION	MISC	TOTAL
NON-FERROUS	176	3	15	0	1	0	0	0	1	1	1	1	1	0	2	1	1	3	0	3	223
METAL CANS	0	46	0	0	0	0	0	2	2	2	0	0	0	0	0	0	2	0	0	0	82
OTHER FAB METAL	4	15	288	1	1	0	1	8	14	8	2	1	6	3	3	9	0	0	8	14	426
ENGINES+TURBIN	0	0	3	28	3	1	0	1	4	4	1	0	0	1	3	3	3	3	8	0	57
CONSTR MACH	0	0	3	7	153	4	0	7	24	2	1	3	3	1	5	6	6	0	2	0	225
FARM MACHINERY	0	0	0	3	9	35	2	2	2	0	0	1	3	0	1	4	4	1	1	1	65
OFFICE MC+COMPUT	0	0	0	0	14	4	78	2	14	1	0	2	13	9	4	1	1	3	10	4	177
SPEC MACHINERY	0	0	7	0	8	6	1	91	8	4	0	1	3	0	2	1	0	0	5	3	164
GENL MACHINERY	1	0	11	1	7	2	1	5	123	4	0	4	2	1	6	2	2	1	7	3	194
OTH NON-EL MC	1	0	5	1	3	1	1	11	11	109	2	2	3	2	1	4	4	1	3	0	153
EL LIGHT+WIRING	1	0	0	1	0	0	1	0	10	2	34	0	4	4	1	1	1	0	0	0	54
EL TRAN EQUIP	1	0	4	0	0	0	0	0	2	1	3	31	1	3	12	1	1	1	0	0	62
RADIO+TV+APPL	1	0	6	6	1	4	2	4	1	4	4	2	115	10	8	4	1	0	3	7	189
ELECTRONICS	0	0	0	1	1	5	2	5	0	1	1	1	12	90	1	3	0	0	4	1	128
OTHER ELEC	5	0	6	3	2	0	2	1	1	2	11	2	9	7	167	6	7	3	10	0	265
COMMUNICATION	0	0	1	0	0	0	1	1	2	2	3	2	8	14	2	62	2	2	2	0	108
MOTOR VEHIC	4	2	12	11	9	14	0	0	10	24	0	1	10	1	4	2	286	13	3	0	424
OTHER TRANSP	1	0	3	0	2	0	0	0	1	1	0	0	0	0	2	1	3	33	2	0	50
PRECISION	0	0	3	0	2	0	5	2	2	2	0	1	1	3	5	2	0	2	161	3	242
MISCELLANEOUS	1	0	7	0	0	1	0	1	1	0	0	2	2	1	0	0	1	1	2	203	239
TOTAL	217	70	441	64	220	72	114	141	234	185	66	54	207	166	245	89	343	71	280	259	8376

CHAPTER 3   — THE MATURING OF FOREIGN SUBSIDIARIES
SECTION 3   -- EXITS VIA MERGER AND REORGANIZATION
TABLE 1   --- BY YEAR AND GEOGRAPHICAL REGION

NO. OF SUBSIDIARIES, BY COUNTRY OR REGION

COUNTRY OR REGION	NO. OF MERGERS DURING YEAR(S)													TOTAL MERGERS
	51-55	56-60	61-65	1966	1967	1968	1969	1970	1971	1972	1973	1974	1975	1951-75
CANADA	19	41	50	18	30	37	47	29	45	28	34	18	18	414
LATIN AMER. (TOTAL)	15	48	66	7	14	34	19	24	26	14	14	23	11	315
C.AM.+CARIB. (TOTAL)	7	30	50	4	9	11	3	7	7	3	2	9	3	145
BAHAMAS	0	0	0	0	1	0	1	2	0	0	0	1	0	5
BERMUDA	0	0	0	0	0	0	0	0	0	0	0	1	1	1
COSTA RICA	0	0	0	0	0	0	0	0	1	0	0	0	0	1
GUATEMALA	0	2	0	0	1	1	0	0	0	1	0	0	0	5
JAMAICA	0	0	0	0	0	0	0	0	0	0	0	0	0	0
MEXICO	6	18	49	4	6	6	2	3	6	1	2	7	1	111
NETH.ANTILLES	0	0	0	0	0	0	0	0	0	0	0	0	0	1
NICARAGUA	0	0	0	0	0	0	0	0	0	1	0	1	0	1
PANAMA	0	3	0	0	1	2	0	1	0	0	0	0	0	8
OTHER C.AM+CAR.	1	7	1	0	0	2	0	1	0	0	0	0	1	13
S.AMERICA (TOTAL)	8	18	16	3	5	23	16	17	19	11	12	14	8	170
BOLIVIA	0	0	0	0	0	0	1	0	0	0	0	0	0	3
CHILE	0	0	0	0	0	0	0	0	0	1	1	0	0	3
COLOMBIA	0	2	3	0	0	12	5	5	4	0	1	3	0	35
ECUADOR	0	0	0	0	0	0	0	0	0	0	1	1	0	2
PERU	0	2	0	0	2	2	0	1	2	0	1	0	1	9
ARGENTINA	2	5	7	1	2	4	1	3	1	1	3	2	1	33
BRAZIL	4	7	4	1	3	2	9	5	8	6	5	7	5	66
URUGUAY	0	0	0	0	0	0	0	0	0	0	0	0	0	0
VENEZUELA	2	2	2	1	0	3	0	3	3	3	1	1	1	22
OTHER S.AMER.	0	2	0	0	0	0	0	0	0	0	0	0	0	2
EUROPE (TOTAL)	25	70	69	31	40	33	38	68	88	62	76	88	36	724
BELGIUM	0	4	0	0	4	1	2	1	2	10	3	4	0	31
FRANCE	4	23	19	4	6	6	3	9	17	10	21	11	2	135
GERMANY	8	4	7	3	1	3	2	10	22	14	11	13	6	104
ITALY	2	5	8	9	6	4	2	16	9	6	3	8	8	86
LUXEMBOURG	0	0	0	0	0	0	0	0	0	0	0	0	0	1
NETHERLANDS	2	3	2	2	5	3	4	4	3	7	1	1	2	41
DENMARK	0	1	0	1	1	0	6	0	0	0	1	3	2	12
IRELAND	0	0	1	0	1	0	1	2	0	0	0	0	2	3
U.K.	8	19	21	8	12	13	14	22	25	7	31	36	14	230
AUSTRIA	0	0	0	1	1	0	0	0	0	0	0	0	0	5
FINLAND	0	1	1	0	0	0	0	0	2	0	0	1	0	2
GREECE	0	0	0	0	0	0	1	0	0	1	1	0	0	4
NORWAY	1	1	0	1	0	0	0	0	1	0	0	0	0	5
PORTUGAL	0	1	1	0	0	0	0	1	1	0	0	0	0	4
SPAIN	0	1	4	1	0	1	1	1	2	1	1	7	1	20
SWEDEN	0	1	1	0	2	2	0	1	0	3	1	1	1	11
SWITZERLAND	0	6	3	2	2	2	2	1	3	3	3	3	0	30
TURKEY	0	0	0	0	2	0	0	0	0	0	0	0	0	0
OTHER EUROPE	0	0	0	0	0	0	0	0	0	0	0	0	0	0

TABLE 3.3.1 (CONTINUED)

COUNTRY OR REGION	NO. OF MERGERS DURING YEAR(S)													TOTAL MERGERS 1951-75
	51-55	56-60	61-65	1966	1967	1968	1969	1970	1971	1972	1973	1974	1975	
N.AFR+M.EAST (TOTAL)	0	2	0	0	0	6	0	0	0	1	1	0	1	11
ALGERIA	0	0	0	0	0	2	0	0	0	0	0	0	0	2
EGYPT	0	1	0	0	0	2	0	0	0	0	0	0	0	3
IRAN	0	1	0	0	0	1	0	0	0	0	0	0	0	2
ISRAEL	0	0	0	0	0	1	0	0	0	0	0	0	0	1
LEBANON	0	0	0	0	0	0	0	0	0	1	0	0	0	1
MOROCCO	0	0	0	0	0	0	0	0	0	0	1	0	0	1
SAUDI ARABIA	0	0	0	0	0	0	0	0	0	0	0	0	1	1
OTHER N.AF+M.E.	0	0	0	0	0	0	0	0	0	0	0	0	0	0
E.+W.AFRICA (TOTAL)	0	2	2	0	2	0	0	6	1	0	1	0	1	15
GHANA	0	0	0	0	0	0	0	0	0	0	0	0	0	0
IVORY COAST	0	0	0	0	0	0	0	0	0	0	0	0	0	0
KENYA	0	0	0	0	0	0	0	0	1	0	0	0	0	1
LIBERIA	0	2	0	0	0	0	0	0	0	0	0	0	1	3
NIGERIA	0	0	0	0	0	0	0	0	0	0	0	0	0	0
ZAIRE	0	0	0	0	0	0	0	0	0	0	0	0	0	0
ZAMBIA	0	0	0	0	2	0	0	6	0	0	1	0	0	9
OTHER E.+W.AFR.	0	0	2	0	0	0	0	0	0	0	0	0	0	2
SOUTH ASIA (TOTAL)	0	0	0	0	0	0	0	1	0	1	0	1	1	4
INDIA	0	0	0	0	0	0	0	1	0	0	0	1	0	2
PAKISTAN	0	0	0	0	0	0	0	0	0	1	0	0	1	2
SRI LANKA	0	0	0	0	0	0	0	0	0	0	0	0	0	0
OTHER S.ASIA	0	0	0	0	0	0	0	0	0	0	0	0	0	0
EAST ASIA (TOTAL)	0	8	0	0	0	5	3	1	1	6	3	4	2	33
HONG KONG	0	1	0	0	0	0	1	0	1	0	0	1	0	3
INDONESIA	0	1	0	0	0	1	1	0	0	0	0	0	0	3
JAPAN	0	1	0	0	0	2	0	1	0	1	1	2	1	9
MALAYSIA	0	1	0	0	0	0	0	0	0	0	0	0	0	1
PHILIPPINES	0	2	0	0	0	1	0	0	0	1	1	0	0	5
SINGAPORE	0	1	0	0	0	0	0	0	0	3	0	0	1	5
S.KOREA	0	1	0	0	0	1	1	0	0	1	0	1	0	5
THAILAND	0	0	0	0	0	0	0	0	0	0	1	0	0	1
TAIWAN	0	0	0	0	0	0	0	0	0	0	0	1	0	1
OTHER E.ASIA	0	0	0	0	0	0	0	0	0	0	0	0	0	0
S.DOMINIONS (TOTAL)	0	7	22	0	15	23	7	8	14	11	8	8	2	125
AUSTRALIA	0	6	14	0	6	12	6	7	5	7	5	7	2	77
NEW ZEALAND	0	0	5	0	1	4	1	0	2	0	1	0	0	14
RHODESIA	0	1	0	0	0	0	0	0	0	0	0	0	0	1
S.AFRICA	0	0	3	0	8	7	0	1	7	3	3	1	0	33
OUTSIDE U.S.(TOTAL)	59	180	209	56	101	138	114	137	175	122	137	142	71	1641

CHAPTER 3   - THE MATURING OF FOREIGN SUBSIDIARIES
SECTION 3   -- EXITS VIA MERGER AND REORGANIZATION
TABLE 2   --- BY YEAR AND PRINCIPAL INDUSTRY

NO. OF SUBSIDIARIES, BY PRINCIPAL INDUSTRY OF SUBSIDIARY AT TIME OF ENTRY INTO PARENT SYSTEM

PRINCIPAL INDUSTRY	NO. OF MERGERS DURING YEAR(S)													TOTAL MERGERS 1951-75
	51-55	56-60	61-65	1966	1967	1968	1969	1970	1971	1972	1973	1974	1975	
BEVERAGES	0	1	0	0	0	0	0	0	0	0	0	1	0	3
TOBACCO	0	0	0	0	0	0	0	0	0	0	1	0	1	1
FOOD	3	7	25	2	5	13	4	4	7	10	17	8	15	120
TEXTILES+APPAREL	2	1	0	0	0	0	1	1	0	0	0	0	0	5
WOOD+FURNITURE	0	0	0	0	0	3	0	2	1	1	0	0	2	9
PAPER	0	9	11	0	7	1	0	1	1	0	1	6	0	37
PRINTING	0	1	1	0	2	2	0	0	0	2	0	0	1	9
INDUSTRIAL CHEM	2	4	2	0	5	3	5	5	5	1	4	1	0	32
PLASTICS	4	1	6	1	5	3	1	3	3	0	2	9	1	39
AGRIC CHEM	0	0	0	0	0	0	2	0	1	0	0	1	0	5
COSMETICS	2	1	2	0	3	4	2	5	2	3	1	4	1	30
DRUGS	2	4	6	4	3	4	0	3	8	1	1	4	1	41
OTHER CHEM	3	2	2	1	1	1	1	5	1	1	1	4	1	23
FABR PLASTICS	0	1	0	0	0	2	0	1	0	0	5	2	0	11
TIRES	0	0	1	0	0	0	0	0	1	0	0	0	0	2
REF PETROLEUM	2	1	1	0	5	2	2	2	2	1	0	4	1	21
OTH PETROLEUM	1	0	0	0	1	2	4	0	0	0	0	1	1	10
LEATHER	0	0	0	0	0	0	0	0	0	0	0	0	0	0
STONE+CLAY+CEMNT	0	1	0	1	0	0	0	2	2	0	0	1	0	5
ABRASIVES	0	3	6	0	0	1	2	2	0	0	0	0	1	15
GLASS	0	0	2	0	0	0	0	0	0	0	1	1	1	5
IRON+STEEL	0	0	0	0	0	0	3	0	0	2	0	2	0	7

163

TABLE 3.3.2 (CONTINUED)

PRINCIPAL INDUSTRY	51-55	56-60	61-65	1966	1967	1968	1969	1970	1971	1972	1973	1974	1975	TOTAL MERGERS 1951-75
NON-FERROUS	0	0	6	0	1	0	1	1	0	2	1	0	0	12
METAL CANS	0	2	2	0	0	0	0	0	0	0	0	0	0	4
OTHER FAB METAL	4	5	6	1	3	0	0	5	8	4	4	4	6	50
ENGINES+TURBIN	0	0	6	0	0	0	0	0	1	0	2	0	1	10
CONSTR MACH	0	2	6	1	2	2	2	1	5	1	0	3	1	26
FARM MACHINERY	0	1	1	1	1	0	4	0	1	0	0	0	0	9
OFFICE MC+COMPUT	2	3	3	4	0	1	0	2	0	2	1	1	1	20
SPEC MACHINERY	0	0	2	0	1	3	0	1	1	0	1	2	0	11
GENL MACHINERY	5	5	5	1	2	3	2	5	0	3	2	4	0	32
OTH NON-EL MC	1	1	2	1	2	1	0	2	3	0	0	3	3	19
EL LIGHT+WIRING	0	1	1	0	0	0	1	0	0	0	0	0	2	5
EL TRAN EQUIP	0	0	0	0	1	0	0	0	0	2	0	0	0	3
RADIO+TV+APPL	0	2	2	1	0	0	1	0	4	3	1	0	0	13
ELECTRONICS	0	0	0	0	0	0	0	0	1	2	0	1	0	4
OTHER ELEC	2	4	2	1	5	0	2	3	3	2	4	3	1	33
COMMUNICATION	1	0	0	2	0	0	0	0	2	0	0	1	1	7
MOTOR VEHIC	1	7	12	1	1	2	2	6	4	7	1	6	6	56
OTHER TRANSP	0	0	0	0	0	1	1	1	0	0	1	1	0	5
PRECISION	2	2	8	1	1	0	2	3	2	2	4	2	0	27
MISCELLANEOUS	7	7	10	1	1	4	3	4	3	5	8	8	0	55
TOTAL	33	78	139	25	58	59	48	61	72	56	65	88	49	831

This page intentionally left blank.

CHAPTER   3   - THE MATURING OF FOREIGN SUBSIDIARIES
SECTION   4   -- EXITS EXCLUDING MERGERS (** "EEM'S" **)
TABLE   1   --- OVERVIEW, BY METHOD OF EXIT

NO. OF SUBSIDIARIES, BY METHOD OF EXIT

| METHOD OF EXIT | NO. OF EEM'S DURING YEAR(S) | | | | | | | | | | | | | TOTAL EEM'S |
	51-55	56-60	61-65	1966	1967	1968	1969	1970	1971	1972	1973	1974	1975	1951-75
SOLD	40	47	82	41	167	110	125	171	146	148	147	158	133	1515
LIQUIDATED	52	80	157	60	151	117	78	103	124	89	124	112	92	1339
EXPROPRIATED	1	54	24	0	3	2	3	2	3	8	9	18	42	169
UNKNOWN	23	26	53	8	8	3	1	1	1	3	0	2	0	129
TOTAL EEM'S	116	207	316	109	329	232	207	277	274	248	280	290	267	3152

CHAPTER 3   - THE MATURING OF FOREIGN SUBSIDIARIES
SECTION 4   -- EXITS EXCLUDING MERGERS (** "EEM'S" **)
TABLE 2   --- BY ACTIVITY OF SUBSIDIARY

NO. OF SUBSIDIARIES, BY ACTIVITY AT ENTRY DATE

PRINCIPAL ACTIVITY	NET FLOW UP TO 31-DEC-50	NO. OF EEM'S DURING YEAR(S)													TOTAL EEM'S 1951-75	TOTAL MERGERS 1951-75	TOTAL EXITS 1951-75
		51-55	56-60	61-65	1966	1967	1968	1969	1970	1971	1972	1973	1974	1975			
MANUFACTURING	947	42	67	127	53	121	105	107	113	131	111	134	148	114	1373	831	2204
SALES	638	29	47	73	32	86	56	39	66	42	66	62	67	73	738	302	1040
EXTRACTION	108	3	13	18	2	6	5	3	13	8	16	16	15	20	138	52	190
OTHER	109	9	20	20	10	39	29	7	23	31	21	31	19	37	296	116	412
UNKNOWN	394	33	60	78	12	77	37	51	62	62	34	37	41	23	607	340	947
TOTAL	2196	116	207	316	109	329	232	207	277	274	248	280	290	267	3152	1641	4793

CHAPTER 3   - THE MATURING OF FOREIGN SUBSIDIARIES
SECTION 4   -- EXITS EXCLUDING MERGERS (** "EEM'S" **)
TABLE 3   --- BY OWNERSHIP OF SUBSIDIARY

NO. OF SUBSIDIARIES, BY PARENT OWNERSHIP AT ENTRY

OWNERSHIP AT ENTRY	NET FLOW UP TO 31-DEC-50	NO. OF EEM'S DURING YEAR(S)													TOTAL EEM'S 1951-75	TOTAL MERGERS 1951-75	TOTAL EXITS 1951-75
		51-55	56-60	61-65	1966	1967	1968	1969	1970	1971	1972	1973	1974	1975			
WHL OWNED: 95-100%	1538	72	153	222	68	201	131	99	146	159	135	181	172	162	1901	1264	3165
MAJ OWNED: 51-94%	185	8	16	18	13	26	27	31	47	34	28	25	29	29	331	129	460
CO-OWNED: 50%	90	5	12	17	8	51	25	23	19	23	22	27	30	16	278	72	350
MIN OWNED: 5-49%	143	7	13	27	10	26	23	27	35	28	32	29	36	42	335	48	383
UNKNOWN	240	24	13	32	10	25	26	27	30	30	31	18	23	18	307	128	435
TOTAL	2196	116	207	316	109	329	232	207	277	274	248	280	290	267	3152	1641	4793

168

CHAPTER 3 - THE MATURING OF FOREIGN SUBSIDIARIES
SECTION 4 -- EXITS EXCLUDING MERGERS (** "EEM'S" **)
TABLE 4 --- BY ENTRY METHOD OF SUBSIDIARY

NO. OF SUBSIDIARIES, BY METHOD OF ENTRY

METHOD OF ENTRY	NET FLOW UP TO 31-DEC-50	NO. OF EEM'S DURING YEAR(S)													TOTAL EEM'S 1951-75	TOTAL MERGERS 1951-75	TOTAL EXITS 1951-75
		51-55	56-60	61-65	1966	1967	1968	1969	1970	1971	1972	1973	1974	1975			
NEWLY FORMED	1230	38	76	122	48	119	97	83	117	82	77	99	111	123	1192	460	1652
ACQUIRED	465	36	49	101	52	128	108	79	126	128	122	154	143	105	1331	906	2237
DESCENDENT	30	1	1	3	0	2	0	0	2	2	2	2	3	1	19	27	46
UNKNOWN	471	41	81	90	9	80	27	45	32	62	47	25	33	38	610	248	858
TOTAL	2196	116	207	316	109	329	232	207	277	274	248	280	290	267	3152	1641	4793

CHAPTER 3 — THE MATURING OF FOREIGN SUBSIDIARIES
SECTION 4 —— EXITS EXCLUDING MERGERS (** "EEM'S" **)
TABLE 5 ——— BY ENTRY DATE OF SUBSIDIARY

NO. OF SUBSIDIARIES, BY ENTRY DATE

ENTRY DATE	NET FLOW UP TO 31-DEC-50	NO. OF EEM'S DURING YEAR(S)													TOTAL EEM'S 1951-75	TOTAL MERGERS 1951-75	TOTAL EXITS 1951-75
		51-55	56-60	61-65	1966	1967	1968	1969	1970	1971	1972	1973	1974	1975			
PRE-1951	2196	103	109	55	19	41	26	35	33	43	48	18	24	28	582	338	920
1951		1	6	6	2	4	2	1	0	2	0	0	0	1	25	21	46
1952		6	12	12	1	31	4	3	4	5	0	1	1	4	84	41	125
1953		3	8	6	2	2	3	4	3	0	0	1	1	3	36	17	53
1954		2	15	7	5	8	5	4	4	2	0	2	5	1	60	27	87
1955		1	7	5	1	10	1	8	6	2	3	1	4	6	55	86	141
1956			16	17	2	13	5	6	3	6	1	4	4	2	79	44	123
1957			16	14	5	21	9	7	4	3	3	3	6	3	94	35	129
1958			12	23	4	11	10	6	8	6	4	1	5	4	94	46	140
1959			2	30	4	8	17	8	5	5	9	6	8	6	108	51	159
1960			4	39	8	26	9	12	12	7	11	6	9	5	148	85	233
1961				38	6	30	15	13	21	12	15	8	6	13	177	67	244
1962				35	14	24	29	10	9	18	10	8	13	5	175	71	246
1963				16	12	17	30	12	18	16	8	16	10	11	166	63	229
1964				10	9	19	23	20	43	27	12	11	19	15	208	110	318
1965				3	7	28	11	21	24	27	17	20	11	15	184	73	257
1966					8	21	12	10	22	12	19	18	15	10	147	76	223
1967						15	20	20	18	25	25	22	17	13	175	81	256
1968							1		27	21	29	39	36	12	165	62	227
1969								7	9	21	15	20	22	26	120	85	205
1970									5	11	9	41	18	26	110	74	184
1971										3	9	24	23	19	78	33	111
1972											1	8	21	12	42	15	57
1973												1	9	9	19	27	46
1974													3	17	20	11	31
1975														1	1	2	3
TOTAL	2196	116	207	316	109	329	232	207	277	274	248	280	290	267	3152	1641	4793

169

CHAPTER 3 - THE MATURING OF FOREIGN SUBSIDIARIES
SECTION 4 -- EXITS EXCLUDING MERGERS (** "EEM'S" **)
TABLE 6 --- BY GEOGRAPHICAL REGION

NO. OF SUBSIDIARIES, BY COUNTRY OR REGION

COUNTRY OR REGION	NET FLOW UP TO 31-DEC-50	NO. OF EEM'S DURING YEAR(S)													TOTAL EEM'S 1951-75	TOTAL MERGERS 1951-75	TOTAL EXITS 1951-75
		51-55	56-60	61-65	1966	1967	1968	1969	1970	1971	1972	1973	1974	1975			
CANADA	441	26	28	55	6	42	36	28	34	41	41	43	33	17	430	414	844
LATIN AMER. (TOTAL)	616	24	96	85	35	72	68	73	65	68	81	38	81	66	852	315	1167
C.AM.+CARIB.(TOTAL)	235	7	70	47	18	25	19	31	28	27	34	16	24	14	360	145	505
BAHAMAS	6	0	0	2	1	4	3	0	2	0	0	0	4	1	16	5	21
BERMUDA	1	0	0	0	0	2	2	0	2	0	0	0	0	1	9	1	10
COSTA RICA	2	0	0	0	0	0	0	4	0	1	1	1	0	2	9	1	10
GUATEMALA	8	0	0	3	0	0	0	0	0	1	1	0	2	2	12	5	17
JAMAICA	4	0	0	0	0	0	1	0	3	0	0	1	0	0	8	0	8
MEXICO	133	3	6	16	8	11	9	20	17	14	12	8	9	6	139	111	250
NETH.ANTILLES	0	0	0	0	0	0	0	0	0	0	4	2	1	0	11	0	11
NICARAGUA	3	1	0	0	0	0	0	0	0	1	1	2	1	0	5	1	6
PANAMA	17	0	4	7	7	7	3	2	6	8	7	0	2	1	54	8	62
OTHER C.AM+CAR.	61	3	60	18	2	1	0	2	0	3	3	3	1	1	97	13	110
S.AMERICA (TOTAL)	381	17	26	38	17	47	49	42	37	41	47	22	57	52	492	170	662
BOLIVIA	11	0	0	1	2	1	1	2	0	2	7	0	0	1	17	0	17
CHILE	28	1	1	0	2	1	3	11	1	2	7	3	5	5	42	3	45
COLOMBIA	58	7	6	6	0	5	4	5	10	3	9	1	2	2	54	35	89
ECUADOR	5	0	1	1	1	0	5	1	0	0	0	0	2	1	12	2	14
PERU	24	7	5	4	2	3	11	3	7	3	2	5	13	2	55	9	64
ARGENTINA	87	7	7	8	6	6	9	6	6	17	4	5	12	15	82	33	115
BRAZIL	87	0	4	0	2	17	10	11	3	0	7	6	12	7	103	66	169
URUGUAY	21	1	3	0	2	1	0	0	1	1	0	1	2	2	14	0	14
VENEZUELA	55	0	3	17	2	13	5	13	1	7	7	13	13	21	108	22	130
OTHER S.AMER.	5	1	1	0	0	1	1	0	0	0	0	0	1	1	5	0	5
EUROPE (TOTAL)	813	46	64	121	52	170	88	74	140	130	98	158	102	95	1338	724	2062
BELGIUM	50	4	2	4	5	10	6	7	7	9	4	10	10	7	82	31	113
FRANCE	110	2	6	13	4	19	13	17	25	14	5	21	17	12	168	135	303
GERMANY	90	4	6	23	7	23	11	11	25	15	12	24	10	17	191	104	295
ITALY	51	8	8	9	8	10	8	6	7	9	9	19	7	8	112	86	198
LUXEMBOURG	1	0	0	1	0	0	2	2	0	2	2	0	0	0	8	1	9
NETHERLANDS	46	2	3	7	5	12	4	4	10	6	6	7	8	7	77	41	118
DENMARK	21	0	3	0	1	5	0	1	2	1	1	5	2	2	31	12	43
IRELAND	10	1	3	1	0	0	1	1	1	0	0	1	2	1	21	3	24
U.K.	276	27	16	47	9	53	19	16	26	35	32	28	29	17	354	230	584
AUSTRIA	15	0	1	1	1	1	1	1	1	4	6	1	1	1	20	5	25
FINLAND	9	0	1	1	0	0	1	1	0	0	0	2	2	1	9	2	11
GREECE	1	0	1	1	2	3	2	0	0	3	0	1	1	1	16	4	20
NORWAY	21	1	1	2	0	3	1	4	4	4	1	4	0	1	21	5	26
PORTUGAL	14	0	4	1	0	0	1	0	7	2	1	1	4	8	17	4	21
SPAIN	32	1	5	3	5	5	4	4	8	6	5	11	4	1	63	20	83
SWEDEN	36	1	1	1	3	7	3	5	1	2	2	5	5	7	38	11	49
SWITZERLAND	25	2	1	7	0	10	9	11	2	11	7	10	5	0	92	30	122
TURKEY	2	0	1	1	1	1	1	0	1	0	1	1	0	1	9	0	9
OTHER EUROPE	3	0	1	0	0	0	1	0	1	1	1	2	2	0	9	0	9

TABLE 3.4.6 (CONTINUED)

COUNTRY OR REGION	NET FLOW UP TO 31-DEC-50	NO. OF EEM'S DURING YEAR(S)													TOTAL EEM'S 1951-75	TOTAL MERGERS 1951-75	TOTAL EXITS 1951-75
		51-55	56-60	61-65	1966	1967	1968	1969	1970	1971	1972	1973	1974	1975			
N.AFR+M.EAST(TOTAL)	45	5	4	9	2	5	9	4	5	4	6	11	7	17	88	11	99
ALGERIA	5	1	0	1	0	2	1	1	1	1	0	1	0	0	8	2	10
EGYPT	7	0	2	1	0	1	0	0	0	0	0	0	0	2	4	3	7
IRAN	0	0	0	1	0	1	2	0	0	1	0	3	2	0	11	2	13
ISRAEL	4	0	1	0	0	0	1	0	0	1	2	0	0	2	5	1	6
LEBANON	0	0	0	0	0	1	0	1	1	1	0	0	1	0	7	1	8
MOROCCO	6	1	1	2	0	0	0	1	0	0	2	3	0	1	12	1	13
SAUDI ARABIA	6	1	0	0	0	0	1	0	0	0	0	0	0	1	3	1	4
OTHER N.AF+M.E.	17	2	0	4	2	0	4	1	3	0	2	5	4	11	38	0	38
E.+W.AFRICA (TOTAL)	15	2	1	4	0	1	3	1	5	6	2	4	13	3	45	15	60
GHANA	1	0	0	0	0	0	2	0	0	0	0	0	1	1	4	4	4
IVORY COAST	0	0	0	0	0	0	0	0	0	0	0	0	1	0	1	0	1
KENYA	1	0	0	0	0	0	1	0	1	1	1	1	0	0	5	1	6
LIBERIA	6	1	0	0	0	1	0	0	0	0	0	2	0	0	4	0	7
NIGERIA	1	0	0	0	0	0	0	0	1	0	0	0	1	0	3	3	3
ZAIRE	1	0	0	0	0	0	0	0	0	0	0	0	2	0	2	0	2
ZAMBIA	3	0	0	1	0	0	0	0	1	3	1	0	2	0	8	0	17
OTHER E.+W.AFR.	2	1	1	3	0	0	0	0	2	2	0	1	6	2	18	2	20
SOUTH ASIA (TOTAL)	29	2	0	4	0	2	5	4	5	0	1	4	5	2	34	4	38
INDIA	22	2	0	2	0	2	4	3	2	0	0	2	5	1	23	2	25
PAKISTAN	4	0	0	2	0	0	1	0	2	0	1	2	0	1	9	2	11
SRI LANKA	3	0	0	0	0	0	0	1	1	0	0	0	0	0	2	0	2
OTHER S.ASIA	0	0	0	0	0	0	0	0	0	0	0	0	0	0	0	0	0
EAST ASIA (TOTAL)	63	4	4	13	7	14	12	8	7	10	7	10	15	29	140	33	173
HONG KONG	1	1	0	1	0	5	2	3	0	1	3	0	0	1	16	3	19
INDONESIA	13	1	3	2	0	0	0	1	0	0	1	0	0	0	8	3	11
JAPAN	12	2	1	3	0	6	2	3	4	6	0	7	13	6	54	9	63
MALAYSIA	4	0	0	3	4	0	3	0	0	0	2	0	0	0	10	1	11
PHILIPPINES	23	0	0	2	2	3	2	1	0	2	0	2	0	2	18	5	23
SINGAPORE	5	0	0	0	1	0	0	0	1	0	0	0	0	1	5	5	7
S.KOREA	0	0	0	0	0	0	0	0	0	1	0	0	0	1	1	1	2
THAILAND	1	0	0	0	0	0	2	0	2	0	1	0	0	5	10	5	15
TAIWAN	3	0	0	1	0	0	1	0	0	0	0	0	1	2	7	1	8
OTHER E.ASIA	1	0	0	1	0	0	0	0	0	0	0	1	1	11	14	0	14
S.DOMINIONS (TOTAL)	174	7	10	25	7	23	11	15	16	15	12	12	34	38	225	125	350
AUSTRALIA	77	2	4	12	6	16	7	7	6	8	7	9	23	30	137	77	214
NEW ZEALAND	30	1	2	2	0	0	0	2	3	0	0	0	1	0	11	14	25
RHODESIA	7	0	1	1	0	2	0	2	1	1	3	0	2	3	16	1	17
S.AFRICA	60	4	3	10	1	5	4	4	6	6	2	3	8	5	61	33	94
OUTSIDE U.S. (TOTAL)	2196	116	207	316	109	329	232	207	277	274	248	280	290	267	3152	1641	4793

CHAPTER 3   - THE MATURING OF FOREIGN SUBSIDIARIES
SECTION 4   -- EXITS EXCLUDING MERGERS (** "EEM'S" **)
TABLE 7   --- BY PRINCIPAL INDUSTRY OF SUBSIDIARY

NO. OF SUBSIDIARIES, BY PRINCIPAL INDUSTRY OF SUBSIDIARY AT TIME OF ENTRY INTO PARENT SYSTEM

PRINCIPAL INDUSTRY	NET FLOW UP TO 31-DEC-50	NO. OF EEM'S DURING YEAR(S) 51-55	56-60	61-65	1966	1967	1968	1969	1970	1971	1972	1973	1974	1975	TOTAL EEM'S 1951-75	TOTAL MERGERS 1951-75	TOTAL EXITS 1951-75
BEVERAGES	26	13	1	1	0	0	0	1	2	2	2	2	10	2	36	3	39
TOBACCO	1	0	0	0	0	0	0	1	0	0	2	0	0	0	1	1	2
FOOD	117	4	16	18	20	19	14	9	11	24	12	21	16	8	192	120	312
TEXTILES+APPAREL	23	0	0	2	2	4	5	3	8	6	10	19	7	14	80	5	85
WOOD+FURNITURE	7	0	1	1	2	2	0	2	0	0	0	3	3	3	14	9	23
PAPER	25	1	3	6	2	7	4	4	3	6	2	8	7	2	55	37	92
PRINTING	5	0	0	0	0	0	1	0	0	0	2	0	3	0	6	9	15
INDUSTRIAL CHEM	54	3	2	12	3	11	7	17	10	10	5	4	0	4	91	32	123
PLASTICS	17	1	0	9	4	18	5	6	10	2	5	3	4	3	70	39	109
AGRIC CHEM	5	1	1	2	1	0	1	2	3	3	3	3	3	1	26	5	31
COSMETICS	42	0	5	7	1	1	6	2	2	5	3	4	1	2	39	30	69
DRUGS	74	1	2	4	1	5	14	6	1	3	2	0	2	3	44	41	85
OTHER CHEM	25	1	2	3	2	4	4	4	8	5	3	3	3	2	44	23	67
FABR PLASTICS	6	0	1	3	0	2	2	4	3	3	1	3	7	3	32	11	43
TIRES	45	1	3	3	0	2	1	0	2	2	1	0	0	2	17	2	19
REF PETROLEUM	30	3	2	2	0	8	0	1	2	0	3	1	1	8	31	21	52
OTH PETROLEUM	14	2	1	0	0	0	3	2	0	0	0	2	3	2	16	10	26
LEATHER	6	0	0	1	0	0	1	0	2	0	0	3	0	0	8	0	8
STONE+CLAY+CEMNT	3	0	1	3	0	1	1	0	0	0	4	1	0	1	12	5	17
ABRASIVES	13	0	0	1	1	0	0	0	2	2	2	0	1	2	11	15	26
GLASS	15	1	2	1	0	0	0	1	1	0	2	0	2	2	12	5	17
IRON+STEEL	3	1	0	1	1	2	0	2	1	2	1	0	1	0	12	7	19

TABLE 3.4.7 (CONTINUED)

PRINCIPAL INDUSTRY	NET FLOW UP TO 31-DEC-50	NO. OF EEM'S DURING YEAR(S)													TOTAL EEM'S 1951-75	TOTAL MERGERS 1951-75	TOTAL EXITS 1951-75
		51-55	56-60	61-65	1966	1967	1968	1969	1970	1971	1972	1973	1974	1975			
NON-FERROUS	19	0	2	3	1	2	2	2	2	4	4	5	6	2	35	12	47
METAL CANS	9	0	2	0	0	1	1	0	1	1	0	0	0	3	9	4	13
OTHER FAB METAL	41	1	3	8	1	1	4	3	7	5	8	2	8	2	53	50	103
ENGINES+TURBIN	3	0	0	1	0	2	0	0	1	3	0	0	1	0	8	10	18
CONSTR MACH	21	0	1	0	0	1	1	1	2	7	0	2	9	2	26	26	52
FARM MACHINERY	4	0	0	0	0	0	0	0	0	0	1	0	1	1	3	9	12
OFFICE MC+COMPUT	33	1	1	3	1	1	1	1	1	0	1	0	2	3	16	20	36
SPEC MACHINERY	17	0	1	1	2	1	1	1	4	2	5	2	1	3	24	11	35
GENL MACHINERY	20	0	0	0	0	1	2	1	1	0	0	2	1	1	9	32	41
OTH NON-EL MC	15	0	0	2	0	0	2	1	0	1	2	2	6	2	18	19	37
EL LIGHT+WIRING	6	0	0	0	0	0	1	2	0	1	1	2	3	1	11	5	16
EL TRAN EQUIP	1	0	0	1	0	0	1	1	3	0	1	3	3	1	14	3	17
RADIO+TV+APPL	14	0	0	4	0	2	4	2	5	5	2	1	4	1	30	13	43
ELECTRONICS	1	0	0	2	0	0	2	2	2	5	0	1	0	3	17	4	21
OTHER ELEC	32	0	0	3	0	1	3	2	1	2	1	7	5	4	29	33	62
COMMUNICATION	18	0	1	0	1	0	1	1	1	3	0	1	1	4	14	7	21
MOTOR VEHIC	33	4	3	6	3	5	4	10	2	4	4	7	7	3	62	56	118
OTHER TRANSP	4	0	0	1	0	0	0	0	0	1	4	4	2	1	13	5	18
PRECISION	15	1	1	1	1	1	1	2	1	2	2	4	1	7	25	27	52
MISCELLANEOUS	85	2	9	11	3	14	5	8	8	8	12	12	10	6	108	55	163
TOTAL	947	42	67	127	53	121	105	107	113	131	111	134	148	114	1373	831	2204

CHAPTER 3   - THE MATURING OF FOREIGN SUBSIDIARIES
SECTION 4   -- EXITS EXCLUDING MERGERS (** "EEM'S" **)
TABLE 8   --- TOTAL EEM'S 1967-75, BY COUNTRY AND INDUSTRY

NO. OF SUBSIDIARIES, BY PRINCIPAL INDUSTRY OF SUBSIDIARY AT TIME OF ENTRY INTO PARENT SYSTEM

COUNTRY OR REGION	BEVERAGES	TOBACCO	FOOD	TXTL+APPRL	WOOD+FURNI / PAPER	PRINTING / PAPER	INDUS-CHEM	AGRIC-CHEM / PLASTIC	COSMETICS	OTHER-CHEM / DRUGS	FABR-PLSTCS	REF-PETRLM / TIRES	OTH-PETRLM	STONE+CLAY+CEMNT / LEATHER	ABRASIVES	IRON / GLASS
CANADA	6	1	31	7	3	1	4	1	2	2	0	0	2	1	1	2
LATIN AMER. (TOTAL)	6	0	37	18	14	2	26	20	8	12	12	10	5	4	2	5
C.AM.+CARIB.(TOTAL)	0	0	13	6	4	0	9	6	4	4	5	3	1	0	0	1
BAHAMAS	0	0	0	1	1	0	9	6	2	3	5	1	0	0	0	0
BERMUDA	0	0	0	0	0	0	0	0	0	0	0	0	0	0	0	0
COSTA RICA	0	0	1	0	0	0	0	0	0	0	0	0	0	0	0	0
GUATEMALA	0	0	2	1	0	0	1	0	0	0	0	1	0	0	0	0
JAMAICA	0	0	1	1	1	0	0	0	0	0	0	0	0	0	0	0
MEXICO	0	0	8	3	1	0	7	6	2	4	4	1	1	0	0	1
NETH.ANTILLES	0	0	0	0	0	0	0	0	0	0	0	0	0	0	0	0
NICARAGUA	0	0	0	0	0	0	0	0	0	0	0	0	0	0	0	0
PANAMA	0	0	0	0	1	0	1	0	0	1	0	0	0	0	0	0
OTHER C.AM+CAR.	0	0	1	0	0	0	0	0	0	0	0	0	0	1	0	0
S.AMERICA (TOTAL)	6	0	24	12	10	2	17	14	4	8	5	3	5	1	2	2
BOLIVIA	1	0	1	1	1	0	2	0	0	0	1	0	1	0	0	0
CHILE	2	0	5	1	0	0	2	0	0	0	1	0	1	0	0	1
COLOMBIA	0	0	2	3	1	0	6	2	0	3	1	0	0	0	0	0
ECUADOR	0	0	1	0	2	0	0	0	0	0	0	0	0	0	0	0
PERU	0	0	9	1	2	0	2	1	0	1	1	0	0	1	0	0
ARGENTINA	3	0	1	0	2	2	5	2	2	2	0	1	1	0	2	1
BRAZIL	0	0	0	0	2	0	8	3	0	3	0	2	0	0	2	0
URUGUAY	0	0	0	0	0	0	1	0	1	0	0	1	0	0	0	0
VENEZUELA	0	0	5	7	0	0	1	0	0	1	0	0	5	0	0	0
OTHER S.AMER.	0	0	0	0	0	0	0	0	0	0	0	0	0	0	0	0
EUROPE (TOTAL)	3	0	50	46	17	3	33	22	7	13	14	16	10	12	3	2
BELGIUM	1	0	3	1	3	3	4	3	1	1	1	3	0	1	1	3
FRANCE	0	0	4	8	1	1	4	2	1	1	3	3	0	1	0	0
GERMANY	0	0	8	7	1	1	7	4	0	1	0	3	4	0	0	0
ITALY	2	0	4	8	5	0	5	4	4	3	1	1	4	0	1	1
LUXEMBOURG	0	0	0	0	0	0	0	0	0	1	0	0	4	0	1	0
NETHERLANDS	0	0	3	3	1	0	2	1	0	5	0	0	0	0	0	0
DENMARK	0	0	5	0	0	0	2	2	1	0	1	1	0	1	0	0
IRELAND	0	0	4	1	1	0	0	0	1	0	2	0	0	3	1	1
U.K.	0	0	10	10	4	1	4	1	2	2	6	2	2	0	0	1
AUSTRIA	0	0	0	0	0	0	0	0	0	0	0	0	0	0	0	0
FINLAND	0	0	0	3	0	0	0	1	0	0	0	0	0	0	0	1
GREECE	0	0	2	0	0	0	0	0	0	1	0	1	0	1	0	0
NORWAY	0	0	2	0	0	0	0	0	0	0	0	0	0	0	0	0
PORTUGAL	0	0	2	0	1	0	1	3	1	0	0	1	0	0	0	0
SPAIN	0	0	2	4	2	0	4	0	2	0	2	0	2	0	0	0
SWEDEN	0	0	2	0	0	0	1	0	0	1	0	0	0	0	0	0
SWITZERLAND	0	0	0	1	0	0	0	0	0	0	0	0	0	0	0	0
TURKEY	0	0	0	0	0	0	0	0	0	1	0	0	0	0	0	1
OTHER EUROPE	0	0	1	0	0	0	0	0	0	0	0	0	0	0	0	0

TABLE   3 . 4 . 8   (CONTINUED)

COUNTRY OR REGION	BEVERAGES	TOBACCO	TXTL+APPRL	FOOD	WOOD+FURNI	PRINTING	PAPER	INDUS-CHEM	PLASTIC	AGRIC-CHEM	COSMETICS DRUGS	OTHER-CHEM	FABR-PLSTCS TIRES	REF-PETRLM	OTH-PETRLM	LEATHER	STONE+CLAY+CEMNT	ABRASIVES GLASS	IRON
N.AFR+M.EAST (TOTAL)	0	0	0	0	0	0	0	1	1	1	0	0	0	4	0	0	0	0	0
ALGERIA	0	0	0	0	0	0	0	0	0	0	0	0	1	1	1	0	0	0	0
EGYPT	0	0	0	0	0	0	0	0	0	0	0	0	0	0	0	0	0	0	0
IRAN	0	0	0	0	0	0	0	0	0	0	0	0	0	1	1	0	0	0	0
ISRAEL	0	0	0	0	0	0	0	0	0	1	0	0	0	0	0	0	0	0	0
LEBANON	0	0	0	0	0	0	0	0	0	0	0	0	0	0	0	0	0	0	0
MOROCCO	0	0	0	0	0	0	0	0	0	0	0	0	0	0	0	0	0	0	0
SAUDI ARABIA	0	0	0	0	0	0	0	0	0	0	0	0	0	2	0	0	0	0	0
OTHER N.AF+M.E.	0	0	0	0	0	0	1	1	0	0	0	0	0	0	0	0	0	0	0
E.+W.AFRICA (TOTAL)	0	0	0	0	0	0	0	1	1	0	1	0	1	1	1	0	0	0	1
GHANA	0	0	0	0	0	0	0	0	0	0	0	0	0	0	0	0	0	0	0
IVORY COAST	0	0	0	0	0	0	0	0	0	0	0	0	0	0	0	0	0	0	0
KENYA	0	0	0	0	0	0	0	1	1	0	0	0	1	0	0	0	0	0	0
LIBERIA	0	0	0	0	0	0	0	0	0	0	0	0	0	0	0	0	0	0	1
NIGERIA	0	0	0	0	0	0	0	0	0	0	1	0	0	0	0	0	0	0	0
ZAIRE	0	0	0	0	0	0	0	0	0	0	0	0	0	0	0	0	0	0	0
ZAMBIA	0	0	0	0	0	0	0	0	0	0	0	0	0	0	0	0	0	0	0
OTHER E.+W.AFR.	0	0	0	0	0	0	0	1	0	0	0	0	0	1	1	0	0	0	0
SOUTH ASIA (TOTAL)	0	0	1	1	0	0	0	0	0	0	3	3	0	0	0	0	0	0	0
INDIA	0	0	0	0	0	0	0	0	0	0	3	3	0	0	1	0	0	0	0
PAKISTAN	0	0	1	1	0	0	0	0	0	0	0	0	0	0	1	0	0	0	0
SRI LANKA	0	0	0	0	0	0	0	0	0	0	0	0	0	0	0	0	0	0	0
OTHER S.ASIA	0	0	0	0	0	0	0	0	0	0	0	0	0	0	0	0	0	0	0
EAST ASIA (TOTAL)	0	0	5	2	2	0	2	5	1	3	3	4	5	2	4	0	0	0	1
HONG KONG	0	0	0	0	1	0	0	0	0	0	0	0	1	0	0	0	0	0	0
INDONESIA	0	0	0	2	0	0	0	1	0	0	0	0	0	0	0	0	0	0	0
JAPAN	0	0	1	2	0	0	1	5	5	0	1	3	3	1	4	0	0	0	1
MALAYSIA	0	0	2	1	1	0	1	0	0	0	0	0	0	0	0	0	0	0	0
PHILIPPINES	0	0	0	0	0	0	1	1	1	0	0	0	1	1	1	0	0	0	0
SINGAPORE	0	0	0	0	0	0	0	0	0	0	0	0	0	0	0	0	0	0	0
S.KOREA	0	0	0	0	0	0	0	0	0	0	0	0	1	0	0	0	0	0	0
THAILAND	0	0	1	1	0	0	0	0	0	1	0	0	0	0	0	0	0	0	0
TAIWAN	0	0	0	0	0	0	0	0	0	0	0	1	0	0	0	0	0	0	0
OTHER E.ASIA	0	0	0	0	0	0	0	0	0	1	1	0	0	0	0	0	0	0	0
S.DOMINIONS (TOTAL)	6	0	10	3	2	0	3	3	5	3	2	2	2	0	1	0	1	2	0
AUSTRALIA	3	0	6	2	1	0	3	3	5	3	1	1	2	1	1	0	0	2	0
NEW ZEALAND	0	0	0	1	0	0	0	0	0	0	0	0	0	1	0	0	0	0	0
RHODESIA	0	0	0	0	0	0	2	0	0	0	0	0	0	0	0	0	0	0	0
S.AFRICA	3	0	4	1	0	0	0	0	0	0	1	0	1	0	0	0	0	0	0
OUTSIDE U.S. (TOTAL)	21	1	134	76	10	43	6	71	56	21	26	36	36	28	10	24	13	7	8	9	8	9

(TABLE CONTINUED ON FOLLOWING PAGES)

TABLE 3.4.8 (CONTINUED)

COUNTRY OR REGION	NON-FERROUS	METAL CANS	FAB-MET	ENGINES	CONSTR-MC	FARM-MC	OFF-MC+COMPUT	SPECL-MC	GENL-MC	OTH-NON-EL-MC	EL-LT+WIRING	EL-TRAN	RAD+TV+APPL	ELECTRONICS	OTH-ELE	COMMUNICATION	MOTOR-VEHIC	OTH-TRN	PRECISION	MISC	TOTAL
CANADA	5	2	2	2	7	0	0	3	0	3	1	5	6	3	3	0	2	2	2	9	139
LATIN AMER. (TOTAL)	6	1	12	1	4	1	1	3	0	4	5	6	6	3	3	2	19	0	5	15	285
C.AM.+CARIB. (TOTAL)	3	0	0	1	1	0	0	0	0	0	0	4	3	2	0	1	4	0	2	3	86
BAHAMAS	0	0	0	0	0	0	0	0	0	0	0	0	0	0	0	0	0	0	0	0	0
BERMUDA	0	0	0	0	0	0	0	0	0	0	0	0	0	0	0	0	0	0	0	0	1
COSTA RICA	0	0	0	0	0	0	0	0	0	0	0	1	1	0	0	0	0	0	0	0	4
GUATEMALA	0	0	0	0	0	0	0	0	0	0	0	0	0	0	0	0	1	0	0	0	5
JAMAICA	0	0	0	0	1	0	0	0	0	0	0	1	1	0	0	0	0	0	0	0	4
MEXICO	3	0	0	1	1	0	0	0	0	2	3	1	1	2	0	1	2	0	1	3	57
NETH.ANTILLES	0	0	0	0	0	0	0	0	0	0	0	0	0	0	0	0	0	0	1	3	2
NICARAGUA	0	0	0	0	0	0	0	0	0	0	0	0	0	0	0	0	0	0	0	0	2
PANAMA	0	0	0	0	0	0	0	0	0	0	0	0	0	0	0	0	0	0	0	0	4
OTHER C.AM+CAR.	0	0	0	0	0	0	0	0	0	0	0	0	0	0	0	0	1	0	0	0	7
S.AMERICA (TOTAL)	3	1	2	0	3	1	1	3	0	4	1	3	3	1	3	1	15	0	3	12	199
BOLIVIA	0	1	0	0	0	1	0	0	0	1	0	0	0	0	0	0	0	0	0	0	4
CHILE	0	0	0	0	0	0	0	0	0	0	0	0	0	0	0	0	2	0	1	3	25
COLOMBIA	1	0	1	0	0	0	1	0	0	1	0	0	0	0	0	0	1	0	1	3	28
ECUADOR	0	0	0	0	0	0	0	0	0	0	0	0	0	0	0	0	0	0	0	0	5
PERU	0	0	0	0	1	0	0	0	0	0	0	0	0	0	0	0	0	0	0	0	18
ARGENTINA	0	0	0	0	0	0	1	1	0	2	1	2	2	1	2	1	5	0	3	3	33
BRAZIL	1	1	1	0	1	0	1	0	0	2	0	1	1	0	0	0	6	0	1	2	49
URUGUAY	0	0	0	0	0	0	0	0	0	0	0	0	0	0	1	0	0	0	0	0	0
VENEZUELA	0	0	0	0	2	0	0	1	0	0	1	0	0	0	0	0	1	0	1	1	36
OTHER S.AMER.	1	0	0	0	0	0	0	0	0	0	0	0	0	0	0	0	0	0	0	0	1
EUROPE (TOTAL)	12	2	21	4	7	1	6	11	6	8	5	6	12	7	14	6	16	7	13	46	478
BELGIUM	1	0	4	0	2	1	0	1	0	0	0	1	2	2	2	0	0	0	1	2	37
FRANCE	1	0	2	1	0	0	2	2	1	2	1	2	6	1	6	3	3	0	2	9	69
GERMANY	1	0	2	0	1	0	1	3	1	6	2	6	2	1	1	3	3	0	5	5	75
ITALY	0	0	1	0	0	0	0	1	0	2	1	1	1	1	2	2	4	0	0	2	54
LUXEMBOURG	0	0	0	0	0	0	0	0	0	0	0	0	0	0	0	1	0	0	0	0	0
NETHERLANDS	0	0	2	0	0	0	1	0	0	0	0	0	0	0	0	0	0	1	1	1	23
DENMARK	0	0	0	0	0	0	0	0	0	0	0	0	0	0	0	0	0	1	1	1	10
IRELAND	0	0	0	0	0	1	0	0	0	0	0	0	0	0	0	0	0	0	1	1	9
U.K.	5	1	5	3	3	1	2	2	0	1	0	2	1	4	4	1	2	1	3	12	116
AUSTRIA	0	0	0	0	0	0	0	0	0	1	0	0	0	0	0	1	0	0	0	2	9
FINLAND	0	0	1	0	0	0	0	0	0	0	0	0	0	0	0	0	0	0	0	0	2
GREECE	0	0	0	0	0	0	0	0	0	0	0	0	0	0	0	0	0	0	1	1	3
NORWAY	4	0	1	0	1	0	0	0	0	0	0	0	0	0	0	0	1	0	0	0	6
PORTUGAL	0	0	0	0	0	0	0	0	0	0	0	0	0	0	0	0	1	1	0	0	6
SPAIN	0	1	1	0	0	0	0	0	0	1	0	0	1	0	0	0	0	0	3	3	33
SWEDEN	0	0	0	0	0	0	0	0	0	0	0	1	0	1	1	0	0	0	1	1	7
SWITZERLAND	0	0	1	0	0	0	0	0	0	0	0	0	0	0	0	2	2	0	0	4	8
TURKEY	0	0	1	0	0	0	0	0	0	0	0	0	0	0	0	0	0	0	1	0	6
OTHER EUROPE	0	0	0	0	0	0	0	0	0	0	0	0	0	0	0	0	0	0	1	2	5

TABLE 3 .4 .8 (CONTINUED)

COUNTRY OR REGION	NON-FERROUS METAL-MC	METAL CANS	FAB-MET	ENGINES	CONSTR-MC	FARM-MC	OFF-MC+COMPUT SPECL-MC	GENL-MC	OTH-NON-EL-MC	EL-LT+WIRING	EL-TRAN	RAD+TV+APPL	OTH-ELE	ELECTRONICS	COMMUNICATION	MOTOR-VEHIC	OTH-TRN	PRECISION	MISC	TOTAL
N.AFR+M.EAST (TOTAL)	2	0	0	0	0	0	0	0	1	0	1	2	1	0	1	1	0	1	1	14
ALGERIA	0	0	0	0	1	0	0	0	0	0	0	0	0	0	0	0	0	0	1	1
EGYPT	0	0	0	0	0	0	0	0	0	0	0	0	0	0	0	0	0	0	0	0
IRAN	0	0	0	0	0	0	0	0	0	0	1	1	0	0	0	1	0	0	0	2
ISRAEL	0	0	0	0	0	0	0	0	0	0	0	0	1	0	1	0	0	0	0	2
LEBANON	0	0	0	0	0	0	0	0	0	0	0	0	0	0	0	1	0	0	1	1
MOROCCO	0	0	0	0	0	0	0	0	0	0	0	0	0	0	0	0	0	0	0	0
SAUDI ARABIA	0	0	0	0	0	0	0	0	0	0	0	0	0	0	0	0	0	0	0	0
OTHER N.AF+M.E.	2	0	0	0	0	0	0	0	0	0	0	1	0	0	0	1	0	0	0	6
E.+W.AFRICA (TOTAL)	0	0	0	0	0	0	0	0	0	0	1	1	1	0	1	1	0	0	1	6
GHANA	0	0	0	0	0	0	0	0	0	0	0	0	1	0	1	1	0	0	1	1
IVORY COAST	0	0	0	0	0	0	0	0	0	0	0	0	0	0	0	0	0	0	0	0
KENYA	0	0	0	0	0	0	0	0	0	0	1	1	0	0	0	0	0	0	0	3
LIBERIA	0	0	0	0	0	0	0	0	0	0	0	0	0	0	0	0	0	0	0	0
NIGERIA	0	0	0	0	0	0	0	0	0	0	0	1	0	0	0	1	0	0	0	1
ZAIRE	0	0	0	0	0	0	0	0	0	0	0	0	0	0	0	0	0	0	0	0
ZAMBIA	0	0	0	0	0	0	0	0	0	0	0	0	0	0	0	0	0	0	0	0
OTHER E.+W.AFR.	0	1	1	0	0	0	0	0	0	0	0	0	0	0	0	0	0	0	0	1
SOUTH ASIA (TOTAL)	0	0	0	0	0	0	1	1	0	0	2	2	0	0	1	1	0	0	1	13
INDIA	0	0	1	0	0	0	1	1	0	0	0	0	0	0	1	1	0	0	1	10
PAKISTAN	0	0	0	0	0	0	0	0	0	0	1	0	0	0	0	0	0	0	0	2
SRI LANKA	0	0	0	0	0	0	0	0	0	0	0	1	0	0	0	0	0	0	0	1
OTHER S.ASIA	0	0	0	0	0	0	0	0	0	0	0	0	0	0	0	0	0	0	0	0
EAST ASIA (TOTAL)	2	2	1	0	2	0	1	1	0	1	0	3	3	3	2	1	2	1	4	67
HONG KONG	0	1	1	0	0	0	0	0	0	0	0	1	1	0	1	0	1	0	3	7
INDONESIA	1	0	0	0	2	0	0	0	1	0	0	0	0	2	0	0	0	0	0	0
JAPAN	0	0	0	0	0	0	1	0	0	1	0	1	0	2	1	1	1	0	1	37
MALAYSIA	0	0	0	0	0	0	0	0	0	0	0	0	0	0	0	0	0	0	0	2
PHILIPPINES	0	0	1	0	0	0	0	0	0	0	0	0	0	0	0	1	0	0	0	6
SINGAPORE	0	0	0	0	0	0	0	0	0	0	0	0	0	0	0	0	0	0	0	1
S.KOREA	0	0	0	0	0	0	0	0	0	0	0	0	1	0	1	1	0	0	0	1
THAILAND	1	0	0	0	0	0	0	0	0	0	0	0	1	0	1	0	0	0	0	5
TAIWAN	0	0	0	0	0	0	0	0	0	0	0	0	0	0	0	0	0	0	0	5
OTHER E.ASIA	0	1	0	0	0	0	0	0	0	0	0	0	0	0	0	0	0	0	0	3
S.DOMINIONS (TOTAL)	2	1	3	0	5	0	1	1	1	1	1	1	3	0	2	6	1	0	6	82
AUSTRALIA	1	0	2	0	4	0	1	1	1	1	1	1	2	0	1	1	1	0	4	56
NEW ZEALAND	0	0	0	0	0	0	0	0	0	0	0	0	0	0	1	0	0	0	0	2
RHODESIA	1	0	0	0	0	0	0	0	0	0	0	0	1	0	1	0	0	0	0	3
S.AFRICA	0	1	1	0	1	0	0	0	0	0	0	0	0	0	0	5	0	0	2	21
OUTSIDE U.S. (TOTAL)	29	7	40	7	25	3	10	20	9	16	11	13	26	15	26	12	46	12	21	83	1084

CHAPTER 3 — THE MATURING OF FOREIGN SUBSIDIARIES
SECTION 5 —— "EXPROPRIATIONS"
TABLE 1 ——— BY YEAR AND GEOGRAPHICAL REGION

NO. OF SUBSIDIARIES, BY COUNTRY OR REGION

COUNTRY OR REGION	NO. OF EXPROPRIATIONS DURING YEAR(S)													TOTAL EXPROPS 1951-75
	51-55	56-60	61-65	1966	1967	1968	1969	1970	1971	1972	1973	1974	1975	
CANADA	1	0	0	0	0	0	0	0	0	0	0	0	0	1
LATIN AMER. (TOTAL)	0	53	18	0	0	2	1	1	3	7	6	11	22	124
C.AM.+CARIB. (TOTAL)	0	53	18	0	0	0	0	0	0	0	0	0	0	71
BAHAMAS	0	0	0	0	0	0	0	0	0	0	0	0	0	0
BERMUDA	0	0	0	0	0	0	0	0	0	0	0	0	0	0
COSTA RICA	0	0	0	0	0	0	0	0	0	0	0	0	0	0
GUATEMALA	0	0	0	0	0	0	0	0	0	0	0	0	0	0
JAMAICA	0	0	0	0	0	0	0	0	0	0	0	0	0	0
MEXICO	0	0	0	0	0	0	0	0	0	0	0	0	0	0
NETH.ANTILLES	0	0	0	0	0	0	0	0	0	0	0	0	0	0
NICARAGUA	0	0	0	0	0	0	0	0	0	0	0	0	0	0
PANAMA	0	0	0	0	0	0	0	0	0	0	0	0	0	0
OTHER C.AM+CAR.	0	53	18	0	0	0	0	0	0	0	0	0	0	71
S.AMERICA (TOTAL)	0	0	0	0	0	2	1	1	3	7	6	11	22	53
BOLIVIA	0	0	0	0	0	0	1	1	0	0	0	0	0	2
CHILE	0	0	0	0	0	0	0	0	3	0	6	0	0	9
COLOMBIA	0	0	0	0	0	0	0	0	0	0	0	0	1	1
ECUADOR	0	0	0	0	0	0	0	0	0	0	0	0	0	0
PERU	0	0	0	0	0	2	0	0	0	7	0	11	0	20
ARGENTINA	0	0	0	0	0	0	0	0	0	0	0	0	1	1
BRAZIL	0	0	0	0	0	0	0	0	0	0	0	0	1	1
URUGUAY	0	0	0	0	0	0	0	0	0	0	0	0	0	0
VENEZUELA	0	0	0	0	0	0	0	0	0	0	0	0	18	18
OTHER S.AMER.	0	0	0	0	0	0	0	0	0	0	0	0	1	1
EUROPE (TOTAL)	0	0	0	0	2	0	0	0	0	0	0	0	0	2
BELGIUM	0	0	0	0	1	0	0	0	0	0	0	0	0	1
FRANCE	0	0	0	0	0	0	0	0	0	0	0	0	0	0
GERMANY	0	0	0	0	1	0	0	0	0	0	0	0	0	1
ITALY	0	0	0	0	0	0	0	0	0	0	0	0	0	0
LUXEMBOURG	0	0	0	0	0	0	0	0	0	0	0	0	0	0
NETHERLANDS	0	0	0	0	0	0	0	0	0	0	0	0	0	0
DENMARK	0	0	0	0	0	0	0	0	0	0	0	0	0	0
IRELAND	0	0	0	0	0	0	0	0	0	0	0	0	0	0
U.K.	0	0	0	0	0	0	0	0	0	0	0	0	0	0
AUSTRIA	0	0	0	0	0	0	0	0	0	0	0	0	0	0
FINLAND	0	0	0	0	0	0	0	0	0	0	0	0	0	0
GREECE	0	0	0	0	0	0	0	0	0	0	0	0	0	0
NORWAY	0	0	0	0	0	0	0	0	0	0	0	0	0	0
PORTUGAL	0	0	0	0	0	0	0	0	0	0	0	0	0	0
SPAIN	0	0	0	0	0	0	0	0	0	0	0	0	0	0
SWEDEN	0	0	0	0	0	0	0	0	0	0	0	0	0	0
SWITZERLAND	0	0	0	0	0	0	0	0	0	0	0	0	0	0
TURKEY	0	0	0	0	0	0	0	0	0	0	0	0	0	0
OTHER EUROPE	0	0	0	0	0	0	0	0	0	0	0	0	0	0

TABLE 3.5.1   (CONTINUED)

COUNTRY OR REGION	NO. OF EXPROPRIATIONS DURING YEAR(S)													TOTAL EXPROPS 1951-75
	51-55	56-60	61-65	1966	1967	1968	1969	1970	1971	1972	1973	1974	1975	
N.AFR+M.EAST (TOTAL)	0	0	4	0	2	0	1	1	0	1	3	3	12	27
ALGERIA	0	0	0	0	2	0	1	0	0	0	0	0	0	3
EGYPT	0	0	1	0	0	0	0	0	0	0	0	0	0	1
IRAN	0	0	0	0	0	0	0	0	0	0	1	0	1	2
ISRAEL	0	0	0	0	0	0	0	0	0	0	0	0	0	0
LEBANON	0	0	0	0	0	0	0	0	0	0	0	0	0	2
MOROCCO	0	0	1	0	0	0	0	0	0	0	0	0	1	1
SAUDI ARABIA	0	0	0	0	0	0	0	0	0	0	0	1	1	2
OTHER N.AF+M.E.	0	0	2	0	0	0	0	1	0	1	2	3	9	18
E.+W.AFRICA (TOTAL)	0	0	0	0	0	0	0	0	0	0	4	0	1	5
GHANA	0	0	0	0	0	0	0	0	0	0	1	0	0	1
IVORY COAST	0	0	0	0	0	0	1	0	0	0	0	0	0	0
KENYA	0	0	0	0	0	0	0	0	0	0	0	0	0	0
LIBERIA	0	0	0	0	0	0	0	0	0	0	0	0	0	0
NIGERIA	0	0	0	0	0	0	1	0	0	0	0	0	0	0
ZAIRE	0	0	0	0	0	0	0	0	0	0	0	0	0	0
ZAMBIA	0	0	0	0	0	0	0	0	0	0	0	1	0	1
OTHER E.+W.AFR.	0	0	0	0	0	0	0	0	0	0	2	0	1	3
SOUTH ASIA (TOTAL)	0	0	0	0	0	0	1	0	0	0	0	0	0	1
INDIA	0	0	0	0	0	0	0	0	0	0	0	0	0	0
PAKISTAN	0	0	0	0	0	0	0	0	0	0	0	0	0	0
SRI LANKA	0	0	0	0	0	0	1	0	0	0	0	0	0	1
OTHER S.ASIA	0	0	0	0	0	0	0	0	0	0	0	0	0	0
EAST ASIA (TOTAL)	0	0	2	0	0	0	0	0	0	0	0	0	4	6
HONG KONG	0	0	0	0	0	0	0	0	0	0	0	0	0	0
INDONESIA	0	0	2	0	0	0	0	0	0	0	0	0	0	2
JAPAN	0	0	0	0	0	0	0	0	0	0	0	0	0	0
MALAYSIA	0	0	0	0	0	0	0	0	0	0	0	0	0	0
PHILIPPINES	0	0	0	0	0	0	0	0	0	0	0	0	0	0
SINGAPORE	0	0	0	0	0	0	0	0	0	0	0	0	0	0
S.KOREA	0	0	0	0	0	0	0	0	0	0	0	0	0	0
THAILAND	0	0	0	0	0	0	0	0	0	0	0	0	0	0
TAIWAN	0	0	0	0	0	0	0	0	0	0	0	0	0	0
OTHER E.ASIA	0	0	0	0	0	0	0	0	0	0	0	0	4	4
S.DOMINIONS (TOTAL)	0	0	0	0	0	0	0	0	0	0	0	0	3	3
AUSTRALIA	0	0	0	0	0	0	0	0	0	0	0	0	0	0
NEW ZEALAND	0	0	0	0	0	0	0	0	0	0	0	0	0	0
RHODESIA	0	0	0	0	0	0	0	0	0	0	0	0	3	3
S.AFRICA	0	0	0	0	0	0	0	0	0	0	0	0	0	0
OUTSIDE U.S. (TOTAL)	1	54	24	0	3	2	3	2	3	8	9	18	42	169

CHAPTER 3 — THE MATURING OF FOREIGN SUBSIDIARIES
SECTION 5 —— "EXPROPRIATIONS"
TABLE 2 ——— BY YEAR AND PRINCIPAL INDUSTRY

NO. OF SUBSIDIARIES, BY PRINCIPAL INDUSTRY OF SUBSIDIARY AT TIME OF ENTRY INTO PARENT SYSTEM

PRINCIPAL INDUSTRY	51-55	56-60	61-65	1966	1967	1968	1969	1970	1971	1972	1973	1974	1975	TOTAL EXPROPS 1951-75
BEVERAGES	0	1	1	0	0	0	0	0	0	0	0	0	0	2
TOBACCO	0	0	0	0	0	0	0	0	0	0	0	0	0	0
FOOD	0	4	2	0	0	0	0	1	0	0	1	4	0	12
TEXTILES+APPAREL	0	0	1	0	0	0	0	0	0	0	0	0	0	1
WOOD+FURNITURE	0	0	0	0	0	0	0	0	0	0	0	0	0	0
PAPER	0	0	1	0	0	0	0	0	0	0	0	2	0	3
PRINTING	0	0	0	0	0	0	0	0	0	0	0	0	0	0
INDUSTRIAL CHEM	0	1	0	0	0	0	0	0	0	1	0	1	0	3
PLASTICS	0	0	0	0	0	0	0	0	0	0	0	1	0	1
AGRIC CHEM	0	1	0	0	0	0	0	0	0	0	0	0	0	1
COSMETICS	0	1	1	0	0	0	0	0	0	0	0	0	0	2
DRUGS	0	1	0	0	0	0	0	0	0	0	0	0	0	1
OTHER CHEM	0	1	0	0	0	0	0	0	0	1	0	0	0	2
FABR PLASTICS	0	0	0	0	0	0	0	0	0	0	0	0	0	0
TIRES	0	2	1	0	0	0	0	0	0	0	0	0	1	4
REF PETROLEUM	0	2	0	0	1	0	0	0	0	0	0	0	8	11
OTH PETROLEUM	0	0	0	0	0	0	0	0	0	0	0	0	1	1
LEATHER	0	0	0	0	0	0	0	0	0	0	0	0	0	0
STONE+CLAY+CEMNT	0	0	0	0	0	0	0	0	0	1	0	0	0	1
ABRASIVES	0	0	0	0	0	0	0	0	0	0	0	0	0	0
GLASS	0	1	0	0	0	0	0	0	0	0	0	0	0	1
IRON+STEEL	0	0	0	0	0	0	0	0	0	0	0	0	0	0

TABLE 3 . 5 . 2 (CONTINUED)

PRINCIPAL INDUSTRY	NO. OF EXPROPRIATIONS DURING YEAR(S)													TOTAL EXPROPS 1951-75
	51-55	56-60	61-65	1966	1967	1968	1969	1970	1971	1972	1973	1974	1975	
NON-FERROUS	0	0	0	0	0	0	0	0	0	0	0	0	1	1
METAL CANS	0	2	0	0	0	0	0	0	0	0	0	0	1	3
OTHER FAB METAL	0	0	2	0	0	0	0	0	0	0	0	0	0	2
ENGINES+TURBIN	0	0	0	0	0	0	0	0	0	0	0	0	0	0
CONSTR MACH	0	0	0	0	0	0	0	0	0	0	0	0	0	0
FARM MACHINERY	0	0	0	0	0	0	0	0	0	0	0	0	0	0
OFFICE MC+COMPUT	0	0	0	0	0	0	0	0	0	0	0	0	0	0
SPEC MACHINERY	0	1	0	0	0	0	0	0	0	0	0	0	0	1
GENL MACHINERY	0	0	0	0	0	0	0	0	0	0	0	0	0	0
OTH NON-EL MC	0	0	0	0	0	0	0	0	0	0	0	0	0	0
EL LIGHT+WIRING	0	0	0	0	0	0	0	0	0	0	0	0	0	0
EL TRAN EQUIP	0	0	0	0	0	0	0	0	0	0	0	0	0	0
RADIO+TV+APPL	0	0	0	0	0	0	0	0	0	0	0	0	0	0
ELECTRONICS	0	0	0	0	0	0	0	0	0	0	0	0	0	0
OTHER ELEC	0	0	1	0	0	0	0	0	0	0	0	0	0	1
COMMUNICATION	0	0	0	0	0	0	0	0	0	0	0	0	1	1
MOTOR VEHIC	0	0	0	0	0	0	0	0	0	0	0	0	0	0
OTHER TRANSP	0	0	0	0	0	0	0	0	0	0	0	0	0	0
PRECISION	0	0	0	0	0	0	0	0	0	0	0	0	0	0
MISCELLANEOUS	0	3	2	0	0	0	0	0	0	1	0	0	1	7
TOTAL	0	21	12	0	1	0	0	1	0	4	1	8	14	62

182

CHAPTER 3   - THE MATURING OF FOREIGN SUBSIDIARIES
SECTION 6   -- METHODS OF EXIT BY PERIOD
TABLE 1   --- BY PRINCIPAL ACTIVITY OF SUBSIDIARY

NO. OF EXITS IN PERIOD, BY ACTIVITY AT ENTRY DATE

(SO=SOLD   LI=LIQUIDATED   MR=MERGED   EX=EXPROPRIATED   UN=UNKNOWN   ALL=TOTAL FOR PERIOD)

PRINCIPAL ACTIVITY	1951-1966						1967-1969						1970-1972						1973-1975					
	SO	LI	MR	EX	UN	ALL	SO	LI	MR	EX	UN	ALL	SO	LI	MR	EX	UN	ALL	SO	LI	MR	EX	UN	ALL
MANUFACTURING	121	120	275	33	15	564	208	120	165	1	4	498	258	90	189	5	2	544	274	98	202	23	1	598
SALES	35	105	66	21	20	247	67	107	71	4	3	252	90	82	101	1	1	275	75	119	64	7	1	266
EXTRACTION	10	23	28	0	3	64	3	9	11	1	1	25	21	11	9	5	0	46	17	13	4	21	0	55
OTHER	7	46	57	2	4	116	32	41	20	0	2	95	31	43	21	1	0	96	33	47	18	7	0	105
UNKNOWN	37	55	78	23	68	261	92	69	86	2	2	251	65	90	114	1	2	272	39	51	62	11	0	163
TOTAL	210	349	504	79	110	1252	402	346	353	8	12	1121	465	316	434	13	5	1233	438	328	350	69	2	1187

CHAPTER 3   - THE MATURING OF FOREIGN SUBSIDIARIES
SECTION 6   -- METHODS OF EXIT BY PERIOD
TABLE 2   --- BY PARENT OWNERSHIP OF SUBSIDIARY

NO. OF EXITS IN PERIOD, BY OWNERSHIP AT ENTRY DATE

(SO=SOLD LI=LIQUIDATED MR=MERGED EX=EXPROPRIATED UN=UNKNOWN ALL=TOTAL FOR PERIOD)

OWNERSHIP AT ENTRY	1951-1966						1967-1969						1970-1972						1973-1975					
	SO	LI	MR	EX	UN	ALL	SO	LI	MR	EX	UN	ALL	SO	LI	MR	EX	UN	ALL	SO	LI	MR	EX	UN	ALL
WHL OWNED: 95-100%	104	269	383	58	84	898	182	236	272	5	8	703	210	222	337	3	5	777	229	247	272	38	1	787
MAJ OWNED: 51- 94%	16	27	43	7	5	98	62	19	21	1	2	105	73	34	43	2	0	152	49	26	22	8	0	105
CO- OWNED: 50%	17	21	17	2	2	59	63	35	14	1	0	113	50	12	13	2	0	77	46	23	28	3	1	101
MIN OWNED: 5- 49%	37	13	11	4	3	68	59	16	15	1	0	91	70	21	14	4	0	109	80	15	8	12	0	115
UNKNOWN	36	19	50	8	16	129	36	40	31	0	2	109	62	27	27	2	0	118	34	17	20	8	0	79
TOTAL	210	349	504	79	110	1252	402	346	353	8	12	1121	465	316	434	13	5	1233	438	328	350	69	2	1187

CHAPTER 3 — THE MATURING OF FOREIGN SUBSIDIARIES
SECTION 6 -- METHODS OF EXIT BY PERIOD
TABLE 3 --- BY GEOGRAPHICAL REGION

NO. OF EXITS IN PERIOD, BY COUNTRY OR REGION

(SO=SOLD LI=LIQUIDATED MR=MERGED EX=EXPROPRIATED UN=UNKNOWN ALL=TOTAL FOR PERIOD)

COUNTRY OR REGION	1951-1966						1967-1969						1970-1972						1973-1975					
	SO	LI	MR	EX	UN	ALL	SO	LI	MR	EX	UN	ALL	SO	LI	MR	EX	UN	ALL	SO	LI	MR	EX	UN	ALL
CANADA	33	64	128	1	17	243	56	48	114	0	2	220	66	49	102	0	1	218	71	22	70	0	0	163
LATIN AMER. (TOTAL)	49	101	136	71	19	376	116	89	67	3	5	280	131	71	64	11	1	278	79	66	48	39	1	233
C.AM.+CARIB. (TOTAL)	20	44	91	71	7	233	40	34	23	0	1	98	49	39	17	0	1	106	19	34	14	0	1	68
BAHAMAS	2	1	0	0	0	3	1	6	2	0	0	9	1	2	0	0	0	3	0	5	1	0	0	6
BERMUDA	0	0	0	0	0	0	1	0	3	0	0	4	1	0	2	0	0	3	0	3	1	0	0	4
COSTA RICA	0	0	0	0	0	0	4	0	0	0	0	4	4	1	0	0	0	5	1	0	0	0	0	1
GUATEMALA	0	3	2	0	0	5	4	0	0	0	0	4	4	1	1	0	0	6	0	2	1	0	0	3
JAMAICA	0	1	0	0	0	1	0	2	0	0	0	2	0	0	0	0	0	0	2	1	0	0	0	3
MEXICO	12	15	77	0	6	110	23	17	14	0	0	54	30	12	10	0	1	53	12	11	10	0	0	33
NETH.ANTILLES	0	0	0	0	0	0	0	0	0	0	0	0	0	4	0	0	0	4	0	6	0	0	0	6
NICARAGUA	0	1	0	0	0	1	0	1	0	0	0	1	1	0	1	0	0	2	0	2	1	0	0	3
PANAMA	4	14	3	0	0	21	4	7	4	0	0	15	7	14	2	0	0	23	0	3	0	0	0	3
OTHER C.AM+CAR.	2	9	9	71	1	92	3	1	0	0	1	5	1	5	1	0	0	7	4	1	0	0	1	6
S.AMERICA (TOTAL)	29	57	45	0	12	143	76	55	44	3	4	182	82	32	47	11	0	172	60	32	34	39	0	165
BOLIVIA	0	3	0	0	0	3	2	5	1	1	0	9	1	0	0	1	0	2	0	1	0	0	0	1
CHILE	0	1	0	0	1	2	2	4	1	1	0	8	4	1	1	4	0	10	2	0	0	6	0	8
COLOMBIA	2	9	5	0	3	19	6	9	16	0	0	31	6	4	9	0	0	19	4	1	3	0	0	8
ECUADOR	1	2	0	0	0	3	5	0	0	0	0	5	2	0	1	0	0	3	1	1	0	0	0	2
PERU	6	2	2	0	0	10	11	2	4	1	0	18	5	1	2	2	0	10	1	0	0	1	0	2
ARGENTINA	5	11	15	0	4	35	9	7	9	0	0	25	20	4	16	2	0	42	6	3	2	11	0	22
BRAZIL	8	9	16	0	1	34	17	14	7	0	2	40	20	7	6	0	0	33	15	5	17	1	0	38
URUGUAY	3	3	0	0	0	6	2	0	0	0	0	2	1	1	0	0	0	2	12	12	0	18	0	42
VENEZUELA	4	15	7	0	3	29	16	14	3	0	1	34	16	4	9	0	0	29	3	1	0	0	0	4
OTHER S.AMER.	0	2	0	0	0	2	6	0	3	0	1	10	7	10	3	2	0	22	16	8	12	2	0	38
EUROPE (TOTAL)	92	137	195	1	53	478	172	158	111	1	1	443	217	149	218	0	2	586	189	165	200	0	1	555
BELGIUM	6	8	4	0	1	19	12	8	7	0	0	27	13	17	3	0	0	33	15	8	11	0	0	34
FRANCE	8	11	50	0	6	75	29	20	15	0	0	64	33	7	40	0	0	80	29	34	21	0	0	84
GERMANY	13	17	22	0	10	62	17	21	13	1	0	52	42	13	46	0	0	101	28	21	32	0	0	81
ITALY	4	15	24	0	7	50	16	13	7	0	0	36	17	11	31	0	0	59	18	16	19	0	0	53
LUXEMBOURG	0	1	0	0	0	1	1	0	0	0	0	1	1	0	2	0	0	3	1	0	0	0	0	1
NETHERLANDS	8	8	9	0	1	26	13	13	6	0	0	32	9	9	14	0	0	32	13	9	6	0	0	28
DENMARK	0	4	2	0	1	7	1	2	0	0	0	3	7	4	2	0	0	13	3	2	2	0	0	7
IRELAND	2	1	1	0	1	5	3	6	4	0	0	13	0	2	1	0	0	3	2	2	7	0	0	11
U.K.	41	39	56	0	19	155	36	52	39	0	0	127	45	47	54	0	1	147	34	40	81	0	0	155
AUSTRIA	0	2	2	0	1	5	1	3	0	0	0	4	7	4	2	0	0	13	2	1	0	0	0	3
FINLAND	0	1	1	1	0	3	1	0	0	0	0	1	0	1	0	0	0	1	2	3	1	0	0	6
GREECE	0	4	0	0	0	4	1	0	0	0	0	1	0	3	2	0	0	5	2	2	1	0	0	5
NORWAY	0	3	4	0	0	7	2	1	2	0	0	5	3	6	1	0	0	10	3	2	0	0	0	5
PORTUGAL	0	5	2	0	0	7	2	2	0	0	0	4	3	2	0	0	0	5	3	2	0	0	0	5
SPAIN	5	2	5	0	0	12	10	5	0	0	0	15	16	4	4	0	0	24	13	10	9	0	0	32
SWEDEN	2	4	2	0	2	10	5	9	2	0	0	16	8	4	4	0	0	16	5	5	0	0	0	10
SWITZERLAND	3	11	11	0	3	28	21	3	15	0	1	40	13	15	7	0	1	36	12	5	10	0	1	28
TURKEY	0	1	0	0	0	1	1	0	0	0	0	1	0	0	3	0	0	3	2	2	0	0	0	4
OTHER EUROPE	0	0	0	0	1	1	0	0	1	0	0	1	0	0	2	0	0	2	2	1	0	0	0	3

TABLE 3.6.3 (CONTINUED)

(SO=SOLD LI=LIQUIDATED MR=MERGED EX=EXPROPRIATED UN=UNKNOWN ALL=TOTAL FOR PERIOD)

COUNTRY OR REGION	1951-1966						1967-1969						1970-1972						1973-1975					
	SO	LI	MR	EX	UN	ALL	SO	LI	MR	EX	UN	ALL	SO	LI	MR	EX	UN	ALL	SO	LI	MR	EX	UN	ALL
N.AFR+M.EAST(TOTAL)	3	10	2	4	3	22	5	10	6	3	0	24	5	8	1	2	0	16	5	12	2	18	0	37
ALGERIA	0	2	0	0	0	2	0	1	2	3	0	6	0	2	1	0	0	3	0	0	0	0	0	0
EGYPT	0	3	1	1	0	4	1	1	2	0	0	3	0	1	0	0	0	1	0	0	1	0	0	0
IRAN	0	0	1	0	0	0	2	1	1	0	0	4	1	1	0	0	0	3	4	4	0	2	0	8
ISRAEL	0	0	1	0	1	2	0	1	0	0	0	1	1	2	0	0	0	2	0	3	0	0	0	3
LEBANON	1	0	0	0	1	4	2	2	0	0	0	4	2	1	1	0	0	3	0	3	1	0	0	5
MOROCCO	1	2	0	1	0	4	0	0	0	0	0	1	1	0	0	0	1	2	0	0	0	1	0	1
SAUDI ARABIA	1	0	0	0	0	4	0	0	1	0	0	2	0	1	0	0	0	3	0	2	0	1	0	1
OTHER N.AF+M.E.	1	4	0	2	1	8	1	5	1	0	0	5	2	2	2	2	0	5	4	2	0	14	0	20
E.+W.AFRICA (TOTAL)	2	4	4	0	1	11	2	3	2	0	0	7	4	8	7	0	1	20	2	13	2	5	0	22
GHANA	0	0	0	0	0	0	0	2	2	0	0	2	0	0	0	0	0	0	0	1	0	1	0	2
IVORY COAST	0	0	0	0	0	0	0	0	0	0	0	0	0	0	0	0	1	0	0	1	0	0	0	1
KENYA	0	0	0	0	0	3	1	0	0	0	0	0	0	3	0	0	0	3	1	1	1	0	0	2
LIBERIA	1	0	2	0	0	3	0	0	0	0	0	1	1	0	0	0	0	0	1	1	1	0	0	3
NIGERIA	0	0	0	0	0	0	0	1	0	0	0	1	0	0	0	0	0	1	0	1	1	0	0	1
ZAIRE	0	0	0	0	0	0	0	0	2	0	0	0	0	0	0	0	1	0	0	1	0	1	0	2
ZAMBIA	1	1	1	0	1	2	1	0	2	0	0	2	3	2	6	0	0	11	2	1	0	0	0	2
OTHER E.+W.AFR.	1	3	1	0	1	6	0	5	0	0	0	5	1	3	1	0	1	5	2	4	0	3	0	9
SOUTH ASIA (TOTAL)	2	3	2	0	1	8	8	2	0	0	0	11	2	4	1	0	0	7	6	5	1	0	0	12
INDIA	1	2	1	0	1	8	7	2	0	1	0	9	1	1	1	0	0	2	5	3	1	0	0	9
PAKISTAN	1	1	1	0	1	5	1	0	0	0	0	1	1	3	0	0	0	4	1	2	0	0	0	3
SRI LANKA	0	0	0	0	0	3	0	0	0	0	0	1	0	0	1	0	0	1	1	2	0	0	0	0
OTHER S.ASIA	0	0	0	0	0	0	0	0	0	0	0	0	0	0	0	0	0	0	0	0	0	0	0	0
EAST ASIA (TOTAL)	10	9	8	2	7	36	17	15	8	0	2	42	16	8	8	0	0	32	32	18	9	4	0	63
HONG KONG	0	1	1	2	1	3	1	8	1	0	1	11	2	1	1	0	0	3	1	0	1	0	0	2
INDONESIA	0	3	1	2	1	3	0	1	1	0	1	13	1	1	3	0	0	1	1	0	3	0	0	0
JAPAN	1	1	1	0	4	7	7	4	2	0	0	13	8	3	3	0	0	14	17	9	3	0	0	29
MALAYSIA	3	4	1	0	4	7	3	1	2	0	0	3	3	0	0	0	0	0	4	0	0	0	0	0
PHILIPPINES	4	0	2	0	0	6	4	1	0	0	1	7	3	1	1	0	1	5	1	0	1	0	0	5
SINGAPORE	1	0	0	0	0	1	0	0	0	1	0	1	0	0	3	0	0	3	1	0	0	0	0	2
S.KOREA	0	0	0	0	0	0	0	0	1	0	0	1	0	1	1	0	0	5	1	0	1	0	0	1
THAILAND	0	0	1	0	1	1	1	1	1	0	0	2	1	1	3	0	0	3	4	2	3	0	0	9
TAIWAN	0	1	1	0	1	2	1	0	0	0	0	1	2	1	0	0	0	3	2	3	0	0	0	2
OTHER E.ASIA	1	0	0	0	0	1	0	0	0	0	0	0	0	0	0	0	0	0	2	7	0	4	0	13
S.DOMINIONS (TOTAL)	19	21	29	0	9	78	26	21	45	0	2	94	24	19	33	0	0	76	54	27	18	3	0	102
AUSTRALIA	8	12	20	0	4	44	18	10	24	0	2	54	14	7	19	0	0	40	45	17	14	0	0	76
NEW ZEALAND	3	0	5	0	2	10	0	2	6	0	0	8	2	2	3	0	0	6	0	1	1	0	0	1
RHODESIA	1	0	0	0	1	2	2	2	0	0	0	4	1	4	0	0	0	5	0	2	0	3	0	6
S.AFRICA	7	9	4	0	2	22	6	7	15	0	0	28	8	6	11	0	0	25	9	7	3	0	0	19
OUTSIDE U.S. (TOTAL)	210	349	504	79	110	1252	402	346	353	8	12	1121	465	316	434	13	5	1233	438	328	350	69	2	1187

CHAPTER 3   - THE MATURING OF FOREIGN SUBSIDIARIES
SECTION 6   -- METHODS OF EXIT BY PERIOD
TABLE 4   --- BY PRINCIPAL INDUSTRY OF SUBSIDIARY

NO. OF EXITS IN PERIOD, BY SUBSIDIARY'S PRINCIPAL INDUSTRY AT TIME OF ENTRY INTO PARENT SYSTEM

(SO=SOLD LI=LIQUIDATED MR=MERGED EX=EXPROPRIATED UN=UNKNOWN ALL=TOTAL FOR PERIOD)

INDUSTRY AT ENTRY	1951-1966						1967-1969						1970-1972						1973-1975					
	SO	LI	MR	EX	UN	ALL	SO	LI	MR	EX	UN	ALL	SO	LI	MR	EX	UN	ALL	SO	LI	MR	EX	UN	ALL
BEVERAGES	12	1	1	2	0	16	1	0	0	0	0	1	5	1	0	0	0	6	13	1	2	0	0	16
TOBACCO	0	0	0	0	0	0	0	1	0	0	0	1	0	0	0	0	0	0	0	0	1	0	0	1
FOOD	28	24	37	6	0	95	33	9	22	0	0	64	33	13	21	1	0	68	32	8	40	5	0	85
TEXTILES+APPAREL	2	1	3	1	0	7	5	7	1	0	0	13	20	4	1	0	0	25	30	10	0	0	0	40
WOOD+FURNITURE	1	2	0	0	1	4	3	1	3	0	0	7	0	0	4	0	0	4	6	0	2	0	0	8
PAPER	6	5	20	1	0	32	10	5	8	0	0	23	7	4	2	0	0	13	11	3	7	2	1	24
PRINTING	0	0	0	0	2	2	1	0	4	0	0	5	2	1	1	0	0	4	2	1	1	0	0	4
INDUSTRIAL CHEM	7	10	8	1	2	28	26	8	13	0	1	48	21	3	6	1	0	31	10	0	5	1	0	16
PLASTICS	8	6	12	0	0	26	18	11	9	0	0	38	15	2	6	0	0	23	9	0	12	1	0	22
AGRIC CHEM	2	1	0	1	1	5	3	0	2	0	0	5	9	2	1	0	0	12	5	2	2	0	0	9
COSMETICS	3	7	5	2	1	18	3	5	9	0	0	17	2	8	10	0	0	20	3	4	6	0	0	13
DRUGS	1	5	16	1	1	24	17	8	7	0	0	32	3	3	12	0	0	18	2	3	6	0	0	11
OTHER CHEM	3	4	8	1	0	16	12	3	3	0	0	18	11	4	6	1	0	22	7	1	6	0	0	14
FABR PLASTICS	0	3	1	0	1	5	5	3	2	0	0	10	7	0	1	0	0	8	11	2	7	0	0	20
TIRES	1	2	1	3	1	8	2	1	0	0	0	3	4	1	1	0	0	6	1	0	0	1	0	2
REF PETROLEUM	3	2	4	2	0	11	7	2	9	0	0	18	4	1	3	0	0	8	1	1	5	8	0	15
OTH PETROLEUM	2	1	1	0	0	4	4	2	7	0	0	13	0	0	0	0	0	0	6	0	2	1	0	9
LEATHER	1	0	0	0	0	1	2	0	0	0	0	2	2	0	0	0	0	2	2	1	0	0	0	3
STONE+CLAY+CEMNT	4	0	2	0	0	6	1	1	0	0	0	2	2	1	2	1	0	6	2	0	1	0	0	3
ABRASIVES	0	2	9	0	0	11	0	0	3	0	0	3	4	2	2	0	0	8	0	3	1	0	0	4
GLASS	2	1	2	1	0	6	1	0	0	0	0	1	3	0	0	0	0	3	3	1	3	0	0	7
IRON+STEEL	1	2	0	0	0	3	1	3	3	0	0	7	3	1	2	0	0	6	1	0	2	0	0	3

TABLE 3.6.4 (CONTINUED)

(SO=SOLD LI=LIQUIDATED MR=MERGED EX=EXPROPRIATED UN=UNKNOWN ALL=TOTAL FOR PERIOD)

INDUSTRY AT ENTRY	1951-1966						1967-1969						1970-1972						1973-1975					
	SO	LI	MR	EX	UN	ALL	SO	LI	MR	EX	UN	ALL	SO	LI	MR	EX	UN	ALL	SO	LI	MR	EX	UN	ALL
NON-FERROUS	2	3	6	0	1	12	4	2	2	0	0	8	8	2	3	0	0	13	11	1	1	1	0	14
METAL CANS	0	0	4	2	0	6	0	2	0	0	0	2	2	0	0	0	0	2	2	0	0	1	0	3
OTHER FAB METAL	4	7	16	2	0	29	3	4	3	0	1	11	13	7	17	0	0	37	7	5	14	0	0	26
ENGINES+TURBIN	0	1	6	0	0	7	1	1	0	0	0	2	3	1	1	0	0	5	1	0	3	0	0	4
CONSTR MACH	0	1	9	0	0	10	1	2	6	0	0	9	5	4	7	0	0	16	9	4	4	0	0	17
FARM MACHINERY	0	0	3	0	0	3	0	0	5	0	0	5	1	0	1	0	0	2	2	0	0	0	0	2
OFFICE MC+COMPUT	1	5	12	0	0	18	2	1	1	0	0	4	1	1	4	0	0	6	4	1	3	0	0	8
SPEC MACHINERY	1	1	2	1	1	6	2	1	4	0	0	7	9	1	2	0	1	13	4	2	3	0	0	9
GENL MACHINERY	0	0	11	0	0	11	1	3	7	0	0	11	1	0	8	0	0	9	2	2	6	0	0	10
OTH NON-EL MC	1	1	5	0	0	7	2	1	3	0	0	6	3	0	5	0	0	8	8	2	6	0	0	16
EL LIGHT+WIRING	0	0	2	0	0	2	1	2	1	0	0	4	2	0	0	0	0	2	4	2	2	0	0	8
EL TRAN EQUIP	0	1	0	0	0	1	0	2	1	0	0	3	4	0	2	0	0	6	5	2	0	0	0	7
RADIO+TV+APPL	2	2	4	0	0	8	3	5	1	0	0	9	7	5	7	0	0	19	1	5	1	0	0	7
ELECTRONICS	1	1	0	0	0	2	3	1	0	0	0	4	6	1	3	0	0	10	3	1	1	0	0	5
OTHER ELEC	0	1	9	1	1	12	3	3	8	0	0	14	3	1	8	0	0	12	12	4	8	0	0	24
COMMUNICATION	1	0	3	0	1	5	1	1	0	0	0	2	2	2	2	0	0	6	3	3	2	0	0	8
MOTOR VEHIC	8	7	21	0	1	37	13	6	5	0	0	24	8	2	17	0	0	27	9	8	13	0	0	30
OTHER TRANSP	1	0	0	0	0	1	0	0	2	0	0	2	5	0	1	0	0	6	5	2	2	0	0	9
PRECISION	2	2	11	0	0	15	2	2	3	0	0	7	3	2	7	0	0	12	7	5	6	0	0	18
MISCELLANEOUS	10	8	19	5	2	44	12	14	8	0	1	35	18	8	12	1	1	40	19	8	16	1	0	44
TOTAL	121	120	275	33	15	564	208	120	165	1	4	498	258	90	189	5	2	544	274	98	202	23	1	598

Financial Statistics
of Foreign Subsidiaries

CHAPTER 4   - FINANCIAL STATISTICS OF FOREIGN SUBSIDIARIES
SECTION 1   -- SALES OF SUBSIDIARIES ACTIVE AT 1-JAN-76
TABLE 1   --- BY PRINCIPAL ACTIVITIES

NO. OF SUBSIDIARIES, BY ACTIVITY IN 1975

PRINCIPAL ACTIVITY	SALES CATEGORY FOR 1975						TOTAL NO. AT 1-JAN-76
	UNDER $1 MILLION	$1-10 MILLION	$10-25 MILLION	$25-100 MILLION	OVER $100 MILLION	UNKNOWN	
MANUFACTURING	528	2043	1108	795	347	954	5775
SALES	656	737	194	127	83	1036	2833
EXTRACTION	32	63	58	38	41	124	356
OTHER	310	73	24	21	14	1535	1977
UNKNOWN	13	6	3	0	2	233	257
TOTAL	1539	2922	1387	981	487	3882	11198

CHAPTER 4 — FINANCIAL STATISTICS OF FOREIGN SUBSIDIARIES
SECTION 1 —— SALES OF SUBSIDIARIES ACTIVE AT 1-JAN-76
TABLE 2 ——— BY OWNERSHIP PATTERNS

NO. OF SUBSIDIARIES, BY PARENT OWNERSHIP IN 1975

OWNERSHIP IN 1975	SALES CATEGORY FOR 1975						TOTAL NO. AT 1-JAN-76
	UNDER $1 MILLION	$1-10 MILLION	$10-25 MILLION	$25-100 MILLION	OVER $100 MILLION	UNKNOWN	
WHL OWNED: 95-100%	1235	2124	948	614	303	2835	8059
MAJ OWNED: 51- 94%	130	315	161	134	72	213	1025
CO- OWNED: 50%	76	214	108	84	25	218	725
MIN OWNED: 5- 49%	84	249	162	144	85	312	1036
UNKNOWN	14	20	8	5	2	304	353
TOTAL	1539	2922	1387	981	487	3882	11198

CHAPTER 4 – FINANCIAL STATISTICS OF FOREIGN SUBSIDIARIES
SECTION 1 -- SALES OF SUBSIDIARIES ACTIVE AT 1-JAN-76
TABLE 3 --- BY METHOD OF ENTRY

NO. OF SUBSIDIARIES, BY METHODS OF ENTRY

METHOD OF ENTRY	SALES CATEGORY FOR 1975						TOTAL NO. AT 1-JAN-76
	UNDER $1 MILLION	$1-10 MILLION	$10-25 MILLION	$25-100 MILLION	OVER $100 MILLION	UNKNOWN	
NEWLY FORMED	861	1550	739	522	273	2071	6016
ACQUIRED	570	1185	554	354	147	1332	4142
DESCENDENT	22	50	29	43	31	41	216
UNKNOWN	86	137	65	62	36	438	824
TOTAL	1539	2922	1387	981	487	3882	11198

CHAPTER 4   - FINANCIAL STATISTICS OF FOREIGN SUBSIDIARIES
SECTION 1   -- SALES OF SUBSIDIARIES ACTIVE AT 1-JAN-76
TABLE 4   --- BY ENTRY DATE

NO. OF SUBSIDIARIES, BY ENTRY DATE

ENTRY DATE	SALES CATEGORY FOR 1975						TOTAL NO. AT 1-JAN-76
	UNDER $1 MILLION	$1-10 MILLION	$10-25 MILLION	$25-100 MILLION	OVER $100 MILLION	UNKNOWN	
PRE-1951	86	224	216	252	177	321	1276
1951	3	23	12	15	11	23	87
1952	17	25	12	13	6	37	110
1953	7	22	12	9	1	22	73
1954	17	34	14	13	9	36	123
1955	12	36	25	23	11	37	144
1956	24	39	31	19	6	61	180
1957	15	41	35	22	4	65	182
1958	15	52	29	19	14	67	196
1959	19	87	46	30	19	77	278
1960	25	103	45	50	21	93	337
1961	31	84	50	49	15	110	339
1962	38	105	54	36	11	101	345
1963	45	126	57	44	18	136	426
1964	43	106	51	35	17	122	374
1965	45	142	67	34	14	145	447
1966	64	167	44	28	15	128	446
1967	112	167	72	44	22	239	656
1968	162	202	76	46	19	274	779
1969	114	197	79	45	20	285	740
1970	98	158	78	39	14	282	669
1971	136	232	59	29	8	330	794
1972	105	155	64	35	6	224	589
1973	117	165	48	22	13	282	647
1974	128	155	45	20	7	233	588
1975	61	75	66	10	9	152	373
TOTAL	1539	2922	1387	981	487	3882	11198

CHAPTER 4   - FINANCIAL STATISTICS OF FOREIGN SUBSIDIARIES
SECTION 1   -- SALES OF SUBSIDIARIES ACTIVE AT 1-JAN-76
TABLE 5   --- BY GEOGRAPHICAL REGION

NO. OF SUBSIDIARIES, BY COUNTRY OR REGION

COUNTRY OR REGION	SALES CATEGORY FOR 1975						TOTAL NO. AT 1-JAN-76
	UNDER $1 MILLION	$1-10 MILLION	$10-25 MILLION	$25-100 MILLION	OVER $100 MILLION	UNKNOWN	
CANADA	153	274	134	121	75	406	1163
LATIN AMER. (TOTAL)	387	707	289	172	58	849	2462
C.AM.+CARIB.(TOTAL)	217	305	124	57	25	452	1180
BAHAMAS	12	2	1	3	3	35	56
BERMUDA	10	4	2	1	2	53	72
COSTA RICA	17	20	2	0	0	6	45
GUATEMALA	21	26	1	4	0	13	65
JAMAICA	4	10	5	4	1	14	38
MEXICO	82	173	90	34	12	161	552
NETH.ANTILLES	8	5	1	1	1	39	55
NICARAGUA	7	11	2	0	0	3	23
PANAMA	32	29	9	2	4	94	170
OTHER C.AM+CAR.	24	25	11	8	2	34	104
S.AMERICA (TOTAL)	170	402	165	115	33	397	1282
BOLIVIA	3	1	1	0	0	5	10
CHILE	10	18	4	3	2	15	52
COLOMBIA	15	67	19	13	4	43	161
ECUADOR	7	14	3	2	1	16	43
PERU	14	34	4	4	2	22	80
ARGENTINA	30	56	35	21	5	60	207
BRAZIL	47	96	69	44	13	106	375
URUGUAY	6	16	2	1	0	14	39
VENEZUELA	34	96	27	26	5	112	300
OTHER S.AMER.	4	4	1	1	1	4	15
EUROPE (TOTAL)	591	1165	659	476	244	1694	4829
BELGIUM	27	82	48	34	15	103	309
FRANCE	66	133	106	63	41	208	617
GERMANY	69	147	105	87	59	221	688
ITALY	40	118	71	46	18	89	382
LUXEMBOURG	5	5	5	3	0	21	39
NETHERLANDS	32	76	44	28	16	110	306
DENMARK	18	36	15	8	3	35	115
IRELAND	20	32	10	2	2	38	104
U.K.	146	226	125	102	49	436	1084
AUSTRIA	16	29	13	8	1	23	90
FINLAND	13	14	4	3	1	11	46
GREECE	10	19	5	4	1	15	54
NORWAY	20	22	13	8	4	25	92
PORTUGAL	7	26	8	2	1	27	71
SPAIN	34	92	47	25	9	91	298
SWEDEN	23	48	20	22	10	68	191
SWITZERLAND	41	44	16	25	10	142	278
TURKEY	1	9	3	5	4	12	34
OTHER EUROPE	3	7	1	1	0	19	31

195

TABLE 4 .1 .5 (CONTINUED)

COUNTRY OR REGION	SALES CATEGORY FOR 1975						TOTAL NO. AT 1-JAN-76
	UNDER $1 MILLION	$1-10 MILLION	$10-25 MILLION	$25-100 MILLION	OVER $100 MILLION	UNKNOWN	
N.AFR+M.EAST (TOTAL)	37	70	16	13	13	115	264
ALGERIA	4	4	1	0	1	4	14
EGYPT	2	2	1	0	3	12	20
IRAN	7	20	3	7	1	29	67
ISRAEL	3	8	2	1	0	6	20
LEBANON	1	10	1	0	0	10	22
MOROCCO	4	13	5	1	0	6	29
SAUDI ARABIA	2	2	1	0	2	15	22
OTHER N.AF+M.E.	14	11	2	4	6	33	70
E.+W.AFRICA (TOTAL)	51	76	31	15	16	132	321
GHANA	1	4	2	1	1	8	17
IVORY COAST	1	3	2	1	1	5	13
KENYA	4	9	1	3	1	9	27
LIBERIA	8	6	3	2	3	23	45
NIGERIA	11	20	3	0	3	20	57
ZAIRE	5	2	6	0	0	13	26
ZAMBIA	12	12	4	3	1	15	47
OTHER E.+W.AFR.	9	20	10	5	6	39	89
SOUTH ASIA (TOTAL)	21	40	23	23	2	35	144
INDIA	8	27	21	18	1	26	101
PAKISTAN	9	12	2	5	1	4	33
SRI LANKA	4	1	0	0	0	4	9
OTHER S.ASIA	0	0	0	0	0	1	1
EAST ASIA (TOTAL)	141	297	123	88	43	312	1004
HONG KONG	16	25	8	6	1	41	97
INDONESIA	9	20	2	3	3	24	61
JAPAN	52	110	66	50	27	121	426
MALAYSIA	9	19	7	2	0	24	61
PHILIPPINES	13	42	13	8	4	28	108
SINGAPORE	19	20	10	6	2	17	74
S.KOREA	2	13	5	2	2	13	37
THAILAND	11	26	5	4	2	14	62
TAIWAN	7	19	6	6	2	19	59
OTHER E.ASIA	3	3	1	1	0	11	19
S.DOMINIONS (TOTAL)	158	293	112	73	36	339	1011
AUSTRALIA	88	159	60	50	24	163	544
NEW ZEALAND	24	46	5	5	3	49	132
RHODESIA	8	9	1	1	0	7	26
S.AFRICA	38	79	46	17	9	120	309
OUTSIDE U.S. (TOTAL)	1539	2922	1387	981	487	3882	11198

CHAPTER 4 - FINANCIAL STATISTICS OF FOREIGN SUBSIDIARIES
SECTION 1 --- SALES OF SUBSIDIARIES ACTIVE AT 1-JAN-76
TABLE 6 --- BY PRINCIPAL INDUSTRY OF SUBSIDIARY

NO. OF SUBSIDIARIES, BY PRINCIPAL INDUSTRY IN 1975

PRINCIPAL INDUSTRY	SALES CATEGORY FOR 1975						TOTAL NO. AT 1-JAN-76
	UNDER $1 MILLION	$1-10 MILLION	$10-25 MILLION	$25-100 MILLION	OVER $100 MILLION	UNKNOWN	
BEVERAGES	12	28	16	9	3	13	81
TOBACCO	1	7	5	8	4	1	26
FOOD	80	244	109	80	24	98	635
TEXTILES+APPAREL	6	41	20	14	1	13	95
WOOD+FURNITURE	8	32	11	5	3	8	67
PAPER	17	78	49	29	7	26	206
PRINTING	29	13	8	4	0	10	64
INDUSTRIAL CHEM	21	62	37	35	11	42	208
PLASTICS	16	51	29	34	6	44	180
AGRIC CHEM	6	21	8	10	1	5	51
COSMETICS	47	135	41	18	8	27	276
DRUGS	41	243	101	50	3	108	546
OTHER CHEM	25	117	74	37	12	44	309
FABR PLASTICS	11	37	20	9	2	16	95
TIRES	0	8	26	39	15	1	89
REF PETROLEUM	4	5	15	36	86	9	155
OTH PETROLEUM	1	12	14	5	3	6	41
LEATHER	2	15	7	0	0	2	26
STONE+CLAY+CEMNT	4	21	13	7	3	15	63
ABRASIVES	11	54	30	11	4	25	135
GLASS	2	27	6	16	2	8	61
IRON+STEEL	2	16	19	10	2	8	57

197

TABLE 4.1.6 (CONTINUED)

PRINCIPAL INDUSTRY	SALES CATEGORY FOR 1975						TOTAL NO. AT 1-JAN-76
	UNDER $1 MILLION	$1-10 MILLION	$10-25 MILLION	$25-100 MILLION	OVER $100 MILLION	UNKNOWN	
NON-FERROUS	8	41	45	39	14	29	176
METAL CANS	2	15	7	7	8	7	46
OTHER FAB METAL	24	128	52	23	3	58	288
ENGINES+TURBIN	3	7	7	5	3	3	28
CONSTR MACH	11	47	39	27	11	18	153
FARM MACHINERY	2	11	3	10	8	1	35
OFFICE MC+COMPUT	1	21	17	18	17	4	78
SPEC MACHINERY	10	40	17	6	1	17	91
GENL MACHINERY	10	54	22	15	0	22	123
OTH NON-EL MC	11	39	22	10	0	27	109
EL LIGHT+WIRING	2	17	5	5	1	4	34
EL TRAN EQUIP	0	21	6	2	0	2	31
RADIO+TV+APPL	13	29	27	25	9	12	115
ELECTRONICS	4	21	23	19	3	20	90
OTHER ELEC	16	71	35	14	5	26	167
COMMUNICATION	3	17	11	12	9	10	62
MOTOR VEHIC	11	75	58	51	47	44	286
OTHER TRANSP	2	6	4	13	0	8	33
PRECISION	13	58	29	19	5	37	161
MISCELLANEOUS	36	58	21	9	3	76	203
TOTAL	528	2043	1108	795	347	954	5775

CHAPTER 4   - FINANCIAL STATISTICS OF FOREIGN SUBSIDIARIES
SECTION 2   -- ASSETS OF SUBSIDIARIES ACTIVE AT 1-JAN-76
TABLE 1   --- BY PRINCIPAL ACTIVITIES

NO. OF SUBSIDIARIES, BY ACTIVITY IN 1975

PRINCIPAL ACTIVITY	ASSETS CATEGORY FOR 1975						TOTAL NO. AT 1-JAN-76
	UNDER $1 MILLION	$1-10 MILLION	$10-25 MILLION	$25-100 MILLION	OVER $100 MILLION	UNKNOWN	
MANUFACTURING	833	2109	849	589	236	1159	5775
SALES	955	463	140	87	36	1152	2833
EXTRACTION	44	82	69	33	36	92	356
OTHER	394	171	55	28	19	1310	1977
UNKNOWN	12	7	0	1	0	237	257
TOTAL	2238	2832	1113	738	327	3950	11198

CHAPTER 4 - FINANCIAL STATISTICS OF FOREIGN SUBSIDIARIES
SECTION 2 -- ASSETS OF SUBSIDIARIES ACTIVE AT 1-JAN-76
TABLE 2 --- BY OWNERSHIP PATTERNS

NO. OF SUBSIDIARIES, BY PARENT OWNERSHIP IN 1975

OWNERSHIP IN 1975	ASSETS CATEGORY FOR 1975						TOTAL NO. AT 1-JAN-76
	UNDER $1 MILLION	$1-10 MILLION	$10-25 MILLION	$25-100 MILLION	OVER $100 MILLION	UNKNOWN	
WHL OWNED: 95-100%	1829	2011	696	446	184	2893	8059
MAJ OWNED: 51- 94%	156	340	144	104	45	236	1025
CO- OWNED: 50%	131	201	84	65	23	221	725
MIN OWNED: 5- 49%	108	265	183	120	74	286	1036
UNKNOWN	14	15	6	3	1	314	353
TOTAL	2238	2832	1113	738	327	3950	11198

200

CHAPTER   4   - FINANCIAL STATISTICS OF FOREIGN SUBSIDIARIES
SECTION   -- ASSETS OF SUBSIDIARIES ACTIVE AT 1-JAN-76
TABLE   3   --- BY METHOD OF ENTRY

NO. OF SUBSIDIARIES, BY METHODS OF ENTRY

METHOD OF ENTRY	ASSETS CATEGORY FOR 1975						TOTAL NO. AT 1-JAN-76
	UNDER $1 MILLION	$1-10 MILLION	$10-25 MILLION	$25-100 MILLION	OVER $100 MILLION	UNKNOWN	
NEWLY FORMED	1260	1544	603	406	180	2023	6016
ACQUIRED	846	1116	400	257	96	1427	4142
DESCENDENT	30	47	29	32	30	48	216
UNKNOWN	102	125	81	43	21	452	824
TOTAL	2238	2832	1113	738	327	3950	11198

CHAPTER 4   - FINANCIAL STATISTICS OF FOREIGN SUBSIDIARIES
SECTION 2   -- ASSETS OF SUBSIDIARIES ACTIVE AT 1-JAN-76
TABLE 4   --- BY ENTRY DATE

NO. OF SUBSIDIARIES, BY ENTRY DATE

ENTRY DATE	ASSETS CATEGORY FOR 1975						TOTAL NO. AT 1-JAN-76
	UNDER $1 MILLION	$1-10 MILLION	$10-25 MILLION	$25-100 MILLION	OVER $100 MILLION	UNKNOWN	
PRE-1951	137	273	223	190	116	337	1276
1951	4	21	14	14	6	28	87
1952	24	20	11	9	3	43	110
1953	7	27	10	7	1	21	73
1954	19	36	9	13	6	40	123
1955	18	37	17	20	7	45	144
1956	31	43	25	15	4	62	180
1957	21	50	27	16	1	67	182
1958	26	58	18	20	6	68	196
1959	36	85	24	23	15	95	278
1960	50	89	39	39	16	104	337
1961	52	94	41	27	13	112	339
1962	70	102	36	25	10	102	345
1963	73	129	40	21	16	147	426
1964	71	96	42	30	9	126	374
1965	77	143	48	25	8	146	447
1966	110	127	39	26	10	134	446
1967	154	160	50	30	14	248	656
1968	207	189	65	34	12	272	779
1969	174	178	61	38	13	276	740
1970	140	151	58	22	12	286	669
1971	197	200	48	27	5	317	794
1972	142	139	54	24	4	226	589
1973	145	159	35	18	3	287	647
1974	172	137	37	13	10	219	588
1975	81	89	42	12	7	142	373
TOTAL	2238	2832	1113	738	327	3950	11198

CHAPTER 4 — FINANCIAL STATISTICS OF FOREIGN SUBSIDIARIES
SECTION 2 -- ASSETS OF SUBSIDIARIES ACTIVE AT 1-JAN-76
TABLE 5 --- BY GEOGRAPHICAL REGION

NO. OF SUBSIDIARIES, BY COUNTRY OR REGION

COUNTRY OR REGION	ASSETS CATEGORY FOR 1975						TOTAL NO. AT 1-JAN-76
	UNDER $1 MILLION	$1-10 MILLION	$10-25 MILLION	$25-100 MILLION	OVER $100 MILLION	UNKNOWN	
CANADA	205	258	125	101	51	423	1163
LATIN AMER. (TOTAL)	531	675	224	121	44	867	2462
C.AM.+CARIB.(TOTAL)	277	297	82	46	20	458	1180
BAHAMAS	14	6	4	1	2	33	56
BERMUDA	9	6	1	1	4	51	72
COSTA RICA	21	17	1	0	0	6	45
GUATEMALA	31	16	2	1	0	15	65
JAMAICA	6	10	2	2	2	16	38
MEXICO	112	184	54	27	5	170	552
NETH.ANTILLES	7	4	2	5	3	34	55
NICARAGUA	11	9	1	0	0	2	23
PANAMA	35	24	5	3	2	101	170
OTHER C.AM+CAR.	31	25	10	6	2	30	104
S.AMERICA (TOTAL)	254	378	142	75	24	409	1282
BOLIVIA	5	1	1	0	0	3	10
CHILE	15	14	4	1	1	17	52
COLOMBIA	32	59	16	10	2	42	161
ECUADOR	13	8	5	1	1	15	43
PERU	20	30	6	0	2	22	80
ARGENTINA	44	59	22	17	4	61	207
BRAZIL	60	103	58	30	13	111	375
URUGUAY	11	8	2	0	0	18	39
VENEZUELA	50	92	27	16	0	115	300
OTHER S.AMER.	4	4	1	0	1	5	15
EUROPE (TOTAL)	917	1151	499	369	151	1742	4829
BELGIUM	55	81	33	25	7	108	309
FRANCE	111	144	78	62	22	200	617
GERMANY	116	162	72	74	38	226	688
ITALY	71	120	51	29	14	97	382
LUXEMBOURG	3	8	4	4	0	20	39
NETHERLANDS	59	74	26	27	10	110	306
DENMARK	33	28	12	2	2	38	115
IRELAND	25	31	5	3	1	39	104
U.K.	190	230	95	87	31	451	1084
AUSTRIA	24	22	12	4	1	27	90
FINLAND	22	8	2	2	0	12	46
GREECE	13	17	5	2	0	17	54
NORWAY	29	19	12	6	2	24	92
PORTUGAL	14	22	3	3	0	29	71
SPAIN	60	86	43	15	5	89	298
SWEDEN	36	43	24	10	6	72	191
SWITZERLAND	48	42	17	10	9	152	278
TURKEY	3	6	5	4	3	13	34
OTHER EUROPE	5	8	0	0	0	18	31

TABLE   4 .2 .5   (CONTINUED)

ASSETS CATEGORY FOR 1975

COUNTRY OR REGION	UNDER $1 MILLION	$1-10 MILLION	$10-25 MILLION	$25-100 MILLION	OVER $100 MILLION	UNKNOWN	TOTAL NO. AT 1-JAN-76
N.AFR+M.EAST(TOTAL)	63	62	18	12	12	97	264
ALGERIA	6	3	1	0	1	4	14
EGYPT	3	2	3	0	1	10	20
IRAN	11	18	5	5	3	25	67
ISRAEL	7	9	0	1	0	3	20
LEBANON	4	9	0	0	0	9	22
MOROCCO	11	8	4	1	0	5	29
SAUDI ARABIA	3	2	0	3	2	12	22
OTHER N.AF+M.E.	18	11	5	2	5	29	70
E.+W.AFRICA (TOTAL)	77	72	25	10	13	124	321
GHANA	2	4	2	1	0	8	17
IVORY COAST	3	4	0	1	1	4	13
KENYA	8	7	1	2	1	8	27
LIBERIA	6	8	3	3	3	22	45
NIGERIA	16	14	4	0	2	21	57
ZAIRE	5	2	3	0	0	14	26
ZAMBIA	16	12	1	2	1	15	47
OTHER E.+W.AFR.	21	19	11	1	5	32	89
SOUTH ASIA (TOTAL)	25	47	21	12	0	39	144
INDIA	12	33	19	8	0	29	101
PAKISTAN	9	12	2	4	0	6	33
SRI LANKA	4	2	0	0	0	3	9
OTHER S.ASIA	0	0	0	0	0	1	1
EAST ASIA (TOTAL)	205	298	105	55	32	309	1004
HONG KONG	26	22	8	3	0	38	97
INDONESIA	14	16	8	5	1	17	61
JAPAN	70	115	49	33	24	135	426
MALAYSIA	15	22	3	0	0	21	61
PHILIPPINES	19	46	11	4	2	26	108
SINGAPORE	24	17	6	4	1	22	74
S.KOREA	4	11	7	0	3	12	37
THAILAND	20	21	3	3	0	15	62
TAIWAN	8	23	8	3	1	16	59
OTHER E.ASIA	5	5	2	0	0	7	19
S.DOMINIONS (TOTAL)	215	269	96	58	24	349	1011
AUSTRALIA	107	145	60	39	20	173	544
NEW ZEALAND	38	35	7	3	0	49	132
RHODESIA	11	6	1	1	0	7	26
S.AFRICA	59	83	28	15	4	120	309
OUTSIDE U.S.(TOTAL)	2238	2832	1113	738	327	3950	11198

CHAPTER 4   - FINANCIAL STATISTICS OF FOREIGN SUBSIDIARIES
SECTION 2   -- ASSETS OF SUBSIDIARIES ACTIVE AT 1-JAN-76
TABLE 6   --- BY PRINCIPAL INDUSTRY OF SUBSIDIARY

NO. OF SUBSIDIARIES, BY PRINCIPAL INDUSTRY IN 1975

PRINCIPAL INDUSTRY	ASSETS CATEGORY FOR 1975						TOTAL NO. AT 1-JAN-76
	UNDER $1 MILLION	$1-10 MILLION	$10-25 MILLION	$25-100 MILLION	OVER $100 MILLION	UNKNOWN	
BEVERAGES	11	24	9	7	0	30	81
TOBACCO	1	5	10	6	1	3	26
FOOD	132	236	84	44	3	136	635
TEXTILES+APPAREL	10	44	18	5	2	16	95
WOOD+FURNITURE	14	34	4	3	3	9	67
PAPER	24	78	34	28	4	38	206
PRINTING	33	8	7	3	0	13	64
INDUSTRIAL CHEM	30	67	30	27	10	44	208
PLASTICS	26	56	26	33	5	34	180
AGRIC CHEM	8	24	8	9	0	2	51
COSMETICS	80	128	20	11	3	34	276
DRUGS	80	238	69	24	1	134	546
OTHER CHEM	34	128	51	24	11	61	309
FABR PLASTICS	17	36	14	7	1	20	95
TIRES	0	18	35	28	6	2	89
REF PETROLEUM	3	10	22	37	74	9	155
OTH PETROLEUM	2	17	9	3	1	9	41
LEATHER	3	19	1	0	0	3	26
STONE+CLAY+CEMNT	5	29	6	7	0	16	63
ABRASIVES	22	52	19	12	2	28	135
GLASS	5	22	8	16	2	8	61
IRON+STEEL	4	22	16	7	1	7	57

TABLE   4 . 2 . 6   (CONTINUED)

ASSETS CATEGORY FOR 1975

PRINCIPAL INDUSTRY	UNDER $1 MILLION	$1-10 MILLION	$10-25 MILLION	$25-100 MILLION	OVER $100 MILLION	UNKNOWN	TOTAL NO. AT 1-JAN-76
NON-FERROUS	16	49	43	24	12	32	176
METAL CANS	2	19	6	6	7	6	46
OTHER FAB METAL	49	123	41	15	0	60	288
ENGINES+TURBIN	2	11	5	3	3	4	28
CONSTR MACH	14	50	28	21	7	33	153
FARM MACHINERY	2	9	7	9	6	2	35
OFFICE MC+COMPUT	4	26	14	16	13	5	78
SPEC MACHINERY	10	42	12	3	0	24	91
GENL MACHINERY	16	55	10	12	0	30	123
OTH NON-EL MC	18	41	11	5	0	34	109
EL LIGHT+WIRING	3	17	5	4	1	4	34
EL TRAN EQUIP	1	22	5	1	0	2	31
RADIO+TV+APPL	18	29	24	22	6	16	115
ELECTRONICS	6	36	14	8	3	23	90
OTHER ELEC	24	73	25	9	4	32	167
COMMUNICATION	9	14	10	11	9	9	62
MOTOR VEHIC	16	84	54	53	27	52	286
OTHER TRANSP	2	6	7	9	0	9	33
PRECISION	25	59	17	11	5	44	161
MISCELLANEOUS	52	49	11	6	3	82	203
TOTAL	833	2109	849	589	236	1159	5775

CHAPTER 4   - FINANCIAL STATISTICS OF FOREIGN SUBSIDIARIES
SECTION 3   --- EQUITY OF SUBSIDIARIES ACTIVE AT 1-JAN-76
TABLE 1   --- BY PRINCIPAL ACTIVITIES

NO. OF SUBSIDIARIES, BY ACTIVITY IN 1975

PRINCIPAL ACTIVITY	EQUITY CATEGORY FOR 1975						TOTAL NO. AT 1-JAN-76
	UNDER $1 MILLION	$1-10 MILLION	$10-25 MILLION	$25-100 MILLION	OVER $100 MILLION	UNKNOWN	
MANUFACTURING	1413	1360	323	190	73	2416	5775
SALES	1237	260	55	28	6	1247	2833
EXTRACTION	87	48	5	17	14	185	356
OTHER	543	107	14	19	7	1287	1977
UNKNOWN	17	5	1	0	0	234	257
TOTAL	3297	1780	398	254	100	5369	11198

CHAPTER 4   - FINANCIAL STATISTICS OF FOREIGN SUBSIDIARIES
SECTION 3   -- EQUITY OF SUBSIDIARIES ACTIVE AT 1-JAN-76
TABLE 2   --- BY OWNERSHIP PATTERNS

NO. OF SUBSIDIARIES, BY PARENT OWNERSHIP IN 1975

OWNERSHIP IN 1975	EQUITY CATEGORY FOR 1975						TOTAL NO. AT 1-JAN-76
	UNDER $1 MILLION	$1-10 MILLION	$10-25 MILLION	$25-100 MILLION	OVER $100 MILLION	UNKNOWN	
WHL OWNED: 95-100%	2597	1143	236	161	57	3865	8059
MAJ OWNED: 51- 94%	257	246	59	38	16	409	1025
CO- OWNED: 50%	213	149	35	13	6	309	725
MIN OWNED: 5- 49%	208	236	65	41	21	465	1036
UNKNOWN	22	6	3	1	0	321	353
TOTAL	3297	1780	398	254	100	5369	11198

CHAPTER   4   - FINANCIAL STATISTICS OF FOREIGN SUBSIDIARIES
SECTION   3   -- EQUITY OF SUBSIDIARIES ACTIVE AT 1-JAN-76
TABLE   --- BY METHOD OF ENTRY

NO. OF SUBSIDIARIES, BY METHODS OF ENTRY

METHOD OF ENTRY	EQUITY CATEGORY FOR 1975						TOTAL NO. AT 1-JAN-76
	UNDER $1 MILLION	$1-10 MILLION	$10-25 MILLION	$25-100 MILLION	OVER $100 MILLION	UNKNOWN	
NEWLY FORMED	1878	974	218	142	62	2742	6016
ACQUIRED	1208	685	146	89	22	1992	4142
DESCENDENT	43	39	14	14	10	96	216
UNKNOWN	168	82	20	9	6	539	824
TOTAL	3297	1780	398	254	100	5369	11198

CHAPTER 4   – FINANCIAL STATISTICS OF FOREIGN SUBSIDIARIES
SECTION 3   –– EQUITY OF SUBSIDIARIES ACTIVE AT 1-JAN-76
TABLE 4   ––– BY ENTRY DATE

NO. OF SUBSIDIARIES, BY ENTRY DATE

ENTRY DATE	EQUITY CATEGORY FOR 1975						TOTAL NO. AT 1-JAN-76
	UNDER $1 MILLION	$1-10 MILLION	$10-25 MILLION	$25-100 MILLION	OVER $100 MILLION	UNKNOWN	
PRE-1951	233	231	94	93	40	585	1276
1951	10	16	7	8	0	46	87
1952	33	15	6	2	0	54	110
1953	20	17	2	2	0	32	73
1954	33	22	5	6	2	55	123
1955	29	23	13	7	2	70	144
1956	44	34	7	4	4	87	180
1957	40	34	7	4	0	97	182
1958	51	35	8	6	2	94	196
1959	73	57	14	7	3	124	278
1960	86	63	19	13	6	150	337
1961	89	67	22	8	2	151	339
1962	106	65	16	3	1	154	345
1963	125	96	16	5	6	178	426
1964	111	67	21	5	2	168	374
1965	125	83	13	7	1	218	447
1966	170	87	12	5	3	169	446
1967	225	106	14	15	3	293	656
1968	266	110	17	10	2	374	779
1969	240	97	14	9	5	375	740
1970	203	89	12	9	5	351	669
1971	294	90	11	7	4	388	794
1972	188	74	14	7	0	306	589
1973	187	71	15	4	1	369	647
1974	218	80	8	4	5	273	588
1975	98	51	11	4	1	208	373
TOTAL	3297	1780	398	254	100	5369	11198

CHAPTER 4 — FINANCIAL STATISTICS OF FOREIGN SUBSIDIARIES
SECTION 3 -- EQUITY OF SUBSIDIARIES ACTIVE AT 1-JAN-76
TABLE 5 --- BY GEOGRAPHICAL REGION

NO. OF SUBSIDIARIES, BY COUNTRY OR REGION

COUNTRY OR REGION	EQUITY CATEGORY FOR 1975						TOTAL NO. AT 1-JAN-76
	UNDER $1 MILLION	$1-10 MILLION	$10-25 MILLION	$25-100 MILLION	OVER $100 MILLION	UNKNOWN	
CANADA	278	157	30	46	18	634	1163
LATIN AMER. (TOTAL)	706	398	75	44	14	1225	2462
C.AM.+CARIB.(TOTAL)	362	167	23	19	9	600	1180
BAHAMAS	16	1	1	1	1	36	56
BERMUDA	12	7	2	2	2	47	72
COSTA RICA	24	10	0	0	0	11	45
GUATEMALA	30	11	0	0	0	24	65
JAMAICA	8	6	0	1	2	21	38
MEXICO	168	96	19	10	1	258	552
NETH.ANTILLES	14	6	0	2	1	32	55
NICARAGUA	11	3	0	0	0	9	23
PANAMA	42	15	1	2	0	110	170
OTHER C.AM+CAR.	37	12	0	1	2	52	104
S.AMERICA (TOTAL)	344	231	52	25	5	625	1282
BOLIVIA	4	0	0	0	0	6	10
CHILE	23	5	1	1	0	22	52
COLOMBIA	47	28	8	2	0	76	161
ECUADOR	15	5	1	1	0	21	43
PERU	27	15	1	0	1	36	80
ARGENTINA	55	43	6	5	0	98	207
BRAZIL	78	79	23	13	3	179	375
URUGUAY	12	3	0	0	0	24	39
VENEZUELA	78	51	12	3	0	156	300
OTHER S.AMER.	5	2	0	0	1	7	15
EUROPE (TOTAL)	1448	782	212	120	49	2218	4829
BELGIUM	92	54	15	6	4	138	309
FRANCE	179	114	33	15	9	267	617
GERMANY	216	145	40	31	12	244	688
ITALY	134	83	10	9	3	143	382
LUXEMBOURG	3	10	3	1	0	22	39
NETHERLANDS	88	42	11	10	4	151	306
DENMARK	52	18	1	2	0	42	115
IRELAND	33	9	2	0	1	59	104
U.K.	291	139	52	30	8	564	1084
AUSTRIA	36	12	5	1	0	36	90
FINLAND	24	3	3	0	0	16	46
GREECE	18	10	2	0	0	24	54
NORWAY	43	15	3	2	0	29	92
PORTUGAL	23	5	1	0	0	42	71
SPAIN	86	58	12	3	2	137	298
SWEDEN	56	23	8	5	1	98	191
SWITZERLAND	61	34	8	5	4	166	278
TURKEY	6	5	3	0	1	19	34
OTHER EUROPE	7	3	0	0	0	21	31

TABLE 4 . 3 . 5 (CONTINUED)

COUNTRY OR REGION	EQUITY CATEGORY FOR 1975						TOTAL NO. AT 1-JAN-76
	UNDER $1 MILLION	$1-10 MILLION	$10-25 MILLION	$25-100 MILLION	OVER $100 MILLION	UNKNOWN	
N.AFR+M.EAST (TOTAL)	98	30	6	1	4	125	264
ALGERIA	6	1	1	0	0	6	14
EGYPT	7	3	0	0	1	9	20
IRAN	21	8	2	0	3	33	67
ISRAEL	8	4	0	0	0	8	20
LEBANON	7	4	0	0	0	11	22
MOROCCO	15	2	3	0	0	9	29
SAUDI ARABIA	4	6	0	0	0	12	22
OTHER N.AF+M.E.	30	2	0	1	0	37	70
E.+W.AFRICA (TOTAL)	114	33	3	7	3	161	321
GHANA	2	3	0	1	0	11	17
IVORY COAST	5	2	1	1	0	4	13
KENYA	11	3	0	0	0	13	27
LIBERIA	7	7	1	1	1	28	45
NIGERIA	23	3	0	0	1	30	57
ZAIRE	7	1	0	0	0	18	26
ZAMBIA	24	4	0	0	1	18	47
OTHER E.+W.AFR.	35	10	1	4	0	39	89
SOUTH ASIA (TOTAL)	34	31	7	3	0	69	144
INDIA	19	25	7	2	0	48	101
PAKISTAN	10	6	0	1	0	16	33
SRI LANKA	5	0	0	0	0	4	9
OTHER S.ASIA	0	0	0	0	0	1	1
EAST ASIA (TOTAL)	324	168	28	13	8	463	1004
HONG KONG	32	15	0	2	0	48	97
INDONESIA	22	7	3	0	0	29	61
JAPAN	127	79	14	9	7	190	426
MALAYSIA	24	7	0	0	0	30	61
PHILIPPINES	29	23	4	1	1	50	108
SINGAPORE	35	10	2	0	0	27	74
S.KOREA	6	5	0	1	0	25	37
THAILAND	25	8	2	0	0	27	62
TAIWAN	16	13	3	0	0	27	59
OTHER E.ASIA	8	1	0	0	0	10	19
S.DOMINIONS (TOTAL)	295	181	37	20	4	474	1011
AUSTRALIA	148	107	27	18	4	240	544
NEW ZEALAND	45	15	4	0	0	68	132
RHODESIA	12	1	1	0	0	12	26
S.AFRICA	90	58	5	2	0	154	309
OUTSIDE U.S. (TOTAL)	3297	1780	398	254	100	5369	11198

CHAPTER 4   - FINANCIAL STATISTICS OF FOREIGN SUBSIDIARIES
SECTION 3   -- EQUITY OF SUBSIDIARIES ACTIVE AT 1-JAN-76
TABLE 6   --- BY PRINCIPAL INDUSTRY OF SUBSIDIARY

NO. OF SUBSIDIARIES, BY PRINCIPAL INDUSTRY IN 1975

PRINCIPAL INDUSTRY	EQUITY CATEGORY FOR 1975						TOTAL NO. AT 1-JAN-76
	UNDER $1 MILLION	$1-10 MILLION	$10-25 MILLION	$25-100 MILLION	OVER $100 MILLION	UNKNOWN	
BEVERAGES	17	11	8	3	0	42	81
TOBACCO	4	9	3	1	0	9	26
FOOD	172	150	20	12	0	281	635
TEXTILES+APPAREL	25	28	5	2	0	35	95
WOOD+FURNITURE	22	19	2	0	0	24	67
PAPER	57	49	12	12	1	75	206
PRINTING	37	4	1	1	0	21	64
INDUSTRIAL CHEM	49	29	12	9	2	107	208
PLASTICS	38	50	21	4	3	64	180
AGRIC CHEM	17	8	5	1	0	20	51
COSMETICS	115	51	4	3	0	103	276
DRUGS	130	112	21	5	1	277	546
OTHER CHEM	73	102	13	9	3	109	309
FABR PLASTICS	32	22	5	1	0	35	95
TIRES	3	31	23	13	1	18	89
REF PETROLEUM	15	22	19	17	30	52	155
OTH PETROLEUM	13	12	2	0	0	14	41
LEATHER	9	8	0	0	0	9	26
STONE+CLAY+CEMNT	9	18	2	2	0	32	63
ABRASIVES	37	44	6	4	1	43	135
GLASS	12	9	8	2	0	30	61
IRON+STEEL	11	16	1	1	0	28	57

213

TABLE   4 . 3 . 6   (CONTINUED)

PRINCIPAL INDUSTRY	EQUITY CATEGORY FOR 1975						TOTAL NO. AT 1-JAN-76
	UNDER $1 MILLION	$1-10 MILLION	$10-25 MILLION	$25-100 MILLION	OVER $100 MILLION	UNKNOWN	
NON-FERROUS	31	47	16	10	4	68	176
METAL CANS	6	10	4	5	0	21	46
OTHER FAB METAL	63	64	10	0	0	151	288
ENGINES+TURBIN	6	8	1	1	1	11	28
CONSTR MACH	28	46	5	8	2	64	153
FARM MACHINERY	7	4	9	6	0	9	35
OFFICE MC+COMPUT	10	16	8	7	5	32	78
SPEC MACHINERY	26	30	3	1	0	31	91
GENL MACHINERY	29	29	4	1	0	60	123
OTH NON-EL MC	32	28	3	1	0	45	109
EL LIGHT+WIRING	7	7	4	1	0	15	34
EL TRAN EQUIP	3	8	0	0	0	20	31
RADIO+TV+APPL	26	30	12	2	2	43	115
ELECTRONICS	25	18	6	2	0	39	90
OTHER ELEC	35	45	6	5	1	75	167
COMMUNICATION	16	11	5	7	4	19	62
MOTOR VEHIC	51	85	25	19	10	96	286
OTHER TRANSP	5	9	1	1	0	17	33
PRECISION	44	40	5	8	1	63	161
MISCELLANEOUS	66	21	3	3	1	109	203
TOTAL	1413	1360	323	190	73	2416	5775

CHAPTER 4 - FINANCIAL STATISTICS OF FOREIGN SUBSIDIARIES
SECTION 4 -- SALES, ASSETS AND EQUITY IN SPECIFIC INDUSTRIES
TABLE 1 --- THE BEVERAGES INDUSTRY (SIC 208)

NO. OF MANUFACTURING SUBSIDIARIES ACTIVE AT 1-JAN-76   (SEE NOTE BELOW)

(CATEGORIES: A=UNDER $1 MILLION B=$1M-$10M C=$10M-$25M D=$25M-$100M E=OVER $100M U=UNKNOWN)

COUNTRY OR REGION	TOTAL NO. AT 1-JAN-76	SALES CATEGORY FOR 1975						ASSETS CATEGORY FOR 1975						EQUITY CATEGORY FOR 1975					
		A	B	C	D	E	U	A	B	C	D	E	U	A	B	C	D	E	U
CANADA	18	0	3	3	2	1	9	0	4	1	2	0	11	0	0	1	1	0	16
C.AM.+CARIB.	9	3	3	3	0	0	0	0	3	0	0	0	6	1	0	0	0	0	8
S.AMERICA	15	3	7	2	3	0	0	3	4	2	1	0	5	3	4	2	0	0	6
EUROPE	20	4	9	3	1	1	2	7	4	2	2	0	5	7	1	2	1	0	9
N.AFR+M.EAST	0	0	0	0	0	0	0	0	0	0	0	0	0	0	0	0	0	0	0
E.+W.AFRICA	3	0	2	1	0	0	0	0	3	0	0	0	0	1	2	0	0	0	0
SOUTH ASIA	1	0	0	0	0	0	1*	0	0	0	0	0	1*	0	0	0	0	0	1*
EAST ASIA	10	1	3	1	2	1	2	1	4	1	2	0	2	4	3	1	1	0	1
S.DOMINIONS	5	1	1	3	0	0	0	0	2	2	0	0	1	1	1	1	0	0	2
OUTSIDE U.S.(TOTAL)	81	12	28	16	8	3	14	11	24	8	7	0	31	17	11	7	3	0	43

(NOTE: IN THIS SECTION SUBSIDIARIES ARE COUNTED ON THE BASIS OF THEIR PRINCIPAL INDUSTRY IN 1975.)

*CLASSIFICATION SUPPRESSED TO AVOID DISCLOSURE OF CONFIDENTIAL DATA

CHAPTER 4 - FINANCIAL STATISTICS OF FOREIGN SUBSIDIARIES
SECTION 4 -- SALES, ASSETS AND EQUITY IN SPECIFIC INDUSTRIES
TABLE 2 ---- THE TOBACCO INDUSTRY (SIC 21)

NO. OF MANUFACTURING SUBSIDIARIES ACTIVE AT 1-JAN-76 (SEE NOTE BELOW)

(CATEGORIES: A=UNDER $1 MILLION B=$1M-$10M C=$10M-$25M D=$25M-$100M E=OVER $100M U=UNKNOWN)

COUNTRY OR REGION	TOTAL NO. AT 1-JAN-76	SALES CATEGORY FOR 1975						ASSETS CATEGORY FOR 1975						EQUITY CATEGORY FOR 1975					
		A	B	C	D	E	U	A	B	C	D	E	U	A	B	C	D	E	U
CANADA	1	0	0	0	0	0	1*	0	0	0	0	0	1*	0	0	0	0	0	1*
C.AM.+CARIB.	5	0	2	2	1	0	0	0	2	2	1	0	0	1	2	0	0	0	2
S.AMERICA	3	0	0	0	2	1	0	0	0	1	2	0	0	0	1	1	0	0	1
EUROPE	10	1	2	2	2	2	1	1	1	3	2	1	2	1	2	1	1	0	5
N.AFR+M.EAST	0	0	0	0	0	0	0	0	0	0	0	0	0	0	0	0	0	0	0
E.+W.AFRICA	1	0	0	0	0	0	1*	0	0	0	0	0	1*	0	0	0	0	0	1*
SOUTH ASIA	2	0	0	0	2	0	0	0	0	2	0	0	0	0	2	0	0	0	0
EAST ASIA	1	0	0	0	0	0	1*	0	0	0	0	0	1*	0	0	0	0	0	1*
S.DOMINIONS	3	0	2	0	1	0	0	0	1	1	0	0	1	1	1	0	0	0	1
OUTSIDE U.S. (TOTAL)	26	1	6	4	8	3	4	1	4	9	5	1	6	3	8	2	1	0	12

(NOTE: IN THIS SECTION SUBSIDIARIES ARE COUNTED ON THE BASIS OF THEIR PRINCIPAL INDUSTRY IN 1975)

*CLASSIFICATION SUPPRESSED TO AVOID DISCLOSURE OF CONFIDENTIAL DATA

CHAPTER 4   - FINANCIAL STATISTICS OF FOREIGN SUBSIDIARIES
SECTION 4   -- SALES, ASSETS AND EQUITY IN SPECIFIC INDUSTRIES
TABLE 3   --- THE FOOD INDUSTRY (SIC 20, EXCLUDING 208)

NO. OF MANUFACTURING SUBSIDIARIES ACTIVE AT 1-JAN-76   (SEE NOTE BELOW)

(CATEGORIES: A=UNDER $1 MILLION   B=$1M-$10M   C=$10M-$25M   D=$25M-$100M   E=OVER $100M   U=UNKNOWN)

COUNTRY OR REGION	TOTAL NO. AT 1-JAN-76	SALES CATEGORY FOR 1975						ASSETS CATEGORY FOR 1975						EQUITY CATEGORY FOR 1975					
		A	B	C	D	E	U	A	B	C	D	E	U	A	B	C	D	E	U
CANADA	83	6	29	13	11	11	13	14	26	9	12	1	21	16	20	4	6	0	37
C.AM.+CARIB.	85	25	34	8	5	1	12	33	29	6	3	0	14	36	20	1	0	0	28
S.AMERICA	89	7	46	20	8	0	8	22	39	10	1	0	17	28	19	1	0	0	41
EUROPE	249	24	75	53	47	11	39	33	90	46	24	2	54	54	60	11	5	0	119
N.AFR+M.EAST	12	2	4	1	1	0	4	2	6	1	0	0	3	2	6	0	0	0	4
E.+W.AFRICA	10	1	4	0	0	0	5	2	3	0	0	0	5	4	0	0	0	0	6
SOUTH ASIA	6	0	4	1	0	0	1	0	4	0	0	0	2	1	1	0	0	0	4
EAST ASIA	44	5	24	4	2	0	9	10	21	4	0	0	9	13	13	0	0	0	18
S.DOMINIONS	57	10	24	9	6	1	7	16	18	8	4	0	11	18	11	3	1	0	24
OUTSIDE U.S.(TOTAL)	635	80	244	109	80	24	98	132	236	84	44	3	136	172	150	20	12	0	281

(NOTE: IN THIS SECTION SUBSIDIARIES ARE COUNTED ON THE BASIS OF THEIR PRINCIPAL INDUSTRY IN 1975)

CHAPTER 4 - FINANCIAL STATISTICS OF FOREIGN SUBSIDIARIES
SECTION 4 -- SALES, ASSETS AND EQUITY IN SPECIFIC INDUSTRIES
TABLE 4 --- THE TEXTILES & APPAREL INDUSTRIES (SIC 22 AND 23)

NO. OF MANUFACTURING SUBSIDIARIES ACTIVE AT 1-JAN-76   (SEE NOTE BELOW)

(CATEGORIES: A=UNDER $1 MILLION B=$1M-$10M C=$10M-$25M D=$25M-$100M E=OVER $100M U=UNKNOWN)

COUNTRY OR REGION	TOTAL NO. AT 1-JAN-76	SALES CATEGORY FOR 1975						ASSETS CATEGORY FOR 1975						EQUITY CATEGORY FOR 1975					
		A	B	C	D	E	U	A	B	C	D	E	U	A	B	C	D	E	U
CANADA	18	0	10	2	4	0	2	2	9	3	1	0	3	5	5	1	1	0	6
C.AM.+CARIB.	6	1	2	2	0	1	0	3	1	1	0	1	0	3	1	1	0	0	1
S.AMERICA	12	2	3	1	2	0	4	2	3	2	1	0	4	3	1	1	0	0	7
EUROPE	43	2	18	12	6	0	5	3	21	10	2	1	6	11	15	2	1	0	14
N.AFR+M.EAST	2	1	1	0	0	0	0	0	1	0	0	0	1	0	0	0	0	0	2
E.+W.AFRICA	0	0	0	0	0	0	0	0	0	0	0	0	0	0	0	0	0	0	0
SOUTH ASIA	2	0	1	0	1	0	0	0	1	1	0	0	0	0	1	0	0	0	1
EAST ASIA	7	0	3	2	1	0	1	0	4	1	1	0	1	2	2	0	0	0	3
S.DOMINIONS	5	0	3	1	0	0	1	0	4	0	0	0	1	1	3	0	0	0	1
OUTSIDE U.S.(TOTAL)	95	6	41	20	14	1	13	10	44	18	5	2	16	25	28	5	2	0	35

(NOTE: IN THIS SECTION SUBSIDIARIES ARE COUNTED ON THE BASIS OF THEIR PRINCIPAL INDUSTRY IN 1975)

CHAPTER 4 - FINANCIAL STATISTICS OF FOREIGN SUBSIDIARIES
SECTION 4 -- SALES, ASSETS AND EQUITY IN SPECIFIC INDUSTRIES
TABLE 5 --- THE WOOD AND FURNITURE INDUSTRIES (SIC 24 AND 25)

NO. OF MANUFACTURING SUBSIDIARIES ACTIVE AT 1-JAN-76   (SEE NOTE BELOW)

(CATEGORIES: A=UNDER $1 MILLION B=$1M-$10M C=$10M-$25M D=$25M-$100M E=OVER $100M U=UNKNOWN)

COUNTRY OR REGION	TOTAL NO. AT 1-JAN-76	SALES CATEGORY FOR 1975						ASSETS CATEGORY FOR 1975						EQUITY CATEGORY FOR 1975					
		A	B	C	D	E	U	A	B	C	D	E	U	A	B	C	D	E	U
CANADA	24	2	9	4	3	3	3	6	9	2	1	3	3	7	7	1	0	0	9
C.AM.+CARIB.	6	3	1	2	0	0	0	3	2	0	0	0	1	3	1	0	0	0	2
S.AMERICA	6	1	4	1	0	0	0	2	4	0	0	0	0	3	2	0	0	0	1
EUROPE	20	1	10	4	1	0	4	2	11	2	1	0	4	7	5	1	0	0	7
N.AFR+M.EAST	1	0	1	0	0	0	0	0	1	0	0	0	0	1	0	0	0	0	0
E.+W.AFRICA	0	0	0	0	0	0	0	0	0	0	0	0	0	0	0	0	0	0	0
SOUTH ASIA	0	0	0	0	0	0	0	0	0	0	0	0	0	0	0	0	0	0	0
EAST ASIA	6	0	4	0	1	0	1	0	4	0	1	0	1	0	2	0	0	0	4
S.DOMINIONS	4	1	3	0	0	0	0	1	3	0	0	0	0	1	2	0	0	0	1
OUTSIDE U.S. (TOTAL)	67	8	32	11	5	3	8	14	34	4	3	3	9	22	19	2	0	0	24

(NOTE: IN THIS SECTION SUBSIDIARIES ARE COUNTED ON THE BASIS OF THEIR PRINCIPAL INDUSTRY IN 1975)

CHAPTER 4 - FINANCIAL STATISTICS OF FOREIGN SUBSIDIARIES
SECTION 4 -- SALES, ASSETS AND EQUITY IN SPECIFIC INDUSTRIES
TABLE 6 --- THE PAPER INDUSTRY (SIC 26)

NO. OF MANUFACTURING SUBSIDIARIES ACTIVE AT 1-JAN-76   (SEE NOTE BELOW)

(CATEGORIES: A=UNDER $1 MILLION B=$1M-$10M C=$10M-$25M D=$25M-$100M E=OVER $100M U=UNKNOWN)

COUNTRY OR REGION	TOTAL NO. AT 1-JAN-76	SALES CATEGORY FOR 1975						ASSETS CATEGORY FOR 1975						EQUITY CATEGORY FOR 1975					
		A	B	C	D	E	U	A	B	C	D	E	U	A	B	C	D	E	U
CANADA	18	2	3	3	6	2	2	3	3	1	5	2	4	3	2	0	2	1	10
C.AM.+CARIB.	20	3	7	3	1	2	4	3	5	3	3	0	6	6	4	0	3	0	7
S.AMERICA	40	2	20	11	3	0	4	3	22	6	4	0	5	8	13	4	0	0	15
EUROPE	76	4	22	25	13	3	9	6	25	19	11	2	13	14	20	6	6	0	30
N.AFR+M.EAST	3	0	3	0	0	0	0	0	3	0	0	0	0	2	0	0	0	0	1
E.+W.AFRICA	5	2	3	0	0	0	0	3	2	0	0	0	0	5	0	0	0	0	0
SOUTH ASIA	0	0	0	0	0	0	0	0	0	0	0	0	0	0	0	0	0	0	0
EAST ASIA	15	0	8	3	2	0	2	1	7	2	1	0	4	4	5	1	0	0	5
S.DOMINIONS	29	4	12	4	4	0	5	5	11	3	4	0	6	15	5	1	1	0	7
OUTSIDE U.S.(TOTAL)	206	17	78	49	29	7	26	24	78	34	28	4	38	57	49	12	12	1	75

(NOTE: IN THIS SECTION SUBSIDIARIES ARE COUNTED ON THE BASIS OF THEIR PRINCIPAL INDUSTRY IN 1975)

CHAPTER   4   - FINANCIAL STATISTICS OF FOREIGN SUBSIDIARIES
SECTION   4   -- SALES, ASSETS AND EQUITY IN SPECIFIC INDUSTRIES
TABLE   7 --- THE PRINTING INDUSTRY (SIC 27)

NO. OF MANUFACTURING SUBSIDIARIES ACTIVE AT 1-JAN-76   (SEE NOTE BELOW)

(CATEGORIES: A=UNDER $1 MILLION B=$1M-$10M C=$10M-$25M D=$25M-$100M E=OVER $100M U=UNKNOWN)

COUNTRY OR REGION	TOTAL NO. AT 1-JAN-76	SALES CATEGORY FOR 1975						ASSETS CATEGORY FOR 1975						EQUITY CATEGORY FOR 1975					
		A	B	C	D	E	U	A	B	C	D	E	U	A	B	C	D	E	U
CANADA	11	3	2	1	1	0	4	4	1	1	1	0	4	5	0	0	1	0	5
C.AM.+CARIB.	4	2	1	1	0	0	0	2	2	0	0	0	0	2	0	0	0	0	2
S.AMERICA	3	3	0	0	0	0	0	3	0	0	0	0	0	3	0	0	0	0	0
EUROPE	35	17	5	5	3	0	5	20	3	5	2	0	5	21	4	1	0	0	9
N.AFR+M.EAST	0	0	0	0	0	0	0	0	0	0	0	0	0	0	0	0	0	0	0
E.+W.AFRICA	0	0	0	0	0	0	0	0	0	0	0	0	0	0	0	0	0	0	0
SOUTH ASIA	0	0	0	0	0	0	0	0	0	0	0	0	0	0	0	0	0	0	0
EAST ASIA	3	0	2	1	0	0	0	0	1	1	0	0	1	1	1	0	0	0	2
S.DOMINIONS	8	4	3	0	0	0	1	4	1	0	0	0	3	5	0	0	0	0	3
OUTSIDE U.S.(TOTAL)	64	29	13	8	4	0	10	33	8	7	3	0	13	37	4	1	1	0	21

(NOTE: IN THIS SECTION SUBSIDIARIES ARE COUNTED ON THE BASIS OF THEIR PRINCIPAL INDUSTRY IN 1975)

CHAPTER 4 - FINANCIAL STATISTICS OF FOREIGN SUBSIDIARIES
SECTION 4 -- SALES, ASSETS AND EQUITY IN SPECIFIC INDUSTRIES
TABLE 8 --- THE INDUSTRIAL CHEMICALS INDUSTRY (SIC 281)

NO. OF MANUFACTURING SUBSIDIARIES ACTIVE AT 1-JAN-76 (SEE NOTE BELOW)

(CATEGORIES: A=UNDER $1 MILLION B=$1M-$10M C=$10M-$25M D=$25M-$100M E=OVER $100M U=UNKNOWN)

COUNTRY OR REGION	TOTAL NO. AT 1-JAN-76	SALES CATEGORY FOR 1975						ASSETS CATEGORY FOR 1975						EQUITY CATEGORY FOR 1975					
		A	B	C	D	E	U	A	B	C	D	E	U	A	B	C	D	E	U
CANADA	20	1	7	1	5	3	3	1	7	2	4	3	3	3	2	0	1	1	13
C.AM.+CARIB.	23	6	5	4	1	0	7	5	7	4	2	0	5	9	2	1	0	0	11
S.AMERICA	19	2	6	1	6	0	4	2	5	2	5	1	4	4	3	3	2	0	7
EUROPE	95	7	25	19	17	6	21	13	28	12	11	4	27	21	16	5	4	1	48
N.AFR+M.EAST	1	0	0	0	0	0	1	0	0	0	0	0	1	0	0	0	0	0	1
E.+W.AFRICA	2	0	0	1	0	0	1	0	1	1	0	0	0	0	0	0	0	0	2
SOUTH ASIA	2	0	1	1	0	0	0	0	2	0	0	0	0	0	0	0	0	0	2
EAST ASIA	31	3	9	10	5	0	4	5	10	9	3	1	3	6	6	2	0	0	17
S.DOMINIONS	15	2	9	0	1	2	1	4	7	0	2	1	1	6	0	1	2	0	6
OUTSIDE U.S. (TOTAL)	208	21	62	37	35	11	42	30	67	30	27	10	44	49	29	12	9	2	107

(NOTE: IN THIS SECTION SUBSIDIARIES ARE COUNTED ON THE BASIS OF THEIR PRINCIPAL INDUSTRY IN 1975)

CHAPTER 4 - FINANCIAL STATISTICS OF FOREIGN SUBSIDIARIES
SECTION 4 -- SALES, ASSETS AND EQUITY IN SPECIFIC INDUSTRIES
TABLE 9 --- THE PLASTICS INDUSTRY (SIC 282)

NO. OF MANUFACTURING SUBSIDIARIES ACTIVE AT 1-JAN-76 (SEE NOTE BELOW)

(CATEGORIES: A=UNDER $1 MILLION B=$1M-$10M C=$10M-$25M D=$25M-$100M E=OVER $100M U=UNKNOWN)

COUNTRY OR REGION	TOTAL NO. AT 1-JAN-76	SALES CATEGORY FOR 1975						ASSETS CATEGORY FOR 1975						EQUITY CATEGORY FOR 1975					
		A	B	C	D	E	U	A	B	C	D	E	U	A	B	C	D	E	U
CANADA	9	0	2	3	3	0	1	0	5	1	2	0	1	1	3	0	0	0	5
C.AM.+CARIB.	20	2	7	3	2	0	6	5	5	4	0	0	6	5	4	2	0	0	9
S.AMERICA	20	3	6	3	3	0	5	4	7	2	4	0	3	5	5	3	1	0	6
EUROPE	76	8	20	12	15	5	16	12	20	6	16	4	18	17	18	8	3	2	28
N.AFR+M.EAST	6	0	2	0	1	0	3	1	3	0	1	1	0	3	1	1	0	1	0
E.+W.AFRICA	1	0	1	0	0	0	0	1	0	0	0	0	0	1	0	0	0	0	0
SOUTH ASIA	3	0	2	1	0	0	0	0	2	1	0	0	0	0	2	0	0	0	1
EAST ASIA	26	2	2	5	5	1	11	2	5	8	6	0	5	3	9	3	0	0	11
S.DOMINIONS	19	1	9	2	5	0	2	1	9	4	4	0	1	3	8	4	0	0	4
OUTSIDE U.S.(TOTAL)	180	16	51	29	34	6	44	26	56	26	33	5	34	38	50	21	4	3	64

(NOTE: IN THIS SECTION SUBSIDIARIES ARE COUNTED ON THE BASIS OF THEIR PRINCIPAL INDUSTRY IN 1975)

CHAPTER 4 - FINANCIAL STATISTICS OF FOREIGN SUBSIDIARIES
SECTION 4 -- SALES, ASSETS AND EQUITY IN SPECIFIC INDUSTRIES
TABLE 10 --- THE AGRICULTURAL CHEMICALS INDUSTRY (SIC 287)

NO. OF MANUFACTURING SUBSIDIARIES ACTIVE AT 1-JAN-76 (SEE NOTE BELOW)

(CATEGORIES: A=UNDER $1 MILLION B=$1M-$10M C=$10M-$25M D=$25M-$100M E=OVER $100M U=UNKNOWN)

COUNTRY OR REGION	TOTAL NO. AT 1-JAN-76	SALES CATEGORY FOR 1975						ASSETS CATEGORY FOR 1975						EQUITY CATEGORY FOR 1975					
		A	B	C	D	E	U	A	B	C	D	E	U	A	B	C	D	E	U
CANADA	4	1	2	0	0	0	1	2	1	0	0	0	1	2	0	0	0	0	2
C.AM.+CARIB.	13	2	8	0	2	0	1	2	7	2	2	0	0	5	1	0	1	0	6
S.AMERICA	12	1	4	5	1	0	1	2	7	2	1	0	0	4	4	0	0	0	4
EUROPE	10	0	4	1	4	1	0	0	4	3	3	0	0	1	0	3	0	0	6
N.AFR+M.EAST	1	0	0	0	0	0	1	0	0	0	0	0	1	0	0	0	0	0	1
E.+W.AFRICA	0	0	0	0	0	0	0	0	0	0	0	0	0	0	0	0	0	0	0
SOUTH ASIA	4	0	0	1	3	0	0	0	1	0	3	0	0	0	2	2	0	0	0
EAST ASIA	6	2	3	0	0	0	1	2	4	0	0	0	0	5	0	0	0	0	1
S.DOMINIONS	1	0	0	0	0	0	1*	0	0	0	0	0	1	0	0	0	0	0	1*
OUTSIDE U.S. (TOTAL)	51	6	21	7	10	1	6	8	24	7	9	0	3	17	7	5	1	0	21

(NOTE: IN THIS SECTION SUBSIDIARIES ARE COUNTED ON THE BASIS OF THEIR PRINCIPAL INDUSTRY IN 1975)

*CLASSIFICATION SUPPRESSED TO AVOID DISCLOSURE OF CONFIDENTIAL DATA

CHAPTER 4 - FINANCIAL STATISTICS OF FOREIGN SUBSIDIARIES
SECTION 4 -- SALES, ASSETS AND EQUITY IN SPECIFIC INDUSTRIES
TABLE 11 --- THE COSMETICS AND SOAP INDUSTRIES (SIC 284)

NO. OF MANUFACTURING SUBSIDIARIES ACTIVE AT 1-JAN-76 (SEE NOTE BELOW)

(CATEGORIES: A=UNDER $1 MILLION B=$1M-$10M C=$10M-$25M D=$25M-$100M E=OVER $100M U=UNKNOWN)

COUNTRY OR REGION	TOTAL NO. AT 1-JAN-76	SALES CATEGORY FOR 1975						ASSETS CATEGORY FOR 1975						EQUITY CATEGORY FOR 1975					
		A	B	C	D	E	U	A	B	C	D	E	U	A	B	C	D	E	U
CANADA	18	4	6	3	2	1	2	4	7	2	1	1	3	5	6	0	1	0	6
C.AM.+CARIB.	36	4	23	3	1	1	4	8	19	2	1	0	6	14	6	1	0	0	15
S.AMERICA	48	7	29	5	4	0	3	18	21	4	0	0	5	20	10	0	0	0	18
EUROPE	100	17	40	22	3	6	12	28	48	4	7	2	11	46	17	2	2	0	33
N.AFR+M.EAST	6	0	5	0	0	0	1	5	0	0	0	0	1	4	0	0	0	0	2
E.+W.AFRICA	9	2	7	0	0	0	0	3	6	0	0	0	0	6	1	0	0	0	2
SOUTH ASIA	5	3	1	0	1	0	0	2	2	1	0	0	0	2	2	0	0	0	1
EAST ASIA	23	6	8	3	5	0	1	6	10	3	2	0	2	10	3	1	1	0	9
S.DOMINIONS	31	4	16	5	2	0	4	6	15	4	0	0	6	8	6	0	0	0	17
OUTSIDE U.S. (TOTAL)	276	47	135	41	18	8	27	80	128	20	11	3	34	115	51	4	3	0	103

(NOTE: IN THIS SECTION SUBSIDIARIES ARE COUNTED ON THE BASIS OF THEIR PRINCIPAL INDUSTRY IN 1975)

CHAPTER   4   - FINANCIAL STATISTICS OF FOREIGN SUBSIDIARIES
SECTION   4   -- SALES, ASSETS AND EQUITY IN SPECIFIC INDUSTRIES
TABLE 12   ---- THE DRUGS INDUSTRY (SIC 283)

NO. OF MANUFACTURING SUBSIDIARIES ACTIVE AT 1-JAN-76   (SEE NOTE BELOW)

(CATEGORIES: A=UNDER $1 MILLION   B=$1M-$10M   C=$10M-$25M   D=$25M-$100M   E=OVER $100M   U=UNKNOWN)

COUNTRY OR REGION	TOTAL NO. AT 1-JAN-76	SALES CATEGORY FOR 1975						ASSETS CATEGORY FOR 1975						EQUITY CATEGORY FOR 1975					
		A	B	C	D	E	U	A	B	C	D	E	U	A	B	C	D	E	U
CANADA	23	2	6	8	5	0	2	1	11	6	2	0	3	3	9	1	0	0	10
C.AM.+CARIB.	54	6	26	14	3	0	5	8	28	8	0	0	10	16	8	1	0	0	29
S.AMERICA	92	6	45	15	7	0	19	12	39	15	2	0	24	17	22	2	1	0	50
EUROPE	213	13	82	42	28	3	45	33	81	29	16	1	53	53	44	12	4	1	99
N.AFR+M.EAST	15	1	10	0	0	0	4	4	6	0	0	0	5	4	2	0	0	0	9
E.+W.AFRICA	12	1	4	1	0	0	6	0	5	0	0	0	7	1	0	0	0	0	11
SOUTH ASIA	23	1	8	5	3	0	6	3	7	5	1	0	7	4	2	1	0	0	16
EAST ASIA	60	7	31	9	2	0	11	8	36	2	2	0	12	19	16	1	0	0	24
S.DOMINIONS	54	4	31	7	2	0	10	11	25	4	1	0	13	13	9	3	0	0	29
OUTSIDE U.S.(TOTAL)	546	41	243	101	50	3	108	80	238	69	24	1	134	130	112	21	5	1	277

(NOTE: IN THIS SECTION SUBSIDIARIES ARE COUNTED ON THE BASIS OF THEIR PRINCIPAL INDUSTRY IN 1975)

CHAPTER 4 - FINANCIAL STATISTICS OF FOREIGN SUBSIDIARIES
SECTION 4 -- SALES, ASSETS AND EQUITY IN SPECIFIC INDUSTRIES
TABLE 13 --- OTHER CHEMICAL INDUSTRIES (OTHER SIC 28)

NO. OF MANUFACTURING SUBSIDIARIES ACTIVE AT 1-JAN-76 (SEE NOTE BELOW)

(CATEGORIES: A=UNDER $1 MILLION B=$1M-$10M C=$10M-$25M D=$25M-$100M E=OVER $100M U=UNKNOWN)

COUNTRY OR REGION	TOTAL NO. AT 1-JAN-76	SALES CATEGORY FOR 1975						ASSETS CATEGORY FOR 1975						EQUITY CATEGORY FOR 1975					
		A	B	C	D	E	U	A	B	C	D	E	U	A	B	C	D	E	U
CANADA	32	8	11	4	3	3	3	7	12	4	2	2	5	9	5	3	1	1	13
C.AM.+CARIB.	26	2	13	6	1	2	2	2	14	5	1	2	2	4	9	0	0	1	12
S.AMERICA	39	5	13	6	8	1	6	5	16	6	4	2	6	11	10	2	3	0	13
EUROPE	135	8	49	38	16	5	19	15	55	24	11	4	26	36	51	6	3	1	38
N.AFR+M.EAST	5	0	2	1	0	0	2	0	2	1	0	0	2	0	3	0	0	0	2
E.+W.AFRICA	0	0	0	0	0	0	0	0	0	0	0	0	0	0	0	0	0	0	0
SOUTH ASIA	6	0	0	2	2	0	2	0	2	1	0	0	3	0	3	0	0	0	3
EAST ASIA	33	0	14	5	7	1	6	2	8	4	6	1	12	6	7	2	2	0	16
S.DOMINIONS	33	2	15	12	0	0	4	3	19	6	0	0	5	7	14	0	0	0	12
OUTSIDE U.S. (TOTAL)	309	25	117	74	37	12	44	34	128	51	24	11	61	73	102	13	9	3	109

(NOTE: IN THIS SECTION SUBSIDIARIES ARE COUNTED ON THE BASIS OF THEIR PRINCIPAL INDUSTRY IN 1975)

CHAPTER 4 - FINANCIAL STATISTICS OF FOREIGN SUBSIDIARIES
SECTION 4 -- SALES, ASSETS AND EQUITY IN SPECIFIC INDUSTRIES
TABLE 14 --- FABRICATED PLASTICS INDUSTRIES (SIC 306 AND 307)

NO. OF MANUFACTURING SUBSIDIARIES ACTIVE AT 1-JAN-76   (SEE NOTE BELOW)

(CATEGORIES: A=UNDER $1 MILLION   B=$1M-$10M   C=$10M-$25M   D=$25M-$100M   E=OVER $100M   U=UNKNOWN)

COUNTRY OR REGION	TOTAL NO. AT 1-JAN-76	SALES CATEGORY FOR 1975						ASSETS CATEGORY FOR 1975						EQUITY CATEGORY FOR 1975					
		A	B	C	D	E	U	A	B	C	D	E	U	A	B	C	D	E	U
CANADA	9	1	2	3	1	0	2	2	2	2	0	0	3	2	2	1	0	0	4
C.AM.+CARIB.	6	0	2	1	1	0	2	1	2	0	1	0	2	2	1	1	0	0	2
S.AMERICA	11	1	7	2	0	0	1	2	7	1	0	0	1	2	3	0	0	0	6
EUROPE	49	5	16	12	6	2	8	7	16	9	5	1	11	18	12	2	1	0	16
N.AFR+M.EAST	0	0	0	0	0	0	0	0	0	0	0	0	0	0	0	0	0	0	0
E.+W.AFRICA	2	0	2	0	0	0	0	1	1	0	0	0	0	2	0	0	0	0	0
SOUTH ASIA	2	1	1	0	0	0	0	1	1	0	0	0	0	1	0	0	0	0	1
EAST ASIA	7	2	1	1	1	0	2	1	1	2	1	0	2	2	0	1	0	0	4
S.DOMINIONS	9	1	6	1	0	0	1	2	6	0	0	0	1	3	4	0	0	0	2
OUTSIDE U.S. (TOTAL)	95	11	37	20	9	2	16	17	36	14	7	1	20	32	22	5	1	0	35

(NOTE: IN THIS SECTION SUBSIDIARIES ARE COUNTED ON THE BASIS OF THEIR PRINCIPAL INDUSTRY IN 1975)

CHAPTER 4 - FINANCIAL STATISTICS OF FOREIGN SUBSIDIARIES
SECTION 4 -- SALES, ASSETS AND EQUITY IN SPECIFIC INDUSTRIES
TABLE 15 --- THE TIRES INDUSTRY (SIC 301)

NO. OF MANUFACTURING SUBSIDIARIES ACTIVE AT 1-JAN-76 (SEE NOTE BELOW)

(CATEGORIES: A=UNDER $1 MILLION B=$1M-$10M C=$10M-$25M D=$25M-$100M E=OVER $100M U=UNKNOWN)

COUNTRY OR REGION	TOTAL NO. AT 1-JAN-76	SALES CATEGORY FOR 1975						ASSETS CATEGORY FOR 1975						EQUITY CATEGORY FOR 1975					
		A	B	C	D	E	U	A	B	C	D	E	U	A	B	C	D	E	U
CANADA	5	0	0	1	0	4	0	0	0	1	1	3	0	0	1	0	3	0	1
C.AM.+CARIB.	8	0	1	3	3	1	0	0	4	1	3	0	0	0	2	2	2	0	2
S.AMERICA	18	0	0	5	10	2	1	0	2	11	3	1	1	1	6	5	2	1	3
EUROPE	28	0	1	6	16	5	0	0	4	8	14	1	1	0	8	10	4	0	6
N.AFR+M.EAST	6	0	1	4	1	0	0	0	1	3	2	0	0	1	3	1	0	0	1
E.+W.AFRICA	5	0	2	3	0	0	0	0	2	3	0	0	0	1	3	0	0	0	1
SOUTH ASIA	3	0	0	2	1	0	0	0	1	2	0	0	0	0	2	0	0	0	1
EAST ASIA	9	0	3	2	3	1	0	0	4	4	0	1	0	0	4	4	0	0	1
S.DOMINIONS	7	0	0	0	5	2	0	0	0	2	5	0	0	0	2	1	2	0	2
OUTSIDE U.S. (TOTAL)	89	0	8	26	39	15	1	0	18	35	28	6	2	3	31	23	13	1	18

(NOTE: IN THIS SECTION SUBSIDIARIES ARE COUNTED ON THE BASIS OF THEIR PRINCIPAL INDUSTRY IN 1975)

CHAPTER 4 - FINANCIAL STATISTICS OF FOREIGN SUBSIDIARIES
SECTION 4 -- SALES, ASSETS AND EQUITY IN SPECIFIC INDUSTRIES
TABLE 16 --- THE PETROLEUM REFINING INDUSTRY (SIC 291)

NO. OF MANUFACTURING SUBSIDIARIES ACTIVE AT 1-JAN-76 (SEE NOTE BELOW)

(CATEGORIES: A=UNDER $1 MILLION B=$1M-$10M C=$10M-$25M D=$25M-$100M E=OVER $100M U=UNKNOWN)

COUNTRY OR REGION	TOTAL NO. AT 1-JAN-76	SALES CATEGORY FOR 1975						ASSETS CATEGORY FOR 1975						EQUITY CATEGORY FOR 1975					
		A	B	C	D	E	U	A	B	C	D	E	U	A	B	C	D	E	U
CANADA	11	0	0	1	2	8	0	0	0	1	3	7	0	0	0	0	2	4	5
C.AM.+CARIB.	15	0	0	3	3	6	3	0	0	4	3	5	3	1	2	1	1	4	6
S.AMERICA	8	1	1	2	1	2	1	1	2	2	1	1	1	1	4	0	0	0	3
EUROPE	74	2	3	6	16	44	3	1	4	10	16	40	3	11	11	8	10	18	16
N.AFR+M.EAST	4	0	0	0	0	4	0	0	0	0	0	4	0	0	0	3	0	0	1
E.+W.AFRICA	8	1	0	1	5	0	1	1	1	3	2	0	1	1	1	0	0	0	6
SOUTH ASIA	3	0	0	0	2	1	0	0	1	0	2	0	0	0	1	1	0	0	1
EAST ASIA	20	0	1	1	3	14	1	0	1	1	5	12	1	1	1	4	2	3	9
S.DOMINIONS	12	0	0	1	4	7	0	0	1	1	5	5	0	0	2	2	2	1	5
OUTSIDE U.S. (TOTAL)	155	4	5	15	36	86	9	3	10	22	37	74	9	15	22	19	17	30	52

(NOTE: IN THIS SECTION SUBSIDIARIES ARE COUNTED ON THE BASIS OF THEIR PRINCIPAL INDUSTRY IN 1975)

CHAPTER 4 - FINANCIAL STATISTICS OF FOREIGN SUBSIDIARIES
SECTION 4 -- SALES, ASSETS AND EQUITY IN SPECIFIC INDUSTRIES
TABLE 17 --- OTHER PETROLEUM INDUSTRIES (OTHER SIC 29)

NO. OF MANUFACTURING SUBSIDIARIES ACTIVE AT 1-JAN-76 (SEE NOTE BELOW)

(CATEGORIES: A=UNDER $1 MILLION B=$1M-$10M C=$10M-$25M D=$25M-$100M E=OVER $100M U=UNKNOWN)

COUNTRY OR REGION	TOTAL NO. AT 1-JAN-76	SALES CATEGORY FOR 1975						ASSETS CATEGORY FOR 1975						EQUITY CATEGORY FOR 1975					
		A	B	C	D	E	U	A	B	C	D	E	U	A	B	C	D	E	U
CANADA	2	0	1	0	0	1	0	0	1	1	0	0	0	1	1	0	0	0	0
C.AM.+CARIB.	4	1	2	1	0	0	0	1	2	0	0	0	1	1	0	0	0	0	3
S.AMERICA	6	0	1	2	3	0	0	0	1	3	1	0	1	0	2	1	0	0	3
EUROPE	14	0	4	6	1	2	1	1	7	3	0	1	2	6	5	1	0	0	2
N.AFR+M.EAST	2	0	1	0	0	0	1	0	1	0	0	0	1	0	1	0	0	0	1
E.+W.AFRICA	3	0	0	1	0	0	2	0	1	0	0	0	2	1	0	0	0	0	2
SOUTH ASIA	0	0	0	0	0	0	0	0	0	0	0	0	0	0	0	0	0	0	0
EAST ASIA	7	0	2	2	1	0	2	0	2	1	2	0	2	2	2	0	0	0	3
S.DOMINIONS	3	0	1	2	0	0	0	0	2	1	0	0	0	2	1	0	0	0	0
OUTSIDE U.S. (TOTAL)	41	1	12	14	5	3	6	2	17	9	3	1	9	13	12	2	0	0	14

(NOTE: IN THIS SECTION SUBSIDIARIES ARE COUNTED ON THE BASIS OF THEIR PRINCIPAL INDUSTRY IN 1975)

CHAPTER 4 - FINANCIAL STATISTICS OF FOREIGN SUBSIDIARIES
SECTION 4 -- SALES, ASSETS AND EQUITY IN SPECIFIC INDUSTRIES
TABLE 18 --- THE LEATHER INDUSTRY (SIC 31)

NO. OF MANUFACTURING SUBSIDIARIES ACTIVE AT 1-JAN-76   (SEE NOTE BELOW)

(CATEGORIES: A=UNDER $1 MILLION B=$1M-$10M C=$10M-$25M D=$25M-$100M E=OVER $100M U=UNKNOWN)

COUNTRY OR REGION	TOTAL NO. AT 1-JAN-76	SALES CATEGORY FOR 1975						ASSETS CATEGORY FOR 1975						EQUITY CATEGORY FOR 1975					
		A	B	C	D	E	U	A	B	C	D	E	U	A	B	C	D	E	U
CANADA	4	0	2	2	0	0	0	0	4	0	0	0	0	0	4	0	0	0	0
C.AM.+CARIB.	1	0	0	0	0	0	1*	0	0	0	0	0	1*	0	0	0	0	0	1*
S.AMERICA	2	0	1	1	0	0	0	0	2	0	0	0	0	1	0	0	0	0	1
EUROPE	15	1	8	4	0	0	2	2	10	1	0	0	2	5	3	0	0	0	7
N.AFR+M.EAST	1	0	0	0	0	0	1*	0	0	0	0	0	1*	0	0	0	0	0	1*
E.+W.AFRICA	0	0	0	0	0	0	0	0	0	0	0	0	0	0	0	0	0	0	0
SOUTH ASIA	0	0	0	0	0	0	0	0	0	0	0	0	0	0	0	0	0	0	0
EAST ASIA	0	0	0	0	0	0	0	0	0	0	0	0	0	0	0	0	0	0	0
S.DOMINIONS	3	0	3	0	0	0	0	0	2	0	0	0	1	2	0	0	0	0	1
OUTSIDE U.S.(TOTAL)	26	1	14	7	0	0	4	2	18	1	0	0	5	8	7	0	0	0	11

(NOTE: IN THIS SECTION SUBSIDIARIES ARE COUNTED ON THE BASIS OF THEIR PRINCIPAL INDUSTRY IN 1975)

*CLASSIFICATION SUPPRESSED TO AVOID DISCLOSURE OF CONFIDENTIAL DATA

CHAPTER 4 - FINANCIAL STATISTICS OF FOREIGN SUBSIDIARIES
SECTION 4 -- SALES, ASSETS AND EQUITY IN SPECIFIC INDUSTRIES
TABLE 19 --- STONE,CLAY AND CEMENT INDUSTRIES (SIC 324 TO 328)

NO. OF MANUFACTURING SUBSIDIARIES ACTIVE AT 1-JAN-76 (SEE NOTE BELOW)

CATEGORIES: A=UNDER $1 MILLION B=$1M-$10M C=$10M-$25M D=$25M-$100M E=OVER $100M U=UNKNOWN

COUNTRY OR REGION	TOTAL NO. AT 1-JAN-76	SALES CATEGORY FOR 1975						ASSETS CATEGORY FOR 1975						EQUITY CATEGORY FOR 1975					
		A	B	C	D	E	U	A	B	C	D	E	U	A	B	C	D	E	U
CANADA	7	1	4	1	0	0	1	1	4	0	0	0	2	1	3	0	0	0	3
C.AM.+CARIB.	7	0	2	2	1	0	2	0	4	1	0	0	2	0	3	0	0	0	4
S.AMERICA	8	0	3	3	0	0	2	0	6	0	0	0	2	1	4	0	0	0	3
EUROPE	27	0	6	5	4	2	10	1	9	4	4	0	9	3	5	1	2	0	16
N.AFR+M.EAST	1	0	0	0	0	0	1*	0	0	0	0	0	1*	0	0	0	0	0	1*
E.+W.AFRICA	0	0	0	0	0	0	0	0	0	0	0	0	0	0	0	0	0	0	0
SOUTH ASIA	1	0	0	0	0	0	1*	0	0	0	0	0	1*	0	0	0	0	0	1
EAST ASIA	7	0	3	2	1	1	0	0	4	1	2	0	0	1	1	1	0	0	4
S.DOMINIONS	5	2	3	0	0	0	0	3	1	0	0	0	1	3	1	0	0	0	1
OUTSIDE U.S.(TOTAL)	63	3	21	13	6	3	17	5	28	6	6	0	18	9	19	2	2	0	32

(NOTE: IN THIS SECTION SUBSIDIARIES ARE COUNTED ON THE BASIS OF THEIR PRINCIPAL INDUSTRY IN 1975)

*CLASSIFICATION SUPPRESSED TO AVOID DISCLOSURE OF CONFIDENTIAL DATA

CHAPTER 4 - FINANCIAL STATISTICS OF FOREIGN SUBSIDIARIES
SECTION 4 -- SALES, ASSETS AND EQUITY IN SPECIFIC INDUSTRIES
TABLE 20 --- ABRASIVES AND ASBESTOS INDUSTRIES (SIC 329)

NO. OF MANUFACTURING SUBSIDIARIES ACTIVE AT 1-JAN-76 (SEE NOTE BELOW)

(CATEGORIES: A=UNDER $1 MILLION B=$1M-$10M C=$10M-$25M D=$25M-$100M E=OVER $100M U=UNKNOWN)

COUNTRY OR REGION	TOTAL NO. AT 1-JAN-76	SALES CATEGORY FOR 1975						ASSETS CATEGORY FOR 1975						EQUITY CATEGORY FOR 1975					
		A	B	C	D	E	U	A	B	C	D	E	U	A	B	C	D	E	U
CANADA	12	2	3	1	3	2	1	4	2	0	4	1	1	4	2	1	2	1	2
C.AM.+CARIB.	9	2	4	1	1	0	1	2	4	2	0	0	1	2	5	1	0	0	1
S.AMERICA	22	3	11	3	1	0	4	5	10	1	1	0	5	6	6	0	0	0	10
EUROPE	61	4	24	17	2	2	12	9	22	11	5	1	13	18	19	4	2	0	18
N.AFR+M.EAST	1	0	0	0	0	0	1	0	0	0	0	0	1	1	0	0	0	0	0
E.+W.AFRICA	1	0	0	0	0	0	1*	0	0	0	0	0	1*	0	0	0	0	0	1*
SOUTH ASIA	3	0	3	0	0	0	0	0	3	0	0	0	0	1	2	0	0	0	0
EAST ASIA	7	0	3	1	1	0	2	0	4	1	0	0	2	1	2	0	0	0	4
S.DOMINIONS	19	0	5	7	3	0	4	1	7	4	2	0	5	3	8	0	0	0	8
OUTSIDE U.S. (TOTAL)	135	11	53	30	11	4	26	21	52	19	12	2	29	36	44	6	4	1	44

(NOTE: IN THIS SECTION SUBSIDIARIES ARE COUNTED ON THE BASIS OF THEIR PRINCIPAL INDUSTRY IN 1975)

*CLASSIFICATION SUPPRESSED TO AVOID DISCLOSURE OF CONFIDENTIAL DATA

CHAPTER 4 - FINANCIAL STATISTICS OF FOREIGN SUBSIDIARIES
SECTION 4 -- SALES, ASSETS AND EQUITY IN SPECIFIC INDUSTRIES
TABLE 21 --- THE GLASS INDUSTRY (SIC 321 TO 323)

NO. OF MANUFACTURING SUBSIDIARIES ACTIVE AT 1-JAN-76 (SEE NOTE BELOW)

(CATEGORIES: A=UNDER $1 MILLION B=$1M-$10M C=$10M-$25M D=$25M-$100M E=OVER $100M U=UNKNOWN)

COUNTRY OR REGION	TOTAL NO. AT 1-JAN-76	SALES CATEGORY FOR 1975						ASSETS CATEGORY FOR 1975						EQUITY CATEGORY FOR 1975					
		A	B	C	D	E	U	A	B	C	D	E	U	A	B	C	D	E	U
CANADA	5	0	2	1	2	0	0	0	2	1	2	0	0	0	0	1	2	0	2
C.AM.+CARIB.	4	1	3	0	0	0	0	3	1	0	0	0	0	3	0	0	0	0	1
S.AMERICA	15	0	6	0	6	0	3	0	5	2	5	0	3	2	2	1	0	0	10
EUROPE	24	0	10	4	3	2	5	0	9	4	4	2	5	4	5	4	0	0	11
N.AFR+M.EAST	0	0	0	0	0	0	0	0	0	0	0	0	0	0	0	0	0	0	0
E.+W.AFRICA	0	0	0	0	0	0	0	0	0	0	0	0	0	0	0	0	0	0	0
SOUTH ASIA	2	0	1	1	0	0	0	1	0	1	0	0	0	1	0	1	0	0	0
EAST ASIA	7	0	4	0	3	0	0	0	4	0	3	0	0	1	2	0	0	0	4
S.DOMINIONS	4	1	1	0	2	0	0	1	1	0	2	0	0	1	0	1	0	0	2
OUTSIDE U.S. (TOTAL)	61	2	27	6	16	2	8	5	22	8	16	2	8	12	9	8	2	0	30

(NOTE: IN THIS SECTION SUBSIDIARIES ARE COUNTED ON THE BASIS OF THEIR PRINCIPAL INDUSTRY IN 1975)

CHAPTER   4   - FINANCIAL STATISTICS OF FOREIGN SUBSIDIARIES
SECTION   4   -- SALES, ASSETS AND EQUITY IN SPECIFIC INDUSTRIES
TABLE 22   ---- THE IRON AND STEEL INDUSTRY (SIC 331 AND 332)

NO. OF MANUFACTURING SUBSIDIARIES ACTIVE AT 1-JAN-76   (SEE NOTE BELOW)

(CATEGORIES: A=UNDER $1 MILLION B=$1M-$10M C=$10M-$25M D=$25M-$100M E=OVER $100M U=UNKNOWN)

COUNTRY OR REGION	TOTAL NO. AT 1-JAN-76	SALES CATEGORY FOR 1975						ASSETS CATEGORY FOR 1975						EQUITY CATEGORY FOR 1975					
		A	B	C	D	E	U	A	B	C	D	E	U	A	B	C	D	E	U
CANADA	6	0	2	1	1	0	2	0	3	0	1	0	2	0	1	0	0	0	5
C.AM.+CARIB.	4	0	1	2	1	0	0	0	3	0	1	0	0	1	2	0	0	0	1
S.AMERICA	7	0	2	2	2	0	1	0	2	3	1	0	1	0	1	0	0	0	6
EUROPE	30	1	10	10	5	2	2	3	12	10	3	1	1	8	10	1	1	0	10
N.AFR+M.EAST	1	0	0	0	0	0	1*	0	0	0	0	0	1*	0	0	0	0	0	1
E.+W.AFRICA	0	0	0	0	0	0	0	0	0	0	0	0	0	0	0	0	0	0	0
SOUTH ASIA	2	0	0	1	0	0	1	0	0	1	0	0	1	0	0	0	0	0	2
EAST ASIA	2	0	1	1	0	0	0	0	2	0	0	0	0	1	1	0	0	0	0
S.DOMINIONS	5	1	0	2	0	0	2	1	0	2	0	0	2	1	1	0	0	0	3
OUTSIDE U.S. (TOTAL)	57	2	16	19	9	2	9	4	22	16	6	1	8	11	16	1	1	0	28

(NOTE: IN THIS SECTION SUBSIDIARIES ARE COUNTED ON THE BASIS OF THEIR PRINCIPAL INDUSTRY IN 1975)

*CLASSIFICATION SUPPRESSED TO AVOID DISCLOSURE OF CONFIDENTIAL DATA

CHAPTER 4 - FINANCIAL STATISTICS OF FOREIGN SUBSIDIARIES
SECTION 4 -- SALES, ASSETS AND EQUITY IN SPECIFIC INDUSTRIES
TABLE 23 --- NON-FERROUS METAL INDUSTRIES (OTHER SIC 33)

NO. OF MANUFACTURING SUBSIDIARIES ACTIVE AT 1-JAN-76 (SEE NOTE BELOW)

(CATEGORIES: A=UNDER $1 MILLION B=$1M-$10M C=$10M-$25M D=$25M-$100M E=OVER $100M U=UNKNOWN)

COUNTRY OR REGION	TOTAL NO. AT 1-JAN-76	SALES CATEGORY FOR 1975						ASSETS CATEGORY FOR 1975						EQUITY CATEGORY FOR 1975					
		A	B	C	D	E	U	A	B	C	D	E	U	A	B	C	D	E	U
CANADA	17	0	5	5	6	1	0	2	4	4	2	2	3	3	5	0	2	0	7
C.AM.+CARIB.	11	0	4	4	2	0	1	0	4	3	3	0	1	1	5	1	1	0	3
S.AMERICA	17	1	4	5	4	1	2	1	5	6	2	1	2	2	5	4	0	1	5
EUROPE	74	3	16	16	20	6	13	7	20	19	12	2	14	12	19	6	5	1	31
N.AFR+M.EAST	4	0	2	1	0	0	1	0	2	1	0	0	1	1	1	0	0	0	2
E.+W.AFRICA	7	0	0	2	2	2	1	0	2	1	2	2	0	1	1	1	1	1	2
SOUTH ASIA	6	1	1	3	1	0	0	1	3	1	1	0	0	3	1	1	0	0	1
EAST ASIA	19	1	8	5	1	1	3	3	8	3	1	1	3	6	7	0	0	0	6
S.DOMINIONS	21	2	1	4	3	3	8	2	1	5	1	4	8	2	3	3	1	1	11
OUTSIDE U.S. (TOTAL)	176	8	41	45	39	14	29	16	49	43	24	12	32	31	47	16	10	4	68

(NOTE: IN THIS SECTION SUBSIDIARIES ARE COUNTED ON THE BASIS OF THEIR PRINCIPAL INDUSTRY IN 1975)

CHAPTER 4 - FINANCIAL STATISTICS OF FOREIGN SUBSIDIARIES
SECTION 4 -- SALES, ASSETS AND EQUITY IN SPECIFIC INDUSTRIES
TABLE 24 ---- THE METAL CANS INDUSTRY (SIC 341)

NO. OF MANUFACTURING SUBSIDIARIES ACTIVE AT 1-JAN-76   (SEE NOTE BELOW)

(CATEGORIES: A=UNDER $1 MILLION B=$1M-$10M C=$10M-$25M D=$25M-$100M E=OVER $100M U=UNKNOWN)

COUNTRY OR REGION	TOTAL NO. AT 1-JAN-76	SALES CATEGORY FOR 1975						ASSETS CATEGORY FOR 1975						EQUITY CATEGORY FOR 1975					
		A	B	C	D	E	U	A	B	C	D	E	U	A	B	C	D	E	U
CANADA	5	1	2	0	0	2	0	1	2	0	0	2	0	1	1	1	0	0	2
C.AM.+CARIB.	6	0	3	2	1	0	0	0	4	2	0	0	0	0	3	0	0	0	3
S.AMERICA	9	0	2	3	3	0	1	0	4	1	3	0	1	1	2	1	1	0	4
EUROPE	17	1	5	1	3	3	4	1	5	2	2	3	4	3	3	2	2	0	7
N.AFR+M.EAST	2	0	1	1	0	0	0	0	2	0	0	0	0	0	1	0	0	0	1
E.+W.AFRICA	1	0	0	0	0	0	1*	0	0	0	0	0	1*	0	0	0	0	0	1
SOUTH ASIA	0	0	0	0	0	0	0	0	0	0	0	0	0	0	0	0	0	0	0
EAST ASIA	3	0	0	0	0	2	1	0	0	1	1	1	0	0	0	0	1	0	2
S.DOMINIONS	3	0	1	0	0	1	1	0	1	0	0	1	1	1	0	0	1	0	1
OUTSIDE U.S.(TOTAL)	46	2	14	7	7	8	8	2	18	6	6	7	7	6	10	4	5	0	21

(NOTE: IN THIS SECTION SUBSIDIARIES ARE COUNTED ON THE BASIS OF THEIR PRINCIPAL INDUSTRY IN 1975)

*CLASSIFICATION SUPPRESSED TO AVOID DISCLOSURE OF CONFIDENTIAL DATA

CHAPTER 4   - FINANCIAL STATISTICS OF FOREIGN SUBSIDIARIES
SECTION 4   -- SALES, ASSETS AND EQUITY IN SPECIFIC INDUSTRIES
TABLE 25 --- OTHER FABRICATED METAL INDUSTRIES (OTHER SIC 34)

NO. OF MANUFACTURING SUBSIDIARIES ACTIVE AT 1-JAN-76   (SEE NOTE BELOW)

(CATEGORIES: A=UNDER $1 MILLION B=$1M-$10M C=$10M-$25M D=$25M-$100M E=OVER $100M U=UNKNOWN)

COUNTRY OR REGION	TOTAL NO. AT 1-JAN-76	SALES CATEGORY FOR 1975						ASSETS CATEGORY FOR 1975						EQUITY CATEGORY FOR 1975					
		A	B	C	D	E	U	A	B	C	D	E	U	A	B	C	D	E	U
CANADA	35	2	17	5	4	1	6	7	13	6	3	0	6	8	6	2	0	0	19
C.AM.+CARIB.	15	3	10	2	0	0	0	5	10	0	0	0	0	7	4	0	0	0	4
S.AMERICA	28	3	13	6	2	0	4	6	12	7	0	0	3	5	5	1	0	0	17
EUROPE	128	4	48	30	16	2	28	9	56	19	12	0	32	16	39	7	0	0	66
N.AFR+M.EAST	5	0	5	0	0	0	0	2	3	0	0	0	0	3	1	0	0	0	1
E.+W.AFRICA	6	1	5	0	0	0	0	3	3	0	0	0	0	3	0	0	0	0	3
SOUTH ASIA	2	0	0	0	0	0	2	0	0	0	0	0	2	0	0	0	0	0	2
EAST ASIA	26	1	16	3	0	0	6	5	13	3	0	0	5	8	4	0	0	0	14
S.DOMINIONS	43	10	14	6	1	0	12	12	13	6	0	0	12	13	5	0	0	0	25
OUTSIDE U.S.(TOTAL)	288	24	128	52	23	3	58	49	123	41	15	0	60	63	64	10	0	0	151

(NOTE: IN THIS SECTION SUBSIDIARIES ARE COUNTED ON THE BASIS OF THEIR PRINCIPAL INDUSTRY IN 1975)

CHAPTER 4 - FINANCIAL STATISTICS OF FOREIGN SUBSIDIARIES
SECTION 4 -- SALES, ASSETS AND EQUITY IN SPECIFIC INDUSTRIES
TABLE 26 --- THE ENGINES AND TURBINES INDUSTRY (SIC 351)

NO. OF MANUFACTURING SUBSIDIARIES ACTIVE AT 1-JAN-76   (SEE NOTE BELOW)

(CATEGORIES: A=UNDER $1 MILLION B=$1M-$10M C=$10M-$25M D=$25M-$100M E=OVER $100M U=UNKNOWN)

COUNTRY OR REGION	TOTAL NO. AT 1-JAN-76	SALES CATEGORY FOR 1975						ASSETS CATEGORY FOR 1975						EQUITY CATEGORY FOR 1975					
		A	B	C	D	E	U	A	B	C	D	E	U	A	B	C	D	E	U
CANADA	5	0	1	2	1	1	0	0	2	1	1	1	0	1	1	0	0	1	2
C.AM.+CARIB.	1	0	0	0	0	0	1*	0	0	0	0	0	1*	0	0	0	0	0	1
S.AMERICA	1	0	0	0	0	0	1	0	0	0	0	0	1	0	0	0	0	0	1
EUROPE	15	2	3	3	3	2	2	1	6	2	2	2	2	4	5	1	1	0	4
N.AFR+M.EAST	0	0	0	0	0	0	0	0	0	0	0	0	0	0	0	0	0	0	0
E.+W.AFRICA	0	0	0	0	0	0	0	0	0	0	0	0	0	0	0	0	0	0	0
SOUTH ASIA	0	0	0	0	0	0	0	0	0	0	0	0	0	0	0	0	0	0	0
EAST ASIA	3	1	1	1	0	0	0	1	1	1	0	0	0	1	1	1	0	0	1
S.DOMINIONS	3	0	1	1	1	0	0	0	1	1	0	0	1	0	1	0	0	0	2
OUTSIDE U.S. (TOTAL)	28	3	6	7	5	3	4	2	10	5	3	3	5	6	8	1	1	1	11

(NOTE: IN THIS SECTION SUBSIDIARIES ARE COUNTED ON THE BASIS OF THEIR PRINCIPAL INDUSTRY IN 1975)

*CLASSIFICATION SUPPRESSED TO AVOID DISCLOSURE OF CONFIDENTIAL DATA

CHAPTER 4 - FINANCIAL STATISTICS OF FOREIGN SUBSIDIARIES
SECTION 4 -- SALES, ASSETS AND EQUITY IN SPECIFIC INDUSTRIES
TABLE 27 --- THE CONSTRUCTION MACHINERY INDUSTRY (SIC 353)

NO. OF MANUFACTURING SUBSIDIARIES ACTIVE AT 1-JAN-76   (SEE NOTE BELOW)

(CATEGORIES: A=UNDER $1 MILLION B=$1M-$10M C=$10M-$25M D=$25M-$100M E=OVER $100M U=UNKNOWN)

COUNTRY OR REGION	TOTAL NO. AT 1-JAN-76	SALES CATEGORY FOR 1975						ASSETS CATEGORY FOR 1975						EQUITY CATEGORY FOR 1975					
		A	B	C	D	E	U	A	B	C	D	E	U	A	B	C	D	E	U
CANADA	25	2	8	4	10	0	1	3	7	3	7	0	5	5	5	2	1	0	12
C.AM.+CARIB.	15	0	12	3	0	0	0	1	10	2	0	0	2	4	6	0	0	0	5
S.AMERICA	16	1	5	5	0	1	4	1	5	4	0	1	5	2	5	1	1	0	7
EUROPE	52	3	8	17	12	6	6	3	14	13	9	3	10	7	18	1	4	1	21
N.AFR.+M.EAST	7	3	2	1	0	0	1	3	2	1	0	0	1	3	1	0	0	0	3
E.+W.AFRICA	1	0	0	0	0	0	1*	0	0	0	0	0	1	0	0	0	0	0	1
SOUTH ASIA	3	0	3	0	0	0	0	0	3	0	0	0	0	0	1	0	0	0	2
EAST ASIA	12	1	0	4	1	2	4	1	2	2	1	2	4	3	2	0	0	1	6
S.DOMINIONS	22	1	8	5	4	2	2	2	7	3	4	1	5	4	8	1	2	0	7
OUTSIDE U.S.(TOTAL)	153	11	46	39	27	11	19	14	50	28	21	7	33	28	46	5	8	2	64

(NOTE: IN THIS SECTION SUBSIDIARIES ARE COUNTED ON THE BASIS OF THEIR PRINCIPAL INDUSTRY IN 1975)

*CLASSIFICATION SUPPRESSED TO AVOID DISCLOSURE OF CONFIDENTIAL DATA

CHAPTER 4 - FINANCIAL STATISTICS OF FOREIGN SUBSIDIARIES
SECTION 4 -- SALES, ASSETS AND EQUITY IN SPECIFIC INDUSTRIES
TABLE 28 --- THE FARM MACHINERY INDUSTRY (SIC 352)

NO. OF MANUFACTURING SUBSIDIARIES ACTIVE AT 1-JAN-76 (SEE NOTE BELOW)

(CATEGORIES: A=UNDER $1 MILLION B=$1M-$10M C=$10M-$25M D=$25M-$100M E=OVER $100M U=UNKNOWN)

COUNTRY OR REGION	TOTAL NO. AT 1-JAN-76	SALES CATEGORY FOR 1975						ASSETS CATEGORY FOR 1975						EQUITY CATEGORY FOR 1975					
		A	B	C	D	E	U	A	B	C	D	E	U	A	B	C	D	E	U
CANADA	2	0	0	0	0	2	0	0	0	0	0	2	0	0	0	0	2	0	0
C.AM.+CARIB.	2	0	0	0	2	0	0	0	0	1	1	0	0	0	0	1	0	0	1
S.AMERICA	4	0	2	1	1	0	0	0	1	1	1	0	1	2	0	1	0	0	1
EUROPE	15	1	4	2	2	6	0	4	2	2	4	4	0	2	1	4	3	0	5
N.AFR+M.EAST	1	0	0	0	0	0	1*	0	0	0	0	0	1*	0	0	0	0	0	1*
E.+W.AFRICA	0	0	0	0	0	0	0	0	0	0	0	0	0	0	0	0	0	0	0
SOUTH ASIA	2	0	1	1	0	0	0	0	1	0	1	0	0	1	0	0	1	0	0
EAST ASIA	2	1	1	0	0	0	0	1	1	0	0	0	0	1	0	0	0	0	1
S.DOMINIONS	7	0	2	0	4	0	1	0	2	2	2	0	1	0	3	3	0	0	1
OUTSIDE U.S. (TOTAL)	35	2	10	3	10	8	1	1	9	6	9	6	3	6	4	9	6	0	10

(NOTE: IN THIS SECTION SUBSIDIARIES ARE COUNTED ON THE BASIS OF THEIR PRINCIPAL INDUSTRY IN 1975)

*CLASSIFICATION SUPPRESSED TO AVOID DISCLOSURE OF CONFIDENTIAL DATA

CHAPTER   4   - FINANCIAL STATISTICS OF FOREIGN SUBSIDIARIES
SECTION   4   -- SALES, ASSETS AND EQUITY IN SPECIFIC INDUSTRIES
TABLE 29   ---- THE OFFICE MACHINES & COMPUTERS INDUSTRY (SIC 357)

NO. OF MANUFACTURING SUBSIDIARIES ACTIVE AT 1-JAN-76   (SEE NOTE BELOW)

(CATEGORIES: A=UNDER $1 MILLION   B=$1M-$10M   C=$10M-$25M   D=$25M-$100M   E=OVER $100M   U=UNKNOWN)

COUNTRY OR REGION	TOTAL NO. AT 1-JAN-76	SALES CATEGORY FOR 1975						ASSETS CATEGORY FOR 1975						EQUITY CATEGORY FOR 1975					
		A	B	C	D	E	U	A	B	C	D	E	U	A	B	C	D	E	U
CANADA	5	0	1	0	2	2	0	1	0	1	2	1	0	1	1	0	1	0	2
C.AM.+CARIB.	6	0	4	1	1	0	0	0	4	1	1	0	0	0	0	1	0	0	5
S.AMERICA	13	0	4	5	2	1	1	0	9	0	2	1	1	0	4	1	1	0	7
EUROPE	35	0	5	7	11	11	1	2	6	9	8	9	1	5	9	4	5	4	8
N.AFR+M.EAST	0	0	0	0	0	0	0	0	0	0	0	0	0	0	0	0	0	0	0
E.+W.AFRICA	0	0	0	0	0	0	0	0	0	0	0	0	0	0	0	0	0	0	0
SOUTH ASIA	1	0	0	0	0	0	1*	0	0	0	0	0	1*	0	0	0	0	0	1
EAST ASIA	13	1	6	1	1	2	2	1	6	0	1	2	3	3	2	0	0	1	7
S.DOMINIONS	5	0	1	2	1	1	0	0	1	2	2	0	0	1	0	2	0	0	2
OUTSIDE U.S. (TOTAL)	78	1	21	16	18	17	5	4	26	13	16	13	6	10	16	8	7	5	32

(NOTE: IN THIS SECTION SUBSIDIARIES ARE COUNTED ON THE BASIS OF THEIR PRINCIPAL INDUSTRY IN 1975)

*CLASSIFICATION SUPPRESSED TO AVOID DISCLOSURE OF CONFIDENTIAL DATA

CHAPTER 4 - FINANCIAL STATISTICS OF FOREIGN SUBSIDIARIES
SECTION 4 -- SALES, ASSETS AND EQUITY IN SPECIFIC INDUSTRIES
TABLE 30 --- THE SPECIAL MACHINERY INDUSTRY (SIC 355)

NO. OF MANUFACTURING SUBSIDIARIES ACTIVE AT 1-JAN-76   (SEE NOTE BELOW)

(CATEGORIES: A=UNDER $1 MILLION B=$1M-$10M C=$10M-$25M D=$25M-$100M E=OVER $100M U=UNKNOWN)

COUNTRY OR REGION	TOTAL NO. AT 1-JAN-76	SALES CATEGORY FOR 1975						ASSETS CATEGORY FOR 1975						EQUITY CATEGORY FOR 1975					
		A	B	C	D	E	U	A	B	C	D	E	U	A	B	C	D	E	U
CANADA	7	1	3	2	0	0	1	3	0	2	0	0	2	2	2	0	0	0	3
C.AM.+CARIB.	4	0	1	0	0	0	3	0	1	0	0	0	3	1	0	0	0	0	3
S.AMERICA	12	2	7	0	1	0	2	2	6	1	0	0	3	3	4	0	0	0	5
EUROPE	56	6	23	12	5	1	9	4	26	9	3	0	14	17	18	3	1	0	17
N.AFR+M.EAST	1	0	1	0	0	0	0	0	1	0	0	0	0	0	1	0	0	0	0
E.+W.AFRICA	0	0	0	0	0	0	0	0	0	0	0	0	0	0	0	0	0	0	0
SOUTH ASIA	0	0	0	0	0	0	0	0	0	0	0	0	0	0	0	0	0	0	0
EAST ASIA	4	1	2	0	0	0	1	1	2	0	0	0	1	2	1	0	0	0	1
S.DOMINIONS	7	0	3	3	0	0	1	0	6	0	0	0	1	1	4	0	0	0	2
OUTSIDE U.S.(TOTAL)	91	10	40	17	6	1	17	10	42	12	3	0	24	26	30	3	1	0	31

(NOTE: IN THIS SECTION SUBSIDIARIES ARE COUNTED ON THE BASIS OF THEIR PRINCIPAL INDUSTRY IN 1975)

CHAPTER 4 - FINANCIAL STATISTICS OF FOREIGN SUBSIDIARIES
SECTION 4 -- SALES, ASSETS AND EQUITY IN SPECIFIC INDUSTRIES
TABLE 31 --- THE GENERAL MACHINERY INDUSTRY (SIC 356)

NO. OF MANUFACTURING SUBSIDIARIES ACTIVE AT 1-JAN-76 (SEE NOTE BELOW)

(CATEGORIES: A=UNDER $1 MILLION B=$1M-$10M C=$10M-$25M D=$25M-$100M E=OVER $100M U=UNKNOWN)

COUNTRY OR REGION	TOTAL NO. AT 1-JAN-76	SALES CATEGORY FOR 1975						ASSETS CATEGORY FOR 1975						EQUITY CATEGORY FOR 1975					
		A	B	C	D	E	U	A	B	C	D	E	U	A	B	C	D	E	U
CANADA	15	0	10	2	1	0	2	0	8	1	1	0	5	1	3	0	1	0	10
C.AM.+CARIB.	11	0	8	0	1	0	2	1	6	0	1	0	3	3	2	0	0	0	6
S.AMERICA	13	4	3	2	1	0	3	5	2	1	1	0	4	5	2	1	0	0	5
EUROPE	61	4	24	11	12	0	10	7	29	6	9	0	10	16	16	3	0	0	26
N.AFR+M.EAST	0	0	0	0	0	0	0	0	0	0	0	0	0	0	0	0	0	0	0
E.+W.AFRICA	1	0	1	0	0	0	0	0	1	0	0	0	0	1	0	0	0	0	0
SOUTH ASIA	1	0	1	0	0	0	0	0	1	0	0	0	0	0	1	0	0	0	0
EAST ASIA	17	1	6	5	0	0	5	2	6	1	0	0	8	1	4	0	0	0	12
S.DOMINIONS	4	1	1	2	0	0	0	1	2	1	0	0	0	2	1	0	0	0	1
OUTSIDE U.S. (TOTAL)	123	10	54	22	15	0	22	16	55	10	12	0	30	29	29	4	1	0	60

(NOTE: IN THIS SECTION SUBSIDIARIES ARE COUNTED ON THE BASIS OF THEIR PRINCIPAL INDUSTRY IN 1975)

CHAPTER   4   - FINANCIAL STATISTICS OF FOREIGN SUBSIDIARIES
SECTION   4   -- SALES, ASSETS AND EQUITY IN SPECIFIC INDUSTRIES
TABLE   32   --- OTHER NON-ELEC MACHINERY INDUSTRIES (OTHER SIC 35)

NO. OF MANUFACTURING SUBSIDIARIES ACTIVE AT 1-JAN-76   (SEE NOTE BELOW)

(CATEGORIES: A=UNDER $1 MILLION   B=$1M-$10M   C=$10M-$25M   D=$25M-$100M   E=OVER $100M   U=UNKNOWN)

COUNTRY OR REGION	TOTAL NO. AT 1-JAN-76	SALES CATEGORY FOR 1975						ASSETS CATEGORY FOR 1975						EQUITY CATEGORY FOR 1975					
		A	B	C	D	E	U	A	B	C	D	E	U	A	B	C	D	E	U
CANADA	12	2	2	2	2	0	4	1	4	0	0	0	7	1	3	0	0	0	8
C.AM.+CARIB.	7	1	0	3	1	0	2	1	2	1	1	0	2	1	2	0	1	0	3
S.AMERICA	11	1	7	1	0	0	2	2	7	0	0	0	2	3	2	0	0	0	6
EUROPE	59	6	20	14	7	0	12	11	20	9	4	0	15	21	15	3	0	0	20
N.AFR+M.EAST	0	0	0	0	0	0	0	0	0	0	0	0	0	0	0	0	0	0	0
E.+W.AFRICA	0	0	0	0	0	0	0	0	0	0	0	0	0	0	0	0	0	0	0
SOUTH ASIA	3	0	2	0	0	0	1	1	1	0	0	0	1	1	1	0	0	0	1
EAST ASIA	6	0	1	2	0	0	3	0	2	1	0	0	3	3	0	0	0	0	3
S.DOMINIONS	11	1	7	0	0	0	3	2	5	0	0	0	4	2	5	0	0	0	4
OUTSIDE U.S.(TOTAL)	109	11	39	22	10	0	27	18	41	11	5	0	34	32	28	3	1	0	45

(NOTE: IN THIS SECTION SUBSIDIARIES ARE COUNTED ON THE BASIS OF THEIR PRINCIPAL INDUSTRY IN 1975)

CHAPTER   4   - FINANCIAL STATISTICS OF FOREIGN SUBSIDIARIES
SECTION   4 -- SALES, ASSETS AND EQUITY IN SPECIFIC INDUSTRIES
TABLE 33 --- ELECTRIC LIGHT & WIRING INDUSTRY (SIC 364)

NO. OF MANUFACTURING SUBSIDIARIES ACTIVE AT 1-JAN-76   (SEE NOTE BELOW)

(CATEGORIES: A=UNDER $1 MILLION B=$1M-$10M C=$10M-$25M D=$25M-$100M E=OVER $100M U=UNKNOWN)

COUNTRY OR REGION	TOTAL NO. AT 1-JAN-76	SALES CATEGORY FOR 1975						ASSETS CATEGORY FOR 1975						EQUITY CATEGORY FOR 1975					
		A	B	C	D	E	U	A	B	C	D	E	U	A	B	C	D	E	U
CANADA	3	0	2	1	0	0	0	0	2	1	0	0	0	0	1	0	0	0	2
C.AM.+CARIB.	5	0	2	0	1	0	2	1	1	0	1	0	2	1	0	1	0	0	3
S.AMERICA	9	2	6	1	0	0	0	2	6	1	0	0	0	4	1	0	0	0	4
EUROPE	10	0	4	1	3	1	1	0	5	0	3	1	1	1	3	3	1	0	2
N.AFR+M.EAST	0	0	0	0	0	0	0	0	0	0	0	0	0	0	0	0	0	0	0
E.+W.AFRICA	0	0	0	0	0	0	0	0	0	0	0	0	0	0	0	0	0	0	0
SOUTH ASIA	3	0	1	2	0	0	0	0	1	2	0	0	0	1	1	0	0	0	1
EAST ASIA	4	0	2	0	1	0	1	0	2	1	0	0	1	0	1	0	0	0	3
S.DOMINIONS	0	0	0	0	0	0	0	0	0	0	0	0	0	0	0	0	0	0	0
OUTSIDE U.S. (TOTAL)	34	2	17	5	5	1	4	3	17	5	4	1	4	7	7	4	1	0	15

(NOTE: IN THIS SECTION SUBSIDIARIES ARE COUNTED ON THE BASIS OF THEIR PRINCIPAL INDUSTRY IN 1975)

CHAPTER 4   - FINANCIAL STATISTICS OF FOREIGN SUBSIDIARIES
SECTION 4   -- SALES, ASSETS AND EQUITY IN SPECIFIC INDUSTRIES
TABLE 34   --- ELEC TRANSMISSION EQUIP INDUSTRY (SIC 361)

NO. OF MANUFACTURING SUBSIDIARIES ACTIVE AT 1-JAN-76   (SEE NOTE BELOW)

(CATEGORIES: A=UNDER $1 MILLION   B=$1M-$10M   C=$10M-$25M   D=$25M-$100M   E=OVER $100M   U=UNKNOWN)

COUNTRY OR REGION	TOTAL NO. AT 1-JAN-76	SALES CATEGORY FOR 1975						ASSETS CATEGORY FOR 1975						EQUITY CATEGORY FOR 1975					
		A	B	C	D	E	U	A	B	C	D	E	U	A	B	C	D	E	U
CANADA	10	0	7	2	1	0	0	0	9	0	1	0	0	0	6	0	0	0	4
C.AM.+CARIB.	0	0	0	0	0	0	0	0	0	0	0	0	0	0	0	0	0	0	0
S.AMERICA	1	0	0	0	0	0	1*	0	0	0	0	0	1*	0	0	0	0	0	1
EUROPE	12	0	7	3	1	0	1	1	6	4	0	0	1	3	0	0	0	0	9
N.AFR+M.EAST	0	0	0	0	0	0	0	0	0	0	0	0	0	0	0	0	0	0	0
E.+W.AFRICA	0	0	0	0	0	0	0	0	0	0	0	0	0	0	0	0	0	0	0
SOUTH ASIA	0	0	0	0	0	0	0	0	0	0	0	0	0	0	0	0	0	0	0
EAST ASIA	2	0	2	0	0	0	0	0	2	0	0	0	0	0	2	0	0	0	2
S.DOMINIONS	6	0	5	0	0	0	1	0	5	0	0	0	1	0	2	0	0	0	4
OUTSIDE U.S. (TOTAL)	31	0	21	5	2	0	3	1	22	4	1	0	3	3	8	0	0	0	20

(NOTE: IN THIS SECTION SUBSIDIARIES ARE COUNTED ON THE BASIS OF THEIR PRINCIPAL INDUSTRY IN 1975)

*CLASSIFICATION SUPPRESSED TO AVOID DISCLOSURE OF CONFIDENTIAL DATA

CHAPTER 4 - FINANCIAL STATISTICS OF FOREIGN SUBSIDIARIES
SECTION 4 -- SALES, ASSETS AND EQUITY IN SPECIFIC INDUSTRIES
TABLE 35 --- RADIO,TV & APPLIANCES INDUSTRIES (SIC 365 AND 363)

NO. OF MANUFACTURING SUBSIDIARIES ACTIVE AT 1-JAN-76 (SEE NOTE BELOW)

(CATEGORIES: A=UNDER $1 MILLION B=$1M-$10M C=$10M-$25M D=$25M-$100M E=OVER $100M U=UNKNOWN)

COUNTRY OR REGION	TOTAL NO. AT 1-JAN-76	SALES CATEGORY FOR 1975						ASSETS CATEGORY FOR 1975						EQUITY CATEGORY FOR 1975					
		A	B	C	D	E	U	A	B	C	D	E	U	A	B	C	D	E	U
CANADA	12	1	4	2	3	2	0	2	3	2	4	1	0	2	2	0	1	0	7
C.AM.+CARIB.	8	1	1	4	2	0	0	1	2	3	1	0	1	1	1	0	1	0	5
S.AMERICA	18	3	7	3	3	0	2	4	7	3	2	0	2	5	5	2	0	0	6
EUROPE	45	3	6	13	10	6	7	4	7	11	10	4	9	8	14	9	0	1	13
N.AFR+M.EAST	2	1	0	0	1	0	0	1	0	0	1	0	0	1	0	0	0	0	1
E.+W.AFRICA	3	1	2	0	0	0	0	2	1	0	0	0	0	3	0	0	0	0	0
SOUTH ASIA	3	2	1	0	0	0	0	2	1	0	0	0	0	2	0	0	0	0	1
EAST ASIA	15	1	5	4	1	1	3	2	5	3	0	1	4	3	4	0	0	1	7
S.DOMINIONS	9	0	3	1	5	0	0	0	3	2	4	0	0	1	4	1	0	0	3
OUTSIDE U.S.(TOTAL)	115	13	29	27	25	9	12	18	29	24	22	6	16	26	30	12	2	2	43

(NOTE: IN THIS SECTION SUBSIDIARIES ARE COUNTED ON THE BASIS OF THEIR PRINCIPAL INDUSTRY IN 1975)

CHAPTER 4 - FINANCIAL STATISTICS OF FOREIGN SUBSIDIARIES
SECTION 4 -- SALES, ASSETS AND EQUITY IN SPECIFIC INDUSTRIES
TABLE 36 --- THE ELECTRONICS INDUSTRY (SIC 367)

NO. OF MANUFACTURING SUBSIDIARIES ACTIVE AT 1-JAN-76   (SEE NOTE BELOW)

(CATEGORIES: A=UNDER $1 MILLION B=$1M-$10M C=$10M-$25M D=$25M-$100M E=OVER $100M U=UNKNOWN)

COUNTRY OR REGION	TOTAL NO. AT 1-JAN-76	SALES CATEGORY FOR 1975						ASSETS CATEGORY FOR 1975						EQUITY CATEGORY FOR 1975					
		A	B	C	D	E	U	A	B	C	D	E	U	A	B	C	D	E	U
CANADA	1	0	0	0	0	0	1*	0	0	0	0	0	1*	0	0	0	0	0	1*
C.AM.+CARIB.	11	2	4	4	0	0	1	2	4	3	0	0	2	4	3	0	0	0	4
S.AMERICA	4	1	0	2	1	0	0	1	0	2	1	0	0	1	1	0	1	0	1
EUROPE	48	1	11	11	12	1	12	2	19	6	6	1	14	12	8	6	1	0	21
N.AFR+M.EAST	0	0	0	0	0	0	0	0	0	0	0	0	0	0	0	0	0	0	0
E.+W.AFRICA	1	0	0	0	0	0	1	0	0	0	0	0	1	0	0	0	0	0	1
SOUTH ASIA	1	0	0	0	1	0	0	0	0	0	0	0	1	0	0	0	0	0	1
EAST ASIA	23	0	5	6	5	2	5	1	12	3	1	2	4	8	5	0	0	0	10
S.DOMINIONS	1	0	0	0	0	0	1	0	0	0	0	0	1	0	0	0	0	0	1
OUTSIDE U.S.(TOTAL)	90	4	20	23	19	3	21	6	35	14	8	3	24	25	17	6	2	0	40

(NOTE: IN THIS SECTION SUBSIDIARIES ARE COUNTED ON THE BASIS OF THEIR PRINCIPAL INDUSTRY IN 1975)

*CLASSIFICATION SUPPRESSED TO AVOID DISCLOSURE OF CONFIDENTIAL DATA

CHAPTER 4 - FINANCIAL STATISTICS OF FOREIGN SUBSIDIARIES
SECTION 4 -- SALES, ASSETS AND EQUITY IN SPECIFIC INDUSTRIES
TABLE 37 --- OTHER ELECTRICAL INDUSTRIES (OTHER SIC 36)

NO. OF MANUFACTURING SUBSIDIARIES ACTIVE AT 1-JAN-76 (SEE NOTE BELOW)

(CATEGORIES: A=UNDER $1 MILLION B=$1M-$10M C=$10M-$25M D=$25M-$100M E=OVER $100M U=UNKNOWN)

COUNTRY OR REGION	TOTAL NO. AT 1-JAN-76	SALES CATEGORY FOR 1975						ASSETS CATEGORY FOR 1975						EQUITY CATEGORY FOR 1975					
		A	B	C	D	E	U	A	B	C	D	E	U	A	B	C	D	E	U
CANADA	12	0	4	3	3	1	1	0	6	2	2	1	1	1	5	1	0	1	4
C.AM.+CARIB.	24	3	13	6	0	0	2	9	10	2	0	0	3	9	6	1	0	0	8
S.AMERICA	27	2	12	6	2	1	4	2	16	2	1	1	5	3	7	0	1	0	16
EUROPE	51	4	13	12	7	3	12	6	12	12	4	2	15	11	11	3	2	0	24
N.AFR+M.EAST	3	0	3	0	0	0	0	1	2	0	0	0	0	1	0	0	0	0	2
E.+W.AFRICA	5	1	4	0	0	0	0	1	4	0	0	0	0	0	2	0	0	0	3
SOUTH ASIA	9	3	2	0	1	0	3	3	2	0	1	0	3	5	0	0	1	0	3
EAST ASIA	22	1	11	8	1	0	1	1	11	7	1	0	2	3	10	1	1	0	7
S.DOMINIONS	14	2	9	0	0	0	3	1	10	0	0	0	3	2	4	0	0	0	8
OUTSIDE U.S. (TOTAL)	167	16	71	35	14	5	26	24	73	25	9	4	32	35	45	6	5	1	75

(NOTE: IN THIS SECTION SUBSIDIARIES ARE COUNTED ON THE BASIS OF THEIR PRINCIPAL INDUSTRY IN 1975.)

CHAPTER 4 - FINANCIAL STATISTICS OF FOREIGN SUBSIDIARIES
SECTION 4 -- SALES, ASSETS AND EQUITY IN SPECIFIC INDUSTRIES
TABLE 38 --- COMMUNICATION EQUIP INDUSTRY (SIC 366)

NO. OF MANUFACTURING SUBSIDIARIES ACTIVE AT 1-JAN-76 (SEE NOTE BELOW)

(CATEGORIES: A=UNDER $1 MILLION B=$1M-$10M C=$10M-$25M D=$25M-$100M E=OVER $100M U=UNKNOWN)

COUNTRY OR REGION	TOTAL NO. AT 1-JAN-76	SALES CATEGORY FOR 1975						ASSETS CATEGORY FOR 1975						EQUITY CATEGORY FOR 1975					
		A	B	C	D	E	U	A	B	C	D	E	U	A	B	C	D	E	U
CANADA	6	1	1	3	0	0	1	1	1	3	0	0	1	1	0	0	0	0	5
C.AM.+CARIB.	4	0	4	0	0	0	0	1	3	0	0	0	0	3	0	0	0	0	1
S.AMERICA	5	0	3	1	0	1	0	1	2	1	0	1	0	2	1	0	1	0	1
EUROPE	36	0	6	5	10	8	7	3	5	4	9	8	7	7	8	4	5	4	8
N.AFR+M.EAST	0	0	0	0	0	0	0	0	0	0	0	0	0	0	0	0	0	0	0
E.+W.AFRICA	2	1	0	1	0	0	0	1	0	1	0	0	0	1	0	0	0	0	1
SOUTH ASIA	0	0	0	0	0	0	0	0	0	0	0	0	0	0	0	0	0	0	0
EAST ASIA	5	1	1	1	0	0	2	1	2	1	0	0	1	1	2	0	0	0	2
S.DOMINIONS	4	0	2	0	2	0	0	1	1	0	2	0	0	1	0	1	1	0	1
OUTSIDE U.S.(TOTAL)	62	3	17	11	12	9	10	9	14	10	11	9	9	16	11	5	7	4	19

(NOTE: IN THIS SECTION SUBSIDIARIES ARE COUNTED ON THE BASIS OF THEIR PRINCIPAL INDUSTRY IN 1975)

CHAPTER 4 - FINANCIAL STATISTICS OF FOREIGN SUBSIDIARIES
SECTION 4 -- SALES, ASSETS AND EQUITY IN SPECIFIC INDUSTRIES
TABLE 39 --- THE MOTOR VEHIC INDUSTRY (SIC 371)

NO. OF MANUFACTURING SUBSIDIARIES ACTIVE AT 1-JAN-76   (SEE NOTE BELOW)

(CATEGORIES: A=UNDER $1 MILLION   B=$1M-$10M   C=$10M-$25M   D=$25M-$100M   E=OVER $100M   U=UNKNOWN)

COUNTRY OR REGION	TOTAL NO. AT 1-JAN-76	SALES CATEGORY FOR 1975						ASSETS CATEGORY FOR 1975						EQUITY CATEGORY FOR 1975					
		A	B	C	D	E	U	A	B	C	D	E	U	A	B	C	D	E	U
CANADA	25	1	2	7	4	6	5	1	3	4	7	3	7	1	4	0	3	3	14
C.AM.+CARIB.	18	1	8	4	1	3	1	2	6	3	3	1	3	3	6	2	1	0	6
S.AMERICA	64	2	19	10	14	10	9	2	22	11	13	7	9	9	20	9	5	2	19
EUROPE	108	1	26	23	20	19	19	5	29	20	24	10	20	25	25	13	8	3	34
N.AFR+M.EAST	3	0	1	1	1	0	0	0	1	1	0	0	1	0	1	0	0	0	2
E.+W.AFRICA	1	0	0	0	0	0	1*	0	0	0	0	0	1*	1	0	0	0	0	1*
SOUTH ASIA	2	1	1	0	0	0	0	1	1	0	0	0	0	1	1	0	0	0	0
EAST ASIA	29	4	6	7	6	3	3	4	9	9	2	2	3	9	12	0	0	2	6
S.DOMINIONS	36	1	11	6	5	6	7	1	12	6	4	4	9	2	16	1	2	0	15
OUTSIDE U.S. (TOTAL)	286	11	74	58	51	47	45	16	83	54	53	27	53	50	85	25	19	10	97

(NOTE: IN THIS SECTION SUBSIDIARIES ARE COUNTED ON THE BASIS OF THEIR PRINCIPAL INDUSTRY IN 1975)

*CLASSIFICATION SUPPRESSED TO AVOID DISCLOSURE OF CONFIDENTIAL DATA

CHAPTER 4 - FINANCIAL STATISTICS OF FOREIGN SUBSIDIARIES
SECTION 4 -- SALES, ASSETS AND EQUITY IN SPECIFIC INDUSTRIES
TABLE 40 --- OTHER TRANSPORTATION INDUSTRIES (OTHER SIC 37)

NO. OF MANUFACTURING SUBSIDIARIES ACTIVE AT 1-JAN-76 (SEE NOTE BELOW)

(CATEGORIES: A=UNDER $1 MILLION B=$1M-$10M C=$10M-$25M D=$25M-$100M E=OVER $100M U=UNKNOWN)

COUNTRY OR REGION	TOTAL NO. AT 1-JAN-76	SALES CATEGORY FOR 1975						ASSETS CATEGORY FOR 1975						EQUITY CATEGORY FOR 1975					
		A	B	C	D	E	U	A	B	C	D	E	U	A	B	C	D	E	U
CANADA	4	0	1	0	3	0	0	0	1	1	2	0	0	0	1	0	1	0	2
C.AM.+CARIB.	3	1	0	0	0	0	2	1	0	0	0	0	2	1	0	0	0	0	2
S.AMERICA	6	0	0	1	1	0	4	0	0	2	1	0	3	1	1	0	0	0	4
EUROPE	18	1	5	3	8	0	1	1	5	4	6	0	2	3	6	1	1	0	8
N.AFR+M.EAST	0	0	0	0	0	0	0	0	0	0	0	0	0	0	0	0	0	0	0
E.+W.AFRICA	0	0	0	0	0	0	0	0	0	0	0	0	0	0	0	0	0	0	0
SOUTH ASIA	1	0	0	0	0	0	1	0	0	0	0	0	1	0	0	0	0	0	1
EAST ASIA	0	0	0	0	0	0	0	0	0	0	0	0	0	0	0	0	0	0	0
S.DOMINIONS	1	0	0	0	0	0	1*	0	0	0	0	0	1	0	0	0	0	0	1*
OUTSIDE U.S. (TOTAL)	33	2	6	4	12	0	9	2	6	7	9	0	9	5	8	1	1	0	18

(NOTE: IN THIS SECTION SUBSIDIARIES ARE COUNTED ON THE BASIS OF THEIR PRINCIPAL INDUSTRY IN 1975)

*CLASSIFICATION SUPPRESSED TO AVOID DISCLOSURE OF CONFIDENTIAL DATA

CHAPTER 4 - FINANCIAL STATISTICS OF FOREIGN SUBSIDIARIES
SECTION 4 -- SALES, ASSETS AND EQUITY IN SPECIFIC INDUSTRIES
TABLE 41 --- PRECISION INSTRUMENTS INDUSTRIES (SIC 38)

NO. OF MANUFACTURING SUBSIDIARIES ACTIVE AT 1-JAN-76 (SEE NOTE BELOW)

(CATEGORIES: A=UNDER $1 MILLION B=$1M-$10M C=$10M-$25M D=$25M-$100M E=OVER $100M U=UNKNOWN)

COUNTRY OR REGION	TOTAL NO. AT 1-JAN-76	SALES CATEGORY FOR 1975						ASSETS CATEGORY FOR 1975						EQUITY CATEGORY FOR 1975					
		A	B	C	D	E	U	A	B	C	D	E	U	A	B	C	D	E	U
CANADA	23	0	10	1	5	1	6	4	6	1	4	1	7	7	2	0	2	0	12
C.AM.+CARIB.	10	1	4	3	0	0	2	3	4	1	0	0	2	6	1	1	0	0	2
S.AMERICA	15	2	9	1	1	0	2	5	6	2	0	0	2	6	6	0	0	0	3
EUROPE	81	6	25	19	9	3	19	9	32	11	4	3	22	18	24	4	4	1	30
N.AFR+M.EAST	3	2	1	0	0	0	0	1	1	0	0	0	1	1	1	0	0	0	1
E.+W.AFRICA	1	0	0	0	0	0	1	0	0	0	0	0	1	0	0	0	0	0	1
SOUTH ASIA	3	0	0	2	1	0	0	0	2	0	1	0	0	0	1	0	1	0	1
EAST ASIA	13	2	4	1	2	0	4	1	4	1	1	0	6	3	3	0	0	0	7
S.DOMINIONS	12	0	5	2	1	1	3	2	4	1	1	1	3	3	2	0	1	0	6
OUTSIDE U.S. (TOTAL)	161	13	58	29	19	5	37	25	59	17	11	5	44	44	40	5	8	1	63

(NOTE: IN THIS SECTION SUBSIDIARIES ARE COUNTED ON THE BASIS OF THEIR PRINCIPAL INDUSTRY IN 1975)

CHAPTER 4 - FINANCIAL STATISTICS OF FOREIGN SUBSIDIARIES
SECTION 4 -- SALES, ASSETS AND EQUITY IN SPECIFIC INDUSTRIES
TABLE 42 --- MISCELLANEOUS INDUSTRIES (SIC 39)

NO. OF MANUFACTURING SUBSIDIARIES ACTIVE AT 1-JAN-76 (SEE NOTE BELOW)

(CATEGORIES: A=UNDER $1 MILLION B=$1M-$10M C=$10M-$25M D=$25M-$100M E=OVER $100M U=UNKNOWN)

COUNTRY OR REGION	TOTAL NO. AT 1-JAN-76	SALES CATEGORY FOR 1975						ASSETS CATEGORY FOR 1975						EQUITY CATEGORY FOR 1975					
		A	B	C	D	E	U	A	B	C	D	E	U	A	B	C	D	E	U
CANADA	30	7	8	1	2	1	11	8	6	1	2	1	12	12	1	1	0	1	15
C.AM.+CARIB.	16	2	5	3	1	0	5	6	3	1	0	0	6	5	1	0	0	0	10
S.AMERICA	15	1	2	0	0	0	12	1	2	0	0	0	12	1	0	0	0	0	14
EUROPE	102	20	31	11	5	1	34	27	29	6	4	1	35	39	12	0	2	0	49
N.AFR+M.EAST	1	0	0	0	0	0	1	0	0	0	0	0	1	0	0	0	0	0	1
E.+W.AFRICA	0	0	0	0	0	0	0	0	0	0	0	0	0	0	0	0	0	0	0
SOUTH ASIA	1	1	0	0	0	0	0	1	0	0	0	0	0	1	0	0	0	0	0
EAST ASIA	19	3	5	4	1	1	5	4	6	1	0	1	7	2	3	1	1	0	12
S.DOMINIONS	19	2	7	2	0	0	8	5	3	2	0	0	9	6	4	1	0	0	8
OUTSIDE U.S. (TOTAL)	203	36	58	21	9	3	76	52	49	11	6	3	82	66	21	3	3	1	109

(NOTE: IN THIS SECTION SUBSIDIARIES ARE COUNTED ON THE BASIS OF THEIR PRINCIPAL INDUSTRY IN 1975)

Employment Statistics of Foreign Subsidiaries

258

DATA BY PRINCIPAL ACTIVITY OF SUBSIDIARY IN 1975

PRINCIPAL ACTIVITY	NO. OF SUBSIDIARIES ACTIVE AT 1-JAN-76	DISTRIBUTION OF SUBSIDIARIES, BY EMPLOYMENT IN 1975 NO. OF EMPLOYEES:					SUBSIDIARIES WITH EMPLOYMENT DATA:	
		1-100	101-1000	1001-10000	OVER 10000	UNKNOWN	NO. ACTIVE AT 1-JAN-76	TOTAL NO. OF EMPLOYEES IN 1975
MANUFACTURING	5775	715	2209	685	42	2124	3651	3667077
SALES	2833	751	280	28	0	1774	1059	157936
EXTRACTION	356	47	44	27	2	236	120	138830
OTHER	1977	179	43	16	3	1736	241	95353
UNKNOWN	257	8	5	0	0	244	13	1449
TOTAL	11198	1700	2581	756	47	6114	5084	4060645

CHAPTER 5 - EMPLOYMENT STATISTICS OF FOREIGN SUBSIDIARIES
SECTION 1 -- OVERVIEW OF ALL SUBSIDIARIES ACTIVE AT 1-JAN-76
TABLE 2 --- BY OWNERSHIP PATTERNS

DATA BY PARENT OWNERSHIP OF SUBSIDIARY IN 1975

OWNERSHIP IN 1975	NO. OF SUBSIDIARIES ACTIVE AT 1-JAN-76	DISTRIBUTION OF SUBSIDIARIES, BY EMPLOYMENT IN 1975 NO. OF EMPLOYEES:					SUBSIDIARIES WITH EMPLOYMENT DATA:	
		1-100	101-1000	1001-10000	OVER 10000	UNKNOWN	NO. ACTIVE AT 1-JAN-76	TOTAL NO. OF EMPLOYEES IN 1975
WHL OWNED: 95-100%	8059	1357	1767	458	24	4453	3606	2429861
MAJ OWNED: 51- 94%	1025	151	333	120	11	410	615	667261
CO- OWNED: 50%	725	100	183	46	3	393	332	204318
MIN OWNED: 5- 49%	1036	86	284	125	9	532	504	741492
UNKNOWN	353	6	14	7	0	326	27	17713
TOTAL	11198	1700	2581	756	47	6114	5084	4060645

CHAPTER 5 - EMPLOYMENT STATISTICS OF FOREIGN SUBSIDIARIES
SECTION 1 -- OVERVIEW OF ALL SUBSIDIARIES ACTIVE AT 1-JAN-76
TABLE 3 --- BY METHOD OF ENTRY

DATA BY METHOD OF ENTRY OF SUBSIDIARY

METHOD OF ENTRY	NO. OF SUBSIDIARIES ACTIVE AT 1-JAN-76	DISTRIBUTION OF SUBSIDIARIES, BY EMPLOYMENT IN 1975 NO. OF EMPLOYEES:					SUBSIDIARIES WITH EMPLOYMENT DATA:	
		1-100	101-1000	1001-10000	OVER 10000	UNKNOWN	NO. ACTIVE AT 1-JAN-76	TOTAL NO. OF EMPLOYEES IN 1975
NEWLY FORMED	6016	1033	1270	358	16	3339	2677	1748333
ACQUIRED	4142	564	1110	324	22	2122	2020	1678735
DESCENDENT	216	25	63	44	9	75	141	487405
UNKNOWN	824	78	138	30	0	578	246	146172
TOTAL	11198	1700	2581	756	47	6114	5084	4060645

CHAPTER 5 - EMPLOYMENT STATISTICS OF FOREIGN SUBSIDIARIES
SECTION 1 -- OVERVIEW OF ALL SUBSIDIARIES ACTIVE AT 1-JAN-76
TABLE 4 --- BY ENTRY DATE

1975 EMPLOYMENT DATA, BY ENTRY DATE OF SUBSIDIARY

ENTRY DATE	NO. OF SUBSIDIARIES ACTIVE AT 1-JAN-76	DISTRIBUTION OF SUBSIDIARIES, BY EMPLOYMENT IN 1975 NO. OF EMPLOYEES:					SUBSIDIARIES WITH EMPLOYMENT DATA:	
		1-100	101-1000	1001-10000	OVER 10000	UNKNOWN	NO. ACTIVE AT 1-JAN-76	TOTAL NO. OF EMPLOYEES IN 1975
PRE-1951	1276	122	385	279	26	464	812	1618720
1951	87	5	29	15	0	38	49	59608
1952	110	14	19	7	0	70	40	24064
1953	73	13	23	7	0	30	43	22452
1954	123	13	40	10	0	60	63	52706
1955	144	23	36	25	1	59	85	94228
1956	180	21	49	10	1	99	81	49814
1957	182	18	52	12	0	100	82	53119
1958	196	31	62	8	0	95	101	44168
1959	278	35	94	23	2	124	154	136745
1960	337	42	117	26	1	151	186	153184
1961	339	52	97	26	0	164	175	94151
1962	345	55	87	16	1	186	159	88735
1963	426	71	120	25	2	208	218	137740
1964	374	59	83	24	1	207	167	118679
1965	447	70	125	21	0	231	216	85883
1966	446	75	112	23	1	235	211	103450
1967	656	118	134	25	1	378	278	145787
1968	779	125	143	36	2	473	306	255206
1969	740	144	143	29	1	423	317	140371
1970	669	108	117	25	3	416	253	144679
1971	794	136	145	16	1	496	298	97995
1972	589	89	115	19	0	366	223	84871
1973	647	91	107	28	1	420	227	113276
1974	588	119	73	13	2	381	207	86829
1975	373	51	74	8	0	240	133	54185
TOTAL	11198	1700	2581	756	47	6114	5084	4060645

CHAPTER 5 - EMPLOYMENT STATISTICS OF FOREIGN SUBSIDIARIES
SECTION 1 --- OVERVIEW OF ALL SUBSIDIARIES ACTIVE AT 1-JAN-76
TABLE 5 --- BY GEOGRAPHICAL REGION

DATA BY COUNTRY OR REGION OF SUBSIDIARY

COUNTRY OR REGION	NO. OF SUBSIDIARIES ACTIVE AT 1-JAN-76	DISTRIBUTION OF SUBSIDIARIES, BY EMPLOYMENT IN 1975 NO. OF EMPLOYEES:					SUBSIDIARIES WITH EMPLOYMENT DATA:	
		1-100	101-1000	1001-10000	OVER 10000	UNKNOWN	NO. ACTIVE AT 1-JAN-76	TOTAL NO. OF EMPLOYEES IN 1975
CANADA	1163	169	261	110	7	616	547	496465
LATIN AMER. (TOTAL)	2462	319	572	149	4	1418	1044	645005
C.AM.+CARIB.(TOTAL)	1180	181	238	41	2	718	462	213625
BAHAMAS	56	4	0	0	0	52	4	55
BERMUDA	72	11	0	0	0	61	11	56
COSTA RICA	45	14	10	1	0	20	25	5391
GUATEMALA	65	23	10	1	0	31	34	7567
JAMAICA	38	4	10	2	0	22	16	6572
MEXICO	552	69	180	33	2	268	284	177948
NETH.ANTILLES	55	8	0	1	0	50	5	1417
NICARAGUA	23	8	3	0	0	12	11	989
PANAMA	170	22	8	0	0	140	30	3322
OTHER C.AM+CAR.	104	22	17	3	0	62	42	10308
S.AMERICA (TOTAL)	1282	138	334	108	2	700	582	431380
BOLIVIA	10	3	0	0	0	7	3	67
CHILE	52	5	14	0	0	30	22	14398
COLOMBIA	161	20	53	9	0	79	82	37893
ECUADOR	43	5	6	0	0	32	11	2380
PERU	80	15	23	3	0	39	41	20292
ARGENTINA	207	24	65	25	0	93	114	86655
BRAZIL	375	29	91	52	2	201	174	209503
URUGUAY	39	6	10	2	0	21	18	4948
VENEZUELA	300	31	68	13	0	188	112	48237
OTHER S.AMER.	15	0	4	1	0	10	5	7007
EUROPE (TOTAL)	4829	785	1136	347	30	2531	2298	2126488
BELGIUM	309	71	92	12	3	131	178	102113
FRANCE	617	95	160	58	6	298	319	340157
GERMANY	688	94	179	67	7	341	347	543110
ITALY	382	57	118	33	1	173	209	146985
LUXEMBOURG	39	2	7	2	0	28	11	7130
NETHERLANDS	306	66	81	11	0	148	158	61841
DENMARK	115	39	22	3	0	51	64	12339
IRELAND	104	20	15	1	0	68	36	12761
U.K.	1084	122	239	108	11	604	480	645136
AUSTRIA	90	17	13	2	0	58	32	10671
FINLAND	46	16	5	0	0	25	21	2485
GREECE	54	14	13	1	0	26	28	6105
NORWAY	92	26	21	3	0	42	50	13245
PORTUGAL	71	10	21	5	0	35	36	15555
SPAIN	298	41	77	22	2	156	142	128161
SWEDEN	191	38	38	10	0	105	86	40780
SWITZERLAND	278	53	25	1	8	192	86	27947
TURKEY	34	1	6	8	0	26	8	8877
OTHER EUROPE	31	3	4	0	0	24	7	1090

263

TABLE 5 .1 .5 (CONTINUED)

COUNTRY OR REGION	NO. OF SUBSIDIARIES ACTIVE AT 1-JAN-76	DISTRIBUTION OF SUBSIDIARIES, BY EMPLOYMENT IN 1975 NO. OF EMPLOYEES:					SUBSIDIARIES WITH EMPLOYMENT DATA:	
		1-100	101-1000	1001-10000	OVER 10000	UNKNOWN	NO. ACTIVE AT 1-JAN-76	TOTAL NO. OF EMPLOYEES IN 1975
N.AFR+M.EAST (TOTAL)	264	32	44	3	0	185	79	25615
ALGERIA	14	2	0	0	0	12	2	70
EGYPT	20	1	0	0	0	16	4	2012
IRAN	67	9	14	2	0	42	25	9199
ISRAEL	20	1	4	1	0	14	6	5324
LEBANON	22	4	6	0	0	12	10	1948
MOROCCO	29	4	10	0	0	15	14	4415
SAUDI ARABIA	22	1	2	0	0	19	3	984
OTHER N.AF+M.E.	70	10	5	0	0	55	15	1663
E.+W.AFRICA (TOTAL)	321	46	39	11	2	223	98	76473
GHANA	17	3	2	2	0	10	7	4967
IVORY COAST	13	1	1	1	0	10	3	2977
KENYA	27	7	9	0	0	11	3	3872
LIBERIA	45	11	3	3	1	27	16	21188
NIGERIA	57	10	9	3	0	36	18	5768
ZAIRE	26	1	5	1	0	19	21	2968
ZAMBIA	47	9	3	0	1	34	7	23842
OTHER E.+W.AFR.	89	4	7	2	0	76	13	10891
SOUTH ASIA (TOTAL)	144	14	45	22	0	63	81	61773
INDIA	101	6	31	21	0	43	58	53012
PAKISTAN	33	5	14	1	0	13	20	8576
SRI LANKA	9	3	0	0	0	6	3	185
OTHER S.ASIA	1	0	0	0	0	1	0	0
EAST ASIA (TOTAL)	1004	158	238	46	2	560	444	316645
HONG KONG	97	19	19	5	0	54	43	17142
INDONESIA	61	8	8	2	0	42	19	8513
JAPAN	426	55	95	19	2	255	171	184747
MALAYSIA	61	9	13	3	0	36	25	14333
PHILIPPINES	108	16	40	6	0	46	62	34076
SINGAPORE	74	23	14	4	0	33	41	14074
S.KOREA	37	5	8	2	0	22	15	8869
THAILAND	62	9	19	0	0	34	28	6528
TAIWAN	59	11	20	5	0	23	36	27805
OTHER E.ASIA	19	2	2	0	0	15	4	558
S.DOMINIONS (TOTAL)	1011	177	246	68	2	518	493	312181
AUSTRALIA	544	109	144	48	2	241	303	209665
NEW ZEALAND	132	23	22	3	0	84	48	11156
RHODESIA	26	6	6	0	0	14	12	2455
S.AFRICA	309	39	74	17	0	179	130	88905
OUTSIDE U.S. (TOTAL)	11198	1700	2581	756	47	6114	5084	4060645

CHAPTER   5
SECTION   1
TABLE   6

- EMPLOYMENT STATISTICS OF FOREIGN SUBSIDIARIES
-- OVERVIEW OF ALL SUBSIDIARIES ACTIVE AT 1-JAN-76
--- BY PRINCIPAL INDUSTRY OF SUBSIDIARY

DATA BY PRINCIPAL INDUSTRY OF SUBSIDIARY IN 1975

PRINCIPAL INDUSTRY	NO. OF SUBSIDIARIES ACTIVE AT 1-JAN-76	DISTRIBUTION OF SUBSIDIARIES, BY EMPLOYMENT IN 1975 NO. OF EMPLOYEES:					SUBSIDIARIES WITH EMPLOYMENT DATA:	
		1-100	101-1000	1001-10000	OVER 10000	UNKNOWN	NO. ACTIVE AT 1-JAN-76	TOTAL NO. OF EMPLOYEES IN 1975
BEVERAGES	81	10	21	5	0	45	36	16354
TOBACCO	26	1	10	10	0	5	21	21277
FOOD	635	78	241	60	0	256	379	225840
TEXTILES+APPAREL	95	12	45	13	0	25	70	41949
WOOD+FURNITURE	67	12	29	8	0	18	49	28795
PAPER	206	17	100	22	0	67	139	96919
PRINTING	64	10	13	4	0	37	27	15205
INDUSTRIAL CHEM	208	38	52	19	0	99	109	66080
PLASTICS	180	20	73	11	0	76	104	47135
AGRIC CHEM	51	16	17	1	0	17	34	8208
COSMETICS	276	77	105	13	0	81	195	57089
DRUGS	546	73	238	19	1	215	331	150367
OTHER CHEM	309	54	123	18	0	114	195	81081
FABR PLASTICS	95	10	41	8	0	36	59	37520
TIRES	89	0	40	47	1	1	88	158820
REF PETROLEUM	155	5	58	24	3	65	90	134970
OTH PETROLEUM	41	5	9	3	0	24	17	6111
LEATHER	26	2	18	0	0	6	20	5388
STONE+CLAY+CEMNT	63	10	22	8	0	23	40	28125
ABRASIVES	135	8	65	17	0	45	90	59291
GLASS	61	4	26	12	1	18	43	63366
IRON+STEEL	57	6	26	6	0	19	38	30309

TABLE 5.1.6 (CONTINUED)

PRINCIPAL INDUSTRY	NO. OF SUBSIDIARIES ACTIVE AT 1-JAN-76	DISTRIBUTION OF SUBSIDIARIES, BY EMPLOYMENT IN 1975 NO. OF EMPLOYEES:					SUBSIDIARIES WITH EMPLOYMENT DATA:	
		1-100	101-1000	1001-10000	OVER 10000	UNKNOWN	NO. ACTIVE AT 1-JAN-76	TOTAL NO. OF EMPLOYEES IN 1975
NON-FERROUS	176	16	73	27	2	58	118	133602
METAL CANS	46	2	14	11	1	18	28	61587
OTHER FAB METAL	288	39	104	18	0	127	161	87180
ENGINES+TURBIN	28	3	8	7	1	9	19	56295
CONSTR MACH	153	23	67	26	0	37	116	95421
FARM MACHINERY	35	3	14	12	0	6	29	50695
OFFICE MC+COMPUT	78	7	28	30	2	11	67	152414
SPEC MACHINERY	91	12	36	5	0	38	53	28879
GENL MACHINERY	123	19	52	15	0	37	86	48241
OTH NON-EL MC	109	19	44	7	0	39	70	35032
EL LIGHT+WIRING	34	3	16	5	1	9	25	33931
EL TRAN EQUIP	31	3	18	3	0	7	24	12485
RADIO+TV+APPL	115	6	42	31	3	33	82	299987
ELECTRONICS	90	5	32	26	1	26	64	89106
OTHER ELEC	167	20	81	15	3	48	119	129284
COMMUNICATION	62	4	16	22	5	15	47	187144
MOTOR VEHIC	286	20	87	67	16	96	190	655253
OTHER TRANSP	33	2	5	8	0	18	15	22204
PRECISION	161	22	57	16	1	65	96	74810
MISCELLANEOUS	203	19	43	6	0	135	68	33328
TOTAL	5775	715	2209	685	42	2124	3651	3667077

266

CHAPTER 5 - EMPLOYMENT STATISTICS OF FOREIGN SUBSIDIARIES
SECTION 2 -- EMPLOYMENT DATA IN SPECIFIC INDUSTRIES
TABLE 1 --- THE BEVERAGES INDUSTRY (SIC 208)

NO. OF MANUFACTURING SUBSIDIARIES ACTIVE AT 1-JAN-76   (SEE NOTE BELOW)

COUNTRY OR REGION	NO. OF SUBSIDIARIES ACTIVE AT 1-JAN-76	DISTRIBUTION OF SUBSIDIARIES, BY EMPLOYMENT IN 1975 NO. OF EMPLOYEES:					SUBSIDIARIES WITH EMPLOYMENT DATA: NO. ACTIVE AT 1-JAN-76	TOTAL NO. OF EMPLOYEES IN 1975
		1-100	101-1000	1001-10000	OVER 10000	UNKNOWN		
CANADA	18	1	6	2	0	9	9	5796
C.AM.+CARIB.	9	0	1	0	0	8	1	120
S.AMERICA	15	1	2	2	0	10	5	3532
EUROPE	20	3	5	1	0	11	9	2989
N.AFR+M.EAST	0	0	0	0	0	0	0	0
E.+W.AFRICA	3	1	1	0	0	1	2	431
SOUTH ASIA	1	0	0	0	0	1*	0	0*
EAST ASIA	10	2	2	0	0	6	4	1188
S.DOMINIONS	5	2	3	0	0	0	5	1508
OUTSIDE U.S.(TOTAL)	81	10	20	5	0	46	35	15564

(NOTE: IN THIS SECTION SUBSIDIARIES ARE COUNTED ON THE BASIS OF THEIR PRINCIPAL INDUSTRY IN 1975)

*CLASSIFICATION SUPPRESSED TO AVOID DISCLOSURE OF CONFIDENTIAL DATA

CHAPTER 5 - EMPLOYMENT STATISTICS OF FOREIGN SUBSIDIARIES
SECTION 2 -- EMPLOYMENT DATA IN SPECIFIC INDUSTRIES
TABLE 2 --- THE TOBACCO INDUSTRY (SIC 21)

NO. OF MANUFACTURING SUBSIDIARIES ACTIVE AT 1-JAN-76   (SEE NOTE BELOW)

COUNTRY OR REGION	NO. OF SUBSIDIARIES ACTIVE AT 1-JAN-76	DISTRIBUTION OF SUBSIDIARIES, BY EMPLOYMENT IN 1975 NO. OF EMPLOYEES:					SUBSIDIARIES WITH EMPLOYMENT DATA:	
		1-100	101-1000	1001-10000	OVER 10000	UNKNOWN	NO. ACTIVE AT 1-JAN-76	TOTAL NO. OF EMPLOYEES IN 1975
CANADA	1	0	0	0	0	1*	0	0*
C.AM.+CARIB.	5	0	4	1	0	0	5	3120
S.AMERICA	3	0	0	3	0	0	3	5500
EUROPE	10	0	3	2	0	5	5	3501
N.AFR+M.EAST	0	0	0	0	0	0	0	0
E.+W.AFRICA	1	0	0	0	0	1*	0	0*
SOUTH ASIA	2	0	0	2	0	0	2	4600
EAST ASIA	1	0	0	0	0	1*	0	0*
S.DOMINIONS	3	1	1	1	0	0	3	1993
OUTSIDE U.S. (TOTAL)	26	1	8	9	0	8	18	18714

(NOTE: IN THIS SECTION SUBSIDIARIES ARE COUNTED ON THE BASIS OF THEIR PRINCIPAL INDUSTRY IN 1975)

*CLASSIFICATION SUPPRESSED TO AVOID DISCLOSURE OF CONFIDENTIAL DATA

CHAPTER 5 - EMPLOYMENT STATISTICS OF FOREIGN SUBSIDIARIES
SECTION 2 -- EMPLOYMENT DATA IN SPECIFIC INDUSTRIES
TABLE 3 --- THE FOOD INDUSTRY (SIC 20, EXCLUDING 208)

NO. OF MANUFACTURING SUBSIDIARIES ACTIVE AT 1-JAN-76   (SEE NOTE BELOW)

COUNTRY OR REGION	NO. OF SUBSIDIARIES ACTIVE AT 1-JAN-76	DISTRIBUTION OF SUBSIDIARIES, BY EMPLOYMENT IN 1975 NO. OF EMPLOYEES:					SUBSIDIARIES WITH EMPLOYMENT DATA:	
		1-100	101-1000	1001-10000	OVER 10000	UNKNOWN	NO. ACTIVE AT 1-JAN-76	TOTAL NO. OF EMPLOYEES IN 1975
CANADA	83	8	26	15	0	34	49	42911
C.AM.+CARIB.	85	13	28	3	0	41	44	14136
S.AMERICA	89	5	38	4	0	42	47	19153
EUROPE	249	27	105	28	0	89	160	110726
N.AFR+M.EAST	12	3	4	0	0	5	7	1032
E.+W.AFRICA	10	2	2	0	0	6	4	1030
SOUTH ASIA	6	0	2	1	0	3	3	1954
EAST ASIA	44	10	15	3	0	16	28	13828
S.DOMINIONS	57	10	21	6	0	20	37	21070
OUTSIDE U.S.(TOTAL)	635	78	241	60	0	256	379	225840

(NOTE: IN THIS SECTION SUBSIDIARIES ARE COUNTED ON THE BASIS OF THEIR PRINCIPAL INDUSTRY IN 1975)

CHAPTER 5 - EMPLOYMENT STATISTICS OF FOREIGN SUBSIDIARIES
SECTION 2 -- EMPLOYMENT DATA IN SPECIFIC INDUSTRIES
TABLE 4 --- THE TEXTILES & APPAREL INDUSTRIES (SIC 22 AND 23)

NO. OF MANUFACTURING SUBSIDIARIES ACTIVE AT 1-JAN-76   (SEE NOTE BELOW)

COUNTRY OR REGION	NO. OF SUBSIDIARIES ACTIVE AT 1-JAN-76	DISTRIBUTION OF SUBSIDIARIES, BY EMPLOYMENT IN 1975 NO. OF EMPLOYEES:					SUBSIDIARIES WITH EMPLOYMENT DATA:	
		1-100	101-1000	1001-10000	OVER 10000	UNKNOWN	NO. ACTIVE AT 1-JAN-76	TOTAL NO. OF EMPLOYEES IN 1975
CANADA	18	3	10	1	0	4	14	5897
C.AM.+CARIB.	6	1	2	2	0	1	5	4858
S.AMERICA	12	1	2	3	0	6	6	4866
EUROPE	43	5	24	5	0	9	34	20687
N.AFR+M.EAST	2	0	1	0	0	1	1	320
E.+W.AFRICA	0	0	0	0	0	0	0	0
SOUTH ASIA	2	0	1	1	0	0	2	2100
EAST ASIA	7	2	3	0	0	2	5	1008
S.DOMINIONS	5	0	2	1	0	2	3	2213
OUTSIDE U.S.(TOTAL)	95	12	45	13	0	25	70	41949

(NOTE: IN THIS SECTION SUBSIDIARIES ARE COUNTED ON THE BASIS OF THEIR PRINCIPAL INDUSTRY IN 1975)

CHAPTER 5 - EMPLOYMENT STATISTICS OF FOREIGN SUBSIDIARIES
SECTION 2 -- EMPLOYMENT DATA IN SPECIFIC INDUSTRIES
TABLE 5 --- THE WOOD AND FURNITURE INDUSTRIES (SIC 24 AND 25)

NO. OF MANUFACTURING SUBSIDIARIES ACTIVE AT 1-JAN-76   (SEE NOTE BELOW)

COUNTRY OR REGION	NO. OF SUBSIDIARIES ACTIVE AT 1-JAN-76	DISTRIBUTION OF SUBSIDIARIES, BY EMPLOYMENT IN 1975 NO. OF EMPLOYEES:					SUBSIDIARIES WITH EMPLOYMENT DATA:	
		1-100	101-1000	1001-10000	OVER 10000	UNKNOWN	NO. ACTIVE AT 1-JAN-76	TOTAL NO. OF EMPLOYEES IN 1975
CANADA	24	4	11	4	0	5	19	14906
C.AM.+CARIB.	6	2	1	1	0	2	4	3098
S.AMERICA	6	1	4	0	0	1	5	1328
EUROPE	20	3	8	2	0	7	13	4884
N.AFR+M.EAST	1	0	1	0	0	0	1	128
E.+W.AFRICA	0	0	0	0	0	0	0	0
SOUTH ASIA	0	0	0	0	0	0	0	0
EAST ASIA	6	1	1	1	0	3	3	3733
S.DOMINIONS	4	1	3	0	0	0	4	718
OUTSIDE U.S.(TOTAL)	67	12	29	8	0	18	49	28795

(NOTE: IN THIS SECTION SUBSIDIARIES ARE COUNTED ON THE BASIS OF THEIR PRINCIPAL INDUSTRY IN 1975)

CHAPTER 5   - EMPLOYMENT STATISTICS OF FOREIGN SUBSIDIARIES
SECTION 2   -- EMPLOYMENT DATA IN SPECIFIC INDUSTRIES
TABLE 6   --- THE PAPER INDUSTRY (SIC 26)

NO. OF MANUFACTURING SUBSIDIARIES ACTIVE AT 1-JAN-76   (SEE NOTE BELOW)

COUNTRY OR REGION	NO. OF SUBSIDIARIES ACTIVE AT 1-JAN-76	DISTRIBUTION OF SUBSIDIARIES, BY EMPLOYMENT IN 1975 NO. OF EMPLOYEES: 1-100	101-1000	1001-10000	OVER 10000	UNKNOWN	SUBSIDIARIES WITH EMPLOYMENT DATA: NO. ACTIVE AT 1-JAN-76	TOTAL NO. OF EMPLOYEES IN 1975
CANADA	18	0	6	6	0	6	12	17270
C.AM.+CARIB.	20	5	6	3	0	6	14	7384
S.AMERICA	40	1	22	2	0	15	25	11993
EUROPE	76	6	39	7	0	24	52	42791
N.AFR+M.EAST	3	0	2	0	0	1	2	700
E.+W.AFRICA	5	1	0	0	0	4	1	40
SOUTH ASIA	0	0	0	0	0	0	0	0
EAST ASIA	15	0	11	0	0	4	11	4268
S.DOMINIONS	29	4	14	4	0	7	22	12473
OUTSIDE U.S.(TOTAL)	206	17	100	22	0	67	139	96919

(NOTE: IN THIS SECTION SUBSIDIARIES ARE COUNTED ON THE BASIS OF THEIR PRINCIPAL INDUSTRY IN 1975)

272

CHAPTER 5 - EMPLOYMENT STATISTICS OF FOREIGN SUBSIDIARIES
SECTION 2 -- EMPLOYMENT DATA IN SPECIFIC INDUSTRIES
TABLE 7 ---- THE PRINTING INDUSTRY (SIC 27)

NO. OF MANUFACTURING SUBSIDIARIES ACTIVE AT 1-JAN-76 (SEE NOTE BELOW)

COUNTRY OR REGION	NO. OF SUBSIDIARIES ACTIVE AT 1-JAN-76	DISTRIBUTION OF SUBSIDIARIES, BY EMPLOYMENT IN 1975 NO. OF EMPLOYEES:					SUBSIDIARIES WITH EMPLOYMENT DATA: NO. ACTIVE AT 1-JAN-76	TOTAL NO. OF EMPLOYEES IN 1975
		1-100	101-1000	1001-10000	OVER 10000	UNKNOWN		
CANADA	11	2	1	1	0	7	4	2615
C.AM.+CARIB.	4	0	2	0	0	2	2	1350
S.AMERICA	3	0	0	0	0	3	0	0
EUROPE	35	7	6	3	0	19	16	9575
N.AFR+M.EAST	0	0	0	0	0	0	0	0
E.+W.AFRICA	0	0	0	0	0	0	0	0
SOUTH ASIA	0	0	0	0	0	0	0	0
EAST ASIA	3	0	2	0	0	1	2	450
S.DOMINIONS	8	1	2	0	0	5	3	1215
OUTSIDE U.S. (TOTAL)	64	10	13	4	0	37	27	15205

(NOTE: IN THIS SECTION SUBSIDIARIES ARE COUNTED ON THE BASIS OF THEIR PRINCIPAL INDUSTRY IN 1975)

CHAPTER   5   - EMPLOYMENT STATISTICS OF FOREIGN SUBSIDIARIES
SECTION   2   -- EMPLOYMENT DATA IN SPECIFIC INDUSTRIES
TABLE   8   --- THE INDUSTRIAL CHEMICALS INDUSTRY (SIC 281)

NO. OF MANUFACTURING SUBSIDIARIES ACTIVE AT 1-JAN-76   (SEE NOTE BELOW)

COUNTRY OR REGION	NO. OF SUBSIDIARIES ACTIVE AT 1-JAN-76	DISTRIBUTION OF SUBSIDIARIES, BY EMPLOYMENT IN 1975 — NO. OF EMPLOYEES:					SUBSIDIARIES WITH EMPLOYMENT DATA: NO. ACTIVE AT 1-JAN-76	TOTAL NO. OF EMPLOYEES IN 1975
		1-100	101-1000	1001-10000	OVER 10000	UNKNOWN		
CANADA	20	5	5	4	0	6	14	15894
C.AM.+CARIB.	23	6	3	2	0	12	11	3845
S.AMERICA	19	1	5	2	0	11	8	6692
EUROPE	95	16	27	5	0	47	48	20165
N.AFR+M.EAST	1	0	0	0	0	1	0	0
E.+W.AFRICA	2	0	0	1	0	1	1	1100
SOUTH ASIA	2	0	2	0	0	0	2	480
EAST ASIA	31	6	9	2	0	14	17	7740
S.DOMINIONS	15	4	1	3	0	7	8	10164
OUTSIDE U.S.(TOTAL)	208	38	52	19	0	99	109	66080

(NOTE: IN THIS SECTION SUBSIDIARIES ARE COUNTED ON THE BASIS OF THEIR PRINCIPAL INDUSTRY IN 1975)

CHAPTER 5 - EMPLOYMENT STATISTICS OF FOREIGN SUBSIDIARIES
SECTION 2 -- EMPLOYMENT DATA IN SPECIFIC INDUSTRIES
TABLE 9 --- THE PLASTICS INDUSTRY (SIC 282)

NO. OF MANUFACTURING SUBSIDIARIES ACTIVE AT 1-JAN-76 (SEE NOTE BELOW)

COUNTRY OR REGION	NO. OF SUBSIDIARIES ACTIVE AT 1-JAN-76	DISTRIBUTION OF SUBSIDIARIES, BY EMPLOYMENT IN 1975 NO. OF EMPLOYEES:					SUBSIDIARIES WITH EMPLOYMENT DATA:	
		1-100	101-1000	1001-10000	OVER 10000	UNKNOWN	NO. ACTIVE AT 1-JAN-76	TOTAL NO. OF EMPLOYEES IN 1975
CANADA	9	1	4	0	0	4	5	2054
C.AM.+CARIB.	20	3	6	1	0	10	10	2774
S.AMERICA	20	3	9	2	0	6	14	8282
EUROPE	76	6	28	6	0	36	40	22391
N.AFR+M.EAST	6	0	3	0	0	3	3	418
E.+W.AFRICA	1	0	0	0	0	1	0	0
SOUTH ASIA	3	0	2	1	0	0	3	2441
EAST ASIA	26	0	13	0	0	13	13	3941
S.DOMINIONS	19	7	8	1	0	3	16	4834
OUTSIDE U.S. (TOTAL)	180	20	73	11	0	76	104	47135

(NOTE: IN THIS SECTION SUBSIDIARIES ARE COUNTED ON THE BASIS OF THEIR PRINCIPAL INDUSTRY IN 1975)

CHAPTER 5 - EMPLOYMENT STATISTICS OF FOREIGN SUBSIDIARIES
SECTION 2 -- EMPLOYMENT DATA IN SPECIFIC INDUSTRIES
TABLE 10 --- THE AGRICULTURAL CHEMICALS INDUSTRY (SIC 287)

NO. OF MANUFACTURING SUBSIDIARIES ACTIVE AT 1-JAN-76   (SEE NOTE BELOW)

COUNTRY OR REGION	NO. OF SUBSIDIARIES ACTIVE AT 1-JAN-76	DISTRIBUTION OF SUBSIDIARIES, BY EMPLOYMENT IN 1975 NO. OF EMPLOYEES:					SUBSIDIARIES WITH EMPLOYMENT DATA:	
		1-100	101-1000	1001-10000	OVER 10000	UNKNOWN	NO. ACTIVE AT 1-JAN-76	TOTAL NO. OF EMPLOYEES IN 1975
CANADA	4	1	0	0	0	3	1	11
C.AM.+CARIB.	13	5	4	0	0	4	9	1475
S.AMERICA	12	5	6	0	0	1	11	2513
EUROPE	10	3	5	0	0	2	8	2537
N.AFR+M.EAST	1	0	0	0	0	1	0	0
E.+W.AFRICA	0	0	0	0	0	0	0	0
SOUTH ASIA	4	0	1	1	0	2	2	1334
EAST ASIA	6	2	0	0	0	4	2	56
S.DOMINIONS	1	0	0	0	0	1*	0	0*
OUTSIDE U.S. (TOTAL)	51	16	16	1	0	18	33	7926

(NOTE: IN THIS SECTION SUBSIDIARIES ARE COUNTED ON THE BASIS OF THEIR PRINCIPAL INDUSTRY IN 1975)

*CLASSIFICATION SUPPRESSED TO AVOID DISCLOSURE OF CONFIDENTIAL DATA

CHAPTER 5 - EMPLOYMENT STATISTICS OF FOREIGN SUBSIDIARIES
SECTION 2 -- EMPLOYMENT DATA IN SPECIFIC INDUSTRIES
TABLE 11 --- THE COSMETICS AND SOAP INDUSTRIES (SIC 284)

NO. OF MANUFACTURING SUBSIDIARIES ACTIVE AT 1-JAN-76   (SEE NOTE BELOW)

COUNTRY OR REGION	NO. OF SUBSIDIARIES ACTIVE AT 1-JAN-76	DISTRIBUTION OF SUBSIDIARIES, BY EMPLOYMENT IN 1975 NO. OF EMPLOYEES:					SUBSIDIARIES WITH EMPLOYMENT DATA: NO. ACTIVE AT 1-JAN-76	TOTAL NO. OF EMPLOYEES IN 1975
		1-100	101-1000	1001-10000	OVER 10000	UNKNOWN		
CANADA	18	2	6	2	0	8	10	5605
C.AM.+CARIB.	36	14	12	2	0	8	28	5516
S.AMERICA	48	11	22	0	0	15	33	7223
EUROPE	100	23	40	8	0	29	71	28114
N.AFR+M.EAST	6	1	1	0	0	4	2	209
E.+W.AFRICA	9	8	1	0	0	0	9	461
SOUTH ASIA	5	2	3	0	0	0	5	1012
EAST ASIA	23	7	8	1	0	7	16	4417
S.DOMINIONS	31	9	12	0	0	10	21	4532
OUTSIDE U.S.(TOTAL)	276	77	105	13	0	81	195	57089

(NOTE: IN THIS SECTION SUBSIDIARIES ARE COUNTED ON THE BASIS OF THEIR PRINCIPAL INDUSTRY IN 1975)

CHAPTER 5 - EMPLOYMENT STATISTICS OF FOREIGN SUBSIDIARIES
SECTION 2 -- EMPLOYMENT DATA IN SPECIFIC INDUSTRIES
TABLE 12 --- THE DRUGS INDUSTRY (SIC 283)

NO. OF MANUFACTURING SUBSIDIARIES ACTIVE AT 1-JAN-76   (SEE NOTE BELOW)

COUNTRY OR REGION	NO. OF SUBSIDIARIES ACTIVE AT 1-JAN-76	DISTRIBUTION OF SUBSIDIARIES, BY EMPLOYMENT IN 1975: NO. OF EMPLOYEES:					SUBSIDIARIES WITH EMPLOYMENT DATA:	
		1-100	101-1000	1001-10000	OVER 10000	UNKNOWN	NO. ACTIVE AT 1-JAN-76	TOTAL NO. OF EMPLOYEES IN 1975
CANADA	23	4	14	0	0	5	18	5243
C.AM.+CARIB.	54	10	25	0	1	18	36	37929
S.AMERICA	92	7	42	6	0	37	55	23256
EUROPE	213	24	93	11	0	85	128	59795
N.AFR+M.EAST	15	0	4	0	0	11	4	841
E.+W.AFRICA	12	3	3	0	0	6	6	815
SOUTH ASIA	23	2	11	2	0	8	15	8685
EAST ASIA	60	12	19	0	0	29	31	6320
S.DOMINIONS	54	11	27	0	0	16	38	7483
OUTSIDE U.S.(TOTAL)	546	73	238	19	1	215	331	150367

(NOTE: IN THIS SECTION SUBSIDIARIES ARE COUNTED ON THE BASIS OF THEIR PRINCIPAL INDUSTRY IN 1975)

278

CHAPTER 5 - EMPLOYMENT STATISTICS OF FOREIGN SUBSIDIARIES
SECTION 2 -- EMPLOYMENT DATA IN SPECIFIC INDUSTRIES
TABLE 13 --- OTHER CHEMICAL INDUSTRIES (OTHER SIC 28)

NO. OF MANUFACTURING SUBSIDIARIES ACTIVE AT 1-JAN-76   (SEE NOTE BELOW)

COUNTRY OR REGION	NO. OF SUBSIDIARIES ACTIVE AT 1-JAN-76	DISTRIBUTION OF SUBSIDIARIES, BY EMPLOYMENT IN 1975 NO. OF EMPLOYEES:					SUBSIDIARIES WITH EMPLOYMENT DATA:	
		1-100	101-1000	1001-10000	OVER 10000	UNKNOWN	NO. ACTIVE AT 1-JAN-76	TOTAL NO. OF EMPLOYEES IN 1975
CANADA	32	6	12	3	0	11	21	13431
C.AM.+CARIB.	26	4	14	1	0	7	19	7479
S.AMERICA	39	5	12	4	0	18	21	10830
EUROPE	135	29	55	7	0	44	91	31375
N.AFR+M.EAST	5	1	1	0	0	3	2	700
E.+W.AFRICA	0	0	0	0	0	0	0	0
SOUTH ASIA	6	0	2	1	0	3	3	3500
EAST ASIA	33	3	13	2	0	15	18	9702
S.DOMINIONS	33	6	14	0	0	13	20	4064
OUTSIDE U.S. (TOTAL)	309	54	123	18	0	114	195	81081

(NOTE: IN THIS SECTION SUBSIDIARIES ARE COUNTED ON THE BASIS OF THEIR PRINCIPAL INDUSTRY IN 1975)

CHAPTER 5 - EMPLOYMENT STATISTICS OF FOREIGN SUBSIDIARIES
SECTION 2 -- EMPLOYMENT DATA IN SPECIFIC INDUSTRIES
TABLE 14 --- FABRICATED PLASTICS INDUSTRIES (SIC 306 AND 307)

NO. OF MANUFACTURING SUBSIDIARIES ACTIVE AT 1-JAN-76 (SEE NOTE BELOW)

COUNTRY OR REGION	NO. OF SUBSIDIARIES ACTIVE AT 1-JAN-76	DISTRIBUTION OF SUBSIDIARIES, BY EMPLOYMENT IN 1975 NO. OF EMPLOYEES:					SUBSIDIARIES WITH EMPLOYMENT DATA:	
		1-100	101-1000	1001-10000	OVER 10000	UNKNOWN	NO. ACTIVE AT 1-JAN-76	TOTAL NO. OF EMPLOYEES IN 1975
CANADA	9	1	6	0	0	2	7	2161
C.AM.+CARIB.	6	1	1	0	0	4	2	901
S.AMERICA	11	0	6	1	0	4	7	2651
EUROPE	49	4	20	5	0	20	29	25377
N.AFR+M.EAST	0	0	0	0	0	0	0	0
E.+W.AFRICA	2	1	1	0	0	0	0	500
SOUTH ASIA	2	0	1	0	0	1	2	200
EAST ASIA	7	2	1	2	0	2	1	3925
S.DOMINIONS	9	1	5	0	0	3	5	1805
OUTSIDE U.S. (TOTAL)	95	10	41	8	0	36	59	37520

(NOTE: IN THIS SECTION SUBSIDIARIES ARE COUNTED ON THE BASIS OF THEIR PRINCIPAL INDUSTRY IN 1975)

CHAPTER 5 - EMPLOYMENT STATISTICS OF FOREIGN SUBSIDIARIES
SECTION 2 -- EMPLOYMENT DATA IN SPECIFIC INDUSTRIES
TABLE 15 --- THE TIRES INDUSTRY (SIC 301)

NO. OF MANUFACTURING SUBSIDIARIES ACTIVE AT 1-JAN-76   (SEE NOTE BELOW)

COUNTRY OR REGION	NO. OF SUBSIDIARIES ACTIVE AT 1-JAN-76	DISTRIBUTION OF SUBSIDIARIES, BY EMPLOYMENT IN 1975 NO. OF EMPLOYEES:					SUBSIDIARIES WITH EMPLOYMENT DATA:	
		1-100	101-1000	1001-10000	OVER 10000	UNKNOWN	NO. ACTIVE AT 1-JAN-76	TOTAL NO. OF EMPLOYEES IN 1975
CANADA	5	0	0	5	0	0	5	21300
C.AM.+CARIB.	8	0	5	3	0	0	8	8510
S.AMERICA	18	0	8	9	0	1	17	25761
EUROPE	28	0	8	19	1	0	28	59590
N.AFR+M.EAST	6	0	5	1	0	0	6	5157
E.+W.AFRICA	5	0	5	0	0	0	5	2701
SOUTH ASIA	3	0	1	2	0	0	3	6001
EAST ASIA	9	0	7	2	0	0	9	15523
S.DOMINIONS	7	0	1	6	0	0	7	14277
OUTSIDE U.S.(TOTAL)	89	0	40	47	1	1	88	158820

(NOTE: IN THIS SECTION SUBSIDIARIES ARE COUNTED ON THE BASIS OF THEIR PRINCIPAL INDUSTRY IN 1975)

CHAPTER 5 - EMPLOYMENT STATISTICS OF FOREIGN SUBSIDIARIES
SECTION 2 -- EMPLOYMENT DATA IN SPECIFIC INDUSTRIES
TABLE 16 --- THE PETROLEUM REFINING INDUSTRY (SIC 291)

NO. OF MANUFACTURING SUBSIDIARIES ACTIVE AT 1-JAN-76 (SEE NOTE BELOW)

COUNTRY OR REGION	NO. OF SUBSIDIARIES ACTIVE AT 1-JAN-76	DISTRIBUTION OF SUBSIDIARIES, BY EMPLOYMENT IN 1975 NO. OF EMPLOYEES:					SUBSIDIARIES WITH EMPLOYMENT DATA: NO. ACTIVE AT 1-JAN-76	TOTAL NO. OF EMPLOYEES IN 1975
		1-100	101-1000	1001-10000	OVER 10000	UNKNOWN		
CANADA	11	0	5	1	2	3	8	32392
C.AM.+CARIB.	15	1	5	1	0	8	7	3292
S.AMERICA	8	1	3	1	0	3	5	3645
EUROPE	74	3	24	17	1	29	45	79318
N.AFR+M.EAST	4	0	0	0	0	4	0	0
E.+W.AFRICA	8	0	3	0	0	5	3	1150
SOUTH ASIA	3	0	1	1	0	1	2	1983
EAST ASIA	20	0	11	2	0	7	13	8670
S.DOMINIONS	12	0	6	1	0	5	7	4520
OUTSIDE U.S.(TOTAL)	155	5	58	24	3	65	90	134970

(NOTE: IN THIS SECTION SUBSIDIARIES ARE COUNTED ON THE BASIS OF THEIR PRINCIPAL INDUSTRY IN 1975)

CHAPTER 5 - EMPLOYMENT STATISTICS OF FOREIGN SUBSIDIARIES
SECTION 2 -- EMPLOYMENT DATA IN SPECIFIC INDUSTRIES
TABLE 17 --- OTHER PETROLEUM INDUSTRIES (OTHER SIC 29)

NO. OF MANUFACTURING SUBSIDIARIES ACTIVE AT 1-JAN-76 (SEE NOTE BELOW)

COUNTRY OR REGION	NO. OF SUBSIDIARIES ACTIVE AT 1-JAN-76	DISTRIBUTION OF SUBSIDIARIES, BY EMPLOYMENT IN 1975 NO. OF EMPLOYEES:					SUBSIDIARIES WITH EMPLOYMENT DATA:	
		1-100	101-1000	1001-10000	OVER 10000	UNKNOWN	NO. ACTIVE AT 1-JAN-76	TOTAL NO. OF EMPLOYEES IN 1975
CANADA	2	0	1	1	0	0	2	1320
C.AM.+CARIB.	4	1	0	0	0	3	1	50
S.AMERICA	6	2	1	0	0	3	3	347
EUROPE	14	2	4	2	0	6	8	3744
N.AFR+M.EAST	2	0	0	0	0	2	0	0
E.+W.AFRICA	3	0	0	0	0	3	0	0
SOUTH ASIA	0	0	0	0	0	0	0	0
EAST ASIA	7	0	2	0	0	5	2	300
S.DOMINIONS	3	0	1	0	0	2	1	350
OUTSIDE U.S.(TOTAL)	41	5	9	3	0	24	17	6111

(NOTE: IN THIS SECTION SUBSIDIARIES ARE COUNTED ON THE BASIS OF THEIR PRINCIPAL INDUSTRY IN 1975)

CHAPTER 5 - EMPLOYMENT STATISTICS OF FOREIGN SUBSIDIARIES
SECTION 2 -- EMPLOYMENT DATA IN SPECIFIC INDUSTRIES
TABLE 18 --- THE LEATHER INDUSTRY (SIC 31)

NO. OF MANUFACTURING SUBSIDIARIES ACTIVE AT 1-JAN-76   (SEE NOTE BELOW)

COUNTRY OR REGION	NO. OF SUBSIDIARIES ACTIVE AT 1-JAN-76	DISTRIBUTION OF SUBSIDIARIES, BY EMPLOYMENT IN 1975 NO. OF EMPLOYEES:					SUBSIDIARIES WITH EMPLOYMENT DATA:	
		1-100	101-1000	1001-10000	OVER 10000	UNKNOWN	NO. ACTIVE AT 1-JAN-76	TOTAL NO. OF EMPLOYEES IN 1975
CANADA	4	0	4	0	0	0	4	1070
C.AM.+CARIB.	1	0	0	0	0	1*	0	0*
S.AMERICA	2	0	1	0	0	1	1	116
EUROPE	15	2	10	0	0	3	12	3337
N.AFR+M.EAST	1	0	0	0	0	1	0	0
E.+W.AFRICA	0	0	0	0	0	0	0	0
SOUTH ASIA	0	0	0	0	0	0	0	0
EAST ASIA	0	0	0	0	0	0	0	0
S.DOMINIONS	3	0	2	0	0	1	2	390
OUTSIDE U.S. (TOTAL)	26	2	17	0	0	7	19	4913

(NOTE: IN THIS SECTION SUBSIDIARIES ARE COUNTED ON THE BASIS OF THEIR PRINCIPAL INDUSTRY IN 1975)

*CLASSIFICATION SUPPRESSED TO AVOID DISCLOSURE OF CONFIDENTIAL DATA

CHAPTER   5   - EMPLOYMENT STATISTICS OF FOREIGN SUBSIDIARIES
SECTION   2   -- EMPLOYMENT DATA IN SPECIFIC INDUSTRIES
TABLE 19 --- STONE,CLAY AND CEMENT INDUSTRIES (SIC 324 TO 328)

NO. OF MANUFACTURING SUBSIDIARIES ACTIVE AT 1-JAN-76   (SEE NOTE BELOW)

COUNTRY OR REGION	NO. OF SUBSIDIARIES ACTIVE AT 1-JAN-76	DISTRIBUTION OF SUBSIDIARIES, BY EMPLOYMENT IN 1975 NO. OF EMPLOYEES:					SUBSIDIARIES WITH EMPLOYMENT DATA:	
		1-100	101-1000	1001-10000	OVER 10000	UNKNOWN	NO. ACTIVE AT 1-JAN-76	TOTAL NO. OF EMPLOYEES IN 1975
CANADA	7	2	1	0	0	4	3	350
C.AM.+CARIB.	7	1	2	1	0	3	4	3001
S.AMERICA	8	1	5	1	0	1	7	3448
EUROPE	27	2	9	5	0	11	16	17973
N.AFR+M.EAST	1	0	0	0	0	1*	0	0*
E.+W.AFRICA	0	0	0	0	0	0	0	0
SOUTH ASIA	1	0	0	0	0	1*	0	0*
EAST ASIA	7	0	3	0	0	4	3	1064
S.DOMINIONS	5	4	1	0	0	0	5	289
OUTSIDE U.S.(TOTAL)	63	10	21	7	0	25	38	26125

(NOTE: IN THIS SECTION SUBSIDIARIES ARE COUNTED ON THE BASIS OF THEIR PRINCIPAL INDUSTRY IN 1975)

*CLASSIFICATION SUPPRESSED TO AVOID DISCLOSURE OF CONFIDENTIAL DATA

CHAPTER 5 - EMPLOYMENT STATISTICS OF FOREIGN SUBSIDIARIES
SECTION 2 -- EMPLOYMENT DATA IN SPECIFIC INDUSTRIES
TABLE 20 --- ABRASIVES AND ASBESTOS INDUSTRIES (SIC 329)

NO. OF MANUFACTURING SUBSIDIARIES ACTIVE AT 1-JAN-76 (SEE NOTE BELOW)

COUNTRY OR REGION	NO. OF SUBSIDIARIES ACTIVE AT 1-JAN-76	DISTRIBUTION OF SUBSIDIARIES, BY EMPLOYMENT IN 1975: NO. OF EMPLOYEES:					SUBSIDIARIES WITH EMPLOYMENT DATA:	
		1-100	101-1000	1001-10000	OVER 10000	UNKNOWN	NO. ACTIVE AT 1-JAN-76	TOTAL NO. OF EMPLOYEES IN 1975
CANADA	12	2	3	4	0	3	9	11619
C.AM.+CARIB.	9	0	6	1	0	2	7	3322
S.AMERICA	22	2	10	3	0	7	15	7032
EUROPE	61	4	28	6	0	23	38	24585
N.AFR+M.EAST	1	0	0	0	0	1*	0	0*
E.+W.AFRICA	1	0	0	0	0	1*	0	0*
SOUTH ASIA	3	0	0	2	0	1	2	3400
EAST ASIA	7	0	3	0	0	4	3	1500
S.DOMINIONS	19	0	13	1	0	5	14	7432
OUTSIDE U.S. (TOTAL)	135	8	63	17	0	47	88	58890

(NOTE: IN THIS SECTION SUBSIDIARIES ARE COUNTED ON THE BASIS OF THEIR PRINCIPAL INDUSTRY IN 1975)

*CLASSIFICATION SUPPRESSED TO AVOID DISCLOSURE OF CONFIDENTIAL DATA

CHAPTER 5 - EMPLOYMENT STATISTICS OF FOREIGN SUBSIDIARIES
SECTION 2 -- EMPLOYMENT DATA IN SPECIFIC INDUSTRIES
TABLE 21 --- THE GLASS INDUSTRY (SIC 321 TO 323)

NO. OF MANUFACTURING SUBSIDIARIES ACTIVE AT 1-JAN-76   (SEE NOTE BELOW)

COUNTRY OR REGION	NO. OF SUBSIDIARIES ACTIVE AT 1-JAN-76	DISTRIBUTION OF SUBSIDIARIES, BY EMPLOYMENT IN 1975 NO. OF EMPLOYEES:					SUBSIDIARIES WITH EMPLOYMENT DATA:	
		1-100	101-1000	1001-10000	OVER 10000	UNKNOWN	NO. ACTIVE AT 1-JAN-76	TOTAL NO. OF EMPLOYEES IN 1975
CANADA	5	0	1	2	0	2	3	5530
C.AM.+CARIB.	4	1	3	0	0	0	4	508
S.AMERICA	15	1	5	5	0	4	11	18124
EUROPE	24	1	11	3	1	8	16	29226
N.AFR+M.EAST	0	0	0	0	0	0	0	0
E.+W.AFRICA	0	0	0	0	0	0	0	0
SOUTH ASIA	2	0	2	0	0	0	2	1180
EAST ASIA	7	1	2	1	0	3	4	2156
S.DOMINIONS	4	0	2	1	0	1	3	6642
OUTSIDE U.S. (TOTAL)	61	4	26	12	1	18	43	63366

(NOTE: IN THIS SECTION SUBSIDIARIES ARE COUNTED ON THE BASIS OF THEIR PRINCIPAL INDUSTRY IN 1975)

CHAPTER 5 - EMPLOYMENT STATISTICS OF FOREIGN SUBSIDIARIES
SECTION 2 -- EMPLOYMENT DATA IN SPECIFIC INDUSTRIES
TABLE 22 --- THE IRON AND STEEL INDUSTRY (SIC 331 AND 332)

NO. OF MANUFACTURING SUBSIDIARIES ACTIVE AT 1-JAN-76 (SEE NOTE BELOW)

COUNTRY OR REGION	NO. OF SUBSIDIARIES ACTIVE AT 1-JAN-76	DISTRIBUTION OF SUBSIDIARIES, BY EMPLOYMENT IN 1975 NO. OF EMPLOYEES:					SUBSIDIARIES WITH EMPLOYMENT DATA: NO. ACTIVE AT 1-JAN-76	TOTAL NO. OF EMPLOYEES IN 1975
		1-100	101-1000	1001-10000	OVER 10000	UNKNOWN		
CANADA	6	1	3	0	0	2	4	1085
C.AM.+CARIB.	4	0	4	0	0	0	4	1570
S.AMERICA	7	0	4	1	0	2	5	2794
EUROPE	30	4	11	5	0	10	20	22876
N.AFR+M.EAST	1	0	0	0	0	1	0	0
E.+W.AFRICA	0	0	0	0	0	0	0	0
SOUTH ASIA	2	0	1	0	0	1	1	600
EAST ASIA	2	0	1	0	0	1	1	248
S.DOMINIONS	5	1	2	0	0	2	3	1136
OUTSIDE U.S.(TOTAL)	57	6	26	6	0	19	38	30309

(NOTE: IN THIS SECTION SUBSIDIARIES ARE COUNTED ON THE BASIS OF THEIR PRINCIPAL INDUSTRY IN 1975)

CHAPTER 5 - EMPLOYMENT STATISTICS OF FOREIGN SUBSIDIARIES
SECTION 2 -- EMPLOYMENT DATA IN SPECIFIC INDUSTRIES
TABLE 23 --- NON-FERROUS METAL INDUSTRIES (OTHER SIC 33)

NO. OF MANUFACTURING SUBSIDIARIES ACTIVE AT 1-JAN-76   (SEE NOTE BELOW)

COUNTRY OR REGION	NO. OF SUBSIDIARIES ACTIVE AT 1-JAN-76	DISTRIBUTION OF SUBSIDIARIES, BY EMPLOYMENT IN 1975 NO. OF EMPLOYEES:					SUBSIDIARIES WITH EMPLOYMENT DATA:	
		1-100	101-1000	1001-10000	OVER 10000	UNKNOWN	NO. ACTIVE AT 1-JAN-76	TOTAL NO. OF EMPLOYEES IN 1975
CANADA	17	5	8	3	0	1	16	12724
C.AM.+CARIB.	11	1	8	1	0	1	10	6107
S.AMERICA	17	1	10	3	0	3	14	14091
EUROPE	74	5	30	9	1	29	45	46243
N.AFR+M.EAST	4	0	3	0	0	1	3	1440
E.+W.AFRICA	7	0	1	2	1	3	4	27363
SOUTH ASIA	6	1	1	1	0	3	3	2120
EAST ASIA	19	0	7	2	0	10	9	6440
S.DOMINIONS	21	3	5	6	0	7	14	17074
OUTSIDE U.S.(TOTAL)	176	16	73	27	2	58	118	133602

(NOTE: IN THIS SECTION SUBSIDIARIES ARE COUNTED ON THE BASIS OF THEIR PRINCIPAL INDUSTRY IN 1975)

CHAPTER 5 - EMPLOYMENT STATISTICS OF FOREIGN SUBSIDIARIES
SECTION 2 -- EMPLOYMENT DATA IN SPECIFIC INDUSTRIES
TABLE 24 --- THE METAL CANS INDUSTRY (SIC 341)

NO. OF MANUFACTURING SUBSIDIARIES ACTIVE AT 1-JAN-76   (SEE NOTE BELOW)

COUNTRY OR REGION	NO. OF SUBSIDIARIES ACTIVE AT 1-JAN-76	DISTRIBUTION OF SUBSIDIARIES, BY EMPLOYMENT IN 1975 NO. OF EMPLOYEES:					SUBSIDIARIES WITH EMPLOYMENT DATA:	
		1-100	101-1000	1001-10000	OVER 10000	UNKNOWN	NO. ACTIVE AT 1-JAN-76	TOTAL NO. OF EMPLOYEES IN 1975
CANADA	5	0	0	2	0	3	2	9100
C.AM.+CARIB.	6	0	3	0	0	3	3	1718
S.AMERICA	9	1	3	2	0	3	6	6150
EUROPE	17	0	6	4	1	6	11	32484
N.AFR+M.EAST	2	0	2	0	0	0	2	1220
E.+W.AFRICA	1	0	0	0	0	1	0	0
SOUTH ASIA	0	0	0	0	0	0	0	0
EAST ASIA	3	0	0	2	0	1	2	6315
S.DOMINIONS	3	1	0	1	0	1	2	4600
OUTSIDE U.S.(TOTAL)	46	2	14	11	1	18	28	61587

(NOTE: IN THIS SECTION SUBSIDIARIES ARE COUNTED ON THE BASIS OF THEIR PRINCIPAL INDUSTRY IN 1975)

CHAPTER 5 - EMPLOYMENT STATISTICS OF FOREIGN SUBSIDIARIES
SECTION 2 -- EMPLOYMENT DATA IN SPECIFIC INDUSTRIES
TABLE 25 --- OTHER FABRICATED METAL INDUSTRIES (OTHER SIC 34)

NO. OF MANUFACTURING SUBSIDIARIES ACTIVE AT 1-JAN-76 (SEE NOTE BELOW)

COUNTRY OR REGION	NO. OF SUBSIDIARIES ACTIVE AT 1-JAN-76	DISTRIBUTION OF SUBSIDIARIES, BY EMPLOYMENT IN 1975 NO. OF EMPLOYEES:					SUBSIDIARIES WITH EMPLOYMENT DATA:	
		1-100	101-1000	1001-10000	OVER 10000	UNKNOWN	NO. ACTIVE AT 1-JAN-76	TOTAL NO. OF EMPLOYEES IN 1975
CANADA	35	9	11	3	0	12	23	11922
C.AM.+CARIB.	15	3	6	0	0	6	9	1777
S.AMERICA	28	6	11	1	0	10	18	5815
EUROPE	128	9	53	13	0	53	75	56297
N.AFR+M.EAST	5	1	1	0	0	3	2	432
E.+W.AFRICA	6	1	0	0	0	5	1	75
SOUTH ASIA	2	0	0	0	0	2	0	0
EAST ASIA	26	3	8	0	0	15	11	3768
S.DOMINIONS	43	7	14	1	0	21	22	7094
OUTSIDE U.S. (TOTAL)	288	39	104	18	0	127	161	87180

(NOTE: IN THIS SECTION SUBSIDIARIES ARE COUNTED ON THE BASIS OF THEIR PRINCIPAL INDUSTRY IN 1975)

CHAPTER 5 - EMPLOYMENT STATISTICS OF FOREIGN SUBSIDIARIES
SECTION 2 -- EMPLOYMENT DATA IN SPECIFIC INDUSTRIES
TABLE 26 --- THE ENGINES AND TURBINES INDUSTRY (SIC 351)

NO. OF MANUFACTURING SUBSIDIARIES ACTIVE AT 1-JAN-76   (SEE NOTE BELOW)

COUNTRY OR REGION	NO. OF SUBSIDIARIES ACTIVE AT 1-JAN-76	DISTRIBUTION OF SUBSIDIARIES, BY EMPLOYMENT IN 1975 — NO. OF EMPLOYEES:					SUBSIDIARIES WITH EMPLOYMENT DATA: NO. ACTIVE AT 1-JAN-76	TOTAL NO. OF EMPLOYEES IN 1975
		1-100	101-1000	1001-10000	OVER 10000	UNKNOWN		
CANADA	5	1	2	2	0	0	5	6150
C.AM.+CARIB.	1	0	0	0	0	1	0	0
S.AMERICA	1	0	0	0	0	1	0	0
EUROPE	15	1	4	4	1	5	10	47856
N.AFR+M.EAST	0	0	0	0	0	0	0	0
E.+W.AFRICA	0	0	0	0	0	0	0	0
SOUTH ASIA	0	0	0	0	0	0	0	0
EAST ASIA	3	1	1	0	0	1	2	450
S.DOMINIONS	3	0	1	1	0	1	2	1839
OUTSIDE U.S.(TOTAL)	28	3	8	7	1	9	19	56295

(NOTE: IN THIS SECTION SUBSIDIARIES ARE COUNTED ON THE BASIS OF THEIR PRINCIPAL INDUSTRY IN 1975)

CHAPTER 5 - EMPLOYMENT STATISTICS OF FOREIGN SUBSIDIARIES
SECTION 2 -- EMPLOYMENT DATA IN SPECIFIC INDUSTRIES
TABLE 27 --- THE CONSTRUCTION MACHINERY INDUSTRY (SIC 353)

NO. OF MANUFACTURING SUBSIDIARIES ACTIVE AT 1-JAN-76   (SEE NOTE BELOW)

COUNTRY OR REGION	NO. OF SUBSIDIARIES ACTIVE AT 1-JAN-76	DISTRIBUTION OF SUBSIDIARIES, BY EMPLOYMENT IN 1975 NO. OF EMPLOYEES:					SUBSIDIARIES WITH EMPLOYMENT DATA:	
		1-100	101-1000	1001-10000	OVER 10000	UNKNOWN	NO. ACTIVE AT 1-JAN-76	TOTAL NO. OF EMPLOYEES IN 1975
CANADA	25	5	10	4	0	6	19	12694
C.AM.+CARIB.	15	2	8	1	0	4	11	3098
S.AMERICA	16	1	5	4	0	6	10	8129
EUROPE	52	5	23	11	0	13	39	49248
N.AFR+M.EAST	7	1	4	0	0	2	5	1954
E.+W.AFRICA	1	0	0	0	0	1	0	0
SOUTH ASIA	3	1	1	1	0	0	3	1683
EAST ASIA	12	3	3	2	0	4	8	4790
S.DOMINIONS	22	5	13	3	0	1	21	13825
OUTSIDE U.S. (TOTAL)	153	23	67	26	0	37	116	95421

(NOTE: IN THIS SECTION SUBSIDIARIES ARE COUNTED ON THE BASIS OF THEIR PRINCIPAL INDUSTRY IN 1975)

CHAPTER 5 - EMPLOYMENT STATISTICS OF FOREIGN SUBSIDIARIES
SECTION 2 -- EMPLOYMENT DATA IN SPECIFIC INDUSTRIES
TABLE 28 --- THE FARM MACHINERY INDUSTRY (SIC 352)

NO. OF MANUFACTURING SUBSIDIARIES ACTIVE AT 1-JAN-76   (SEE NOTE BELOW)

COUNTRY OR REGION	NO. OF SUBSIDIARIES ACTIVE AT 1-JAN-76	DISTRIBUTION OF SUBSIDIARIES, BY EMPLOYMENT IN 1975 NO. OF EMPLOYEES:					SUBSIDIARIES WITH EMPLOYMENT DATA:	
		1-100	101-1000	1001-10000	OVER 10000	UNKNOWN	NO. ACTIVE AT 1-JAN-76	TOTAL NO. OF EMPLOYEES IN 1975
CANADA	2	0	0	2	0	0	2	8100
C.AM.+CARIB.	2	0	1	1	0	0	2	2047
S.AMERICA	4	1	2	1	0	0	4	3560
EUROPE	15	1	6	6	0	2	13	29873
N.AFR+M.EAST	1	0	0	0	0	1	0	0
E.+W.AFRICA	0	0	0	0	0	0	0	0
SOUTH ASIA	2	0	0	1	0	1	1	3000
EAST ASIA	2	1	0	0	0	1	1	55
S.DOMINIONS	7	0	5	1	0	1	6	4060
OUTSIDE U.S. (TOTAL)	35	3	14	12	0	6	29	50695

(NOTE: IN THIS SECTION SUBSIDIARIES ARE COUNTED ON THE BASIS OF THEIR PRINCIPAL INDUSTRY IN 1975)

CHAPTER   5   - EMPLOYMENT STATISTICS OF FOREIGN SUBSIDIARIES
SECTION   2   -- EMPLOYMENT DATA IN SPECIFIC INDUSTRIES
TABLE 29 --- THE OFFICE MACHINES & COMPUTERS INDUSTRY (SIC 357)

NO. OF MANUFACTURING SUBSIDIARIES ACTIVE AT 1-JAN-76   (SEE NOTE BELOW)

COUNTRY OR REGION	NO. OF SUBSIDIARIES ACTIVE AT 1-JAN-76	DISTRIBUTION OF SUBSIDIARIES, BY EMPLOYMENT IN 1975 NO. OF EMPLOYEES:					SUBSIDIARIES WITH EMPLOYMENT DATA: NO. ACTIVE AT 1-JAN-76	TOTAL NO. OF EMPLOYEES IN 1975
		1-100	101-1000	1001-10000	OVER 10000	UNKNOWN		
CANADA	5	0	2	3	0	0	5	14730
C.AM.+CARIB.	6	0	5	1	0	0	6	3230
S.AMERICA	13	1	6	4	0	2	11	12115
EUROPE	35	4	10	16	2	3	32	95556
N.AFR+M.EAST	0	0	0	0	0	0	0	0
E.+W.AFRICA	0	0	0	0	0	0	0	0
SOUTH ASIA	1	0	0	0	0	1*	0	0*
EAST ASIA	13	2	3	3	0	5	8	18565
S.DOMINIONS	5	0	2	2	0	1	4	5118
OUTSIDE U.S.(TOTAL)	78	7	28	29	2	12	66	149314

(NOTE: IN THIS SECTION SUBSIDIARIES ARE COUNTED ON THE BASIS OF THEIR PRINCIPAL INDUSTRY IN 1975)

*CLASSIFICATION SUPPRESSED TO AVOID DISCLOSURE OF CONFIDENTIAL DATA

CHAPTER 5 - EMPLOYMENT STATISTICS OF FOREIGN SUBSIDIARIES
SECTION 2 -- EMPLOYMENT DATA IN SPECIFIC INDUSTRIES
TABLE 30 --- THE SPECIAL MACHINERY INDUSTRY (SIC 355)

NO. OF MANUFACTURING SUBSIDIARIES ACTIVE AT 1-JAN-76   (SEE NOTE BELOW)

COUNTRY OR REGION	NO. OF SUBSIDIARIES ACTIVE AT 1-JAN-76	DISTRIBUTION OF SUBSIDIARIES, BY EMPLOYMENT IN 1975 NO. OF EMPLOYEES:					SUBSIDIARIES WITH EMPLOYMENT DATA:	
		1-100	101-1000	1001-10000	OVER 10000	UNKNOWN	NO. ACTIVE AT 1-JAN-76	TOTAL NO. OF EMPLOYEES IN 1975
CANADA	7	2	2	0	0	3	4	1022
C.AM.+CARIB.	4	0	1	0	0	3	1	125
S.AMERICA	12	0	4	1	0	7	5	3898
EUROPE	56	8	26	4	0	18	38	22493
N.AFR+M.EAST	1	0	0	0	0	1	0	0
E.+W.AFRICA	0	0	0	0	0	0	0	0
SOUTH ASIA	0	0	0	0	0	0	0	0
EAST ASIA	4	1	0	0	0	3	1	31
S.DOMINIONS	7	1	3	0	0	3	4	1310
OUTSIDE U.S. (TOTAL)	91	12	36	5	0	38	53	28879

(NOTE: IN THIS SECTION SUBSIDIARIES ARE COUNTED ON THE BASIS OF THEIR PRINCIPAL INDUSTRY IN 1975)

CHAPTER   5   - EMPLOYMENT STATISTICS OF FOREIGN SUBSIDIARIES
SECTION   2   -- EMPLOYMENT DATA IN SPECIFIC INDUSTRIES
TABLE 31   --- THE GENERAL MACHINERY INDUSTRY (SIC 356)

NO. OF MANUFACTURING SUBSIDIARIES ACTIVE AT 1-JAN-76   (SEE NOTE BELOW)

COUNTRY OR REGION	NO. OF SUBSIDIARIES ACTIVE AT 1-JAN-76	DISTRIBUTION OF SUBSIDIARIES, BY EMPLOYMENT IN 1975 NO. OF EMPLOYEES:					SUBSIDIARIES WITH EMPLOYMENT DATA:	
		1-100	101-1000	1001-10000	OVER 10000	UNKNOWN	NO. ACTIVE AT 1-JAN-76	TOTAL NO. OF EMPLOYEES IN 1975
CANADA	15	5	6	1	0	3	12	3392
C.AM.+CARIB.	11	2	4	1	0	4	7	2872
S.AMERICA	13	1	5	0	0	7	6	2832
EUROPE	61	8	27	13	0	13	48	35359
N.AFR+M.EAST	0	0	0	0	0	0	0	0
E.+W.AFRICA	1	0	1	0	0	0	1	243
SOUTH ASIA	1	0	1	0	0	0	1	800
EAST ASIA	17	2	6	0	0	9	8	2251
S.DOMINIONS	4	1	2	0	0	1	3	492
OUTSIDE U.S.(TOTAL)	123	19	52	15	0	37	86	48241

(NOTE: IN THIS SECTION SUBSIDIARIES ARE COUNTED ON THE BASIS OF THEIR PRINCIPAL INDUSTRY IN 1975)

CHAPTER 5   – EMPLOYMENT STATISTICS OF FOREIGN SUBSIDIARIES
SECTION 2   -- EMPLOYMENT DATA IN SPECIFIC INDUSTRIES
TABLE 32 --- OTHER NON-ELEC MACHINERY INDUSTRIES (OTHER SIC 35)

NO. OF MANUFACTURING SUBSIDIARIES ACTIVE AT 1-JAN-76   (SEE NOTE BELOW)

COUNTRY OR REGION	NO. OF SUBSIDIARIES ACTIVE AT 1-JAN-76	DISTRIBUTION OF SUBSIDIARIES, BY EMPLOYMENT IN 1975 NO. OF EMPLOYEES:					SUBSIDIARIES WITH EMPLOYMENT DATA:	
		1-100	101-1000	1001-10000	OVER 10000	UNKNOWN	NO. ACTIVE AT 1-JAN-76	TOTAL NO. OF EMPLOYEES IN 1975
CANADA	12	2	4	2	0	4	8	3896
C.AM.+CARIB.	7	1	3	1	0	2	5	3413
S.AMERICA	11	0	6	0	0	5	6	2805
EUROPE	59	12	26	4	0	17	42	22589
N.AFR+M.EAST	0	0	0	0	0	0	0	0
E.+W.AFRICA	0	0	0	0	0	0	0	0
SOUTH ASIA	3	0	2	0	0	1	2	755
EAST ASIA	6	0	1	0	0	5	1	600
S.DOMINIONS	11	4	2	0	0	5	6	974
OUTSIDE U.S. (TOTAL)	109	19	44	7	0	39	70	35032

(NOTE: IN THIS SECTION SUBSIDIARIES ARE COUNTED ON THE BASIS OF THEIR PRINCIPAL INDUSTRY IN 1975)

CHAPTER   5   - EMPLOYMENT STATISTICS OF FOREIGN SUBSIDIARIES
SECTION   2   -- EMPLOYMENT DATA IN SPECIFIC INDUSTRIES
TABLE   33 --- ELECTRIC LIGHT & WIRING INDUSTRY (SIC 364)

NO. OF MANUFACTURING SUBSIDIARIES ACTIVE AT 1-JAN-76   (SEE NOTE BELOW)

COUNTRY OR REGION	NO. OF SUBSIDIARIES ACTIVE AT 1-JAN-76	DISTRIBUTION OF SUBSIDIARIES, BY EMPLOYMENT IN 1975 NO. OF EMPLOYEES:					SUBSIDIARIES WITH EMPLOYMENT DATA:	
		1-100	101-1000	1001-10000	OVER 10000	UNKNOWN	NO. ACTIVE AT 1-JAN-76	TOTAL NO. OF EMPLOYEES IN 1975
CANADA	3	0	3	0	0	0	3	1326
C.AM.+CARIB.	5	0	2	0	0	3	2	931
S.AMERICA	9	2	5	0	0	2	7	2359
EUROPE	10	1	4	2	1	2	8	23994
N.AFR+M.EAST	0	0	0	0	0	0	0	0
E.+W.AFRICA	0	0	0	0	0	0	0	0
SOUTH ASIA	3	0	1	2	0	0	3	2641
EAST ASIA	4	0	1	1	0	2	2	2680
S.DOMINIONS	0	0	0	0	0	0	0	0
OUTSIDE U.S. (TOTAL)	34	3	16	5	1	9	25	33931

(NOTE: IN THIS SECTION SUBSIDIARIES ARE COUNTED ON THE BASIS OF THEIR PRINCIPAL INDUSTRY IN 1975)

CHAPTER 5   - EMPLOYMENT STATISTICS OF FOREIGN SUBSIDIARIES
SECTION 2   -- EMPLOYMENT DATA IN SPECIFIC INDUSTRIES
TABLE 34 --- ELEC TRANSMISSION EQUIP INDUSTRY (SIC 361)

NO. OF MANUFACTURING SUBSIDIARIES ACTIVE AT 1-JAN-76   (SEE NOTE BELOW)

COUNTRY OR REGION	NO. OF SUBSIDIARIES ACTIVE AT 1-JAN-76	DISTRIBUTION OF SUBSIDIARIES, BY EMPLOYMENT IN 1975 NO. OF EMPLOYEES: 1-100	101-1000	1001-10000	OVER 10000	UNKNOWN	SUBSIDIARIES WITH EMPLOYMENT DATA: NO. ACTIVE AT 1-JAN-76	TOTAL NO. OF EMPLOYEES IN 1975
CANADA	10	1	6	2	0	1	9	5337
C.AM.+CARIB.	0	0	0	0	0	0	0	0
S.AMERICA	1	0	0	0	0	1*	0	0*
EUROPE	12	1	8	1	0	2	10	4733
N.AFR+M.EAST	0	0	0	0	0	0	0	0
E.+W.AFRICA	0	0	0	0	0	0	0	0
SOUTH ASIA	0	0	0	0	0	0	0	0
EAST ASIA	2	0	0	0	0	2	0	0
S.DOMINIONS	6	1	3	0	0	2	4	1715
OUTSIDE U.S.(TOTAL)	31	3	17	3	0	8	23	11785

(NOTE: IN THIS SECTION SUBSIDIARIES ARE COUNTED ON THE BASIS OF THEIR PRINCIPAL INDUSTRY IN 1975)

*CLASSIFICATION SUPPRESSED TO AVOID DISCLOSURE OF CONFIDENTIAL DATA

CHAPTER 5 - EMPLOYMENT STATISTICS OF FOREIGN SUBSIDIARIES
SECTION 2 -- EMPLOYMENT DATA IN SPECIFIC INDUSTRIES
TABLE 35 --- RADIO,TV & APPLIANCES INDUSTRIES (SIC 365 AND 363)

NO. OF MANUFACTURING SUBSIDIARIES ACTIVE AT 1-JAN-76   (SEE NOTE BELOW)

COUNTRY OR REGION	NO. OF SUBSIDIARIES ACTIVE AT 1-JAN-76	DISTRIBUTION OF SUBSIDIARIES, BY EMPLOYMENT IN 1975 NO. OF EMPLOYEES:					SUBSIDIARIES WITH EMPLOYMENT DATA:	
		1-100	101-1000	1001-10000	OVER 10000	UNKNOWN	NO. ACTIVE AT 1-JAN-76	TOTAL NO. OF EMPLOYEES IN 1975
CANADA	12	3	6	3	0	0	12	11484
C.AM.+CARIB.	8	0	4	2	0	2	6	7976
S.AMERICA	18	1	5	3	0	9	9	11510
EUROPE	45	2	16	15	2	10	35	173870
N.AFR+M.EAST	2	0	0	1	0	1	1	4500
E.+W.AFRICA	3	0	1	0	0	2	1	600
SOUTH ASIA	3	0	1	0	0	2	1	650
EAST ASIA	15	0	4	3	1	7	8	81416
S.DOMINIONS	9	0	5	4	0	0	9	7981
OUTSIDE U.S.(TOTAL)	115	6	42	31	3	33	82	299987

(NOTE: IN THIS SECTION SUBSIDIARIES ARE COUNTED ON THE BASIS OF THEIR PRINCIPAL INDUSTRY IN 1975)

CHAPTER 5 - EMPLOYMENT STATISTICS OF FOREIGN SUBSIDIARIES
SECTION 2 -- EMPLOYMENT DATA IN SPECIFIC INDUSTRIES
TABLE 36 --- THE ELECTRONICS INDUSTRY (SIC 367)

NO. OF MANUFACTURING SUBSIDIARIES ACTIVE AT 1-JAN-76   (SEE NOTE BELOW)

COUNTRY OR REGION	NO. OF SUBSIDIARIES ACTIVE AT 1-JAN-76	DISTRIBUTION OF SUBSIDIARIES, BY EMPLOYMENT IN 1975 NO. OF EMPLOYEES:					SUBSIDIARIES WITH EMPLOYMENT DATA:	
		1-100	101-1000	1001-10000	OVER 10000	UNKNOWN	NO. ACTIVE AT 1-JAN-76	TOTAL NO. OF EMPLOYEES IN 1975
CANADA	1	0	0	0	0	1*	1	0*
C.AM.+CARIB.	11	0	4	3	0	4	7	5307
S.AMERICA	4	1	1	2	0	0	4	3955
EUROPE	48	3	17	13	1	14	34	45182
N.AFR+M.EAST	0	0	0	0	0	0	0	0
E.+W.AFRICA	1	0	0	0	0	1	0	0
SOUTH ASIA	1	0	0	0	0	1*	0	0*
EAST ASIA	23	1	8	8	0	6	17	33532
S.DOMINIONS	1	0	0	0	0	1	0	0
OUTSIDE U.S. (TOTAL)	90	5	30	26	1	28	62	87976

(NOTE: IN THIS SECTION SUBSIDIARIES ARE COUNTED ON THE BASIS OF THEIR PRINCIPAL INDUSTRY IN 1975)

*CLASSIFICATION SUPPRESSED TO AVOID DISCLOSURE OF CONFIDENTIAL DATA

CHAPTER 5 - EMPLOYMENT STATISTICS OF FOREIGN SUBSIDIARIES
SECTION 2 -- EMPLOYMENT DATA IN SPECIFIC INDUSTRIES
TABLE 37 --- OTHER ELECTRICAL INDUSTRIES (OTHER SIC 36)

NO. OF MANUFACTURING SUBSIDIARIES ACTIVE AT 1-JAN-76 (SEE NOTE BELOW)

COUNTRY OR REGION	NO. OF SUBSIDIARIES ACTIVE AT 1-JAN-76	DISTRIBUTION OF SUBSIDIARIES, BY EMPLOYMENT IN 1975 NO. OF EMPLOYEES:					SUBSIDIARIES WITH EMPLOYMENT DATA: NO. ACTIVE AT 1-JAN-76	TOTAL NO. OF EMPLOYEES IN 1975
		1-100	101-1000	1001-10000	OVER 10000	UNKNOWN		
CANADA	12	1	7	1	1	2	10	23221
C.AM.+CARIB.	24	5	13	0	0	6	18	4836
S.AMERICA	27	1	11	5	0	10	17	21617
EUROPE	51	6	22	8	2	13	38	66460
N.AFR+M.EAST	3	1	1	0	0	1	2	210
E.+W.AFRICA	5	0	4	0	0	1	4	810
SOUTH ASIA	9	1	4	0	0	4	5	1495
EAST ASIA	22	0	14	1	0	7	15	8364
S.DOMINIONS	14	5	5	0	0	4	10	2271
OUTSIDE U.S.(TOTAL)	167	20	81	15	3	48	119	129284

(NOTE: IN THIS SECTION SUBSIDIARIES ARE COUNTED ON THE BASIS OF THEIR PRINCIPAL INDUSTRY IN 1975)

CHAPTER 5 - EMPLOYMENT STATISTICS OF FOREIGN SUBSIDIARIES
SECTION 2 -- EMPLOYMENT DATA IN SPECIFIC INDUSTRIES
TABLE 38 --- COMMUNICATION EQUIP INDUSTRY (SIC 366)

NO. OF MANUFACTURING SUBSIDIARIES ACTIVE AT 1-JAN-76 (SEE NOTE BELOW)

COUNTRY OR REGION	NO. OF SUBSIDIARIES ACTIVE AT 1-JAN-76	DISTRIBUTION OF SUBSIDIARIES, BY EMPLOYMENT IN 1975: NO. OF EMPLOYEES:					SUBSIDIARIES WITH EMPLOYMENT DATA:	
		1-100	101-1000	1001-10000	OVER 10000	UNKNOWN	NO. ACTIVE AT 1-JAN-76	TOTAL NO. OF EMPLOYEES IN 1975
CANADA	6	0	3	2	0	1	5	5044
C.AM.+CARIB.	4	0	2	0	0	2	2	820
S.AMERICA	5	1	1	2	0	1	4	8795
EUROPE	36	1	7	14	5	9	27	161563
N.AFR+M.EAST	0	0	0	0	0	0	0	0
E.+W.AFRICA	2	1	0	1	0	0	2	1523
SOUTH ASIA	0	0	0	0	0	0	0	0
EAST ASIA	5	1	2	1	0	1	4	3387
S.DOMINIONS	4	0	1	2	0	1	3	6012
OUTSIDE U.S.(TOTAL)	62	4	16	22	5	15	47	187144

(NOTE: IN THIS SECTION SUBSIDIARIES ARE COUNTED ON THE BASIS OF THEIR PRINCIPAL INDUSTRY IN 1975)

CHAPTER 5   - EMPLOYMENT STATISTICS OF FOREIGN SUBSIDIARIES
SECTION 2   -- EMPLOYMENT DATA IN SPECIFIC INDUSTRIES
TABLE 39   --- THE MOTOR VEHIC INDUSTRY (SIC 371)

NO. OF MANUFACTURING SUBSIDIARIES ACTIVE AT 1-JAN-76   (SEE NOTE BELOW)

COUNTRY OR REGION	NO. OF SUBSIDIARIES ACTIVE AT 1-JAN-76	DISTRIBUTION OF SUBSIDIARIES, BY EMPLOYMENT IN 1975 NO. OF EMPLOYEES:					SUBSIDIARIES WITH EMPLOYMENT DATA: NO. ACTIVE AT 1-JAN-76	TOTAL NO. OF EMPLOYEES IN 1975
		1-100	101-1000	1001-10000	OVER 10000	UNKNOWN		
CANADA	25	2	7	7	3	6	19	79691
C.AM.+CARIB.	18	0	9	4	0	5	13	18876
S.AMERICA	64	2	16	22	2	22	42	105912
EUROPE	108	9	38	23	8	30	78	357697
N.AFR+M.EAST	3	0	1	1	0	1	2	2400
E.+W.AFRICA	1	0	0	0	0	1	0	0
SOUTH ASIA	2	0	1	0	0	1	1	250
EAST ASIA	29	3	7	3	1	15	14	22128
S.DOMINIONS	36	4	8	7	2	15	21	68299
OUTSIDE U.S. (TOTAL)	286	20	87	67	16	96	190	655253

(NOTE: IN THIS SECTION SUBSIDIARIES ARE COUNTED ON THE BASIS OF THEIR PRINCIPAL INDUSTRY IN 1975)

CHAPTER 5   - EMPLOYMENT STATISTICS OF FOREIGN SUBSIDIARIES
SECTION 2   -- EMPLOYMENT DATA IN SPECIFIC INDUSTRIES
TABLE 40 --- OTHER TRANSPORTATION INDUSTRIES (OTHER SIC 37)

NO. OF MANUFACTURING SUBSIDIARIES ACTIVE AT 1-JAN-76   (SEE NOTE BELOW)

COUNTRY OR REGION	NO. OF SUBSIDIARIES ACTIVE AT 1-JAN-76	DISTRIBUTION OF SUBSIDIARIES, BY EMPLOYMENT IN 1975 NO. OF EMPLOYEES:					SUBSIDIARIES WITH EMPLOYMENT DATA:	
		1-100	101-1000	1001-10000	OVER 10000	UNKNOWN	NO. ACTIVE AT 1-JAN-76	TOTAL NO. OF EMPLOYEES IN 1975
CANADA	4	0	2	2	0	0	4	4359
C.AM.+CARIB.	3	0	0	0	0	3	0	0
S.AMERICA	6	0	1	0	0	5	1	767
EUROPE	18	2	2	5	0	9	9	15078
N.AFR+M.EAST	0	0	0	0	0	0	0	0
E.+W.AFRICA	0	0	0	0	0	0	0	0
SOUTH ASIA	1	0	0	0	0	1	0	0
EAST ASIA	0	0	0	0	0	0	0	0
S.DOMINIONS	1	0	0	0	0	1*	0*	0*
OUTSIDE U.S. (TOTAL)	33	2	5	7	0	19	14	20204

(NOTE: IN THIS SECTION SUBSIDIARIES ARE COUNTED ON THE BASIS OF THEIR PRINCIPAL INDUSTRY IN 1975)

*CLASSIFICATION SUPPRESSED TO AVOID DISCLOSURE OF CONFIDENTIAL DATA

CHAPTER 5 - EMPLOYMENT STATISTICS OF FOREIGN SUBSIDIARIES
SECTION 2 -- EMPLOYMENT DATA IN SPECIFIC INDUSTRIES
TABLE 41 --- PRECISION INSTRUMENTS INDUSTRIES (SIC 38)

NO. OF MANUFACTURING SUBSIDIARIES ACTIVE AT 1-JAN-76   (SEE NOTE BELOW)

COUNTRY OR REGION	NO. OF SUBSIDIARIES ACTIVE AT 1-JAN-76	DISTRIBUTION OF SUBSIDIARIES, BY EMPLOYMENT IN 1975: NO. OF EMPLOYEES:					SUBSIDIARIES WITH EMPLOYMENT DATA: NO. ACTIVE AT 1-JAN-76	TOTAL NO. OF EMPLOYEES IN 1975
		1-100	101-1000	1001-10000	OVER 10000	UNKNOWN		
CANADA	23	4	5	5	0	9	14	10822
C.AM.+CARIB.	10	2	7	0	0	1	9	2917
S.AMERICA	15	1	3	1	0	10	5	3747
EUROPE	81	10	33	7	1	30	51	47279
N.AFR+M.EAST	3	1	0	0	0	2	1	5
E.+W.AFRICA	1	0	0	0	0	1	0	0
SOUTH ASIA	3	0	1	1	0	1	2	1938
EAST ASIA	13	3	3	0	0	7	6	1053
S.DOMINIONS	12	1	5	2	0	4	8	7049
OUTSIDE U.S. (TOTAL)	161	22	57	16	1	65	96	74810

(NOTE: IN THIS SECTION SUBSIDIARIES ARE COUNTED ON THE BASIS OF THEIR PRINCIPAL INDUSTRY IN 1975)

CHAPTER 5 - EMPLOYMENT STATISTICS OF FOREIGN SUBSIDIARIES
SECTION 2 -- EMPLOYMENT DATA IN SPECIFIC INDUSTRIES
TABLE 42 --- MISCELLANEOUS INDUSTRIES (SIC 39)

NO. OF MANUFACTURING SUBSIDIARIES ACTIVE AT 1-JAN-76 (SEE NOTE BELOW)

COUNTRY OR REGION	NO. OF SUBSIDIARIES ACTIVE AT 1-JAN-76	DISTRIBUTION OF SUBSIDIARIES, BY EMPLOYMENT IN 1975 NO. OF EMPLOYEES:					SUBSIDIARIES WITH EMPLOYMENT DATA:	
		1-100	101-1000	1001-10000	OVER 10000	UNKNOWN	NO. ACTIVE AT 1-JAN-76	TOTAL NO. OF EMPLOYEES IN 1975
CANADA	30	3	5	2	0	20	10	7463
C.AM.+CARIB.	16	3	4	0	0	9	7	1288
S.AMERICA	15	0	1	0	0	14	1	227
EUROPE	102	10	24	3	0	65	37	17616
N.AFR+M.EAST	1	0	0	0	0	1	0	0
E.+W.AFRICA	0	0	0	0	0	0	0	0
SOUTH ASIA	1	0	0	0	0	1	0	0
EAST ASIA	19	0	5	1	0	13	6	4990
S.DOMINIONS	19	3	4	0	0	12	7	1744
OUTSIDE U.S. (TOTAL)	203	19	43	6	0	135	68	33328

(NOTE: IN THIS SECTION SUBSIDIARIES ARE COUNTED ON THE BASIS OF THEIR PRINCIPAL INDUSTRY IN 1975)

Ownership Patterns

CHAPTER 6 - OWNERSHIP PATTERNS
SECTION 1 -- AN OVERVIEW
TABLE 1 --- BY PRINCIPAL ACTIVITY AT ENTRY DATE

NO. OF SUBSIDIARIES, BY PRINCIPAL ACTIVITY AND PARENT OWNERSHIP AT ENTRY DATE

ACTIVITY / PAR.OWN.	NET FLOW UP TO 31-DEC-50	NO. OF ENTRIES DURING YEAR(S)													TOTAL ENTRIES 1951-75	TOTAL EXITS 1951-75	NET FLOW UP TO 1-JAN-76
		51-55	56-60	61-65	1966	1967	1968	1969	1970	1971	1972	1973	1974	1975			
MANUFACTURING:TOTAL	947	419	960	1612	343	437	546	471	416	446	381	375	269	204	6879	2204	5622
WHL (95-100%)	629	252	523	769	178	248	383	317	270	292	257	226	159	118	3992	1268	3353
MAJ (51- 94%)	98	53	136	252	49	62	68	39	51	56	48	39	32	26	911	250	759
CO- (50%)	42	35	100	225	42	50	41	43	41	48	38	43	27	24	757	224	575
MIN (5- 49%)	87	50	134	237	55	56	46	50	52	45	37	62	48	36	908	262	733
UNKNOWN	91	29	67	129	19	21	8	22	2	5	1	5	3	0	311	200	202
SALES :TOTAL	638	237	480	810	149	299	271	240	233	263	159	187	200	101	3629	1040	3227
WHL (95-100%)	504	195	388	617	114	246	240	210	196	227	127	150	158	77	2945	804	2645
MAJ (51- 94%)	41	14	21	53	4	18	11	7	13	11	12	16	5	3	188	66	163
CO- (50%)	15	5	30	48	9	13	11	7	12	12	11	7	13	10	190	65	140
MIN (5- 49%)	24	15	17	47	14	12	12	14	12	10	7	10	21	11	195	38	181
UNKNOWN	54	8	24	45	8	10	5	1	0	3	2	4	3	0	111	67	98
EXTRACTION :TOTAL	108	58	67	73	14	27	29	44	19	30	11	12	32	14	430	190	348
WHL (95-100%)	63	30	44	46	10	17	19	29	10	16	6	7	22	7	263	104	222
MAJ (51- 94%)	9	14	7	7	3	3	4	4	2	0	2	3	4	2	54	28	35
CO- (50%)	9	2	1	3	0	4	1	1	2	2	0	0	1	2	21	8	22
MIN (5- 49%)	14	10	7	10	2	2	3	6	5	11	3	2	5	2	68	26	56
UNKNOWN	13	2	8	7	1	1	2	3	0	0	0	0	0	0	24	24	13
OTHER :TOTAL	109	124	181	272	64	85	120	125	134	124	81	104	95	54	1563	412	1260
WHL (95-100%)	72	104	144	194	41	64	101	104	105	103	64	82	73	42	1216	306	982
MAJ (51- 94%)	8	4	6	25	9	9	10	10	15	0	0	9	7	1	116	42	82
CO- (50%)	7	4	0	14	3	3	5	7	8	6	7	6	7	3	85	12	80
MIN (5- 49%)	6	2	9	19	6	6	4	3	9	7	0	7	8	8	100	27	79
UNKNOWN	16	6	12	20	3	3	0	1	2	1	0	0	0	0	46	25	37
UNKNOWN :TOTAL	394	151	269	458	99	64	40	65	51	42	14	15	23	3	1294	947	741
WHL (95-100%)	270	112	204	333	70	42	28	45	38	31	13	13	21	2	952	683	539
MAJ (51- 94%)	29	10	20	40	4	4	2	3	7	2	0	1	0	0	96	74	51
CO- (50%)	17	10	20	17	4	1	2	3	0	4	2	0	0	0	53	41	29
MIN (5- 49%)	12	5	10	25	16	4	0	4	2	2	1	0	2	0	48	30	30
UNKNOWN	66	14	32	43	16	15	7	10	4	3	0	1	0	1	145	119	92
ALL :TOTAL	2196	989	1957	3225	669	912	1006	945	853	905	646	693	619	376	13795	4793	11198
WHL (95-100%)	1538	693	1303	1959	413	617	771	705	614	669	467	478	433	246	9368	3165	7741
MAJ (51- 94%)	185	99	190	377	71	94	96	96	88	77	62	68	48	32	1365	460	1090
CO- (50%)	90	56	150	307	61	71	61	63	63	72	62	56	50	40	1106	350	846
MIN (5- 49%)	143	82	173	338	77	80	58	77	80	75	58	81	82	58	1319	383	1079
UNKNOWN	240	59	141	244	47	50	20	37	8	12	3	10	6	0	637	435	442

CHAPTER 6 — OWNERSHIP PATTERNS
SECTION 1 —— AN OVERVIEW
TABLE 2 ——— BY METHOD OF ENTRY

NO. OF SUBSIDIARIES, BY METHOD OF ENTRY AND PARENT OWNERSHIP AT ENTRY DATE

METH.ENTRY/PAR.OWN.	NET FLOW UP TO 31-DEC-50	51-55	56-60	61-65	1966	1967	1968	1969	1970	1971	1972	1973	1974	1975	TOTAL ENTRIES 1951-75	TOTAL EXITS 1951-75	NET FLOW UP TO 1-JAN-76
NEWLY FORMED :TOTAL	1230	507	1009	1430	288	366	423	437	402	388	282	307	365	234	6438	1652	6016
WHL (95-100%)	936	363	692	856	189	248	326	338	293	282	194	211	247	165	4404	1045	4295
MAJ (51- 94%)	93	58	90	141	23	30	38	28	31	26	24	27	26	17	559	166	486
CO- (50%)	41	28	85	195	33	44	29	29	41	38	35	29	39	25	650	171	520
MIN (5- 49%)	72	43	93	145	34	30	24	34	35	36	28	39	49	27	617	140	549
UNKNOWN	88	15	49	93	9	14	6	8	2	6	1	1	4	0	208	130	166
ACQUIRED :TOTAL	465	301	645	1314	309	457	534	452	403	479	319	354	212	135	5914	2237	4142
WHL (95-100%)	253	199	398	794	174	319	409	327	289	363	242	245	156	76	3991	1512	2732
MAJ (51- 94%)	57	25	75	190	44	61	56	31	21	29	21	37	20	14	682	226	513
CO- (50%)	30	17	47	89	27	23	26	31	21	29	21	24	9	15	379	133	276
MIN (5- 49%)	53	35	73	166	41	45	31	38	38	37	23	40	25	30	622	211	464
UNKNOWN	72	25	52	75	23	9	12	24	5	4	1	1	8	0	240	155	157
DESCENDENT :TOTAL	30	7	20	36	2	19	29	15	17	16	23	11	30	7	232	46	216
WHL (95-100%)	18	6	13	25	0	15	22	10	11	8	15	7	19	5	156	29	145
MAJ (51- 94%)	2	1	3	4	0	1	1	1	1	2	4	2	2	1	26	0	28
CO- (50%)	3	0	1	1	0	1	2	0	1	4	0	2	1	1	15	5	13
MIN (5- 49%)	4	0	1	2	1	1	3	2	3	1	4	0	8	1	26	4	26
UNKNOWN	3	0	2	4	1	0	0	2	0	0	0	0	0	0	9	8	4
UNKNOWN :TOTAL	471	174	283	445	70	70	20	41	31	22	22	21	12	0	1211	858	824
WHL (95-100%)	331	125	200	284	50	35	14	30	21	16	16	15	11	0	817	579	569
MAJ (51- 94%)	33	15	22	42	4	2	0	2	2	2	2	2	1	0	98	68	63
CO- (50%)	16	11	17	22	1	2	3	3	0	1	1	1	0	0	62	41	37
MIN (5- 49%)	14	4	6	25	4	4	1	3	4	1	3	2	0	0	54	28	40
UNKNOWN	77	19	38	72	14	27	2	3	4	2	1	1	0	0	180	142	115
ALL :TOTAL	2196	989	1957	3225	669	912	1006	945	853	905	646	693	619	376	13795	4793	11198
WHL (95-100%)	1538	693	1303	1959	413	617	771	705	614	669	467	478	433	246	9368	3165	7741
MAJ (51- 94%)	185	99	190	377	71	94	96	63	88	77	62	68	48	32	1365	460	1090
CO- (50%)	90	56	150	307	61	71	61	63	63	56	56	56	50	40	1106	350	846
MIN (5- 49%)	143	82	173	338	77	80	58	77	80	75	58	81	82	58	1319	383	1079
UNKNOWN	240	59	141	244	47	50	20	37	8	12	3	10	6	0	637	435	442

NO. OF ENTRIES DURING YEAR(S) — columns 1966 through 1975.

CHAPTER 6   - OWNERSHIP PATTERNS
SECTION 2   -- COMPARISON OF NET FLOW AND STOCK
TABLE 1   --- BY PRINCIPAL ACTIVITY IN 1975

NO. OF SUBSIDIARIES ACTIVE AT 1-JAN-76

ACTIVITY IN 1975	TOTAL NO. AT 1-JAN-76	PARENT OWNERSHIP AT ENTRY DATE					PARENT OWNERSHIP IN 1975				
		95-100%	51-94%	50%	5-49%	UNKNOWN	95-100%	51-94%	50%	5-49%	UNKNOWN
MANUFACTURING	5775	3434	770	580	754	237	3758	743	518	703	53
SALES	2833	2312	148	136	157	80	2388	134	118	167	26
EXTRACTION	356	229	31	25	54	17	238	37	17	60	4
OTHER	1977	1596	119	88	102	72	1567	102	67	98	143
UNKNOWN	257	170	22	17	12	36	108	9	5	8	127
TOTAL	11198	7741	1090	846	1079	442	8059	1025	725	1036	353

CHAPTER 6 — OWNERSHIP PATTERNS
SECTION 2 -- COMPARISON OF NET FLOW AND STOCK
TABLE 2 --- BY METHOD OF ENTRY

NO. OF SUBSIDIARIES ACTIVE AT 1-JAN-76

METHOD OF ENTRY	TOTAL NO. AT 1-JAN-76	PARENT OWNERSHIP AT ENTRY DATE					PARENT OWNERSHIP IN 1975				
		95-100%	51-94%	50%	5-49%	UNKNOWN	95-100%	51-94%	50%	5-49%	UNKNOWN
NEWLY FORMED	6016	4295	486	520	549	166	4387	520	450	554	105
ACQUIRED	4142	2732	513	276	464	157	2931	432	229	402	148
DESCENDENT	216	145	28	13	26	4	149	25	16	25	1
UNKNOWN	824	569	63	37	40	115	592	48	30	55	99
TOTAL	11198	7741	1090	846	1079	442	8059	1025	725	1036	353

CHAPTER 6 - OWNERSHIP PATTERNS
SECTION 2 -- COMPARISON OF NET FLOW AND STOCK
TABLE 3 --- BY GEOGRAPHICAL REGION

NO. OF SUBSIDIARIES ACTIVE AT 1-JAN-76

COUNTRY OR REGION	TOTAL NO. AT 1-JAN-76	PARENT OWNERSHIP AT ENTRY DATE					PARENT OWNERSHIP IN 1975				
		95-100%	51-94%	50%	5-49%	UNKNOWN	95-100%	51-94%	50%	5-49%	UNKNOWN
CANADA	1163	969	52	46	58	38	979	47	42	51	44
LATIN AMER. (TOTAL)	2462	1643	260	159	300	100	1686	259	132	293	92
C.AM.+CARIB. (TOTAL)	1180	818	100	75	144	43	827	93	74	151	35
BAHAMAS	56	44	2	5	4	1	48	1	3	3	1
BERMUDA	72	68	1	2	1	0	69	0	2	1	0
COSTA RICA	45	32	7	3	1	2	35	7	2	1	0
GUATEMALA	65	41	10	3	7	4	45	9	4	6	1
JAMAICA	38	22	7	3	6	0	21	6	3	8	0
MEXICO	552	331	55	41	101	24	330	47	44	108	23
NETH.ANTILLES	55	51	0	1	1	2	53	0	1	1	0
NICARAGUA	23	9	5	4	3	2	9	8	3	3	0
PANAMA	170	149	2	8	5	6	141	3	9	7	10
OTHER C.AM+CAR.	104	71	11	6	14	2	76	12	3	13	0
S.AMERICA (TOTAL)	1282	825	160	84	156	57	859	166	58	142	57
BOLIVIA	10	7	2	0	1	0	7	1	0	2	0
CHILE	52	34	9	4	4	1	32	9	2	6	3
COLOMBIA	161	91	13	22	28	7	101	15	16	22	7
ECUADOR	43	28	5	2	6	2	31	7	2	3	0
PERU	80	54	12	7	6	1	47	16	2	12	3
ARGENTINA	207	149	19	5	21	13	151	22	1	17	16
BRAZIL	375	236	52	26	45	16	255	45	25	35	15
URUGUAY	39	32	2	0	3	2	31	3	0	5	0
VENEZUELA	300	181	45	18	41	15	192	46	10	40	12
OTHER S.AMER.	15	13	1	0	0	0	12	2	0	0	1
EUROPE (TOTAL)	4829	3447	487	334	367	194	3650	419	271	332	157
BELGIUM	309	236	19	25	19	10	253	16	18	19	3
FRANCE	617	340	136	39	86	16	368	115	32	82	20
GERMANY	688	481	71	49	50	37	539	50	41	40	18
ITALY	382	263	52	21	30	16	270	52	20	24	16
LUXEMBOURG	39	32	1	2	2	2	35	1	1	2	0
NETHERLANDS	306	234	21	22	17	12	258	12	13	18	5
DENMARK	115	92	8	5	3	7	101	6	2	3	3
IRELAND	104	93	2	4	3	2	93	2	4	4	1
U.K.	1084	844	56	73	58	53	870	55	56	45	58
AUSTRIA	90	67	9	5	7	2	72	8	3	7	0
FINLAND	46	39	3	0	3	1	43	1	0	1	1
GREECE	54	33	6	3	7	5	36	5	2	9	2
NORWAY	92	75	9	2	4	2	74	8	2	7	1
PORTUGAL	71	43	11	3	8	6	47	9	3	10	2
SPAIN	298	138	50	59	40	11	149	48	55	34	12
SWEDEN	191	156	7	14	11	3	161	5	12	9	4
SWITZERLAND	278	242	16	6	5	9	247	12	5	4	10
TURKEY	34	18	8	2	6	0	14	12	2	6	0
OTHER EUROPE	31	21	2	0	8	0	20	2	0	8	1

TABLE 6.2.3 (CONTINUED)

COUNTRY OR REGION	TOTAL NO. AT 1-JAN-76	PARENT OWNERSHIP AT ENTRY DATE					PARENT OWNERSHIP IN 1975				
		95-100%	51-94%	50%	5-49%	UNKNOWN	95-100%	51-94%	50%	5-49%	UNKNOWN
N.AFR+M.EAST(TOTAL)	264	144	39	23	49	9	145	40	19	56	4
ALGERIA	14	8	2	0	3	1	6	4	0	3	1
EGYPT	20	11	4	4	3	1	12	5	2	1	0
IRAN	67	32	7	8	18	2	30	7	7	23	0
ISRAEL	20	6	7	1	5	1	7	7	1	5	0
LEBANON	22	16	3	1	1	1	17	2	1	1	1
MOROCCO	29	13	5	4	6	1	12	4	1	9	0
SAUDI ARABIA	22	8	4	4	6	0	12	3	4	4	0
OTHER N.AF+M.E.	70	50	7	1	10	2	49	8	3	10	2
E.+W.AFRICA (TOTAL)	321	221	34	13	41	12	222	44	8	37	10
GHANA	17	9	2	1	2	3	9	5	1	1	1
IVORY COAST	13	7	2	0	3	1	8	2	0	3	0
KENYA	27	18	3	3	2	1	8	3	2	3	1
LIBERIA	45	37	1	0	6	1	18	16	0	5	3
NIGERIA	57	38	12	3	2	2	35	16	2	3	1
ZAIRE	26	20	3	0	3	0	21	2	0	2	1
ZAMBIA	47	28	5	1	10	3	31	7	0	8	1
OTHER E.+W.AFR.	89	64	6	5	13	1	65	7	3	12	2
SOUTH ASIA (TOTAL)	144	60	30	13	37	4	48	36	12	47	1
INDIA	101	40	12	13	32	4	28	17	12	43	1
PAKISTAN	33	14	14	0	5	0	13	16	0	4	1
SRI LANKA	9	6	3	0	0	0	7	2	0	4	0
OTHER S.ASIA	1	0	1	0	0	0	0	1	0	0	0
EAST ASIA (TOTAL)	1004	537	84	186	150	47	552	97	186	144	25
HONG KONG	97	78	3	9	2	5	81	4	9	2	1
INDONESIA	61	37	16	1	4	3	37	18	1	3	2
JAPAN	426	141	16	144	102	23	144	26	142	97	17
MALAYSIA	61	46	8	1	2	4	48	8	2	2	1
PHILIPPINES	108	73	15	2	12	6	76	13	1	15	3
SINGAPORE	74	58	5	2	7	3	62	3	1	6	3
S.KOREA	37	11	4	14	8	0	11	4	15	7	0
THAILAND	62	42	11	4	4	1	43	10	4	5	0
TAIWAN	59	36	7	7	7	2	36	11	7	5	0
OTHER E.ASIA	19	15	0	2	2	0	14	0	2	2	1
S.DOMINIONS (TOTAL)	1011	720	104	72	77	38	777	83	55	76	20
AUSTRALIA	544	369	67	45	39	24	407	49	32	45	11
NEW ZEALAND	132	100	11	11	5	5	104	11	8	6	3
RHODESIA	26	19	1	1	4	1	18	3	0	3	2
S.AFRICA	309	232	25	15	29	8	248	20	15	22	4
OUTSIDE U.S. (TOTAL)	11198	7741	1090	846	1079	442	8059	1025	725	1036	353

CHAPTER 6   - OWNERSHIP PATTERNS
SECTION 2   -- COMPARISON OF NET FLOW AND STOCK
TABLE 4   --- FOR MANUFACTURING SUBSIDIARIES, BY REGION

NO. OF MANUFACTURING SUBSIDIARIES ACTIVE AT 1-JAN-76

COUNTRY OR REGION	TOTAL NO. AT 1-JAN-76	PARENT OWNERSHIP AT ENTRY DATE					PARENT OWNERSHIP IN 1975				
		95-100%	51-94%	50%	5-49%	UNKNOWN	95-100%	51-94%	50%	5-49%	UNKNOWN
CANADA	594	499	31	28	18	18	518	34	21	13	8
LATIN AMER. (TOTAL)	1325	724	205	107	232	57	778	212	100	218	17
C.AM.+CARIB. (TOTAL)	542	289	76	47	108	22	297	78	50	109	8
BAHAMAS	5	3	0	0	2	0	3	0	1	1	0
BERMUDA	0	0	0	0	0	0	0	0	0	0	0
COSTA RICA	23	12	6	2	1	2	15	6	1	1	0
GUATEMALA	34	16	7	2	5	4	20	7	3	4	0
JAMAICA	20	7	7	1	5	0	7	6	2	5	0
MEXICO	364	202	42	32	76	12	204	41	34	78	7
NETH.ANTILLES	6	5	0	0	0	1	6	0	0	0	0
NICARAGUA	13	2	4	2	4	1	2	6	2	3	0
PANAMA	27	20	1	4	2	0	15	2	5	4	1
OTHER C.AM+CAR.	50	22	9	4	13	2	25	10	2	13	0
S.AMERICA (TOTAL)	783	435	129	60	124	35	481	134	50	109	9
BOLIVIA	2	1	1	0	0	0	1	1	0	0	0
CHILE	30	15	8	3	4	0	20	6	1	3	0
COLOMBIA	104	51	11	14	22	6	59	11	16	18	0
ECUADOR	23	13	3	1	5	1	14	6	1	2	0
PERU	38	20	8	4	5	1	12	14	1	11	0
ARGENTINA	130	87	13	3	18	9	92	18	0	14	6
BRAZIL	255	141	44	23	36	11	164	39	22	28	2
URUGUAY	21	16	1	0	3	1	15	2	0	3	1
VENEZUELA	176	88	40	12	30	6	101	36	9	30	0
OTHER S.AMER.	4	3	0	0	1	0	3	1	0	0	0
EUROPE (TOTAL)	2427	1537	328	221	238	103	1733	294	183	198	19
BELGIUM	159	105	16	17	14	7	119	14	12	13	1
FRANCE	354	167	94	28	54	11	198	82	23	48	3
GERMANY	398	264	49	35	32	18	307	41	28	19	3
ITALY	231	142	42	18	19	10	158	42	15	15	1
LUXEMBOURG	13	13	0	0	0	0	12	1	0	0	0
NETHERLANDS	128	91	13	10	9	5	103	9	5	9	2
DENMARK	40	31	4	2	2	1	36	2	1	0	1
IRELAND	61	52	2	4	2	1	52	2	4	3	0
U.K.	565	425	28	49	36	27	466	30	40	24	5
AUSTRIA	32	20	5	2	3	2	24	4	1	3	0
FINLAND	7	5	1	0	1	0	6	0	0	1	0
GREECE	31	16	3	2	6	4	20	2	1	6	2
NORWAY	26	19	4	1	1	1	20	3	1	2	0
PORTUGAL	37	19	7	1	5	5	24	5	1	7	0
SPAIN	192	69	40	37	38	8	86	37	37	32	0
SWEDEN	73	49	7	12	4	1	52	5	11	4	1
SWITZERLAND	47	36	7	2	0	2	39	6	2	0	0
TURKEY	21	9	6	1	5	0	6	9	1	5	0
OTHER EUROPE	12	5	0	0	7	0	5	0	0	7	0

317

TABLE 6.2.4 (CONTINUED)

COUNTRY OR REGION	TOTAL NO. AT 1-JAN-76	PARENT OWNERSHIP AT ENTRY DATE					PARENT OWNERSHIP IN 1975				
		95-100%	51-94%	50%	5-49%	UNKNOWN	95-100%	51-94%	50%	5-49%	UNKNOWN
N.AFR+M.EAST(TOTAL)	100	31	22	12	31	4	30	21	12	37	0
ALGERIA	4	3	0	0	1	0	3	0	0	1	0
EGYPT	2	0	2	0	0	0	0	2	0	0	0
IRAN	33	8	4	6	14	1	6	3	6	18	0
ISRAEL	16	5	6	1	4	0	5	6	1	4	0
LEBANON	10	6	3	0	1	0	7	2	0	1	0
MOROCCO	17	5	2	2	6	1	4	4	2	7	0
SAUDI ARABIA	6	0	2	2	2	0	0	2	2	2	0
OTHER N.AF+M.E.	12	4	2	1	3	2	5	2	1	4	0
E.+W.AFRICA (TOTAL)	91	48	14	6	16	7	50	22	3	16	0
GHANA	6	2	2	0	0	2	2	4	0	0	0
IVORY COAST	6	2	1	0	2	1	3	2	0	1	0
KENYA	16	8	2	3	2	1	9	3	2	2	0
LIBERIA	0	0	0	1	0	0	0	0	0	0	0
NIGERIA	20	11	4	2	2	2	11	7	0	2	0
ZAIRE	11	9	2	0	0	0	9	2	0	0	0
ZAMBIA	15	8	2	0	4	1	8	2	0	5	0
OTHER E.+W.AFR.	17	8	1	2	6	0	8	2	1	6	0
SOUTH ASIA (TOTAL)	111	32	28	12	36	3	23	32	11	45	0
INDIA	82	24	12	12	31	3	14	16	11	41	0
PAKISTAN	23	6	12	0	5	0	6	13	0	4	0
SRI LANKA	5	2	3	0	0	0	3	2	0	0	0
OTHER S.ASIA	1	0	1	0	0	0	0	1	0	0	0
EAST ASIA (TOTAL)	568	204	63	144	128	29	220	69	148	124	7
HONG KONG	27	19	1	4	1	2	21	1	4	1	0
INDONESIA	27	10	12	1	3	1	11	11	1	3	1
JAPAN	275	48	10	114	87	16	51	17	117	85	5
MALAYSIA	30	18	7	0	2	3	19	7	1	2	1
PHILIPPINES	68	40	13	2	10	3	45	10	1	12	0
SINGAPORE	35	27	0	1	5	2	30	0	1	4	0
S.KOREA	28	5	3	12	8	0	5	9	13	7	0
THAILAND	35	17	10	4	3	1	18	9	4	4	0
TAIWAN	40	19	7	6	7	1	18	11	6	5	0
OTHER E.ASIA	3	1	0	0	2	0	2	0	0	1	0
S.DOMINIONS (TOTAL)	559	359	79	50	55	16	406	59	40	52	2
AUSTRALIA	310	191	52	30	26	11	221	37	22	29	1
NEW ZEALAND	70	45	9	8	4	4	52	7	7	4	0
RHODESIA	13	9	1	1	2	0	9	2	0	2	0
S.AFRICA	166	114	17	11	23	1	124	13	11	17	1
OUTSIDE U.S.(TOTAL)	5775	3434	770	580	754	237	3758	743	518	703	53

CHAPTER 6 - OWNERSHIP PATTERNS
SECTION 2 -- COMPARISON OF NET FLOW AND STOCK
TABLE 5 --- BY PRINCIPAL INDUSTRY

NO. OF MANUFACTURING SUBSIDIARIES ACTIVE AT 1-JAN-76, BY PRINCIPAL INDUSTRY IN 1975

PRINCIPAL INDUSTRY	TOTAL NO. AT 1-JAN-76	PARENT OWNERSHIP AT ENTRY DATE					PARENT OWNERSHIP IN 1975				
		95-100%	51-94%	50%	5-49%	UNKNOWN	95-100%	51-94%	50%	5-49%	UNKNOWN
BEVERAGES	81	65	9	4	3	0	61	10	4	3	3
TOBACCO	26	9	9	0	6	2	10	9	0	7	0
FOOD	635	394	118	61	46	16	435	89	66	35	10
TEXTILES+APPAREL	95	51	11	15	14	4	57	10	12	15	1
WOOD+FURNITURE	67	47	6	6	7	1	48	7	6	5	1
PAPER	206	89	38	43	35	1	107	36	35	28	0
PRINTING	64	47	7	1	5	4	52	5	3	4	0
INDUSTRIAL CHEM	208	96	26	40	38	8	104	20	39	43	2
PLASTICS	180	71	21	38	32	18	86	22	33	35	4
AGRIC CHEM	51	26	6	7	10	2	33	5	6	7	0
COSMETICS	276	232	19	9	9	7	238	23	8	6	1
DRUGS	546	408	71	33	14	20	430	66	28	12	10
OTHER CHEM	309	164	32	45	53	15	176	38	45	49	1
FABR PLASTICS	95	56	15	12	10	2	63	12	11	9	0
TIRES	89	41	17	2	13	16	43	31	2	13	0
REF PETROLEUM	155	69	17	20	43	6	75	13	20	46	1
OTH PETROLEUM	41	22	6	6	7	0	26	3	6	6	0
LEATHER	26	20	1	2	2	1	21	2	2	1	0
STONE+CLAY+CEMNT	63	29	7	9	15	3	35	6	8	14	0
ABRASIVES	135	73	19	14	26	3	82	22	12	18	1
GLASS	61	20	11	14	14	2	24	9	15	13	0
IRON+STEEL	57	27	13	6	10	1	34	9	5	9	0

TABLE 6.2.5 (CONTINUED)

PRINCIPAL INDUSTRY	TOTAL NO. AT 1-JAN-76	PARENT OWNERSHIP AT ENTRY DATE					PARENT OWNERSHIP IN 1975				
		95-100%	51-94%	50%	5-49%	UNKNOWN	95-100%	51-94%	50%	5-49%	UNKNOWN
NON-FERROUS	176	83	25	22	44	2	88	27	19	42	0
METAL CANS	46	17	5	5	16	3	24	7	1	14	0
OTHER FAB METAL	288	180	27	32	40	9	200	29	25	34	0
ENGINES+TURBIN	28	15	3	3	6	1	18	2	3	5	0
CONSTR MACH	153	84	29	12	23	5	102	23	7	20	1
FARM MACHINERY	35	19	2	1	13	0	21	3	0	11	0
OFFICE MC+COMPUT	78	61	6	2	5	4	64	5	4	3	2
SPEC MACHINERY	91	64	9	5	8	5	70	10	3	8	0
GENL MACHINERY	123	74	13	13	16	7	78	13	12	19	1
OTH NON-EL MC	109	70	8	10	15	6	78	10	5	15	1
EL LIGHT+WIRING	34	14	9	2	8	1	16	9	2	7	0
EL TRAN EQUIP	31	24	4	0	2	1	24	5	0	2	0
RADIO+TV+APPL	115	82	16	4	8	5	84	17	3	9	2
ELECTRONICS	90	69	5	9	6	1	71	6	8	5	0
OTHER ELEC	167	91	21	12	23	20	100	28	9	30	0
COMMUNICATION	62	42	6	4	2	8	45	9	3	4	1
MOTOR VEHIC	286	138	39	27	71	11	153	46	20	64	3
OTHER TRANSP	33	19	2	2	7	3	21	2	3	7	0
PRECISION	161	109	29	7	13	3	123	19	5	13	1
MISCELLANEOUS	203	123	33	21	16	10	138	26	20	13	6
TOTAL	5775	3434	770	580	754	237	3758	743	518	703	53

CHAPTER 6 - OWNERSHIP PATTERNS
SECTION 3 -- IN SPECIFIC INDUSTRIES, BY REGION AND ENTRY PERIOD
TABLE 1 --- THE BEVERAGES INDUSTRY (SIC 208)

NO. OF SUBSIDIARIES MANUFACTURING IN THIS INDUSTRY AT TIME OF ENTRY INTO PARENT SYSTEM

PERIOD OF ENTRY AND PARENT OWNERSHIP AT ENTRY DATE

(WHL=WHOLLY OWNED,95-100%   MA=MAJORITY,51-94%   CO=50%   MI=MINORITY,5-49%   UN=UNKNOWN   ALL=TOTAL FOR PERIOD)

REGION	1951-1966						1967-1969						1970-1972						1973-1975					
	WHL	MA	CO	MI	UN	ALL	WHL	MA	CO	MI	UN	ALL	WHL	MA	CO	MI	UN	ALL	WHL	MA	CO	MI	UN	ALL
CANADA	3	0	0	0	0	3	7	0	0	0	0	7	11	0	0	0	0	11	1	1	0	0	0	2
C.AM.+CARIB.	1	2	0	0	0	3	1	0	0	0	0	1	6	1	0	0	0	7	0	0	1	0	0	1
S.AMERICA	6	5	1	0	0	12	3	5	0	0	0	8	1	1	0	0	0	2	0	0	0	1	0	1
EUROPE	8	1	0	0	1	10	8	2	1	0	0	11	2	0	1	0	0	3	2	0	0	1	0	3
N.AFR+M.EAST	0	0	0	0	0	0	0	0	0	0	0	0	0	0	0	0	0	0	0	0	0	0	0	0
E.+W.AFRICA	2	0	0	0	0	2	0	0	0	0	0	0	1	0	0	0	0	1	0	0	0	0	0	0
SOUTH ASIA	1	1	0	0	0	2	0	0	0	0	0	0	0	0	0	0	0	0	0	0	0	0	0	0
EAST ASIA	4	2	1	0	0	7	1	0	0	0	0	1	0	0	0	0	0	0	2	0	1	1	0	4
S.DOMINIONS	6	1	0	0	0	7	2	0	0	0	0	2	7	0	0	0	0	7	1	0	0	0	0	1
OUTSIDE U.S.(TOTAL)	31	12	2	0	1	46	22	7	1	0	0	30	28	2	1	0	0	31	6	1	2	3	0	12

CHAPTER 6 - OWNERSHIP PATTERNS
SECTION 3 -- IN SPECIFIC INDUSTRIES, BY REGION AND ENTRY PERIOD
TABLE 2 ---- THE TOBACCO INDUSTRY (SIC 21)

NO. OF SUBSIDIARIES MANUFACTURING IN THIS INDUSTRY AT TIME OF ENTRY INTO PARENT SYSTEM

PERIOD OF ENTRY AND PARENT OWNERSHIP AT ENTRY DATE

(WHL=WHOLLY OWNED,95-100% MA=MAJORITY,51-94% CO=50% MI=MINORITY,5-49% UN=UNKNOWN ALL=TOTAL FOR PERIOD)

REGION	1951-1966						1967-1969						1970-1972						1973-1975					
	WHL	MA	CO	MI	UN	ALL	WHL	MA	CO	MI	UN	ALL	WHL	MA	CO	MI	UN	ALL	WHL	MA	CO	MI	UN	ALL
CANADA	2	0	0	0	0	2	0	0	0	0	0	0	0	0	0	0	0	0	0	0	0	0	0	0
C.AM.+CARIB.	0	0	0	0	0	0	0	0	0	1	0	1	1	1	0	1	0	2	1	1	0	0	0	2
S.AMERICA	3	2	0	0	1	6	0	0	0	0	0	0	0	0	0	0	0	0	0	1	0	0	0	1
EUROPE	1	1	0	0	0	2	2	0	0	0	0	2	2	0	0	2	0	4	0	0	0	0	0	0
N.AFR+M.EAST	0	0	0	0	0	0	0	0	0	0	0	0	0	0	0	0	0	0	0	0	0	0	0	0
E.+W.AFRICA	0	0	0	0	0	0	0	0	0	0	1	1	0	0	0	0	0	0	0	0	0	0	0	0
SOUTH ASIA	0	0	0	0	0	0	0	0	0	2	0	2	0	0	0	0	0	0	0	0	0	0	0	0
EAST ASIA	0	0	0	0	0	0	0	0	0	0	0	0	0	1	0	0	0	1	0	0	0	0	0	0
S.DOMINIONS	1	1	0	0	0	2	1	0	0	0	0	1	0	1	0	0	0	1	0	0	0	0	0	0
OUTSIDE U.S.(TOTAL)	7	4	0	0	1	12	3	0	0	3	1	7	2	3	0	3	0	8	1	2	0	0	0	3

322

CHAPTER 6 - OWNERSHIP PATTERNS
SECTION 3 -- IN SPECIFIC INDUSTRIES, BY REGION AND ENTRY PERIOD
TABLE 3 --- THE FOOD INDUSTRY (SIC 20, EXCLUDING 208)

NO. OF SUBSIDIARIES MANUFACTURING IN THIS INDUSTRY AT TIME OF ENTRY INTO PARENT SYSTEM

PERIOD OF ENTRY AND PARENT OWNERSHIP AT ENTRY DATE

(WHL=WHOLLY OWNED,95-100% MA=MAJORITY,51-94% CO=50% MI=MINORITY,5-49% UN=UNKNOWN ALL=TOTAL FOR PERIOD)

REGION	1951-1966						1967-1969						1970-1972						1973-1975					
	WHL	MA	CO	MI	UN	ALL	WHL	MA	CO	MI	UN	ALL	WHL	MA	CO	MI	UN	ALL	WHL	MA	CO	MI	UN	ALL
CANADA	48	5	4	1	0	58	32	0	3	0	0	35	33	0	2	0	0	35	8	0	0	0	0	8
C.AM.+CARIB.	36	16	9	8	4	73	10	7	4	3	0	24	12	3	4	2	0	21	3	4	1	0	0	8
S.AMERICA	32	24	3	9	2	70	9	3	0	2	0	14	6	2	0	1	0	9	7	0	2	1	0	10
EUROPE	87	36	17	9	5	154	69	13	4	5	5	96	38	13	1	3	2	57	25	2	5	1	1	34
N.AFR+M.EAST	3	1	1	0	0	5	1	1	0	0	0	2	0	0	1	0	0	1	1	1	1	0	0	3
E.+W.AFRICA	1	1	0	0	0	2	4	1	1	0	0	6	1	0	1	0	0	2	0	0	0	0	0	0
SOUTH ASIA	0	0	0	1	0	1	0	0	0	0	0	0	0	1	1	1	0	3	0	0	0	0	0	0
EAST ASIA	7	8	4	8	1	28	1	3	2	1	1	8	1	2	3	4	0	10	4	0	3	0	0	7
S.DOMINIONS	23	5	5	1	3	37	7	3	0	0	0	10	7	3	1	1	0	12	2	0	0	1	0	3
OUTSIDE U.S.(TOTAL)	237	96	43	37	15	428	133	31	14	11	6	195	98	24	14	12	2	150	50	7	12	3	1	73

CHAPTER 6 - OWNERSHIP PATTERNS
SECTION 3 -- IN SPECIFIC INDUSTRIES, BY REGION AND ENTRY PERIOD
TABLE 4 --- THE TEXTILES & APPAREL INDUSTRIES (SIC 22 AND 23)

NO. OF SUBSIDIARIES MANUFACTURING IN THIS INDUSTRY AT TIME OF ENTRY INTO PARENT SYSTEM

PERIOD OF ENTRY AND PARENT OWNERSHIP AT ENTRY DATE

(WHL=WHOLLY OWNED,95-100% MA=MAJORITY,51-94% CO=50% MI=MINORITY,5-49% UN=UNKNOWN ALL=TOTAL FOR PERIOD)

REGION	1951-1966						1967-1969						1970-1972						1973-1975					
	WHL	MA	CO	MI	UN	ALL	WHL	MA	CO	MI	UN	ALL	WHL	MA	CO	MI	UN	ALL	WHL	MA	CO	MI	UN	ALL
CANADA	11	0	1	1	0	13	1	0	2	1	0	4	4	0	2	1	0	7	1	0	0	0	0	1
C.AM.+CARIB.	5	2	1	2	0	10	1	0	0	0	0	1	2	0	1	0	0	3	1	0	0	0	0	1
S.AMERICA	9	1	3	3	3	19	0	1	0	0	0	1	1	0	0	0	0	1	2	0	0	2	0	4
EUROPE	30	2	11	3	5	51	21	1	1	1	0	24	17	5	0	1	0	23	5	0	0	1	0	6
N.AFR+M.EAST	0	1	0	0	0	1	0	0	0	0	0	0	1	0	0	0	0	1	0	0	0	1	0	1
E.+W.AFRICA	0	0	0	0	0	0	0	0	0	0	0	0	0	0	0	0	0	0	0	0	0	0	0	0
SOUTH ASIA	0	0	1	0	0	1	0	0	0	0	0	0	0	0	0	0	0	0	0	0	0	0	0	0
EAST ASIA	0	0	1	1	0	2	1	0	1	0	0	2	0	1	3	0	0	4	0	0	0	0	0	0
S.DOMINIONS	1	0	1	2	0	4	2	0	0	0	0	2	0	0	0	0	0	0	0	1	0	2	0	3
OUTSIDE U.S.(TOTAL)	56	6	19	12	8	101	26	2	4	2	0	34	25	6	6	2	0	39	9	1	0	6	0	16

CHAPTER 6   - OWNERSHIP PATTERNS
SECTION 3   -- IN SPECIFIC INDUSTRIES, BY REGION AND ENTRY PERIOD
TABLE 5   --- THE WOOD AND FURNITURE INDUSTRIES (SIC 24 AND 25)

NO. OF SUBSIDIARIES MANUFACTURING IN THIS INDUSTRY AT TIME OF ENTRY INTO PARENT SYSTEM

PERIOD OF ENTRY AND PARENT OWNERSHIP AT ENTRY DATE

(WHL=WHOLLY OWNED, 95-100%) MA=MAJORITY, 51-94% CO=50% MI=MINORITY, 5-49% UN=UNKNOWN ALL=TOTAL FOR PERIOD)

REGION	1951-1966						1967-1969						1970-1972						1973-1975					
	WHL	MA	CO	MI	UN	ALL	WHL	MA	CO	MI	UN	ALL	WHL	MA	CO	MI	UN	ALL	WHL	MA	CO	MI	UN	ALL
CANADA	6	1	0	2	0	9	8	0	1	0	1	10	7	0	1	0	0	8	2	0	0	0	0	2
C.AM.+CARIB.	0	2	1	1	0	4	1	1	0	0	0	2	0	0	0	0	0	0	1	0	0	0	0	1
S.AMERICA	2	0	0	1	0	3	2	0	0	0	0	2	0	0	1	0	0	1	1	0	0	0	0	1
EUROPE	6	2	5	0	1	14	1	1	1	1	0	4	6	1	0	0	0	7	3	0	0	1	0	4
N.AFR+M.EAST	0	0	0	0	0	0	0	0	0	0	0	0	0	0	0	0	0	0	0	0	0	1	0	1
E.+W.AFRICA	0	0	0	0	0	0	0	0	0	0	0	0	0	0	0	0	0	0	0	0	0	0	0	0
SOUTH ASIA	0	0	0	0	0	0	0	0	0	0	0	0	0	0	0	1	0	1	0	0	0	0	0	0
EAST ASIA	2	0	0	1	0	3	0	0	0	0	0	0	3	0	0	0	0	3	0	0	0	0	0	0
S.DOMINIONS	3	0	0	0	0	3	1	0	1	0	0	2	2	0	0	0	0	2	2	0	0	0	0	2
OUTSIDE U.S. (TOTAL)	19	5	6	4	2	36	13	2	3	1	1	20	18	1	2	1	0	22	9	0	2	0	0	11

CHAPTER 6 - OWNERSHIP PATTERNS
SECTION 3 -- IN SPECIFIC INDUSTRIES, BY REGION AND ENTRY PERIOD
TABLE 6 --- THE PAPER INDUSTRY (SIC 26)

NO. OF SUBSIDIARIES MANUFACTURING IN THIS INDUSTRY AT TIME OF ENTRY INTO PARENT SYSTEM

PERIOD OF ENTRY AND PARENT OWNERSHIP AT ENTRY DATE

(WHL=WHOLLY OWNED,95-100% MA=MAJORITY,51-94% CO=50% MI=MINORITY,5-49% UN=UNKNOWN ALL=TOTAL FOR PERIOD)

REGION	1951-1966						1967-1969						1970-1972						1973-1975					
	WHL	MA	CO	MI	UN	ALL	WHL	MA	CO	MI	UN	ALL	WHL	MA	CO	MI	UN	ALL	WHL	MA	CO	MI	UN	ALL
CANADA	18	4	0	5	1	28	4	0	1	0	0	5	2	0	0	0	0	2	0	0	0	0	0	0
C.AM.+CARIB.	8	2	3	5	0	18	0	0	0	2	1	3	3	0	2	0	0	5	3	0	0	1	0	4
S.AMERICA	9	6	5	10	3	33	4	2	0	0	0	6	1	1	2	0	0	4	2	1	2	1	0	6
EUROPE	19	15	11	5	1	51	12	1	2	0	0	15	12	3	5	2	0	22	7	3	3	2	0	15
N.AFR+M.EAST	0	0	2	0	0	2	0	0	0	0	0	0	0	0	0	1	0	1	0	0	0	0	0	0
E.+W.AFRICA	1	0	1	1	0	3	0	0	0	2	0	2	0	0	0	0	0	0	0	0	0	0	0	0
SOUTH ASIA	0	1	0	0	0	1	0	0	0	0	0	0	0	0	0	0	0	0	0	0	0	0	0	0
EAST ASIA	2	3	3	2	1	11	0	1	2	1	0	4	2	0	0	0	0	2	0	0	1	0	0	1
S.DOMINIONS	27	0	4	7	0	38	4	2	3	0	1	10	0	0	0	2	0	2	0	0	0	0	0	0
OUTSIDE U.S.(TOTAL)	84	31	29	35	6	185	24	6	8	5	2	45	20	4	9	5	0	38	12	4	6	4	0	26

CHAPTER 6   - OWNERSHIP PATTERNS
SECTION 3   -- IN SPECIFIC INDUSTRIES, BY REGION AND ENTRY PERIOD
TABLE   7   --- THE PRINTING INDUSTRY (SIC 27)

NO. OF SUBSIDIARIES MANUFACTURING IN THIS INDUSTRY AT TIME OF ENTRY INTO PARENT SYSTEM

PERIOD OF ENTRY AND PARENT OWNERSHIP AT ENTRY DATE

(WHL=WHOLLY OWNED,95-100%   MA=MAJORITY,51-94%   CO=50%   MI=MINORITY,5-49%   UN=UNKNOWN   ALL=TOTAL FOR PERIOD)

REGION	1951-1966						1967-1969						1970-1972						1973-1975					
	WHL	MA	CO	MI	UN	ALL	WHL	MA	CO	MI	UN	ALL	WHL	MA	CO	MI	UN	ALL	WHL	MA	CO	MI	UN	ALL
CANADA	3	0	0	0	0	3	5	0	0	0	0	5	3	0	0	0	0	3	0	0	0	0	0	0
C.AM.+CARIB.	2	0	0	1	0	3	1	0	0	0	0	1	1	0	0	0	0	1	0	0	0	1	0	1
S.AMERICA	1	0	1	1	0	3	3	0	0	0	0	3	1	0	0	0	0	1	0	0	0	0	0	0
EUROPE	8	4	0	3	2	17	14	1	0	1	0	16	8	0	0	0	0	8	1	1	0	0	0	2
N.AFR+M.EAST	0	0	0	0	0	0	0	0	0	0	0	0	0	0	0	0	0	0	0	0	0	0	0	0
E.+W.AFRICA	0	0	0	0	0	0	0	0	0	1	0	1	0	0	0	0	0	0	0	0	0	0	0	0
SOUTH ASIA	0	0	0	0	0	0	0	0	0	0	0	0	0	0	0	0	0	0	0	0	0	0	0	0
EAST ASIA	1	0	1	0	0	2	0	0	0	0	0	0	1	0	0	0	0	1	1	0	1	0	0	2
S.DOMINIONS	4	0	1	0	0	5	4	0	0	0	0	4	0	0	0	0	0	0	0	0	0	0	0	0
OUTSIDE U.S.(TOTAL)	19	4	3	5	2	33	27	1	0	2	0	30	14	0	0	0	0	14	2	1	1	1	0	5

CHAPTER 6   - OWNERSHIP PATTERNS
SECTION 3   -- IN SPECIFIC INDUSTRIES, BY REGION AND ENTRY PERIOD
TABLE 8   --- THE INDUSTRIAL CHEMICALS INDUSTRY (SIC 281)

NO. OF SUBSIDIARIES MANUFACTURING IN THIS INDUSTRY AT TIME OF ENTRY INTO PARENT SYSTEM

PERIOD OF ENTRY AND PARENT OWNERSHIP AT ENTRY DATE

(WHL=WHOLLY OWNED,95-100%   MA=MAJORITY,51-94%   CO=50%   MI=MINORITY,5-49%   UN=UNKNOWN   ALL=TOTAL FOR PERIOD)

REGION	1951-1966						1967-1969						1970-1972						1973-1975					
	WHL	MA	CO	MI	UN	ALL	WHL	MA	CO	MI	UN	ALL	WHL	MA	CO	MI	UN	ALL	WHL	MA	CO	MI	UN	ALL
CANADA	18	2	2	1	2	25	6	0	0	0	1	7	1	0	0	1	0	2	1	0	1	0	0	2
C.AM.+CARIB.	15	4	2	12	3	36	2	1	0	1	0	4	2	0	0	2	0	4	3	1	0	3	0	7
S.AMERICA	13	7	5	3	5	33	4	0	2	1	0	7	1	0	1	0	0	2	1	0	1	1	0	3
EUROPE	35	20	27	10	4	96	14	2	6	3	0	25	24	3	5	2	0	34	10	0	2	4	0	16
N.AFR+M.EAST	2	0	0	3	0	5	1	0	0	0	0	1	0	0	0	0	0	0	0	1	1	0	0	2
E.+W.AFRICA	0	0	0	0	0	0	1	0	0	0	0	1	0	0	0	0	0	0	0	0	0	0	0	0
SOUTH ASIA	0	2	0	0	0	2	0	0	0	1	0	1	0	0	0	0	0	0	0	0	0	0	0	0
EAST ASIA	3	2	6	5	2	18	3	1	3	3	0	10	1	1	3	2	0	7	2	0	2	0	0	4
S.DOMINIONS	5	3	7	1	4	20	3	0	1	1	0	5	3	0	0	1	0	4	1	0	0	0	0	1
OUTSIDE U.S.(TOTAL)	91	40	49	35	20	235	34	4	12	10	1	61	32	4	9	8	0	53	18	2	6	9	0	35

CHAPTER 6   - OWNERSHIP PATTERNS
SECTION 3   -- IN SPECIFIC INDUSTRIES, BY REGION AND ENTRY PERIOD
TABLE 9   --- THE PLASTICS INDUSTRY (SIC 282)

NO. OF SUBSIDIARIES MANUFACTURING IN THIS INDUSTRY AT TIME OF ENTRY INTO PARENT SYSTEM

PERIOD OF ENTRY AND PARENT OWNERSHIP AT ENTRY DATE

WHL=WHOLLY OWNED,95-100%   MA=MAJORITY,51-94%   CO=50%   MI=MINORITY,5-49%   UN=UNKNOWN   ALL=TOTAL FOR PERIOD

REGION	1951-1966						1967-1969						1970-1972						1973-1975					
	WHL	MA	CO	MI	UN	ALL	WHL	MA	CO	MI	UN	ALL	WHL	MA	CO	MI	UN	ALL	WHL	MA	CO	MI	UN	ALL
CANADA	12	3	1	1	0	17	2	0	0	0	0	2	4	0	0	0	0	4	5	0	0	0	0	5
C.AM.+CARIB.	6	4	2	6	3	21	0	1	1	1	1	4	2	2	2	2	0	8	0	0	1	1	0	2
S.AMERICA	12	5	8	2	7	34	5	1	0	0	0	6	0	2	1	2	2	7	1	1	0	1	0	3
EUOPE	38	10	17	19	8	92	20	3	2	0	1	26	11	2	2	1	0	16	11	0	3	0	0	14
N.AFR+M.EAST	0	1	0	0	0	1	0	1	0	0	0	1	0	1	0	1	0	2	0	0	0	1	0	1
E.+W.AFRICA	1	0	0	0	1	2	0	0	0	0	0	0	0	0	0	0	0	0	1	0	0	0	0	1
SOUTH ASIA	0	1	0	2	1	4	0	0	0	0	0	0	0	0	0	0	0	0	0	0	0	0	0	0
EAST ASIA	4	1	9	8	1	23	0	0	4	0	1	5	2	1	2	1	0	6	3	0	3	4	1	11
S.DOMINIONS	9	7	3	3	3	25	4	1	0	0	0	5	3	0	1	1	0	5	0	0	1	0	0	1
OUTSIDE U.S.(TOTAL)	82	32	40	41	24	219	31	7	7	1	3	49	22	8	8	8	2	48	21	1	8	7	1	38

CHAPTER 6 - OWNERSHIP PATTERNS
SECTION 3 -- IN SPECIFIC INDUSTRIES, BY REGION AND ENTRY PERIOD
TABLE 10 --- THE AGRICULTURAL CHEMICALS INDUSTRY (SIC 287)

NO. OF SUBSIDIARIES MANUFACTURING IN THIS INDUSTRY AT TIME OF ENTRY INTO PARENT SYSTEM

PERIOD OF ENTRY AND PARENT OWNERSHIP AT ENTRY DATE

REGION	(WHL=WHOLLY OWNED,95-100%) 1951-1966						MA=MAJORITY,51-94% CO=50% 1967-1969						MI=MINORITY,5-49% UN=UNKNOWN 1970-1972						ALL=TOTAL FOR PERIOD 1973-1975					
	WHL	MA	CO	MI	UN	ALL	WHL	MA	CO	MI	UN	ALL	WHL	MA	CO	MI	UN	ALL	WHL	MA	CO	MI	UN	ALL
CANADA	2	0	1	0	0	3	2	0	0	0	0	2	0	0	0	0	0	0	1	0	0	0	0	1
C.AM.+CARIB.	2	1	1	4	0	8	3	0	0	0	0	3	3	0	0	1	0	4	1	0	1	1	0	3
S.AMERICA	3	2	4	0	3	12	3	0	0	0	0	3	2	0	0	0	0	2	2	0	0	0	0	2
EUROPE	3	8	2	3	1	17	4	0	0	0	1	5	1	0	1	0	0	2	1	0	0	0	0	1
N.AFR+M.EAST	1	1	0	1	0	3	0	0	0	0	0	0	0	0	0	0	0	0	0	0	0	0	0	0
E.+W.AFRICA	3	0	0	0	0	3	0	0	0	0	0	0	0	0	0	0	0	0	0	0	0	0	0	0
SOUTH ASIA	2	0	0	2	0	4	0	0	0	0	0	0	0	0	0	0	0	0	0	0	0	0	0	0
EAST ASIA	1	1	1	0	0	3	1	1	0	3	1	6	0	0	1	0	0	1	1	0	1	0	0	2
S.DOMINIONS	5	0	1	0	0	6	1	1	0	0	1	3	1	0	0	1	0	2	0	0	0	0	0	0
OUTSIDE U.S. (TOTAL)	22	13	10	10	4	59	14	2	0	3	3	22	7	0	2	2	0	11	6	0	2	1	0	9

CHAPTER 6 - OWNERSHIP PATTERNS
SECTION 3 -- IN SPECIFIC INDUSTRIES, BY REGION AND ENTRY PERIOD
TABLE 11 --- THE COSMETICS AND SOAP INDUSTRIES (SIC 284)

NO. OF SUBSIDIARIES MANUFACTURING IN THIS INDUSTRY AT TIME OF ENTRY INTO PARENT SYSTEM

PERIOD OF ENTRY AND PARENT OWNERSHIP AT ENTRY DATE

(WHL=WHOLLY OWNED,95-100% MA=MAJORITY,51-94% CO=50% MI=MINORITY,5-49% UN=UNKNOWN ALL=TOTAL FOR PERIOD)

REGION	1951-1966						1967-1969						1970-1972						1973-1975					
	WHL	MA	CO	MI	UN	ALL	WHL	MA	CO	MI	UN	ALL	WHL	MA	CO	MI	UN	ALL	WHL	MA	CO	MI	UN	ALL
CANADA	12	0	0	1	1	14	6	0	0	0	0	6	7	0	0	0	0	7	2	0	0	0	0	2
C.AM.+CARIB.	15	1	1	0	2	19	9	0	0	0	0	9	6	0	0	0	0	6	3	0	0	0	0	3
S.AMERICA	18	3	1	0	2	24	5	0	0	0	0	5	6	1	0	0	0	7	10	1	0	0	0	11
EUROPE	56	4	4	4	3	71	20	1	2	1	1	25	34	5	2	0	0	41	14	3	1	1	0	19
N.AFR+M.EAST	6	0	0	0	0	6	1	0	0	0	0	1	1	0	1	0	0	2	1	0	0	0	0	1
E.+W.AFRICA	3	0	0	0	0	3	2	2	0	0	0	4	1	0	0	0	0	1	1	0	0	0	0	1
SOUTH ASIA	1	2	0	1	0	4	2	0	0	0	0	2	0	0	0	0	0	0	0	0	0	0	0	0
EAST ASIA	9	0	2	0	1	12	4	2	1	0	0	7	2	1	0	1	0	4	2	1	1	1	0	5
S.DOMINIONS	15	0	2	0	1	18	6	0	0	0	0	6	10	1	0	0	0	11	6	0	0	0	0	6
OUTSIDE U.S. (TOTAL)	135	10	10	6	10	171	55	5	3	1	1	65	67	8	3	1	0	79	39	5	2	2	0	48

CHAPTER 6 - OWNERSHIP PATTERNS
SECTION 3 -- IN SPECIFIC INDUSTRIES, BY REGION AND ENTRY PERIOD
TABLE 12 --- THE DRUGS INDUSTRY (SIC 283)

NO. OF SUBSIDIARIES MANUFACTURING IN THIS INDUSTRY AT TIME OF ENTRY INTO PARENT SYSTEM

PERIOD OF ENTRY AND PARENT OWNERSHIP AT ENTRY DATE

WHL=WHOLLY OWNED,95-100% MA=MAJORITY,51-94% CO=50% MI=MINORITY,5-49% UN=UNKNOWN ALL=TOTAL FOR PERIOD

REGION	1951-1966						1967-1969						1970-1972						1973-1975					
	WHL	MA	CO	MI	UN	ALL	WHL	MA	CO	MI	UN	ALL	WHL	MA	CO	MI	UN	ALL	WHL	MA	CO	MI	UN	ALL
CANADA	15	2	0	1	3	21	9	0	0	0	0	9	1	0	0	0	0	1	0	0	0	0	0	0
C.AM.+CARIB.	26	0	2	0	1	29	9	3	0	0	1	13	3	1	0	0	0	4	0	0	0	0	0	0
S.AMERICA	38	7	2	1	4	52	13	1	1	0	1	16	9	1	0	0	0	10	8	2	0	0	0	10
EUROPE	73	13	4	6	5	101	51	4	1	3	3	62	23	4	0	1	0	28	16	3	1	1	0	21
N.AFR+M.EAST	4	1	2	0	0	7	4	1	0	1	0	6	0	0	0	0	0	0	0	0	2	0	0	2
E.+W.AFRICA	3	0	0	0	0	3	1	0	0	0	0	1	4	0	0	0	0	4	3	0	0	0	0	3
SOUTH ASIA	6	8	2	3	0	19	2	1	0	2	0	5	1	0	0	0	0	1	1	1	0	0	0	2
EAST ASIA	10	5	5	0	2	22	11	0	3	0	1	15	4	4	3	0	1	12	3	0	1	0	0	4
S.DOMINIONS	24	4	3	0	0	31	10	1	0	0	1	12	6	1	0	0	0	7	1	0	0	0	0	1
OUTSIDE U.S.(TOTAL)	199	40	20	11	15	285	110	11	5	6	7	139	51	11	3	1	1	67	32	6	2	3	0	43

CHAPTER   6   - OWNERSHIP PATTERNS
SECTION   3   -- IN SPECIFIC INDUSTRIES, BY REGION AND ENTRY PERIOD
TABLE 13 --- OTHER CHEMICAL INDUSTRIES (OTHER SIC 28)

NO. OF SUBSIDIARIES MANUFACTURING IN THIS INDUSTRY AT TIME OF ENTRY INTO PARENT SYSTEM

PERIOD OF ENTRY AND PARENT OWNERSHIP AT ENTRY DATE

(WHL=WHOLLY OWNED,95-100%   MA=MAJORITY,51-94%   CO=50%   MI=MINORITY,5-49%   UN=UNKNOWN   ALL=TOTAL FOR PERIOD)

REGION	1951-1966						1967-1969						1970-1972						1973-1975					
	WHL	MA	CO	MI	UN	ALL	WHL	MA	CO	MI	UN	ALL	WHL	MA	CO	MI	UN	ALL	WHL	MA	CO	MI	UN	ALL
CANADA	10	0	0	2	1	13	9	0	0	0	0	9	5	0	2	0	0	7	6	0	0	0	0	6
C.AM.+CARIB.	7	2	1	4	0	14	1	1	2	0	0	4	3	1	0	6	0	10	0	0	0	0	0	0
S.AMERICA	14	5	1	3	0	23	4	2	0	2	0	8	0	5	2	0	0	7	7	1	2	4	0	14
EUROPE	32	13	10	8	2	65	18	5	6	3	1	33	21	4	6	0	0	31	21	5	4	2	0	32
N.AFR+M.EAST	1	0	0	0	0	1	1	1	0	0	0	2	0	1	0	0	0	1	0	0	2	0	0	2
E.+W.AFRICA	0	0	0	0	0	0	0	0	0	0	0	0	0	0	0	0	0	0	0	0	0	0	0	0
SOUTH ASIA	0	0	0	1	0	1	0	0	0	0	0	0	0	0	0	0	0	0	0	0	0	2	0	2
EAST ASIA	2	3	2	6	0	13	1	1	2	1	0	5	4	1	4	2	0	11	2	0	0	1	0	3
S.DOMINIONS	3	2	0	4	0	9	6	0	2	1	0	9	6	1	0	2	0	9	4	0	1	2	0	7
OUTSIDE U.S.(TOTAL)	69	25	14	28	3	139	40	10	12	7	1	70	39	13	14	10	0	76	40	6	9	11	0	66

CHAPTER 6 - OWNERSHIP PATTERNS
SECTION 3 -- IN SPECIFIC INDUSTRIES, BY REGION AND ENTRY PERIOD
TABLE 14 --- FABRICATED PLASTICS INDUSTRIES (SIC 306 AND 307)

NO. OF SUBSIDIARIES MANUFACTURING IN THIS INDUSTRY AT TIME OF ENTRY INTO PARENT SYSTEM

PERIOD OF ENTRY AND PARENT OWNERSHIP AT ENTRY DATE

(WHL=WHOLLY OWNED,95-100%   MA=MAJORITY,51-94%   CO=50%   MI=MINORITY,5-49%   UN=UNKNOWN   ALL=TOTAL FOR PERIOD)

REGION	1951-1966						1967-1969						1970-1972						1973-1975					
	WHL	MA	CO	MI	UN	ALL	WHL	MA	CO	MI	UN	ALL	WHL	MA	CO	MI	UN	ALL	WHL	MA	CO	MI	UN	ALL
CANADA	7	0	0	0	1	8	4	0	0	1	0	5	3	1	1	0	0	5	4	0	0	0	1	5
C.AM.+CARIB.	2	0	3	2	0	7	2	0	0	0	0	2	3	0	0	1	0	4	0	0	0	0	0	0
S.AMERICA	1	0	0	4	1	6	3	0	2	0	0	5	1	1	0	1	0	3	1	1	1	0	0	3
EUROPE	11	1	8	5	0	25	13	4	2	1	0	20	22	1	2	1	0	26	13	1	1	0	0	15
N.AFR+M.EAST	0	2	0	0	0	2	0	0	0	0	0	0	0	0	0	0	0	0	0	0	0	0	0	0
E.+W.AFRICA	0	0	1	0	0	1	1	1	0	0	0	2	0	0	0	0	0	0	1	0	0	1	0	2
SOUTH ASIA	0	1	0	0	0	1	0	0	0	0	0	0	0	0	1	0	0	1	0	0	0	0	0	0
EAST ASIA	1	0	1	0	2	4	1	0	0	3	0	4	1	1	3	0	0	5	0	0	0	0	0	0
S.DOMINIONS	2	2	0	0	0	4	3	1	0	0	0	4	4	0	0	1	0	5	2	1	0	0	0	3
OUTSIDE U.S.(TOTAL)	24	6	13	11	4	58	27	6	4	5	0	42	34	4	7	4	0	49	21	3	1	2	1	28

CHAPTER 6 - OWNERSHIP PATTERNS
SECTION 3 -- IN SPECIFIC INDUSTRIES, BY REGION AND ENTRY PERIOD
TABLE 15 --- THE TIRES INDUSTRY (SIC 301)

NO. OF SUBSIDIARIES MANUFACTURING IN THIS INDUSTRY AT TIME OF ENTRY INTO PARENT SYSTEM

PERIOD OF ENTRY AND PARENT OWNERSHIP AT ENTRY DATE

WHL=WHOLLY OWNED,95-100% MA=MAJORITY,51-94% CO=50% MI=MINORITY,5-49% UN=UNKNOWN ALL=TOTAL FOR PERIOD

REGION	1951-1966 WHL	MA	CO	MI	UN	ALL	1967-1969 WHL	MA	CO	MI	UN	ALL	1970-1972 WHL	MA	CO	MI	UN	ALL	1973-1975 WHL	MA	CO	MI	UN	ALL
CANADA	1	0	0	0	0	1	1	0	0	0	0	1	0	0	0	0	0	0	0	0	0	0	0	0
C.AM.+CARIB.	1	0	0	1	3	5	0	0	0	0	0	0	0	0	0	0	0	0	0	0	0	0	0	0
S.AMERICA	2	0	0	2	1	5	0	0	0	0	0	0	0	0	0	0	0	0	1	1	0	0	0	2
EUROPE	5	3	0	2	5	15	0	0	0	0	0	0	4	0	0	0	0	4	0	0	0	0	0	0
N.AFR+M.EAST	0	2	0	0	2	4	0	0	0	0	0	0	0	1	0	0	0	1	0	0	0	1	0	1
E.+W.AFRICA	1	0	0	0	0	1	0	2	0	1	0	3	1	0	0	0	0	1	0	0	0	0	0	0
SOUTH ASIA	0	1	0	0	0	1	0	0	0	0	0	0	0	0	0	0	0	0	0	0	0	0	0	0
EAST ASIA	0	1	0	1	0	2	0	2	0	0	0	2	0	1	0	0	0	1	0	0	0	0	0	0
S.DOMINIONS	0	1	0	1	1	3	0	0	0	0	0	0	0	0	0	0	0	0	0	0	0	0	0	0
OUTSIDE U.S.(TOTAL)	10	8	0	7	12	37	1	4	0	1	0	6	5	2	0	0	0	7	1	1	0	1	0	3

CHAPTER 6 — OWNERSHIP PATTERNS
SECTION 3 -- IN SPECIFIC INDUSTRIES, BY REGION AND ENTRY PERIOD
TABLE 16 --- THE PETROLEUM REFINING INDUSTRY (SIC 291)

NO. OF SUBSIDIARIES MANUFACTURING IN THIS INDUSTRY AT TIME OF ENTRY INTO PARENT SYSTEM

PERIOD OF ENTRY AND PARENT OWNERSHIP AT ENTRY DATE

(WHL=WHOLLY OWNED,95-100% MA=MAJORITY,51-94% CO=50% MI=MINORITY,5-49% UN=UNKNOWN ALL=TOTAL FOR PERIOD)

REGION	1951-1966						1967-1969						1970-1972						1973-1975					
	WHL	MA	CO	MI	UN	ALL	WHL	MA	CO	MI	UN	ALL	WHL	MA	CO	MI	UN	ALL	WHL	MA	CO	MI	UN	ALL
CANADA	1	3	0	1	0	5	1	0	0	0	0	1	0	0	0	0	0	0	1	0	0	0	0	1
C.AM.+CARIB.	3	1	0	0	0	4	2	1	1	2	0	5	1	0	0	2	0	3	1	0	0	1	0	2
S.AMERICA	4	0	1	1	0	6	0	0	1	1	0	2	1	0	0	0	0	1	0	0	0	0	0	0
EUROPE	20	5	5	5	5	40	5	0	2	6	0	13	6	0	1	1	0	8	2	0	1	4	0	7
N.AFR+M.EAST	1	0	2	1	2	6	0	0	0	0	0	0	0	0	0	0	0	0	0	0	1	1	0	2
E.+W.AFRICA	1	0	0	4	0	5	0	0	0	2	0	2	0	0	0	3	0	3	0	0	0	0	0	0
SOUTH ASIA	0	0	0	3	0	3	0	0	0	0	0	0	0	0	0	0	0	0	0	0	0	0	0	0
EAST ASIA	3	1	4	3	0	11	4	0	2	1	0	7	0	1	2	1	0	4	0	0	0	0	0	0
S.DOMINIONS	3	2	1	0	0	6	0	0	1	3	0	4	0	0	0	1	0	1	0	0	0	0	0	0
OUTSIDE U.S.(TOTAL)	36	12	13	18	7	86	12	1	6	15	0	34	8	1	3	8	0	20	4	0	2	6	0	12

CHAPTER 6 - OWNERSHIP PATTERNS
SECTION 3 -- IN SPECIFIC INDUSTRIES, BY REGION AND ENTRY PERIOD
TABLE 17 --- OTHER PETROLEUM INDUSTRIES (OTHER SIC 29)

NO. OF SUBSIDIARIES MANUFACTURING IN THIS INDUSTRY AT TIME OF ENTRY INTO PARENT SYSTEM

PERIOD OF ENTRY AND PARENT OWNERSHIP AT ENTRY DATE

(WHL=WHOLLY OWNED,95-100% MA=MAJORITY,51-94% CO=50% MI=MINORITY,5-49% UN=UNKNOWN ALL=TOTAL FOR PERIOD)

REGION	1951-1966						1967-1969						1970-1972						1973-1975					
	WHL	MA	CO	MI	UN	ALL	WHL	MA	CO	MI	UN	ALL	WHL	MA	CO	MI	UN	ALL	WHL	MA	CO	MI	UN	ALL
CANADA	4	2	0	0	0	6	0	0	0	0	0	0	0	0	0	0	0	0	1	0	0	0	0	1
C.AM.+CARIB.	1	0	0	2	0	3	0	0	0	0	0	0	2	0	0	0	0	2	0	0	0	1	0	1
S.AMERICA	6	1	0	1	2	10	0	0	0	1	0	1	1	0	0	0	0	1	0	0	0	0	0	0
EUROPE	11	1	12	3	1	28	0	0	2	0	0	2	2	0	2	2	0	6	0	2	1	0	0	3
N.AFR+M.EAST	0	0	0	0	0	0	1	0	1	1	0	3	0	0	0	0	0	0	0	0	0	0	0	0
E.+W.AFRICA	1	0	0	0	0	1	0	1	0	0	0	1	0	0	1	1	0	2	0	0	0	0	0	0
SOUTH ASIA	0	0	2	1	0	3	0	0	0	0	0	0	0	0	0	0	0	0	0	0	0	0	0	0
EAST ASIA	0	1	1	4	0	6	3	0	0	3	0	6	1	0	0	0	0	1	0	0	0	0	0	0
S.DCMINIONS	1	0	3	0	0	4	2	0	1	0	0	3	0	0	0	0	0	0	1	0	0	0	0	1
OUTSIDE U.S.(TOTAL)	24	5	18	11	3	61	6	1	4	5	0	16	6	0	3	3	0	12	2	2	1	1	0	6

CHAPTER 6   - OWNERSHIP PATTERNS
SECTION 3   -- IN SPECIFIC INDUSTRIES, BY REGION AND ENTRY PERIOD
TABLE 18   ---- THE LEATHER INDUSTRY (SIC 31)

NO. OF SUBSIDIARIES MANUFACTURING IN THIS INDUSTRY AT TIME OF ENTRY INTO PARENT SYSTEM

PERIOD OF ENTRY AND PARENT OWNERSHIP AT ENTRY DATE

(WHL=WHOLLY OWNED,95-100%   MA=MAJORITY,51-94%   CO=50%   MI=MINORITY,5-49%   UN=UNKNOWN   ALL=TOTAL FOR PERIOD)

REGION	1951-1966						1967-1969						1970-1972						1973-1975					
	WHL	MA	CO	MI	UN	ALL	WHL	MA	CO	MI	UN	ALL	WHL	MA	CO	MI	UN	ALL	WHL	MA	CO	MI	UN	ALL
CANADA	2	0	0	0	0	2	1	0	0	0	0	1	0	0	0	0	0	0	2	0	0	0	0	2
C.AM.+CARIB.	0	0	0	0	0	0	0	0	0	0	0	0	0	0	0	0	0	0	0	0	1	0	0	1
S.AMERICA	0	0	0	0	0	0	0	0	0	0	0	0	0	0	0	0	0	0	0	0	0	0	0	0
EUROPE	5	1	1	1	1	9	2	0	1	1	0	4	1	0	0	0	0	1	1	0	0	0	0	1
N.AFR+M.EAST	0	0	0	0	0	0	0	0	0	0	0	0	1	0	0	0	0	1	0	0	0	0	0	0
E.+W.AFRICA	0	0	1	0	0	1	0	0	0	0	0	0	0	0	0	0	0	0	0	0	0	0	0	0
SOUTH ASIA	0	0	0	0	0	0	0	0	0	0	0	0	0	0	0	0	0	0	0	0	0	0	0	0
EAST ASIA	0	0	0	0	0	0	0	0	0	0	0	0	0	0	0	0	0	0	0	0	0	0	0	0
S.DOMINIONS	1	0	0	0	0	1	0	0	0	0	0	0	0	0	0	0	0	0	0	0	0	1	0	1
OUTSIDE U.S.(TOTAL)	8	1	2	1	1	13	3	0	1	1	0	5	2	0	0	0	0	2	3	0	1	1	0	5

CHAPTER 6 - OWNERSHIP PATTERNS
SECTION 3 -- IN SPECIFIC INDUSTRIES, BY REGION AND ENTRY PERIOD
TABLE 19 --- STONE,CLAY AND CEMENT INDUSTRIES (SIC 324 TO 328)

NO. OF SUBSIDIARIES MANUFACTURING IN THIS INDUSTRY AT TIME OF ENTRY INTO PARENT SYSTEM

PERIOD OF ENTRY AND PARENT OWNERSHIP AT ENTRY DATE

(WHL=WHOLLY OWNED,95-100%   MA=MAJORITY,51-94%   CO=50%   MI=MINORITY,5-49%   UN=UNKNOWN   ALL=TOTAL FOR PERIOD)

REGION	1951-1966						1967-1969						1970-1972						1973-1975					
	WHL	MA	CO	MI	UN	ALL	WHL	MA	CO	MI	UN	ALL	WHL	MA	CO	MI	UN	ALL	WHL	MA	CO	MI	UN	ALL
CANADA	3	0	0	0	0	3	1	0	0	0	0	1	0	0	0	0	0	0	4	0	0	0	0	4
C.AM.+CARIB.	2	2	0	0	0	4	0	1	1	0	0	2	0	0	0	0	0	0	0	1	0	0	0	1
S.AMERICA	0	1	0	2	3	6	4	0	0	1	0	5	0	0	0	1	0	1	0	0	0	0	0	0
EUROPE	7	0	0	1	2	10	6	1	0	1	2	10	7	1	3	0	0	11	1	0	1	1	0	3
N.AFR+M.EAST	0	0	0	0	0	0	0	0	0	0	0	0	0	0	0	0	0	0	0	0	0	1	0	1
E.+W.AFRICA	0	0	0	0	0	0	0	0	0	0	0	0	0	0	0	0	0	0	0	0	0	0	0	0
SOUTH ASIA	0	0	0	2	0	2	0	0	0	0	0	0	0	0	1	0	0	1	0	0	0	0	0	0
EAST ASIA	0	0	0	2	0	2	0	1	0	0	0	1	0	0	0	0	0	0	1	0	0	0	0	1
S.DOMINIONS	3	0	1	0	0	4	0	0	0	0	0	0	1	0	0	0	0	1	0	0	0	0	0	0
OUTSIDE U.S.(TOTAL)	15	3	1	7	5	31	11	3	1	2	2	19	8	1	4	1	0	14	6	1	2	2	0	10

CHAPTER 6   - OWNERSHIP PATTERNS
SECTION 3   -- IN SPECIFIC INDUSTRIES, BY REGION AND ENTRY PERIOD
TABLE 20 --- ABRASIVES AND ASBESTOS INDUSTRIES (SIC 329)

NO. OF SUBSIDIARIES MANUFACTURING IN THIS INDUSTRY AT TIME OF ENTRY INTO PARENT SYSTEM

PERIOD OF ENTRY AND PARENT OWNERSHIP AT ENTRY DATE

(WHL=WHOLLY OWNED, 95-100%   MA=MAJORITY, 51-94%   CO=50%   MI=MINORITY, 5-49%   UN=UNKNOWN   ALL=TOTAL FOR PERIOD)

REGION	1951-1966						1967-1969						1970-1972						1973-1975					
	WHL	MA	CO	MI	UN	ALL	WHL	MA	CO	MI	UN	ALL	WHL	MA	CO	MI	UN	ALL	WHL	MA	CO	MI	UN	ALL
CANADA	4	0	0	0	0	4	3	0	0	0	1	4	4	0	0	0	0	4	0	0	0	0	0	0
C.AM.+CARIB.	3	0	1	2	0	6	0	0	0	1	0	1	1	0	1	0	0	2	0	0	0	0	0	0
S.AMERICA	4	1	1	3	0	9	2	1	0	1	0	4	5	1	0	0	0	6	3	0	0	0	0	3
EUROPE	18	4	2	4	1	29	7	3	1	2	0	13	12	4	5	3	0	24	6	0	2	1	1	10
N.AFR+M.EAST	0	1	0	1	0	2	0	0	0	0	0	0	0	0	0	0	0	0	0	0	0	0	0	0
E.+W.AFRICA	0	0	0	1	0	1	0	0	0	0	0	0	0	0	0	0	0	0	0	0	0	0	0	0
SOUTH ASIA	0	0	0	1	0	1	0	0	0	0	0	0	0	0	1	0	0	1	0	0	0	0	0	0
EAST ASIA	0	0	0	5	0	5	0	0	0	1	0	1	1	0	2	2	0	5	0	0	1	0	0	1
S.DOMINIONS	1	2	1	0	0	4	1	2	1	0	0	4	1	0	2	1	0	2	1	0	1	1	0	3
OUTSIDE U.S. (TOTAL)	30	8	5	17	1	61	13	6	2	5	1	27	24	5	9	6	0	44	10	0	4	2	1	17

CHAPTER   6   - OWNERSHIP PATTERNS
SECTION   3   -- IN SPECIFIC INDUSTRIES, BY REGION AND ENTRY PERIOD
TABLE 21 --- THE GLASS INDUSTRY (SIC 321 TO 323)

NO. OF SUBSIDIARIES MANUFACTURING IN THIS INDUSTRY AT TIME OF ENTRY INTO PARENT SYSTEM

PERIOD OF ENTRY AND PARENT OWNERSHIP AT ENTRY DATE

REGION	(WHL=WHOLLY OWNED,95-100%						MA=MAJORITY,51-94%						CO=50%						MI=MINORITY,5-49%						UN=UNKNOWN						ALL=TOTAL FOR PERIOD)					
	1951-1966						1967-1969						1970-1972						1973-1975																		
	WHL	MA	CO	MI	UN	ALL	WHL	MA	CO	MI	UN	ALL	WHL	MA	CO	MI	UN	ALL	WHL	MA	CO	MI	UN	ALL
CANADA	1	0	0	0	0	1	2	0	0	0	0	2	0	0	0	0	0	0	1	0	1	0	0	2
C.AM.+CARIB.	1	0	0	1	0	2	1	0	3	0	0	4	0	0	0	0	0	0	0	0	0	0	0	0
S.AMERICA	4	3	1	2	0	10	1	0	0	0	0	1	3	1	0	0	0	4	1	1	0	0	0	2
EUROPE	5	4	2	2	0	13	2	2	3	1	0	8	4	1	0	2	0	7	1	2	0	0	0	3
N.AFR+M.EAST	0	0	0	0	0	0	0	0	0	0	0	0	0	0	0	0	0	0	0	0	0	0	0	0
E.+W.AFRICA	0	0	0	0	0	0	0	0	0	0	0	0	0	0	0	0	0	0	0	0	0	0	0	0
SOUTH ASIA	0	0	0	2	0	2	0	0	0	1	0	1	0	0	0	0	0	0	0	0	0	0	0	0
EAST ASIA	0	0	1	2	0	3	0	0	0	0	0	0	0	0	0	1	0	1	1	0	1	1	0	3
S.DOMINIONS	1	0	2	1	0	4	0	0	0	0	0	0	1	0	1	1	0	3	0	0	0	0	0	0
OUTSIDE U.S.(TOTAL)	12	7	6	9	1	35	6	2	6	2	0	16	8	2	1	4	0	15	4	3	2	1	0	10

CHAPTER 6 - OWNERSHIP PATTERNS
SECTION 3 -- IN SPECIFIC INDUSTRIES, BY REGION AND ENTRY PERIOD
TABLE 22 --- THE IRON AND STEEL INDUSTRY (SIC 331 AND 332)

NO. OF SUBSIDIARIES MANUFACTURING IN THIS INDUSTRY AT TIME OF ENTRY INTO PARENT SYSTEM

PERIOD OF ENTRY AND PARENT OWNERSHIP AT ENTRY DATE

(WHL=WHOLLY OWNED,95-100% MA=MAJORITY,51-94% CO=50% MI=MINORITY,5-49% UN=UNKNOWN ALL=TOTAL FOR PERIOD)

REGION	1951-1966 WHL	MA	CO	MI	UN	ALL	1967-1969 WHL	MA	CO	MI	UN	ALL	1970-1972 WHL	MA	CO	MI	UN	ALL	1973-1975 WHL	MA	CO	MI	UN	ALL
CANADA	2	0	0	0	0	2	2	0	0	0	0	2	2	0	0	0	0	2	1	1	0	0	0	2
C.AM.+CARIB.	0	0	0	0	0	0	0	0	0	0	0	0	0	0	0	0	0	0	0	0	0	1	0	1
S.AMERICA	0	0	2	2	0	4	4	1	0	0	0	5	1	1	0	0	0	2	0	0	0	1	0	1
EUROPE	2	2	1	0	1	6	6	3	2	1	1	13	3	3	1	0	0	7	5	1	1	2	0	9
N.AFR+M.EAST	0	0	0	0	0	0	0	0	0	0	0	0	0	0	0	0	0	0	0	0	0	1	0	1
E.+W.AFRICA	0	0	0	1	0	1	0	0	0	0	0	0	0	0	0	0	0	0	0	0	0	0	0	0
SOUTH ASIA	0	0	0	0	0	0	0	0	0	0	0	0	0	0	0	0	0	0	0	1	0	1	0	2
EAST ASIA	0	0	0	0	0	0	0	1	0	0	0	1	0	0	0	1	0	1	0	0	0	0	0	0
S.DOMINIONS	1	0	0	0	0	1	2	0	0	0	0	2	0	0	0	1	0	1	0	0	0	1	0	1
OUTSIDE U.S.(TOTAL)	5	2	3	3	1	14	14	5	2	1	1	23	6	4	1	2	0	13	6	3	1	7	0	17

CHAPTER 6   - OWNERSHIP PATTERNS
SECTION 3   -- IN SPECIFIC INDUSTRIES, BY REGION AND ENTRY PERIOD
TABLE   23   --- NON-FERROUS METAL INDUSTRIES (OTHER SIC 33)

NO. OF SUBSIDIARIES MANUFACTURING IN THIS INDUSTRY AT TIME OF ENTRY INTO PARENT SYSTEM

PERIOD OF ENTRY AND PARENT OWNERSHIP AT ENTRY DATE

(WHL=WHOLLY OWNED,95-100%)   MA=MAJORITY,51-94%   CO=50%   MI=MINORITY,5-49%   UN=UNKNOWN   ALL=TOTAL FOR PERIOD

REGION	1951-1966						1967-1969						1970-1972						1973-1975					
	WHL	MA	CO	MI	UN	ALL	WHL	MA	CO	MI	UN	ALL	WHL	MA	CO	MI	UN	ALL	WHL	MA	CO	MI	UN	ALL
CANADA	11	1	2	1	1	16	3	1	0	0	1	5	3	0	0	0	0	3	1	0	0	0	0	1
C.AM.+CARIB.	0	2	0	3	0	5	0	0	0	1	0	1	0	0	0	0	0	0	0	0	0	2	0	2
S.AMERICA	3	4	1	5	0	13	4	0	0	3	0	7	0	1	0	0	0	1	1	0	1	0	0	2
EUROPE	18	3	10	4	0	35	14	4	3	5	1	27	13	1	2	2	0	18	6	0	0	1	0	7
N.AFR+M.EAST	0	0	1	1	0	2	0	0	0	2	0	2	0	0	0	0	0	0	0	0	0	1	0	1
E.+W.AFRICA	0	2	0	0	0	2	1	0	0	1	0	3	2	0	0	1	0	3	0	0	0	0	0	0
SOUTH ASIA	1	0	0	1	0	2	0	0	0	0	0	0	0	0	1	0	0	1	0	0	0	0	0	0
EAST ASIA	0	1	0	5	1	7	0	1	2	2	0	5	3	1	1	3	0	8	0	0	1	3	0	4
S.DOMINIONS	3	5	2	0	3	13	6	0	2	1	0	9	1	0	2	1	0	4	1	0	0	0	0	1
OUTSIDE U.S.(TOTAL)	36	18	16	20	5	95	28	6	7	15	2	58	22	3	6	7	0	38	9	0	1	8	0	18

CHAPTER 6 - OWNERSHIP PATTERNS
SECTION 3 -- IN SPECIFIC INDUSTRIES, BY REGION AND ENTRY PERIOD
TABLE 24 --- THE METAL CANS INDUSTRY (SIC 341)

NO. OF SUBSIDIARIES MANUFACTURING IN THIS INDUSTRY AT TIME OF ENTRY INTO PARENT SYSTEM

PERIOD OF ENTRY AND PARENT OWNERSHIP AT ENTRY DATE

(WHL=WHOLLY OWNED,95-100% MA=MAJORITY,51-94% CO=50% MI=MINORITY,5-49% UN=UNKNOWN ALL=TOTAL FOR PERIOD)

REGION	1951-1966						1967-1969						1970-1972						1973-1975					
	WHL	MA	CO	MI	UN	ALL	WHL	MA	CO	MI	UN	ALL	WHL	MA	CO	MI	UN	ALL	WHL	MA	CO	MI	UN	ALL
CANADA	3	1	1	1	1	7	1	0	0	0	0	1	0	0	0	0	0	0	1	0	0	0	0	1
C.AM.+CARIB.	3	3	0	0	2	8	2	0	0	0	0	2	0	0	0	0	0	0	0	0	0	1	0	1
S.AMERICA	3	1	0	2	0	6	0	1	0	1	0	2	0	0	0	0	0	0	1	0	0	1	0	2
EUROPE	0	0	0	4	0	4	5	1	1	1	0	8	1	0	0	0	0	1	0	0	0	0	0	0
N.AFR+M.EAST	0	0	0	1	0	1	0	0	0	0	0	0	0	0	0	0	0	0	0	0	0	0	0	0
E.+W.AFRICA	1	0	0	0	0	1	1	0	0	0	0	1	2	0	0	0	0	2	0	0	0	0	0	0
SOUTH ASIA	0	0	0	0	0	0	0	0	0	0	0	0	0	0	0	0	0	0	0	0	0	0	0	0
EAST ASIA	0	1	0	1	1	3	0	1	0	1	0	2	0	0	0	0	0	0	0	0	0	0	0	0
S.DOMINIONS	2	0	0	0	0	2	1	0	0	0	0	1	1	0	0	0	0	1	0	0	0	0	0	0
OUTSIDE U.S.(TOTAL)	12	6	1	9	4	32	10	3	1	3	0	17	4	0	0	0	0	4	2	0	0	2	0	4

CHAPTER 6   - OWNERSHIP PATTERNS
SECTION 3   -- IN SPECIFIC INDUSTRIES, BY REGION AND ENTRY PERIOD
TABLE 25   --- OTHER FABRICATED METAL INDUSTRIES (OTHER SIC 34)

NO. OF SUBSIDIARIES MANUFACTURING IN THIS INDUSTRY AT TIME OF ENTRY INTO PARENT SYSTEM

PERIOD OF ENTRY AND PARENT OWNERSHIP AT ENTRY DATE

(WHL=WHOLLY OWNED,95-100%   MA=MAJORITY,51-94%   CO=50%   MI=MINORITY,5-49%   UN=UNKNOWN   ALL=TOTAL FOR PERIOD)

REGION	1951-1966						1967-1969						1970-1972						1973-1975					
	WHL	MA	CO	MI	UN	ALL	WHL	MA	CO	MI	UN	ALL	WHL	MA	CO	MI	UN	ALL	WHL	MA	CO	MI	UN	ALL
CANADA	27	1	3	1	2	34	18	0	0	0	0	18	9	0	0	0	0	9	11	0	0	0	1	12
C.AM.+CARIB.	8	2	1	5	0	16	1	0	0	1	2	4	3	1	1	0	0	5	0	0	0	1	0	1
S.AMERICA	5	1	0	7	1	14	4	3	2	0	0	9	2	1	0	1	0	4	1	2	1	5	0	9
EUROPE	43	9	9	6	10	77	33	2	4	7	1	47	36	3	1	7	0	47	24	1	2	7	0	34
N.AFR+M.EAST	0	0	0	1	0	1	0	0	0	0	0	0	0	1	0	1	0	2	0	0	0	0	0	0
E.+W.AFRICA	1	0	0	0	0	1	1	0	0	0	0	1	2	0	0	0	0	2	0	0	0	0	0	0
SOUTH ASIA	1	2	0	1	0	4	0	0	0	0	0	0	0	0	1	0	0	1	0	1	0	2	0	3
EAST ASIA	0	1	0	3	1	5	3	2	3	2	0	10	5	0	2	0	0	7	2	1	2	1	0	6
S.DOMINIONS	5	0	1	2	3	11	14	3	2	2	0	21	8	2	2	1	0	13	3	0	0	0	0	3
OUTSIDE U.S.(TOTAL)	90	16	14	26	17	163	74	10	11	12	3	110	65	8	7	10	0	90	41	5	5	16	1	68

CHAPTER 6 - OWNERSHIP PATTERNS
SECTION 3 -- IN SPECIFIC INDUSTRIES, BY REGION AND ENTRY PERIOD
TABLE 26 --- THE ENGINES AND TURBINES INDUSTRY (SIC 351)

NO. OF SUBSIDIARIES MANUFACTURING IN THIS INDUSTRY AT TIME OF ENTRY INTO PARENT SYSTEM

PERIOD OF ENTRY AND PARENT OWNERSHIP AT ENTRY DATE

(WHL=WHOLLY OWNED,95-100% MA=MAJORITY,51-94% CO=50% MI=MINORITY,5-49% UN=UNKNOWN ALL=TOTAL FOR PERIOD)

REGION	1951-1966						1967-1969						1970-1972						1973-1975					
	WHL	MA	CO	MI	UN	ALL	WHL	MA	CO	MI	UN	ALL	WHL	MA	CO	MI	UN	ALL	WHL	MA	CO	MI	UN	ALL
CANADA	5	0	1	0	0	6	0	0	0	0	0	0	0	0	0	0	0	0	0	0	0	0	0	0
C.AM.+CARIB.	0	1	0	0	0	1	0	0	0	0	0	0	0	0	0	0	0	0	0	0	0	0	0	0
S.AMERICA	0	2	0	0	0	2	2	0	0	0	0	2	0	0	0	0	0	0	0	0	0	0	0	0
EUROPE	10	1	2	3	2	18	7	0	0	0	0	7	1	1	0	1	0	3	2	0	1	1	0	4
N.AFR+M.EAST	0	0	0	0	0	0	0	0	0	0	0	0	0	0	0	0	0	0	0	0	0	0	0	0
E.+W.AFRICA	0	0	0	0	0	0	0	0	0	0	0	0	0	0	0	0	0	0	0	0	0	0	0	0
SOUTH ASIA	0	0	0	0	0	0	0	0	0	0	0	0	0	0	0	0	0	0	0	0	0	0	0	0
EAST ASIA	0	1	0	0	0	1	0	0	0	1	0	1	2	0	0	0	0	2	0	0	1	1	0	2
S.DOMINIONS	1	0	0	0	0	1	0	0	0	1	0	1	0	0	0	0	0	0	0	0	0	0	0	0
OUTSIDE U.S. (TOTAL)	16	5	3	3	2	29	9	0	0	2	0	11	3	1	0	1	0	5	2	0	2	2	0	6

CHAPTER 6   - OWNERSHIP PATTERNS
SECTION 3   -- IN SPECIFIC INDUSTRIES, BY REGION AND ENTRY PERIOD
TABLE 27   ---- THE CONSTRUCTION MACHINERY INDUSTRY (SIC 353)

NO. OF SUBSIDIARIES MANUFACTURING IN THIS INDUSTRY AT TIME OF ENTRY INTO PARENT SYSTEM

PERIOD OF ENTRY AND PARENT OWNERSHIP AT ENTRY DATE

(WHL=WHOLLY OWNED,95-100%)   MA=MAJORITY,51-94%   CO=50%   MI=MINORITY,5-49%   UN=UNKNOWN   ALL=TOTAL FOR PERIOD

REGION	1951-1966						1967-1969						1970-1972						1973-1975					
	WHL	MA	CO	MI	UN	ALL	WHL	MA	CO	MI	UN	ALL	WHL	MA	CO	MI	UN	ALL	WHL	MA	CO	MI	UN	ALL
CANADA	13	1	1	0	0	15	11	3	0	0	0	14	4	0	0	0	0	4	2	0	0	0	0	2
C.AM.+CARIB.	3	1	1	2	0	7	0	1	0	1	1	3	1	1	1	0	0	3	2	0	0	0	0	2
S.AMERICA	2	2	1	1	1	7	5	3	0	2	0	10	4	0	0	1	0	5	1	1	0	1	0	3
EUROPE	16	5	3	4	4	32	11	1	1	0	0	13	7	5	2	4	0	18	3	1	0	7	0	11
N.AFR+M.EAST	0	0	0	0	0	0	0	1	0	0	0	1	0	0	0	0	0	0	1	2	1	1	0	5
E.+W.AFRICA	0	0	0	0	0	0	0	0	0	0	0	0	0	0	0	0	0	0	0	0	0	0	0	0
SOUTH ASIA	1	0	1	0	0	2	0	0	0	0	0	0	0	0	0	0	0	0	0	0	0	0	0	0
EAST ASIA	0	0	2	1	0	3	0	0	0	2	0	2	1	0	1	3	0	5	4	0	1	1	0	6
S.DOMINIONS	7	1	3	0	0	11	5	2	0	1	0	8	1	1	1	1	0	4	4	1	0	0	0	5
OUTSIDE U.S.(TOTAL)	42	10	12	8	5	77	32	11	1	6	1	51	18	7	5	9	0	39	17	5	2	10	0	34

CHAPTER 6 - OWNERSHIP PATTERNS
SECTION 3 -- IN SPECIFIC INDUSTRIES, BY REGION AND ENTRY PERIOD
TABLE 28 --- THE FARM MACHINERY INDUSTRY (SIC 352)

NO. OF SUBSIDIARIES MANUFACTURING IN THIS INDUSTRY AT TIME OF ENTRY INTO PARENT SYSTEM

PERIOD OF ENTRY AND PARENT OWNERSHIP AT ENTRY DATE

WHL=WHOLLY OWNED,95-100% MA=MAJORITY,51-94% CO=50% MI=MINORITY,5-49% UN=UNKNOWN ALL=TOTAL FOR PERIOD

REGION	1951-1966						1967-1969						1970-1972						1973-1975					
	WHL	MA	CO	MI	UN	ALL	WHL	MA	CO	MI	UN	ALL	WHL	MA	CO	MI	UN	ALL	WHL	MA	CO	MI	UN	ALL
CANADA	1	0	0	0	0	1	1	0	0	0	0	1	0	0	0	0	0	0	0	0	0	0	0	0
C.AM.+CARIB.	0	0	0	0	1	1	0	0	0	0	0	0	0	0	0	0	0	0	0	0	0	0	0	0
S.AMERICA	1	0	2	2	0	5	0	0	0	0	1	1	0	0	0	0	0	0	0	1	0	0	0	1
EUROPE	6	3	0	6	3	18	0	0	0	1	0	1	1	0	0	2	0	3	3	0	0	2	0	5
N.AFR+M.EAST	0	1	0	0	0	1	0	0	0	1	0	1	0	0	0	0	0	0	0	0	0	0	0	0
E.+W.AFRICA	0	0	0	0	0	0	0	0	0	0	0	0	0	0	0	0	0	0	0	0	0	0	0	0
SOUTH ASIA	0	0	0	1	0	1	0	0	0	0	0	0	0	0	0	1	0	1	0	0	0	0	0	0
EAST ASIA	0	0	0	0	0	0	0	0	0	0	0	0	1	0	0	0	0	1	1	0	0	0	0	1
S.DOMINIONS	2	2	1	1	0	6	0	0	0	0	0	0	1	0	0	1	0	2	0	0	0	0	0	0
OUTSIDE U.S. (TOTAL)	10	6	3	10	4	33	1	0	0	2	1	4	3	0	0	4	0	7	4	1	0	2	0	7

CHAPTER 6 - OWNERSHIP PATTERNS
SECTION 3 -- IN SPECIFIC INDUSTRIES, BY REGION AND ENTRY PERIOD
TABLE 29 ---- THE OFFICE MACHINES & COMPUTERS INDUSTRY (SIC 357)

NO. OF SUBSIDIARIES MANUFACTURING IN THIS INDUSTRY AT TIME OF ENTRY INTO PARENT SYSTEM

PERIOD OF ENTRY AND PARENT OWNERSHIP AT ENTRY DATE

(WHL=WHOLLY OWNED,95-100%   MA=MAJORITY,51-94%   CO=50%   MI=MINORITY,5-49%   UN=UNKNOWN   ALL=TOTAL FOR PERIOD)

REGION	1951-1966						1967-1969						1970-1972						1973-1975					
	WHL	MA	CO	MI	UN	ALL	WHL	MA	CO	MI	UN	ALL	WHL	MA	CO	MI	UN	ALL	WHL	MA	CO	MI	UN	ALL
CANADA	5	0	0	0	0	5	2	0	0	0	0	2	1	0	0	0	0	1	1	0	0	0	0	1
C.AM.+CARIB.	2	1	0	0	0	3	1	0	0	0	0	1	0	0	0	0	0	0	2	0	0	0	0	2
S.AMERICA	3	1	0	0	0	4	0	0	0	0	0	0	0	0	0	0	0	0	0	1	0	0	0	1
EUROPE	11	1	0	2	0	14	9	1	1	1	0	12	8	2	0	0	0	10	1	0	0	0	0	1
N.AFR+M.EAST	0	0	0	0	0	0	0	0	0	0	0	0	0	0	0	0	0	0	0	0	0	0	0	0
E.+W.AFRICA	0	0	0	0	0	0	0	0	0	0	0	0	0	0	0	0	0	0	0	0	0	0	0	0
SOUTH ASIA	0	1	0	1	0	2	0	0	0	0	0	0	0	0	0	0	0	0	0	0	0	0	0	0
EAST ASIA	0	1	0	2	0	3	0	0	0	1	0	1	4	0	1	0	0	5	3	0	1	1	0	5
S.DOMINIONS	1	0	0	0	0	1	1	0	0	0	0	1	1	0	0	0	0	1	2	0	0	0	0	2
OUTSIDE U.S. (TOTAL)	22	5	0	5	0	32	13	1	1	2	0	17	14	2	1	0	0	17	9	1	1	1	0	12

CHAPTER 6 - OWNERSHIP PATTERNS
SECTION 3 -- IN SPECIFIC INDUSTRIES, BY REGION AND ENTRY PERIOD
TABLE 30 --- THE SPECIAL MACHINERY INDUSTRY (SIC 355)

NO. OF SUBSIDIARIES MANUFACTURING IN THIS INDUSTRY AT TIME OF ENTRY INTO PARENT SYSTEM

PERIOD OF ENTRY AND PARENT OWNERSHIP AT ENTRY DATE

(WHL=WHOLLY OWNED,95-100%) (MA=MAJORITY,51-94%) (CO=50%) (MI=MINORITY,5-49%) (UN=UNKNOWN) (ALL=TOTAL FOR PERIOD)

REGION	1951-1966						1967-1969						1970-1972						1973-1975					
	WHL	MA	CO	MI	UN	ALL	WHL	MA	CO	MI	UN	ALL	WHL	MA	CO	MI	UN	ALL	WHL	MA	CO	MI	UN	ALL
CANADA	4	0	1	0	0	5	3	0	0	0	0	3	3	0	0	0	0	3	1	0	0	0	0	1
C.AM.+CARIB.	0	0	2	1	0	3	2	0	0	0	0	2	1	0	0	0	0	1	2	0	0	0	0	2
S.AMERICA	1	0	0	4	0	5	0	1	0	0	0	1	0	0	0	0	0	0	3	0	0	3	0	6
EUROPE	20	4	3	5	5	37	8	2	0	0	0	10	9	2	1	1	1	14	17	1	0	1	1	20
N.AFR+M.EAST	0	0	0	0	0	0	0	0	0	1	0	1	0	0	0	1	0	1	0	0	0	0	0	0
E.+W.AFRICA	0	0	0	0	0	0	0	0	0	0	0	0	0	0	0	0	0	0	0	0	0	0	0	0
SOUTH ASIA	0	0	0	0	0	0	1	0	0	0	0	1	0	0	0	0	0	0	0	0	0	0	0	0
EAST ASIA	0	1	0	1	1	3	0	0	1	0	0	1	0	0	1	0	0	1	0	0	1	0	0	1
S.DOMINIONS	4	0	1	0	1	6	2	0	0	0	0	2	0	0	0	0	0	0	0	1	0	1	0	2
OUTSIDE U.S.(TOTAL)	29	5	7	11	7	59	16	3	1	1	0	21	13	2	2	2	1	20	23	2	1	5	1	32

CHAPTER 6   - OWNERSHIP PATTERNS
SECTION 3   -- IN SPECIFIC INDUSTRIES, BY REGION AND ENTRY PERIOD
TABLE 31   --- THE GENERAL MACHINERY INDUSTRY (SIC 356)

NO. OF SUBSIDIARIES MANUFACTURING IN THIS INDUSTRY AT TIME OF ENTRY INTO PARENT SYSTEM

PERIOD OF ENTRY AND PARENT OWNERSHIP AT ENTRY DATE

(WHL=WHOLLY OWNED,95-100%   MA=MAJORITY,51-94%   CO=50%   MI=MINORITY,5-49%   UN=UNKNOWN   ALL=TOTAL FOR PERIOD)

REGION	1951-1966						1967-1969						1970-1972						1973-1975					
	WHL	MA	CO	MI	UN	ALL	WHL	MA	CO	MI	UN	ALL	WHL	MA	CO	MI	UN	ALL	WHL	MA	CO	MI	UN	ALL
CANADA	14	0	0	1	1	16	9	0	1	0	0	10	4	0	0	0	0	4	1	0	0	0	0	1
C.AM.+CARIB.	2	1	1	2	1	7	4	0	0	1	0	5	1	0	0	0	0	1	4	0	0	0	0	4
S.AMERICA	2	1	0	2	0	5	3	1	2	0	0	6	1	1	0	0	0	2	0	0	2	0	0	2
EUROPE	15	2	3	1	6	27	18	5	0	2	0	25	16	4	0	4	0	24	11	5	0	1	0	17
N.AFR+M.EAST	0	0	1	0	0	1	0	0	0	0	0	0	0	0	0	0	0	0	0	0	0	0	0	0
E.+W.AFRICA	0	0	0	0	0	0	0	0	0	0	0	0	0	0	0	0	0	0	0	0	0	0	0	0
SOUTH ASIA	2	0	0	0	0	2	1	0	0	0	0	1	0	0	0	0	0	0	0	0	0	1	0	1
EAST ASIA	0	0	0	1	0	1	0	0	1	3	0	4	1	0	3	4	0	8	0	0	3	1	0	4
S.DOMINIONS	5	0	1	1	1	8	5	0	0	2	2	9	1	0	0	0	0	1	0	0	0	0	0	0
OUTSIDE U.S. (TOTAL)	40	4	6	8	9	67	40	6	4	7	3	60	24	5	3	8	0	40	16	5	5	3	0	29

CHAPTER 6   - OWNERSHIP PATTERNS
SECTION 3   -- IN SPECIFIC INDUSTRIES, BY REGION AND ENTRY PERIOD
TABLE 32   --- OTHER NON-ELEC MACHINERY INDUSTRIES (OTHER SIC 35)

NO. OF SUBSIDIARIES MANUFACTURING IN THIS INDUSTRY AT TIME OF ENTRY INTO PARENT SYSTEM

PERIOD OF ENTRY AND PARENT OWNERSHIP AT ENTRY DATE

(WHL=WHOLLY OWNED,95-100%   MA=MAJORITY,51-94%   CO=50%   MI=MINORITY,5-49%   UN=UNKNOWN   ALL=TOTAL FOR PERIOD)

REGION	1951-1966						1967-1969						1970-1972						1973-1975					
	WHL	MA	CO	MI	UN	ALL	WHL	MA	CO	MI	UN	ALL	WHL	MA	CO	MI	UN	ALL	WHL	MA	CO	MI	UN	ALL
CANADA	9	1	1	0	0	11	9	0	0	0	0	9	3	1	0	0	0	4	7	0	0	0	0	7
C.AM.+CARIB.	2	1	0	4	0	7	1	0	0	0	1	2	0	0	0	0	0	0	3	0	0	0	0	3
S.AMERICA	2	1	0	2	0	5	4	1	0	1	0	6	1	2	0	1	0	4	2	0	1	2	0	5
EUROPE	13	2	2	5	8	30	18	2	2	0	1	23	20	2	0	1	0	23	5	2	0	2	0	9
N.AFR+M.EAST	0	0	0	0	0	0	0	0	0	0	0	0	0	0	0	0	0	0	0	0	0	0	0	0
E.+W.AFRICA	0	0	0	0	0	0	0	0	0	0	0	0	0	0	0	0	0	0	0	0	0	0	0	0
SOUTH ASIA	1	0	1	0	0	2	1	0	0	0	0	1	0	0	0	1	0	1	0	0	0	0	0	0
EAST ASIA	0	0	1	1	1	3	0	0	0	1	0	1	1	0	1	0	0	2	0	0	0	1	0	1
S.DOMINIONS	3	0	1	2	2	8	4	0	0	2	0	6	1	1	3	0	0	5	1	0	0	0	0	1
OUTSIDE U.S. (TOTAL)	30	5	6	14	11	66	37	3	2	4	2	48	26	6	4	3	0	39	18	2	1	5	0	26

CHAPTER 6   - OWNERSHIP PATTERNS
SECTION 3   -- IN SPECIFIC INDUSTRIES, BY REGION AND ENTRY PERIOD
TABLE 33   --- ELECTRIC LIGHT & WIRING INDUSTRY (SIC 364)

NO. OF SUBSIDIARIES MANUFACTURING IN THIS INDUSTRY AT TIME OF ENTRY INTO PARENT SYSTEM

PERIOD OF ENTRY AND PARENT OWNERSHIP AT ENTRY DATE

(WHL=WHOLLY OWNED,95-100%   MA=MAJORITY,51-94%   CO=50%   MI=MINORITY,5-49%   UN=UNKNOWN   ALL=TOTAL FOR PERIOD)

REGION	1951-1966						1967-1969						1970-1972						1973-1975					
	WHL	MA	CO	MI	UN	ALL	WHL	MA	CO	MI	UN	ALL	WHL	MA	CO	MI	UN	ALL	WHL	MA	CO	MI	UN	ALL
CANADA	6	1	0	0	0	7	1	0	0	0	0	1	1	0	0	0	0	1	0	0	0	0	0	0
C.AM.+CARIB.	3	0	0	1	0	4	1	0	0	1	0	2	0	1	0	0	0	1	0	1	0	0	0	1
S.AMERICA	4	0	0	1	1	6	2	1	0	0	0	3	2	1	0	0	0	3	0	1	1	0	0	2
EUROPE	1	2	1	2	1	7	2	1	0	1	0	4	6	0	0	0	0	6	2	1	1	0	0	4
N.AFR+M.EAST	0	0	0	0	0	0	0	0	0	0	0	0	0	0	0	0	0	0	0	0	0	0	0	0
E.+W.AFRICA	0	0	0	0	0	0	0	0	0	0	0	0	0	0	0	0	0	0	0	0	0	0	0	0
SOUTH ASIA	0	0	0	3	0	3	0	0	0	0	0	0	0	0	0	0	0	0	0	0	0	0	0	0
EAST ASIA	1	1	0	1	0	3	0	0	0	1	0	1	1	0	1	0	0	2	0	0	0	1	0	1
S.DOMINIONS	0	0	0	0	3	3	0	1	0	0	0	1	0	0	0	0	0	0	0	0	0	0	0	0
OUTSIDE U.S.(TOTAL)	15	4	1	8	5	33	6	3	0	3	0	12	10	2	1	0	0	13	2	3	2	1	0	8

CHAPTER 6 - OWNERSHIP PATTERNS
SECTION 3 -- IN SPECIFIC INDUSTRIES, BY REGION AND ENTRY PERIOD
TABLE 34 --- ELEC TRANSMISSION EQUIP INDUSTRY (SIC 361)

NO. OF SUBSIDIARIES MANUFACTURING IN THIS INDUSTRY AT TIME OF ENTRY INTO PARENT SYSTEM

PERIOD OF ENTRY AND PARENT OWNERSHIP AT ENTRY DATE

(WHL=WHOLLY OWNED,95-100% MA=MAJORITY,51-94% CO=50% MI=MINORITY,5-49% UN=UNKNOWN ALL=TOTAL FOR PERIOD)

REGION	1951-1966						1967-1969						1970-1972						1973-1975					
	WHL	MA	CO	MI	UN	ALL	WHL	MA	CO	MI	UN	ALL	WHL	MA	CO	MI	UN	ALL	WHL	MA	CO	MI	UN	ALL
CANADA	6	1	0	0	0	7	2	0	0	0	0	2	1	0	0	0	0	1	3	0	0	0	0	3
C.AM.+CARIB.	2	1	0	0	1	4	1	1	0	0	0	2	0	0	0	0	0	0	0	0	0	0	0	0
S.AMERICA	0	1	0	0	0	1	2	0	0	0	0	2	0	1	0	0	0	1	0	0	0	0	0	0
EUROPE	8	1	2	0	2	13	3	0	0	0	0	3	13	2	0	0	0	15	0	0	0	0	0	0
N.AFR+M.EAST	0	0	0	0	0	0	0	0	0	0	0	0	0	0	0	0	0	0	0	0	0	0	0	0
E.+W.AFRICA	0	0	0	0	0	0	0	0	0	0	0	0	0	0	0	0	0	0	0	0	0	0	0	0
SOUTH ASIA	0	0	0	0	0	0	0	0	0	0	0	0	0	0	0	0	0	0	0	0	0	0	0	0
EAST ASIA	0	0	1	0	0	1	0	0	0	1	0	1	0	0	0	0	0	0	0	0	0	0	0	0
S.DOMINIONS	2	0	0	0	0	2	1	0	0	0	0	1	2	0	0	0	0	2	1	1	0	0	0	2
OUTSIDE U.S. (TOTAL)	18	4	2	1	3	28	9	1	0	1	0	11	16	3	0	0	0	19	4	1	0	0	0	5

CHAPTER 6 - OWNERSHIP PATTERNS
SECTION 3 -- IN SPECIFIC INDUSTRIES, BY REGION AND ENTRY PERIOD
TABLE 35 --- RADIO,TV & APPLIANCES INDUSTRIES (SIC 365 AND 363)

NO. OF SUBSIDIARIES MANUFACTURING IN THIS INDUSTRY AT TIME OF ENTRY INTO PARENT SYSTEM

PERIOD OF ENTRY AND PARENT OWNERSHIP AT ENTRY DATE

(WHL=WHOLLY OWNED,95-100%   MA=MAJORITY,51-94%   CO=50%   MI=MINORITY,5-49%   UN=UNKNOWN   ALL=TOTAL FOR PERIOD)

REGION	1951-1966						1967-1969						1970-1972						1973-1975					
	WHL	MA	CO	MI	UN	ALL	WHL	MA	CO	MI	UN	ALL	WHL	MA	CO	MI	UN	ALL	WHL	MA	CO	MI	UN	ALL
CANADA	5	1	0	0	0	6	7	0	0	0	0	7	3	0	0	0	0	3	3	0	0	0	0	3
C.AM.+CARIB.	7	1	1	0	1	10	1	0	0	1	0	2	0	0	0	0	0	0	3	0	0	0	0	3
S.AMERICA	8	0	1	0	1	10	1	1	0	1	0	3	2	0	0	2	0	4	0	0	0	0	0	0
EUROPE	19	10	3	1	3	36	11	2	1	1	0	15	9	1	0	1	0	11	5	1	0	1	0	7
N.AFR+M.EAST	0	0	1	0	0	1	1	0	0	1	0	2	0	0	0	0	0	0	0	0	0	0	0	0
E.+W.AFRICA	1	2	0	0	0	3	0	1	0	0	0	1	1	0	0	0	0	1	0	1	0	0	0	1
SOUTH ASIA	1	1	0	1	0	3	0	0	0	2	0	2	0	0	1	1	0	2	0	0	0	0	0	0
EAST ASIA	5	0	1	1	1	8	1	1	0	0	0	2	4	0	0	0	0	4	1	0	2	1	0	4
S.DOMINIONS	3	0	0	0	0	3	0	0	0	0	0	0	0	0	0	0	0	0	0	0	0	0	0	0
OUTSIDE U.S. (TOTAL)	49	15	7	3	6	80	22	5	1	6	0	34	19	1	1	4	0	25	12	2	2	2	0	18

CHAPTER 6   - OWNERSHIP PATTERNS
SECTION 3   -- IN SPECIFIC INDUSTRIES, BY REGION AND ENTRY PERIOD
TABLE 36   --- THE ELECTRONICS INDUSTRY (SIC 367)

NO. OF SUBSIDIARIES MANUFACTURING IN THIS INDUSTRY AT TIME OF ENTRY INTO PARENT SYSTEM

PERIOD OF ENTRY AND PARENT OWNERSHIP AT ENTRY DATE

(WHL=WHOLLY OWNED,95-100%   MA=MAJORITY,51-94%   CO=50%   MI=MINORITY,5-49%   UN=UNKNOWN   ALL=TOTAL FOR PERIOD)

REGION	1951-1966						1967-1969						1970-1972						1973-1975					
	WHL	MA	CO	MI	UN	ALL	WHL	MA	CO	MI	UN	ALL	WHL	MA	CO	MI	UN	ALL	WHL	MA	CO	MI	UN	ALL
CANADA	3	0	0	1	0	4	1	0	0	0	0	1	0	0	0	0	0	0	2	0	0	0	0	2
C.AM.+CARIB.	2	1	0	0	0	3	2	0	0	1	0	3	3	0	0	0	0	3	9	1	0	0	0	10
S.AMERICA	2	0	0	2	0	4	1	0	0	0	0	1	1	0	0	0	0	1	0	0	0	0	0	0
EUROPE	10	5	3	3	0	21	9	2	1	1	0	13	14	2	1	2	0	19	7	2	0	0	0	9
N.AFR+M.EAST	0	0	0	0	0	0	0	0	0	0	0	0	0	0	0	0	0	0	0	0	0	0	0	0
E.+W.AFRICA	1	0	0	0	0	1	0	0	0	1	0	1	0	0	0	0	0	0	0	0	0	0	0	0
SOUTH ASIA	0	0	0	0	0	0	0	0	0	0	0	0	0	0	0	0	0	0	0	0	0	0	0	0
EAST ASIA	1	0	0	4	0	5	6	2	2	0	0	10	6	1	1	1	0	9	5	0	4	0	0	9
S.DOMINIONS	0	0	0	2	1	3	0	0	0	1	0	1	1	0	0	0	0	1	0	0	0	0	0	0
OUTSIDE U.S. (TOTAL)	19	6	3	12	1	41	19	4	3	4	0	30	25	3	2	3	0	33	23	3	4	0	0	30

CHAPTER 6 - OWNERSHIP PATTERNS
SECTION 3 -- IN SPECIFIC INDUSTRIES, BY REGION AND ENTRY PERIOD
TABLE 37 --- OTHER ELECTRICAL INDUSTRIES (OTHER SIC 36)

NO. OF SUBSIDIARIES MANUFACTURING IN THIS INDUSTRY AT TIME OF ENTRY INTO PARENT SYSTEM

PERIOD OF ENTRY AND PARENT OWNERSHIP AT ENTRY DATE

(WHL=WHOLLY OWNED,95-100% MA=MAJORITY,51-94% CO=50% MI=MINORITY,5-49% UN=UNKNOWN ALL=TOTAL FOR PERIOD)

REGION	1951-1966						1967-1969						1970-1972						1973-1975					
	WHL	MA	CO	MI	UN	ALL	WHL	MA	CO	MI	UN	ALL	WHL	MA	CO	MI	UN	ALL	WHL	MA	CO	MI	UN	ALL
CANADA	9	1	0	0	1	11	4	0	0	0	0	4	3	0	0	0	0	3	3	0	0	0	0	3
C.AM.+CARIB.	9	1	1	3	5	19	2	0	0	1	0	3	4	0	0	0	0	4	1	0	0	1	0	2
S.AMERICA	5	0	1	3	2	11	4	2	1	0	0	7	8	1	0	1	0	10	2	1	1	0	0	4
EUROPE	9	3	3	2	2	19	15	1	0	2	2	20	23	2	0	4	0	29	11	0	2	3	0	16
N.AFR+M.EAST	0	1	0	0	0	1	1	0	0	0	0	1	0	0	0	0	0	0	0	1	0	1	0	2
E.+W.AFRICA	0	0	0	0	0	0	1	0	0	0	2	3	0	1	0	0	0	1	1	0	0	0	0	1
SOUTH ASIA	0	0	2	0	1	3	0	1	0	0	0	1	0	1	1	0	0	2	0	0	0	1	0	1
EAST ASIA	2	0	3	2	6	13	1	2	2	2	0	7	5	0	2	1	0	8	2	0	2	1	0	5
S.DOMINIONS	2	1	0	1	0	4	3	0	0	0	1	4	2	1	1	1	0	5	2	0	0	0	0	2
OUTSIDE U.S. (TOTAL)	36	7	10	11	17	81	31	6	3	5	5	50	45	6	4	7	0	62	22	2	5	7	0	36

CHAPTER 6 - OWNERSHIP PATTERNS
SECTION 3 -- IN SPECIFIC INDUSTRIES, BY REGION AND ENTRY PERIOD
TABLE 38 --- COMMUNICATION EQUIP INDUSTRY (SIC 366)

NO. OF SUBSIDIARIES MANUFACTURING IN THIS INDUSTRY AT TIME OF ENTRY INTO PARENT SYSTEM

PERIOD OF ENTRY AND PARENT OWNERSHIP AT ENTRY DATE

(WHL=WHOLLY OWNED,95-100% MA=MAJORITY,51-94% CO=50% MI=MINORITY,5-49% UN=UNKNOWN ALL=TOTAL FOR PERIOD)

REGION	1951-1966						1967-1969						1970-1972						1973-1975					
	WHL	MA	CO	MI	UN	ALL	WHL	MA	CO	MI	UN	ALL	WHL	MA	CO	MI	UN	ALL	WHL	MA	CO	MI	UN	ALL
CANADA	4	0	0	0	1	5	1	0	0	0	0	1	0	0	0	0	0	0	2	0	0	0	0	2
C.AM.+CARIB.	0	0	0	0	0	0	0	1	1	0	0	2	0	0	0	0	0	0	2	0	0	0	0	2
S.AMERICA	1	0	0	0	0	1	1	0	0	0	0	1	2	1	0	0	0	3	1	0	1	0	0	2
EUROPE	12	2	1	1	0	16	12	3	0	0	0	15	3	2	1	2	0	8	2	0	0	0	0	2
N.AFR+M.EAST	0	0	0	0	0	0	0	0	0	1	0	1	0	0	0	0	0	0	0	0	0	0	0	0
E.+W.AFRICA	0	0	0	0	0	0	0	1	0	0	0	1	0	0	0	0	0	0	1	0	0	0	0	1
SOUTH ASIA	0	0	0	0	0	0	0	0	0	0	0	0	0	0	0	0	0	0	0	0	0	0	0	0
EAST ASIA	2	0	0	0	1	3	2	0	0	0	0	2	1	0	0	0	0	1	0	2	1	1	0	4
S.DOMINIONS	2	0	0	0	0	2	0	0	0	0	0	0	0	0	0	0	0	0	1	0	0	0	0	1
OUTSIDE U.S.(TOTAL)	21	2	1	1	2	27	16	5	1	1	0	23	6	3	1	2	0	12	9	2	2	1	0	14

358

CHAPTER 6 - OWNERSHIP PATTERNS
SECTION 3 -- IN SPECIFIC INDUSTRIES, BY REGION AND ENTRY PERIOD
TABLE 39 --- THE MOTOR VEHIC INDUSTRY (SIC 371)

NO. OF SUBSIDIARIES MANUFACTURING IN THIS INDUSTRY AT TIME OF ENTRY INTO PARENT SYSTEM

PERIOD OF ENTRY AND PARENT OWNERSHIP AT ENTRY DATE

(WHL=WHOLLY OWNED,95-100%   MA=MAJORITY,51-94%   CO=50%   MI=MINORITY,5-49%   UN=UNKNOWN   ALL=TOTAL FOR PERIOD)

REGION	1951-1966						1967-1969						1970-1972						1973-1975					
	WHL	MA	CO	MI	UN	ALL	WHL	MA	CO	MI	UN	ALL	WHL	MA	CO	MI	UN	ALL	WHL	MA	CO	MI	UN	ALL
CANADA	17	2	0	3	2	24	6	0	0	0	0	6	10	1	0	0	0	11	4	1	0	1	2	8
C.AM.+CARIB.	5	3	2	9	3	22	0	0	0	2	0	2	1	0	0	1	0	2	1	0	0	2	0	3
S.AMERICA	16	8	9	14	4	51	6	5	3	3	0	17	3	2	3	3	0	11	3	1	1	6	1	12
EUROPE	29	10	4	24	3	70	20	2	0	3	1	26	24	4	5	5	0	38	17	5	3	5	0	30
N.AFR+M.EAST	1	0	0	0	0	1	1	0	0	0	0	1	0	0	0	0	0	0	0	1	0	1	0	2
E.+W.AFRICA	0	0	1	0	0	1	0	0	0	0	0	0	1	0	0	0	0	1	0	0	0	0	0	0
SOUTH ASIA	0	1	2	1	1	5	0	0	0	0	0	0	0	0	0	0	0	0	0	0	0	0	0	0
EAST ASIA	1	0	1	2	2	6	1	0	0	4	0	5	3	2	3	6	0	14	1	0	3	0	0	4
S.DOMINIONS	7	8	2	2	1	20	10	1	1	0	0	12	3	0	0	1	0	4	6	2	2	1	0	11
OUTSIDE U.S.(TOTAL)	76	32	21	55	16	200	44	8	4	12	1	69	45	9	11	16	0	81	32	10	9	16	3	70

CHAPTER 6   - OWNERSHIP PATTERNS
SECTION 3   -- IN SPECIFIC INDUSTRIES, BY REGION AND ENTRY PERIOD
TABLE 40   --- OTHER TRANSPORTATION INDUSTRIES (OTHER SIC 37)

NO. OF SUBSIDIARIES MANUFACTURING IN THIS INDUSTRY AT TIME OF ENTRY INTO PARENT SYSTEM

PERIOD OF ENTRY AND PARENT OWNERSHIP AT ENTRY DATE

(WHL=WHOLLY OWNED,95-100%   MA=MAJORITY,51-94%   CO=50%   MI=MINORITY,5-49%   UN=UNKNOWN   ALL=TOTAL FOR PERIOD)

REGION	1951-1966						1967-1969						1970-1972						1973-1975					
	WHL	MA	CO	MI	UN	ALL	WHL	MA	CO	MI	UN	ALL	WHL	MA	CO	MI	UN	ALL	WHL	MA	CO	MI	UN	ALL
CANADA	2	1	0	2	0	5	2	1	0	0	0	3	1	0	0	0	0	1	2	0	0	0	0	2
C.AM.+CARIB.	0	0	0	1	0	1	1	0	0	0	0	1	0	0	0	0	0	0	1	0	0	1	0	2
S.AMERICA	0	0	0	0	0	0	0	1	0	0	0	1	1	0	0	1	0	2	1	0	0	2	0	3
EUROPE	1	2	1	2	1	7	5	1	1	2	0	9	9	1	1	0	0	11	4	0	0	2	0	6
N.AFR+M.EAST	0	0	0	0	0	0	0	0	0	0	0	0	0	0	0	0	0	0	0	0	0	0	0	0
E.+W.AFRICA	0	0	0	0	0	0	0	0	0	0	0	0	0	0	0	0	0	0	0	0	0	0	0	0
SOUTH ASIA	0	0	0	0	0	0	0	0	0	0	0	0	0	0	0	0	0	0	0	0	0	1	0	1
EAST ASIA	0	0	0	0	0	0	1	0	1	0	0	2	0	0	0	0	0	0	0	0	0	0	0	0
S.DOMINIONS	1	0	0	1	1	3	0	0	0	0	0	0	1	0	0	0	0	1	0	0	0	0	0	0
OUTSIDE U.S. (TOTAL)	4	3	1	6	2	16	9	3	2	2	0	16	12	1	1	1	0	15	8	0	0	6	0	14

359

CHAPTER 6   - OWNERSHIP PATTERNS
SECTION 3   -- IN SPECIFIC INDUSTRIES, BY REGION AND ENTRY PERIOD
TABLE 41   --- PRECISION INSTRUMENTS INDUSTRIES (SIC 38)

NO. OF SUBSIDIARIES MANUFACTURING IN THIS INDUSTRY AT TIME OF ENTRY INTO PARENT SYSTEM

PERIOD OF ENTRY AND PARENT OWNERSHIP AT ENTRY DATE

(WHL=WHOLLY OWNED,95-100%   MA=MAJORITY,51-94%   CO=50%   MI=MINORITY,5-49%   UN=UNKNOWN   ALL=TOTAL FOR PERIOD)

REGION	1951-1966						1967-1969						1970-1972						1973-1975					
	WHL	MA	CO	MI	UN	ALL	WHL	MA	CO	MI	UN	ALL	WHL	MA	CO	MI	UN	ALL	WHL	MA	CO	MI	UN	ALL
CANADA	10	0	0	0	0	10	5	0	0	0	0	5	8	0	0	0	0	8	4	0	0	0	0	4
C.AM.+C&RIB.	5	0	0	0	0	5	2	0	0	0	0	2	2	0	0	0	0	2	1	0	0	0	0	1
S.AMERICA	9	1	3	1	0	14	2	2	0	0	0	4	4	4	0	0	0	8	1	0	1	1	0	3
EUROPE	44	7	1	4	2	58	20	2	1	1	0	24	31	4	0	1	0	36	23	3	2	5	0	33
N.AFR+M.EAST	0	0	0	0	0	0	0	1	0	0	0	1	0	0	0	0	0	0	0	1	0	1	0	2
E.+W.AFRICA	0	0	0	0	0	0	0	0	0	0	0	0	1	0	0	0	0	1	0	0	0	0	0	0
SOUTH ASIA	1	1	0	0	0	2	0	0	0	1	0	1	0	0	0	1	0	1	0	0	0	0	0	0
EAST ASIA	0	0	0	0	0	0	0	0	2	2	1	5	4	0	1	0	0	5	1	1	0	2	0	4
S.DOMINIONS	4	1	0	0	0	5	4	1	0	0	0	5	4	1	0	0	0	5	0	1	0	0	0	1
OUTSIDE U.S.(TOTAL)	73	10	4	5	2	94	33	6	3	4	1	47	54	9	1	2	0	66	30	6	3	9	0	48

CHAPTER 6 - OWNERSHIP PATTERNS
SECTION 3 -- IN SPECIFIC INDUSTRIES, BY REGION AND ENTRY PERIOD
TABLE 42 --- MISCELLANEOUS INDUSTRIES (SIC 39)

NO. OF SUBSIDIARIES MANUFACTURING IN THIS INDUSTRY AT TIME OF ENTRY INTO PARENT SYSTEM

PERIOD OF ENTRY AND PARENT OWNERSHIP AT ENTRY DATE

WHL=WHOLLY OWNED,95-100% MA=MAJORITY,51-94% CO=50% MI=MINORITY,5-49% UN=UNKNOWN ALL=TOTAL FOR PERIOD

REGION	1951-1966						1967-1969						1970-1972						1973-1975					
	WHL	MA	CO	MI	UN	ALL	WHL	MA	CO	MI	UN	ALL	WHL	MA	CO	MI	UN	ALL	WHL	MA	CO	MI	UN	ALL
CANADA	5	0	0	1	0	6	7	0	1	0	0	8	7	1	0	0	1	9	1	0	3	0	0	4
C.AM.+CARIB.	2	1	0	0	0	3	1	0	0	0	0	1	1	1	0	1	0	3	0	0	0	1	0	1
S.AMERICA	7	3	1	0	1	12	1	1	0	0	0	2	0	0	0	1	0	1	0	1	0	0	0	1
EUROPE	17	2	3	2	5	29	15	3	1	1	0	20	20	4	0	2	0	26	5	5	0	1	0	11
N.AFR+M.EAST	1	0	0	0	0	1	0	0	0	1	0	1	0	0	0	0	0	0	0	0	0	0	0	0
E.+W.AFRICA	2	0	1	0	0	3	0	0	0	0	0	0	0	0	0	0	0	0	0	0	0	0	0	0
SOUTH ASIA	0	0	0	1	0	1	0	0	0	0	0	0	0	0	0	0	0	0	0	0	0	0	0	0
EAST ASIA	5	0	0	0	0	5	0	0	1	1	0	2	2	0	0	1	0	3	0	1	2	1	0	4
S.DOMINIONS	4	1	1	1	2	9	6	1	2	0	0	9	1	1	0	0	0	2	3	0	0	0	0	3
OUTSIDE U.S. (TOTAL)	43	7	6	5	8	69	30	5	5	3	0	43	31	7	0	5	1	44	9	7	5	3	0	24

CHAPTER 6 — OWNERSHIP PATTERNS
SECTION 4 -- FLOW OF JOINT VENTURES
TABLE 1 --- MAJORITY-OWNED (51-94%) BY PARENT, AT ENTRY DATE

NO. OF SUBSIDIARIES, BY COUNTRY OR REGION

COUNTRY OR REGION	NET FLOW UP TO 31-DEC-50	NO. OF ENTRIES DURING YEAR(S)													TOTAL ENTRIES 1951-75	TOTAL EXITS 1951-75	NET FLOW UP TO 1-JAN-76
		51-55	56-60	61-65	1966	1967	1968	1969	1970	1971	1972	1973	1974	1975			
CANADA	14	14	14	20	3	4	4	3	3	3	2	2	1	0	73	35	52
LATIN AMER. (TOTAL)	60	24	69	88	17	29	28	11	18	13	16	16	9	11	349	149	260
C.AM.+CARIB. (TOTAL)	23	6	16	45	10	10	9	6	7	6	5	5	2	5	132	55	100
BAHAMAS	0	0	0	1	0	0	1	1	1	0	0	0	0	0	4	2	2
BERMUDA	0	0	0	0	0	1	0	0	0	0	0	1	0	0	2	1	1
COSTA RICA	0	0	0	2	0	1	1	0	0	1	1	1	1	1	9	2	7
GUATEMALA	1	0	2	7	0	0	0	2	0	0	0	1	0	0	12	3	10
JAMAICA	0	0	0	4	1	0	1	1	0	0	1	1	0	0	9	2	7
MEXICO	15	4	13	25	5	4	6	2	3	3	2	2	2	0	71	31	55
NETH.ANTILLES	0	0	0	0	1	0	0	0	0	0	0	0	0	0	1	1	0
NICARAGUA	0	0	0	2	1	0	0	0	0	1	1	1	0	0	6	1	5
PANAMA	0	0	0	1	0	0	0	0	0	0	1	1	0	0	3	1	2
OTHER C.AM+CAR.	7	1	1	6	0	3	0	0	1	0	0	0	0	3	15	11	11
S.AMERICA (TOTAL)	37	18	53	43	7	19	19	5	11	7	11	11	7	6	217	94	160
BOLIVIA	5	0	1	1	0	0	0	0	2	0	0	0	1	1	6	9	2
CHILE	2	1	2	5	0	4	2	0	0	0	0	0	1	2	17	10	9
COLOMBIA	2	2	7	9	2	0	1	0	0	1	0	1	0	1	24	13	13
ECUADOR	0	0	2	1	0	1	0	0	0	0	0	1	2	0	7	2	5
PERU	5	0	4	3	1	3	2	1	1	1	0	1	0	0	17	10	12
ARGENTINA	6	2	6	9	1	2	3	2	0	1	0	0	0	0	26	13	19
BRAZIL	8	7	12	6	2	9	5	2	3	4	4	8	3	0	65	21	52
URUGUAY	0	0	0	1	0	0	1	0	0	0	0	0	1	0	3	1	2
VENEZUELA	9	6	19	7	1	0	5	2	5	0	5	0	1	0	51	15	45
OTHER S.AME.	0	0	0	1	0	0	0	0	0	0	0	0	0	0	1	0	1
EUROPE (TOTAL)	88	30	64	187	33	38	43	31	50	38	24	30	20	12	600	201	487
BELGIUM	5	1	3	8	2	2	3	0	4	0	1	1	2	1	28	14	19
FRANCE	16	11	17	43	8	17	14	8	17	10	6	10	9	4	174	54	136
GERMANY	10	5	13	26	5	4	7	6	8	8	6	4	2	1	95	34	71
ITALY	4	1	6	26	5	2	8	5	5	5	2	2	2	1	70	22	52
LUXEMBOURG	0	0	0	1	0	0	0	0	0	0	0	0	0	0	1	0	1
NETHERLANDS	5	0	3	11	1	0	0	3	2	1	0	1	0	0	22	6	21
DENMARK	2	0	0	1	1	0	0	0	1	1	0	3	0	0	7	1	8
IRELAND	0	0	0	2	0	0	0	0	0	0	0	0	1	0	3	1	2
U.K.	31	5	8	17	2	4	3	1	7	2	1	0	3	2	55	30	56
AUSTRIA	4	0	1	2	1	1	0	0	0	2	1	0	0	1	9	4	9
FINLAND	2	0	0	2	0	0	0	0	0	0	0	0	0	0	2	1	3
GREECE	0	2	0	5	0	1	0	2	1	1	0	0	0	0	12	6	6
NORWAY	3	0	1	0	1	1	0	1	1	1	1	0	0	0	7	1	9
PORTUGAL	1	1	5	3	0	1	0	0	1	1	0	0	0	0	12	2	11
SPAIN	4	1	2	18	6	6	3	3	1	3	3	6	3	2	57	11	50
SWEDEN	1	0	3	4	0	0	0	0	0	2	0	0	0	0	9	3	7
SWITZERLAND	0	0	0	10	1	1	1	4	3	3	1	0	0	0	24	8	16
TURKEY	0	3	0	5	1	0	0	1	1	0	0	0	0	0	11	3	8
OTHER EUROPE	0	1	0	1	0	0	0	0	0	0	0	0	0	0	2	0	2

TABLE 6 .4 .1 (CONTINUED)

NO. OF ENTRIES DURING YEAR(S)

COUNTRY OR REGION	NET FLOW UP TO 31-DEC-50	51-55	56-60	61-65	1966	1967	1968	1969	1970	1971	1972	1973	1974	1975	TOTAL ENTRIES 1951-75	TOTAL EXITS 1951-75	NET FLOW UP TO 1-JAN-76
N.AFR+M.EAST(TOTAL)	2	4	4	13	3	2	4	1	0	5	3	2	5	4	50	13	39
ALGERIA	0	1	1	0	0	0	0	0	0	0	0	1	1	0	3	1	2
EGYPT	0	0	0	0	0	1	0	0	0	0	0	0	0	2	4	0	4
IRAN	0	0	0	2	0	0	1	0	0	1	0	0	0	1	8	1	7
ISRAEL	0	0	2	2	2	1	2	0	0	2	0	0	0	0	8	1	7
LEBANON	0	0	0	4	1	0	1	0	0	0	0	1	0	0	7	4	3
MOROCCO	0	0	0	2	1	0	0	0	0	1	2	0	0	0	7	2	5
SAUDI ARABIA	0	1	0	0	0	0	0	1	0	0	0	0	1	1	4	0	4
OTHER N.AF+M.E.	2	1	0	3	0	0	0	0	0	1	1	0	3	0	9	4	7
E.+W.AFRICA (TOTAL)	0	8	3	8	1	4	6	3	3	1	3	3	1	1	45	11	34
GHANA	0	0	1	0	0	1	0	0	0	0	0	0	0	0	2	0	2
IVORY COAST	0	0	1	0	0	1	0	0	0	0	0	0	0	0	2	0	2
KENYA	0	0	0	1	0	0	1	1	0	0	1	0	0	0	4	1	3
LIBERIA	0	0	0	0	0	0	0	0	0	0	0	0	1	0	1	0	1
NIGERIA	0	1	0	3	0	0	1	1	2	1	1	1	0	1	12	0	12
ZAIRE	0	0	0	0	0	1	0	1	0	0	1	0	0	0	3	0	3
ZAMBIA	0	6	1	2	1	0	2	0	0	0	0	0	0	0	12	7	5
OTHER E.+W.AFR.	0	1	0	2	0	1	2	0	1	0	0	2	0	0	9	3	6
SOUTH ASIA (TOTAL)	2	2	9	10	2	0	1	1	1	1	0	3	0	0	30	2	30
INDIA	1	2	3	4	1	0	1	0	0	0	0	2	0	0	13	2	12
PAKISTAN	1	0	4	6	1	0	0	0	1	1	0	0	0	0	13	0	14
SRI LANKA	0	0	2	0	0	0	0	1	0	0	0	0	0	0	3	0	3
OTHER S.ASIA	0	0	0	0	0	0	0	0	0	0	0	1	0	0	1	0	1
EAST ASIA (TOTAL)	3	6	13	16	5	10	5	7	8	8	10	9	4	2	103	22	84
HONG KONG	0	0	1	1	1	1	0	0	0	0	0	0	0	0	4	1	3
INDONESIA	0	0	0	1	0	2	0	4	0	5	2	2	3	1	17	1	16
JAPAN	2	1	2	3	2	2	0	0	1	1	1	5	0	0	19	5	16
MALAYSIA	0	1	1	2	0	0	3	0	0	0	2	0	0	1	9	1	8
PHILIPPINES	1	4	6	4	1	3	0	0	1	0	1	0	1	0	20	6	15
SINGAPORE	0	0	0	0	0	0	0	1	2	0	2	0	0	0	4	0	4
S.KOREA	0	0	0	0	0	1	0	0	2	1	0	0	0	0	4	0	4
THAILAND	0	0	2	3	1	2	2	2	1	0	2	1	0	1	15	4	11
TAIWAN	0	0	1	1	0	1	0	0	1	1	0	1	0	0	8	1	7
OTHER E.ASIA	0	0	0	1	0	0	0	1	1	0	0	1	0	0	3	3	0
S.DOMINIONS (TOTAL)	16	11	14	35	6	7	6	7	6	8	4	3	6	2	115	27	104
AUSTRALIA	10	8	11	23	4	3	3	4	5	3	2	1	4	2	73	16	67
NEW Z'ALAND	3	0	1	4	0	2	0	0	1	0	0	1	0	0	9	1	11
RHODESIA	0	1	0	0	1	0	0	0	0	0	0	0	0	0	2	1	1
S.AFRICA	3	2	2	8	1	2	3	3	0	5	2	1	2	0	31	9	25
OUTSIDE U.S. (TOTAL)	185	99	190	377	71	94	96	63	88	77	62	68	48	32	1365	460	1090

CHAPTER 6 — OWNERSHIP PATTERNS
SECTION 4 -- FLOW OF JOINT VENTURES
TABLE 2 --- CO-OWNED (50%) BY PARENT, AT ENTRY DATE

NO. OF SUBSIDIARIES, BY COUNTRY OR REGION

COUNTRY OR REGION	NET FLOW UP TO 31-DEC-50	51-55	56-60	61-65	NO. OF ENTRIES DURING YEAR(S)										TOTAL ENTRIES 1951-75	TOTAL EXITS 1951-75	NET FLOW UP TO 1-JAN-76
					1966	1967	1968	1969	1970	1971	1972	1973	1974	1975			
CANADA	11	5	5	14	3	3	3	5	6	4	2	4	0	2	56	21	46
LATIN AMER. (TOTAL)	35	15	32	58	11	22	8	8	8	12	7	9	9	8	207	83	159
C.AM.+CARIB. (TOTAL)	6	5	12	26	4	11	4	3	4	7	4	3	6	4	93	24	75
BAHAMAS	1	1	1	0	0	0	0	0	1	0	1	0	0	0	4	0	5
BERMUDA	0	0	1	1	0	0	0	0	0	1	0	0	0	1	4	2	2
COSTA RICA	0	0	1	3	0	0	0	0	0	1	0	0	0	0	4	1	3
GUATEMALA	1	0	1	2	0	1	0	0	1	0	0	0	0	0	3	1	3
JAMAICA	0	0	0	2	0	1	0	0	0	0	0	1	0	0	5	2	3
MEXICO	1	4	5	11	2	9	3	3	3	3	3	1	3	1	51	11	41
NETH.ANTILLES	0	0	0	0	1	0	1	0	0	0	0	1	0	0	4	3	1
NICARAGUA	0	0	2	1	2	0	0	0	0	1	0	1	1	0	8	5	3
PANAMA	2	0	2	5	0	0	0	0	0	0	0	0	2	0	9	4	6
OTHER C.AM+CAR.	1	0	2	5	0	0	0	0	0	0	0	0	0	0	9	4	6
S.AMERICA (TOTAL)	29	10	20	32	7	11	4	5	4	5	3	6	3	4	114	59	84
BOLIVIA	1	0	2	0	0	1	0	0	1	0	0	0	0	0	1	2	0
CHILE	1	0	2	2	1	1	0	0	0	0	0	0	0	0	7	4	4
COLOMBIA	14	0	3	8	2	1	1	0	2	1	0	1	0	0	19	11	22
ECUADOR	0	0	0	0	1	1	0	0	0	0	0	0	0	0	3	1	2
PERU	0	1	3	1	1	2	0	0	0	0	0	0	0	0	8	1	7
ARGENTINA	4	2	5	5	2	2	0	0	0	0	0	0	0	0	16	15	5
BRAZIL	4	3	2	11	0	3	3	3	3	3	2	5	3	2	38	16	26
URUGUAY	0	0	0	0	1	0	1	0	0	0	0	0	0	0	0	0	0
VENEZUELA	5	3	5	5	1	1	2	2	0	0	0	0	0	1	22	9	18
OTHER S.AMER.	0	0	0	0	1	0	0	0	0	0	0	0	0	0	0	0	0
EUROPE (TOTAL)	30	17	84	152	30	21	35	25	23	21	24	22	19	13	486	182	334
BELGIUM	0	1	7	6	3	3	4	3	2	0	4	1	1	3	35	10	25
FRANCE	2	3	12	22	3	1	3	4	1	4	2	7	2	2	62	27	39
GERMANY	7	4	16	17	3	1	5	4	4	4	3	4	2	0	69	20	49
ITALY	1	2	9	15	1	2	3	3	1	1	2	1	0	0	40	21	21
LUXEMBOURG	0	0	0	1	1	0	0	0	0	0	0	0	0	0	3	1	2
NETHERLANDS	3	2	3	14	2	0	0	2	1	0	0	0	0	1	30	11	22
DENMARK	0	0	1	7	1	0	0	0	0	0	0	0	0	0	8	3	5
IRELAND	0	0	0	1	0	0	0	1	0	0	0	0	0	0	4	0	4
U.K.	13	4	28	32	6	6	8	4	7	7	5	3	0	3	113	53	73
AUSTRIA	3	0	0	0	1	0	0	0	0	0	0	0	1	0	2	0	5
FINLAND	0	0	0	1	0	0	0	0	0	0	0	0	1	0	0	1	0
GREECE	0	0	1	1	0	1	0	0	0	0	0	0	0	0	4	1	3
NORWAY	0	0	2	2	0	0	0	1	0	0	0	0	0	0	4	2	2
PORTUGAL	1	0	0	0	1	1	0	1	0	0	0	0	1	0	4	2	3
SPAIN	0	1	4	24	11	4	5	0	3	7	6	3	9	2	79	20	59
SWEDEN	0	0	1	5	0	0	1	1	0	0	2	2	1	2	16	2	14
SWITZERLAND	0	0	0	3	0	0	1	2	2	0	1	1	0	0	10	4	6
TURKEY	0	0	0	0	0	0	2	0	0	0	0	0	0	0	2	0	2
OTHER EUROPE	0	0	0	1	0	0	0	0	0	0	0	0	0	0	1	1	0

TABLE 6 .4 .2 (CONTINUED)

COUNTRY OR REGION	NET FLOW UP TO 31-DEC-50	NO. OF ENTRIES DURING YEAR(S)													TOTAL ENTRIES 1951-75	TOTAL EXITS 1951-75	NET FLOW UP TO 1-JAN-76
		51-55	56-60	61-65	1966	1967	1968	1969	1970	1971	1972	1973	1974	1975			
N.AFR+M.EAST (TOTAL)	5	2	4	7	2	4	0	0	0	2	0	1	2	3	27	9	23
ALGERIA	0	0	0	0	0	0	0	0	0	0	0	0	0	0	0	0	0
EGYPT	1	0	1	0	0	1	0	0	0	0	0	0	0	1	3	0	4
IRAN	0	1	2	2	2	2	0	0	0	0	0	0	1	0	10	2	8
ISRAEL	0	1	0	0	0	0	0	0	0	0	0	0	0	0	1	0	1
LEBANON	1	0	0	1	0	0	0	0	0	0	0	0	0	0	1	1	1
MOROCCO	0	0	0	1	0	0	0	0	0	1	0	1	1	0	4	0	4
SAUDI ARABIA	2	0	0	0	0	1	0	0	0	1	0	0	0	1	3	1	4
OTHER N.AF+M.E.	1	0	1	3	0	0	0	0	0	0	0	0	0	1	5	5	1
E.+W.AFRICA (TOTAL)	0	1	1	5	2	0	0	3	2	1	2	0	0	1	18	5	13
GHANA	0	1	0	1	0	0	0	0	0	0	0	0	0	0	2	1	1
IVORY COAST	0	0	0	0	0	0	0	0	0	0	0	0	0	0	0	0	0
KENYA	0	0	1	1	0	0	0	1	1	0	0	0	0	0	4	1	3
LIBERIA	0	0	0	1	0	0	0	0	0	0	0	0	0	0	1	0	1
NIGERIA	0	0	0	0	0	0	0	1	1	1	0	0	0	0	3	0	3
ZAIRE	0	0	0	0	0	0	0	0	0	0	0	0	0	0	0	0	0
ZAMBIA	0	0	0	2	0	0	0	0	0	0	0	0	0	0	2	1	1
OTHER E.+W.AFR.	0	0	0	0	2	0	0	1	0	0	2	0	0	1	6	2	4
SOUTH ASIA (TOTAL)	1	0	0	9	1	0	0	1	2	2	0	0	0	0	15	3	13
INDIA	1	0	0	9	1	0	0	1	2	2	0	0	0	0	15	3	13
PAKISTAN	0	0	0	0	0	0	0	0	0	0	0	0	0	0	0	0	0
SRI LANKA	0	0	0	0	0	0	0	0	0	0	0	0	0	0	0	0	0
OTHER S.ASIA	0	0	0	0	0	0	0	0	0	0	0	0	0	0	0	0	0
EAST ASIA (TOTAL)	1	9	7	34	8	12	11	18	16	24	16	19	18	10	202	17	186
HONG KONG	0	0	0	1	2	2	1	2	1	0	1	0	1	0	11	2	9
INDONESIA	0	0	0	0	0	0	0	0	0	0	0	0	1	0	1	0	1
JAPAN	0	8	7	31	6	8	4	11	13	19	13	17	11	8	156	12	144
MALAYSIA	1	0	0	0	0	0	0	0	0	0	0	1	0	0	1	1	1
PHILIPPINES	0	1	0	1	0	0	0	0	0	0	0	0	1	0	3	1	2
SINGAPORE	0	0	0	0	0	0	0	0	1	0	1	0	0	0	2	0	2
S.KOREA	0	0	0	0	0	0	4	4	0	3	0	0	3	0	14	0	14
THAILAND	0	0	0	0	0	0	1	1	0	0	0	1	0	1	4	0	4
TAIWAN	0	0	0	0	0	2	1	0	1	2	0	0	1	0	7	0	7
OTHER E.ASIA	0	0	0	1	0	0	0	0	0	0	1	0	0	1	3	1	2
S.DOMINIONS (TOTAL)	7	7	16	28	4	9	4	4	6	6	5	1	2	3	95	30	72
AUSTRALIA	3	3	10	18	1	7	4	2	6	3	2	1	2	2	61	19	45
NEW ZEALAND	1	2	2	5	0	0	0	0	0	0	0	0	0	1	10	0	11
RHODESIA	1	0	0	0	0	0	0	0	0	0	0	0	0	0	0	0	1
S.AFRICA	2	2	4	5	3	2	0	2	0	3	3	0	0	0	24	11	15
OUTSIDE U.S. (TOTAL)	90	56	150	307	61	71	61	63	63	72	56	56	50	40	1106	350	846

CHAPTER 6 - OWNERSHIP PATTERNS
SECTION 4 -- FLOW OF JOINT VENTURES
TABLE 3 --- MINORITY-OWNED (5-498) BY PARENT, AT ENTRY DATE

NO. OF SUBSIDIARIES, BY COUNTRY OR REGION

COUNTRY OR REGION	NET FLOW UP TO 31-DEC-50	51-55	56-60	61-65	NO. OF ENTRIES DURING YEAR(S)										TOTAL ENTRIES 1951-75	TOTAL EXITS 1951-75	NET FLOW UP TO 1-JAN-76
					1966	1967	1968	1969	1970	1971	1972	1973	1974	1975			
CANADA	10	11	10	21	5	2	4	2	3	3	1	1	8	0	71	23	58
LATIN AMER. (TOTAL)	45	23	63	89	27	18	14	15	20	22	14	19	24	22	370	115	300
C.AM.+CARIB. (TOTAL)	14	5	26	41	17	9	8	9	12	16	7	6	11	8	175	45	144
BAHAMAS	0	0	1	1	1	0	0	0	1	0	0	0	0	0	4	0	4
BERMUDA	0	0	1	1	0	0	0	0	0	0	0	0	0	0	2	1	1
COSTA RICA	0	0	0	2	0	1	0	0	0	0	0	0	0	0	3	2	1
GUATEMALA	0	0	2	1	2	0	0	1	0	1	0	1	0	0	8	1	7
JAMAICA	2	0	1	2	2	0	0	0	0	0	0	0	0	0	5	1	6
MEXICO	8	2	16	30	10	8	5	3	7	16	6	5	10	5	123	30	101
NETH.ANTILLES	0	0	0	0	0	0	0	0	1	0	0	0	0	0	1	0	1
NICARAGUA	0	0	1	2	1	0	0	0	0	0	0	0	0	0	4	0	4
PANAMA	2	2	1	2	1	0	0	1	0	0	0	0	0	0	7	4	5
OTHER C.AM+CAR.	2	1	4	2	0	0	2	2	2	0	1	0	1	3	18	6	14
S.AMERICA (TOTAL)	31	18	37	48	10	9	6	6	8	6	7	13	13	14	195	70	156
BOLIVIA	0	0	0	1	0	0	0	0	0	0	0	0	0	0	1	0	1
CHILE	7	0	0	1	0	2	0	0	1	0	0	1	0	0	5	8	4
COLOMBIA	6	4	8	11	1	0	0	0	0	2	2	1	1	2	32	10	28
ECUADOR	1	0	3	5	0	1	0	0	0	0	2	0	0	0	11	6	6
PERU	1	5	3	1	0	1	0	1	1	1	0	0	0	0	9	4	6
ARGENTINA	3	3	3	13	3	1	1	0	3	0	0	0	1	0	28	10	21
BRAZIL	9	4	10	3	2	0	0	2	1	0	3	8	8	8	51	15	45
URUGUAY	2	1	0	1	0	0	0	0	0	0	0	1	0	0	3	2	3
VENEZUELA	2	1	11	12	4	0	0	3	2	2	2	2	3	3	53	14	41
OTHER S.AMER.	0	0	1	0	1	0	0	0	0	0	0	0	0	0	2	1	1
EUROPE (TOTAL)	59	25	55	122	27	32	18	28	31	26	22	30	23	18	457	149	367
BELGIUM	5	0	2	6	2	2	2	2	6	3	2	0	1	1	26	12	19
FRANCE	24	4	13	36	5	7	3	6	8	3	6	8	4	3	106	44	86
GERMANY	7	4	10	18	4	6	2	4	1	5	1	1	2	2	60	17	50
ITALY	2	3	7	12	3	3	0	0	1	3	1	1	2	2	40	12	30
LUXEMBOURG	0	0	0	2	1	0	0	0	0	0	0	0	0	0	3	1	2
NETHERLANDS	2	2	2	6	1	1	0	0	2	2	1	0	2	0	21	6	17
DENMARK	1	1	0	0	2	1	0	0	0	1	0	0	0	0	5	3	3
IRELAND	0	0	0	2	0	0	0	0	0	1	1	1	0	0	4	1	3
U.K.	15	7	11	11	3	4	2	4	3	3	3	9	3	5	68	25	58
AUSTRIA	0	0	0	1	0	0	0	1	1	1	0	0	1	0	9	2	7
FINLAND	0	0	1	3	0	2	0	0	1	0	0	0	1	0	3	0	3
GREECE	0	0	0	2	1	0	1	1	0	0	1	2	1	1	8	1	7
NORWAY	0	0	0	1	0	0	0	1	2	1	0	2	0	0	7	3	4
PORTUGAL	1	1	1	1	0	0	4	0	2	2	1	2	6	0	9	2	8
SPAIN	1	5	6	13	4	4	4	3	0	1	1	5	6	1	51	12	40
SWEDEN	1	0	0	2	0	1	0	1	1	2	1	0	1	1	11	1	11
SWITZERLAND	0	0	1	2	1	0	0	1	1	1	0	0	0	0	8	3	5
TURKEY	0	0	0	4	0	1	0	0	2	0	0	0	0	0	7	1	6
OTHER EUROPE	0	0	0	0	1	1	0	0	0	3	2	1	1	2	11	3	8

TABLE 6.4.3 (CONTINUED)

COUNTRY OR REGION	NET FLOW UP TO 31-DEC-50	NO. OF ENTRIES DURING YEAR(S) 51-55	56-60	61-65	1966	1967	1968	1969	1970	1971	1972	1973	1974	1975	TOTAL ENTRIES 1951-75	TOTAL EXITS 1951-75	NET FLOW UP TO 1-JAN-76
N.AFR+M.EAS (TOTAL)	9	2	4	9	3	3	3	4	3	3	2	9	8	4	57	17	49
ALGERIA	0	0	1	1	0	0	1	0	1	1	0	0	0	0	4	1	3
EGYPT	0	0	0	0	0	0	0	0	0	0	0	0	0	0	0	0	0
IRAN	0	1	0	2	1	1	0	1	0	0	2	3	7	2	21	3	18
ISRAEL	1	0	0	1	0	1	0	2	1	1	0	1	0	0	5	1	5
LEBANON	0	0	0	1	0	0	0	0	0	0	0	0	0	0	2	1	1
MOROCCO	0	0	0	0	0	0	0	0	0	1	0	2	0	0	6	0	6
SAUDI ARABIA	2	0	0	0	0	0	1	0	1	0	0	0	1	2	4	0	6
OTHER N.AF+M.E.	6	1	3	3	2	1	1	1	0	0	0	3	1	0	15	11	10
E.+W.AFRICA (TOTAL)	0	7	3	11	2	4	5	2	4	4	0	2	3	1	48	7	41
GHANA	0	0	0	0	0	2	1	0	0	0	0	0	0	0	3	1	3
IVORY COAST	0	0	0	3	0	0	0	0	0	0	0	0	0	0	3	0	2
KENYA	0	0	1	0	0	0	0	0	0	0	0	0	0	0	2	0	2
LIBERIA	0	0	0	1	0	0	1	1	1	0	0	0	2	1	6	0	6
NIGERIA	0	0	0	2	0	0	0	0	0	2	0	0	0	0	3	1	2
ZAIRE	0	0	0	1	1	0	0	0	0	1	0	0	0	0	3	0	3
ZAMBIA	0	6	0	0	0	0	1	1	1	1	0	1	0	0	11	1	10
OTHER E.+W.AFR.	0	1	2	4	1	2	2	2	2	0	2	2	1	0	17	4	13
SOUTH ASIA (TOTAL)	0	2	10	17	1	2	4	1	1	1	1	0	1	2	46	9	37
INDIA	0	2	9	15	1	1	1	1	0	1	4	4	1	2	39	7	32
PAKISTAN	0	0	1	2	0	1	2	0	1	1	0	0	0	0	6	1	5
SRI LANKA	0	0	0	0	0	1	0	1	0	0	0	0	0	0	1	1	0
OTHER S.ASIA	0	0	0	0	0	0	0	0	0	0	0	0	0	0	0	0	0
EAST ASIA (TOTAL)	5	6	11	53	10	12	9	17	10	14	12	9	11	7	181	36	150
HONG KONG	0	0	0	0	1	0	0	0	1	1	0	1	0	0	3	1	2
INDONESIA	0	0	0	1	1	0	0	0	0	1	0	1	1	0	4	0	4
JAPAN	4	6	9	45	5	8	6	14	4	11	8	4	1	3	124	26	102
MALAYSIA	0	0	0	0	0	0	0	0	0	0	0	1	0	1	3	1	2
PHILIPPINES	0	0	1	5	1	1	0	1	0	0	1	1	0	2	14	1	12
SINGAPORE	0	0	0	0	0	2	0	2	2	0	0	1	3	0	8	1	7
S.KOREA	0	0	0	1	2	0	1	0	0	0	1	0	2	0	8	0	8
THAILAND	0	0	0	1	1	1	1	1	2	0	1	0	0	1	6	2	4
TAIWAN	0	0	1	0	0	0	0	0	1	0	1	1	1	1	8	1	7
OTHER E.ASIA	1	0	0	0	0	1	1	1	0	0	0	1	1	0	3	2	2
S.DOMINIONS (TOTAL)	15	6	17	16	2	7	1	8	8	2	7	7	4	4	89	27	77
AUSTRALIA	10	3	10	8	1	4	0	3	6	1	4	2	3	3	47	18	39
NEW ZEALAND	1	1	1	0	0	0	0	1	1	0	0	2	0	1	5	1	5
RHODESIA	0	2	0	0	0	0	0	1	0	0	0	0	1	1	4	0	4
S.AFRICA	4	1	6	8	1	3	1	3	1	1	3	4	1	0	33	8	29
OUTSIDE U.S. (TOTAL)	143	82	173	338	77	80	58	77	80	75	58	81	82	58	1319	383	1079

CHAPTER 6   - OWNERSHIP PATTERNS
SECTION 4   -- FLOW OF JOINT VENTURES
TABLE 4   --- MANUFACTURING SUBSIDIARIES,MAJORITY-OWNED AT ENTRY

NO. OF SUBSIDIARIES, BY PRINCIPAL INDUSTRY OF SUBSIDIARY AT TIME OF ENTRY INTO PARENT SYSTEM

PRINCIPAL INDUSTRY	NET FLOW UP TO 31-DEC-50	NO. OF ENTRIES DURING YEAR(S)													TOTAL ENTRIES 1951-75	TOTAL EXITS 1951-75	NET FLOW UP TO 1-JAN-76
		51-55	56-60	61-65	1966	1967	1968	1969	1970	1971	1972	1973	1974	1975			
BEVERAGES	1	0	2	3	3	1	6	0	1	0	1	0	1	0	18	5	14
TOBACCO	0	1	1	1	1	0	0	0	1	0	1	0	2	0	9	0	9
FOOD	8	1	26	52	11	12	10	8	9	8	6	0	1	6	150	42	116
TEXTILES+APPAREL	3	1	1	4	0	1	0	0	3	1	1	0	0	0	13	6	10
WOOD+FURNITURE	1	0	0	3	0	0	0	0	0	0	1	0	0	0	4	1	4
PAPER	4	9	5	12	4	2	2	1	2	2	0	0	1	3	43	10	37
PRINTING	1	0	1	2	1	0	1	0	0	0	0	1	0	0	6	1	6
INDUSTRIAL CHEM	12	2	15	18	3	2	1	0	1	0	1	1	0	1	46	21	37
PLASTICS	2	4	2	16	1	3	2	1	1	4	0	0	0	0	34	6	30
AGRIC CHEM	0	0	1	3	3	0	2	0	0	0	0	0	0	0	9	6	3
COSMETICS	3	0	3	0	0	1	1	2	2	4	0	1	2	1	17	3	17
DRUGS	5	3	18	18	1	6	4	1	2	6	1	3	1	1	65	11	59
OTHER CHEM	1	4	5	12	2	4	2	1	2	4	5	2	0	2	45	13	33
FABR PLASTICS	0	0	1	2	1	1	3	1	3	0	0	0	1	0	15	4	11
TIRES	1	0	3	4	1	2	1	1	0	0	2	0	0	1	15	0	16
REF PETROLEUM	3	1	3	7	1	1	0	0	0	0	0	0	0	0	13	6	10
OTH PETROLEUM	0	1	0	2	0	0	1	0	0	0	0	0	0	0	4	1	3
LEATHER	2	0	0	1	0	0	0	0	0	0	0	0	0	0	1	2	1
STONE+CLAY+CEMNT	1	0	2	2	0	2	2	1	2	0	0	0	1	0	7	2	6
ABRASIVES	1	3	3	0	1	1	1	2	2	3	0	0	0	0	17	5	13
GLASS	1	0	1	5	0	1	0	1	0	1	1	2	1	0	13	2	12
IRON+STEEL	0	0	0	1	0	2	1	0	0	2	2	1	2	0	11	1	10

369

TABLE 6 .4 .4 (CONTINUED)

PRINCIPAL INDUSTRY	NET FLOW UP TO 31-DEC-50	NO. OF ENTRIES DURING YEAR(S)													TOTAL ENTRIES 1951-75	TOTAL EXITS 1951-75	NET FLOW UP TO 1-JAN-76
		51-55	56-60	61-65	1966	1967	1968	1969	1970	1971	1972	1973	1974	1975			
NON-FERROUS	5	2	5	10	0	0	1	3	0	0	1	0	0	0	22	9	18
METAL CANS	0	0	4	1	0	1	0	0	0	0	0	0	0	0	6	3	3
OTHER FAB METAL	7	3	3	7	1	0	5	4	2	3	1	5	0	0	34	10	31
ENGINES+TURBIN	0	0	1	3	1	0	0	0	1	0	0	0	0	0	6	4	2
CONSTR MACH	3	1	3	3	0	8	2	1	1	2	4	0	3	2	30	6	27
FARM MACHINERY	0	0	1	5	0	0	0	0	0	0	0	0	0	0	6	3	3
OFFICE MC+COMPUT	3	2	2	0	1	0	0	0	1	0	0	0	0	1	7	3	7
SPEC MACHINERY	2	1	0	2	1	2	0	1	2	0	0	1	1	0	11	1	12
GENL MACHINERY	4	1	0	2	0	2	1	1	0	1	1	3	2	0	14	3	15
OTH NON-EL MC	2	0	1	3	0	1	1	0	1	1	2	0	1	0	11	2	11
EL LIGHT+WIRING	0	1	0	3	0	0	1	1	1	0	1	1	2	0	11	2	9
EL TRAN EQUIP	0	0	2	2	0	0	0	0	0	0	0	0	0	1	7	2	5
RADIO+TV+APPL	1	3	1	8	3	1	1	0	1	0	0	0	1	1	20	10	11
ELECTRONICS	0	0	1	3	1	1	1	0	1	0	1	2	0	0	11	4	7
OTHER ELEC	3	0	1	3	0	1	3	1	2	0	3	1	1	0	16	3	16
COMMUNICATION	3	0	0	1	0	0	0	1	2	0	1	2	0	0	6	3	6
MOTOR VEHIC	2	3	8	17	3	3	2	2	3	1	5	5	2	2	56	8	50
OTHER TRANSP	1	1	1	1	1	0	2	0	0	0	0	0	0	0	6	3	4
PRECISION	2	0	1	4	4	1	2	1	1	3	4	1	3	1	26	6	22
MISCELLANEOUS	10	5	10	6	0	0	5	3	4	6	1	5	2	3	50	17	43
TOTAL	98	53	136	252	49	62	68	39	51	56	48	39	32	26	911	250	759

CHAPTER 6   - OWNERSHIP PATTERNS
SECTION 4   -- FLOW OF JOINT VENTURES
TABLE 5   --- MANUFACTURING SUBSIDIARIES, CO-OWNED AT ENTRY

NO. OF SUBSIDIARIES, BY PRINCIPAL INDUSTRY OF SUBSIDIARY AT TIME OF ENTRY INTO PARENT SYSTEM

PRINCIPAL INDUSTRY	NET FLOW UP TO 31-DEC-50	NO. OF ENTRIES DURING YEAR(S)													TOTAL ENTRIES 1951-75	TOTAL EXITS 1951-75	NET FLOW UP TO 1-JAN-76
		51-55	56-60	61-65	1966	1967	1968	1969	1970	1971	1972	1973	1974	1975			
BEVERAGES	0	0	0	0	2	0	0	0	0	0	0	0	1	0	6	1	5
TOBACCO	0	0	0	0	0	0	1	0	0	0	1	1	0	0	0	0	0
FOOD	4	5	10	18	7	8	1	5	4	5	5	3	5	1	77	20	61
TEXTILES+APPAREL	3	0	3	13	3	1	0	3	1	5	0	0	0	0	29	16	16
WOOD+FURNITURE	0	0	1	4	1	0	1	1	2	2	0	0	0	0	10	3	7
PAPER	2	4	6	18	1	3	3	2	2	5	0	0	2	2	48	12	38
PRINTING	0	0	0	2	1	0	0	0	0	0	0	0	0	0	3	1	2
INDUSTRIAL CHEM	7	3	20	20	1	3	4	3	3	2	2	1	1	3	66	30	43
PLASTICS	1	2	7	19	2	0	3	2	1	4	2	2	2	3	49	17	33
AGRIC CHEM	1	1	1	7	0	0	0	0	0	0	0	0	2	0	13	6	8
COSMETICS	0	1	0	4	3	0	2	0	0	2	2	1	0	0	13	1	12
DRUGS	6	2	1	14	1	2	0	2	1	0	2	2	0	3	27	5	28
OTHER CHEM	0	1	2	6	3	5	2	3	2	4	4	3	2	3	40	7	33
FABR PLASTICS	0	1	0	9	1	0	0	3	2	3	1	0	0	0	20	9	11
TIRES	3	0	0	0	0	0	0	0	0	0	0	0	0	0	0	2	1
REF PETROLEUM	3	5	4	3	0	0	4	0	1	1	0	1	0	1	20	7	16
OTH PETROLEUM	1	0	7	8	2	2	0	1	0	1	1	1	0	1	24	7	18
LEATHER	0	0	0	0	1	0	1	0	0	0	0	1	0	0	3	1	2
STONE+CLAY+CEMNT	0	0	0	1	0	0	1	0	0	0	3	1	0	0	6	0	6
ABRASIVES	0	1	2	0	1	2	0	0	3	3	0	0	1	2	15	2	13
GLASS	0	0	2	1	2	4	2	0	0	0	1	2	0	0	14	1	13
IRON+STEEL	0	0	0	2	0	1	1	1	1	0	0	1	0	0	6	2	4

TABLE 6 . 4 . 5 (CONTINUED)

PRINCIPAL INDUSTRY	NET FLOW UP TO 31-DEC-50	NO. OF ENTRIES DURING YEAR(S)													TOTAL ENTRIES 1951-75	TOTAL EXITS 1951-75	NET FLOW UP TO 1-JAN-76
		51-55	56-60	61-65	1966	1967	1968	1969	1970	1971	1972	1973	1974	1975			
NON-FERROUS	0	1	9	5	0	2	1	4	1	2	1	0	1	0	27	7	20
METAL CANS	0	0	0	1	0	0	1	0	0	0	0	0	0	0	2	0	2
OTHER FAB METAL	1	0	5	7	1	2	4	5	2	2	2	1	1	2	33	6	28
ENGINES+TURBIN	0	0	0	3	0	0	0	0	0	0	0	0	2	0	5	2	3
CONSTR MACH	2	1	2	7	0	0	0	1	2	2	0	0	1	0	16	5	13
FARM MACHINERY	0	0	0	1	1	0	0	0	0	0	0	0	0	0	2	0	2
OFFICE MC+COMPUT	1	0	0	0	0	0	1	0	1	1	0	1	0	0	3	2	2
SPEC MACHINERY	0	1	0	5	0	1	0	0	1	1	0	1	0	0	10	5	5
GENL MACHINERY	0	1	0	3	1	1	2	1	1	0	1	2	0	1	14	2	12
OTH NON-EL MC	0	0	2	1	2	0	2	0	2	1	1	1	0	0	11	2	9
EL LIGHT+WIRING	0	0	0	1	0	0	0	0	0	1	0	1	0	0	3	1	2
EL TRAN EQUIP	0	0	1	0	1	0	0	0	0	0	0	0	0	0	2	1	1
RADIO+TV+APPL	0	1	1	5	0	0	1	0	0	0	0	0	0	1	9	5	4
ELECTRONICS	0	0	0	3	0	2	1	0	1	1	0	3	1	0	12	1	11
OTHER ELEC	2	2	4	4	0	1	0	0	2	1	1	1	2	1	19	6	15
COMMUNICATION	0	0	0	1	0	1	0	0	1	0	0	0	1	0	4	1	3
MOTOR VEHIC	0	0	5	14	2	4	0	0	4	1	5	5	0	3	43	14	29
OTHER TRANSP	0	0	1	0	0	0	0	2	0	0	1	0	0	0	4	3	1
PRECISION	0	0	0	3	0	0	1	1	0	0	1	2	1	0	9	1	8
MISCELLANEOUS	5	2	4	12	2	5	1	4	1	1	2	5	1	0	40	10	35
TOTAL	42	35	100	225	42	50	41	43	41	48	38	43	27	24	757	224	575

CHAPTER 6   - OWNERSHIP PATTERNS
SECTION 4   -- FLOW OF JOINT VENTURES
TABLE 6   --- MANUFACTURING SUBSIDIARIES, MINORITY-OWNED AT ENTRY

NO. OF SUBSIDIARIES, BY PRINCIPAL INDUSTRY OF SUBSIDIARY AT TIME OF ENTRY INTO PARENT SYSTEM

PRINCIPAL INDUSTRY	NET FLOW UP TO 31-DEC-50	NO. OF ENTRIES DURING YEAR(S)													TOTAL ENTRIES 1951-75	TOTAL EXITS 1951-75	NET FLOW UP TO 1-JAN-76
		51-55	56-60	61-65	1966	1967	1968	1969	1970	1971	1972	1973	1974	1975			
BEVERAGES	1	0	0	0	0	0	0	0	0	0	0	2	1	0	3	0	4
TOBACCO	0	0	0	0	0	0	3	0	0	3	0	0	0	0	6	0	6
FOOD	6	4	11	14	8	5	2	4	4	2	4	1	0	2	61	23	44
TEXTILES+APPAREL	2	0	5	4	0	1	1	0	1	0	0	3	1	1	17	4	15
WOOD+FURNITURE	1	0	1	2	0	1	0	1	0	0	0	2	0	0	6	0	7
PAPER	5	4	10	16	3	1	1	3	3	2	0	2	0	2	47	9	43
PRINTING	0	1	0	0	4	0	0	1	1	0	0	1	0	0	7	2	5
INDUSTRIAL CHEM	5	4	11	11	8	1	5	1	1	4	2	1	4	2	55	15	45
PLASTICS	1	3	9	23	2	1	0	0	0	3	4	0	4	2	51	17	35
AGRIC CHEM	0	1	2	5	1	2	1	0	0	1	0	0	0	1	14	4	10
COSMETICS	0	0	1	2	1	0	0	1	0	0	1	1	1	0	8	2	6
DRUGS	1	2	3	3	0	0	1	1	0	1	0	0	2	1	14	3	12
OTHER CHEM	4	3	11	11	1	3	3	1	2	3	3	3	4	3	51	17	38
FABR PLASTICS	1	1	0	5	1	2	0	1	0	2	0	1	1	0	14	5	10
TIRES	12	3	1	3	0	1	0	0	0	0	0	0	0	1	9	7	14
REF PETROLEUM	3	0	7	10	1	3	6	6	5	1	1	0	4	2	46	7	42
OTH PETROLEUM	2	0	2	4	2	4	0	1	1	0	0	1	0	0	15	5	12
LEATHER	0	0	0	1	0	0	1	0	0	0	0	1	0	0	3	1	2
STONE+CLAY+CEMNT	1	1	3	2	1	0	0	1	1	0	0	2	0	0	11	3	9
ABRASIVES	3	3	2	6	5	4	0	0	2	1	1	1	0	1	26	4	25
GLASS	8	2	1	3	2	0	0	2	1	1	0	1	0	0	13	7	14
IRON+STEEL	0	0	1	2	0	0	1	0	1	1	0	1	2	3	12	3	9

TABLE 6.4.6 (CONTINUED)

PRINCIPAL INDUSTRY	NET FLOW UP TO 31-DEC-50	NO. OF ENTRIES DURING YEAR(S)													TOTAL ENTRIES 1951-75	TOTAL EXITS 1951-75	NET FLOW UP TO 1-JAN-76
		51-55	56-60	61-65	1966	1967	1968	1969	1970	1971	1972	1973	1974	1975			
NON-FERROUS	0	0	9	6	2	3	5	5	3	3	0	1	3	3	42	10	32
METAL CANS	5	1	1	4	1	0	1	1	0	0	0	0	1	1	11	4	12
OTHER FAB METAL	0	1	4	17	1	3	1	1	3	3	2	8	3	2	49	10	39
ENGINES+TURBIN	1	0	0	0	1	0	1	1	0	0	0	2	0	0	5	0	6
CONSTR MACH	0	0	3	3	1	2	0	1	4	1	2	1	6	1	25	4	21
FARM MACHINERY	0	1	1	5	0	0	0	2	2	1	0	0	1	0	13	2	11
OFFICE MC+COMPUT	1	0	1	4	0	0	0	1	0	0	0	0	0	0	6	4	3
SPEC MACHINERY	1	1	3	6	1	1	0	0	1	1	0	4	0	0	18	6	13
GENL MACHINERY	3	2	0	2	1	2	1	2	1	4	2	2	0	0	19	3	19
OTH NON-EL MC	1	0	0	8	2	1	0	1	2	0	0	1	1	0	16	3	14
EL LIGHT+WIRING	1	0	2	2	0	2	0	0	0	0	0	0	1	0	7	0	8
EL TRAN EQUIP	0	0	0	1	0	0	0	1	0	0	0	0	0	0	2	0	2
RADIO+TV+APPL	0	0	0	1	0	4	1	1	3	0	0	0	1	0	11	3	8
ELECTRONICS	0	3	5	3	0	1	1	0	1	1	1	0	0	0	16	7	9
OTHER ELEC	3	1	0	7	1	0	2	1	5	1	1	3	3	1	26	10	19
COMMUNICATION	2	0	1	0	0	0	0	0	1	0	0	0	0	0	2	3	1
MOTOR VEHIC	7	4	14	32	2	4	2	6	1	2	11	9	1	4	92	30	69
OTHER TRANSP	0	0	4	0	0	0	0	0	1	0	0	3	0	0	8	3	5
PRECISION	2	0	1	3	0	0	2	1	0	0	1	3	2	1	14	6	10
MISCELLANEOUS	4	4	4	6	2	4	4	2	2	4	1	1	1	2	37	16	25
TOTAL	87	50	134	237	55	56	46	50	52	45	37	62	48	36	908	262	733

374

CHAPTER 6   - OWNERSHIP PATTERNS
SECTION 5   -- OUTSIDE OWNERS IN 1975
TABLE 1   --- BY PRINCIPAL ACTIVITY IN 1975

NO. OF SUBSIDIARIES ACTIVE AT 1-JAN-76

ACTIVITY IN 1975	CATEGORY OF PRINCIPAL OUTSIDE OWNER, AND PERCENTAGE OWNED BY PRINCIPAL OUTSIDE OWNER, IN 1975																					
	LOCAL PRIVATE					LOCAL STATE					FOREIGN PRIVATE					WIDELY DISPERSED					UN-KNOWN	WHOLLY OWNED BY PARENT
	5-49	50	51-94	UNK	TOT	5-49	50	51-94	UNK	TOT	5-49	50	51-94	UNK	TOT	5-49	50	51-94	UNK	TOT		
MANUFACTURING	230	243	166	45	684	35	18	22	6	81	72	42	19	10	143	52	9	41	13	115	994	3758
SALES	39	40	21	6	106	5	6	3	1	15	25	19	7	2	53	2	3	10	2	17	254	2388
EXTRACTION	10	5	9	3	27	8	2	3	1	14	10	4	2	3	19	0	0	1	0	1	57	238
OTHER	15	22	18	2	57	7	3	1	0	11	11	6	3	0	20	1	1	6	1	9	313	1567
UNKNOWN	2	0	0	0	2	0	0	0	0	0	0	0	1	1	2	0	0	0	0	0	145	108
TOTAL	296	310	214	56	876	55	29	29	8	121	118	71	32	16	237	55	13	58	16	142	1763	8059

CHAPTER 6   - OWNERSHIP PATTERNS
SECTION 5   -- OUTSIDE OWNERS IN 1975
TABLE 2   --- BY METHOD OF ENTRY

NO. OF SUBSIDIARIES ACTIVE AT 1-JAN-76

METHOD OF ENTRY	CATEGORY OF PRINCIPAL OUTSIDE OWNER, AND PERCENTAGE OWNED BY PRINCIPAL OUTSIDE OWNER, IN 1975																				UN-KNOWN	WHOLLY OWNED BY PARENT
	LOCAL PRIVATE					LOCAL STATE					FOREIGN PRIVATE					WIDELY DISPERSED						
	5-49	50	51-94	UNK	TOT	5-49	50	51-94	UNK	TOT	5-49	50	51-94	UNK	TOT	5-49	50	51-94	UNK	TOT		
NEWLY FORMED	173	222	120	17	532	49	26	20	2	97	72	50	16	13	151	27	5	31	5	68	781	4387
ACQUIRED	113	66	83	33	295	6	3	5	4	18	30	15	14	3	62	21	7	24	9	61	775	2931
DESCENDENT	2	6	3	2	13	0	0	3	1	4	4	3	0	0	7	6	1	2	1	10	33	149
UNKNOWN	8	16	8	4	36	0	0	1	1	2	12	3	2	0	17	1	0	1	1	3	174	592
TOTAL	296	310	214	56	876	55	29	29	8	121	118	71	32	16	237	55	13	58	16	142	1763	8059

CHAPTER 6   - OWNERSHIP PATTERNS
SECTION 5   -- OUTSIDE OWNERS IN 1975
TABLE 3   --- BY GEOGRAPHICAL REGION

NO. OF SUBSIDIARIES ACTIVE AT 1-JAN-76

CATEGORY OF PRINCIPAL OUTSIDE OWNER, AND PERCENTAGE OWNED BY PRINCIPAL OUTSIDE OWNER, IN 1975

COUNTRY OR REGION	LOCAL PRIVATE					LOCAL STATE					FOREIGN PRIVATE					WIDELY DISPERSED					UN-KNOWN	WHOLLY OWNED BY PARENT
	5-49	50	51-94	UNK	TOT	5-49	50	51-94	UNK	TOT	5-49	50	51-94	UNK	TOT	5-49	50	51-94	UNK	TOT		
CANADA	9	16	4	1	30	1	1	1	0	3	10	5	1	2	18	10	1	1	0	12	121	979
LATIN AMER. (TOTAL)	51	42	82	13	188	13	1	5	0	19	27	13	8	3	51	18	5	17	5	45	473	1686
C.AM.+CARIB. (TOTAL)	20	20	42	5	87	6	1	3	0	10	13	4	4	3	24	8	4	12	4	28	204	827
BAHAMAS	0	0	0	0	0	0	0	0	0	0	1	1	0	0	2	0	0	0	0	0	6	48
BERMUDA	0	0	0	0	0	0	0	0	0	0	0	1	0	0	2	0	0	0	0	0	3	69
COSTA RICA	0	0	0	1	1	0	0	0	0	0	4	0	0	1	5	0	0	0	1	1	3	35
GUATEMALA	1	2	0	2	3	1	0	0	0	1	2	0	0	0	2	0	1	0	0	3	11	45
JAMAICA	2	0	2	2	5	0	0	1	0	2	0	0	0	0	3	2	0	0	0	0	7	21
MEXICO	16	14	37	2	69	0	0	1	0	1	0	2	2	0	3	5	3	9	2	19	130	330
NETH.ANTILLES	0	0	0	0	0	0	0	0	0	0	0	0	0	0	0	0	0	9	0	1	8	53
NICARAGUA	1	0	1	0	2	3	0	0	0	3	0	0	0	0	0	0	0	1	0	1	0	9
PANAMA	0	3	1	0	4	0	0	0	0	0	0	1	0	0	2	0	1	1	1	2	21	141
OTHER C.AM+CAR.	1	1	1	0	3	1	1	1	0	3	3	1	2	1	7	1	0	1	0	2	13	76
S.AMERICA (TOTAL)	31	22	40	8	101	7	0	2	0	9	14	9	4	0	27	10	1	5	1	17	269	859
BOLIVIA	1	0	0	1	1	0	0	0	0	0	0	0	1	0	1	1	1	0	0	1	1	7
CHILE	5	5	1	0	3	1	0	0	0	2	0	0	0	0	1	1	0	0	0	0	13	32
COLOMBIA	1	6	6	1	16	0	0	0	0	0	0	2	0	0	2	1	0	3	0	5	37	101
ECUADOR	4	1	0	0	5	1	0	0	0	1	1	0	0	0	1	0	1	0	1	1	3	31
PERU	2	0	0	3	5	1	0	0	0	3	3	0	1	0	4	1	0	0	0	1	20	47
ARGENTINA	11	1	6	0	9	3	0	0	0	2	4	5	1	0	4	2	0	2	0	4	39	151
BRAZIL	1	10	14	5	40	2	0	0	0	0	4	0	0	0	10	3	1	0	0	3	65	255
URUGUAY	1	0	0	0	1	0	0	0	0	2	0	0	1	0	0	0	0	0	0	1	6	31
VENEZUELA	5	5	10	1	21	0	1	0	0	1	2	0	1	0	3	1	0	1	0	0	83	192
OTHER S.AMER.	0	0	0	0	0	0	0	0	0	0	0	0	0	0	0	1	1	0	0	1	2	12
EUROPE (TOTAL)	112	106	50	17	285	10	10	9	4	33	48	30	16	3	97	10	2	17	5	34	730	3650
BELGIUM	2	3	1	1	7	0	1	0	0	1	3	4	3	0	9	0	1	0	0	0	39	253
FRANCE	32	12	12	7	63	5	0	3	0	8	13	4	2	1	20	2	1	4	1	7	151	368
GERMANY	17	21	6	3	47	5	1	1	1	4	5	8	3	0	17	0	0	1	1	2	79	539
ITALY	13	9	1	1	24	1	1	1	2	5	5	1	3	1	3	4	0	1	1	6	74	270
LUXEMBOURG	0	0	0	0	0	2	0	0	0	5	0	0	0	0	2	0	0	0	0	0	2	35
NETHERLANDS	5	2	2	1	10	0	0	0	0	0	6	2	2	0	10	0	2	0	0	2	26	258
DENMARK	1	1	0	0	2	0	0	0	0	0	1	2	0	0	1	0	0	1	0	0	11	101
IRELAND	0	1	1	0	2	0	0	0	0	1	1	0	1	0	1	1	0	0	0	1	17	93
U.K.	17	22	13	0	52	1	0	0	0	1	5	6	3	1	15	3	0	4	1	8	138	870
AUSTRIA	1	1	0	0	2	0	0	0	0	0	2	0	0	0	2	0	0	0	0	2	12	72
FINLAND	0	0	0	0	0	0	1	0	1	1	0	0	0	0	0	0	1	0	1	0	2	43
GREECE	1	2	2	0	4	1	0	0	1	1	2	0	0	0	2	0	0	0	0	1	10	36
NORWAY	2	2	1	0	5	0	1	0	0	1	0	0	0	0	0	1	0	1	0	1	17	74
PORTUGAL	1	2	3	0	6	1	0	0	1	4	3	1	0	0	4	0	1	0	0	2	17	47
SPAIN	16	22	6	2	46	0	0	1	0	1	3	1	0	0	2	1	1	2	0	3	92	149
SWEDEN	0	7	0	1	8	0	1	0	1	0	3	1	1	0	10	0	0	0	0	1	18	161
SWITZERLAND	0	0	1	0	2	0	0	1	0	3	3	3	0	0	7	0	1	0	0	1	24	247
TURKEY	2	0	2	2	5	1	1	1	0	3	1	1	0	1	2	0	0	0	0	0	10	14
OTHER EUROPE	2	0	0	0	2	0	0	3	0	3	0	0	0	0	0	0	0	0	1	1	6	20

TABLE 6.5.3 (CONTINUED)

CATEGORY OF PRINCIPAL OUTSIDE OWNER, AND PERCENTAGE OWNED BY PRINCIPAL OUTSIDE OWNER, IN 1975

COUNTRY OR REGION	LOCAL PRIVATE					LOCAL STATE					FOREIGN PRIVATE					WIDELY DISPERSED					UN-KNOWN	WHOLLY OWNED BY PARENT
	5-49	50	51-94	UNK	TOT	5-49	50	51-94	UNK	TOT	5-49	50	51-94	UNK	TOT	5-49	50	51-94	UNK	TOT	KNOWN	PARENT
N.AFR+M.EAST(TOTAL)	11	3	11	1	26	9	10	5	1	25	4	1	1	0	6	0	1	3	2	6	56	145
ALGERIA	1	0	0	0	1	1	2	1	0	2	0	1	1	0	1	0	0	0	0	0	4	6
EGYPT	0	0	0	0	0	0	1	0	0	2	1	0	1	0	1	0	0	0	0	0	5	12
IRAN	2	2	2	0	8	5	5	1	1	12	1	0	0	0	1	0	2	3	1	3	13	30
ISRAEL	4	0	2	0	6	2	0	1	0	2	0	1	0	0	1	0	0	0	0	0	4	7
LEBANON	1	0	2	0	3	1	0	0	0	0	1	0	0	0	1	0	1	1	0	2	4	17
MOROCCO	1	0	2	0	3	0	1	1	0	3	0	0	0	0	1	0	0	0	1	0	8	12
SAUDI ARABIA	2	1	1	0	4	0	2	0	0	4	0	0	0	0	0	0	0	0	0	0	2	12
OTHER N.AF+M.E.	0	0	2	1	3	0	0	0	0	0	1	0	0	0	1	0	1	0	1	1	16	49
E.+W.AFRICA (TOTAL)	7	3	5	1	16	13	3	2	0	18	11	3	1	3	18	0	0	1	0	1	46	222
GHANA	0	0	0	0	0	2	0	0	0	2	2	3	0	0	2	0	0	0	0	0	4	9
IVORY COAST	0	0	1	0	1	1	0	0	0	1	3	0	0	0	3	0	0	0	0	0	0	8
KENYA	1	1	0	0	2	1	0	0	0	1	0	0	0	0	3	0	0	0	0	0	4	18
LIBERIA	1	0	0	0	1	0	2	0	0	3	1	0	0	1	3	0	0	0	0	0	6	35
NIGERIA	2	0	0	1	4	3	0	0	0	3	0	0	0	0	1	0	0	0	0	0	14	35
ZAIRE	0	0	0	0	0	2	0	0	0	2	1	0	0	0	0	0	0	1	0	0	2	21
ZAMBIA	1	0	3	0	4	0	0	1	0	1	1	2	0	0	3	0	0	0	0	0	8	31
OTHER E.+W.AFR.	2	2	1	0	5	4	1	1	0	6	3	1	0	1	5	0	0	0	0	0	8	65
SOUTH ASIA (TOTAL)	13	5	4	1	23	3	4	4	0	7	1	0	0	1	2	3	1	6	0	10	54	48
INDIA	8	5	3	1	17	1	4	4	0	5	1	0	0	1	2	3	1	6	0	10	39	28
PAKISTAN	5	0	1	0	6	1	0	0	0	1	0	0	0	0	0	0	0	0	0	0	13	13
SRI LANKA	0	0	0	0	0	0	0	0	0	1	0	0	0	0	0	0	0	0	0	0	2	7
OTHER S.ASIA	0	0	0	0	0	1	0	0	0	1	0	0	0	0	0	0	0	0	0	0	0	0
EAST ASIA (TOTAL)	62	108	42	16	228	5	4	3	3	15	7	10	1	1	19	10	0	6	2	18	172	552
HONG KONG	2	2	0	0	4	0	0	0	3	1	0	0	0	0	1	10	0	6	2	18	11	81
INDONESIA	8	0	0	1	9	1	0	0	0	2	2	1	1	1	2	0	0	0	0	0	11	37
JAPAN	36	94	35	8	173	1	0	0	0	3	2	3	0	0	6	1	0	2	0	5	95	144
MALAYSIA	3	0	0	3	3	1	0	0	0	0	0	1	1	0	1	1	0	1	0	2	6	48
PHILIPPINES	2	1	5	0	11	0	0	0	0	1	1	0	0	0	1	0	0	0	0	3	17	76
SINGAPORE	1	0	1	2	3	0	0	0	0	0	1	0	0	0	1	0	0	0	0	0	7	62
S.KOREA	3	6	0	1	12	0	3	0	0	1	0	0	0	0	0	2	0	1	0	0	9	11
THAILAND	5	0	0	1	6	2	0	0	0	5	1	1	0	0	1	2	2	2	0	0	8	43
TAIWAN	2	3	1	0	7	0	0	0	1	3	0	1	0	0	2	3	0	0	0	0	6	36
OTHER E.ASIA	0	0	0	0	0	0	0	0	0	0	0	3	0	0	3	0	0	0	0	0	2	14
S.DOMINIONS (TOTAL)	31	27	16	6	80	1	0	0	0	1	10	9	4	3	26	4	3	7	2	16	111	777
AUSTRALIA	16	17	11	2	46	0	0	0	0	0	6	7	4	2	19	1	3	3	1	8	64	407
NEW ZEALAND	8	2	1	0	11	0	0	0	0	0	0	0	0	0	1	1	1	1	1	3	13	104
RHODESIA	1	0	0	0	1	0	0	0	0	0	1	1	0	0	2	1	0	0	0	1	4	18
S.AFRICA	6	8	4	4	22	1	0	0	0	1	3	1	0	0	4	1	0	3	0	4	30	248
OUTSIDE U.S.(TOTAL)	296	310	214	56	876	55	29	29	8	121	118	71	32	16	237	55	13	58	16	142	1763	8059

CHAPTER 6   – OWNERSHIP PATTERNS
SECTION 5   -- OUTSIDE OWNERS IN 1975
TABLE 4   --- FOR MANUFACTURING SUBSIDIARIES, BY REGION

NO. OF MANUFACTURING SUBSIDIARIES ACTIVE AT 1-JAN-76

CATEGORY OF PRINCIPAL OUTSIDE OWNER, AND PERCENTAGE OWNED BY PRINCIPAL OUTSIDE OWNER, IN 1975

COUNTRY OR REGION	LOCAL PRIVATE 5-49	50	51-94	UNK	TOT	LOCAL STATE 5-49	50	51-94	UNK	TOT	FOREIGN PRIVATE 5-49	50	51-94	UNK	TOT	WIDELY DISPERSED 5-49	50	51-94	UNK	TOT	UN-KNOWN	WHOLLY OWNED BY PARENT
CANADA	3	8	3	1	15	0	0	0	0	0	3	1	0	0	4	10	0	1	0	11	46	518
LATIN AMER. (TOTAL)	45	31	60	11	147	12	1	3	0	16	22	10	4	3	39	17	5	14	5	41	304	778
C.AM.+CARIB. (TOTAL)	19	12	30	5	66	5	1	1	0	7	9	2	3	3	17	7	4	10	4	25	130	297
BAHAMAS	0	0	0	0	0	1	0	0	0	0	0	0	0	0	0	0	0	0	0	0	2	3
BERMUDA	0	0	0	0	0	0	0	0	0	0	0	0	0	0	0	0	0	0	0	0	0	0
COSTA RICA	0	0	0	1	1	0	0	0	0	0	3	0	1	0	4	0	0	1	0	1	2	15
GUATEMALA	0	0	1	0	1	0	0	0	0	0	2	0	0	0	2	1	0	0	0	1	1	20
JAMAICA	2	0	1	2	5	0	0	0	0	0	1	0	1	0	2	0	0	0	0	0	7	7
MEXICO	15	10	25	2	52	0	0	0	0	0	1	1	0	0	2	4	3	8	2	17	89	204
NETH.ANTILLES	0	0	0	0	0	0	0	0	0	0	1	0	1	0	2	0	0	0	0	0	0	6
NICARAGUA	1	0	1	0	2	3	0	0	0	3	0	0	0	0	0	0	0	1	0	1	5	2
PANAMA	0	1	1	0	2	0	1	0	0	1	0	0	0	0	0	1	0	0	0	1	8	15
OTHER C.AM+CAR.	1	0	1	0	2	1	0	1	1	3	2	1	1	1	5	1	1	0	0	2	12	25
S.AMERICA (TOTAL)	26	19	30	6	81	7	0	2	0	9	13	8	1	0	22	10	1	4	1	16	174	481
BOLIVIA	1	0	0	0	1	0	0	0	0	0	0	0	0	0	0	1	0	0	0	1	0	1
CHILE	1	0	0	0	1	1	0	0	0	0	0	1	0	0	1	0	0	0	0	0	4	20
COLOMBIA	4	5	4	0	13	0	0	2	0	2	0	2	0	0	2	1	1	2	1	5	25	59
ECUADOR	1	1	2	0	4	1	0	0	0	0	1	0	0	0	1	1	0	0	0	1	2	14
PERU	4	0	0	1	5	3	0	0	0	1	2	0	0	0	2	0	0	1	0	1	15	12
ARGENTINA	1	1	6	0	8	0	0	0	0	0	4	0	0	0	4	2	0	1	0	3	23	92
BRAZIL	9	8	9	4	30	2	0	0	0	2	4	5	1	0	10	3	0	0	0	3	46	164
URUGUAY	1	0	0	0	1	0	0	0	0	0	0	0	0	0	0	1	0	0	0	1	4	15
VENEZUELA	4	4	8	1	17	0	0	0	0	1	2	0	0	0	2	0	0	0	0	0	55	101
OTHER S.AMER.	0	0	0	0	0	0	0	0	0	0	0	0	0	0	0	1	0	0	0	1	0	3
EUROPE (TOTAL)	88	77	43	14	222	3	5	7	3	18	21	17	10	2	50	9	2	8	2	21	383	1733
BELGIUM	1	2	1	1	5	0	0	1	0	1	2	2	2	0	6	1	0	2	0	3	28	119
FRANCE	23	11	11	5	50	1	1	0	0	2	7	4	3	0	14	2	0	2	0	4	85	198
GERMANY	14	16	5	2	37	0	1	2	0	3	4	2	0	0	6	0	0	2	0	2	46	307
ITALY	11	7	1	1	20	0	1	0	0	1	0	2	1	0	3	4	1	1	0	6	42	158
LUXEMBOURG	0	0	0	0	0	0	1	1	0	2	0	0	0	0	0	0	1	0	0	1	1	12
NETHERLANDS	5	0	2	1	8	0	0	0	0	0	1	2	1	0	4	0	0	1	0	1	12	103
DENMARK	1	0	0	0	1	0	0	0	0	0	0	0	0	0	0	0	0	0	0	0	3	36
IRELAND	0	1	1	0	2	0	0	0	0	0	1	0	0	0	1	0	0	0	0	0	5	52
U.K.	11	17	8	0	36	0	0	1	0	1	2	3	1	0	6	0	0	0	0	0	52	466
AUSTRIA	0	0	0	0	0	0	0	0	0	0	0	0	0	0	0	1	0	0	0	1	6	24
FINLAND	0	0	0	0	0	0	0	1	0	1	0	0	0	0	0	1	0	0	0	1	1	6
GREECE	1	0	2	0	3	0	0	0	0	0	0	2	0	0	2	0	0	0	0	0	5	20
NORWAY	1	1	1	0	2	0	0	0	0	0	0	0	0	0	0	0	0	0	0	0	4	20
PORTUGAL	1	0	3	0	4	1	1	0	0	2	0	0	0	0	0	0	0	0	0	0	9	24
SPAIN	15	16	6	2	39	0	0	1	0	1	3	0	1	0	4	0	0	0	0	0	59	86
SWEDEN	0	6	1	0	7	0	0	0	0	0	0	0	0	2	2	0	0	0	2	2	10	52
SWITZERLAND	0	0	0	0	0	1	0	0	2	3	1	0	0	0	1	0	0	0	0	0	7	39
TURKEY	2	0	1	2	5	0	0	0	0	0	0	1	0	0	1	0	0	0	0	0	6	6
OTHER EUROPE	2	0	0	0	2	0	0	0	1	1	0	0	0	0	0	0	0	0	0	0	2	5

TABLE 6.5.4 (CONTINUED)

CATEGORY OF PRINCIPAL OUTSIDE OWNER, AND PERCENTAGE OWNED BY PRINCIPAL OUTSIDE OWNER, IN 1975

COUNTRY OR REGION	LOCAL PRIVATE 5-49	50	51-94	UNK	TOT	LOCAL STATE 5-49	50	51-94	UNK	TOT	FOREIGN PRIVATE 5-49	50	51-94	UNK	TOT	WIDELY DISPERSED 5-49	50	51-94	UNK	TOT	UN-KNOWN	WHOLLY OWNED BY PARENT
N.AFR+M.EAST(TOTAL)	8	3	8	0	19	7	5	4	1	17	2	1	0	0	3	0	0	3	2	5	26	30
ALGERIA	0	0	0	0	0	1	0	0	0	1	0	0	0	0	0	0	0	0	0	0	0	3
EGYPT	0	0	0	0	0	0	0	0	0	0	1	0	0	0	1	0	0	0	0	0	1	0
IRAN	2	2	4	0	8	3	3	1	1	8	0	0	0	0	0	0	0	2	1	3	8	6
ISRAEL	3	0	2	0	5	2	0	0	0	2	0	0	0	0	0	0	0	0	0	0	3	5
LEBANON	1	0	0	0	1	0	0	0	0	0	1	0	0	0	1	0	0	0	0	0	2	7
MOROCCO	1	0	2	0	3	1	2	0	0	3	0	1	0	0	1	0	0	1	0	1	5	4
SAUDI ARABIA	1	1	0	0	2	0	0	3	0	3	0	0	0	0	0	0	0	0	0	0	1	0
OTHER N.AF+M.E.	0	0	0	0	0	0	0	0	0	0	0	0	0	0	0	0	0	0	1	1	6	5
E.+W.AFRICA (TOTAL)	1	2	3	1	7	6	3	2	0	11	6	2	0	2	10	0	1	0	0	1	12	50
GHANA	0	0	0	0	0	2	1	0	0	3	1	0	0	0	1	0	1	0	0	1	1	2
IVORY COAST	0	0	0	0	0	1	0	0	0	1	2	0	0	0	2	0	0	0	0	0	2	3
KENYA	0	1	0	0	1	1	0	0	0	1	0	0	0	1	1	0	0	0	0	0	1	9
LIBERIA	0	0	0	0	0	0	2	1	0	3	0	0	0	0	0	0	0	0	0	0	0	1
NIGERIA	0	0	0	1	1	2	0	0	0	2	0	0	0	0	0	0	0	0	0	0	6	11
ZAIRE	0	0	0	0	0	0	0	0	0	0	0	0	0	0	0	0	0	0	0	0	1	9
ZAMBIA	0	1	1	0	2	0	0	1	0	1	2	1	0	0	3	0	0	0	0	0	0	8
OTHER E.+W.AFR.	1	0	2	0	3	0	0	0	0	0	1	1	0	1	3	0	0	0	0	0	1	8
SOUTH ASIA (TOTAL)	13	5	4	1	23	3	0	4	0	7	1	0	0	1	2	2	1	6	0	9	47	23
INDIA	8	5	3	1	17	1	0	4	0	5	1	0	0	1	2	2	1	6	0	9	35	14
PAKISTAN	5	0	1	0	6	1	0	0	0	1	0	0	0	0	0	0	0	0	0	0	10	6
SRI LANKA	0	0	0	0	0	0	0	0	0	0	0	0	0	0	0	0	0	0	0	0	2	3
OTHER S.ASIA	0	0	0	0	0	1	0	0	0	1	0	0	0	0	0	0	0	0	0	0	0	0
EAST ASIA (TOTAL)	47	94	38	13	192	4	4	2	2	12	7	5	0	1	13	10	0	5	2	17	114	220
HONG KONG	0	0	0	0	0	0	0	0	0	0	0	1	0	0	1	0	0	0	0	0	6	21
INDONESIA	5	0	0	1	6	0	0	0	0	0	0	1	0	0	1	0	0	0	0	0	9	11
JAPAN	28	84	34	6	152	1	1	0	1	3	3	3	0	0	6	1	0	3	0	4	59	51
MALAYSIA	2	0	0	0	2	1	0	0	0	1	0	0	0	0	0	3	0	0	0	3	6	19
PHILIPPINES	2	2	2	1	7	0	0	0	0	0	1	0	0	0	1	0	0	0	0	0	12	45
SINGAPORE	1	0	0	0	1	0	0	0	0	0	1	0	0	0	1	0	0	0	0	0	3	30
S.KOREA	3	6	1	2	12	0	3	2	0	5	0	0	0	0	0	2	0	0	1	3	6	5
THAILAND	4	0	1	0	5	0	0	0	0	0	1	0	0	1	2	0	0	1	0	1	7	18
TAIWAN	2	3	1	1	7	2	0	0	1	3	1	0	0	0	1	3	0	1	1	5	6	18
OTHER E.ASIA	0	0	0	0	0	0	0	0	0	0	0	0	0	0	0	1	0	0	0	1	0	2
S.DOMINIONS (TOTAL)	25	23	7	4	59	0	0	0	0	0	10	6	4	2	22	4	1	3	2	10	62	406
AUSTRALIA	15	15	4	1	35	0	0	0	0	0	6	4	4	1	15	1	1	1	1	4	35	221
NEW ZEALAND	4	2	1	0	7	0	0	0	0	0	0	1	0	0	1	1	0	1	1	3	7	52
RHODESIA	1	0	0	0	1	0	0	0	0	0	1	0	0	1	2	1	0	0	0	1	0	9
S.AFRICA	5	6	2	3	16	0	0	0	0	0	3	1	0	0	4	1	0	1	0	2	20	124
OUTSIDE U.S. (TOTAL)	230	243	166	45	684	35	18	22	6	81	72	42	19	10	143	52	9	41	13	115	994	3758

CHAPTER 6   - OWNERSHIP PATTERNS
SECTION 5   -- OUTSIDE OWNERS IN 1975
TABLE 5   --- BY PRINCIPAL INDUSTRY

NO. OF MANUFACTURING SUBSIDIARIES ACTIVE AT 1-JAN-76, BY PRINCIPAL INDUSTRY IN 1975

CATEGORY OF PRINCIPAL OUTSIDE OWNER, AND PERCENTAGE OWNED BY PRINCIPAL OUTSIDE OWNER, IN 1975

PRINCIPAL INDUSTRY	LOCAL PRIVATE					LOCAL STATE					FOREIGN PRIVATE					WIDELY DISPERSED					UN-KNOWN	WHOLLY OWNED BY PARENT
	5-49	50	51-94	UNK	TOT	5-49	50	51-94	UNK	TOT	5-49	50	51-94	UNK	TOT	5-49	50	51-94	UNK	TOT		
BEVERAGES	0	1	1	0	2	0	0	0	0	0	0	0	0	0	0	2	0	2	0	4	14	61
TOBACCO	1	0	1	1	3	1	0	0	0	1	0	0	0	1	0	0	0	1	0	0	12	10
FOOD	32	26	7	4	69	1	3	0	0	4	5	2	1	1	9	5	1	1	1	8	110	435
TEXTILES+APPAREL	5	5	7	1	18	0	0	0	0	0	1	0	0	0	1	0	0	0	0	0	19	57
WOOD+FURNITURE	3	4	0	2	9	0	0	0	0	0	0	1	0	0	1	0	0	0	0	0	9	48
PAPER	19	18	3	0	40	2	0	1	0	3	3	8	0	0	11	4	2	6	0	12	33	107
PRINTING	2	1	0	1	4	0	1	0	0	1	1	0	0	0	1	0	0	0	0	0	6	52
INDUSTRIAL CHEM	7	19	6	1	34	0	0	2	0	2	2	5	2	1	10	2	0	2	2	6	52	104
PLASTICS	14	22	9	1	46	3	2	2	0	7	2	1	1	1	5	1	1	3	0	5	31	86
AGRIC CHEM	2	2	1	0	5	2	1	3	0	6	0	1	0	0	0	1	0	0	0	1	6	33
COSMETICS	5	3	1	1	10	3	0	0	0	3	1	1	0	0	2	0	0	0	0	0	23	238
DRUGS	16	16	1	1	34	3	0	0	0	3	0	1	0	0	1	3	0	0	0	3	75	430
OTHER CHEM	8	18	9	5	40	1	3	1	0	5	7	5	3	0	15	4	0	5	3	12	61	176
FABR PLASTICS	1	5	5	0	11	0	0	0	1	1	1	0	0	0	0	1	0	0	1	1	18	63
TIRES	3	1	6	3	13	8	0	2	0	10	2	0	0	0	2	6	0	2	0	8	13	43
REF PETROLEUM	6	11	3	0	20	4	5	4	3	16	10	2	2	4	18	3	0	6	0	9	17	75
OTH PETROLEUM	1	3	1	0	5	0	0	1	0	1	2	1	0	0	3	0	0	0	0	0	6	26
LEATHER	1	0	0	0	1	0	0	0	0	0	0	0	0	0	0	0	0	0	0	0	4	21
STONE+CLAY+CEMNT	4	2	3	1	10	0	0	0	0	0	0	4	0	0	4	0	0	0	0	0	14	35
ABRASIVES	9	6	5	1	21	0	0	0	0	0	4	0	0	1	6	0	1	0	0	1	25	82
GLASS	3	8	5	0	16	0	0	0	0	0	1	2	1	0	4	1	4	1	0	5	12	24
IRON+STEEL	4	0	0	3	7	0	1	0	0	1	2	0	3	0	5	0	0	0	0	0	10	34

TABLE 6 .5 .5 (CONTINUED)

CATEGORY OF PRINCIPAL OUTSIDE OWNER, AND PERCENTAGE OWNED BY PRINCIPAL OUTSIDE OWNER, IN 1975

PRINCIPAL INDUSTRY	LOCAL PRIVATE					LOCAL STATE					FOREIGN PRIVATE					WIDELY DISPERSED					UN-KNOWN	WHOLLY OWNED BY PARENT
	5-49	50	51-94	UNK	TOT	5-49	50	51-94	UNK	TOT	5-49	50	51-94	UNK	TOT	5-49	50	51-94	UNK	TOT		
NON-FERROUS	12	3	10	0	25	2	1	1	0	4	7	2	2	1	12	3	0	1	1	5	42	88
METAL CANS	0	1	4	0	5	0	0	0	0	0	4	0	0	0	4	0	0	0	1	1	12	24
OTHER FAB METAL	5	7	9	2	23	1	0	2	0	3	1	3	0	0	4	1	0	2	0	3	55	200
ENGINES+TURBIN	1	2	1	0	4	0	0	0	0	0	0	0	0	0	0	0	0	0	0	0	6	18
CONSTR MACH	8	6	6	1	21	0	0	0	0	0	2	0	0	0	2	1	0	0	1	1	27	102
FARM MACHINERY	1	0	4	0	5	0	1	0	0	1	0	0	0	0	0	2	0	1	0	3	5	21
OFFICE MC+COMPUT	1	4	1	1	7	0	0	0	0	0	0	0	0	0	0	1	0	0	0	1	6	64
SPEC MACHINERY	1	2	2	0	5	0	0	0	0	0	1	1	1	0	2	0	0	0	0	0	14	70
GENL MACHINERY	5	7	6	2	20	0	0	0	0	0	0	0	0	0	2	1	0	1	0	2	23	78
OTH NON-EL MC	2	1	5	0	8	0	1	0	0	1	1	0	0	1	2	0	0	0	0	0	20	78
EL LIGHT+WIRING	4	3	1	0	8	0	0	0	0	0	2	0	0	0	2	1	0	1	0	2	6	16
EL TRAN EQUIP	0	0	2	0	2	0	0	0	0	0	0	0	0	0	0	0	0	0	0	0	5	24
RADIO+TV+APPL	4	1	1	2	8	0	0	0	0	0	0	0	0	1	1	2	0	2	0	4	18	84
ELECTRONICS	2	3	2	0	7	0	0	0	0	0	2	0	0	0	2	0	0	0	0	0	10	71
OTHER ELEC	7	7	9	1	24	1	0	0	0	1	4	0	1	0	5	1	0	3	2	6	31	100
COMMUNICATION	0	1	0	0	1	2	0	0	0	2	0	1	0	0	1	0	0	0	0	0	13	45
MOTOR VEHIC	12	10	23	5	50	0	0	1	2	3	3	1	1	0	5	7	0	4	0	11	64	153
OTHER TRANSP	3	2	1	1	7	0	0	0	0	0	0	0	1	0	1	0	0	1	0	1	3	21
PRECISION	10	3	4	2	19	1	0	1	0	2	0	1	0	0	0	0	0	0	0	0	17	123
MISCELLANEOUS	6	9	1	1	17	1	0	0	0	0	1	0	0	0	1	0	0	0	0	0	47	138
TOTAL	230	243	166	45	684	35	18	22	6	81	72	42	19	10	143	52	9	41	13	115	994	3758

CHAPTER 6 - OWNERSHIP PATTERNS
SECTION 5 -- OUTSIDE OWNERS IN 1975
TABLE 6 --- BY SALES OF SUBSIDIARY IN 1975

NO. OF SUBSIDIARIES ACTIVE AT 1-JAN-76

SALES IN 1975	CATEGORY OF PRINCIPAL OUTSIDE OWNER, AND PERCENTAGE OWNED BY PRINCIPAL OUTSIDE OWNER, IN 1975																						
	LOCAL PRIVATE					LOCAL STATE					FOREIGN PRIVATE					WIDELY DISPERSED					UN-KNOWN	WHOLLY OWNED BY PARENT
	5-49	50	51-94	UNK	TOT	5-49	50	51-94	UNK	TOT	5-49	50	51-94	UNK	TOT	5-49	50	51-94	UNK	TOT		
UNDER $1 MILLION	33	39	29	4	105	2	3	1	0	6	9	4	3	2	18	3	0	4	0	7	168	1235
$1-10 MILLION	94	98	75	12	279	15	4	6	0	25	21	18	5	2	46	20	8	11	5	44	404	2124
$10-25 MILLION	67	53	32	8	160	7	4	6	1	18	13	11	7	6	37	6	1	11	2	20	204	948
$25-100 MILLION	33	35	32	13	113	6	6	5	2	19	19	8	2	4	33	13	2	12	6	33	169	614
OVER $100 MILLION	20	13	13	9	55	6	4	4	4	18	20	6	5	0	31	13	0	6	2	21	59	303
UNKNOWN	49	72	33	10	164	19	8	7	1	35	36	24	10	2	72	0	2	14	1	17	759	2835
TOTAL	296	310	214	56	876	55	29	29	8	121	118	71	32	16	237	55	13	58	16	142	1763	8059

Chapter Seven

Exports and Intrasystem Sales

CHAPTER 7   - EXPORTS AND INTRA-SYSTEM SALES
SECTION 1   -- OVERVIEW OF ALL SUBSIDIARIES ACTIVE AT 1-JAN-76
TABLE 1   --- BY PRINCIPAL ACTIVITIES

NO. OF SUBSIDIARIES, BY PRINCIPAL ACTIVITY IN 1975

PRINCIPAL ACTIVITY	TOTAL NO. AT 1-JAN-76	LEVEL OF EXPORTS IN 1975 (AS PERCENTAGE OF SUBSIDIARY'S SALES)				LEVEL OF INTRA-SYSTEM SALES IN 1975 (AS PERCENTAGE OF SUBSIDIARY'S SALES)			
		0-9%	10-50%	51-100%	UNKNOWN	0-9%	10-50%	51-100%	UNKNOWN
MANUFACTURING	5775	2596	872	362	1945	2979	403	351	2042
SALES	2833	1397	99	178	1159	1488	62	99	1184
EXTRACTION	356	73	22	108	153	72	33	92	159
OTHER	1977	312	16	27	1622	295	14	47	1621
UNKNOWN	257	5	2	1	249	6	1	0	250
TOTAL	11198	4383	1011	676	5128	4840	513	589	5256

CHAPTER 7   - EXPORTS AND INTRA-SYSTEM SALES
SECTION 1   -- OVERVIEW OF ALL SUBSIDIARIES ACTIVE AT 1-JAN-76
TABLE 2   --- BY OWNERSHIP PATTERNS

NO. OF SUBSIDIARIES, BY PARENT OWNERSHIP IN 1975

OWNERSHIP IN 1975	TOTAL NO. AT 1-JAN-76	LEVEL OF EXPORTS IN 1975 (AS PERCENTAGE OF SUBSIDIARY'S SALES)				LEVEL OF INTRA-SYSTEM SALES IN 1975 (AS PERCENTAGE OF SUBSIDIARY'S SALES)			
		0-9%	10-50%	51-100%	UNKNOWN	0-9%	10-50%	51-100%	UNKNOWN
WHL OWNED: 95-100%	8059	3139	720	530	3670	3453	392	450	3764
MAJ OWNED: 51- 94%	1025	481	126	63	355	551	54	54	366
CO- OWNED: 50%	725	303	64	33	325	317	29	40	339
MIN OWNED: 5- 49%	1036	433	98	48	457	496	34	41	465
UNKNOWN	353	27	3	2	321	23	4	4	322
TOTAL	11198	4383	1011	676	5128	4840	513	589	5256

CHAPTER 7   - EXPORTS AND INTRA-SYSTEM SALES
SECTION 1   -- OVERVIEW OF ALL SUBSIDIARIES ACTIVE AT 1-JAN-76
TABLE 3   --- BY METHOD OF ENTRY

NO. OF SUBSIDIARIES, BY METHOD OF ENTRY

METHOD OF ENTRY	TOTAL NO. AT 1-JAN-76	LEVEL OF EXPORTS IN 1975 (AS PERCENTAGE OF SUBSIDIARY'S SALES)				LEVEL OF INTRA-SYSTEM SALES IN 1975 (AS PERCENTAGE OF SUBSIDIARY'S SALES)			
		0-9%	10-50%	51-100%	UNKNOWN	0-9%	10-50%	51-100%	UNKNOWN
NEWLY FORMED	6016	2448	503	406	2659	2664	287	344	2721
ACQUIRED	4142	1582	425	219	1916	1805	180	179	1978
DESCENDENT	216	97	36	8	75	112	20	9	75
UNKNOWN	824	256	47	43	478	259	26	57	482
TOTAL	11198	4383	1011	676	5128	4840	513	589	5256

CHAPTER 7 - EXPORTS AND INTRA-SYSTEM SALES
SECTION 1 -- OVERVIEW OF ALL SUBSIDIARIES ACTIVE AT 1-JAN-76
TABLE 4 --- BY ENTRY DATE

NO. OF SUBSIDIARIES, BY ENTRY DATE OF SUBSIDIARY

ENTRY DATE	TOTAL NO. AT 1-JAN-76	LEVEL OF EXPORTS IN 1975 (AS PERCENTAGE OF SUBSIDIARY'S SALES)				LEVEL OF INTRA-SYSTEM SALES IN 1975 (AS PERCENTAGE OF SUBSIDIARY'S SALES)			
		0-9%	10-50%	51-100%	UNKNOWN	0-9%	10-50%	51-100%	UNKNOWN
PRE-1951	1276	568	184	75	449	635	95	73	473
1951	87	35	13	3	36	36	11	1	39
1952	110	44	10	7	49	43	7	10	50
1953	73	35	10	4	24	38	8	3	24
1954	123	53	19	13	38	55	20	7	41
1955	144	62	16	7	59	72	6	11	55
1956	180	75	19	12	74	74	12	16	78
1957	182	59	21	13	89	70	11	14	87
1958	196	78	23	15	80	92	13	4	87
1959	278	121	35	22	100	130	24	19	105
1960	337	131	40	25	141	147	23	15	152
1961	339	140	23	23	153	157	12	20	150
1962	345	147	35	16	147	157	18	19	151
1963	426	149	63	34	180	181	25	32	188
1964	374	158	31	16	169	171	14	24	165
1965	447	170	36	30	211	192	14	31	210
1966	446	212	35	26	173	236	18	18	174
1967	656	249	49	41	317	275	21	37	323
1968	779	323	46	31	379	336	19	36	388
1969	740	269	54	49	368	295	31	42	372
1970	669	224	49	39	357	247	20	36	366
1971	794	279	54	46	415	300	30	34	430
1972	589	206	37	24	322	235	7	15	332
1973	647	213	44	42	348	231	21	33	362
1974	588	233	37	41	277	267	14	28	279
1975	373	150	28	22	173	168	19	11	175
TOTAL	11198	4383	1011	676	5128	4840	513	589	5256

CHAPTER 7   - EXPORTS AND INTRA-SYSTEM SALES
SECTION 1   -- OVERVIEW OF ALL SUBSIDIARIES ACTIVE AT 1-JAN-76
TABLE 5   --- BY SALES OF SUBSIDIARY IN 1975

NO. OF SUBSIDIARIES, BY SALES CATEGORY IN 1975

SALES IN 1975	TOTAL NO. AT 1-JAN-76	LEVEL OF EXPORTS IN 1975 (AS PERCENTAGE OF SUBSIDIARY'S SALES)				LEVEL OF INTRA-SYSTEM SALES IN 1975 (AS PERCENTAGE OF SUBSIDIARY'S SALES)			
		0-9%	10-50%	51-100%	UNKNOWN	0-9%	10-50%	51-100%	UNKNOWN
UNDER $1 MILLION	1539	1009	66	50	414	1014	22	75	428
$1-10 MILLION	2922	1713	329	211	669	1877	150	180	715
$10-25 MILLION	1387	675	239	140	333	809	121	101	356
$25-100 MILLION	981	446	221	107	207	559	117	82	223
OVER $100 MILLION	487	211	118	84	74	253	77	68	89
UNKNOWN	3882	329	38	84	3431	328	26	83	3445
TOTAL	11198	4383	1011	676	5128	4840	513	589	5256

CHAPTER 7 - EXPORTS AND INTRA-SYSTEM SALES
SECTION 1 -- OVERVIEW OF ALL SUBSIDIARIES ACTIVE AT 1-JAN-76
TABLE 6 --- BY GEOGRAPHICAL REGION

NO. OF SUBSIDIARIES, BY COUNTRY OR REGION

COUNTRY OR REGION	TOTAL NO. AT 1-JAN-76	LEVEL OF EXPORTS IN 1975 (AS PERCENTAGE OF SUBSIDIARY'S SALES)				LEVEL OF INTRA-SYSTEM SALES IN 1975 (AS PERCENTAGE OF SUBSIDIARY'S SALES)			
		0-9%	10-50%	51-100%	UNKNOWN	0-9%	10-50%	51-100%	UNKNOWN
CANADA	1163	487	95	37	544	500	59	48	556
LATIN AMER. (TOTAL)	2462	1066	152	129	1115	1127	72	145	1118
C.AM.+CARIB.(TOTAL)	1180	435	85	102	558	486	43	91	560
BAHAMAS	56	15	1	4	37	15	2	1	38
BERMUDA	72	16	1	8	57	5	2	10	55
COSTA RICA	45	16	12	6	11	26	2	4	13
GUATEMALA	65	36	8	5	16	42	2	2	19
JAMAICA	38	12	6	6	14	16	1	6	15
MEXICO	552	272	40	31	209	280	22	38	212
NETH.ANTILLES	55	9	0	3	43	8	0	2	43
NICARAGUA	23	9	2	2	10	11	0	2	10
PANAMA	170	25	8	22	115	41	4	14	111
OTHER C.AM+CAR.	104	35	8	15	46	42	6	12	44
S.AMERICA (TOTAL)	1282	631	67	27	557	641	29	54	558
BOLIVIA	10	4	0	1	5	4	0	4	6
CHILE	52	29	0	2	21	28	2	4	18
COLOMBIA	161	74	16	3	68	80	4	9	68
ECUADOR	43	19	1	4	19	20	1	5	17
PERU	80	44	2	2	32	44	1	2	33
ARGENTINA	207	107	15	0	85	105	9	8	85
BRAZIL	375	198	22	5	150	197	7	15	156
URUGUAY	39	19	0	2	18	20	0	0	19
VENEZUELA	300	133	11	5	151	140	5	7	148
OTHER S.AMER.	15	4	0	3	8	3	0	4	8
EUROPE (TOTAL)	4829	1641	562	316	2310	1953	287	198	2391
BELGIUM	309	63	58	44	144	119	19	23	148
FRANCE	617	214	92	21	290	249	44	14	310
GERMANY	688	265	87	30	306	297	39	29	323
ITALY	382	161	45	22	154	178	34	15	155
LUXEMBOURG	39	5	0	12	22	6	0	10	22
NETHERLANDS	306	87	38	36	145	125	21	18	142
DENMARK	115	50	8	8	49	52	5	3	55
IRELAND	104	34	12	20	38	46	10	9	39
U.K.	1084	296	148	50	590	348	73	41	622
AUSTRIA	90	41	13	4	32	50	2	3	35
FINLAND	46	29	1	0	16	30	2	0	14
GREECE	54	26	1	1	26	28	0	3	23
NORWAY	92	36	7	8	41	39	8	3	42
PORTUGAL	71	34	0	3	34	34	0	4	33
SPAIN	298	134	20	12	132	144	8	10	136
SWEDEN	191	77	15	9	97	87	5	6	97
SWITZERLAND	278	62	15	37	164	92	16	3	164
TURKEY	34	20	2	2	10	20	0	3	11
OTHER EUROPE	31	7	0	4	20	9	0	2	20

TABLE 7 .1 .6 (CONTINUED)

COUNTRY OR REGION	TOTAL NO. AT 1-JAN-76	LEVEL OF EXPORTS IN 1975 (AS PERCENTAGE OF SUBSIDIARY'S SALES)				LEVEL OF INTRA-SYSTEM SALES IN 1975 (AS PERCENTAGE OF SUBSIDIARY'S SALES)			
		0-9%	10-50%	51-100%	UNKNOWN	0-9%	10-50%	51-100%	UNKNOWN
N.AFR+M.EAST(TOTAL)	264	107	14	26	117	128	4	16	116
ALGERIA	14	8	0	2	4	9	0	1	4
EGYPT	20	5	0	2	13	6	1	1	13
IRAN	67	38	1	2	26	39	1	2	25
ISRAEL	20	5	4	0	11	9	0	0	11
LEBANON	22	8	2	2	10	12	0	0	10
MOROCCO	29	16	2	1	10	18	0	1	10
SAUDI ARABIA	22	5	2	4	11	6	2	3	11
OTHER N.AF+M.E.	70	22	3	13	32	29	1	8	32
E.+W.AFRICA (TOTAL)	321	116	20	36	149	125	14	27	155
GHANA	17	7	1	1	8	7	0	1	9
IVORY COAST	13	3	0	3	7	3	1	2	7
KENYA	27	13	3	2	9	17	0	1	9
LIBERIA	45	9	0	13	23	9	2	10	24
NIGERIA	57	23	4	3	27	26	1	3	27
ZAIRE	26	7	2	3	14	8	2	0	16
ZAMBIA	47	14	4	4	25	16	4	2	25
OTHER E.+W.AFR.	89	40	6	7	36	39	4	8	38
SOUTH ASIA (TOTAL)	144	84	8	2	50	86	4	3	51
INDIA	101	57	5	1	38	59	2	1	39
PAKISTAN	33	20	3	1	9	21	2	1	9
SRI LANKA	9	6	0	0	3	5	0	1	3
OTHER S.ASIA	1	1	0	0	0	1	0	0	0
EAST ASIA (TOTAL)	1004	429	80	89	406	468	33	83	420
HONG KONG	97	21	9	20	47	33	5	9	50
INDONESIA	61	25	1	8	27	26	1	6	28
JAPAN	426	209	38	11	168	216	11	23	176
MALAYSIA	61	24	4	5	28	26	1	6	28
PHILIPPINES	108	50	9	7	42	53	3	10	42
SINGAPORE	74	26	9	21	18	33	5	15	21
S.KOREA	37	17	2	1	17	19	1	0	17
THAILAND	62	36	1	2	23	36	0	4	22
TAIWAN	59	17	7	12	23	22	6	9	22
OTHER E.ASIA	19	4	0	2	13	4	0	1	14
S.DOMINIONS (TOTAL)	1011	453	80	41	437	453	40	69	449
AUSTRALIA	544	240	46	26	232	242	26	35	241
NEW ZEALAND	132	72	3	0	57	72	2	1	57
RHODESIA	26	12	5	1	8	14	2	3	8
S.AFRICA	309	129	26	14	140	125	11	30	143
OUTSIDE U.S.(TOTAL)	11198	4383	1011	676	5128	4840	513	589	5256

392

CHAPTER 7   - EXPORTS AND INTRA-SYSTEM SALES
SECTION 2   -- MANUFACTURING SUBSIDIARIES ACTIVE AT 1-JAN-76
TABLE 1   --- BY PRINCIPAL INDUSTRY

NO. OF SUBSIDIARIES, BY PRINCIPAL INDUSTRY IN 1975

PRINCIPAL INDUSTRY	TOTAL NO. AT 1-JAN-76	LEVEL OF EXPORTS IN 1975 (AS PERCENTAGE OF SUBSIDIARY'S SALES)				LEVEL OF INTRA-SYSTEM SALES IN 1975 (AS PERCENTAGE OF SUBSIDIARY'S SALES)			
		0-9%	10-50%	51-100%	UNKNOWN	0-9%	10-50%	51-100%	UNKNOWN
BEVERAGES	81	43	12	5	21	45	7	6	23
TOBACCO	26	15	3	4	4	20	2	0	4
FOOD	635	363	56	32	184	371	26	37	201
TEXTILES+APPAREL	95	40	15	11	29	57	4	6	28
WOOD+FURNITURE	67	44	8	2	13	50	2	1	14
PAPER	206	112	40	7	47	114	6	36	50
PRINTING	64	38	5	2	19	41	3	1	19
INDUSTRIAL CHEM	208	78	28	14	88	98	13	8	89
PLASTICS	180	80	19	8	73	96	9	9	66
AGRIC CHEM	51	32	4	9	6	38	4	4	5
COSMETICS	276	165	41	9	61	189	14	6	67
DRUGS	546	236	75	27	208	277	26	23	220
OTHER CHEM	309	141	50	12	106	166	28	11	104
FABR PLASTICS	95	42	11	5	37	53	2	5	35
TIRES	89	68	12	2	7	72	7	3	7
REF PETROLEUM	155	76	27	10	42	57	14	37	47
OTH PETROLEUM	41	23	1	0	17	20	2	6	13
LEATHER	26	12	3	4	7	13	0	3	10
STONE+CLAY+CEMNT	63	30	10	1	22	38	3	1	21
ABRASIVES	135	63	19	8	45	71	13	3	48
GLASS	61	29	9	4	19	38	3	0	20
IRON+STEEL	57	26	5	2	24	25	2	4	26

TABLE 7.2.1 (CONTINUED)

PRINCIPAL INDUSTRY	TOTAL NO. AT 1-JAN-76	LEVEL OF EXPORTS IN 1975 (AS PERCENTAGE OF SUBSIDIARY'S SALES)				LEVEL OF INTRA-SYSTEM SALES IN 1975 (AS PERCENTAGE OF SUBSIDIARY'S SALES)			
		0-9%	10-50%	51-100%	UNKNOWN	0-9%	10-50%	51-100%	UNKNOWN
NON-FERROUS	176	35	42	11	88	47	32	7	90
METAL CANS	46	24	6	0	16	27	3	0	16
OTHER FAB METAL	288	117	47	20	104	143	16	12	117
ENGINES+TURBIN	28	7	4	6	11	13	0	3	12
CONSTR MACH	153	63	34	21	35	89	15	7	42
FARM MACHINERY	35	19	9	3	4	20	8	3	4
OFFICE MC+COMPUT	78	34	26	11	7	35	22	15	6
SPEC MACHINERY	91	23	21	8	39	30	9	7	45
GENL MACHINERY	123	49	27	5	42	62	11	5	45
OTH NON-EL MC	109	38	23	4	44	46	15	2	46
EL LIGHT+WIRING	34	12	3	1	18	16	1	0	17
EL TRAN EQUIP	31	13	3	0	15	15	0	0	16
RADIO+TV+APPL	115	47	16	15	37	48	10	18	39
ELECTRONICS	90	10	19	23	38	20	11	24	35
OTHER ELEC	167	83	31	12	41	103	9	10	45
COMMUNICATION	62	7	9	6	40	16	4	4	38
MOTOR VEHIC	286	125	40	12	109	138	14	11	123
OTHER TRANSP	33	11	3	2	17	10	1	2	20
PRECISION	161	70	32	12	47	93	12	4	52
MISCELLANEOUS	203	53	24	12	114	59	20	7	117
TOTAL	5775	2596	872	362	1945	2979	403	351	2042

CHAPTER 7 - EXPORTS AND INTRA-SYSTEM SALES
SECTION 2 -- MANUFACTURING SUBSIDIARIES ACTIVE AT 1-JAN-76
TABLE 2 --- BY OWNERSHIP PATTERNS

NO. OF SUBSIDIARIES, BY PARENT OWNERSHIP IN 1975

OWNERSHIP IN 1975	TOTAL NO. AT 1-JAN-76	LEVEL OF EXPORTS IN 1975 (AS PERCENTAGE OF SUBSIDIARY'S SALES)				LEVEL OF INTRA-SYSTEM SALES IN 1975 (AS PERCENTAGE OF SUBSIDIARY'S SALES)			
		0-9%	10-50%	51-100%	UNKNOWN	0-9%	10-50%	51-100%	UNKNOWN
WHL OWNED: 95-100%	3758	1647	600	279	1232	1889	314	259	1296
MAJ OWNED: 51- 94%	743	364	119	41	219	434	42	39	228
CO- OWNED: 50%	518	234	60	18	206	245	26	25	222
MIN OWNED: 5- 49%	703	336	90	23	254	398	18	26	261
UNKNOWN	53	15	3	1	34	13	3	2	35
TOTAL	5775	2596	872	362	1945	2979	403	351	2042

CHAPTER 7   - EXPORTS AND INTRA-SYSTEM SALES
SECTION 2   -- MANUFACTURING SUBSIDIARIES ACTIVE AT 1-JAN-76
TABLE 3   --- BY METHOD OF ENTRY

NO. OF SUBSIDIARIES, BY METHOD OF ENTRY

METHOD OF ENTRY	TOTAL NO. AT 1-JAN-76	LEVEL OF EXPORTS IN 1975 (AS PERCENTAGE OF SUBSIDIARY'S SALES)				LEVEL OF INTRA-SYSTEM SALES IN 1975 (AS PERCENTAGE OF SUBSIDIARY'S SALES)			
		0-9%	10-50%	51-100%	UNKNOWN	0-9%	10-50%	51-100%	UNKNOWN
NEWLY FORMED	2760	1324	412	196	828	1487	221	174	878
ACQUIRED	2620	1089	394	147	990	1294	151	138	1037
DESCENDENT	140	65	33	5	37	82	14	7	37
UNKNOWN	255	118	33	14	90	116	17	32	90
TOTAL	5775	2596	872	362	1945	2979	403	351	2042

CHAPTER 7   - EXPORTS AND INTRA-SYSTEM SALES
SECTION 2   -- MANUFACTURING SUBSIDIARIES ACTIVE AT 1-JAN-76
TABLE 4   --- BY ENTRY DATE

NO. OF SUBSIDIARIES, BY ENTRY DATE OF SUBSIDIARY

ENTRY DATE	TOTAL NO. AT 1-JAN-76	LEVEL OF EXPORTS IN 1975 (AS PERCENTAGE OF SUBSIDIARY'S SALES)				LEVEL OF INTRA-SYSTEM SALES IN 1975 (AS PERCENTAGE OF SUBSIDIARY'S SALES)			
		0-9%	10-50%	51-100%	UNKNOWN	0-9%	10-50%	51-100%	UNKNOWN
PRE-1951	712	357	169	42	144	424	85	38	165
1951	49	23	11	0	15	23	8	0	18
1952	52	20	10	2	20	21	5	4	22
1953	36	20	9	2	5	23	7	1	5
1954	61	33	16	2	10	32	16	2	11
1955	69	32	13	2	22	39	4	6	20
1956	88	52	17	4	15	53	10	5	20
1957	77	35	18	6	18	46	8	4	19
1958	93	47	19	8	19	55	11	2	25
1959	158	73	32	10	43	83	19	7	49
1960	200	96	37	12	55	106	20	9	65
1961	178	88	22	14	54	97	12	17	52
1962	182	92	29	10	51	102	15	13	52
1963	221	88	57	17	59	109	22	24	66
1964	195	95	27	12	61	107	12	19	57
1965	230	102	30	18	80	126	9	19	76
1966	231	127	30	12	62	146	12	8	65
1967	298	125	42	18	113	150	13	23	112
1968	410	177	39	21	173	195	11	23	181
1969	371	156	44	25	146	176	21	26	148
1970	322	121	39	23	139	141	17	22	142
1971	388	156	46	27	159	173	24	22	169
1972	342	132	33	17	160	157	7	11	167
1973	345	122	33	28	162	133	11	25	176
1974	263	125	26	22	90	146	9	19	89
1975	204	102	24	8	70	116	15	2	71
TOTAL	5775	2596	872	362	1945	2979	403	351	2042

CHAPTER 7 - EXPORTS AND INTRA-SYSTEM SALES
SECTION 2 -- MANUFACTURING SUBSIDIARIES ACTIVE AT 1-JAN-76
TABLE 5 --- BY SALES OF SUBSIDIARY IN 1975

NO. OF SUBSIDIARIES, BY SALES CATEGORY IN 1975

SALES IN 1975	TOTAL NO. AT 1-JAN-76	LEVEL OF EXPORTS IN 1975 (AS PERCENTAGE OF SUBSIDIARY'S SALES)				LEVEL OF INTRA-SYSTEM SALES IN 1975 (AS PERCENTAGE OF SUBSIDIARY'S SALES)			
		0-9%	10-50%	51-100%	UNKNOWN	0-9%	10-50%	51-100%	UNKNOWN
UNDER $1 MILLION	528	307	40	22	159	315	14	33	166
$1-10 MILLION	2043	1150	278	117	498	1269	115	121	538
$10-25 MILLION	1108	539	215	88	266	666	97	61	284
$25-100 MILLION	795	357	203	69	166	451	106	55	183
OVER $100 MILLION	347	142	111	43	51	179	58	46	64
UNKNOWN	954	101	25	23	805	99	13	35	807
TOTAL	5775	2596	872	362	1945	2979	403	351	2042

CHAPTER 7   - EXPORTS AND INTRA-SYSTEM SALES
SECTION 2   -- MANUFACTURING SUBSIDIARIES ACTIVE AT 1-JAN-76
TABLE 6   --- BY GEOGRAPHICAL REGION

NO. OF SUBSIDIARIES, BY COUNTRY OR REGION

COUNTRY OR REGION	TOTAL NO. AT 1-JAN-76	LEVEL OF EXPORTS IN 1975 (AS PERCENTAGE OF SUBSIDIARY'S SALES)				LEVEL OF INTRA-SYSTEM SALES IN 1975 (AS PERCENTAGE OF SUBSIDIARY'S SALES)			
		0-9%	10-50%	51-100%	UNKNOWN	0-9%	10-50%	51-100%	UNKNOWN
CANADA	594	300	84	16	194	327	42	22	203
LATIN AMER. (TOTAL)	1325	748	136	59	382	802	57	73	393
C.AM.+CARIB. (TOTAL)	542	284	74	50	134	323	34	45	140
BAHAMAS	5	3	0	0	2	3	0	0	2
BERMUDA	0	0	0	0	0	0	0	0	0
COSTA RICA	23	9	11	1	2	18	2	0	3
GUATEMALA	34	21	8	2	3	27	1	1	5
JAMAICA	20	10	4	1	5	15	0	0	5
MEXICO	364	205	36	27	96	211	22	32	99
NETH.ANTILLES	6	2	0	3	1	1	2	2	1
NICARAGUA	13	8	1	1	3	9	0	1	3
PANAMA	27	4	7	5	11	12	2	2	11
OTHER C.AM+CAR.	50	22	7	10	11	27	5	7	11
S.AMERICA (TOTAL)	783	464	62	9	248	479	23	28	253
BOLIVIA	2	1	0	0	1	1	0	0	1
CHILE	30	21	0	0	9	21	1	2	6
COLOMBIA	104	58	15	1	30	64	3	5	32
ECUADOR	23	12	1	1	9	14	0	2	7
PERU	38	26	1	0	11	26	0	0	12
ARGENTINA	130	81	15	0	34	81	9	6	34
BRAZIL	255	153	21	2	79	156	6	8	85
URUGUAY	21	12	0	2	7	13	0	0	8
VENEZUELA	176	98	9	2	67	101	4	4	67
OTHER S.AMER.	4	2	0	1	1	2	0	1	1
EUROPE (TOTAL)	2427	820	489	211	907	1072	241	147	967
BELGIUM	159	22	45	30	62	65	13	16	65
FRANCE	354	128	88	18	120	164	40	10	140
GERMANY	398	153	81	20	144	187	38	21	152
ITALY	231	93	43	19	76	111	28	15	77
LUXEMBOURG	13	0	0	12	1	1	1	10	1
NETHERLANDS	128	30	30	21	47	58	17	9	44
DENMARK	40	12	6	5	17	14	3	3	20
IRELAND	61	15	11	18	17	26	9	9	17
U.K.	565	170	133	34	228	219	65	29	252
AUSTRIA	32	12	6	1	13	14	1	2	15
FINLAND	7	2	0	0	5	2	1	0	4
GREECE	31	14	0	1	16	15	0	3	13
NORWAY	26	6	5	6	9	10	4	1	11
PORTUGAL	37	15	0	3	19	15	0	4	18
SPAIN	192	102	19	10	61	111	8	8	65
SWEDEN	73	23	10	2	38	29	5	2	37
SWITZERLAND	47	6	10	7	24	12	8	1	26
TURKEY	21	13	2	0	6	13	0	2	6
OTHER EUROPE	12	4	0	4	4	6	0	2	4

TABLE 7.2.6 (CONTINUED)

COUNTRY OR REGION	TOTAL NO. AT 1-JAN-76	LEVEL OF EXPORTS IN 1975 (AS PERCENTAGE OF SUBSIDIARY'S SALES)				LEVEL OF INTRA-SYSTEM SALES IN 1975 (AS PERCENTAGE OF SUBSIDIARY'S SALES)			
		0-9%	10-50%	51-100%	UNKNOWN	0-9%	10-50%	51-100%	UNKNOWN
N.AFR+M.EAST(TOTAL)	100	51	12	7	30	65	3	2	30
ALGERIA	4	2	0	1	1	3	0	0	1
EGYPT	2	2	0	1	1	1	0	0	1
IRAN	33	26	1	0	6	26	1	0	6
ISRAEL	16	3	4	0	9	7	0	0	9
LEBANON	10	2	2	2	4	6	0	0	4
MOROCCO	17	12	1	1	3	13	0	1	3
SAUDI ARABIA	6	3	2	0	1	3	2	0	1
OTHER N.AF+M.E.	12	3	2	2	5	6	0	1	5
E.+W.AFRICA (TOTAL)	91	45	11	7	28	51	4	6	30
GHANA	6	4	1	0	1	4	0	0	2
IVORY COAST	6	0	0	2	4	0	1	1	4
KENYA	16	10	2	1	3	12	0	1	3
LIBERIA	0	0	0	0	0	0	0	0	0
NIGERIA	20	11	3	0	6	13	1	0	6
ZAIRE	11	5	1	0	5	6	0	0	5
ZAMBIA	11	7	2	2	4	8	2	1	4
OTHER E.+W.AFR.	17	8	2	2	5	8	0	3	6
SOUTH ASIA (TOTAL)	111	70	8	2	31	72	4	3	32
INDIA	82	50	5	1	26	52	2	1	27
PAKISTAN	23	15	3	1	4	16	2	1	4
SRI LANKA	5	4	0	0	1	3	0	1	1
OTHER S.ASIA	1	1	0	0	0	1	0	0	0
EAST ASIA (TOTAL)	568	264	64	46	194	287	23	54	204
HONG KONG	27	3	2	9	13	6	0	5	14
INDONESIA	27	17	0	0	10	16	0	0	11
JAPAN	275	141	36	5	93	149	8	17	101
MALAYSIA	30	13	3	2	12	16	1	0	11
PHILIPPINES	68	37	9	2	20	40	2	6	20
SINGAPORE	35	7	5	16	7	9	4	12	10
S.KOREA	28	15	2	1	10	17	1	0	10
THAILAND	35	19	1	1	14	20	0	3	12
TAIWAN	40	10	6	10	14	13	5	9	13
OTHER E.ASIA	3	2	0	0	1	1	0	0	2
S.DOMINIONS (TOTAL)	559	298	68	14	179	303	29	44	183
AUSTRALIA	310	161	40	10	99	169	19	19	103
NEW ZEALAND	70	40	2	0	28	41	2	0	27
RHODESIA	13	5	5	0	3	7	0	3	3
S.AFRICA	166	92	21	4	49	86	8	22	50
OUTSIDE U.S.(TOTAL)	5775	2596	872	362	1945	2979	403	351	2042

CHAPTER 7   - EXPORTS AND INTRA-SYSTEM SALES
SECTION 3   -- BY REGION AND PRINCIPAL INDUSTRY IN 1975
TABLE 1   --- "EXPORT SUBSIDIARIES"

NO. OF MANUFACTURING SUBSIDIARIES ACTIVE AT 1-JAN-76, WITH EXPORTS GREATER THAN 10% OF SALES IN 1975

COUNTRY OR REGION	BEVERAGES	TOBACCO	FOOD	TXTL+APPRL	WOOD+FURNI PAPER	PRINTING	INDUS-CHEM PLASTIC	AGRIC-CHEM	COSMETICS	DRUGS	OTHER-CHEM	FABR-PLSTCS TIRES	REF-PETRLM OTH-PETRLM	LEATHER	STONE+CLAY+CEMNT ABRASIVES	GLASS	IRON
CANADA	5	0	8	3	2	1	5	2	3	3	2	0	2	0	3	0	1
LATIN AMER. (TOTAL)	3	2	13	1	7	0	7	8	11	23	9	1	9	0	2	2	0
C.AM.+CARIB. (TOTAL)	1	2	10	1	4	0	5	6	9	13	3	1	6	1	0	0	0
BAHAMAS	0	0	0	0	0	0	0	0	0	0	0	0	0	1	0	0	0
BERMUDA	0	0	0	0	0	0	0	0	0	0	0	0	0	0	0	0	0
COSTA RICA	0	0	2	0	0	0	0	1	0	1	0	0	0	0	0	0	0
GUATEMALA	0	0	2	0	1	0	0	0	0	1	0	0	0	0	0	0	0
JAMAICA	0	0	1	0	0	0	1	0	2	1	0	0	0	1	0	0	0
MEXICO	1	1	1	1	1	0	3	2	2	5	3	0	0	0	0	0	0
NETH.ANTILLES	0	1	0	0	0	0	0	1	0	0	0	0	1	1	0	0	0
NICARAGUA	0	0	1	0	1	0	0	0	0	0	0	0	0	0	0	0	0
PANAMA	0	0	2	0	0	0	0	1	3	4	1	0	2	0	0	0	0
OTHER C.AM+CAR.	0	1	1	0	1	0	1	1	2	1	0	0	3	0	0	0	0
S.AMERICA (TOTAL)	2	0	3	0	3	0	2	2	2	10	6	0	3	0	2	2	0
BOLIVIA	0	0	0	0	0	0	0	0	0	0	0	0	0	0	0	0	0
CHILE	0	0	0	0	0	0	0	0	0	0	0	0	0	0	0	0	0
COLOMBIA	0	0	1	0	0	0	0	2	0	4	1	0	1	0	1	1	0
ECUADOR	0	0	0	0	0	0	0	0	0	0	0	0	0	0	0	0	0
PERU	0	0	1	0	0	0	0	0	0	1	0	0	1	0	1	1	0
ARGENTINA	0	0	0	0	1	0	1	0	0	2	3	0	0	0	0	0	0
BRAZIL	1	0	1	0	1	0	1	0	1	1	1	0	0	0	0	0	0
URUGUAY	1	0	0	0	0	0	0	0	0	0	0	0	0	0	0	0	0
VENEZUELA	0	0	0	0	1	0	0	0	0	2	1	0	2	0	0	0	0
OTHER S.AMER.	0	0	0	0	0	0	0	0	0	0	0	0	0	0	0	0	0
EUROPE (TOTAL)	5	5	47	19	17	3	23	3	27	58	43	10	18	4	18	9	6
BELGIUM	1	1	7	4	3	0	9	0	2	6	9	1	3	0	4	2	1
FRANCE	0	0	4	1	4	0	0	1	9	11	9	0	3	0	4	0	0
GERMANY	0	0	7	1	2	0	2	0	1	6	6	2	3	1	2	3	4
ITALY	0	1	2	1	2	0	2	1	1	5	6	0	4	1	1	1	1
LUXEMBOURG	0	0	0	0	0	0	0	0	0	0	0	1	0	0	1	1	0
NETHERLANDS	0	1	8	3	1	1	4	0	1	1	5	1	4	0	1	0	0
DENMARK	0	0	4	0	0	0	0	1	1	0	1	0	1	0	0	1	0
IRELAND	0	0	4	1	1	0	2	0	0	6	1	0	0	0	1	0	0
U.K.	1	0	6	3	1	2	5	0	8	15	12	4	2	1	3	2	0
AUSTRIA	0	0	0	0	1	0	0	0	0	1	0	0	0	1	0	0	0
FINLAND	0	0	0	0	0	0	0	0	0	0	0	0	0	0	0	0	0
GREECE	0	0	1	0	0	0	2	0	0	0	0	1	0	0	0	0	0
NORWAY	0	0	0	0	0	0	0	0	0	0	0	0	0	0	1	0	0
PORTUGAL	0	0	1	1	0	0	1	0	0	2	2	0	0	0	0	0	0
SPAIN	2	1	1	0	0	0	0	0	2	1	1	0	1	0	1	0	0
SWEDEN	0	1	0	1	1	0	0	0	0	4	0	1	0	0	0	0	0
SWITZERLAND	1	0	2	1	1	0	0	0	1	0	0	0	0	0	0	0	0
TURKEY	1	0	0	0	0	0	0	0	0	0	0	0	0	0	1	0	0
OTHER EUROPE	0	0	0	0	1	0	0	1	1	0	0	0	0	0	0	0	0

TABLE 7.3.1 (CONTINUED)

COUNTRY OR REGION	BEVERAGES	TOBACCO	FOOD	TXTL+APPRL	WOOD+FURNI	PAPER	PRINTING	INDUS-CHEM	PLASTIC	AGRIC-CHEM COSMETICS	OTHER-CHEM DRUGS	FABR-PLSTCS TIRES	OTHER-CHEM	REF-PETRLM TIRES	REF-PETRLM	OTH-PETRLM	STONE+CLAY+CEMNT LEATHER	ABRASIVES	STONE+CLAY+CEMNT	IRON GLASS	IRON
N.AFR+M.EAST (TOTAL)	0	0	2	1	0	1	0	0	1	0	2	3	0	0	1	4	0	1	0	0	0	0
ALGERIA	0	0	0	0	0	0	0	0	0	0	0	0	0	0	0	1	0	0	0	0	0	0
EGYPT	0	0	0	0	0	0	0	0	0	0	0	0	0	0	0	0	0	0	0	0	0	0
IRAN	0	0	0	0	0	0	0	0	0	0	0	0	0	0	0	0	0	0	0	0	0	0
ISRAEL	0	0	1	0	0	0	0	0	0	0	0	0	0	0	0	0	0	1	0	0	0	0
LEBANON	0	0	1	0	0	0	0	0	1	0	2	3	0	0	1	0	0	0	0	0	0	0
MOROCCO	0	0	0	0	0	0	0	0	0	0	0	0	0	0	0	0	0	0	0	0	0	0
SAUDI ARABIA	0	0	0	0	0	1	0	0	0	0	0	0	0	0	0	2	0	0	0	0	0	0
OTHER N.AF+M.E.	0	0	0	1	0	1	0	0	0	0	0	0	0	1	0	1	0	0	0	0	0	0
E.+W.AFRICA (TOTAL)	0	0	3	0	0	3	0	0	0	0	1	3	0	0	0	2	0	0	0	0	0	0
GHANA	0	0	0	0	0	0	0	0	0	0	0	0	0	0	0	0	0	0	0	0	0	0
IVORY COAST	0	0	0	0	0	0	0	0	0	0	0	0	0	0	0	0	0	0	0	0	0	0
KENYA	0	0	2	0	0	0	0	0	0	0	0	0	0	0	0	1	0	0	0	0	0	0
LIBERIA	0	0	0	0	0	0	0	0	0	0	0	0	0	0	0	0	0	0	0	0	0	0
NIGERIA	0	0	0	0	0	0	0	0	0	0	0	2	0	0	0	0	0	0	0	0	0	0
ZAIRE	0	0	0	0	0	0	0	0	0	0	0	1	0	1	0	0	0	0	0	0	0	0
ZAMBIA	0	0	0	0	0	1	0	0	0	0	1	0	0	0	0	0	0	0	0	0	1	0
OTHER E.+W.AFR.	0	0	1	0	0	2	0	0	0	0	0	0	0	1	0	1	0	0	0	0	0	0
SOUTH ASIA (TOTAL)	0	0	1	0	0	0	0	0	0	0	0	2	0	0	0	0	0	0	0	0	0	0
INDIA	0	0	1	0	0	0	0	0	0	0	0	1	1	0	0	0	0	0	0	0	0	0
PAKISTAN	0	0	1	0	0	0	0	0	0	0	0	1	1	0	0	0	0	0	0	0	0	0
SRI LANKA	0	0	0	0	0	0	0	0	0	0	0	0	0	0	0	0	0	0	0	0	0	0
OTHER S.ASIA	0	0	0	0	0	0	0	0	0	0	0	0	0	0	0	0	0	0	0	0	0	0
EAST ASIA (TOTAL)	3	0	6	1	0	3	1	5	2	1	4	4	5	2	2	2	0	0	1	0	0	0
HONG KONG	0	0	1	0	0	0	0	0	0	0	0	0	1	0	0	0	0	0	0	0	0	0
INDONESIA	0	0	0	0	0	0	0	0	0	0	0	0	0	0	0	0	0	0	0	0	0	0
JAPAN	0	0	0	1	0	1	0	3	0	0	1	0	4	1	1	1	0	0	0	0	0	0
MALAYSIA	0	0	3	0	0	1	0	0	0	1	1	2	0	0	0	0	0	0	0	0	0	0
PHILIPPINES	2	0	2	0	0	1	0	0	0	0	0	1	4	0	0	0	0	0	0	0	0	0
SINGAPORE	0	0	0	0	0	0	0	0	0	0	1	1	0	0	0	0	0	0	0	0	1	0
S.KOREA	1	0	0	0	0	1	0	1	0	0	1	0	0	1	1	0	0	0	0	0	0	0
THAILAND	0	0	0	0	0	0	0	1	0	0	0	0	0	1	0	0	0	0	0	0	0	0
TAIWAN	0	0	0	0	0	1	0	1	2	0	0	1	0	1	1	1	0	0	0	0	0	0
OTHER E.ASIA	0	0	0	0	0	0	0	0	0	0	0	0	0	0	0	0	0	0	0	0	0	0
S.DOMINIONS (TOTAL)	1	0	8	1	0	14	2	2	2	2	2	6	3	2	1	0	0	1	1	4	1	0
AUSTRALIA	1	0	6	0	0	1	1	2	1	1	4	4	2	0	0	0	0	1	1	3	1	0
NEW ZEALAND	0	0	1	1	0	0	0	0	0	0	0	1	0	0	0	0	0	0	0	0	0	0
RHODESIA	0	0	0	0	0	3	0	0	0	0	0	0	0	1	0	0	0	0	0	0	0	0
S.AFRICA	0	0	1	0	0	11	1	0	0	0	0	1	1	1	1	0	0	1	0	0	0	0
OUTSIDE U.S. (TOTAL)	17	7	88	26	10	47	7	42	27	13	50	102	62	16	14	37	1	7	11	27	13	7

(TABLE CONTINUED ON FOLLOWING PAGES)

TABLE 7 .3 .1 (CONTINUED)

COUNTRY OR REGION	NON-FERROUS METAL	METAL CANS	FAB-MET	ENGINES	CONSTR-MC	FARM-MC	OFF-MC+COMPUT	SPECL-MC	GENL-MC	OTH-NON-EL-MC	EL-LT+WIRING	EL-TRAN	RAD+TV+APPL	ELECTRONICS	OTH-ELE	COMMUNICATION	MOTOR-VEHIC	OTH-TRN	PRECISION	MISC	TOTAL
CANADA	7	2	9	2	7	2	0	5	2	3	0	0	2	0	2	0	5	1	4	2	100
LATIN AMER. (TOTAL)	7	1	7	0	6	0	7	3	1	4	0	1	0	7	8	11	5	9	2	7	195
C.AM.+CARIB. (TOTAL)	3	1	3	0	5	0	3	0	0	2	0	0	5	4	9	4	4	0	4	5	124
BAHAMAS	0	0	0	0	0	0	0	0	0	0	0	0	0	0	0	0	0	0	0	0	0
BERMUDA	0	0	0	0	0	0	0	0	0	0	0	0	0	0	0	0	0	0	0	0	0
COSTA RICA	0	1	0	0	0	0	0	0	0	0	0	0	2	0	2	0	0	0	2	1	12
GUATEMALA	0	1	1	0	0	0	0	1	1	1	0	0	0	0	0	0	0	0	1	0	10
JAMAICA	2	0	1	0	0	0	3	0	0	0	0	0	0	0	0	0	0	0	0	0	5
MEXICO	0	0	1	0	5	0	0	1	0	0	0	4	6	6	4	4	4	2	2	2	63
NETH.ANTILLES	0	0	0	0	0	0	0	0	0	0	0	0	0	0	0	0	0	0	0	0	3
NICARAGUA	0	0	0	0	0	0	0	0	0	0	0	0	0	0	0	0	0	0	0	0	2
PANAMA	0	0	0	0	0	0	0	0	0	0	0	0	0	0	0	0	0	0	0	0	12
OTHER C.AM+CAR.	1	0	0	0	0	0	0	0	0	1	0	1	1	0	0	0	0	0	0	2	17
S.AMERICA (TOTAL)	4	0	4	0	1	0	4	3	0	2	0	2	2	1	0	1	5	0	3	0	71
BOLIVIA	0	0	0	0	0	0	0	0	0	0	0	0	0	0	0	0	0	0	0	0	0
CHILE	0	0	0	0	0	0	0	0	0	0	0	0	0	0	0	0	0	0	0	0	0
COLOMBIA	1	0	2	0	0	0	0	0	0	0	0	0	0	0	0	0	0	0	0	0	16
ECUADOR	0	0	0	0	0	0	0	0	0	0	0	0	0	0	0	1	0	0	0	0	2
PERU	0	0	0	0	0	0	0	0	0	0	0	0	0	0	0	0	0	0	0	0	1
ARGENTINA	0	0	1	0	0	0	1	0	1	1	0	1	1	1	0	2	1	0	0	0	15
BRAZIL	0	0	1	0	1	0	3	3	0	0	0	1	1	0	0	2	2	0	0	0	23
URUGUAY	0	0	0	0	0	0	0	0	0	0	0	0	0	0	0	0	0	0	0	0	2
VENEZUELA	2	0	0	0	0	0	0	0	0	0	0	0	0	0	0	1	1	0	0	0	11
OTHER S.AMER.	1	0	0	0	0	0	0	0	0	0	0	1	1	0	0	0	0	0	0	0	1
EUROPE (TOTAL)	24	3	43	5	28	9	21	24	23	19	2	3	12	19	20	8	30	2	29	21	700
BELGIUM	2	0	2	1	2	1	1	1	1	1	0	0	1	0	3	2	3	0	3	0	75
FRANCE	1	0	2	1	8	2	2	2	5	3	1	0	7	2	7	0	7	0	7	1	106
GERMANY	2	1	4	1	5	2	7	4	3	3	1	1	6	2	4	1	6	2	4	3	101
ITALY	1	0	5	0	4	0	2	2	2	3	0	0	1	4	1	1	2	2	4	1	62
LUXEMBOURG	0	0	1	0	2	0	0	0	0	0	0	0	0	1	1	0	0	0	1	0	12
NETHERLANDS	4	1	3	0	2	1	0	1	0	1	0	0	0	0	4	0	4	0	3	0	51
DENMARK	0	1	1	0	0	0	1	0	0	1	0	0	0	2	0	0	1	0	0	0	11
IRELAND	0	0	1	1	0	1	0	1	0	0	0	0	2	0	1	1	1	0	1	1	29
U.K.	8	0	11	1	5	2	2	8	6	6	1	1	2	5	7	2	7	0	7	10	167
AUSTRIA	0	0	0	0	0	0	0	0	0	0	0	0	0	0	1	0	0	0	2	0	7
FINLAND	0	0	0	0	0	0	0	0	0	0	0	0	0	0	0	0	0	0	0	0	0
GREECE	0	0	0	0	0	0	0	0	0	0	0	0	0	0	0	0	0	0	0	0	1
NORWAY	4	0	3	0	0	0	0	0	0	0	0	0	0	0	1	0	0	0	0	0	11
PORTUGAL	0	0	0	0	0	0	0	0	0	0	0	0	1	1	0	0	0	0	1	1	3
SPAIN	1	1	6	0	1	0	0	1	1	1	0	0	0	1	2	2	3	0	1	1	29
SWEDEN	1	0	1	0	1	1	1	0	0	1	0	0	1	1	0	0	1	0	0	0	12
SWITZERLAND	1	0	0	0	1	1	1	1	0	0	0	0	0	0	0	0	1	0	1	1	17
TURKEY	0	0	1	0	0	0	0	0	0	1	1	0	0	0	0	0	0	0	0	0	2
OTHER EUROPE	0	0	0	0	0	0	0	0	0	0	0	0	0	1	0	0	0	0	0	0	4

TABLE 7.3.1 (CONTINUED)

COUNTRY OR REGION	NON-FERROUS	METAL CANS FAB-MET	ENGINES	CONSTR-MC FARM-MC	OFF-MC+COMPUT	SPECL-MC GENL-MC	OTH-NON-EL-MC	EL-LT+WIRING EL-TRAN	RAD+TV+APPL	ELECTRONICS OTH-ELE	COMMUNICATION	MOTOR-VEHIC OTH-TRN	PRECISION	MISC	TOTAL
N.AFR+M.EAST(TOTAL)	1	0	0	0	2	0	0	0	0	0	0	0	0	0	19
ALGERIA	0	0	0	0	0	0	0	0	0	0	0	0	0	0	1
EGYPT	0	0	0	0	1	0	0	0	0	0	0	0	0	0	1
IRAN	1	0	0	0	0	0	0	0	0	0	0	0	0	0	1
ISRAEL	0	0	0	0	0	0	0	0	0	0	0	0	0	0	4
LEBANON	0	0	0	0	0	0	0	0	0	0	0	0	0	0	4
MOROCCO	0	0	0	0	0	0	0	0	0	0	0	0	0	0	2
SAUDI ARABIA	0	0	0	0	0	0	0	0	0	0	0	0	0	0	2
OTHER N.AF+M.E.	0	0	0	0	1	0	0	0	0	0	0	0	0	0	4
E.+W.AFRICA (TOTAL)	3	0	0	0	0	0	0	1	1	2	1	1	0	0	18
GHANA	0	0	0	0	0	0	0	1	1	1	0	1	0	0	1
IVORY COAST	1	0	0	0	0	0	0	0	0	1	0	0	0	0	2
KENYA	0	0	0	0	0	0	0	0	0	0	1	0	0	0	3
LIBERIA	0	0	0	0	0	0	0	0	0	0	0	0	0	0	0
NIGERIA	0	0	0	0	0	0	0	0	0	0	0	0	0	0	3
ZAIRE	0	0	0	0	0	0	0	0	0	0	0	0	0	0	1
ZAMBIA	2	0	0	0	0	0	0	0	0	0	0	0	0	0	4
OTHER E.+W.AFR.	0	0	0	0	0	0	0	0	0	0	0	0	0	0	4
SOUTH ASIA (TOTAL)	2	0	0	1	1	0	0	1	1	1	0	1	0	0	10
INDIA	1	0	0	1	1	0	0	0	0	1	0	1	0	0	6
PAKISTAN	1	0	0	0	0	0	0	1	1	0	0	0	0	0	4
SRI LANKA	0	0	0	0	0	0	0	0	0	0	0	0	0	0	0
OTHER S.ASIA	0	0	0	0	0	0	0	0	0	0	0	0	0	0	0
EAST ASIA (TOTAL)	4	5	2	4	1	5	1	3	1	7	14	7	2	5	110
HONG KONG	0	2	0	1	0	1	0	3	1	7	7	0	0	0	11
INDONESIA	0	0	0	0	0	0	0	0	0	3	0	0	0	1	10
JAPAN	0	0	0	2	0	3	0	1	0	0	0	1	4	3	41
MALAYSIA	1	0	0	1	0	0	1	0	1	1	1	0	0	0	5
PHILIPPINES	1	1	0	0	0	1	0	1	0	2	2	0	0	0	11
SINGAPORE	2	0	1	0	0	0	0	0	0	4	3	0	0	0	21
S.KOREA	0	1	0	0	0	0	0	1	0	0	0	0	0	0	3
THAILAND	0	0	0	0	0	0	0	0	0	6	0	1	0	0	2
TAIWAN	0	0	0	0	0	0	0	0	0	6	0	1	0	0	16
OTHER E.ASIA	0	0	0	0	0	0	0	0	0	0	0	0	0	0	0
S.DOMINIONS (TOTAL)	5	0	3	1	7	0	2	1	2	2	0	0	2	3	82
AUSTRALIA	4	0	3	1	4	0	2	1	2	2	0	0	2	2	50
NEW ZEALAND	0	0	0	0	0	0	0	0	0	0	0	0	0	0	2
RHODESIA	0	0	0	0	0	0	0	0	0	0	0	0	0	0	5
S.AFRICA	1	0	0	0	3	0	0	0	0	0	0	0	0	1	25
OUTSIDE U.S.(TOTAL)	53	6	67	10	55	12	37	29	32	27	4	3	31	42	1234

CHAPTER 7 - EXPORTS AND INTRA-SYSTEM SALES
SECTION 3 -- BY REGION AND PRINCIPAL INDUSTRY IN 1975
TABLE 2 --- "INTRA-SYSTEM SALES SUBSIDIARIES"

NO. OF MANUFACTURING SUBSIDIARIES ACTIVE AT 1-JAN-76, WITH INTRA-SYSTEM SALES GREATER THAN 10% OF TOTAL SALES IN 1975

COUNTRY OR REGION	BEVERAGES	TOBACCO	FOOD	TXTL+APPRL	WOOD+FURNI PAPER	PRINTING PAPER	INDUS-CHEM PLASTIC	AGRIC-CHEM PLASTIC	COSMETICS	DRUGS	OTHER-CHEM FABR-PLSTCS	TIRES	REF-PETRLM OTH-PETRLM	LEATHER	STONE+CLAY+CEMNT ABRASIVES	GLASS	IRON
CANADA	1	0	9	3	1	1	1	0	1	2	0	1	5	0	3	0	0
LATIN AMER. (TOTAL)	4	0	5	2	6	0	6	4	6	5	7	0	7	3	0	1	1
C.AM.+CARIB. (TOTAL)	2	0	3	1	1	0	5	2	3	4	4	0	6	1	0	1	0
BAHAMAS	0	0	0	0	0	0	0	0	0	0	0	0	0	0	0	0	0
BERMUDA	0	0	0	0	0	0	0	0	0	0	0	0	0	0	0	0	0
COSTA RICA	0	0	0	0	1	0	1	0	1	0	0	0	0	0	0	0	0
GUATEMALA	0	0	0	0	0	0	1	0	0	0	0	0	0	0	0	0	0
JAMAICA	2	0	0	1	0	0	0	0	0	0	0	0	0	0	0	0	0
MEXICO	0	0	1	0	0	0	3	1	1	2	3	0	2	0	0	1	0
NETH.ANTILLES	0	0	0	0	0	0	0	2	0	0	0	0	2	0	0	0	0
NICARAGUA	0	0	1	0	0	0	0	1	1	1	1	0	0	0	0	0	0
PANAMA	0	0	0	0	0	0	0	2	0	1	0	0	2	0	0	0	0
OTHER C.AM+CAR.	0	0	2	0	0	0	0	0	0	0	0	0	0	0	0	0	0
S.AMERICA (TOTAL)	2	0	2	1	5	0	2	2	3	3	3	0	3	2	0	0	1
BOLIVIA	0	0	0	0	0	0	0	0	0	0	0	0	1	0	0	0	0
CHILE	0	0	0	0	0	0	0	0	0	0	0	0	1	0	0	0	0
COLOMBIA	0	0	0	0	1	0	1	0	1	1	1	0	0	1	0	0	1
ECUADOR	0	0	1	0	0	0	0	0	0	0	0	0	1	0	0	0	0
PERU	0	0	0	0	2	0	0	0	0	0	0	0	0	0	0	0	0
ARGENTINA	2	0	1	1	1	0	1	0	1	1	1	0	0	2	0	0	0
BRAZIL	0	0	0	0	1	0	0	0	1	1	1	0	1	0	0	0	0
URUGUAY	0	0	0	0	0	0	0	0	0	0	0	0	0	0	0	0	0
VENEZUELA	0	0	0	0	0	1	0	0	0	0	1	0	1	0	0	0	0
OTHER S.AMER.	0	0	0	0	0	0	0	0	0	0	0	0	0	0	0	0	0
EUROPE (TOTAL)	5	2	30	4	12	2	10	8	12	33	29	7	21	3	11	2	4
BELGIUM	1	0	2	0	2	0	2	0	1	3	1	1	2	1	2	0	0
FRANCE	0	0	2	0	1	0	1	0	1	3	1	1	2	1	2	0	1
GERMANY	1	0	4	0	2	1	1	0	1	4	4	1	5	1	1	0	1
ITALY	0	1	3	3	2	0	1	1	1	5	4	2	2	0	1	1	1
LUXEMBOURG	0	0	0	0	0	0	0	0	0	0	0	0	0	0	0	0	0
NETHERLANDS	0	0	4	1	2	0	2	0	1	0	4	1	0	0	1	0	0
DENMARK	0	0	2	0	0	0	0	0	1	4	1	0	4	0	0	0	0
IRELAND	0	0	3	0	0	1	0	0	0	6	7	3	0	1	2	0	0
U.K.	1	0	5	0	3	1	2	0	2	6	7	2	1	0	4	1	2
AUSTRIA	0	0	0	0	1	0	0	0	0	0	0	0	1	0	0	0	0
FINLAND	0	0	0	0	0	0	0	0	0	0	0	0	0	0	0	0	0
GREECE	0	0	1	0	0	0	0	0	0	1	1	0	0	0	1	0	0
NORWAY	0	0	0	0	0	0	0	0	0	0	0	0	1	0	0	0	0
PORTUGAL	2	0	1	0	0	0	0	0	0	2	1	0	0	0	0	0	0
SPAIN	0	1	1	0	0	1	1	0	1	2	1	1	2	0	1	0	0
SWEDEN	0	0	0	0	0	0	0	0	0	0	0	0	0	0	0	0	0
SWITZERLAND	0	0	2	0	0	0	0	0	0	2	2	0	0	0	0	0	0
TURKEY	0	0	0	0	0	0	0	0	0	0	0	0	0	0	0	0	0
OTHER EUROPE	0	0	0	0	1	0	0	0	1	0	0	0	0	0	0	0	0

TABLE 7 . 3 . 2 (CONTINUED)

COUNTRY OR REGION	BEVERAGES	TOBACCO	FOOD	TXTL+APPRL	WOOD+FURNI	PAPER	PRINTING	INDUS-CHEM	PLASTIC	AGRIC-CHEM	COSMETICS	DRUGS	OTHER-CHEM	FABR-PLSTCS	TIRES	REF-PETRLM	OTH-PETRLM	LEATHER	STONE+CLAY+CEMNT	ABRASIVES	GLASS	IRON
N.AFR+M.EAST (TOTAL)	0	0	1	0	0	1	0	0	0	0	0	1	0	0	0	2	0	0	0	0	0	0
ALGERIA	0	0	1	0	0	1	0	0	0	0	0	0	0	0	0	0	0	0	0	0	0	0
EGYPT	0	0	0	0	0	0	0	0	0	0	0	0	0	0	0	0	0	0	0	0	0	0
IRAN	0	0	0	0	0	0	0	0	0	0	0	0	0	0	0	0	0	0	0	0	0	0
ISRAEL	0	0	0	0	0	0	0	0	0	0	0	0	0	0	0	0	0	0	0	0	0	0
LEBANON	0	0	0	0	0	0	0	0	0	0	0	0	0	0	0	0	0	0	0	0	0	0
MOROCCO	0	0	1	0	0	0	0	0	0	0	0	0	0	0	0	0	0	0	0	0	0	0
SAUDI ARABIA	0	0	0	0	0	0	0	0	0	0	0	0	0	0	0	0	0	0	0	0	0	0
OTHER N.AF+M.E.	0	0	0	0	0	1	0	0	0	0	0	0	0	0	0	2	0	0	0	0	0	0
E.+W.AFRICA (TOTAL)	0	0	2	0	0	2	0	0	0	1	0	1	0	0	0	1	0	0	0	0	0	0
GHANA	0	0	2	0	0	2	0	0	0	0	0	0	0	0	0	0	0	0	0	0	0	0
IVORY COAST	0	0	0	0	0	0	0	0	0	0	0	0	0	0	0	0	0	0	0	0	0	0
KENYA	0	0	1	0	0	0	0	0	0	0	0	0	0	0	0	0	0	0	0	0	0	0
LIBERIA	0	0	0	0	0	0	0	0	0	0	0	0	0	0	0	0	0	0	0	0	0	0
NIGERIA	0	0	0	0	0	0	0	0	0	1	0	1	0	0	0	0	0	0	0	0	0	0
ZAIRE	0	0	0	0	0	0	0	0	0	0	0	0	0	0	0	0	0	0	0	0	0	0
ZAMBIA	0	0	0	0	0	1	0	0	0	0	0	0	0	0	0	0	0	0	0	0	0	0
OTHER E.+W.AFR.	0	0	1	0	0	1	0	0	0	0	0	0	0	0	0	1	0	0	0	0	0	0
SOUTH ASIA (TOTAL)	0	0	1	0	0	0	0	0	0	0	0	1	0	0	0	0	0	0	0	0	0	0
INDIA	0	0	1	0	0	0	0	0	0	0	0	1	0	0	0	0	0	0	0	0	0	0
PAKISTAN	0	0	1	0	0	0	0	0	0	0	0	0	0	0	0	0	0	0	0	0	0	0
SRI LANKA	0	0	0	0	0	0	0	0	0	0	0	0	0	0	0	0	0	0	0	0	0	0
OTHER S.ASIA	0	0	0	0	0	0	0	0	0	0	0	0	0	0	0	0	0	0	0	0	0	0
EAST ASIA (TOTAL)	2	0	5	1	1	0	0	0	2	1	0	3	1	0	0	8	2	0	0	0	0	0
HONG KONG	0	0	0	0	0	0	0	0	0	0	0	0	1	0	0	0	0	0	0	0	0	0
INDONESIA	1	0	0	0	1	0	0	0	0	0	0	0	1	0	0	0	0	0	0	0	0	0
JAPAN	0	0	0	1	0	0	0	0	0	1	0	0	0	0	0	5	2	0	0	0	0	0
MALAYSIA	1	0	3	0	0	0	0	0	0	0	0	1	0	0	0	0	0	0	0	0	0	0
PHILIPPINES	1	0	1	0	0	0	0	0	0	0	0	0	0	0	0	2	0	0	0	0	0	0
SINGAPORE	0	0	0	0	0	0	0	0	0	0	0	0	0	0	0	2	0	0	0	0	0	0
S.KOREA	0	0	1	0	0	0	0	0	0	0	0	0	0	0	0	0	0	0	0	0	0	0
THAILAND	0	0	0	0	0	0	0	0	2	0	0	0	0	0	0	0	0	0	0	0	0	0
TAIWAN	0	0	0	0	0	0	0	0	0	0	0	1	0	0	0	0	0	0	0	0	0	0
OTHER E.ASIA	0	0	0	0	0	0	0	0	0	0	0	1	0	0	0	0	0	0	0	0	0	0
S.DOMINIONS (TOTAL)	1	0	10	0	0	16	1	4	2	2	2	2	2	0	1	7	0	1	1	2	0	1
AUSTRALIA	1	0	6	0	0	2	0	3	2	1	1	1	1	1	0	3	0	0	1	0	0	1
NEW ZEALAND	0	0	1	0	0	0	0	1	2	0	0	0	0	0	0	0	0	0	0	0	0	0
RHODESIA	0	0	0	0	0	3	0	0	0	0	0	0	0	0	0	0	0	0	0	0	0	0
S.AFRICA	0	0	3	0	0	11	1	0	0	0	1	1	1	0	1	4	0	1	0	2	0	0
OUTSIDE U.S. (TOTAL)	13	2	63	10	3	42	4	21	18	8	20	49	39	7	10	51	8	3	4	16	3	6

(TABLE CONTINUED ON FOLLOWING PAGES)

406

TABLE   7 .3 .2   (CONTINUED)

COUNTRY OR REGION	NON-FERROUS METAL	CANS	FAB-MET	ENGINES	CONSTR-MC	FARM-MC	OFF-MC+COMPUT SPECL-MC	GENL-MC	OTH-NON-EL-MC	EL-LT+WIRING	EL-TRAN	RAD+TV+APPL	ELECTRONICS OTH-ELE	COMMUNICATION	MOTOR-VEHIC	OTH-TRN	PRECISION	MISC	TOTAL
CANADA	4	1	5	1	2	2	2	2	2	0	0	1	8	0	2	0	0	3	64
LATIN AMER. (TOTAL)	7	2	4	0	3	1	9	0	3	0	0	6	8	3	4	2	2	3	130
C.AM.+CARIB. (TOTAL)	2	1	2	0	3	0	4	0	2	0	0	3	6	3	2	2	1	3	79
BAHAMAS	0	0	0	0	0	0	0	0	0	0	0	0	0	0	0	0	1	0	0
BERMUDA	0	0	0	0	0	0	0	0	0	0	0	0	0	0	0	0	0	0	0
COSTA RICA	0	0	0	0	0	0	0	0	0	0	0	0	0	0	0	0	0	0	2
GUATEMALA	0	0	0	0	0	0	0	0	0	0	0	0	0	0	0	0	0	1	2
JAMAICA	1	1	0	0	0	0	0	0	0	0	0	0	0	0	0	0	1	0	0
MEXICO	0	1	1	0	3	0	4	0	2	0	0	3	5	3	2	2	0	1	54
NETH.ANTILLES	0	0	0	0	0	0	0	0	0	0	0	0	0	0	0	0	2	0	4
NICARAGUA	0	0	0	0	0	0	0	0	0	0	0	0	0	0	0	0	0	0	1
PANAMA	0	0	0	0	0	0	0	0	0	0	0	0	0	0	0	0	0	0	4
OTHER C.AM+CAR.	1	0	1	0	0	0	0	0	0	0	0	0	1	0	0	0	0	1	12
S.AMERICA (TOTAL)	5	1	2	0	0	1	5	0	1	0	0	3	2	3	2	0	0	0	51
BOLIVIA	0	0	0	0	0	0	0	0	0	0	0	0	0	0	0	0	1	0	0
CHILE	1	0	0	0	0	0	0	0	0	0	0	1	0	1	0	0	0	0	3
COLOMBIA	1	1	0	0	0	0	0	0	0	0	0	0	0	0	0	0	0	0	8
ECUADOR	0	0	0	0	0	0	1	0	0	0	0	0	0	0	0	0	0	0	2
PERU	0	0	0	0	0	0	0	0	0	0	0	0	0	0	0	0	0	0	0
ARGENTINA	0	0	1	0	0	1	2	0	0	0	0	1	1	1	1	0	0	0	15
BRAZIL	0	0	0	0	0	0	0	0	0	0	0	1	1	0	1	0	1	0	14
URUGUAY	0	0	0	0	0	0	0	0	0	0	0	0	0	0	0	0	0	0	0
VENEZUELA	2	0	0	0	0	0	0	0	0	0	0	0	0	0	0	0	0	0	8
OTHER S.AMER.	1	0	0	0	0	0	0	0	0	0	0	0	0	0	0	0	0	0	1
EUROPE (TOTAL)	15	0	13	2	13	7	16	15	13	11	0	9	13	6	16	1	12	16	388
BELGIUM	0	0	2	0	3	1	1	4	1	1	0	0	0	1	0	0	2	2	29
FRANCE	1	0	0	0	3	1	2	2	0	1	0	1	2	0	3	0	2	2	50
GERMANY	2	0	2	1	2	2	5	3	2	2	0	3	1	0	2	0	3	3	59
ITALY	1	0	0	0	2	0	2	0	3	3	0	1	1	1	2	1	3	2	43
LUXEMBOURG	0	0	1	0	0	1	0	0	1	0	0	0	0	0	0	0	2	1	11
NETHERLANDS	2	0	0	0	0	0	3	0	0	0	0	0	2	1	0	0	0	0	26
DENMARK	0	0	1	0	0	1	0	0	0	1	0	1	0	0	1	0	1	1	6
IRELAND	0	0	1	0	0	0	0	0	0	1	0	0	1	0	1	0	0	0	18
U.K.	6	0	5	1	2	1	1	6	2	2	0	2	5	2	8	3	3	4	94
AUSTRIA	0	0	0	0	0	0	0	0	0	0	0	0	0	0	0	0	1	1	3
FINLAND	0	0	0	0	0	0	0	0	0	0	0	0	0	0	0	0	0	0	1
GREECE	2	0	0	0	0	0	0	0	0	0	0	0	0	0	0	0	0	0	3
NORWAY	0	0	1	0	0	0	0	0	0	0	0	0	0	0	0	0	0	0	5
PORTUGAL	1	0	0	0	0	1	0	0	1	1	0	1	1	1	1	0	0	1	4
SPAIN	0	0	2	0	0	1	1	0	0	0	0	0	0	0	0	0	1	1	16
SWEDEN	0	0	0	0	0	0	0	0	0	0	0	1	1	1	1	1	1	1	7
SWITZERLAND	0	0	0	0	1	0	1	0	0	0	0	0	0	0	0	0	1	0	9
TURKEY	0	0	0	0	1	0	0	0	0	0	0	0	0	0	0	0	0	0	2
OTHER EUROPE	0	0	0	0	0	0	0	0	0	0	0	0	0	0	0	0	0	0	2

TABLE 7.3.2 (CONTINUED)

COUNTRY OR REGION	NON-FERROUS	METAL CANS FAB-MET	ENGINES	CONSTR-MC	OFF-MC+COMPUT FARM-MC	SPECL-MC	GENL-MC	OTH-MC	OTH-NON-EL-MC	EL-LT+WIRING	EL-TRAN	RAD+TV+APPL	ELECTRONICS	OTH-ELE	COMMUNICATION	MOTOR-VEHIC	OTH-TRN	PRECISION	MISC	TOTAL
N.AFR+M.EAST (TOTAL)	1	0	0	0	0	0	0	0	0	2	0	0	0	0	0	0	0	0	0	5
ALGERIA	0	0	0	0	0	0	0	0	0	0	0	0	0	0	0	0	0	0	0	0
EGYPT	0	0	0	0	0	0	0	0	0	0	0	0	0	0	0	0	0	0	0	0
IRAN	1	0	0	0	0	0	0	0	0	0	0	0	0	0	0	0	0	0	0	1
ISRAEL	0	0	0	0	0	0	0	0	0	0	0	0	0	0	0	0	0	0	0	0
LEBANON	0	0	0	0	0	0	0	0	0	0	0	0	0	0	0	0	0	0	0	0
MOROCCO	0	0	0	0	0	0	0	0	0	0	0	0	0	0	0	0	1	0	0	1
SAUDI ARABIA	0	0	0	0	0	0	0	0	0	1	0	0	0	0	0	0	1	0	0	2
OTHER N.AF+M.E.	0	0	0	0	0	0	0	0	0	1	0	0	0	0	0	0	0	0	0	1
E.+W.AFRICA (TOTAL)	3	0	0	0	0	0	0	0	0	2	1	0	0	0	1	0	0	0	0	10
GHANA	0	0	0	0	0	0	0	0	0	0	0	0	0	0	0	0	0	0	0	0
IVORY COAST	1	0	0	0	0	0	0	0	0	0	1	0	0	0	0	0	0	0	0	2
KENYA	0	0	0	0	0	0	0	0	0	1	0	0	0	0	0	0	0	0	0	1
LIBERIA	0	0	0	0	0	0	0	0	0	0	0	0	0	0	0	0	0	0	0	0
NIGERIA	0	0	0	0	0	0	0	0	0	0	0	0	0	0	1	0	0	0	0	1
ZAIRE	0	0	0	0	0	0	0	0	0	0	0	0	0	0	0	0	0	0	0	0
ZAMBIA	2	0	0	0	0	0	0	0	0	0	0	0	0	0	0	0	0	0	0	3
OTHER E.+W.AFR.	0	0	0	0	0	0	0	0	0	1	0	0	0	0	0	0	0	0	0	3
SOUTH ASIA (TOTAL)	2	0	0	0	0	0	0	0	0	2	1	0	0	1	0	0	0	0	0	7
INDIA	1	0	0	0	0	0	0	0	0	1	1	0	0	1	0	0	0	0	0	3
PAKISTAN	1	0	0	0	0	0	0	0	0	1	0	0	0	0	0	0	0	0	0	3
SRI LANKA	0	0	0	0	0	0	0	0	0	0	0	0	0	0	0	0	0	0	0	1
OTHER S.ASIA	0	0	0	0	0	0	0	0	0	0	0	0	0	0	0	0	0	0	0	0
EAST ASIA (TOTAL)	2	4	0	1	1	8	0	1	1	9	1	0	13	4	2	2	1	0	1	77
HONG KONG	0	1	0	0	1	1	0	0	0	3	1	0	0	0	0	0	0	0	1	7
INDONESIA	0	0	0	0	0	0	0	0	0	0	0	0	0	0	0	0	0	0	0	0
JAPAN	0	2	0	1	0	6	1	0	1	2	0	0	2	0	0	2	0	0	2	25
MALAYSIA	1	0	0	0	0	0	0	0	0	0	0	0	2	0	0	0	0	0	0	3
PHILIPPINES	1	0	0	0	0	1	0	0	0	1	0	0	4	3	0	0	0	0	0	8
SINGAPORE	0	1	0	0	0	0	0	0	0	0	0	0	1	0	1	0	0	0	0	16
S.KOREA	0	0	0	0	0	0	0	0	0	1	0	0	0	1	0	0	0	0	0	1
THAILAND	0	0	0	0	0	0	0	0	0	2	0	0	6	1	0	1	0	0	0	3
TAIWAN	0	0	0	0	0	0	0	0	0	0	0	0	0	1	1	1	0	0	0	14
OTHER E.ASIA	0	0	0	0	0	0	0	0	0	0	0	0	0	0	0	0	0	0	0	0
S.DOMINIONS (TOTAL)	5	2	0	3	0	2	0	0	0	1	0	0	1	0	0	2	0	1	3	73
AUSTRALIA	4	1	0	2	0	2	0	0	0	0	0	0	0	0	0	2	0	1	1	38
NEW ZEALAND	0	0	0	0	0	0	0	0	0	0	0	0	0	0	0	0	0	0	0	2
RHODESIA	0	0	0	0	0	0	0	0	0	0	0	0	0	0	0	0	0	0	0	3
S.AFRICA	1	1	0	1	0	0	0	0	0	0	0	0	0	0	0	0	0	0	2	30
OUTSIDE U.S. (TOTAL)	39	3	28	3	22	11	37	16	16	17	1	0	28	35	19	8	25	3	16	754

Chapter Eight

Extraction and Exploration Activity

CHAPTER   8   - EXTRACTION AND EXPLORATION ACTIVITY
SECTION   1   -- EXTRACTION SUBSIDIARIES
TABLE   1   --- PROLIFERATION BY GEOGRAPHICAL REGION

NO. OF SUBSIDIARIES, BY REGION

REGION	TOTAL NO. AT 31-DEC-50	NO. OF ENTRIES DURING YEAR(S)													TOTAL ENTRIES 1951-75	TOTAL EXITS 1951-75	NET FLOW UP TO 1-JAN-76
		51-55	56-60	61-65	1966	1967	1968	1969	1970	1971	1972	1973	1974	1975			
CANADA	18	13	16	15	2	9	11	7	2	2	3	1	3	2	86	43	61
C.AM.+CARIB.	36	6	13	11	2	2	2	5	2	12	4	3	2	1	65	41	60
S.AMERICA	18	6	14	15	4	4	5	8	2	6	1	0	4	3	72	36	54
EUROPE	3	4	6	7	0	2	3	4	2	4	1	1	17	3	54	9	48
N.AFR+M.EAST	10	11	7	4	1	2	1	1	1	1	0	2	0	0	31	20	21
E.+W.AFRICA	5	11	5	5	3	3	2	6	4	1	0	2	1	2	45	19	31
SOUTH ASIA	0	0	0	0	0	0	0	0	0	0	0	0	0	0	0	0	0
EAST ASIA	8	1	1	2	1	2	2	4	4	3	1	1	3	1	26	7	27
S.DOMINIONS	10	6	5	14	1	3	3	9	2	1	2	2	2	2	51	15	46
OUTSIDE U.S. (TOTAL)	108	58	67	73	14	27	29	44	19	30	11	12	32	14	430	190	348

CHAPTER 8   - EXTRACTION AND EXPLORATION ACTIVITY
SECTION 1   -- EXTRACTION SUBSIDIARIES
TABLE 2   --- PROLIFERATION BY OWNERSHIP PATTERNS

NO. OF SUBSIDIARIES, BY PARENT OWNERSHIP AT ENTRY

OWNERSHIP AT ENTRY	TOTAL NO. AT 31-DEC-50	NO. OF ENTRIES DURING YEAR(S)													TOTAL ENTRIES 1951-75	TOTAL EXITS 1951-75	NET FLOW UP TO 1-JAN-76
		51-55	56-60	61-65	1966	1967	1968	1969	1970	1971	1972	1973	1974	1975			
WHL OWNED: 95-100%	63	30	44	46	10	17	19	29	10	16	6	7	22	7	263	104	222
MAJ OWNED: 51- 94%	9	14	7	7	1	3	4	4	2	1	2	3	4	2	54	28	35
CO- OWNED: 50%	9	2	1	3	0	4	1	2	2	2	0	0	1	3	21	8	22
MIN OWNED: 5- 49%	14	10	7	10	2	2	3	6	5	11	3	2	5	2	68	26	56
UNKNOWN	13	2	8	7	1	1	2	3	0	0	0	0	0	0	24	24	13
TOTAL	108	58	67	73	14	27	29	44	19	30	11	12	32	14	430	190	348

CHAPTER 8   - EXTRACTION AND EXPLORATION ACTIVITY
SECTION 1   -- EXTRACTION SUBSIDIARIES
TABLE 3   --- EXITS EXCLUDING MERGERS (* "EEM'S" *) BY REGION

NO. OF SUBSIDIARIES, BY REGION

REGION	TOTAL NO. ACTIVE AT 31-DEC-50	NO. OF EEM'S DURING YEAR(S)													TOTAL EEM'S 1951-75	TOTAL MERGERS 1951-75	TOTAL EXITS 1951-75
		51-55	56-60	61-65	1966	1967	1968	1969	1970	1971	1972	1973	1974	1975			
CANADA	18	0	4	4	0	0	3	0	7	1	5	5	2	1	32	11	43
C.AM.+CARIB.	36	1	2	4	1	0	0	0	3	2	2	1	2	1	19	22	41
S.AMERICA	18	1	2	4	0	4	1	2	0	2	6	2	3	6	33	3	36
EUROPE	3	0	0	1	0	0	0	1	0	1	0	2	2	0	7	2	9
N.AFR+M.EAST	10	0	2	1	0	0	1	0	2	0	1	3	1	6	17	3	20
E.+W.AFRICA	5	1	1	2	0	0	0	0	1	1	0	1	4	0	11	8	19
SOUTH ASIA	0	0	0	0	0	0	0	0	0	0	0	0	0	0	0	0	0
EAST ASIA	8	0	0	0	1	0	0	0	0	1	1	0	1	1	5	2	7
S.DOMINIONS	10	0	2	2	0	2	0	0	0	0	1	2	0	5	14	1	15
OUTSIDE U.S.(TOTAL)	108	3	13	18	2	6	5	3	13	8	16	16	15	20	138	52	190

CHAPTER 8   - EXTRACTION AND EXPLORATION ACTIVITY
SECTION 1   -- EXTRACTION SUBSIDIARIES
TABLE 4   --- BY REGION AND OWNERSHIP CHANGES

NO. OF SUBSIDIARIES ACTIVE AT 1-JAN-76

REGION	TOTAL NO. AT 1-JAN-76	PARENT OWNERSHIP AT ENTRY DATE					PARENT OWNERSHIP IN 1975				
		95-100%	51-94%	50%	5-49%	UNKNOWN	95-100%	51-94%	50%	5-49%	UNKNOWN
CANADA	61	37	6	5	12	1	39	4	4	13	1
C.AM.+CARIB.	54	36	5	2	11	0	32	5	1	16	0
S.AMERICA	61	40	8	3	8	2	45	8	0	8	0
EUROPE	64	50	1	4	5	4	48	5	4	4	3
N.AFR+M.EAST	22	16	0	3	2	1	15	2	1	4	0
E.+W.AFRICA	28	12	5	3	7	1	14	7	3	4	0
SOUTH ASIA	0	0	0	0	0	0	0	0	0	0	0
EAST ASIA	32	21	4	2	1	4	23	5	2	2	0
S.DOMINIONS	34	17	2	3	8	4	22	1	2	9	0
OUTSIDE U.S.(TOTAL)	356	229	31	25	54	17	238	37	17	60	4

CHAPTER 8 — EXTRACTION AND EXPLORATION ACTIVITY
SECTION 1 —— EXTRACTION SUBSIDIARIES
TABLE 5 ——— BY REGION AND OUTSIDE OWNERSHIP IN 1975

NO. OF SUBSIDIARIES ACTIVE AT 1-JAN-76

REGION	CATEGORY OF PRINCIPAL OUTSIDE OWNER, AND PERCENTAGE OWNED BY PRINCIPAL OUTSIDE OWNER, IN 1975																				UN-KNOWN	WHOLLY OWNED BY PARENT
	LOCAL PRIVATE					LOCAL STATE					FOREIGN PRIVATE					WIDELY DISPERSED						
	5-49	50	51-94	UNK	TOT	5-49	50	51-94	UNK	TOT	5-49	50	51-94	UNK	TOT	5-49	50	51-94	UNK	TOT		
CANADA	5	1	1	0	7	1	0	1	0	2	2	1	1	1	5	0	0	0	0	0	8	39
C.AM.+CARIB.	0	0	1	0	1	1	2	0	0	3	2	0	0	0	2	0	0	1	0	1	15	32
S.AMERICA	0	0	3	1	4	0	0	0	0	0	1	0	1	0	2	0	0	0	0	0	10	45
EUROPE	1	1	0	0	2	0	0	0	0	0	2	2	0	0	4	0	0	0	0	0	10	48
N.AFR+M.EAST	0	0	0	0	0	1	0	2	0	3	2	0	0	0	2	0	0	0	0	0	2	15
E.+W.AFRICA	1	1	0	0	2	4	0	0	0	4	1	0	0	0	1	0	0	0	0	0	7	14
SOUTH ASIA	0	0	0	0	0	0	0	0	0	0	0	0	0	0	0	0	0	0	0	0	0	0
EAST ASIA	2	1	0	0	3	1	0	0	1	2	0	1	0	1	2	0	0	0	0	0	2	23
S.DOMINIONS	1	1	4	2	8	0	0	0	0	0	0	0	0	1	1	0	0	0	0	0	3	22
OUTSIDE U.S. (TOTAL)	10	5	9	3	27	8	2	3	1	14	10	4	2	3	19	0	0	1	0	1	57	238

415

CHAPTER 8 - EXTRACTION AND EXPLORATION ACTIVITY
SECTION 1 -- EXTRACTION SUBSIDIARIES
TABLE 6 --- BY REGION AND FINANCIAL DATA FOR 1975

NO. OF SUBSIDIARIES ACTIVE AT 1-JAN-76

(CATEGORIES: A=UNDER $1 MILLION B=$1M-$10M C=$10M-$25M D=$25M-$100M E=OVER $100M U=UNKNOWN)

REGION	TOTAL NO. AT 1-JAN-76	SALES CATEGORY FOR 1975						ASSETS CATEGORY FOR 1975						EQUITY CATEGORY FOR 1975					
		A	B	C	D	E	U	A	B	C	D	E	U	A	B	C	D	E	U
CANADA	61	8	9	13	3	9	19	7	8	20	5	7	14	10	6	2	4	3	36
C.AM.+CARIB.	54	5	14	6	8	2	19	6	19	2	3	3	21	14	11	0	2	2	25
S.AMERICA	61	5	12	10	5	6	23	10	16	9	6	4	16	18	10	0	3	1	29
EUROPE	64	8	12	8	7	7	22	12	12	8	6	7	19	21	8	1	2	3	29
N.AFR+M.EAST	22	0	0	3	3	7	9	1	2	7	3	5	4	12	0	0	1	2	7
E.+W.AFRICA	28	1	6	6	2	5	8	2	9	6	2	5	4	4	3	0	3	1	17
SOUTH ASIA	0	0	0	0	0	0	0	0	0	0	0	0	0	0	0	0	0	0	0
EAST ASIA	32	3	6	5	4	1	13	4	8	9	4	0	7	5	6	1	0	0	20
S.DOMINIONS	34	2	4	7	6	4	11	2	8	8	4	5	7	3	4	1	2	2	22
OUTSIDE U.S.(TOTAL)	356	32	63	58	38	41	124	44	82	69	33	36	92	87	48	5	17	14	185

CHAPTER 8   - EXTRACTION AND EXPLORATION ACTIVITY
SECTION 1   -- EXTRACTION SUBSIDIARIES
TABLE 7   --- BY PARENT OWNERSHIP AND FINANCIAL DATA FOR 1975

NO. OF SUBSIDIARIES ACTIVE AT 1-JAN-76

(CATEGORIES: A=UNDER $1 MILLION   B=$1M-$10M   C=$10M-$25M   D=$25M-$100M   E=OVER $100M   U=UNKNOWN)

OWNERSHIP IN 1975	TOTAL NO. AT 1-JAN-76	SALES CATEGORY FOR 1975						ASSETS CATEGORY FOR 1975						EQUITY CATEGORY FOR 1975					
		A	B	C	D	E	U	A	B	C	D	E	U	A	B	C	D	E	U
WHL OWNED: 95-100%	238	23	47	41	24	18	85	34	61	47	22	15	59	62	32	3	6	8	127
MAJ OWNED: 51- 94%	37	6	5	7	4	10	5	4	9	7	3	9	5	8	7	0	6	2	14
CO- OWNED: 50%	17	0	2	3	3	3	6	1	3	4	3	2	4	2	0	1	0	2	12
MIN OWNED: 5- 49%	60	3	8	7	7	10	25	5	9	11	5	10	20	15	9	1	5	2	28
UNKNOWN	4	0	1	0	0	0	3	0	0	0	0	0	4	0	0	0	0	0	4
TOTAL	356	32	63	58	38	41	124	44	82	69	33	36	92	87	48	5	17	14	185

CHAPTER 8 - EXTRACTION AND EXPLORATION ACTIVITY
SECTION 2 -- EXPLORATION SUBSIDIARIES
TABLE 1 --- PROLIFERATION BY GEOGRAPHICAL REGION

NO. OF SUBSIDIARIES, BY REGION

REGION	NET FLOW UP TO 31-DEC-50	NO. OF ENTRIES DURING YEAR(S)													TOTAL ENTRIES 1951-75	TOTAL EXITS 1951-75	NET FLOW UP TO 1-JAN-76
		51-55	56-60	61-65	1966	1967	1968	1969	1970	1971	1972	1973	1974	1975			
CANADA	4	3	8	3	0	1	0	0	1	0	0	0	1	0	17	5	16
C.AM.+CARIB.	1	6	4	6	0	0	4	0	1	3	0	0	2	2	28	3	26
S.AMERICA	7	3	2	2	0	1	2	2	3	0	0	1	1	1	18	3	22
EUROPE	1	3	5	11	0	0	0	1	2	2	2	5	2	6	39	7	33
N.AFR+M.EAST	2	2	4	1	0	1	0	1	2	1	4	4	1	0	21	2	21
E.+W.AFRICA	1	4	1	4	1	2	1	4	3	3	1	4	4	1	33	3	31
SOUTH ASIA	0	0	0	1	0	0	0	0	0	0	0	0	0	0	1	0	1
EAST ASIA	2	1	0	1	1	1	1	2	0	1	3	3	2	0	16	2	16
S.DOMINIONS	1	1	4	5	1	0	1	4	0	4	2	0	1	0	23	3	21
OUTSIDE U.S. (TOTAL)	19	23	28	34	3	6	9	14	12	14	12	17	14	10	196	28	187

CHAPTER 8   – EXTRACTION AND EXPLORATION ACTIVITY
SECTION 2   -- EXPLORATION SUBSIDIARIES
TABLE 2   --- BY REGION AND ASSETS IN 1975

NO. OF SUBSIDIARIES ACTIVE AT 1-JAN-76

| REGION | ASSETS CATEGORY FOR 1975 | | | | | | TOTAL NO. AT 1-JAN-76 |
	UNDER $1 MILLION	$1-10 MILLION	$10-25 MILLION	$25-100 MILLION	OVER $100 MILLION	UNKNOWN	
CANADA	5	1	1	0	0	9	16
C.AM.+CARIB.	11	3	1	0	0	11	26
S.AMERICA	3	3	0	0	2	14	22
EUROPE	5	4	5	1	0	18	33
N.AFR+M.EAST	3	7	2	0	0	9	21
E.+W.AFRICA	6	3	3	1	1	17	31
SOUTH ASIA	1	0	0	0	0	0	1
EAST ASIA	1	4	1	1	0	9	16
S.DOMINIONS	4	5	2	1	0	9	21
OUTSIDE U.S.(TOTAL)	39	30	15	4	3	96	187

Questionnaires

The following questionnaires are those used in the collection of data on the foreign subsidiaries of U.S. parent systems. The first questionnaire, labeled "Questionnaire for Updating Existing U.S. Subsidiary Data," applies to those subsidiaries included in the original study of U.S. multinational enterprises.

The original study covered the foreign subsidiaries of each parent system from year of entry to 1967. If a subsidiary was in the data base derived from that study, and if it had not departed from its parent system prior to 1967, then the first questionnaire, known as the "short form," was used to collect data for that subsidiary. The data from the "short form" were then merged with the subsidiary's records from the original data base to form a complete entry in the new data base used for this book. The new data base contains approximately 8,650 such entries.

The second questionnaire, labeled "Questionnaire for Subsidiaries Formed After 1967," applies to subsidiaries that entered their parent systems after 1967. This questionnaire, known as the "long form," contains additional information relevant to the subsidiary's status at the time of entry into its parent system. About 7,400 long forms were completed in the course of collecting the data used in this book.

The third questionnaire, labeled "Addendum Form for Pre-1967 Subsidiaries not on EMY 1," was used in the event that a subsidiary was discovered that had in reality entered its parent system before 1967, but that had not been included in the original data base. For such subsidiaries, a "long form" plus an "addendum form" were completed to collect data comparable to those entered for existing subsidiaries from the original data base. About 400 such subsidiaries were identified and entered in the new data base.

The data base used for this book also contains 2,750 entries from the original EMY 1 data bank, which represent subsidiaries that left their respective parent systems before 1967. The final form, known as a "parent form," was used to collect data on each parent system. One such form was completed and entered for each of the 180 parent systems in the sample. The seven page questionnaire used to collect data for the original 1967 data base is not shown here.

**QUESTIONNAIRE FOR UPDATING EXISTING
U.S. SUBSIDIARY DATA (short form)**

1. Name of system (ultimate U.S. parent) _____   _____
2. Name of subsidiary, as of 1967 _____   _____
2a. Most recent name of subject, if not 2. _____   _____
3. Country of incorporation of subsidiary. _____   _____
4. If subsidiary left the system:
    a) Year _____
    b) Method (check one)
        1) Sold . . . . ☐
        2) Confiscated or expropriated . . . . ☐
        3) Liquidated, function terminated . . . . ☐
        4) Liquidated, function continued by other means . . . . ☐
    c) If function continued, list successor subsidiaries:

    _____   _____
    _____   _____

5. Primary activity in 1974:
    a) Year for which data apply, if not 1974 _____   _____
    b) Principal activity; check only one box. If any manufacturing, check #1.
        1) Manufacturing (some manufacturing is known) . . . . ☐
        2) Research and development. . . . . ☐
        3) Sales or service (includes marketing, repair and maintenance,
           transport, storage, or finance). . . . . ☐
        4) Extraction (includes extraction of all raw materials, plus
           farming or fishing) . . . . ☐
        5) Holding (principal activity consists of owning and adminis-
           tering subsidiaries) . . . . ☐
        6) Other (please specify) _____   . . . . ☐
        7) Inactive . . . . ☐   _____
6. Products manufactured in 1974, if any. List principal products first, on the
   basis of sales volume.
    a) If not 1974, list year for which data apply _____   _____

    b) List products:
        1) _____   _____
        2) _____   _____
        3) _____   _____
        4) _____   _____
        5) _____   _____
        6) _____   _____
7. Ownership in 1974:
    a) If not 1974, list year for which data apply _____   _____
    b) Immediate parent(s) in system: _____   _____

    c) Percentage ownership by immediate parent(s): _____   _____

8. Outside ownership in 1974:
    a) If not 1974, list year for which data apply _____   _____
    b) Outside owner category (check one): 1st outside owner 2nd outside owner
        1) a locally controlled private enterprise. . . . ☐ . . . . . ☐   _____
        2) a local state agency or state enterprise . . . ☐ . . . . . ☐

(name 3) a foreign-controlled private enterprise ... ☐ ..... ☐ _____

below) 4) stock is widely dispersed .... ☐ ..... ☐ _____

    c) Percentage ownership by outside owners _____ _____ _____

9. Financial statistics (check one box each for sales, assets, and equity. The year for which data apply should be listed next to each entry):

	Sales _____	Assets _____	Equity _____	
1) less than $1 million	☐	☐	☐	_____
2) between $1 and $10 m	☐	☐	☐	_____
3) between $10 and $25m	☐	☐	☐	_____
4) between $25 and $100m	☐	☐	☐	_____
5) more than $100m	☐	☐	☐	_____

10. Number of employees _____ Year _____

11. Principal market of sales (check one):

    1) less than 10% of sales are exported .... ☐

    2) between 10% and 50% of sales are exported .... ☐

    3) more than 50% of sales are exported .... ☐ _____

12. Principal customer of sales (check one):

    1) less than 10% sales are to parent or affiliates in system . ☐

    2) between 10% and 50% of sales are within system ..... ☐

    3) more than 50% of sales are within system .... ☐

COMMENTS OR ADDITIONAL INFORMATION:

FOR OFFICE USE ONLY:

    Other Parent Systems:

QUESTIONNAIRE FOR SUBSIDIARIES FORMED AFTER 1967 (long form)

1. Name of system (ultimate U.S. parent)

   _____   _____

2. Most recent name of subsidiary

   _____   _____

3. Subsidiary's country of incorporation

   _____   _____

4. Nation of primary activity, if not (3)

   _____   _____

5. Year subsidiary entered system _____   _____

6. How subsidiary entered system (check one)
   1) Newly formed . . . . [____]
   2) Merger or break-up of older subsidiaries . . . . [____]
   3) Acquired existing company directly . . . . [____]
   4) Acquired through acquisition of another firm . . . . [____] _____

7. If subsidiary left the system:
   a) Year _____   _____
   b) Method of departure (check one)
      1) Sold . . . . [____]
      2) Confiscated. . . . . [____]
      3) Liquidated, function ended
         . . . . [____]
      4) Liquidated, function continued by other means . . . [____] _____
   c) If function continued, successor subsidiaries _____   _____

   _____

8. Nature of principal activity at entry date (check one):
   1) Manufacturing (if any manufacturing, check this box . . . . . . [____]
   2) Research and development. . . [____]
   3) Sales or service (includes marketing, repair and maintenance, transport, storage, or finance)
      . . . . [____]
   4) Extraction (all raw material extraction, plus farming and fishing) . . . . [____]
   5) Holding (principal activity consists of owning and administering subsidiaries . . . . . [____]
   6) Other (specify) _____ [____]
   7) Inactive _____ [____]

9. Principal activity in 1974
   a) Year of data, if not 1974 _____
   b) Principal activity (list number from question 8) _____

10. Products manufactured at entry, if any. Principal products first.
    1) _____   _____
    2) _____   _____
    3) _____   _____
    4) _____   _____
    5) _____   _____
    6) _____   _____

11. Products manufactured in 1974, if any. Year, if not 1974 ____   _____
    1) _____   _____
    2) _____   _____
    3) _____   _____
    4) _____   _____
    5) _____   _____
    6) _____   _____

12. Ownership of the subsidiary:
    a) At entry date
       1) Name of immediate parent(s) in system
          a) _____   _____
          b) _____   _____
       2) % ownership by above parent(s) **
          by a) _____   _____
          by b) _____   _____
    b) In 1974 (if another year, list) _____   _____
       1) Name of immediate parent(s) in system
          a) _____   _____
          b) _____   _____
       2) % ownership by above parent(s):
          by a) _____   _____
          by b) _____   _____
    c) Total system ownership in 1974
       1) If not 1974, list year ___   _____
       2) Total % ownership ___   _____

13. Outside ownership at entry:
    a) Category of outside owner(s)   1st outside owner   2nd outside owner
        1) a locally controlled private enterprise . . . . ☐ . . . . . ☐
(name 2) a local state agency or state enterprise . . . . ☐ . . . . . ☐
below) 3) a foreign-controlled private enterprise . . . . ☐ . . . . . ☐
        4) stock is widely dispersed . . . . ☐ . . . . . ☐
    b) Percentage ownership held by outside owner(s) _____
14. Outside ownership in 1974:   Year, if not 1974 _____
    a) Category of outside owner(s)   1st outside owner   2nd outside owner
        1) a locally controlled private enterprise. . . . . ☐ . . . . . ☐
        2) a local state agency or state enterprise . . . . ☐ . . . . . ☐
(name 3) a foreign-controlled private enterprise . . . . ☐ . . . . . ☐
below) 4) stock is widely dispersed . . . . ☐ . . . . . ☐
    b) Percentage ownership held by outside owner(s) _____
15. Financial statistics (check one box for sales, assets, and equity each. List
    year for which data apply in space next to each).

	Sales _____	Assets _____	Equity _____
1) less than $1 million	☐	. . . . ☐	. . . . . ☐
2) from $1 to $10m	☐	. . . . ☐	. . . . . ☐
3) from $10 to $25 m.	☐	. . . . ☐	. . . . . ☐
4) from $25 to $100m	☐	. . . . ☐	. . . . . ☐
5) more than $100 m	☐	. . . . ☐	. . . . . ☐

16. Number of employees _____ Year _____
17. Principal market of sales (check one):
    1) less than 10% of sales are exported . . . . ☐
    2) between 10% and 50% of sales are exported . . . . ☐
    3) more than 50% of sales are exported . . . . ☐
18. Principal customer of sales (check one):
    1) less than 10% of sales are to parent or
       affiliates in the system . . . . ☐
    2) between 10% and 50% of sales are within the
       system . . . . ☐
    3) more than 50% of sales are within the system . . . . ☐
COMMENTS OR ADDITIONAL INFORMATION:

FOR OFFICE USE ONLY:
OTHER PARENT SYSTEMS

ADDENDUM FORM FOR PRE-1967 SUBSIDIARIES NOT ON EMY 1

1. Primary activity in:
                                                                 1957   1966
   1) Manufacturing (if any manufacturing, check this box). . . ☐ . . . . . . ☐
   2) Research and development. . . . . ☐ . . . . . . ☐
   3) Sales or service (includes marketing, repair and
       maintenance, transport, storage, or finance) . . . . ☐ . . . . . . ☐
   4) Extraction (all raw material extraction, plus
       farming and fishing) . . . . ☐ . . . . . . ☐
   5) Holding (principal activity consists of
       owning and administering subsidiaries . . . . ☐ . . . . . . ☐
   6) Other (specify)_____ . . . . ☐ . . . . . . ☐
   7) Inactive . . . . ☐ . . . . . . ☐
2. Products manufactured in 1957:   in 1966
   1) _____
   2) _____
   3) _____
   4) _____
   5) _____
   6) _____
3. Ownership in 1957:
   1) Immediate parent(s) and percentage ownership

   Ownership in 1966:
   1) Immediate parent(s) and percentage ownership

5. Outside ownership: in 1957   in 1966
   a) category of outside owner
      1. a locally controlled private enterprise. . . . . ☐ . . . . ☐
      2. a local state agency or state enterprise . . . . ☐ . . . . ☐
      3. a foreign-controlled private enterprise . . . . ☐ . . . . ☐
      4. stock is widely dispersed . . . . ☐ . . . . ☐
   b) Percentage ownership held by outside owner _____

PARENT SYSTEM QUESTIONNAIRE

Please use consolidated data.
1. Name of system _____
2. Address of headquarters _____
   (street, city, country) _____
3. Financial statistics (from *Fortune 500* directory)
   Sales ($ '000) _____
   Assets ($ '000) _____
   Net Profit ($ '000) _____
   Invested Capital ($ '000) _____
4. Number of employees _____
5. Complete list of products made by system in
   home country only. (3 digit SIC codes, and
   names of product categories; please give as
   detailed a list as possible)

   _____   _____   _____
   _____   _____   _____
   _____   _____   _____

6. Primary SIC industry of system (3 digit code from SEC disclosure) _____
7. Average wage rate paid by company ($ per year/person) _____
8. Total wages paid (labor cost) _____
9. R and D expenditures _____
10. Number of R and D workers _____
11. Advertising expenditures _____
12. Total sales outside home country _____
13. Total export sales from home country _____
14. Number of employees outside home country _____

Information Sources

The following reference list represents the major public sources used in gathering data on the parent systems and their subsidiaries. While the availability of published information on the activities of multinational enterprises has dramatically improved in recent years, much of the information used in the preparation of this book was derived from direct interviews with the firms themselves.

SOURCES OF INFORMATION FOR COMPANY RESEARCH

I. Company Publications
   1. Annual reports for parent system
   2. 10–K reports to the Securities and Exchange Commission
   3. Prospectuses
   4. Separate annual reports for foreign subsidiaries

II. Periodical Indexes
   1. *Funk and Scott International Index*
   2. *Funk and Scott Corporation Index*
   3. *New York Times Index*
   4. *Wall Street Journal Index*
   5. *Business Periodicals Index*

III. Directories
   1. *Jane's Major Companies of Europe*
   2. *Kompass registers*
      (for the U.K., Holland, France, Brazil, Belgium, Denmark, Norway, Spain, Germany, Hong Kong, and Singapore)
   3. *Dun and Bradstreet International*
   4. *Directory of American Business in Germany*, by Paul Baudler
   5. *Who Owns Whom*, for the U.K., North America, Europe, and the Far East
   6. *1975, The Financial Times International Business Yearbook*
   7. *Yearbook of Lebanese Companies*
   8. *List of American Firms in France*
   9. Lists of largest firms in various countries—for Denmark, Norway, Belgium, Switzerland, France, U.K., Germany, Sweden, Japan, Canada, Colombia, Australia, Finland, Spain, Italy, and Greece, such as *President Directory (Japan)*

427

10. *Dun and Bradstreet of Canada Report*
11. U.S. Bureau of International Commerce, *American Firms, Subsidiaries and Affiliates*
12. *Brazil Report*
13. *American Chamber of Commerce Report for Brazil*
14. *Moody's Industrial Manual*
15. *Export Directory for Colombia*
16. *BOAC Japan Directory*
17. *Standard and Poor's Guide to American Businesses*
18. *Kothari's Economic Guide to India*
19. *Philippine Financial Directory*
20. *American Chamber of Commerce Report for Australia*
21. *Beerman's Guide to South Africa*
22. *Commerce in Belgium*
23. *Kayser-Roth Financial Survey*
24. *Financial Dynamics*
25. Industry sources, such as *Chemical Guide to Europe, Mining Yearbook*

IV. Books
1. Business history books
2. Books on specific companies

In the EMY data bank, products manufactured by foreign subsidiaries are classified at the 4 digit SIC level. For the purposes of this book, the manufacturing SIC codes were aggregated into 42 broad industry groups. The method of aggregations appears below.

Industry Group	*SIC Codes*
The Beverages Industry	208
The Tobacco Industry	21
The Food Industry	20 , excluding 208
The Textiles and Apparel Industries	22 and 23
The Wood and Furniture Industries	24 and 25
The Paper Industry	26
The Printing Industry	27
The Industrial Chemicals Industry	281
The Plastics Industry	282
The Agricultural Chemicals Industry	287
The Cosmetics and Soaps Industries	284
The Drugs Industry	283
Other Chemical Industries	Other 28
Fabricated Plastics Industries	306 and 307
The Tire Industry	301
The Petroleum Refining Industry	291
Other Petroleum Industries	Other 29
The Leather Industry	31
Stone, Clay, and Cement Industries	324–328
Abrasives and Asbestos Industries	329
The Glass Industry	321–323
The Iron and Steel Industry	331–332
Non-ferrous Metal Industries	Other 33
The Metal Can Industry	341
Other Fabricated Metal Industries	Other 34
The Engines and Turbines Industry	351
The Construction Machinery Industry	353
The Farm Machinery Industry	352
The Office Machine and Computer Industry	357
The Special Machinery Industry	355
The General Machinery Industry	356
Other Non-electrical Machinery Industries	Other 35
Electric Light and Wiring Industry	364
Electric Transmission Equipment Industry	361
Radio, TV, and Appliances Industries	363 and 365

The Electronics Industry   367
Other Electrical Industries   Other 36
Communication Equipment Industry   366
The Motor Vehicle Industry   371
Other Transportation Industries   37
Precision Instruments Industries   38
Miscellaneous Industries   39